CONCORDIA UNIVERSITY
D103.B77   C001 V
MEN AND CENTURIES OF EUROPEAN CIVIL

3 4211 000020187

History of Europe

A History of Russia
SIR BERNARD PARES

The German People
VEIT VALENTIN

The British People 1746–1946
G. D. H. COLE AND RAYMOND POSTGATE

The Evolution of the French People
CHARLES M. SEIGNOBOS

The Rise of European Civilization
CHARLES M. SEIGNOBOS

A History of Modern Europe
THAD W. RIKER

THESE ARE *Bozoi Books*, PUBLISHED IN NEW YORK BY
Alfred A. Knopf

Men & Centuries
of
EUROPEAN CIVILIZATION

Men and Centuries

OF

European Civilization

LOUISE FARGO BROWN

and

GEORGE BARR CARSON, JR.

NEW YORK
ALFRED · A · KNOPF
1948

THIS IS A BORZOI BOOK,
PUBLISHED BY ALFRED A. KNOPF, INC.

COPYRIGHT *1948 by Louise Fargo Brown and George B. Carson, Jr. All rights reserved. No part of this book may be reproduced in any form without permission in writing from the publisher, except by a reviewer who may quote brief passages and reproduce not more than three illustrations in a review to be printed in a magazine or newspaper. Manufactured in the United States of America. Published simultaneously in Canada by The Ryerson Press.*

FIRST EDITION

Preface

THIS BOOK takes its form from a definite conception of what a student should carry away from the introductory college course in European history. The authors believe he should have gained enough familiarity with a definite body of information to make it a permanent part of his mental equipment. He should have had the opportunity to read some of the great historical sources in full and others in part, and to make the acquaintance of leading authorities in different fields. He should have laid the foundations for a critical method of reading and using historical material.

If all of this is to be done in the limited time at a student's disposal, the text-book must absorb only a small portion of his time and employ it effectively. The book should contain only those facts which today are generally recognized as essential. It should present them in such a way as to arouse the student's interest in each period, and to impel him to read further to satisfy his curiosity. It should be a guide, not an encyclopedia. In recent years books based on the theory that they ought to be encyclopedic have supplanted the brief text-book. They aim at the inclusion of all the facts a student needs in order to pass an examination in the course, and they do not awaken his desire to read further, even if he has the time. These three- and four-pound volumes deprive the student of his rightful opportunity to become literate in history.

The problem of presenting clearly a subject so complicated as European history is far from simple. We have not followed the usual topical plan, which fails to give a sense of continuous development or to put political events in the frame of an evolving society. Separate chapters on the arts, and on institutional development, inserted here and there among chapters of political narrative do not help toward understanding the spirit of an age, or the connection between different aspects of human activity. Our clue to arrangement came from two circumstances known to every experienced teacher: first, students confronted with a body of unfamiliar facts have difficulty in seizing the time element, even when the facts are assiduously buttressed by dates. The second circumstance is that the human aspect of history is the most interesting to students, and consequently the events they are most likely to remember are those connected with individuals who have aroused their interest.

The plan of this book has been based on these observations. Certain important individuals have been selected from each century—usually one from the first half and another from the latter half. In the chapter which bears his name, the student is told enough of the essentials to awaken an interest in the historical character and to understand the period in which he lived. The political history of the times is also related in this chapter, and wherever it can be logically done connections are established between events and individuals. The lifetime of a human being is, however, too brief for showing the development of institutions, which always spans several generations at least. History is a continuous process, of course, and yet it must be divided for purposes of study. A division into centuries is the one which best preserves and emphasizes the principle of continuity. It is the traditional division for studying the development of the arts, and lends itself equally well to describing the progress of social and political institutions. Consequently, a section on the century as a whole precedes the semi-biographical chapters. In this section the chief aspects of the century are summarized; conditions, institutions, progress in science and the arts are all considered, and also such political events as can be treated there more appropriately than in the separate chapters. In short, these sections on centuries enable us to understand the great figures of history in their time and place, and the semi-biographical chapters tell the events that occurred when they were alive.

It is not the function of a text-book to paint the portrait of a man so that he will come alive. Something more truly educational can be done in the text-book by sketching an outline of the picture, and by telling the student where he should look for material with which to paint the picture for himself. For this purpose, selections have been made from historical sources with the idea of giving him some clues. The reading lists have been drawn up to provide a wide variety of books, and to acquaint the student with those which will give him the most useful bibliographical aid in carrying on independent study.

Preface [ix

The inclusion of source readings assures the instructor that his students have in their possession a common body of materials for discussion in class. Wherever sources have been published in a handy edition, extracts are taken from that edition in the hope that students may wish to acquire the book and read it as a whole.

The authors wish to express their indebtedness for criticisms and suggestions to Dr. Geneva Drinkwater, Professor G. P. Cuttino, Professor Harold J. Grimm, and to members of the Department of History of Vassar College. Aid with the illustrations was generously given by Professors Richard Krautheimer and Adolf Katzenellenbogen of the Department of Art of Vassar College, and by Dr. Guido Schonberger and Mrs. Charles Brophy of the Institute of Fine Arts of New York University.

L. F. B.

G. B. C.

Contents

PART I. *The Fourth and Fifth Centuries*   3
  Ch. 1   THE WORLD OF ST. AUGUSTINE   17
  Ch. 2   THE WORLD OF APOLLINARIS SIDONIUS   26
  READINGS:
    St. Augustine, *Confessions* · 33
      The City of God · 36
    Apollinaris Sidonius, *Letters* · 40

PART II. *The Sixth Century*   47
  Ch. 3   THE WORLD OF JUSTINIAN   54
  Ch. 4   THE WORLD OF ST. GREGORY THE GREAT   62
  READINGS:
    Procopius of Caesarea, *History of the Wars* · 67
      Secret History: Anecdota · 68
    Pope Gregory I, *The Dialogues* · 71
      Pastoral Care · 72
      Correspondence · 72

PART III. *The Seventh Century*   79
  Ch. 5   THE WORLD OF MOHAMMED AND THE FIRST FIVE CALIPHS   84
  READINGS:
    The Koran · 91

Contents

PART IV. *The Eighth Century*   97

    Ch. 6   THE WORLD OF THE VENERABLE BEDE   104

    Ch. 7   THE WORLD OF CHARLEMAGNE   111

    READINGS:

        Bede, *The Ecclesiastical History of the English Nation* · 118

        Eginhard, *Life of Charlemagne* · 124

PART V. *The Ninth Century*   131

    Ch. 8   THE WORLD OF JOHN SCOTUS ERIGENA   136

    Ch. 9   THE WORLD OF ALFRED   142

    READINGS:

        Xanten, St. Vaast, and Fulda Annals · 147

        John Scotus Erigena, Translation of the *De Coelesti Hierarchia* · 148

        De Divisione Naturae · 149

        King Alfred, Preface to the *Dialogues* of Gregory the Great · 152

        Preface to the *Pastoral Care* · 153

        Interpolations in *The Consolations of Boethius* · 153

        Translation of *The Seven Books of Orosius* · 155

        Preface to the "Blooms" or *Soliloquies* of St. Augustine · 156

PART VI. *The Tenth Century*   161

    Ch. 10   THE WORLD OF OTTO I   170

    Ch. 11   THE WORLD OF GERBERT (SILVESTER II)   176

    READINGS:

        Liudprand of Cremona, *Antapodosis* · 182

        De Legatione Constantinopolitana · 184

        Richer, *Account of the Election of Hugh Capet* · 185

        Gerbert, *Letters* · 187

Contents [xiii

PART VII. *The Eleventh Century* 193

  Ch. 12 THE WORLD OF LANFRANC 201

READINGS:

    A Shire-moot in Herefordshire · 209
    William of Malmesbury, *Lanfranc and William the Conqueror* · 210
    William the Conqueror, *Letter to Pope Gregory VII* · 214
    Mandate for Dividing the Civil and Church Courts · 214

PART VIII. *The Twelfth Century* 219

  Ch. 13 THE WORLD OF ST. BERNARD OF CLAIRVAUX 233

  Ch. 14 THE WORLD OF FREDERICK BARBAROSSA 243

READINGS:

    Urban II, *Speech at the Council of Clermont* · 248
    Abbot Suger, *Poem on the Doors of the Central West Portal* · 250
    On What Was Done under His Administration · 250
    St. Bernard of Clairvaux, *Letters* · 252
    Frederick I, *Letters* · 255
    The Stirrup Episode · 257

PART IX. *The Thirteenth Century* 261

  Ch. 15 THE WORLD OF INNOCENT III 268

  Ch. 16 THE WORLD OF FREDERICK II 275

  Ch. 17 THE WORLD OF DANTE 279

READINGS:

    Innocent III, *Answer Concerning the Inderdict* · 285
    St. Francis of Assisi, *Canticle of the Sun* · 286
    Will · 287
    Matthew Paris's English History · 289
    Salimbene, *Chronicle* · 290

xiv] *Contents*

> Dante, *De Vulgari Eloquentia* · 294
> *The Divine Comedy: Inferno* · 295
> *The Divine Comedy: Purgatorio* · 297

PART X. *The Fourteenth Century*   301

  Ch. 18   THE WORLD OF JOHN WYCLIFFE   305

READINGS:

> *Bull of Pope Gregory XI against John Wycliffe* · 313
> *Wycliffe's Reply to the Summons of Pope Urban VI* · 315

PART XI. *The Fifteenth Century*   321

  Ch. 19   THE WORLD OF JACQUES COEUR   328

  Ch. 20   THE WORLD OF LORENZO THE MAGNIFICENT   336

READINGS:

> *Complaint of Charles VII* · 341
> *Letter of the Sultan to Charles VII* · 342
> *Description of Coeur's Dress* · 343
> Lorenzo dei Medici, *Carnival Song* · 344
> *Letter to His Son* · 345

PART XII. *The Sixteenth Century*   351

  Ch. 21   THE WORLD OF ERASMUS   357

  Ch. 22   THE WORLD OF JOHN CALVIN   363

  Ch. 23   THE WORLD OF ELIZABETH OF ENGLAND   370

READINGS:

> Erasmus, *Letters* · 376
> John Calvin, *Institutes* · 379
> Queen Elizabeth, *Letters* · 384
> *Speech Proroguing the Parliament* · 386

PART XIII. *The Seventeenth Century*   391

  Ch. 24   THE WORLD OF GALILEO   398

Contents [xv

Ch. 25 THE WORLD OF ISAAC NEWTON   408

READINGS:
    Galileo, *The Siderial Messenger* · 425
        System of the World · 426
    Sir Isaac Newton, *Principia* · 428

PART XIV. *The Eighteenth Century*   435

Ch. 26 THE WORLD OF BENJAMIN FRANKLIN   442

Ch. 27 THE WORLD OF NAPOLEON BONAPARTE   454

READINGS:
    Benjamin Franklin, *Letters and Papers* · 469
        Respecting Alterations in the Constitution of Pennsylvania · 471
    Napoleon Bonaparte, *Letters* · 473

PART XV. *The Nineteenth Century*   481

Ch. 28 THE WORLD OF CHARLES DARWIN   489

Ch. 29 THE WORLD OF JEAN JAURÈS   499

READINGS:
    Charles Darwin, *Autobiography* · 515
    Jean Jaurès, *Writings* · 518

PART XVI. *The Twentieth Century*   523

Ch. 30 THE WORLD OF NIKOLAI LENIN   528

Ch. 31 THE WORLD OF WINSTON CHURCHILL   547

Ch. 32 OUR WORLD   555

READINGS:
    Nikolai Lenin, *Letters* · 573
    Winston Churchill, *Dunkirk* · 578
        Their Finest Hour · 580

Bibliography   585

Index   *follows page* 628

Illustrations

IN TEXT

	PAGE
Roman altar in Britain	15
Fourth century relief from Constantinople	24
Bronze lamp in shape of basilica	43
The world as imagined by Cosmos Indicopleustes, a Greek monk	52
St. Sophia	61
Votive crown of a seventh century Visogothic king	82
Saxon church at Bradford on Avon	102
Part of Celtic cross at Jedburgh	110
Diadem of Charlemagne	128
Drawing of a ship, from an English manuscript	135
Group of Saxon warriors	140
Gold ornament, inscribed "Alfred had me made"	157
Bishop giving a blessing	169
A monk being driven from the presence of a king	174
A house of the period, from an English manuscript influenced by Utrecht Psalter	190
Ploughman with wheeled plow, from Cademon illustration	200
The coronation of a king in the days of William the Conqueror	215
The building of a church	231
Seal of St. Bernard	241

	PAGE
Twelfth century ship, from a manuscript in the British Museum	257
Chinese drawing of the thirteenth century showing loom	266
A bishop ordaining a priest, from a manuscript made early in Innocent's lifetime	273
Battle scene, from a manuscript in the British Museum	278
Drawing from the Luttrell Psalter, showing harrowing with a horse wearing a padded collar	298
Drawing of the fourteenth century, showing quilling wheel for winding a bobbin	304
Coat of arms of Edward III	316
Leonardo da Vinci's devices for wheel and pinions, swinging and rotary motion, and gears	327
Large ship and small boat of the fifteenth century	334
Illustration from a medical book	347
Frontispiece by Albrecht Durer	356
Siege of Boulogne by Henry VIII	362
Witches on their way to a sabbath	368
Map of the world from Pedro de Medina's *Arte de Navigar*, Valladolid, 1545	387
Engraving by the French artist Jacques Callot	397
Monumental brass of an English knight and his lady, about 1630	407
Engraving of the first Eddystone Lighthouse	431
Engraving made in 1717 showing a steam pump used in mines	441
The British House of Commons, sitting in 1741-42	453
Medal issued by Napoleon to commemorate the invasion of England which he planned in 1804	477
The first English steam engine used for a passenger train	488
Engraving of early steamboat, 1813	498
The "Christmas tree" which regulates the flow of oil from a well	527
Automobile of 1912	545
Official seal and emblem of the United Nations	572

Illustrations [xix

PLATES

FACING PAGE

PLATE I. *Fourth & Fifth Centuries*   39a
Head of Christ
Arch of Constantine, Rome
Relief from Arch of Titus

PLATE II. *Fourth & Fifth Centuries*   39b
Pharaoh's Feast
Mosaic from a Roman Villa
Head of a Roman Emperor
Old St. Peter's Church, Rome

PLATE III. *Sixth Century*   69a
Mosaic Portrait of Justinian
Interior of the Church of Hagia Sophia, Constantinople
Mosaic of Empress Theodora and Attendants

PLATE IV. *Sixth Century*   69b
Byzantine Ivory Carving of the Nativity
Resurrection of Lazarus
Arming of David by Saul
Church of St. Apollinare in Classe, Ravenna

PLATE V. *Seventh Century*   107a
King Ibn Saud
Ancient Arabs
Dome of the Rock, Jerusalem
Baptistery of St. John, Poitiers

PLATE VI. *Seventh Century*   107b
Page from *Homilies* of St. Augustine
An English Stone Church
Frankish Buckle
Frankish Chatelaine

PLATE VII. *Eighth Century*   121a
Page from an English Psalter
Page from Lindisfarne Gospels
Page from the Book of Kells
Mosque of Cordoba, Spain

FACING PAGE

PLATE VIII. *Eighth Century* 121b
 Equestrian Statue of Charlemagne
 Moslem Carving in Wood
 Chapel of Charlemagne
 Porch of Monastery, Lorsch

PLATE IX. *Ninth Century* 127a
 Page from the Bible of Charles the Bald
 Viking Ship
 Beaten Gold Manuscript Cover

PLATE X. *Ninth Century* 127b
 Page from the Utrecht Psalter
 Crystal of Lothair
 Church of Santa Maria de Naranco, Oviedo, Spain

PLATE XI. *Tenth Century* 157a
 Otto I
 Illustration from the Stuttgart Psalter
 Byzantine Ivory Carving
 Abbey Church of Gernrode, Germany

PLATE XII. *Tenth Century* 157b
 King David Playing the Organ
 Emblems of the Evangelists
 Otto III Receiving Gifts

PLATE XIII. *Eleventh Century* 187a
 Adam and Eve Driven from Paradise
 Landing Scene from the Bayeux Tapestry
 Relief from Bronze Doors of St. Michael's Church, Hildesheim
 Church of St. Etienne, Caen

PLATE XIV. *Eleventh Century* 187b
 Abbey of Cluny
 Abbey of Monte Cassino
 Church of St. Sophia, Novgorod
 Apse of Speyer Cathedral

PLATE XV. *Twelfth Century* 217a
 Tympanum of the Cathedral of Autun
 Murder of Thomas à Becket
 Abbey Church of St. Denis

Illustrations [xxi]

FACING PAGE

PLATE XVI. *Twelfth Century*   217b
Imperial Seal of Frederick I
Stone Sculpture of Shepherds, Chartres Cathedral
Stone Sculpture of Aristotle, Chartres Cathedral
Nave of Durham Cathedral

PLATE XVII. *Thirteenth Century*   279a
Gold Augustal of Frederick II
Apse of Reims Cathedral
Nave of Chartres Cathedral
Cloth Hall, Ypres

PLATE XVIII. *Thirteenth Century*   279b
Dante
Presentation of Jesus in the Temple
Crusades of Louis IX

PLATE XIX. *Fourteenth Century*   309a
Page from the Wycliffe Bible
Christ and St. John
Marienburg Castle
Cathedral of Palma, Majorca

PLATE XX. *Fourteenth Century*   309b
Banquet Scene from an Illuminated Manuscript
Ivory Relief of a Tournament

PLATE XXI. *Fifteenth Century*   339a
House of Jacques Coeur, Bourges
Illustration from Nuremberg Chronicle
Illustration from Chronicles of Rouen

PLATE XXII. *Fifteenth Century*   339b
Lorenzo dei Medici and Friends
Devices for Raising a Drawbridge
Gattemalata
The Sacrament of Baptism

PLATE XXIII. *Sixteenth Century*   369a
Erasmus
Calvin
Illustration from *Der Weiss König*
Hampton Court Palace

	FACING PAGE
PLATE XXIV. *Sixteenth Century*	369b

    Queen Elizabeth
    Tomb of the Medici
    Machine for Removing Water from a Mine
    Breughel's *Spring*

PLATE XXV. *Seventeenth Century*   431a

    Galileo
    James, Duke of York
    Church of Santa Agnese, Rome
    Ruben's *The Wolf Hunt*

PLATE XXVI. *Seventeenth Century*   431b

    Isaac Newton
    Ostade's *Saying Grace*
    East India Company Ships
    Printing Shop

PLATE XXVII. *Eighteenth Century*   461a

    Benjamin Franklin
    Chippendale Secretary
    Watteau's *Company in a Park*

PLATE XXVIII. *Eighteenth Century*   461b

    Napoleon
    Palace of Sans Souci
    David's *Oath of the Tennis Court*

PLATE XXIX. *Nineteenth Century*   491a

    Charles Darwin
    Delacroix's *Liberty Leading the People*
    Daumier's *Uprising*
    The Crystal Palace

PLATE XXX. *Nineteenth Century*   491b

    Jean Jaurès
    Rodin's *The Hand of God*
    Monet's *Le Port d'Honfleur*
    Paris Opera House

Illustrations [xxiii

FACING PAGE

PLATE XXXI. *Twentieth Century* 521a
Nikolai Lenin
Harvesting in Russia
Brancusi's *Bird in Flight*
Country House near Paris

PLATE XXXII. *Twentieth Century* 521b
Moore's *Tube Shelter Perspective*
Cyclotron
Signing the United Nations Charter

MAPS

	PAGE
The Roman Empire (Fourth Century)	5
The Carolingian, Byzantine and Mohammedan Empires (About 800)	99
Feudal Europe (About 1200)	221
Europe (About 1500)	323
Europe (After 1648. Peace of Westphalia)	411
Europe (After the Congress of Vienna)	465
Europe (At the beginning of the 20th Century)	511
Europe (Between 1919 and 1938)	565

PART I

The Fourth and Fifth Centuries

CHRONOLOGY

325 Council of Nicæa
c. 370 St. Jerome's translation of the Bible (Vulgate)
374 Ambrose, Bishop of Milan
376 Goths pass the Danube into the Empire
406 Germanic passage of the Rhine in force
410 Alaric's Sack of Rome
416 Visigoths in Spain
429 Vandals in Africa
430 Death of St. Augustine
433 Attila, leader of the Huns
438 Theodosian Code
453 Death of Attila
c. 463 Death of St. Patrick of Ireland
476 Romulus Augustulus deposed, last Roman emperor in the west; Odoacer becomes King in Italy
481 Clovis becomes King of the Franks
493 Theodoric becomes ruler in Italy
496 Baptism of Clovis

PART I

The Fourth and Fifth Centuries

EUROPEAN history since earliest times has been characterized by movements of peoples seeking to better the conditions under which they lived. The migrating groups have been united by loyalties ranging all the way from simple tribal feeling to the strong sentiments of modern nationalism. The roots of these loyalties have been common interests, tastes, and habits, as well as a common language. In pursuit of their interests these groups have made war upon each other from the time when they used stone axes until the day when armed divisions moved with tanks into Poland. Between wars they developed what we know as Western civilization.

The nature of the lands over which these groups moved and in which they settled and grew into nations exerted great influence upon them. The physical map shows how Europe divides roughly into two main parts. The great northern plain extends across the continent and into Asia by the gap between the Ural Mountains and the Caspian Sea. The rivers crossing this plain provide excellent means of communication between the seaboard and the interior, but there are few mountain ranges to offer defensible frontiers north of the Alps. The plain has been for ages the scene of mass movements of peoples, generally westward. After each invasion, conquerors and conquered intermingled, except for small groups who fled to remote districts and remained unassimilated. The Mediterranean region is strikingly different in character. There plateaus and mountain ranges surround the great sea which provides a natural highway. The ancient civilizations were located in this region, which is relatively isolated by physical barriers: in Africa, to the south of the coast region by mountains and other obstacles; in Europe to the north by the great chain of the Alps and lesser ranges stretching eastward to the Black Sea. The Alps have always been a formidable but not an insurmountable barrier between the two regions of Europe.

This book begins with the fourth and fifth centuries of the Christian era because in the fifth century the people of the great northern plain—who had already been widely penetrated by the ideas, faith, and ways of life which had been developed in the Mediterranean area—began to play a decisive part in Western civilization. That civilization had, in some fields, been brought during the fifth century before the Christian era to the highest point it has ever developed. The intervening period must be briefly surveyed.

The Greeks, whose legendary history tells of an invasion from the north, settled in the rocky peninsula that still bears their name and on the islands and eastern shore of the Aegean Sea. There they came in touch with the civilizations that had developed in the valleys of the Nile and of the Tigris and Euphrates, and brought a new civilization into being. Their art and architecture have never been surpassed in dignity and beauty; their literature and philosophy are today a precious heritage; and they made great progress in scientific theory. Their characteristic political achievement was the city-state (*polis*), an independent city governed by its citizens. Although our word democracy comes from the Greek words meaning government by the people, the citizens of a *polis* were a comparatively small group bound by a special loyalty, who dominated subject people and slaves. Until the rise of Alexander of Macedon there was no Greek empire to challenge the sovereignty of the city-state. One of the greatest military conquerors of history, Alexander united West (the Greek world based on the city-state) and East (the Asiatic empire of the ancient Persians based on the cult of an emperor-god), and introduced two radically new concepts which became integral features of all later empires in Europe. To replace the *polis,* with its local sovereignty and limited citizenship, Alexander planned a *cosmopolis,* a universal city embracing all the civilized people of the world and extending citizenship to all free men. He united the varied groups in his universal city-state only by adopting the characteristic of Asiatic monarchies in which the ruler is deified. This conception gave universality to his rule, for if the ruler is a god he can be equally worshipped by all men. In the eastern world this was

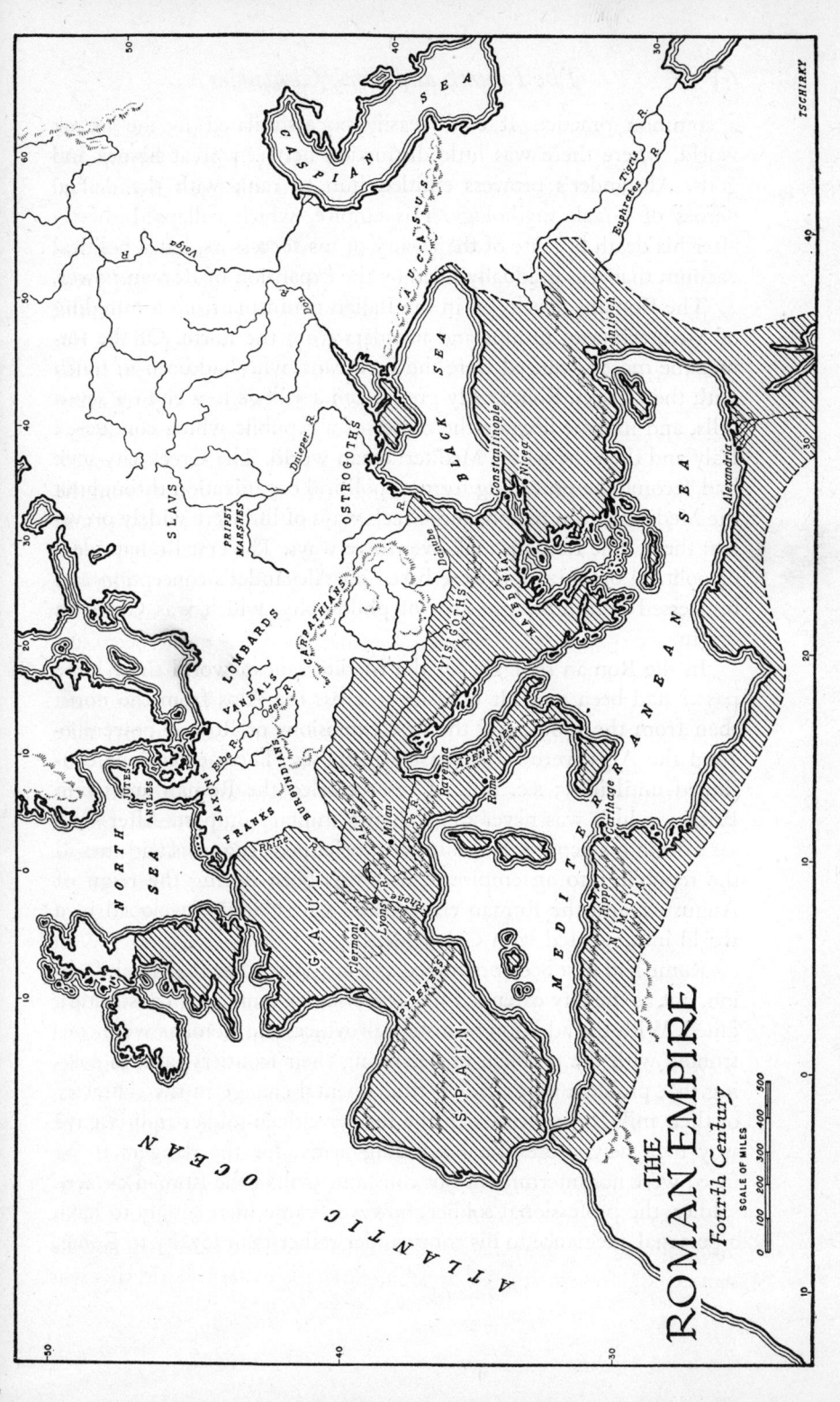

a common practice. It could easily be assimilated in the Greek world, where there was little distinction between great heroes and gods. Alexander's prowess entitled him to rank with the deified heroes of Greek mythology. His empire, which collapsed shortly after his death because of the rivalry of his successors, left a political vacuum that was gradually filled by the expansion of Roman power.

The Romans developed in the Italian peninsula from a mingling of Mediterranean groups and invaders from the north. Of the former the most advanced were the Etruscans, who had been in touch with the Greeks. Rome early grew from a village to a city on seven hills, and in time became the center of a republic which conquered Italy and then the whole Mediterranean world. The Greek city-state had become the prevailing form of political organization throughout the Mediterranean region, and Greek ways of life were widely prevalent there. The Romans took over these ways. The best Roman ideas of political organization were based on Alexander's conception and buttressed by the Stoic system of philosophy, which was Greek in origin.

In the Roman struggle for the Mediterranean world the Alpine passes had been used. It is easier to cross the Alps from the north than from the south, and the first extensions of Roman power beyond the Alps were for defensive purposes. These extensions continued until in 55 B.C. Julius Caesar carried the Roman arms into Britain, which was never more than a military outpost. After Caesar's death his nephew had himself proclaimed Augustus and turned the republic into an empire. Christ was born during the reign of Augustus, and the Roman empire and Christianity developed in a world impregnated with Greek ideas.

Rome had first been organized as a city-state after the Greek fashion, but as the city extended its territories its municipal constitution failed. With the addition of distant provinces the Romans were confronted with the problem of defending their frontiers; and in solving that problem they made a fundamental change in the character of their military institutions. The former citizen-soldier militia gave way to a new professional standing army, for the dangers to be faced were not intermittent but constant. Unlike the Roman citizen-soldier, the professional soldier, however, came increasingly to have a personal allegiance to his commander rather than loyalty to Rome.

The commanders thus became masters of Roman legions and, when they realized their power, masters of Rome. During the last century before Christ a succession of such commanders with political ambitions fastened the habit of military dictatorship on the city-state of Rome, which was trying to rule an empire.

Under military dictatorship—or Caesarism as it was called after the most successful dictators—the Roman empire took on unity and gradually adopted the characteristics which had made Alexander's empire a universal state. Caesarism helped to eliminate internal strife and factional rivalry because the people were equally subject to the dictator. As in Alexander's model, the Roman Empire became a church as well as a state. In the old city-state civic worship had been customary; in an empire state, worship of the emperor was logical. Since there was a personal emperor, his worship provided the cohesive principle uniting the disparate peoples of the Mediterranean world under the rule of Rome. As there rose to power emperors who were not Roman, and later not even Italian, citizenship was gradually extended to their native provinces, diminishing the privileges first of Rome and then of Italy. The Empire thus became a leveling force in which nationality (i.e., linguistic or cultural heritage) and social status blended into a common allegiance, until in 212 A.D. universal citizenship was proclaimed for all freeborn men. The government was also unified. Imperial government in Rome began as a dual affair, with autarchy in the administration of military and financial matters but with a respect for old constitutional institutions. By 300 A.D., however, the rights of local institutions had been infringed so much that the Roman Empire had many of the aspects of oriental despotism.

While these internal changes were taking place, the Romans were coping with the problem of the northern barbarians. At the beginning of the Christian era the Roman frontier lay along the Rhine and Danube rivers, with an outpost in Britain. The last invaders of western Europe to come under Roman rule had been a short, dark people who in modern times have been called Celts. The Romans knew the Celts of Spain as Iberians, those of France as Gauls, and those of England as Britons. After conquering each, they assumed the responsibility of defending them against the most recent invaders, whom the Roman writers called Germans.

These latest migrants were a tall, fair-haired, blue-eyed people who had come from the shores of the Baltic Sea.[1] They made their slow and laborious way through dense forests and across great rivers, and when they were checked at the Roman frontier they settled between the Rhine and the Elbe. The Romans traded with them, exchanging wine and olive oil for cattle, amber, slaves, and hides, and fought the groups that breached the frontier.

What manner of men were these newcomers? Various theories have been based on the description of Tacitus, a celebrated Roman historian who wrote at the end of the first century A.D. In the late nineteenth century English historians used his description to trace British democracy to the Germanic tribes of the central European forests. In the twentieth century, German historians found in Tacitus's primitive nature-worshippers the leadership principle and the source of German valor. In the light of more objective research the Germanic tribes appear to have had a society far from democratic. They divided their land according to the social standing of families, although all had rights in the undivided wasteland and forests. The work, except fighting, was done by slaves. The assembly of the folk which chose the leaders was a gathering of the fighting men and they elected these leaders from a certain family, traditionally royal. Large landholders lived with their families on the land, while tenants and slaves who cultivated it lived near them in villages. The land was ploughed in long narrow strips with a wheeled plow drawn by oxen, and fields were either left fallow every alternate year or planted on a system of two-field rotation. By the fourth century, when these invaders began to come into the Roman empire in large numbers, their habits must have changed in many respects, but the land hunger which had set in motion their first migrations has never been sated.

The Germanic tribes along the lower Rhine called themselves Franks, those along the North Sea and in Denmark, Angles, Jutes,

---

[1] Groups that have been isolated for a long period are likely to perpetuate certain physical traits, such as the fair hair and blue eyes of these Baltic folk. The same results come when for religious reasons a group discourages intermarriage with other groups, as in the case of the Jews. These physical types should not be confused with racial differences. The idea of race is sometimes wrongly connected with a word like Semitic, which applies solely to the language group to which Arabic, Hebrew, and Sanskrit belong. Race is based upon certain hereditary characteristics such as type of hair and color of skin. Scientists disagree as to the origin of these differences, but they do agree that there is no inferior or superior race.

and Saxons. Early in the third century other Germanic groups, whose ancestors had come from Scandinavia, began to move about on the outskirts of the Roman empire, increasing the pressure on the frontiers. Goths moved all the way south from the Baltic coasts into the region north of the Black Sea, where they separated into two branches known to the Romans as Visigoths and Ostrogoths. Burgundians settled along the upper Rhine. In the fourth century these peoples moved again because of the pressure of the Huns, savage Asiatic horsemen who entered Europe through the Ural gap, conquered the Ostrogoths, and pushed the Visigoths toward the Danube.

Undisguised despotism had grown rapidly in the late third century as a result of invasions from without and internal social disorders which almost destroyed the Empire. Having stabilized the frontiers on the line of the Rhine and the Danube, the emperors strove to provide military defense against the steady pressure of barbarian peoples beyond. Since the foundation of the imperial office was military dictatorship, the emperors were absolutely dependent on the army. Once the army became aware of its own power, a crisis arose in the imperial organization: the soldiers would continue to support an emperor only in return for concessions to themselves. Selling their allegiance became very profitable to the soldiers; and from 235 to 270 A.D. the army made and unmade so many emperors that the imperial office was cheapened. In an effort to check the declining religious veneration of the emperors, eastern cults were welcomed at Rome. The Emperor Aurelian encouraged Mithraism, which identified the ruler with the sun god, and some enactments indicate that he expected from his subjects the blind prostration which was accorded the gods among oriental peoples.

At the end of the third and the beginning of the fourth century the Empire was saved from further disintegration only by the efforts of two able rulers, Diocletian (284–305) and Constantine (306–337). With Diocletian there were established two emperors, one residing in the East and another in the West, with a hierarchy of officials under each. Their most important duty was to maintain the armies with funds raised through an elaborate system of taxes, heavier than any the Empire had ever known. To facilitate collection of taxes and to keep up the production of food and manufactured goods, society hardened into a caste system in which every man was bound to his father's status and occupation. Diocletian thus built up an intricate, unified bureaucratic state and left as his legacy to the Roman world a fully developed system of both central and local administration. Although he saved the empire, Diocletian forgot that the state was a man-made creation to serve man's needs, not an all-devouring abstraction to whose interests men must be subordinated. By the time of his death the Roman idea of empire embodied the conception of a single universal state, a single universal citizenship, and a single universal, centralized administration. The remaining facet of the Roman conception of empire was to be added later, though the idea behind it already existed—a single universal religion.

Roman ideas of empire spread through the Mediterranean world and became the heritage of all European peoples. The extension of Roman civilization was largely unconscious, not a matter of deliberate policy, and this perhaps best explains its permanent influence. The splendid roads, reaching to the remotest frontiers, which the emperors constructed as a matter of military necessity were highways for trade and ideas as well as armies. Free trade throughout the empire, with the Mediterranean Sea serving as the greatest link in the system of communications, diffused the advantages of Roman civilization to every part of the ancient world. The ships bringing products of the civilized world to Rome brought also the ideas and philosophies of outlying regions. The interchange of goods and ideas was made easier by the general adoption of a universal language, or at most two languages which were common currency—Greek in the East and Latin throughout the West. Latin was not the least part of the legacy of Rome to later ages, since the modern Romance languages are derived from the colloquial Latin of the later Roman Empire, modified by the barbarian invaders and by time, and the written language of the educated Romans, pagan and Christian, was universal among educated people of the Middle Ages.

Even while the unity of the Roman Empire, however, was making possible the spread of Roman civilization, society in the later Empire was changing; Diocletian's reforms had deprived men of initiative, literature became sterile, philosophy had all but disappeared, and art had degenerated into formalism. In a troubled world religion took the direction of a yearning for assurance of a better life after death. The great oriental religions offered such assurance, and by Constantine's day spiritual aspiration for some firm moral

The Fourth and Fifth Centuries [11

basis for life had become a major problem of the Roman world. Diocletian's state was based on the principle of fear, and each individual was fixed in his niche with an all-pervading central administration to supervise his activity. Constantine perfected this system and gave it a valid moral basis by an alliance with Christianity. He thereby rounded out the Roman conception of empire by integrating with it the spiritual strength of the most powerful of the oriental religions.

Roman civilization gave Christianity its great opportunity. Ease of communication, though advantageous to a proselyting religion, would hardly have been sufficient had not Rome stood in dire need of a new cult to replace nearly defunct emperor-worship as a cement for empire. Rome could have absorbed Christianity, as she had so many philosophies, but Christianity required an undivided allegiance. It refused to compromise and to share pre-eminence with Roman state religion or even with formal emperor-worship. Christianity was persecuted for this, not for its doctrine or practices. Persecution, however, strengthened Christianity, giving Christians a consciousness of their uniqueness in Roman society, compelling them to recognize their brotherhood, and making doubly welcome the material aid which Christian congregations gave their members in obedience to the injunction of Christ. The strength of Christianity, demonstrated under persecution, was an important consideration with Constantine, who gave the religion legal existence, and thus enabled it to conquer Rome.

To Rome Christianity owed not only its opportunity, but its organization as the Christian Church. The hierarchical priesthood was modeled upon the framework of the old Roman religion with the Pontifex Maximus at its head; the constitution of the church was based on the imperial centralized Roman state; and the canon law incorporated the principles of Roman jurisprudence. The ritual absorbed many of the features of Roman cults and incorporated local festivals to strengthen the loyalty of new adherents to Christianity, and the very terminology of the church comes directly from the language of Rome. Even Christian Church architecture was indebted to Rome. But if Rome could give to Christianity organization, ritual, terminology, these were not religion. That was something Christianity could give to Rome.

Christianity gave to Rome a fundamental change in the conception of empire by stressing the spiritual as against the political. Diocletian's consolidation of imperial unity had made the state the basis of life. With the adoption of Christianity the church became the basis of life. The imposition by Diocletian of hereditary status, with heavy obligations in state services and state dues, removed voluntary support for the state and left only fear. In order to survive in a world permeated with the Stoic thought of the ancient Greek and Roman philosophers, an empire needed a religious cult with a universal appeal. Emperor-worship had once sufficed, but its appeal was gone. Christianity had the requisite qualifications, for it was not jealously guarded by the people among whom it originated, but was evangelistic and stressed the inclusion of Gentiles. Even more advantageous from the standpoint of a Roman emperor seeking a moral authority on which to base state control, in temporal matters Christianity deferred to the political powers. The apostle Paul, to whom much of the early spread of Christianity must be credited, had emphasized the dualism which became standard Christian teaching —there were matters of the spirit or the soul, in which the church spoke with the voice of God, and there were matters of the body, in which the political authorities spoke with the voice of God, for they had been ordained by His will. One of the greatest political texts of the Middle Ages was in the thirteenth chapter of Paul's epistle to the Romans, where he affirmed, "the powers that be are ordained of God. Whosoever resisteth the power resisteth the ordinance of God."

By allying itself with Christianity the empire gained unity on the basis of common allegiance to the Christian creed. The emperors, the church taught, were the powers ordained by God to rule over men's temporal affairs in a Christian society. During the century following the reign of Constantine, Christianity became universal, backed as it was by all the advantages of a universal empire. From a minority creed (estimates vary, but Christians numbered perhaps no more than one-tenth of the population of the Empire at the beginning of Constantine's reign), Christianity expanded to become the religion of the civilized Roman world; and as Christianity grew, so did the universal church, believed to be ordained of God to rule over men's spiritual affairs. Graeco-Roman civilization had been primarily political and men's interest had been concentrated on the fleeting life of this world. The universal Christian church stressed the religious

The Fourth and Fifth Centuries [13]

motive, and directed interest toward everlasting life in the next world.

The growth of the Christian commonwealth under the later Roman Empire, then, was largely a shift in attitude. Outwardly the principal modification in Roman imperial control was caused by the gradual infiltration of the barbarians from across the frontiers and their piecemeal absorption of provinces of the Empire which they converted into barbarian kingdoms. The Emperor Theodosius I (379-395) established the pattern by which the barbarian kingdoms were eventually set up. According to a usage already established, a group of Visigoths attacked by the Huns who were pouring into Russia had been allowed to cross the Danube as allies (*foederati*) and take refuge in the Empire. Cheated by Roman officials, they revolted, and won a great victory at Adrianople (378). Theodosius confirmed their status as *foederati,* conferred upon the barbarian leader (a king among his own people) the title of *patricius,* which characterized the Roman noble, and supplied him with funds to pay soldiers who were to be used for defensive purposes.

Groups of Franks and Burgundians had long since crossed the Rhine, into regions from which the inhabitants had fled because the local government did not provide them protection, and many barbarians were to be found far within the borders of the Empire. When Roman generals had fought and defeated Germanic tribes who made trouble at the frontiers, they settled their captives as *coloni* in places where agricultural labor was needed. *Coloni* were farm laborers who theoretically were freemen but actually were attached to the plots of land for which they paid rent in money, services, or produce. Retired soldiers, too, were entitled to become *coloni,* and many of these were Germanic tribesmen. They had been recruited in large numbers into the Roman armies, for military service had fallen into disrepute among the Romans, long accustomed to the more luxurious life of towns. Sons of Germanic chieftains, brought up as hostages in Roman cities, grew up to admire Roman customs, while Germanic ways affected Roman habits; blonde wigs were fashionable among the ladies, and the traditional loose toga of ancient Rome was modified. Flowing robes were increasingly left to the clergy, and despite prohibitory legislation the trousers of the barbarian came into vogue.

The traditional date of the fall of the Roman Empire has been the year 476 A.D., when there ceased to be a Roman emperor in the West. Some of the misconceptions about the events of the fourth and fifth centuries in the Roman Empire are due to a classic of historical literature, *The Decline and Fall of the Roman Empire,* written by Edward Gibbon, an English rationalist of the eighteenth century. It is generally agreed today that the Germanic invasions were not regarded by contemporaries as the calamities they appear to be in the pages of Gibbon, but that several centuries of peaceful penetration led the way toward amalgamation of the peoples. In fact it is a little misleading to say the Roman Empire fell at all. Since the time of Diocletian the Empire had been divided for administrative purposes into an eastern and a western branch, and Constantine had founded an eastern capital at Constantinople, on the site of the ancient Greek colony of Byzantium. Emperors at Constantinople continued until the fifteenth century. The church in the East recognized the emperor as its head, and was administered as a department of the state, a tradition later passed on to Russian tsars and Turkish sultans. In the West no resident emperor ruled after 476, nor was there an imperial capital, imperial citizenship, or centralized imperial administration. Politically, the Roman Empire in the West collapsed, but if it is regarded as a universal Christian community—and this it was by the late fifth century—there was no fall. That Christian community produced for itself a spiritual ruler in the pope, and preserved its essential unity through the Middle Ages.

The fourth and fifth centuries were, therefore, a great formative period in the growth of Christianity. Its institutional form became channeled and began to take on the characteristics that can be seen in the church today; and its doctrines also were being elaborated by the great theologians who have come to be known as the Fathers of the church. One of the most influential of these was St. Augustine, bishop of Hippo in North Africa, whose ideas are even today effective forces. As St. Augustine lived in the last half of the fourth century and the first three decades of the fifth, the events of that period may conveniently be recalled in connection with his career. He was a child in the days when the Emperor Julian tried to dam the current of Christian expansion in Roman society and revive paganism; he was in his twenties when the Visigoths were allowed to settle within the Empire, and his thinking was profoundly affected by the barbarian invasions of Italy and Africa which took place between 406 and 430, the year of his death.

Apollinaris Sidonius is a convenient, though far less eminent, figure to connect with the events of the latter part of the fifth century. A well-born citizen of Gaul, one of the most thoroughly Latinized provinces of the Roman empire, Sidonius illustrates the way of life of the fifth-century Roman noble. In his later years he was a bishop, burdened with the manifold duties and responsibilities of an ecclesiastical leader at a time when the church was a haven in the troubled world of the barbarian migrations. His letters are a vital source of information on the habits of the nobility, the bishops, and the barbarian leaders; the style in which they are written, a pompous effort to galvanize into life the language of an earlier age, shows the intellectual degradation of the period. Sidonius's serene disregard of all classes of society save his own underlines Professor Rostovzeff's idea that Rome declined because the benefits of her

ROMAN ALTAR IN BRITAIN

(From *A Student's History of England* by Samuel R. Gardiner, Longmans Green, London, 1897.)

civilization were not extended beyond the dominant class in the state.

At the end of the fifth century, though Constantine's successors ruled on in Constantinople and the East, in the West many barbarian kings wielded independent authority in former provinces of the Roman empire. Western Europe had entered on that long period of political decentralization known as the Middle Ages, when the universal church provided the only unity and served as the principal link with the past. True, the church rejected much of the scientific thought of the Greeks and Romans as dangerous to its intellectual domination, and theology ruled as queen of the sciences, but exiled heretics preserved much of the knowledge of the ancients. The universal church also came to the momentous decision that heresy must be stamped out, and, despite the lesson of its own early experience, left a fearful legacy of persecution. The prayers of the church, however, expressed hope for the end of wars and the establishment of universal justice on earth through the power of Christian faith. Christianity upheld the ideas that were necessary if a union of peoples were ever to be achieved: Christian charity, the equality of all men, the duty of citizens to be subject to government, and of government to give justice to all its citizens. The fifth century, in other words, saw the bringing together of Graeco-Roman civilization, the Germanic peoples, and the Christian church—the elements out of which modern civilization was to be fused.

CHAPTER 1

The World of St. Augustine
[354–430]

~~~~~~~~~~~~~~~~~~~~~~~~~~~~~~~~~~~~

ST. AUGUSTINE was a native of the African province of Numidia and spent his early years in a part of the Roman empire hardly touched by the ferment of barbarian migrations in northern Europe. His world was still the Roman world. From the African desert and the Persian Gulf to the Scottish border, the Rhine, and the Danube ran magnificent roads where public posting stations made travel easy and rapid for those able to afford it. Trade, in luxuries at least, still flourished in the regions bordering on the Mediterranean, whither the fabrics and spices of distant China and India were brought by stages to Constantinople or the Levantine ports or Alexandria and then were carried to Italy, to Gaul, and to Iberia. In each city a bishop, elected by the people to serve as the chief administrative officer of the church, guided his Christian flock, performed Christian rites, denounced heretics, and looked with disapproval at the smoke that rose from a dwindling number of pagan altars. Following a centuries-old custom, the populace of the city of Rome and other great towns of the Empire were kept docile in an authoritarian state through being pampered by food doles and huge public spectacles. Christianity ultimately banished the gladiatorial games, but in the vast circuses and theaters horse races were held, wild animals fought each other, and players enacted dance-pantomimes to the accompaniment of relatively primitive instruments of music and rhythm—the tibia, the syrinx, the lyre, cymbals, and heel-tapping.

The Roman world of St. Augustine was run for the benefit of a small dominant class of nobility who owned a great part of the land. They spent much of their time on their large estates, which were worked by slaves or peasants bound to the soil. In the towns lived a middle class which had once prospered through commercial enterprise and had enjoyed a wide degree of self-government. But in the mid fourth century, when the status of every individual in the Empire had become hereditary, those town dwellers who were eligible for municipal office (*curiales*) had been made responsible not only for city government but for the collection of the heavy taxes by which the imperial organization was supported. Crushed by their duties—their personal fortunes had to be used to meet deficits in tax collection—the *curiales* lost both wealth and initiative to nobles and imperial officials. Into this class of *curiales* Augustine was born, since his father was a minor official in Thagaste, a town in Algeria. Only by borrowing from a wealthy friend could the father afford to send his son to the famous schools at Carthage and give him the best education available. Augustine became familiar with the classic writers of ancient Rome—the prose of Cicero, whose thought influenced him throughout his life, the poetry of Vergil, the encyclopedic works of Varro—and in translation some of the writings of the Greek philosophers Plato and Aristotle. Since rhetoric was the most popular study of the age, Augustine became a teacher of rhetoric when his education was finished. He lectured to budding lawyers first in his native town, then in Carthage, later in Rome, and finally in Milan. There he came under the influence of Ambrose, the vigorous bishop of Milan who was not only furthering the work of the church by his learned and persuasive sermons but also demonstrating by his energetic administration that the church offered a possible remedy for an increasingly evident economic, social, and political decline in the western half of the Empire.

Of the several factors contributing to the decline of the Empire in the West, not the least was the administrative division which left the city of Rome in a peripheral rather than a central position. The eastern territory of the Empire extended to a line running roughly north and south through the Balkan Peninsula. Rome was therefore on the extreme edge of the western portion of the Empire, and the province of Gaul occupied a far more strategic position. Not only was Gaul centrally located, but the major problem of defense in the West was the Rhine frontier. The shift in the political and military center of gravity led to a gradual growth of provincial at the expense of imperial sovereignty in such provinces as Gaul. The symptoms of decline were not limited to the waning military prestige of the imperial office in the West; a slow disintegration of the administrative machinery set in as the wealthy and powerful noble families moved their residences from their town houses to great country estates. In this movement can be discerned the roots of later feudalism, for a personal relationship developed between the peasant cultivator bound to the soil and the wealthy resident owner whose political influence or wealth could secure him protection. In the law courts, where once the imperial Roman law had been free to all who wished to share its advantages, corruption was widespread by the end of the fourth century and influence or bribes were as important as a just cause in winning a decision.

The exodus of wealthy families also drained the resources of the cities, and contributed to the decline of trade, which was becoming more and more limited to local markets. Where once the great landed estates had been scientifically farmed to produce large cash crops which could be profitably marketed in the great cities that imported food on a large scale, the now resident owners began to shift toward production for self-sufficiency. In abandoning their luxurious but parasitic town life they no longer needed a constant flow of cash; far more important was a large number of dependents that could make a family almost a law unto itself on its estates. To fulfill the wants of the estates' inhabitants, production was more diversified, and many bulk products were removed from the trade lanes. The field was left to the Levantine merchants who increasingly dominated the luxury market.

While the towns and imperial administration declined, the church was growing wealthy. Constantine had encouraged the custom of giving grants of land to the church and favors to the clergy, and his successors followed suit. The clergy was established as a privileged class. Land was one of the principal fields of investment, and pious citizens who wished to aid the church and store up good deeds for themselves gave or bequeathed their land to the church. The administration of this property was in the hands of the higher clergy, and the bishop came to be a figure fully as important in the control of land and of the tenants or peasants bound to the soil who went with it, as any great lay lord. Bishops were not only the spiritual leaders of the Christian commonwealth but temporal leaders as well, since the bishop was a great landlord and protected a large number of dependents. Popular election of bishops helped to guarantee that only men of ability and integrity served as heads of the dioceses. However, since bishops were frequently chosen from great noble families because only they had experience in managing vast properties, there was often a marked similarity in outlook between the bishop and the lay lord. As bishops more and more took on the character of the most influential leaders in the diocese in temporal as well as spiritual affairs, there was a tendency for the position of the clergy to become more and more worldly.

The church was able to attract outstanding talent because the conditions of service competed very favorably with those of the imperial organization. Little security accompanied the high offices of the imperial service for much depended on personal whim and winning the favor of the emperor, to say nothing of the limited opportunity due to the contraction of the imperial administration in the latter fourth century. In the church, however, men had the advantage of life security and every possibility of quick promotion, since the church was a growing institution with a steadily expanding demand for personnel and with a mushrooming accumulation of wealth. Such conditions could attract a character so remarkable as Ambrose of Milan, who was a layman at the time of his episcopal election. A lawyer, Ambrose took a great interest in the problem of justice and set a potent precedent for the extension of ecclesiastical jurisdiction in civil affairs. Bishops had the prestige that enabled them to secure fair trials even in the most corrupt imperial courts; and by using his influence for the poor and the weak, the widow and the orphan, Ambrose set the example for a continuing church championship of the downtrodden. In part because of Ambrose the church developed a tradition of hospitality to strangers and sanctuary for the oppressed. After status had become fixed, an individual unknown in the community was suspected of being a fugitive from the law, but Ambrose offered him asylum, recognizing that he might also be a refugee from injustice.

The leading role of the church in temporal affairs was greatly enhanced by the invasions of the fifth century. About the year 400 the Gothic conqueror Alaric led his people over the vulnerable passes of the Julian Alps into northern Italy and ravaged the countryside. He was finally defeated and temporarily withdrew from the Italian peninsula, but the frightened imperial leaders paid a disastrous price for a brief respite. Because of the threat to Italy and to Rome itself troops were withdrawn from Britain and from the Rhine frontier in Gaul, and the way was opened for the invasions of Gaul which began in the year 406. Among the principal invaders were the Vandals, who pillaged their way through Gaul and into Spain, and eventually crossed over to Africa, where they established a Vandal kingdom. By opening Gaul to the barbarians the emperor had abandoned the role of imperial defender of the provinces, and the civilian population had to be armed for self-defense. The bishops frequently became the principal local protectors of the flocks, organizing military defense, elaborating the theory of a just war (i.e., against the pagan or heretical invaders), and, when the invaders had passed, devoting the great resources of the church to the problems of reconstruction.

As the barbarians began to absorb one after another of the Roman provinces of the West, they respected the church's property in most instances, and the resources of the church soon rivaled and then surpassed those of the emperor. Because of the comparatively small numbers involved in the migrations, the change brought about by the establishment of barbarian kingdoms was not extensive and was largely non-violent. (Approximately 80,000 Vandals crossed from Spain to Africa.) The church was the leading institution which the barbarians encountered and could not be destroyed easily because it was so universally established in the lives of citizens and it did not fall directly before military defeat, as did purely political institutions. Furthermore, the church was the only responsible organization which offered barbarian conquerors who wished to co-operate with it an alternative to rule by martial law. The former alliance between church and state was continued within the barbarian kingdoms, and the bishops remained a vital part of the society of western Europe. As spiritual leaders they comforted their flocks in the trials of the invasions, but they also represented material strength in the face of attack since their palaces offered refuge and their provisions helped prevent famine when the scourge had passed.

In his *Confessions,* one of the world's great autobiographies, St. Augustine related the steps by which he entered into the current of Christian activity. Not a Christian until he reached maturity, he went through periods of intense interest in many of the leading philosophical movements of his day. This inevitably influenced his articulation of Christian doctrine when he ultimately became a famous preacher and controversialist in the church. For many years before his conversion he was a Manichean, believing in the philosophical dualism that personified both the powers of evil and the powers of good and holding that the former controlled the body. This was also the belief of Mithraism, the oriental cult which the Emperor Aurelian had encouraged and which became widely popular before Christianity spread. Plato had believed in the warfare of soul and body; and St. Paul, in his first efforts to organize Christian doctrine, had accepted that idea, for he was Greek trained. The doctrines of Plato, however, had been transformed in the third century into the mystical philosophy of Neo-Platonism, which emphasized monotheism but taught that the nature of the one true god might be found in a variety of earthly revelations. Dissatisfied with the Manicheans, Augustine had turned to Neo-Platonism. Finally he came under the influence of Ambrose's preaching at Milan. Augustine was no stranger to Christianity, since his dearly loved mother was a Christian and his pagan father was finally converted, but only after much searching of soul did he decide to become a Christian himself.

The conversion of Augustine took place in the year 387 when he was thirty-three years old, four years before the Emperor Theodosius reversed the traditional Roman policy of toleration in religious worship and made Christianity virtually the state religion. Now Christians themselves had in the past been persecuted on political grounds, and Christianity owed much of its proselyting success to an astute policy of taking over festivals, usages, and shrines of rival faiths; nevertheless, when the step which Theodosius took in 391—probably under the influence of the powerful Ambrose—assured the church of supremacy, it turned energetically to the suppression of paganism. Thus Augustine became a Christian just when Christianity was engaged in an active program of controversy both with the survivals of paganism without the church and heresies within. Many of the practices which Christianity had adopted during its rise were called into question. In the earlier years a Christian art greatly influenced by the East had developed; churches built in Egypt and Syria had domes and barrel vaults and were decorated with mosaics; music and even dancing were used in the ritual.[1] It was still a moot question whether Christians should study pagan authors, though the Fathers of the church, scholars themselves, were inclined to approve, provided the authors were chosen with discretion. Augustine himself believed that "He that is a good and true Christian will understand that his Lord has spoken in whatsoever words he finds the truth." Shortly after his conversion he began a series of textbooks on the nine liberal arts that Varro had given as the pattern of Latin education: grammar, rhetoric, dialectic, arithmetic, geometry, astronomy, music, medicine, architecture. The plan remained unfinished, but the treatise on music, which has come down to us, shows remarkable technical knowledge and is our chief single source of information about early church music.

The church did not long permit a man of Augustine's erudition and intellectual capacity to avoid sharing in the responsibilities of church administration. He was ordained in 391 by the bishop of Hippo (the modern seaport of Bone, between Bizerte and Algiers), whom he succeeded as bishop five years later. Augustine was fixed for life in Hippo, since custom in Africa forbade the moving of bishops from one diocese to another, and he began the great period of writing and controversy which was to make him one of the greatest of the church Fathers. In the course of his pastoral duties he found time to produce a great body of doctrinal writing in which he dealt with such subjects as the nature of matter, the problem of evil, and the possibility of understanding God's plan for the universe. He developed authoritatively some of the ideas which had come into Christianity from Judaism, especially the guilt of the children of Adam and the necessity for atonement. Much of Augustine's writing was aimed at confuting heresies, and in the course of his arguments he was not always consistent. Men were later to find in his writings both the doctrine of predestination, by which God chooses in advance those who will be saved, and free will, by which He allows man himself to affect that momentous decision. Augustine also did not hesitate to invade the economic field, for he forbade the taking of interest and laid down the doctrine of the just price, thereby establishing principles which the church diligently promoted for many centuries. In his first years of controversy Augustine disapproved the

[1] The type of Christ which became permanent in Western art was established by the fourth century. See Plate I, Fig. 1.

use of force against heretics, but finding them stiff-necked and obstinate, he came to feel after much experience that the state might use compulsion against the few to save the people as a whole from error.

Augustine believed that history was the unrolling of God's plan and that the Roman empire represented only a moment in that plan. He expressed this idea in his most famous work, the *City of God,* written as a result of the events of the year 410. In that year Alaric and his Goths finally seized and sacked Rome. The cry arose that this judgment had come upon the Eternal City because it had deserted its ancient pagan gods—a notion which Augustine set out to disprove. To him the eternal city was a city not built by hands but a universal city of God, made up of all who served the Lord. The book fulfilled its purpose as an answer to the pagan argument, but its great significance came at a later period; as time went on the City of God came to be identified in the minds of the faithful with the organized Christian church. This conception for centuries governed the attitude of the church toward the state. Although the state was an institution divinely sanctioned for the correction of men's bodies, it partook of the sinful nature of man who created it, and could approach virtue only if it submitted to the guidance of the church.

Although he wrote and labored and preached in his diocese for more than thirty years, Augustine never lost the freshness of his youth; all his writings were charged with inexhaustible vitality. His reasoning was that of a mind grounded in ancient philosophy, and he transmitted to later ages the classical spirit infused with Christian ideas. He stands pre-eminent among the other great men who were

FOURTH CENTURY RELIEF FROM
CONSTANTINOPLE

(From *Les Arts de la Moyen Age* by Paul Lacroix. Paris, 1873. Courtesy of New York Public Library.)

his contemporaries: St. Jerome, the hermit and author of the standard Latin translation of the Bible (the Vulgate); St. Ambrose, the many-sided defender of the church; the Emperor Theodosius; the barbarian leader Alaric. When St. Augustine died in 430, during the siege of Hippo by the Vandals, his writings were a legacy which proved more influential in the ages that followed his than those of any of the other Fathers of the church.

CHAPTER 2

The World of Apollinaris Sidonius

[c. 431 – c. 488]

~~~~~~~~~~

APOLLINARIS SIDONIUS, a Gallo-Roman count, was born within a year or two of the death of St. Augustine. He played no important part in history, but his letters give the best account we have of the life of a Roman noble and a Christian bishop in the period when the authority of Rome broke down in the West and the Germanic peoples assumed control. He was a man of kindly and tolerant nature, with a host of friends, to whom he wrote accounts of his travels, his various luxurious homes, and the manners and appearance of the barbarian chieftains with whom he came in contact. Sidonius believed with all his heart in the Roman state, which for centuries had given peace and prosperity to the people within its borders. His title of count (*comes*) was apparently an honorary one, but the importance of his family is attested to by the fact that he served for a year as prefect of the city of Rome, responsible for the importation of doles of food for the populace, and that he was the son-in-law of an emperor. Sidonius had his town house in his native city of Lyons, in central Gaul, but lived by preference in one of his villas, with its library, baths, sunrooms and heated rooms, its provisions for hunting, hawking, and ball.[1] Esteemed by his friends as a poet, he wrote in the elaborate and stilted style of the age, and his poems contain many references to the new barbarian kingdoms as well as panegyrics for three emperors.

The emergence of these barbarian kingdoms was inevitable when the emperors, during the latter fourth century, began entrusting the

[1] For a representation of hunting on a late Roman estate, see Plate II, Fig. 3.

supreme military command to barbarians. The career of Alaric the Goth was the story of an ambitious barbarian whose hopes of an important command in the imperial service had been disappointed; his various campaigns in Italy were efforts to secure recognition. Stilicho the Vandal, commander of the imperial armies at the beginning of the fifth century, was faced by a shortage of troops to defend the frontiers, and in the hope of regaining Alaric's services, he temporized with Alaric instead of crushing him. The confusion of the years that followed Alaric's successful demonstration of independent action, when Rome itself was sacked, encouraged other barbarian groups to emulate the example of the Goths. The ability of the Emperor Theodosius, which had enabled him to keep some check on the disintegration of Roman administration in the West, did not appear in his successors. Until the region in which he lived was threatened, Sidonius himself apparently took with equanimity the establishment of barbarian kingdoms around him, for his letters scarcely indicate that he was conscious of the Empire's decline. By Sidonius' day a large proportion of the Germanic invaders had lived for generations within the empire, and had discontinued many of their old customs with their acceptance of the Christian faith and the standards of their Roman neighbors. On the other hand, the pictures he gives of barbarian chieftains do show some startling contrasts with the patrician behavior of himself and his friends.

The spread of barbarian influence was accelerated in the mid fifth century by the appearance of the Huns in western Europe. After driving the Visigoths into the eastern Empire in the fourth century, these Asiatic nomads had established themselves north of the Danube. In 434 Attila, an unprepossessing Hun of great ability, became their leader, spread his authority through what is now modern Austria, Hungary, Romania, and southern Russia, and even extorted tribute from the emperor at Constantinople. In 451, when Sidonius was about twenty, Attila swept into Gaul with an assortment of Huns and subject peoples. At that time a Visigothic kingdom, with Toulouse as its capital, occupied the south; a Burgundian kingdom lay in the Rhone valley; the Salian Franks were in the north, on the lower Rhine; and the Ripuarian Franks were on the middle Rhine. Between Frank and Visigoth lay the region still governed directly by the emperor. The imperial governor summoned the Salian Franks and the Burgundians, as *foederati*, to come to his aid, secured the Visigothic king as an ally, and thus brought about the defeat of the Huns in the battle of Chalons. The importance of this victory has been overestimated, but the Huns subsequently withdrew, invading Italy on their way eastward; and two years later, with the death of Attila (453), the Hunnish empire collapsed. A few bands of Huns remained along the lower Danube, but the fate of the rest is unknown. Probably more Huns were mingled with the Germans who settled within the Empire than has usually been recognized.

Sidonius was much impressed by these events and actually began a history of them, which he never completed as he was soon absorbed in politics. His prefecture in Rome, a dozen years after the death of Attila, marked the zenith of his political career, but his administrative talents found scope in the church when he was elected bishop of Clermont-Ferrand in Gaul. He took with great seriousness his manifold episcopal duties, which included hearing complaints, adjusting quarrels, administering justice both civil and ecclesiastical, helping to govern his city, managing the vast episcopal estates, and taking part in episcopal elections to insure that suitable candidates should be chosen.

The Germanic power was still spreading throughout the West. The Germanic peoples usually came into the Empire in confederations, and their kings were as a rule proud to receive the title of *patricius* and to exercise power as nominal delegates of the emperor. The invaders demanded a certain proportion of the land, usually two-thirds, and settled in the country, avoiding the cities. Authorities still differ on the extent to which life was continuous in the cities. In the country, however, they usually, if not invariably, avoided the Roman villas and had new dwellings built. They had an insufficient number of laborers and a certain amount of tillage came to be carried on by tenants who worked out their rents on the proprietor's land. The invaders had brought their heavy ploughs, without which extensive cultivation in northern Europe would have been impossible. They introduced new crops: rye, oats, and hops. They used butter where the Romans used olive oil; barrels and tubs instead of the skins and earthenware of the Romans. Other innovations, either Germanic or Asiatic, were the use of skis, of furs and of felt, and the stirrup, without which feudal cavalry could not have developed. The invaders were not at a stage of development which permitted

The World of Apollinaris Sidonius [29

them to profit by the technological skills of the Romans. Roads and bridges fell into disrepair; the great aqueducts which had supplied the cities with water were no longer in use. The one mechanical invention which the barbarians took over was the water-mill, which to some extent was used instead of the quern or hand mill for grinding grain.

The Germanic infiltration was not always peaceful; the year after the withdrawal of the Huns the Vandals, who had established their power in Algiers and had taken to piracy, crossed to Italy and sacked Rome. Their name, like that of the Goths, came to stand for the destruction of civilized values. The Roman garrisons had been withdrawn from Britain, and bands of Angles, Jutes, and Saxons from the Elbe region made incursions there. The legends of King Arthur echo the struggles of the Christianized Britons against these Germanic invaders. The Visigoths were increasing their holdings in Gaul; Sidonius, younger and more vigorous than was Augustine when the Vandals attacked Hippo, gave courage to the defenders of Clermont through several sieges of his episcopal city. When finally the Emperor ceded all Auvergne to the Visigoths, Sidonius secured from them permission to continue as bishop.

The variety of activities in which Sidonius engaged as a bishop, together with the fact that he continued in his office by sufferance of the barbarian rulers, suggests that the institutional organization of the church was still incomplete. The bishops were in practice independent, except for the recognition of political authorities. The process of subjecting all bishops to a single head of the church was accelerated in Sidonius's day by the need of preserving unity in the Christian commonwealth in the face of political disintegration. As long as there had been a universal imperial authority, the emperors could act to maintain unity; with the gradual elimination of the emperors' power in the West, the church there needed to develop its own head.

The problem of maintaining unity in the church was as old as its legal position in the Empire. In the time of Constantine Christians had been divided on the doctrine of the Trinity and the emperor had called the Christian leaders to the first general council of the church (at Nicea, in 325) in an effort to restore unity. At the council of Nicea the followers of Athanasius, one of the Fathers, asserted the equality of the persons of the Trinity (Father, Son, and

Holy Ghost), which the followers of Arius denied. The council declared Arianism a heresy and adopted the Nicene creed, which expressed the orthodox interpretation of Christian faith. Arianism was not extirpated; it enjoyed brief periods of orthodoxy under Arian emperors, and during one such period the Goths were converted. Christianity in the Arian form then spread from the Goths to most of the Germanic groups except the Franks, Angles, and Saxons. Since to the orthodox clergy an Arian heretic was worse than a pagan, the barbarian peoples had to be reconverted when they occupied the western Empire.

Other councils were called by succeeding emperors in the struggle against heresy. These assemblies established the orthodox creed, and also finally decided on the canonical books of the Christian Bible. Christianity, therefore, was well provided with fundamental texts, but disputes were constantly arising out of the interpretation of those texts, and the recognition of some supreme judicial authority for their settlement was vitally needed. The general councils, which represented the consensus of the whole church, seemed impracticable: the bishops were busy men and could hardly afford to spend half their time traveling to innumerable conciliar sessions. Furthermore, councils were assembled at times and places specified by the emperor, and this conceivably might at some time place the church under the power of the state in matters of faith and dogma.

In addition to the restrictions imposed by decrees of the general councils limitation of the independence of bishops developed from the precedents which attributed a special importance or special sanctity to certain bishoprics. The bishops of provincial capitals in the empire exercised a certain moral force over the other bishops in the province because of the importance of their dioceses. Some such authority was needed, as all recognized, if only to insure against irresponsibility in the selection or behavior of bishops. Other bishoprics enjoyed high prestige because of their antiquity. By the beginning of the fifth century the bishops of Rome, Alexandria, Antioch, and Constantinople generally enjoyed the highest respect, though a particularly able bishop in some other diocese (for example, Ambrose of Milan) might temporarily outshine one of them. So long as the bishops enjoyed wide autonomy heresy was difficult to check; the continued progress of Arianism in the fourth century after its condemnation by the council of Nicea was proof enough of that. Arian and orthodox bishops threw their flocks into confusion by excommunicating each other. A court of appeal continuously in session was needed, and in the absence of a church-wide body such as the council, disputes were often submitted to the bishop of Rome, or the patriarch—as the bishops of great towns in the East were usually called—of Alexandria, of Antioch, or of Constantinople.

By the fifth century it was clear that if the church were to preserve its unity as an institution it should have a sovereign head, since Arianism persisted and was being spread by the invaders. If the general council was not acceptable, and the emperor was undesirable because of the fear of lay dictation in spiritual matters, the choice was bound to fall on one of the great bishoprics. A struggle for supremacy ensued. In this struggle Rome had great advantages, for although Rome had lost her position as a political center of the Empire, she was still strategically centered in the Christian world. Furthermore, she was the only one of the four greatest bishoprics that was located in the western Empire, whereas the eastern Empire divided its support between three great patriarchs. There was also some precedent for regarding the Roman bishop as the primate of Christendom because of the traditions about the founding of the church in the capital by St. Peter. The bishops of Rome were always ready to press the Petrine argument, by which they stood as the residuary legatees of the power of Christ on earth. They quoted the scriptural text in which Christ says, "Thou art Peter, and upon this rock I will build my church . . . and I will give unto thee the keys of the kingdom of heaven" (Matthew xvi, 18-19). They took the lead in support of the Nicene Creed and orthodoxy, and more than once they were supported by emperors. The bishops of Rome regarded it as their duty, as successors of Peter, to assume the leadership of the church. Consequently they were very aggressive in asserting their sovereignty; they encouraged the submission of disputes to Rome as a supreme court of appeal, they undertook at the same time to interpret the decrees of general councils, and finally they pre-empted the right to depose bishops and veto episcopal elections.

By eliminating imperial authority in the West, the barbarian invasions materially assisted general recognition of the primacy of the bishops of Rome. Constantinople remained the eastern capital, a center of flourishing trade in a region almost unaffected by the forces which were bringing about the collapse of imperial power in the West, for the barbarians had never entered the city or closed the trade routes. In Italy, where the imperial army had become more and more an army of Germanic tribesmen as the fifth century progressed, the troops made and unmade emperors. In 476 a group of soldiers chose Odoacer, one of their number, as king, and he deposed the boy emperor Romulus Augustulus, who was himself a usurper. Odoacer granted the soldiers a third of the land of Italy, sent the imperial insignia to the emperor at Constantinople, and was allowed to govern Italy with the title of *patricius*. Although the importance of these events has been exaggerated by later writers who sought an exact date for the "fall of Rome," there was not another emperor in the West until the year 800. Lacking a universal political head, western Europe developed in its place solidarity under a single ecclesiastical head, the bishops of Rome—or as they came to be called by the Roman populace from a Latin word applied to bishops, *papa,* or pope.

Sidonius, Roman official and Christian bishop, was one of many noble Romans who, living in the most thoroughly Romanized province of the Empire, by his way of life demonstrated to the Germanic people around him the age's standards of civilized living, and the role of a Christian bishop. He represented the social and political importance of the landed proprietor and the official of the church, an importance which was to be carried over into the new society which was slowly evolving under new conditions. If Sidonius lived until 486 he knew that the heathen Franks in northern Gaul under their new king Clovis had conquered the last part of Gaul directly governed by a Roman official and had extended the Frankish kingdom to the Loire River. Thereafter the imperial Roman power existed in Constantinople alone. Since the election of emperors in the West had ceased, the Roman church, with the papacy at its head, remained the principal unifying force in a jumble of Germanic kingdoms.

[THE FOURTH AND FIFTH CENTURIES]

Readings

~~~~~~

St. Augustine

CONFESSIONS *

[These extracts show Augustine's insight into human psychology. For his remarkable portrait of his mother, his philosophy, his deep religious feeling, the *Confessions* should be read as a whole.]

Thou didst sometime fashion me. Thus there received me the comforts of woman's milk. . . . Afterwards I began to smile; first in sleep, then waking: for so it was told me of myself, and I believed it; for we see the like in other infants, though of myself I remember it not. Thus, little by little, I became conscious where I was; and to have a wish to express my wishes to those who could contend them, and I could not; for the wishes were within me and they without; nor could they by any sense of theirs enter within my spirit. So I flung about at random limbs and voice, making the few signs I could and such as I could, like, though in truth very little like, what I wished. And when I was not presently obeyed, (my wishes being hurtful or unintelligible,) then I was indignant with my elders for not submitting to me, with those owing me no service, for not serving me; and avenged myself on them by tears. Such have I learnt infants to be from observing them; and that I was myself such, they, all unconscious, have shewn me better than my nurses who knew it. . . . Next I was put to school to get learning, in which I (poor wretch) knew not what use there was; and yet, if idle in learning, I was beaten. For this was judged right by our forefathers; and many, passing the same course before us framed for us weary

* Taken from *Everyman's Library;* translated by E. B. Pusey (1838), following William Watts (1650), published by E. P. Dutton & Co., Inc., New York.

[33

paths through which we were fain to pass; multiplying toil and grief upon the sons of Adam. . . . And yet we sinned, in writing or reading or studying less than was exacted of us. For we wanted not, O Lord, memory or capacity, whereof Thy will gave enough for our age; but our sole delight was play; and for this we were punished by those who yet themselves were doing the like. But elder folks' idleness is called "business"; that of boys, being really the same, is punished by those elders; and none commiserates either boys or men. For will any of sound discretion approve of my being beaten as a boy because by playing at ball I made less progress in studies which I was to learn, only that as a man I might play more unbeseemingly? And what else did he who beat me? who, if worsted in some trifling discussion with his fellow-tutor, was more embittered and jealous than I when beaten at ball by a play-fellow?

[from Book I, sections vi, ix]

Theft is punished by Thy law, O Lord, and the law written in the hearts of men, which iniquity itself effaces not. For what thief will abide a thief? not even a rich thief, one stealing through want. Yet I lusted to thieve and did it, compelled by no hunger nor poverty but through a cloyedness of well-doing and a pamperedness of iniquity. For I stole that of which I had enough, and much better. Nor cared I to enjoy what I stole, but joyed in the theft and sin itself. A pear tree there was near our vineyard, laden with fruit, tempting neither for colour nor taste. To shake and rob this some lewd young fellows of us went, late one night, (having according to our pestilent custom prolonged our sports in the streets till then,) and took huge loads, not for our eating, but to fling to the very hogs, having only tasted them. . . . Fair were those pears, but not them did my wretched soul desire; for I had store of better, and those I gathered only that I might steal. For, when gathered, I flung them away, my only feast therein being my own sin, which I was pleased to enjoy. For if aught of those pears came within my mouth, what sweetened it was the sin. . . . alone, I had never committed that theft, wherein what I stole pleased me not, but that I stole; nor had it alone liked me to do it, nor had I done it. O friendship too unfriendly! thou incomprehensible inveigler of the soul, thou greediness to do mischief out of mirth and wantonness, thou thirst of others' loss, without lust of my own gain or revenge: but when it is said, "Let's go, let's do it," we are ashamed not to be shameless.

[from Book II, sections iv, vi, ix]

And what did it profit me, that scarce twenty years old, a book of Aristotle which they call the ten Predicaments, falling into my hands, (on whose very name I hung, as on something great and divine, so often as my rhetoric master of Carthage, and others accounted learned, mouthed it with cheeks bursting with pride,) I read and understood it unaided? . . . . And what did it profit me, that all the books I could procure of the so-called liberal arts I, the vile slave of vile affections, read by myself and understood? And I delighted in them but knew not whence came all that therein was true or certain. For I had my back to the light and my face to the things enlightened; whence my face, with which I discerned the things enlightened, itself was not enlightened. Whatever was written, either on rhetoric or logic, geometry, music, and arithmetic, by myself without much difficulty or any instructor, I understood, Thou knowest O Lord my God; because both quickness of understanding and acuteness in discerning is Thy gift: yet did I not thence sacrifice to Thee. . . .

[from Book IV, section xvi]

I joyed also that the old Scriptures of the Law and the Prophets were laid before me, not now to be perused with that eye to which before they seemed absurd, when I reviled Thy holy ones for so thinking, whereas indeed they thought not so: and with joy I heard Ambrose in his sermons to the people, oftentimes most diligently recommend this text for a rule, *The letter killeth but the Spirit giveth life;* whilst he drew aside the mystic veil, laying open spiritually what according to the letter seemed to teach something unsound; teaching herein nothing that offended me, though he taught what I knew not as yet whether it were true. For I kept my heart from assenting to any thing, fearing to fall headlong; but by hanging in suspense I was the worse killed. For I wished to be as assured of the things I saw not, as I was that seven and three are ten. . . . Then Thou, O Lord, little by little with most tender and most merciful hand, touching and composing my heart didst persuade me—considering what innumerable things I believed which I saw not, nor was present while they were done, as so many things in secular history, so many reports of places and of cities which I had not seen; so many of friends, so many of physicians, so many continually of other men, which unless we should believe, we should do nothing at all in this life; lastly, with how unshaken an assurance I believed of what parents I was born, which I could not know had

I not believed upon hearsay—considering all this, Thou didst persuade me that not they who believed Thy Books, (which Thou hast established in so great authority among almost all nations,) but they who believed them not, were to be blamed; . . .

[from Book VI, sections iv, v]

. . . For many of my years (some twelve) had now run out with me since my nineteenth, when, upon the reading of Cicero's Hortensius I was stirred to an earnest love of wisdom; and still I was deferring to reject mere earthly felicity, and give myself to search out that whereof not the finding only, but the very search, was to be preferred to the treasures and kingdoms of the world, though already found, and to the pleasures of the body, though spread around me at my will. But I wretched, most wretched, in the very commencement of my early youth had begged chastity of Thee, and said, "Give me chastity and continency, only not yet". . . .

[from Book VIII, sections vii, xii]

THE CITY OF GOD *

[These extracts from St. Augustine's most important work show his preoccupation with problems that are still unsolved: divisions between groups; war and peace; the advent of a better world.]

Difference of language, an impediment to human society. The miseries of the justest wars.

After the city, follows the whole world, wherein the third kind of human society is resident, the first being in the house, and the second in the city. Now the world is as a flood of waters, the greater, the more dangerous: and first of all difference of language divides man from man. For if two meet, who perchance light upon some accident craving their abiding together, and conference, if neither of them can understand the other, you may sooner make two brute beasts of two several kinds, sociable to one another than these two men. For when they would commune together, their tongues do not agree, which being so, all the other helps of nature are nothing: so that a man had rather be with his own dog, than with another man of a strange language. But the great western Babylon endeavours to

---

* Reprinted by permission of J. M. Dent and Sons, Ltd., from *Temple Classics*, one-volume edition, translated by John Healey.

communicate her language to all the lands she has subdued, to procure a fuller society, and a greater abundance of interpreters on both sides. It is true, but how many lives has this cost! and suppose that done, the worst is not past: for although she never wanted stranger nations against whom to lead her forces, yet this large extension of her empire procured greater wars than those, named civil and confederate wars, and these were they that troubled the souls of mankind both in their heat, with desire to see them extinct, and in their pacification, with fear to see them renewed. If I should stop to recite the massacres, and the extreme effects hereof, as I might (though I cannot do it as I should) the discourse would be infinite. Yea, but a wise man, say they, will wage none but just war. He will not! As if the very remembrance that himself is man, ought not to procure his greater sorrow in that he has cause of just war, and must needs wage them, which if they were not just, were not for him to deal in, so that a wise man should never have war: for it is the other men's wickedness that works his cause just that he ought to deplore, whether ever it produce wars or not: wherefore he that does but consider with compassion all those extremes of sorrow and bloodshed, must needs say that this is a mystery, but he that endures them without a sorrowful emotion, or thought thereof, is far more wretched to imagine he has the bliss of a god, when he has lost the natural feeling of a man.

[*from Book XV, chapter 7*]

That the bloodiest war's chief aim is peace: the desire of which is natural in man.

Who will not confess this with me, who marks man's affairs, and the general form of nature? For joy and peace are desired alike of all men. The warrior would but conquer: war's aim is nothing but glorious peace: what is victory but a suppression of resistants, which being done, peace follows? So that peace is war's purpose, the scope of all military discipline, and the limit at which all just contentions level. All men seek peace by war, but none seek war by peace. For they that perturb the peace they live in, do it not for hate of it, but to shew their power in alteration of it. They would not disannul it, but they would have it as they like; and though they break into seditions from the rest, yet must they hold a peaceful force with their fellows that are engaged with them, or else they shall never effect what they intend. Even the thieves themselves that molest all the world besides them, are at peace amongst themselves. . . . the very wild beasts (part of whose brutishness they place in him), do preserve a peace each with other in their kind, begetting, breeding, and living together amongst themselves, being otherwise the insociable births of the deserts: I speak not here of sheep, deer, pigeons, starlings or bees, but of lions, foxes, eagles, and owls. For what tiger is there that does not purr over her young ones, and fawn upon them in their tenderness? What kite is there, though he fly solitarily about for his prey, but will seek his female, build his nest, sit his eggs, feed his young, and assist his mate in her motherly duty, all that in him lies? Far stronger are the bands that bind man unto society, and peace with all that are peaceable: the worst men of all do fight for their fellows' quietness, and would (if it lay in their power) reduce all into a distinct form of state, drawn by themselves, whereof they would be the heads, which could never be, but by a coherence either through fear or love. For herein is perverse pride an imitator of the goodness of God, having equality of others with itself under Him, and laying a yoke of obedience upon its fellows, under itself, instead of Him: thus hates it the just peace of God, and builds an unjust one for itself. Yet can it not but love peace, for no vice however unnatural, can pull nature up by the roots. But he that can discern between good and bad, and between order and confusion, may soon distinguish the godly peace from the wicked. . . .

[*from Book XV, chapter 12*]

The grounds of the concord and discord between the cities of heaven and earth

. . . . The faithless, "worldly city" aims at earthly peace, and settles the self therein, only to have an uniformity of the citizens' wills in matters only pertaining to mortality. And the "Heavenly City," or rather that part thereof which is as yet a pilgrim on earth and lives by faith, uses this peace also: as it should, it leaves this mortal life, wherein such a peace is requisite, and therefore lives (while it is here on earth) as if it were in captivity, and having received the promise of redemption, and divers spiritual gifts as seals thereof, it willingly obeys such laws of the "temporal city" as order the things pertaining to the sustenance of this mortal life, to the end that both the cities might observe a peace in such things as are pertinent hereunto. . . . This "celestial society" while it is here on earth, increases itself out of all languages, never respecting the temporal laws that are made against so good and religious a practice; yet not breaking but observing their diversity in divers nations, all which do tend unto the preservation of earthly peace, if they oppose not the adoration of one only God. . . . This peace is that unto which the pilgrim in faith refers the other which he has here in his pilgrimage, and then lives he according to faith, when all that he does for the obtaining hereof is by himself referred unto God, and his neighbour withal, because being a citizen, he must not be all for himself, but sociable in his life and actions.

[*from Book XV, chapter 17*]

The peace of God's enemies, useful to the piety of His friends as long as their earthly pilgrimage lasts.

Wherefore, as the soul is the flesh's life, so is God the beatitude of man, as the Hebrew's holy writ affirms: "Blessed is the people whose God is the Lord;" wretched then are they that are strangers to that God, and yet have those a king of allowable peace, but that they shall not have for ever, because they used it not well when they had it. But that they should have it in this life is for our good also; because that during our commixture with Babylon, we ourselves make use of her peace, and faith does free the people of God at length out of her, yet so, as in the meantime we live as pilgrims in her. And therefore the apostle admonished the Church, to pray for the kings and potentates of that earthly city, adding this reason, "That we may lead a quiet life in all godliness and charity." And the prophet Jeremiah, foretelling the captivity of God's ancient people, commanding them (from the Lord) to go peaceably and patiently to Babylon, advised them also to pray, saying, "For in her peace shall be your peace," meaning that temporal peace which is common both to good and bad.

[*from Book XV, chapter 26*]

PLATE I

Fourth & Fifth Centuries

FIGURE 1. *Head of Christ, from a fourth century fresco in one of the Roman catacombs. The Roman Christian artist was brought up in the naturalistic tradition of Roman art, but he gradually developed, from the stylized Semitic art of Syria and Asia, features which increased the hieratic aspect of his representations of the figure. Consequently, while the technique of this painting is similar to that of the frescoes of Pompeii, the character of the impressive head with beard and flowing hair is not classical but Eastern. This type was to become the accepted one for representations of Christ.*

FIGURE 2. *Arch of Constantine, Rome. This is the most effective of the arches which Roman emperors erected to perpetuate the memory of their military achievements. Many of its sculptures are taken from other arches, but they are well integrated in the sumptuous decorations. The tripartite type of arch was to be revived during the so-called Carolingian Renaissance in the porch of the monastery at Lorsch. (See Plate VIII, Fig. 4.) The nineteenth century saw revivals of the triumphal arch, notably the Arc de Triomphe in Paris and the arch in Washington Square, New York.*

FIGURE 3. *Second century relief from the Arch of Titus, showing the realistic Roman method of recording historical events as a continuous process. This relief displays the sacred vessels that were taken from the Temple after the conquest of Jerusalem in 70 A.D. Some of the treasures, including the great candelabrum, were carried from Rome to Africa by the Vandals in 455, thence to Constantinople by Justinian's general Belisarius and finally returned to the Jews. (See extract from Procopius, p. 67.) Note the sense of forward movement which the sculptor secured by his use of planes.* [*Alinari photograph*]

PLATE II

Fourth & Fifth Centuries

FIGURE 1. *Pharaoh's feast.* This illustration is from a manuscript known as the Vienna Genesis, probably made in Asia Minor in the late fifth century after an earlier model. Thus it still reflects the naturalistic mode of late Roman art. Scriptural illustrations were treated as historical records, but contemporary costume was used and events were pictured as if continuous. Pharaoh's feast is represented as a Roman banquet such as Apollinaris Sidonius described in his letters. The guests recline and are entertained by players on musical instruments.

FIGURE 2. *Mosaic showing boar hunting, from a late Roman villa in North Africa.* The Romans were given to decorating the floors of their villas with mosaics. These mosaics frequently represented scenes from outdoor life, which for the Roman citizen of the leisure class was the same whether in Africa or in Gaul.

FIGURE 3. *Head from colossal statue of a Roman emperor, perhaps Valentinian I, found at Barletta in Apulia.* This is a fine example of late Roman portraiture which was influenced by Eastern tradition. The artist wished to increase the impressiveness of an imperial portrait by a strictly frontal pose. He directed the head stiffly forward; the eyes, looking straight ahead, were fixed on the indefinite distance. The carving is simple, details are suppressed, and only the essential features are blocked in.

FIGURE 4. *Reconstruction of the old St. Peter's Church in Rome.* This was the most important church in Christendom from the fourth century until the sixteenth, when it was torn down to make way for the present structure. This type of Christian church was probably derived from the Roman basilica, a rectangular building in which the Romans transacted business or held courts of law, but was modified to suit its new functions. The church was approached by a peristyle through which the worshipper entered the atrium or courtyard. Beyond this was the narthex, a wide porch, the farthest point to which the unbaptized were allowed to go. In the interior, the semicircular apse at the end where the judges had sat in the Roman basilica, now accommodated the altar of the Christian church. The churchgoer's eye was directed to the altar at the eastern end by the regular rhythm of the columns which supported the walls of the nave. Like the nave, the side aisle additions were covered by simple truss roofs. An even light was achieved by numerous windows. To provide additional room for the clergy a transept was erected at the eastern end, giving the building the shape of a cross.

Apollinaris Sidonius

LETTERS*

[The first letter pictures the life of Gallo-Roman nobles between 460 and 470 A.D. Sidonius, in his thirties, had received his title of count from one of the emperors whose panegyric he had written, and was living a country life, temporarily withdrawn from politics. His next entry into politics won him the prefectship of Rome. The second letter was written shortly before he was made bishop of Clermont-Ferrand. The barbarian prince he describes was probably a Frank, seen at Lyons on his way to marry a Burgundian princess. The verses were written in the year 478, after Sidonius's imprisonment by Euric, the Burgundian king. They were enclosed in a letter to a friend at Euric's court, and presumably aided in securing Euric's permission to return to his diocese.]

To his friend Domitius [461–7]

To your question why, having got as far as Nimes, I still leave your hospitality expectant, I reply by giving the reason for my delayed return. I will even dilate upon the causes of my dilatoriness, for I know that what I enjoy is your enjoyment too. The fact is, I have passed the most delightful time in the most beautiful country in the company of Tonantius Ferreolus and Apollinaris, the most charming hosts in the world. Their estates march together; their houses are not far apart; and the extent of intervening ground is just too far for a walk and just too short to make the ride worth while. The hills above the houses are under vines and olives; they might be Nysa and Aracynthus, famed in song. The view from one villa is over a wide flat country, that from the other over woodland; yet different though their situations are, the eye derives equal pleasure from both. But enough of sites; I have now to unfold the order of my entertainment. Sharp scouts were posted to look out for our return; and not only were the roads patrolled by men from each estate, but even winding short-cuts and sheep-tracks were under observation, to make it quite impossible for us to elude the friendly ambush. Into this of course we fell, no unwilling prisoners; and our captors instantly made us swear to dismiss every idea of continuing our journey until a whole week had elapsed. And so every morning began with a flattering rivalry between the two hosts, as to which

* Reprinted by permission of Oxford University Press, from *The Letters of Sidonius*, translated by O. M. Dalton.

of their kitchens should first smoke for the refreshment of their guest; nor, though I am personally related to one, and connected through my relatives with the other, could I manage by alternation to give them quite equal measure, since age and the dignity of prefectorian rank gave Ferreolus a prior right of invitation over and above his other claims. From the first moment we were hurried from one pleasure to another. Hardly had we entered the vestibule of either house when we saw two opposed pairs of partners in the ball-game repeating each other's movements as they turned in wheeling circles; in another place one heard the rattle of dice boxes and the shouts of the contending players; in yet another, were books in abundance ready to your hand; you might have imagined yourself among the shelves of some grammarian, or the tiers of the Athenaeum, or a bookseller's towering cases. They were so arranged that the devotional works were near the ladies' seats; where the master sat were those ennobled by the great style of Roman eloquence. The arrangement had this defect, that it separated certain books by certain authors in manner as near to each other as in matter they are far apart. Thus Augustine writes like Varro, and Horace like Prudentius; but you had to consult them on different sides of the room. Turranius Rufinus' interpretation of Adamantius Origen was eagerly examined by the readers of theology among us; according to our several points of view, we had different reasons to give for the censure of this Father by certain of the clergy as too trenchant a controversialist and best avoided by the prudent; but the translation is so literal and yet renders the spirit of the work so well, that neither Apuleius' version of Plato's *Phaedo,* nor Cicero's of the *Ctesiphon* of Demosthenes is more admirably adapted to the use and rule of our Latin tongue. While we were engaged in these discussions as fancy prompted each, appears an envoy from the cook to warn us that the moment of bodily refreshment is at hand. And in fact the fifth hour had just elapsed, proving that the man was punctual, had properly marked the advance of the hours upon the water-clock. The dinner was short, but abundant, served in the fashion affected in senatorial houses where inveterate usage prescribes numerous courses on very few dishes, though to afford variety, roast alternated with stew. Amusing and instructive anecdotes accompanied our potations; wit went with the one sort, and learning with the other. To be brief, we were entertained with decorum, refinement, and good cheer. After dinner, if we were at Vorocingus (the name of one estate) we walked over to our quarters and our own belongings. If at Prusianum, as the other is called, [the young] Tonantius and his brothers turned out of their beds for us because we could not be always dragging our gear about: they are surely the elect among the nobles of our own age. The siesta over, we took a short ride to sharpen our jaded appetites for supper. . . .

[*from Book II, letter ix*]

To his friend Domnicius [c. 470]

You take such pleasure in the sight of arms and those who wear them, that I can imagine your delight if you could have seen the young prince Sigismer on his way to the palace of his father-in-law in the guise of a bridegroom or suitor in all the pomp and bravery of the tribal fashion. His own steed with its caparisons, other steeds laden with flashing gems, paced before and after; but the conspicuous interest in the procession centred in the prince himself, as with a charming modesty he went afoot amid his bodyguard and footmen, in flame-red mantle, with much glint of ruddy gold, and gleam of snowy silken tunic, his fair hair, red cheeks and white skin according with the three hues of his equipment. But the chiefs and allies who bore him company were dread of aspect, even thus on peace intent. Their feet were laced in boots of bristly hide reaching to the heels; ankles and legs were exposed. They wore high tight tunics of varied color hardly descending to their bare knees, the sleeves covering only the upper arm. Green mantles they had with crimson borders; baldrics supported swords hung from their shoulders, and pressed on sides covered with cloaks of skin secured by brooches. No small part of their adornment consisted of their arms; in their hands they grasped barbed spears and missile axes; their left sides were guarded by shields, which flashed with tawny golden bosses and snowy silver borders, betraying at once their wealth and their good taste. Though the business in hand was wedlock, Mars was no whit less prominent in all this pomp than Venus. Why need I say more? Only your presence was wanting to the full enjoyment of so fine a spectacle. For when I saw that you had missed the things you love to see, I longed to have you with me in all the impatience of your longing soul. Farewell.

[*from Book IV, letter xx*]

. . . . Twice has the moon risen upon me prisoned here; and but once have I been received into the presence. For scant leisure has the King even for himself, since all the subjugated earth awaits his nod. We see in his courts the blue-eyed Saxon, lord of the seas, but a timid landsman here. The razor's keen blade, content no more to hold its usual course round the head's extremity, with clean strokes shearing to the skin, drives the margin of the hair back from his brow, till the head looks smaller and the visage longer. We see thee, aged Sygambrian warrior, the back of thy head shaven in sign of thy defeat; but now thou guidest the new-grown locks to the old neck again. Here strolls the Herulian with his glaucous cheeks, inhabitant of Ocean's furthest shore, and of one complexion with its weedy deeps. Here the Burgundian bends his seven feet of stature on suppliant knee, imploring peace. Here the Ostrogoth finds a powerful patron, and crushing the Hun beyond his border, triumphs at home only through his homage to this mighty patron. And here, O Roman, thou also seekest thy protection; if the Great Bear menaces commotion, and the Scythian hordes advance, the strong arm of Euric is invoked, that Garonne, drawing power from the Mars who loves his banks, may bring defence to the dwindled stream of Tiber. Here the Parthian Arsacid himself asks grace to hold, a tributary, his high hall of Susa. He perceives in the regions of the Bosphorus dread war arise with all its enginery, nor hopes that Persia, dismayed at the mere sound of conflict, shall avail to guard alone Euphrates' bank. He who boasts himself kin with stars and near allied to Phoebus, even he becomes a simple mortal, and descends to lowly supplication. . . .

[*from Book VIII, letter ix*]

BRONZE LAMP IN SHAPE OF BASILICA

(From *Storia dell 'arte,* Vol. 52, by P. R. Garrucci, 1879. Courtesy of New York Public Library.)

PART II

The Sixth Century

CHRONOLOGY

511 Death of Clovis; division of Frankish kingdom
527 Justinian becomes Emperor in East
529 Closing of Athenian schools; migration of pagan Greek philosophy to East
— Justinian's Code
— St. Benedict's Rule
— Monte Cassino founded
533 Justinian's Digest
537 Construction of St. Sophia in Constantinople
c. 565 Founding of Iona by St. Columba
568 Lombards in Italy, end of first great period of Germanic invasions
c. 570 Birth of the prophet Mohammed
590 Gregory the Great becomes Pope
597 Mission of St. Augustine to Britain

PART II

The Sixth Century

~~~~~~~~~~~~~~~~~~~~

DURING the sixth century a tremendous effort was made by emperors, barbarian rulers, popes, and other churchmen to stabilize society in the Christian world. There continued to be a considerable surface shifting of political rule in the West, a backwash perhaps of the great wave of barbarian invasions of the preceding century. Warring kingdoms of Angles and Saxons jockeyed for power in Britain, but Britons survived along the Irish Sea, in the mountains of Wales, and across the English Channel in Brittany. The southern shores of the Bay of Biscay were occupied by Sueves and Basques, but in the remainder of the Iberian peninsula and Gaul the Vandal, Gothic, Burgundian, and Frankish kings ruled. The conversion of the Frankish king Clovis to orthodox Christianity in the last decade of the fifth century earned him the wholehearted support of the Gallo-Roman clergy against his rivals, the Arian Visigoths, and Clovis was able to present his occupation of their kingdom in Aquitaine as a just war against heretics. Clerical support was similarly useful to Clovis's sons when they overthrew the Burgundian kingdom in the upper Rhine valley and extended Frankish rule to the upper Danube.

Beyond the Danube and the Elbe a new migratory group, the Slavs, had been moving into regions vacated by the Huns and those Germanic tribes who had moved westward. Originating in the forests and marshes between the Carpathian Mountains and the Pripet River, the Slavs developed a primitive agriculture in the upper Vistula and the upper Dnieper valleys, and some of them came into conflict with Germanic groups to the west, beginning a hostility between Slav and German which has become a historic tradition. The new pressure in central Europe created by this conflict and by

[47

the incursions of the Asiatic Avars was one of the factors which prompted the Lombards, a Germanic people, to cross the Alps into northern Italy (c. 570). The Lombards were the last great Germanic invaders of the Roman Empire.

The effects of Germanic invasions had been similar everywhere. Barbarian chieftains established themselves on the land of Roman proprietors, lived in rude comfort upon the labor of workers who became bound to the soil, and perpetuated the organization of late-Roman society in which the great landholders had been a dominant class. In general the methods of cultivation in use on the great Roman estates were continued, although the Germanic peoples kept their heavy ploughs, which had been developed for the heavier soils of the north. The Germanic chieftains bore less severely upon the slaves than Roman overseers had done, so that the slave class was gradually elevated in the social scale. Free labor, however, was correspondingly depressed, as the independent farmer found competition with the great estate impossible and surrendered first his land and then his liberty of movement to the powerful landlord in return for protection and security. Thus was produced the serf, neither slave nor free, a man who had the use of his small portion of soil but who was legally bound to it.

In their conquests Germanic kings took for themselves the former imperial lands and usually granted a part of them to followers, with the understanding that those so rewarded owed military service in return. The crown lands were immune from visitation by public officials, and since this immunity frequently accompanied grants made to subjects, many landowners were rulers as well as proprietors. This facilitated the substitution, in whole or in part, of Germanic law for Roman law in western Europe, and in many places codes were written down for use in the surviving Roman courts. These codes reveal that the Germanic peoples regarded law as something personal, varying with the position of the individual in society. In a culture that regards law as a personal matter, crime becomes not the concern of the society as a whole but an offense between the culprit and his victim. Owing to the dependence of primitive societies on the family unit, the relatives of the injured invariably adopted his cause and retaliated against the offender or his relatives, and the blood-feud resulted. As a device for doing away with the blood-feud the Germanic tribes developed the wergeld, which was the value of a man's life or limb, computed in money or goods and varying with his position in society. Every offense could then be compounded by payment of an appropriate fine to the injured or his heirs; guilt or innocence was determined by compurgation, some form of ordeal, or the judgment of battle. In compurgation the accused swore his innocence and produced supporters to swear they thought he was a man whose oath should be credited; the requisite number of oath-helpers varied with the social position of the accused. The ordeal was based on the assumption that God would intervene so that fire would not burn an innocent man nor water, that pure element, receive a guilty one.

Of the Germanic groups on the Continent only the Franks were to have a permanent or very extensive kingdom. They had never abandoned their early homes on the Rhine, and had expanded their power west and south. The Frankish king Clovis gave his officials the titles of duke and count, which had been used by the late Roman officials; the duties of the dukes were primarily military, of the counts judicial and administrative. Clovis endeavored to keep up the Roman system of taxation, but the sources upon which it had been based dwindled as the great imperial roads decayed and trade evaporated, towns shrank, and the large landowners were more and more isolated on their estates.

General diffusion of Germanic custom and law in the barbarian kingdoms of the West gave to western Europe a certain underlying coherence despite political disunity. At the same time certain aspects of the old Roman conception of universality were being preserved by the eastern Empire and by the Christian church. The Emperor Justinian (527–565) nearly succeeded for a time in his grand design of winning back the West and resurrecting the old Roman Empire. He made the Mediterranean once again a Roman lake, only to see his efforts defeated in the end by the ruinous cost of his conquests. Justinian's permanent contribution to European history, however, was his great work of codification of Roman law, in which he attempted to give final definition to the proper conduct of individuals as citizens in the state. The Justinian code, coming precisely at the period when Germanic law was spreading in the West and threatening to blot out the Roman practice, passed on to later ages one of the greatest contributions of Roman genius.

Justinian also contributed at least indirectly to the development of the papacy during the sixth century. When his plans for imperial conquest collapsed, he retained southern Italy; thus differences between southern and northern Italy, already in existence because of variations in soil and climate, were accentuated when the Lombard kingdom was established. Between the two powers the papacy had an opportunity to develop, and it was Pope Gregory I who dominated the latter half of the century as Justinian had the earlier. With Gregory I may be associated a certain change in outlook which developed in the West, based on the substitution of the miraculous for the rational as a dominant influence in men's thinking. Along with this changed outlook came a wide spread of the monastic life, which Gregory encouraged.

The earliest monastic life was originally an Eastern phenomenon. Very devout individuals adopted the practice of withdrawing from society to devote themselves wholly to the contemplation of God's greatness, and their own unworthiness, and to the renunciation of worldly pleasures for the purification of their souls. With the passing of persecution and the accompanying martyrdom in the West, monasticism became increasingly popular because it provided a substitute. The idea of suffering, in imitation of the founder of Christianity who suffered for all men, had a potent influence in the minds of many people; when Christians were no longer abused by their fellow men because of their faith, they could abuse themselves by accepting the ascetic life of a monk. Singly or in groups an increasing number of people deliberately set out to live the holiest possible life in this world as a preparation for the next. Women flocked to convents and men to monasteries. The conjunction in popular thinking between monks and miracles came in part from the reputation for sanctity acquired by many of the monks and the established traditions of unusual events associated with such holy men. St. Martin of Tours, a fourth-century monk, was celebrated alike for his asceticism and his ability to work miracles. Since there was no rule of behavior for monks, most of them were quite independent unless they joined some group which lived apart in a special monastic community.

By the sixth century monastic life had gradually undergone a shift from complete independence and extreme asceticism to obedience and moderation. The need for discipline and order among monks increased when the barbarian invasions encouraged people to seek the refuge of a holy life. An outstanding figure in the development of regularity in monastic practice was Honoratus, who organized a very successful monastery at Lerins in southern Gaul. He insisted that his monks become students and scholars as well as ascetics. Honoratus later became bishop of Arles, and his monastery was in some respects almost a school for bishops, since many of his monks were elected to episcopal office. More and more in the period of the barbarian invasions people looked upon the monastery as a place of security, and persons of wealth and scholarly tastes took refuge in the cloister. As monastic life was considered a holy life, there was a tendency to believe that God would take care of His own; there would be justice for monks as servants of God, even if miracles were necessary to effect it.

Codification of the rules governing monastic conduct was accomplished in the sixth century by St. Benedict of Nursia, whose early reputation was that of a holy man and a worker of miracles. The practice of leaving the world in order to seek God had become a sufficiently general impulse to warrant some universal attempt to regulate monastic life, and St. Benedict's "Holy Rule" may possibly have been written by papal request. There was certainly precedent for a code, since the Justinian Code was in preparation or completed when the Benedictine Rule was written; and a short time before, a learned churchman, Dionysius, had codified the work of the church councils and papal decrees. The Benedictine Rule drew from the contemporary codes and previous rules for individual monasteries, but St. Benedict's code was intended to be universally applied. Its general acceptance—it has been the basic rule for monastic life, though sometimes modified by later monastic orders—meant that by the end of the sixth century Christian Europe was provided with a definite set of principles to govern the behavior of men as citizens (Justinian Code), as clerics or bishops (Dionysian Code), and as monks (Benedictine Rule).

With the introduction of regular discipline into monastic life, the functions of monasteries began to take on a little of the worldly tinge that had already affected the church and the secular clergy. On the other hand, monasteries developed into major centers of learning and important repositories of the classics of ancient culture. They also acquired wealth by gift or bequest as had the early church, and they often profited by receiving the worldly goods of rich neophytes, since those entering upon monastic life took the vow of poverty. For a long time much of the personnel of monasteries was drawn from the middle and upper classes of society, which meant that lands, serfs, and even slaves fell under the control of monastic communities. Not a few abbots, as the heads of monasteries were called, dispensed quite as much wealth as bishops and exercised a comparable influence in society.

Gregory I encouraged the adoption of the Benedictine Rule and was influential in its dispersion over Europe, thereby contributing to the preservation of the learning and culture of which monasteries were the chief custodians for the next few centuries. Monastic learning, of course, had its limitations; where the thinking of St. Augustine and other Fathers of the church was grounded upon classical authors and followed rational lines even when dealing with mysteries, the thinking of the men of the sixth century proceeded from their confidence in the miraculous. Gregory I himself was an administrator rather than a scholar and drew his entire system of doctrine from the writings of St. Augustine; but since classical thought had not molded his mind, he distrusted its influence, and his writings stressed the fear of Hell rather than the contemplation

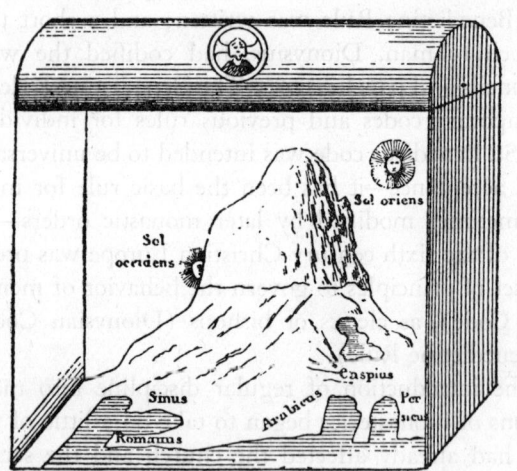

THE WORLD AS IMAGINED BY COSMAS INDI-
COPLEUSTES, A GREEK MONK

(From *Astronomical Myths* by J. F. Blake. London, 1877. Courtesy of New York Public Library.)

of God's grace. He preferred the allegorical to the literal interpretation of the Bible and had unbounded reverence for the miraculous powers of relics of the saints. The cult of saints and a liking for allegory as a literary form were persistent characteristics of the ages following Gregory I.

At the end of the sixth century Christian Europe displayed a growing solidarity and stability in its religious organization; patterns of Christian behavior were becoming more or less fixed according to the great codes. But the universality of the Christian commonwealth was limited to social, intellectual, or spiritual factors; the political universality of imperial Rome was still lacking—and still being sought. The eastern Empire had failed to reconquer the West and never threatened to do so again. No barbarian kingdom had yet succeeded in dominating the West. The papacy, with increased prestige at the end of the century, appeared to represent the greatest potential force in the West and, unless imperial power should be revived there, to stand on the threshold of a career in temporal as well as spiritual leadership.

CHAPTER 3

The World of Justinian

[483 – 565]

~~~~~~~~

WHILE the successful barbarian general, Odoacer, who had deposed the last Roman emperor in the West, was ruling in Italy, in Macedonia there was growing up a peasant boy who was to win fame as the Emperor Justinian. He became famous partly because he had a capacity for hard work and a dogged determination to be a great emperor, partly because he was well-served. Justinian was provided with an education through his uncle, Justin, a soldier who had risen high in the imperial service and had adopted him. When Justin became emperor at Constantinople Justinian developed into the power behind the throne and became emperor himself upon his uncle's death in 527. Behind Justinian's pleasant manner lay infirmity of will, cowardice, suspicion and superstition, but he was guided through the greater part of his reign by his wife Theodora, a woman of great talents, and as emperor he was the head of a splendidly working bureaucracy, and could command the services of experts.

During Justinian's youth the exploits of two men of action who possessed the qualities of courage and hardihood which he lacked drew his attention—Clovis the Frank and Theodoric the Ostrogoth, who were building strong independent kingdoms. It is not strange that when Justinian became emperor he longed to undo their work, but he was too cautious to attack the kingdom of the Franks, so distant from his own center of power and with its firm foundation on the clergy's approval. Clovis, who had made himself king of all the Franks by trickery and murder and had overthrown the Roman governor in Gaul, adopted orthodox Christianity and then marched against the Arian Visigoths. With the help of the Burgundian king, whom he had made a tributary, Clovis drove the Visigoths from Aquitaine and ruled a kingdom that extended from the Rhine to the Pyrenees. Making Paris the seat of his residence, Clovis gave a further demonstration of his piety by building a great church there. When he died in 511, the Frankish kingdom was weakened because it was divided—in accordance with Frankish custom—among his sons.

Meanwhile Theodoric the Ostrogoth had built up an important kingdom in Italy. As a youth Theodoric had lived as a hostage in Constantinople, where he had been enormously impressed by Roman customs and law and the distinctive culture which was beginning to flourish there, known as Byzantine from Byzantium, the ancient name of the eastern capital. In 489 he had invaded Italy with his army, having been promised the regency if he should succeed in conquering Odoacer. After Odoacer had been defeated and slain, Theodoric established an Ostrogothic kingdom, and his position in Italy was recognized by the emperor, who awarded him the title of *patricius*. Much in the policy of this Goth could be approved from Constantinople. Theodoric proceeded to make his capital, Ravenna, a city glorious after the Byzantine model. Like other Arian rulers, he was tolerant; he refused to have the orthodox persecuted, and halted attacks upon the Jews, saying: "We cannot enjoin religion, for no one can be forced to believe against his will." As Odoacer had done, Theodoric made use of the Roman administrative forms. In ways he could not foresee, his desire to preserve Graeco-Roman civilization was accomplished by three of his contemporaries, two of whom were in his service: Boethius, Cassiodorus, and Benedict of Nursia.

Boethius, who was Theodoric's Master of the Offices, had definite theories of education, which helped to carry over the use of some of the ancient classics into the medieval era. In the generation after St. Augustine an African scholar, Martianus Capella, had written an allegory called *The Marriage of Mercury and Philosophy,* in which he introduced seven of the original nine liberal arts, leaving out medicine and architecture (see p. 23). Seven they were to remain: Boethius called arithmetic, geometry, music, and astronomy the fourfold path to learning (*quadrivium*) and wrote treatises on the first three. These, with Capella's book and the grammars of Donatus and Priscian, became the basis of education in western

Europe, and it then became the fashion to call grammar, rhetoric, and dialectic the *trivium,* introductory to the *quadrivium.*

Boethius's ambition was to harmonize the ideas of Plato and Aristotle. He began by translating and commenting upon the *Logic* of Aristotle, deliberately using in his translation a flexible Latin which became the foundation of medieval Latin. Many generations of men who enjoy arguments have been fascinated by the problem of "universals" which Boethius raised: the question as to whether general ideas, such as "church" or "faith" have real existence or are merely convenient names. Boethius did not take sides on this question, but in his theological treatises he expressed the belief that it was possible, as the Greek philosophers had claimed, to arrive at truth by the use of reason. Toward the end of Theodoric's reign Boethius was thrown into prison on suspicion of treasonable correspondence with the Emperor Justin. He was condemned to death, and while awaiting execution wrote his famous *Consolation of Philosophy,* a book filled with the spirit of classical antiquity; it was destined to be one of the most popular books of the next twelve centuries, and was influential in the field of art as well as of thought.

Boethius's successor, Cassiodorus, wrote Theodoric's letters in an elaborate Latin style such as had been affected by Apollinaris Sidonius. When Cassiodorus retired from the royal service, he became a monk and founded a monastery where he gathered a great library. He set his monks to copying books, and gave himself to writing and teaching. He wrote a handbook of the seven liberal arts for use in the monastery school, a handbook which showed the influence of Boethius's treatises; and he lived out his very long life in devotion to classical literature, which he admired, and Christian literature, which he reverenced.

The services of these two noble Romans to learning were unwittingly supplemented by the work of another Roman of noble family, Benedict of Nursia, who was born among the Sabine Hills at about the time Clovis became king of the Franks and who was educated in Rome. Dissatisfied with what his biographer, Pope Gregory the Great, caller "ignorant learning," and appalled by the immorality about him, he decided to adopt the ascetic life. Beginning as a hermit, he practiced every form of bodily deprivation and torture he could devise. Then he became the head of a small community of monks, and finally he founded the monastery of Monte Cassino, on a hilltop midway between Rome and Naples, which through the centuries has been destroyed and rebuilt and destroyed again. The famous *Rule* Benedict framed has been the basis of monastic life from that day to this. Having personally experienced and observed the unfortunate physical and psychological results of extreme asceticism, he drew up his rule on the common-sense principle of moderation.

The Benedictine Rule was a regime suited to all sorts and conditions of men, and was adopted widely in monasteries and convents. Occasional fasting was prescribed, but wholesome food was the standard and work was esteemed a way of praising God. The monks elected one of their number to rule them for life as their abbot; his decisions were final, but before making them he was obliged to consult with the whole community in important matters, or with the senior monks in less important questions. Monks were not allowed to wander from one monastery to another, but were obliged to become permanent members of one community, and the details of their daily life were prescribed in the Rule. By retiring early, monks had usually enjoyed seven or eight hours of unbroken sleep before they arose at about two o'clock for the office of vigils, which included scripture reading as well as prayer and psalm-singing. After the office of matins at dawn and prime at sunrise came six to twelve hours of manual labor before they broke their fast at twelve or three. During the meals one of the brothers read aloud; afterwards came a period of rest and individual reading, followed by more labor until the evening meal. At dusk the day was closed by vespers and compline. Daily reading of the Scriptures and the Fathers was enjoined; and for this purpose every monastery came to have its library. Since books had to be made by hand, tablets and pens were distributed to each monk. It is not certain whether Cassiodorus used the Benedictine Rule in his monastery, but the copying of manuscripts which Cassiodorus favored came to be an accepted monastic activity, although it does not seem to have been a part of Benedict's plan. Because of such copying, treasures of ancient thought accumulated in monastery libraries, side by side with the works of the Fathers, to be read by monks of studious tastes and rediscovered by other men centuries later.

Justinian succeeded his uncle as emperor the year following the death of Theodoric (526). At that time the territory directly ruled from Constantinople included the eastern Balkans, Greece, Asia Minor, Syria, Armenia, Palestine, and Egypt; and although the emperor's subjects were for the most part Greeks, Egyptians, Armenians, Syrians, and Jews, the official language was still Latin. Indirectly the emperor still claimed to rule the West through the barbarian kings who, when they established their kingdoms, had accepted the title *patricius* from the emperors. Justinian believed that his duty was to turn his shadowy authority in the West into reality and to make orthodox Christianity supreme. He sent out armies under skilled commanders who overthrew the Vandal rulers of Africa and wrested part of Spain from the Visigoths.

In Italy, where Theodoric's successors were fighting each other, Justinian decided to intervene. The valley of the Po was ravaged by the barbarians who served as *foederati* in the imperial armies, Rome was taken and retaken, many Italian cities were reduced to ruins, and Italy was finally conquered—but only after twenty-five years of bitter struggle. The overthrow of the Ostrogothic kingdom was followed by the infiltration of Slavs and of Asiatic nomads into the Balkans, and, although Justinian's armies drove out some of them, the descendants of those who remained are there today. The Emperor also found it necessary to spend men and treasure in wars with Persia during the latter part of his reign. On Justinian's accession the Empire had been at war with Persia and Justinian had made peace. Justinian's aggression in Europe, however, made the Persian monarch fear that in time he too would be attacked; and in 540 he launched what would today be called a preventive war, which lasted with periods of truce until 562, when Justinian bought an expensive peace.

The enormous cost of these wars laid a heavy burden upon the finances of the Empire. A fortunate disclosure of the Chinese secret of the silk-worm led to a government monopoly which brought in great revenue, and the imperial capital remained a place of luxurious living. The splendid geographical location of Constantinople gave the Byzantine Empire an economic strength which enabled it to survive great shocks. Constantinople was, and is, at a great crossroads of trade routes. Justinian's policies for increasing the glory of the empire, however, created among the poor a discontent which was ready to break out when any favorable occasion appeared.

Politics in Constantinople was rent with the factional strife of

The World of Justinian

two parties whose rivalry was most openly expressed in the chariot races which they sponsored at the Hippodrome, center of social life for the capital. The parties took their names from the colors borne by their horses—Blues and Greens—and the Hippodrome was occasionally the scene of ugly riots staged by the rivals. Once Justinian enraged both factions, and a riot in the Hippodrome grew into a revolt so menacing that the emperor in a panic decided to flee for his life. Theodora saved his career by urging him to defend his throne to the death, reminding him: "Empire is a fair winding-sheet."

As emperor, Justinian was also the effective head of the Eastern church in matters of government and doctrine. It became tradition in the Byzantine Empire to administer the church as a branch of the state, a procedure which had far-reaching consequences when, centuries later, Byzantine missionaries converted the Slavs of eastern Europe. Justinian himself was shrewd in making use of missionaries for diplomatic purposes. Determined to stamp out heresy in his own dominions, he stirred up religious animosities among neighbor peoples to further his own plans, a kind of state craft too well known in that region before and since. After the death of Theodora, the emperor became more and more absorbed in religious matters. He had been deeply devoted to her and had associated her with himself as ruler, not merely as titular empress. The last seventeen years of Justinian's reign were far from glorious, since he neglected political affairs, and his subjects were both impatient for his demise and reluctant to face the possibility of civil war after his death. The worst disadvantage of the imperial system was the failure to solve the problem of peaceful succession.

In response to Justinian's pride in the imperial dignity which led him to encourage the arts, the city of Constantinople developed a unique culture which reflected the influence of the East, whence its power now derived. The great church of St. Sophia, in which the problem of crowning a square building with a round dome was successfully solved, remains the finest monument to the skill of Byzantine architects. All their buildings were decorated in the magnificent style which Byzantine artists had developed from Greek, Syrian, Coptic, Persian, and Mesopotamian originals. Byzantine mosaics were made with colored glass instead of bits of stone, so that Byzantine interiors blazed with color. Jewelers, sculptors, and workers in ivory produced masterpieces of elaborate workmanship. An impressive, hieratic character was given to Byzantine art by the fact that religious influence provided the underlying motif. Byzantine architecture, widely copied in the East, was not at once popular in the West; but Byzantine art, with its formal patterns and elaborate designs, later had a marked effect upon Western art. In the city of Ravenna, the seat of the imperial representative in the West, there are fine examples of the architectural style, evolved over several centuries, which was to become the standard type of the Christian church. Developed from the Roman law court (the basilica), this was a rectangular building with a semicircular projection at one end called an apse, with a roof supported by rows of pillars dividing the interior into a central nave, and with aisles on either side. The interiors of these Ravenna churches provided excellent examples of the sculptured architectural detail and mosaics of Justinian's day.[1]

The influence of Justinian upon letters was not beneficent. He closed the schools of Athens, where Greek philosophy was still taught on a pagan basis, and thenceforth learning in the East was expected to conform to Christian ideas. Educated persons continued to study the classics, however, and when, after Justinian died, Greek became the official language, Byzantine education and learning became predominantly Greek.

Justinian's name is chiefly memorable in the field of law. The Roman law had developed from primitive stages into a great system based on abstract principles, and was applicable to peoples in all stages of development. In the course of centuries of legislation the Roman law had become so complicated that its administration was almost impossible. Justinian had the statute law consolidated (*Codex Justinianus*), the commentaries and judicial opinions digested (*Digests* or *Pandects*), and a manual (*Institutes*) for law students approved; combined with Justinian's own legislation (*Novellae*) these form the famous *Corpus Juris,* the body of law. The superstructure of the greater part of modern European law has been built upon the foundation of the *Corpus Juris,* with its recognition of the principles that all men are equal before the law, and that the people are the ultimate source of power.

The world of Justinian was a world which, after the failure of his imperial plans, was finally broken into two parts. Clovis laid the

[1] See Plate V, Fig. 4.

foundation of power for the Franks, with whom lay the political future of the West, while Theodoric provided the soil in which Boethius and Cassiodorus sowed the seeds of ancient culture. Benedict of Nursia framed a pattern of Christian life into which could be fitted the preservation of learning. Justinian saved the Roman law and fostered a new culture, the Byzantine, which was to flourish for nearly a thousand years. In his endeavor to mend the breach between East and West, however, he destroyed the Ostrogothic kingdom in northern Italy and cleared the way for the Lombards. In the interim between the downfall of the Ostrogoths and the rise of the Lombards a field was provided for the extension of papal authority by one of the ablest of the popes, Gregory I, called the Great.

ST. SOPHIA

(From *L'Art Byzantin* by C. Bayet. 1883)

CHAPTER 4

The World of St. Gregory the Great

[c. 540–604]

~~~~~~~~~~~~~~~~~~~~~~~~~~~~~

POPE GREGORY I belonged to one of the great families of the city of Rome and grew up amid the sieges and devastation of Justinian's wars against the Ostrogoths. When his father died, Gregory was prefect of Rome, and shortly afterward he gave up his inheritance, turned the family home into a monastery, and lived there as a monk for several years. Then he was for six years a papal envoy to Constantinople, a valuable post of observation for a future administrator. Returning to Italy, he ruled his monastery as abbot until in 590 he was compelled, against his wishes, to accept election as pope. Paul the Deacon, historian of the Lombards, has left an account of a contemporary portrait of Gregory at the height of his power. It showed a stoutish man of medium height and good figure, with a large head and oval face, dark hair hanging down halfway over the ears, and two curls over the high, broad forehead, below which small yellow-brown eyes with full underlids were set under arching brows. Gregory had an aquiline nose, full red lips, a ruddy complexion, and a prominent chin somewhat sparsely covered by a tawny beard. His expression was mild, and he had exquisite hands, with long tapering fingers. By nature a man of great geniality and simplicity, he was a cheerful perpetrator of puns, approached practical problems in the mood of a modern man of business, and possessed remarkable administrative powers.

Although Gregory called himself "servant of the servants of God," he had a most exalted view of the papal office. The austerities he had practiced as a monk had ruined his health, and for the rest of his life he suffered from acute indigestion and other ailments, but he never allowed this fact to interfere with his constant activity. As the successor of St. Peter he considered himself the defender of the Roman populace, the supreme authority in the church, the director of Christian missions, the arbiter of faith and doctrine. In the first category he was called upon to defend Rome against the Lombards, who were among the fiercest of the Germanic invaders of the Empire. Justinian had at first admitted them and used their help to drive the Ostrogoths from Italy. In 568 the Lombards occupied the greater part of the valley of the Po, made Pavia their capital, spread south through Tuscany, and founded the great duchies of Spoleto and Benevento.

The effects of Lombard settlement followed lines that can be traced in the other Germanic kingdoms, except that as the Lombards were absorbed slowly into the population of northern Italy, the bishops who ruled the cities prevented the decay that had followed in the towns of the western kingdoms.

Through the diplomacy of Gregory the Lombards were kept from settling in the region about Rome, and the great pope also paved the way for their conversion to orthodoxy by acting as moderator between them and the Italian clergy. In Rome itself Gregory reorganized the municipal government, and carried on public works for which he paid from revenues of church lands. The custom of bequeathing land to the church as a means of saving one's soul had made all bishops landed proprietors, but the territories that had thus accrued to the papacy were especially extensive, and were scattered over all Italy, Sicily, Corsica, Africa, and Sardinia. Gregory developed a remarkable system of administration for these estates, known as the Patrimony of St. Peter, and from the sixth century onward they produced a great income.

In his role of supreme authority in the church, Gregory was notably successful in securing recognition of papal control, encouraging appeals to the Roman court (*curia*) from eastern as well as western churches. He also maintained a policy which ultimately led to the claim that monasteries were under the direct authority of the pope, rather than of local bishops. He reformed monasteries, introducing the Benedictine Rule where it did not obtain. As the rulers of Vandal Africa and Visigothic Spain gave up the Arian heresy, they were led to recognize the papal supremacy. With the

Franks, however, where Clovis had built up what was practically a national church, Gregory was obliged to exercise his influence indirectly through Clovis's successors.

Gregory's most famous achievement in his encouragement of missionary effort was in England. The Angles, Jutes, and Saxons had stamped out Christianity in Britain, but fleeing Christians had carried the faith into Ireland, and there St. Patrick in the fifth century introduced an independent, eastern type of monasticism which became very popular. The Irish monasteries which sprang up were centers of poetry, learning, and art; they became famous for the production of manuscripts illuminated in the richly ornamental style of the Celts. There was great missionary zeal among these monks: the Irish monk St. Columba migrated to the island of Iona, off the Scottish coast, and founded a monastery which became the center of Celtic Christianity; his disciples did a notable work of conversion in Scotland and northern England. Another Irish "dove," St. Columban, founded Luxeuil and other monasteries in the land of the Franks, and Bobbio in Italy.

Since southern England had remained heathen, Pope Gregory sent thither in 597 a group of monks who succeeded in converting the ruler of Kent, the kingdom nearest to the Continent. The residence of the king of Kent was Canterbury (from "Kentish burgh"); and as the successful mission was led by a second saintly Augustine he is known as St. Augustine of Canterbury to distinguish him from his greater predecessor. As a matter of course the Kentish church, unlike the missions in the north, recognized the papal supremacy. The story of Augustine's mission and the subsequent conversion of the other kings in England was charmingly told in the following century by the English monk Bede, in his *Ecclesiastical History of the English Nation*. Bede also tells the story of the *gesiths* (royal companions) who decided to murder their king when on his conversion he declared that henceforth he would love his enemies; naturally the only recourse for such a king was to forsake the world and enter a monastery.

Apparently more kings exchanged the crown for the cowl and the throne for the cell, in England than on the Continent, if we are to judge by Gregory of Tours' *History of the Franks*. This Gregory, who became bishop of Tours, provided in his *History* our great source for the study of life in Gaul during the last half of the sixth century. His native city was a place of pilgrimage because of the presence, just outside the walls, of a wonder-working shrine at the tomb of St. Martin, the celebrated fourth-century monk. Gregory relates that he himself was cured of a fever at the shrine. He came of a family of churchmen and was educated by one of them, his uncle, who as bishop of Clermont-Ferrand was a successor of Apollinaris Sidonius. Just as we have in Sidonius's letters our best picture of Gallo-Roman society in the latter half of the fifth century, so we have in Gregory's *History* the reflection of the same society a hundred years later, when the Franks had imposed their rule upon the Gallo-Romans, and the two elements were blending. The clergy, assiduous in their support of the orthodox Franks, greatly aided this blending; and the *History of the Franks,* in its stories of Clovis and his successors, reveals the complaisant attitude of the Christian prelate toward murder and other crimes committed by rulers who protected the church and duly partook of its sacraments.

The wonder-working tomb of St. Martin of Tours was characteristic of the emphasis on the miraculous in the sixth-century mind. From early days, conversions to Christianity had been facilitated by the fact that the church shared with heathen a belief in evil spirits, whose machinations could be set at naught by appropriate spells, incantations, and charms. Relics provided a satisfactory substitute for amulets, and miracles for magic. Churchmen fought the practice of magic without denying its validity; they emphasized the greater efficacy of miracles. Pope Gregory did yeoman service in this field, for the miraculous was his favorite subject and his writings are filled with accounts of miracles, related in the utmost detail. His biography of St. Benedict of Nursia showed the founder of the Benedictine rule to be a prodigious worker of miracles. The most famous story of the miraculous connected with Pope Gregory's career is that of the vision of an angel sheathing his sword above the Emperor Hadrian's tomb in Rome, which ever since has been called the Castle of St. Angelo. Apparently there was no story about angels or demons that Pope Gregory did not consider worthy of recording for the edification of the faithful, and he was equally assiduous in providing churches with relics of the saints. His zeal that the Scriptures should be works of edification led him to stress their allegorical interpretation. He made much of the terrors of Hell; yet at the same time—perhaps naturally, since he was a man of compassionate nature—he first among the Fathers of the church dilated at length upon Purgatory, that great intermediary realm between Heaven and Hell where souls not free of all sin are purged and sent to eternal bliss, while souls damned beyond redemption are consigned to everlasting punishment.

For reasons which are not exactly clear, Gregory's name has come to be associated with music through the "Gregorian Chant," the plain song, a blending of Greek and oriental elements which had long been in use in Christian ritual. Perhaps he realized its religious value and gave encouragement to the further development of a musical setting to reproduce the moods evoked by the steps in the sacrifice of the mass, the greatest miracle of the church. Perhaps also he did something to further the work of The Schola Cantorum, the famous school of music at Rome.

Although Pope Gregory I was a prolific writer, he was not a great scholar. His Latin style shows a great falling away from classical standards, and he feared the pagan influence of classical authors, counselling instead the study of the Fathers. He had an enormous admiration, unfortunately not always accompanied by understanding, for the ideas of St. Augustine. Gregory ranks with the Fathers, but his sobriquet "the Great" is due to his extension of papal authority over areas where it had not previously been recognized; he is regarded as the founder of papal supremacy throughout the West. The world of Gregory I was a world full of violence, but it was also a world in which all men took for granted that miracles might at any moment affect the course of their daily lives, and a world in which a great new missionary movement carried on by monks was bringing more kingdoms into the Christian fold by peaceful conquest. Christianity was to have need of these accessions, because in the next century there arose a new faith whose rivalry eventually threatened the conquest of Europe—the religion of Islam, taught by the prophet Mohammed.

[THE SIXTH CENTURY]

Readings

Procopius of Caesarea

[Procopius of Caesarea was the private secretary of Justinian's general Belisarius, and accompanied him on his campaigns. He also lived many years at Justinian's court. His *History of the Wars* is objective; the *Secret History* is so filled with venom against Justinian and Theodora that for the most part it cannot be taken seriously. Portions do, however, suggest authentic traits.]

HISTORY.OF.THE.WARS*

Belisarius, upon reaching Byzantium with Gelimer and the Vandals, was counted worthy to receive such honours, as in former times were assigned to those generals of the Romans who had won the greatest and most noteworthy victories. And a period of about six hundred years had now passed since anyone had attained these honours, except, indeed, Titus and Trajan, and such other emperors as had led armies against some barbarian nation and had been victorious. For he displayed the spoils and slaves from the war in the midst of the city and led a procession which the Romans call a "triumph," not, however, in the ancient manner, but going on foot from his own house to the hippodrome and then again from the barriers until he reached the place where the imperial throne is. And there was booty,—first of all, whatever articles are wont to be set apart for the royal service,—thrones of gold and carriages in which it is customary for a king's consort to ride, and much jewelry made of precious stones, and golden drinking cups, and all the other things which are useful for the royal table. And there was also silver weighing many thousands of talents and all the royal treasure amounting to an exceedingly great sum (for Gizeric had despoiled

* Reprinted by permission of Harvard University Press from Procopius, *History of the Wars* and *Secret History*, H. B. Dewing, editor (Loeb Classical Library).

the Palatium in Rome, as has been said in the preceding narrative), and among these were the treasures of the Jews, which Titus, the son of Vespasian, together with certain others, had brought to Rome after the capture of Jerusalem. And one of the Jews, seeing these things, approached one of those known to the emperor and said: "These treasures I think it inexpedient to carry into the palace in Byzantium. Indeed, it is not possible for them to be elsewhere than in the place where Solomon, the king of the Jews, formerly placed them. For it is because of these that Gizeric captured the palace of the Romans, and that now the Roman army has captured that of the Vandals." When this had been brought to the ears of the Emperor, he became afraid and quickly sent everything to the sanctuaries of the Christians in Jerusalem. And there were slaves in the triumph, among whom was Gelimer himself, wearing some sort of a purple garment upon his shoulders, and all his family, and as many of the Vandals as were very tall and fair of body. And when Gelimer reached the hippodrome and saw the emperor sitting upon a lofty seat and the people standing on either side and realized as he looked about in what an evil plight he was, he neither wept nor cried out, but ceased not saying over in the words of the Hebrew scripture: "Vanity of vanities, all is vanity." And when he came before the emperor's seat, they stripped off the purple garment, and compelled him to fall prone on the ground and do obeisance to the Emperor Justinian. This also Belisarius did, as being a suppliant of the emperor along with him. And the Emperor Justinian and the Empress Theodora presented the children of Ilderic and his offspring and all those of the family of the Emperor Valentinian with sufficient sums of money, and to Gelimer they gave lands not to be despised in Galatia and permitted him to live there together with his family. However, Gelimer was by no means enrolled among the patricians, since he was unwilling to change from the faith of Arius.

[*from Book IV, section 9*]

SECRET HISTORY: ANECDOTA*

... And while Justinian was such as I have described in respect to his character in general, he still shewed himself approachable and kindly to those who came in contact with him; and no man whatever had the experience of being excluded from access to him, but

* *Ibid.*

on the contrary he was never angry even with those who failed to observe decorum as to standing or speaking in his presence. However, he did not, on that account, blush before any of those destined to be ruined by him. Indeed he never allowed himself to shew anger, either, or exasperation, and thus to reveal his feelings to those who had given offence, but with gentle mien and with lowered brows and in a restrained voice he would give orders for the death of thousands of innocent men, for the dismantling of cities, and for the confiscation of all monies to the Treasury. And one would infer from this characteristic that he had the spirit of a lamb. Yet if any-one sought to intercede through prayers and supplications for those who had given offence and thus to gain for them forgiveness, then, "enraged and showing his teeth," he would seem to be ready to burst, so that no one of those who were supposed to be intimate with him had any hope after that of getting the desired pardon.

And while he seemed to have a firm belief as regards Christ, yet even this was for the ruin of his subjects. For he permitted the priests with comparative freedom to outrage their neighbours, and if they plundered the property of the people whose lands adjoined theirs, he would congratulate them, thinking that thus he was shewing reverence for the Deity. And in adjudicating such cases, he considered that he was acting in a pious manner if any man in the name of religion succeeded by his argument in seizing something that did not belong to him, and, having won the case, went his way. For he thought that justice consisted in the priests' prevailing over their antagonists. And he himself, upon acquiring by means which were entirely improper the estates of persons either living or deceased and immediately dedicating them to one of the Churches, would feel pride in this pretence of piety, his object, however, being that title in these estates should not revert to the injured owners. . . .

And he was not given to sleep, as a general thing, and he never filled himself to repletion with either food or drink, but he usually just touched the food with the tips of his fingers and went his way. For such matters seemed to him a kind of side-issue imposed upon him by Nature, for he often actually remained without food two days and nights, especially when the time before the festival called Easter led that way. For on that occasion he many times abstained from food for two days, as has been said, and insisted upon living on a little water and certain wild plants, and after sleeping perhaps

PLATE III

Sixth Century

FIGURE 1. *Mosaic portrait of Justinian from the Church of St. Apollinare Nuovo, Ravenna. This is undoubtedly a contemporary portrait, as is another, less benevolent in expression, in the central-type Church of St. Vitale, Ravenna, which also was built in Justinian's lifetime.*

[*Alinari photograph*]

FIGURE 2. *Interior of the Church of Hagia Sophia, or the Divine Wisdom, at Constantinople. The exterior is plain and simple; it was upon the interior that the architect concentrated his skill in decoration. The great feature of the church is the enormous central dome, which rests upon four great piers, yet appears to float because of the row of windows just below the dome. The light from the windows and the hundreds of lamps which illuminate the interior makes the mosaics and marble incrustations glitter so that the solidity of the walls seems dissolved and space appears to float mysteriously. Procopius wrote: "Whoever enters there to worship perceives at once that it is not by any human strength or skill, but by the favor of God, that this whole work has been perfected."*

FIGURE 3. *Mosaic from the Church of St. Vitale, Ravenna, showing the Empress Theodora with attendants. The dark and light bands on the garments of the men indicate that they are officials of the palace. A mosaic on the opposite wall respresents Justinian similarly attended. Presumably the two mosaics represent the emperor and empress offering gifts at the dedication ceremonies of the church. These mosaics use the Eastern design of figures in immobile poses with fixed stares. The principle of balance has given way to the principle of a patterned rhythm.*

PLATE IV

Sixth Century

FIGURE 1. *Byzantine ivory carving of the Nativity, from the so-called throne of Maximian. Maximian was Archbishop of Ravenna from 546 to 556. This archepiscopal throne, or* cathedra, *is covered with elaborate carvings on small plates. Large-scale sculpture in the round was disappearing, and ivory carving was the chief means of perpetuating the sculptural tradition. The fact that these carvings were from the nature of the material small and easily transportable facilitated the spread of the Byzantine style throughout Europe.*

FIGURE 2. *Resurrection of Lazarus, from a manuscript in Rossano Cathedral. This manuscript was produced in Asia Minor and, like the Theodora mosaic, shows how the hieratic nonrepresentational style of the Orient was carrying Christian art away from the naturalistic, three-dimensional Graeco-Roman tradition. The Lazarus scene is two-dimensional, with emphasis on the expressive quality of heads and hands which stand out as clear silhouettes against the purple-tinted background. The observer is transported to a world of unreality, where the resurrection of the dead becomes possible.*

FIGURE 3. *Silver plate from Cyprus, representing the arming of David by Saul. This is one of a set of plates in the Metropolitan Museum of Art which depict scenes from the life of David in a lively, realistic fashion, untouched by Eastern stylization. They are representations of historical scenes but the persons concerned are clothed in the costume of the artist's day. The armor is the armor of the sixth century Roman soldier. Note the convention of giving biblical personages haloes.*
[*Courtesy of the Metropolitan Museum of Art, New York*]

FIGURE 4. *Interior of the Church of St. Apollinare in Classe, Ravenna. This basilica follows the type of early Christian basilicas but the mosaic decoration has become more abstract. In the mosaics of the apse, St. Apollinare stands with raised hands below a jeweled cross at which three sheep are gazing. These sheep stand for the three disciples who accompanied Christ to the Mount of Olives. The scene represents the transfiguration. The twelve sheep below stand for the twelve apostles. Note the columns of the nave and the altar in the apse. The walls of the clerestory above the roofs of the aisles, pierced by windows, follow the plan of St. Peter's at Rome. (See Plate II, Fig. 4.) This was ultimately to become the standard form of the Christian church, but other forms were long popular.*

one hour he would spend the rest of the time walking about constantly. . . .

[*from Chapter XIII*]

Now for Justinian it was rather easy to manage everything, not only because of his easy-going disposition, but also because he rarely slept, as has been stated, and was the most accessible person in the world. For even men of low estate and altogether obscure had complete freedom, not merely to come before this tyrant, but also to converse with him and to enjoy confidential relations with him. The Empress, on the other hand, could not be approached even by one of the magistrates, except at the expense of much time and labour, but, actually, they all had to wait constantly upon her convenience with a servile kind of assiduity, waiting in a small and stuffy anteroom for an endless time. For it was a risk beyond bearing for any one of the officials to be absent. And they stood there constantly upon the tips of their toes, each one straining to hold his head higher than the persons next to him, in order that the eunuchs when they came out might see him. And some of them were summoned at last, after many days, and going in to her presence in great fear they very quickly departed, having simply done obeisance and having touched the instep of each of her feet with the tips of their lips. For there was no opportunity to speak or to make any request unless she bade them to do so. For the Government had sunk into a servile condition, having her as slave-instructor. Thus the Roman State was being ruined partly by the tyrant, who seemed too good-natured, and partly by Theodora, who was harsh and exceedingly difficult. For whereas in the good-nature of the one there was instability, in the difficult nature of the other there was a bar to action. . . .

[*from Chapter XV*]

And among the innovations of Justinian and Theodora in the administration of the Government there is also the following. In ancient times the Senate, as it came into the Emperor's presence, was accustomed to do obeisance in the following manner. Any man of patrician rank saluted him on the right breast. And the Emperor would kiss him on the head and then dismiss him; but all the rest first bent the right knee to the Emperor and then withdrew. The Empress, however, it was not at all customary to salute. But in the case of Justinian and Theodora, all the other members of the

Senate and those as well who held the rank of Patricians, whenever they entered into their presence, would prostrate themselves to the floor, flat on their faces, and holding their hands and feet stretched far out they would touch with their lips one foot of each before rising. For even Theodora was not disposed to forego this testimony to her dignity, she who acted as though the Roman Empire lay at her feet, but was by no means averse to receiving even the ambassadors of the Persians and of the other barbarians and to bestowing upon them presents of money, a thing which had never happened since the beginning of time. . . .

[from Chapter XXX]

Pope Gregory I

THE DIALOGUES*

[Gregory relates tales of miracles to his deacon, Peter, whose questions and comments adorn the tale and provide the author with opportunities to point the moral.]

Of Aequitius, abbat in the Province of Valeria, as related by Fortunatus, abbat of the monastery called Cicero's Bath

Among many examples of miraculous power, it is recorded that upon a certain day one of the nuns of the monastery, going into the garden, saw a lettuce that liked her, and forgetting to bless it before with the sign of the cross greedily did she eat it. Whereupon she was suddenly possessed with the devil, fell down to the ground, and was painfully tormented. Word in all haste was carried to Aequitius, desiring him quickly to visit the afflicted woman and to help her with his prayers. So soon as he came into the garden, the devil that was entered into her began, by her tongue as it were, to excuse himself, saying, What have I done? What have I done? I was sitting there upon the lettuce, and she came and did eat me. But the man of God in great zeal commanded him to depart, and

---

* From translation in the seventeenth century by an English Catholic, quoted by G. F. Browne, *King Alfred's Books*. By permission of The Macmillan Company, publishers.

not to tarry longer in the servant of Almighty God, and the devil straightway went out, not presuming any more to touch her.

[*from I–4*]

PASTORAL CARE*

[It is worth observing that in this work, which became the handbook of the clergy in dealing with their flocks, Gregory advises adapting the method to suit the group, and especially stresses the reconciling of the poor with their lot as far as possible.]

Men are to be admonished one way, in another way women. Men are to be taught more seriously and severely, women more lightly; that the men may aspire to a greater burden, and the women brought on by gentle treatment.

The young are to be taught in one way, in another way the old; because the young are more often made useful with zealous admonition, and the old with mild entreaties, as it is written in the law: "Rebuke not the old man, but entreat him as thy father."

The poor are to be admonished in one way, in another way the rich. The poor are to be consoled and cheered, lest they despair too much by reason of their hardships. . . .

CORRESPONDENCE †

[The first of these letters shows that image-worship was already an issue. The second shows St. Gregory's feeling which was the same as that of all the orthodox clergy about the Arian heresy; it also reflects his enthusiasm for relics. The tone of the letter of St. Columbanus, the founder of continental monasteries, is refreshingly independent. There is no better account extant of the Celtic Christian's position as to reckoning the date of Easter: adherence to the Greek tradition, fortified by the name of St. Jerome.]

To Serenus, Bishop of Marseilles

That we have been so long in sending a letter to your Fraternity attribute not to sluggishness, but to press of business. . . . Furthermore we notify to you that it has come to our ears that your Fra-

* Reprinted by permission of Oxford University Press from the translation of King Alfred's version of the *Pastoral Care* of Gregory into modern English by Henry Sweet.

† From *A Select Library of Nicene and Post-Nicene Fathers* (Second Series, Volume 13), translated by James Barmby.

ternity, seeing certain adorers of images, broke and threw down these same images in Churches. And we commend you indeed for your zeal against anything made with hands being an object of adoration; but we signify to you that you ought not to have broken these images. For pictorial representation is made use of in Churches for this reason; that such as are ignorant of letters may at least read by looking at the walls what they cannot read in books. Your Fraternity therefore should have both preserved the images and prohibited the people from adoration of them, to the end that both those who are ignorant of letters might have wherewith to gather a knowledge of the history, and that the people might by no means sin by adoration of a pictorial representation.

[*from Book IX, letter 105*]

To Recarred, King of the Visigoths (c. 598)

I cannot express in words, most excellent son, how much I am delighted with thy work and thy life. For on hearing of the power of a new miracle in our days, to wit that the whole nation of the Goths has through thy Excellency been brought over from the error of Arian heresy to the firmness of a right faith, one is disposed to exclaim with the prophet, *This is the change wrought by the right hand of the Most High* (*Ps. lxxvi. 11*). For whose breast, even though stony, would not, on hearing of so great a work, soften in praises of Almighty God and love of thy Excellency? As for me, I declare that it delights me often to tell these things that have been done through you to my sons who resort to me, and often together with them to admire. These things also for the most part stir me up against myself, in that I languish sluggish and unprofitable in listless ease, while kings are labouring in the gathering together of souls for the gains of the heavenly country. . . . Further, how gladly the blessed Peter, Prince of the Apostles, has accepted the gifts of your Excellency your very life witnesses evidently to all. For it is written, *The vows of the righteous are his delight* (*Prov. xv. 8*). For indeed in the judgment of Almighty God it is not what is given, but by whom it is given, that is regarded. . . .

The very government also of your kingdom in relation to your subjects ought to be tempered with moderation, lest power steal upon your mind. For a kingdom is ruled well when the glory of reigning does not dominate the disposition. Care also is to be taken that wrath creep not in, lest whatever is lawful to be done be done too hastily. For wrath, even when it prosecutes the faults of delinquents, ought not to go before the mind as a mistress, but attend as a handmaid behind the back of reason, that it may come to the front when bidden. For, if once it begins to have possession of the mind, it accounts as just what it does cruelly. For hence it is written, *The wrath of man worketh not the righteousness of God* (*Jam. 1, 20*). Hence again it is said, *Let every man be swift to hear, but slow to speak, and slow to wrath* (*Ib. 19*). However I doubt not that under the guidance of God you observe all these things. Still, now that an opportunity of admonition has arisen, I join myself furtively to your good deeds, so that what you do though not admonished you may not do alone, having an admonisher to boot. Now may Almighty God protect you in all your doings by the stretching out of His heavenly arm, and grant you prosperity in the present life, and after a course of many years eternal joys.

We have sent you a small key from the most sacred body of the blessed apostle Peter to convey his blessing, containing iron from his chains, that what had bound his neck for martyrdom may loose yours from all sins. We have given also to the bearer of these presents, to be offered to you, a cross in which there is some of the wood of the Lord's cross, and hairs of the blessed John the Baptist, from which you may ever have the succour of our Saviour through the intercession of His forerunner.

Moreover, we have sent to our most reverend brother and fellow-bishop Leander a pallium from the See of the blessed Apostle Peter, which we owe both to ancient custom, and to your character, and to his goodness and gravity. . . .

[*from Book IX, letter 122*]

St. Columbanus to Gregory

. . . . I am pleased to think, O holy pope, that it will seem to thee nothing extravagant to be interrogated about Easter, according to that canticle, *Ask thy father, and he will shew thee; thine elders and they will tell thee* (*Deut. xxxii, 7*). . . .

What, then, dost thou say concerning Easter on the 21st or 22nd day of the moon, which (with thy peace be it said) is proved by many calculators not to be Easter, but in truth a time of darkness? For it is not unknown, as I believe, to thy Efficiency, how Anatolius (a man of wonderful learning, as says Saint Hieronymus, extracts from whose writings Eusebius, bishop of Caesarea, inserted in his Ecclesiastical History, and Saint Hieronymus praised this same work about Easter in his catalogue) disputes with strong disapprobation about this age of the moon. . . .

Do not, I pray thee, in such a question trust to humility only or to gravity, which are often deceived. *Better* by far *is a living dog* in this problem *than a dead lion* (Eccles. ix, 4). For a living saint may correct what had not been corrected by another who came before him. For know thou that by our masters and the Irish ancients, who were philosophers and most wise computists in constructing calculations, Victorius was not received, but held rather worthy of ridicule or of excuse than as carrying authority. Wherefore to me, as a timid stranger rather than as a sciolist, afford the support of thy judgment, and disdain not to send us speedily the suffrage of thy Placability for assuaging this tempest which surrounds us; since, after so many authors whom I have read, I am not satisfied with that one sentence of those bishops who say only, *We ought not to keep the Passover with the Jews.* . . .

Let, then, thy Vigilence take thought that, in approving the faith of one of the two authors aforesaid who are mutually opposed to each other, there be no dissonance, when thou pronouncest thy opinion, between thee and Hieronymus, lest we should be on all sides in a strait, as to whether we should agree with thee or with him. Spare the weak in this matter, lest thou exhibit the scandal of diversity. For I frankly acknowledge to thee that any one who goes against the authority of Saint Hieronymus will be one to be repudiated as a heretic among the churches of the West: for they accommodate their faith in all respects unhesitatingly to him with regard to the divine Scriptures. But let this suffice with respect to Easter. . . .

I have read thy book containing the Pastoral Rule, short in style, lengthy in teaching, full of mysteries; and acknowledge it to be a work sweeter than honey to one that is in need. . . . It was for me to provoke, to interrogate, to request: it is for thee not to refuse what thou hast received freely, to put thy talent out to use, to give to him that asks the bread of doctrine, as Christ enjoins. Peace be to thee and thine; pardon my forwardness, blessed pope, in that I have written so boldly; and I pray thee in thy holy prayers to our common Lord to pray for me, a most vile sinner. I think it quite superfluous to commend to thee my people, whom the Saviour judges fit to be received, as walking in His name; and if, as I have heard from thy holy Candidus, thou shouldest be disposed to say in reply that things confirmed by ancient usage cannot be changed, error is manifestly ancient; but truth which reproves it is ever more ancient still.

[*from Book IX, letter 127*]

PART III

The Seventh Century

CHRONOLOGY

610–41 Reign of Heraclius I
615 Death of St. Columban, founder of Bobbio
622 Hegira; flight of Mohammed from Mecca to Medina
627 Conversion of Northumbria to Christianity
632 Death of Mohammed
634 Omar Caliph
636 Death of Isidore of Seville
642 Fall of Alexandria to Arabs
661 Beginning of Ommiad caliphate at Damascus
664 Synod of Whitby
678 Missions to Frisia

PART III

The Seventh Century

~~~~~~~~~~~~~~~~~~~~~~~~~~~~~~~~~~~~~~

THE large-scale Germanic migrations which ended in the sixth century had been set in motion by the nomad Huns. They were followed in the seventh by another nomad movement equally significant, that of the Arabs. Although the Germanic peoples abandoned their primitive faith for the religion of those whom they conquered, the conquering Arabs spread their new faith, Mohammedanism, which has ever since been one of the great religions of the world. They swept through Arabia, Syria, Persia, Egypt, and north Africa, reached the gates of Constantinople, and seized strategic islands in the Mediterranean. Their swift success was due to several factors; the new religion which served as inspiration for the conquests arose at a time when economic necessity was driving the Arabs toward expansion, and wars between the Byzantine and Persian empires had weakened both to such an extent that the only great powers in the East which might have checked the Arabs failed to do so.

Mohammedanism was based on Judaism and Christianity, and had a code of behavior excellently adapted to a nomadic people. The policy of the Mohammedan empire toward conquered peoples was equally well adapted to its society of traders: the conquered were generally allowed to retain their own religion, language, and customs if they wished, and trade followed conquest. Prosperity accompanied increasing trade, and a prosperous society could afford the luxury of polygamy and the increase of population that accompanied it. Conversion to the new religion, when not forcible, was encouraged by making non-Moslems subject to special taxation and regarding only Moslems as equal before the law. There were neither nobles nor clergy to dominate the lives of the poor. The Mohammedan faith, unlike other Oriental religions, did not teach a sense of guilt and the necessity for atonement, nor did it hold up an ascetic ideal.

While the Moslem empire was developing in Asia and north Africa, the Franks, aided by the Christian clergy, were preparing for leadership in European affairs. The Frankish system of dividing a kingdom among the rulers' heirs had led to the break-up of the empire built by Clovis. Reunited and redivided under his descendants, called Merovingians after an ancestor of Clovis, it was the scene of continual turmoil in which three fairly distinct kingdoms were prominent: Neustria in central and western Gaul, Austrasia along the Rhine, and Burgundy in the Rhone valley. When the rulers of these states were not fighting each other they were fighting their neighbors: the Bretons, descendants of those Britons who had fled to Brittany to escape the Angles and Saxons; the Basques, a pre-Celtic people from the Iberian peninsula; the Slavs, who had built up a temporary empire in central Europe with Bohemia as the core; and the Avars, Mongol horsemen from Asia who invariably defeated the Frankish foot-soldiers.

During the fratricidal conflicts of Clovis's successors Frankish society was taking on new forms that reflected a mingling of Germanic and Roman institutions. One of the Germanic customs which had been described by Tacitus was the *comitatus,* or war band, which consisted of a group of young men sworn to die if necessary to defend their leader. In times of peace these young warriors feasted at their leader's board, rode abroad with him, and generally added to his importance; in war he rewarded them with shares of booty and conquered land. This relationship had points of similarity with the Roman *patrocinium,* in which a small landholder, to gain the protection of a great noble, surrendered the ownership of his land, receiving it back *in precario.* This meant that the former smallholder still had the use of his land but paid rent for it. The new owner also expected his tenant's aid in defense, if needed, and thus he became more powerful. The church, too, adopted the custom of letting out land *in precario,* which reverted on the death of the tenant, frequently with additions due to the tenant's anxiety to save his soul. A similar relationship developed among the great landholders and their rulers, since those who served the king expected the grant of a benefice (*beneficium*), which might be land, a remunerative office, a privilege or exemption. (To obtain a benefice a man went through the ceremony of commendation, in which he declared himself the king's man, bound to give military service.) Because the kings ordinarily gave office and power to members of their household, their personal servants, the official who came to have the greatest influence was the mayor of the palace, who was originally the king's chief steward. This office tended to become hereditary and its possessor, like other nobles, a great landholder.

The unit of landholding was the villa, an estate which may or may not have been originally a Roman villa. Part of the land was kept as the domain (*demesne*) of the lord and was reserved for his subsistence, while the remainder was for that of his dependents. The lord's residence, or that of his steward, stood on the domain, and its arable part was cultivated by peasants whose labor was rent for the huts they occupied and the fields from which they wrung a meager livelihood. The lord usually maintained a mill, a wine press, and a forge, and there was a church or chapel to which the lord nominated a priest. Some of the tenants were artisans who made the few indispensable tools, and the villa was largely a self-sufficient economic unit. Traveling merchants and a few simple industries in the shrunken towns supplied what goods the villa could not, and products of the soil in excess of the villa's needs were sold or bartered in the nearest market town.

Some of the social changes taking place in the West were also in progress in the East, although the freeman was not entirely replaced by the serf; and towns and trade continued to flourish. The Emperor Heraclius recognized the military value of the peasants in his dominions and instituted a system of land grants to free peasants for which military service was due. As only the eldest son was obliged to be a soldier, the others tilled the land; this system gave back to the empire its old citizen army and made possible the survival of a free peasantry when in western Europe the peasants were becoming bound to the soil.

Certain ethnic changes in the character of the Balkan population also occurred in the seventh century. When Heraclius became emperor, the Slovenes, a branch of the Slavs who had moved into the empire in the sixth century, were living in Carniola and along the Adriatic coast as far as Greece. Because they menaced Constantinople, Heraclius invited two other Slavic groups, the Serbs and the Croats, who were living in the region of the Carpathians, to enter

The Seventh Century

the Balkan peninsula, and then settled them in such a way that they divided the Slovenes. Thus the Balkans became a Slav land, but occupied by disparate groups which in that rugged and mountainous country clung to their separate traditions. Later in the century came the Bulgars (a people akin to the Turks of central Asia), who mingled with the Slavs and accepted their language but preserved a few definite characteristics of their own.

The papal power underwent no very startling changes in the seventh century; no prelate of Gregory I's stature appeared. Northern England was brought into the circle of papal obedience when the king of Northumbria chose papal instead of Celtic Christianity

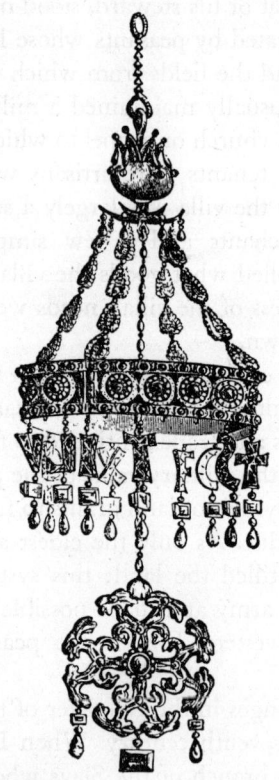

VOTIVE CROWN OF A SEVENTH CENTURY VISOGOTHIC KING

(From *Les Arts de la Moyen Age,* by Paul Lacroix. Paris, 1873. Courtesy of New York Public Library.)

at the Synod, or council, of Whitby in 664. Celtic Christianity, however, survived political defeat; throughout Europe classical culture was declining except in the Celtic churches in the British Isles and Celtic foundations on the Continent. In Celtic monasteries the classics were still studied, the rich art of the Celts was perpetuated in Britain, and in due time flowered in a magnificent style of manuscript illumination. Artistic activity was greatest where Celtic influences were felt, but considerable artistic skill was shown by the Franks in the use of niello work; buckles and other metal objects decorated in this way have survived.[1] In building, the Frankish kings sometimes employed capable builders; witness the Baptistery of St. John at Poitiers, which carried on the Roman tradition. The tradition for Moslem architecture was established by the domed Mosque of the Rock at Jerusalem built over the rock upon which the Temple of Solomon was thought to have been built.[2]

While unobtrusive but far-reaching social changes were taking place in Europe the more spectacular activities of the Arabs dominated the century, and the figure of Mohammed towers above that of any of his contemporaries. Under the Prophet and his immediate successors the religion of Islam was founded, propagated, and systematized. The basis for a powerful Moslem empire was established in the lands around the eastern and southern shores of the Mediterranean. At the end of the seventh century the wave of Mohammedan conquest was still rolling westward, ready to pour into the Iberian peninsula and Gaul in a colossal—and almost successful—effort to turn the flank of Christian Europe. This it was to be the destiny of the Franks to defeat.

[1] See Plate VI, Fig. 3.
[2] See Plate V, Figs. 3, 4.

CHAPTER 5

The World of Mohammed and the First Five Caliphs

[c. 570–682]

~~~~~~~~~~~~~~~~~~~~~~~~~~~~~~~~~~~~~

THE Arabian peninsula is a vast plateau region, about one-third the size of the United States, mainly desert and surrounded by mountains. Between the mountains and the sea is a narrow strip of coastal land, much of it very fertile. For centuries the peninsula had been a thoroughfare for peoples, mostly Semitic, who had eddied across the deserts and through the mountains. In the valleys of the Nile and Tigris-Euphrates these ancient peoples had built the civilizations upon which that of the Greeks was based. In Arabia itself civilizations had risen and fallen, but for a thousand years before Mohammed the land lay quiet. Those Arabs who settled in the coast and mountain regions built towns and traded; their nomadic brethren, the Bedouin Arabs, roamed the ageless desert, across which crawled caravans in the immemorial fashion of the East, laden with frankincense, spices, and rich goods.

By the sixth century the desert oases gave insufficient pasturage to the flocks of a people increasing in numbers, and there was growing unrest among them. The Bedouin Arabs of the seventh century were like the Bedouins of today; nomads with a fierce hatred of change, proud and independent, wise in the knowledge the desert-dweller needs, fond of poetry and story-telling, and with the fatalism bred of a natural environment in which man and his works fade into insignificance. Their unit of organization was the family, and next in importance to the family came the tribe. Climate and geography combined to make life a constant struggle, not only with the elements but with other tribes for the scant resources of the oases.

The temptation sometimes must have been very strong to plunder caravans or even to raid the coastal zone.

The most progressive region of the coastal zone was the district on the Red Sea known as the Hedjaz. Political organization in the cities of the Hedjaz had not progressed much beyond the tribal stage, but an important trade had developed in which goods came by ship from India and the Orient, to be carried inland to Mecca, whence the caravans started across the desert to Syria. Jews in large numbers had settled in the towns of the coastal zone, and there were some Christian merchants, but the more advanced religious views of these groups had little affected the paganism of the Arabs, except perhaps to pave the way for monotheism. The town of Mecca provided the chief unity in religion that existed among the Arabs because it possessed a famous shrine, containing a sacred stone called the Kaaba and other objects, and to this shrine Arabs made annual pilgrimages.

Mecca was the birthplace of the prophet Mohammed. Orphaned as a child, he grew up to travel with the caravans first in the employ of others, then as a merchant himself. It is reported that he was a kindly man, a dreamer, fond of children and animals. Even when he became a great leader he lived in the utmost simplicity, milking his goat and mending his own clothes. First as a traveling merchant, then as a man of leisure with a rich wife, he talked with Jews and Christians and became familiar with the contents of their Scriptures. He abandoned the fetish-worship of his people for a belief in one God who rewarded the righteous with paradise and cast the wicked into a burning hell. Eventually he came to the conclusion that God had chosen him to be a prophet, the successor of Moses and of Jesus. He gathered a band of followers, and since the Meccans in general reviled him he removed to the neighboring town of Medina. The traditional date of this removal, known as the Hegira (622 A.D.), marks the beginning of the new Moslem calendar.

At Medina Mohammed gave form to his new faith, which had the merit of great simplicity. He failed to convert the Jews but was successful with the rest of the population and with the Bedouins of the desert, to whom he gave an outlet for their restlessness by authorizing them to make war upon the caravans that came from Mecca. The attacks were justified on the ground that the Meccans had refused the true faith, and immediately brought on reprisals.

The war which ensued ended with Mohammed's triumphant return in 630 to Mecca, where he purged the shrine, incorporated certain of the traditional ceremonies into his faith, and allowed Mecca to remain a pilgrimage center.

Mohammed called his faith Islam, "submission to God," and his followers were called Moslems, "those who have submitted." The Moslem creed proclaimed "There is but one God, and Mohammed is his prophet," and the believer's religious duties were equally simple: prayer five times daily, alms-giving, fasting through the holy month of Ramadan, and if possible a pilgrimage to Mecca. It is noteworthy that the principal function of the church was judicial and administrative; it was not a necessary intermediary to assist the believer toward salvation, as in the Christian world, nor did it provide the social services of the Christian church. Mohammed retained the family as the basic cell of social organization, and held it responsible for all its members, with the important addition of alms-giving as a major duty of the faithful for the relief of the indigent. A Moslem was supposed to be honorable in his dealings, to protect the weak, to avoid strong drink, and to wash before praying. The emphasis on washing is a noteworthy characteristic in a code designed for a desert people. In a society with the family and tribal organization of the Arabs unattached females were inadmissible, and in view of the traditional chattel position of women among Eastern peoples the authorization of polygamy probably represented a step in advance—the Prophet permitted the believer as many as four wives.

Mohammedanism, like its rivals Judaism and Christianity, has its sacred writings, known as the Koran; this holy book expresses the will of God (whom the Arabs call Allah) revealed through the prophet Mohammed. The revelations were dictated by Mohammed following sudden trances or seizures (which perhaps were epileptic) to which he was subject and which rendered him unconscious. At least in his later years he seems to have been able to bring on his trances at will. The Koran is a difficult book to use, since the revelations, when collected, were simply arranged according to length, but it is often possible to distinguish the Prophet's earlier utterances by their clarity and directness. The later sayings, revealed when Mohammed was appealed to in times of crisis and obliged to produce an inspired judgment, bear unmistakable reference to definite situations. The Koran is not only the final authority for the theology of Islam, but also the fundamental source of social and legal practice in the Mohammedan world.

After the taking of Mecca most of the Arabs of the peninsula accepted the Moslem faith. Mohammed died in 632 and Abu Bekr, one of his earliest followers, was chosen his successor as caliph, or leader of the faithful. Abu Bekr assembled and arranged the revelations of the prophet, which had been taken down on palm leaves, stones, and bits of bone, as well as on papyrus and parchment. After this arrangement was made definitive by the next caliph, the Koran remained unchanged. Abu Bekr also proclaimed the Holy War, which became the fifth duty of every Moslem.

Abu Bekr's holy war fell at a propitious moment when the Persian and Byzantine empires were exhausted by a long series of wars. Justinian's successors had often been able to do little more than defend Constantinople against the attacks that stemmed from Slav and Avar settlements in the Balkans and the lower Danube valley. During Mohammed's lifetime, however, the Emperor Heraclius (610–641) was more aggressive. An emperor of great ability, Heraclius reformed taxation and military organization, instituted agricultural improvements, and endeavored to check the flow of lands into the control of the church. He repelled the Slavs and Avars on the north and also succeeded in driving the Persians from Syria and Egypt. These provinces had suffered much in changing hands repeatedly during the Byzantine-Persian wars, and there was great dissatisfaction with the tax system Heraclius developed. Justinian had once tried to stamp out heresy in Syria and Egypt, but it still flourished, and although Heraclius was less bigoted the compromise doctrine which he worked out with the aid of the patriarch of Constantinople was rejected. When the Moslems appeared, the inhabitants gave no aid to the imperial armies.

The caliph Abu Bekr who proclaimed the Holy War ruled only two years, but in those years he was able to unify the Arabs, so that his successor, Omar (634–644) could begin the war in earnest. Omar met with dazzling success; after conquering Syria and Armenia he overthrew the Persian king, then overran Egypt, and from these great stretches of conquered territory the Arabs easily recruited auxiliary forces for still further expansion. They also took to the sea, captured the island of Cyprus, and threatened Constantinople with their fleet. But under Othman, the third caliph (644–656), dissension arose and Islam was split into two sects, partly as a result of dissatisfaction over the favor Othman showed to his relatives, the Ommiad family. The rising Mohammedan empire had quickly outrun the situations foreseen in the Koran, and when it became necessary to find authority for new decisions not specifically provided in the divine revelation the leaders had recourse to the words and the deeds of the Prophet himself. These had been recorded by the members of his family and other close disciples, and made up the Sunna, which came to be considered authoritative when a problem could not be settled directly by the Koran. Differences arose in the interpretation of the Sunna, however, and these were brought to a head when Ali, the cousin and son-in-law of Mohammed, was elected to succeed Othman as caliph. The two sects which appeared in the Islamic world were the Sunnites, who accepted the validity of all the Sunna, and the Shiites, who took the narrower view that only those acts and words recorded by the Prophet's immediate family were to be accepted. The Sunnites triumphed, setting up the Ommiad Caliphate at Damascus in 661, and the Sunnite interpretation has remained the orthodox Mohammedan view, though the Shiites enjoyed occasional prominence in parts of the Moslem world. Under the first Ommiad caliph (661–680) Arab rule was spread westward to Algeria and eastward beyond the borders of India. The successors of Heraclius were able to defend Constantinople and hold the eastern gateway to Christian Europe, but beyond that they were helpless.

Meanwhile, the West could boast of little either in the way of imperial strength or cultural progress. The Merovingian monarchs of the Frankish kingdoms were supine and left the management of affairs to their palace mayors, who were regarded as the real leaders and the chief representatives of the great nobles or landholders. There was little enough royal administration in any case; kingdoms were the king's personal estate and managed like any other great noble's holdings. There was no regular system of taxation, since armies were provided by tenants who owed military service; the cost of justice was paid by the fines levied; and all local matters were handled by the nobles on their own estates. Count Pepin of Landen, the palace mayor of Austrasia, was the founder of a family which in the next century was to supplant the Merovingian line. Late in the seventh century his grandson, Pepin of Heristal, succeeded in defeating the palace mayor of Neustria and once more reunited the Frankish dominions. Pepin devoted much energy to weakening the power of the other great nobles but the task was difficult, for it was a period of rude manners and violent behavior in which the life of the nobility had little similarity to that of the generation of Apollinaris Sidonius. Learning was in abeyance, even in the church, for Gregory the Great had discouraged classical studies and taught that the devil and his minions were to be fought by miracle and exorcism rather than by reason. Only in the monasteries where the Irish tradition ruled and in Spain were the works of the pagan Greeks and Romans studied. The Visigothic conquerors of Spain, a comparatively small group, had been thoroughly Romanized, and their kings encouraged scholarship. Bishop Isidore of Seville, a man twenty years younger than Pope Gregory, produced in his *Etymologies* the only European work of learning the age could boast. Isidore intended it to be a compendium of human knowledge, and it became in fact the encyclopedia of the Middle Ages, but its value lay in the classical works that were embedded in it; the *Etymologies* themselves were childish guesses, taken from various authorities.

In England, as the missionaries of the Roman tradition progressed northward and those of the Celtic tradition progressed southward, conflict became inevitable. The followers of Augustine used the Roman system of reckoning Easter, while the Irish used a more ancient system; there were other minor differences.[1] The effectiveness of the basis upon which the doctrine of papal supremacy had been erected was demonstrated by the success of the Roman over the Celtic church at the Synod of Whitby (664). This synod was called because of a clash between Celtic and Roman Christianity in Northumbria, which had become the leading English kingdom, and after both sides had been heard, the king decided for Rome on the ground that the pope had the keys of Heaven. Thenceforth England was in the circle of activity that took prelates to and from Rome, linking the island with Continental movements, and the English kingdoms with each other. Some years after the Synod of Whitby the pope sent to England as archbishop of Canterbury a learned Greek, Theodore of Tarsus, who, aided by another scholar, the African monk Hadrian, organized the English church in the Roman tradition. They established a famous school at Canterbury, and

[1] See letter of St. Columban, p. 74.

Hadrian encouraged the founding of monasteries and the introduction of the Benedictine rule. Two Benedictine monasteries were founded at Wearmouth and Jarrow, near Durham, by a Northumbrian named Benedict Biscop, who stocked them with books which he brought from Italy. Since Celtic foundations such as Lindisfarne, on the North Sea, also continued to be centers of literary and artistic activity, the mingled Celtic and Roman tradition continued in England.

The world of Mohammed was a world in which the affairs of Europe played a minor part. True, the Synod of Whitby opened the way for the extension of Roman authority in England; in the land of the Franks the first steps were taken toward the establishment of a new ruling house; in eastern Europe the Byzantine emperors achieved the successful defense of Constantinople against all comers. But the light of learning and of culture burned low, kept from extinction only by the unheralded labor of unknown monks and a few noteworthy individuals such as Theodore of Tarsus and Isidore of Seville. It was the Arabs, aglow with the fire of a new faith, who brought forth the developments which were to be among the most significant for the future of Europe. The vast empire they established along the southern Mediterranean created a civilization which was to preserve for the modern world the Greek science and other learning of the ancients, neglected alike by the Christian church and the untutored Germanic kings and nobles in the West.

[THE SEVENTH CENTURY]

Readings

~~~~~~~~~~~~~~~~~~~~~~~~~~~~~~

The Koran *

[This arrangement of the Suras is supposed to be chronological. These are some of the earlier Suras containing fundamental ideas and practices.]

TITLE

In the Name of God, the Compassionate, the Merciful

Praise be to God, Lord of the worlds!
The compassionate, the merciful!
King on the day of reckoning!
Thee *only* do we worship, and to Thee do we cry for help.
Guide Thou us on the straight path.
The path of those to whom Thou has been gracious;—with whom thou art not angry, and who go not astray.

[from Sura 1]

THE INEVITABLE

In the Name of God, the Compassionate, the Merciful

When the day that must come shall have come suddenly,
None shall treat that sudden coming as a lie:
Day that shall abase! Day that shall exalt!
When the earth shall be shaken with a shock,
And the mountains shall be crumbled with a crumbling,
And shall become scattered dust,
And into three bands shall ye be divided:

---

*Taken from *Everyman's Library*; translated from the Arabic by J. M. Rodwell, published by E. P. Dutton & Co., Inc., New York.

[91

Then the people of the right hand—Oh! how happy shall be the people of the right hand!
And the people of the left hand—Oh! how wretched shall be the people of the left hand!
And they who were foremost *on earth*—the foremost still.
These are they who shall be brought nigh to God,
In gardens of delight;
A crowd of the former
And few of the latter generations;
On inwrought couches
Reclining on them face to face:
Aye-blooming youths go round about to them
With goblets and ewers and a cup of flowing wine;
Their brows ache not from it, nor fails the sense:
And with such fruits as shall please them best,
And with flesh of such birds, as they shall long for:
And theirs shall be the Houris, with large dark eyes, like pearls hidden in their shells,
In recompense of their labours past.
No vain discourse shall they hear therein, nor charge of sin,
But only the cry, "Peace! Peace!" . . .

But the people of the left hand—oh! how wretched shall be the people of the left hand!
Amid pestilential winds and in scalding water,
And in the shadow of a black smoke,
Not cool, and horrid to behold.
For they truly, ere this, were blessed with worldly goods,
But persisted in heinous sin,
And were wont to say,
"What! after we have died, and become dust and bones, shall we be raised?
And our fathers, the men of yore?"
Say: Aye, the former and the latter:
Gathered shall they all be for the time of a known day. . . .

[*from Sura 56*]

The Cow

. . . . There is no piety in turning your faces toward the east or the west, but he is pious who believeth in God, and the last day, and the angels, and the Scriptures, and the prophets; who for the love of God disburseth his wealth to his kindred, and to the orphans, and to the needy, and the wayfarer, and those who ask, and for ransoming; who observeth prayer, and payeth the legal alms, and who is of those who are faithful to their engagements when they have engaged in them, and patient under ills and hardships, and in time of trouble: these are they who are just, and these are they who fear the Lord.

.... They will ask thee concerning wine and games of chance. Say: In both is great sin, and advantage also, to men; but their sin is greater than their advantage. They will ask thee also what they shall bestow in alms:

Say: What ye can spare. Thus God sheweth you his signs that ye may ponder. ...

Let there be no compulsion in Religion. Now is the right way made distinct from error. Whoever therefore shall deny Thagout [1] and believe in God—he will have taken hold on a strong handle that shall not be broken: and God is He who Heareth, Knoweth.

God is the patron of believers: He shall bring them out of darkness into light:

As to those who believe not, their patrons are Thagout: they shall bring them out of light into darkness: they shall be given over to the fire: they shall abide therein for ever. ...

God will not burden any soul beyond its power. It shall enjoy the good which it hath acquired and shall bear the evil for the acquirement of which it laboured. O our Lord! punish us not if we forget, or fall into sin; O our Lord! and lay not on us a load like that which thou hast laid on those who have been before us; O our Lord! and lay not on us that for which we have not strength: but blot out our sins and forgive us, and have pity on us. Thou art our protector: give us victory therefore over the infidel nations.

[*from Sura 2*]

Women

In the Name of God, the Compassionate, the Merciful

.... Worship God, and join not aught with Him in worship. Be good to parents, and to kindred, and to orphans, and to the poor, and to a neighbour, whether kinsman or new-comer, and to a fellow traveller, and to the wayfarer, and to the slaves whom your right hands hold; verily, God loveth not the proud, the vain boaster,

[1] An idol.

Who are niggardly themselves, and bid others be niggards, and hide away what God of his bounty hath given them. We have made ready a shameful chastisement for the unbelievers,

And for those who bestow their substance in alms to be seen of men, and believe not in God and in the last day. Whoever hath Satan for his companion, an evil companion hath he! . . . .

[from Sura 4]

The Table

In the Name of God, the Compassionate, the Merciful

. . . . O Believers! when ye address yourselves to prayer, wash your faces, and your hands up to the elbow, and wipe your heads, and your feet to the ankles.

And if ye have become unclean, then purify yourselves. But if ye are sick, or on a journey, or if one of you come from the place of retirement, or if ye have touched women, and ye find no water, then take clean sand and rub your faces and your hands with it. God desireth not to lay a burden upon you, but he desireth to purify you, and He would fill up the measure of His favour upon you, that ye may ge grateful. . . .

Unto God belongeth the sovereignty of the Heavens and of the Earth, and of all that they contain; and He hath power over all things.

[from Sura 5]

PART IV

The Eighth Century

CHRONOLOGY

711 Mohammedans cross to Spain
725 Emperor Leo III provokes the iconoclastic controversy
731 Bede's *Ecclesiastical History of the English Nation* completed
732 Northernmost penetration of Mohammedans in France marked by victory of Charles Martel
750 Beginning of the Abassid caliphate
754 Pepin crowned king of Franks by pope
— Death of St. Boniface, organizer of the church in Germany
756 Spanish caliphate (Ommiad) founded
771 Charlemagne rules alone in the Frankish kingdom
772 Beginning of Charlemagne's campaigns against Saxons
774 Charlemagne destroys the Lombard kingdom in Italy
778 Incident of Roncesvalles during Charlemagne's withdrawal over the Pyrenees after intervention in Spain. Foundation for legends of the Song of Roland
786 Harun-al-Rashid Caliph
793 Sack of Lindisfarne by Northmen

PART IV

The Eighth Century

THE spectacular rise of the Mohammedan empire in the seventh century continued into the eighth with scarcely diminished momentum, until the Moslem power far surpassed in extent the territorial conquests of Rome. Aided by Berber auxiliaries from the recently conquered north African provinces, the Arabs crossed the Strait of Gibraltar into Spain, overthrew the Visigothic kingdom to set up their own government with Cordova as a capital, then crossed the Pyrenees and laid Gaul waste as far as the Loire River. At the other extreme of their vast empire the Arabs penetrated India and occupied the greater part of the valley of the Indus. They even reached the borders of China, and established control over the important trade routes by which oriental silks were carried into Europe.

The Arabs were an adaptable people, borrowing what appealed to them from the cultures of the peoples they conquered. In return the Arabs contributed their own genius for mathematics, their amazingly flexible language, and highly personalized social structure, to build up a new civilization known as Saracen, from which the western world was to borrow in its turn. The Mohammedan conquerors of the Iberian peninsula made Spain a garden spot by improving the irrigation methods introduced by the Romans, planting orchards and gardens, and raising rice and sugar cane. The Berber auxiliaries who had aided the conquest settled in the mountain regions, where they raised cattle and planted olive groves. In the East the Arabs received a great stimulus from the new ideas with which they came into contact. In the eighth century the Chinese had brought their art to perhaps its most lovely development, were perfecting block printing, and were making advances in the study of mathematics

[97

and astronomy. Greek writings had been carried to Persia in the fifth century by Nestorian Christians driven from Constantinople as heretics. These Christian heretics in Persia frequented a learned academy where they met Persian, Indian, and Syrian scholars; and, when Justinian closed the schools of Athens, they were joined by other refugees skilled in Greek learning. When the Moslems conquered Persia they gave full encouragement to this academy; and stimulated by Chinese, Indian, and Greek survivals in Persia, Moslem science developed rapidly in the latter eighth century until Bagdad became a great scientific center. Moslem artisans learned from captured Chinese workmen the art of making paper, their potters revived the ancient Persian mode of glazing pottery, their architects developed new architectural forms from existing foundations, and the Saracen civilization flourished as one of the world's great cultures.

That the Moslem empire and the Saracen civilization did not become established, even temporarily, north of the Pyrenees was due to the new vigor displayed by the Franks in the eighth century. In a battle at Tours, fought just one hundred years after the death of Mohammed, the Moslems were defeated and soon compelled to withdraw to Spain. The leader of the victorious Franks was the famous Charles Martel (Charles the Hammer), illegitimate son of Pepin of Heristal but mayor of the palace in the Frankish kingdom by right of conquest. His descendants were the Carolingian family, under whom was created a Frankish empire which made possible, at the end of the century, the revival of the imperial title in the West. The Carolingian empire represented the final fusion of the Germanic, Roman, and Christian traditions which were the basic elements of medieval civilization.

The vitality of the Roman tradition was evident from its survival despite the obliteration of imperial power in the West by the Germanic kingdoms. For a long time the barbarian kings ruled as kings *de facto* with a gnawing consciousness that they were not fully kings *de jure*. This was to a certain extent overcome by the granting of the title *patricius* from the emperors at Constantinople and by the recognition which the orthodox clergy gave to Clovis and his successors among the Franks. The Roman tradition was also traceable in the persistent division of the Frankish kingdom into two segments no matter how often it was reunited. Central Gaul had a Gallo-Roman population and language, to which the Franks were

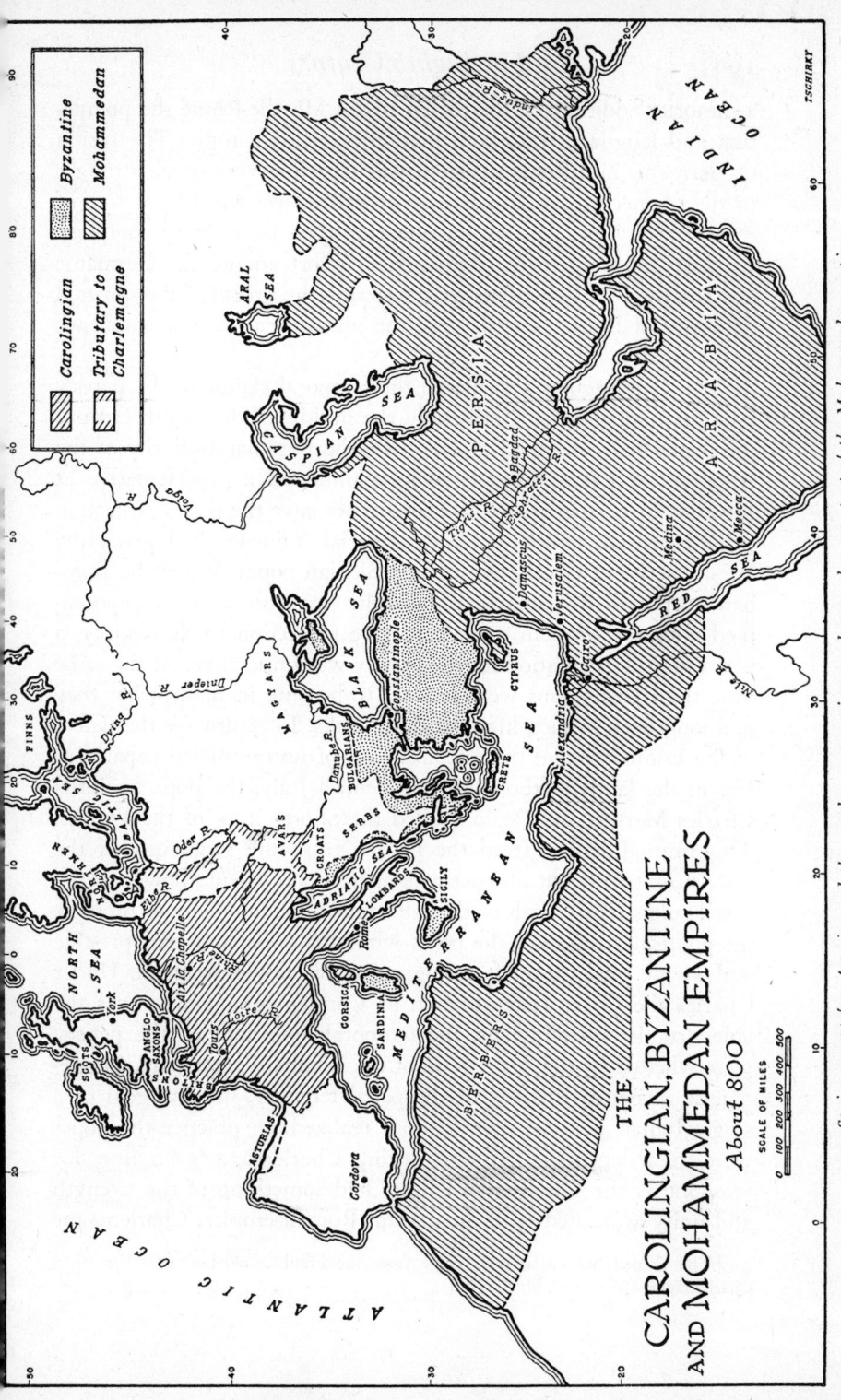

a minority addition. In the region of the Moselle-Rhine the population and language were both predominantly Teutonic. The fusion of Germanic and Roman custom was therefore very much stronger in the former region and had to be carried eastward by a sort of reverse migration, first by missionaries, then by military conquest. By their encouragement of missionary effort among the Germanic heathen the Frankish rulers were fostering the spread of the spiritual authority of Rome as well, since the missionaries taught obedience to the papacy.

The Carolingians also placed the temporal claims of the papacy on a permanent basis. Until about the middle of the eighth century the popes had continued to recognize the nominal authority of the emperors at Constantinople, who maintained a representative at Ravenna in northern Italy and sometimes gave the popes protection from barbarian attacks. Indeed, imperial influence had given the West a series of Greek, Syrian, and Sicilian popes. When the Lombards captured Ravenna (751), and the emperors were too preoccupied with the Moslem menace to give protection to the papacy, a new political orientation for the papacy was imperative. At the same time the Carolingians were seeking to become in name what they had long been in fact, kings of the Franks. In return for the defeat of the Lombards and the establishment of untrammeled papal control in the lands of the church in central Italy, the pope anointed Charles Martel's son Pepin (called the Short) king of the Franks. This mutual service freed the papacy from the suzerainty of the eastern emperor, but also set a dangerous precedent: powerful political rulers from north of the Alps tended to intervene to preserve the political position of the pope, while the pope conferred prestige and divine blessing on fostering rulers by crowning them. Under Charles the Great (later known as Charlemagne[1]) who was the ablest of the Carolingians, the temporal ambitions of the papacy were whetted by the destruction of the Lombard monarchy. Charlemagne increased the size of the papal territory, but the goal of a single Italian political unit was not realized. In practice the popes were in a dependent position during Charlemagne's lifetime, for temporarily the Carolingian empire had something of the strength and unity associated with the ancient Roman empire. Charlemagne

---

[1] The French, who take their name from the Franks, called Charles the Great Charlemagne (from *Carolus Magnus*).

was even able to intervene in Spain to protect the kingdom of Asturias, founded by Christian refugees in the mountains of the north, during its precarious beginnings. He thus left a Christian nucleus in the Mohammedan peninsula to begin the work of reconquest.

When Charlemagne had created an empire, the imperial title was resurrected in the West. This revival of interest in a Roman emperor in the West was partly due to the emphasis on classical learning at Charlemagne's court by the monastic scholars whom he patronized. Men of learning identified the interests of both Christianity and civilization with imperial Rome. The political circumstances were exceptionally favorable at the end of the eighth century when the pope, on that memorable Christmas Day of the year 800, crowned Charlemagne as a Roman emperor. At the time there was no emperor in the East, but there was an empress, the notorious Irene. For a woman to occupy such a position was abhorrent to the mind of the East and contrary to all tradition, East or West. Charlemagne was therefore immediately recognized as an equal by the Empress Irene in the hope of strengthening her own position through Western acceptance. The pope's action had been prompted by the need for protection, newly demonstrated by an attempt on his life in Rome itself. Charlemagne was reluctant to receive the honor, from the pope, a reluctance fully justified by the developments of later centuries. He resented the pope's presumption and implied superiority to the temporal power of the emperor, and he must have foreseen the probable difficulty of maintaining the title among his heirs. In view of Frankish custom, the Carolingian empire would have to end with Charlemagne, for it would be divided among his sons.

The activities of the Carolingians in their defense and extension of the Frankish kingdom led to institutional changes. All freemen among the Franks owed military service to the king; they served on foot and were expected to provide their own food and equipment. In fighting the Moslems Charles Martel learned the value of cavalry, but since cavalry required special and expensive equipment he had to make a change in the system of service to bring a Frankish cavalry into being. Some of the lands of the church were taken over for distribution as benefices to warriors, who were bound in return to provide mounted men for the service; the church retained title to the land and received a part of the income. This action strengthened the connection between landholding and military service. In the days of Charlemagne warfare was practically continuous, and in order not to withdraw too many men from productive labor several men were allowed to club together and furnish equipment for one of their number. When those to be equipped for the campaign were ready to leave they were allowed to follow their local landholder instead of a royal official to the field of battle. This custom increased the landholder's authority and influence, and in these innovations the relationship characteristic of the institution later called feudalism is discernible.

It is a singular fact about the eighth century that much of its intellectual activity produced works of transmission rather than original contributions. The Arabs continued the spread of Islam, and because of the eclectic spirit which they displayed in the face of new ideas, preserved much that was of value among the people they conquered. The unification of a great part of Europe by the Carolingians together with an increase in the power of the church and the papacy were important factors in passing on the Roman and Christian traditions to the Germanic and other peoples beyond the Rhine. Charlemagne's desire to reestablish the glories of ancient Rome stimulated the building of churches within the empire. Although his chapel at Aachen was a rotunda, the basilica as developed

SAXON CHURCH AT BRADFORD ON AVON

(From *A Student's History of England* by Samuel Gardiner. Longmans Green, London, 1897.)

at Ravenna was the form most frequently chosen, and became the model for later churches.

Since the transmission of sixth- and seventh-century versions of ancient learning was the chief mark of intellectual activity in western Europe, a logical guide through the first part of the eighth century is the celebrated English monk known as the Venerable Bede, for he not only worked to transmit learning but excelled as a recorder of the spirit of his age. Events of the remainder of the century crystallize about the figure of Charlemagne. Upon the foundation laid by his predecessors, Charlemagne built an integrated kingdom which took on the status of an empire as the century closed. Its political institutions were the heritage of succeeding centuries.

CHAPTER 6

The World of the Venerable Bede

[673-735]

~~~~~~~~~~~~~~

WHEN the Angles, Saxons, and Jutes invaded Britain they found no such firmly established Roman customs as had impressed the invaders of the Continent. Britain had always been an outpost, and by the time the invaders arrived it was a poorly defended one, in which the partially Romanized Britons were easily scattered. Consequently Germanic institutions continued without essential modification, notably in the folk moot (meeting) as a device to settle local affairs. Roman influence was not reintroduced until the days of St. Augustine of Canterbury. Therefore the early development of the English people occurred under circumstances different from those among the several Germanic groups on the Continent. In the Roman provinces of Europe the invaders found themselves a minority in a Romanized society; in Britain the situation was reversed. Roman influence on English folkways began with ecclesiastics, trained in the Roman tradition, who came to be the advisers of English kings. In so far as there was a difference in the traditions of Christian Rome and imperial Rome, the Roman influence in England was that of the former. The classical spirit made its way into England through the monastic foundations of Celtic Christianity and their tradition of scholarship. Although the Synod of Whitby resulted in the supremacy of the Roman church, Celtic scholarship had been well established on English soil, and English monks were accustomed to cross to Irish monasteries for study. Thus the English monk Bede benefited by two streams of learning: that of Celtic Ireland and that of Christian Rome.

The only material world this gifted scholar knew was a few miles of English countryside between York and Lindisfarne, yet he brought to his tasks of studying, teaching, and writing in the monasteries of Wearmouth and Jarrow, learning and ability beyond that of most scholars of his day. Bede was born in the kingdom of Northumbria, on the lands of the monastery of Wearmouth. When he was seven years old he was put under the care of its learned founder and abbot, Benedict Biscop. From that time, as Bede said toward the end of his life, "I have taken delight always either to learn, or to teach, or to write." He was soon transferred from Wearmouth to Jarrow, the new monastery nearby, but since the two were administered as one foundation, the books which Benedict Biscop had brought from the Continent were shared. By the time Bede grew up, the collection had doubled and under his fostering care it increased to still more respectable proportions. Since he also probably borrowed from libraries at Canterbury and Lindisfarne, he had at his disposal greater facilities than many Continental scholars who lived near more famous centers of learning. Bede was taught Latin, Greek, and some Hebrew by men who had studied under Theodore of Tarsus and Hadrian. While he was in his teens, Northumbria was devastated by the plague, and all those at Jarrow who were sufficiently trained to carry on the services died except the abbot and Bede. The two carried on until the community could be built up again, but then a period of warfare among the several English kingdoms set in which lasted the rest of Bede's life, and English society entered upon an unhappy period. Bede continued his studies, however, and in due time became monk, deacon, and priest, devoting all his free time to teaching and writing.

Bede was 38 when the Arab army, reinforced by Berbers, crossed from Africa to the rock of Gibraltar, which perpetuates the leader's name (Gebel Tarik, Tarik's hill), and began the conquest of Spain. Between that date (711) and 732 the Moslem armies pushed everything before them, and devout Christians in Europe had some justification for considering Charles Martel's victory over the invaders at Tours a miraculous intervention. Bede was so impressed when the news reached him that he seems to have reopened his *Ecclesiastical History of the English Nation,* finished in 731, to insert in his account of the year 729: "At what time the Saracens, like a very sore plague, wasted France with pitiful destruction, and themselves not long after were justly punished in the same country for their disbelief." Bede did not record as a corresponding example of divine retribution the repulse of a Moslem force before Constantinople in 718, when the Spanish Moslems had crossed the Pyrenees and Islam threatened to crush Christendom in a giant pincer movement. Perhaps Bede would not have recognized the hand of God in the triumph of a heretic: the emperor who saved Constantinople, and thus Europe, from the Moslem was Leo the Isaurian.

The Emperor Leo deserves to rank with the great Byzantine rulers, for he not only beat off the Mohammedan threat but initiated a series of internal reforms that gave the empire strength to withstand all external shocks for another two or three centuries. His agrarian and commercial policies put the empire on a sound economic basis by supporting the free peasantry, checking the growth of serfdom, and abolishing the pernicious system of collecting taxes in advance. Leo, however, brought upon himself a torrent of opposition by taxing monastic property. Denunciation of the Emperor reached epic proportions when Leo, greatly troubled by the increase in the use of images as objects of devotion, decreed that all representations of sacred personages be banished from churches on the ground that prayers before them were image-worship. Pope Gregory II declared this policy of iconoclasm a dangerous heresy and Leo was anathematized, whereupon the Emperor attempted to withdraw certain provinces from the control of the papacy and began a serious breach between the churches of the East and West.

In the controversy over images the papacy added to its authority as the champion of orthodoxy and the enemy of heresy. The influence of the church and the papacy was further expanded in the eighth century by the ecclesiastical policy of the Carolingians, which showed a remarkable continuity. Since the time of Clovis the Franks had used the clergy in support of their territorial aggrandizement, and the Carolingians fully understood the value of Christianity in softening the warlike habits of their neighbors and preparing them for conquest. Pepin of Heristal approved and assisted the mission of Willibrord (d. 738), an English monk armed with the papal blessing and a goodly assortment of relics, who worked to convert the Frisians along the North Sea coast. A second English monk, Boniface (680-754), did a notable missionary work among the heathen east of the Rhine, with the active encouragement of Charles Martel. These English monks accepted the Roman tradition and therefore were agents for the spread of papal authority; Pope Gregory II made

Boniface bishop of Hesse and Thuringia, and authorized him to organize the Frankish church. Boniface took a special oath of submission to the pope—and when he was later made archbishop imposed on every bishop under his charge a similar oath—binding him to be obedient to all papal commands, to hold an annual council, and to oblige archbishops to receive the *pallium,* their badge of office, from the pope.

The spread of the faith among the heathen was accelerated by the encouragement of adoration of the saints and by the generous distribution of relics. Boniface did not neglect the more solid work of organization, however; he founded a number of monasteries, of which the most famous was Fulda in Bavaria, and had schools established in the monasteries to train local lads for the priesthood. The monasteries were put under the authority of the pope and compelled to accept the Benedictine Rule. Irish monks who refused to give up their stricter regime and independent foundations were driven out, carrying their learning and artistic skill to other lands. The monks of Boniface's monasteries cut down forest trees to clear land, dispelling the fears of the peasants that bad luck would attend encroachment on the realm of their ancient pagan gods, and the monastic acres became demonstration centers for improved agricultural methods. As the monks encouraged settlement, towns grew in their neighborhood. The organization of the church by Boniface in Bavaria, Austrasia, and Neustria under the aegis of Rome meant extension of the study and use of Latin for carrying on the services, and he fostered the translation of works of devotion into Germanic dialects, thus as time went on helping the growth of a vernacular literature. Like the vernacular poetry that was springing up in England in the same period, this literature reflected the spirit in which these Germanic folk accepted the Christian faith: it was the spirit of the *comitatus* and the king's *gesiths*—loyalty to a leader. They accepted Christ as the leader who would reward their devotion with the joys of heaven when the campaign was ended.

Bede's interests centered in the cloister, rather than in the mission. His attention was focused on making the Scriptures intelligible, and he devoted many volumes to explanation and interpretation, citing Jerome, Ambrose, Augustine, and Gregory the Great. He also wrote some works of a secular nature: a glossary of Latin words compiled for his students, and a treatise on metre, in which

PLATE V

Seventh Century

FIGURE 1. *Photograph of Abdul Aziz Ibn Saud, present king of Saudi Arabia.* [*Courtesy of Black Star Publishing Company, Inc., New York*]

FIGURE 2. *These two Arabs lived in 2000 B.C. and 1500 B.C. The striking similarities in features and even in growth and trimming of the beard between these Arabs and the king of Saudi Arabia make it clear that the Arab type has come down unchanged through many centuries of life in the Arabian desert, and that we can make a likely guess as to the appearance of Mohammed.*
[*From* The Ancient Egyptians *by* T. Elliott Smith. *Harper and Brothers, New York, 1911*]

FIGURE 3. *Dome of the Rock, Jerusalem. Also known as the Mosque of Omar. This mosque was built over the rock upon which the Temple had been built. The Moslems believe that from it Mohammed made his flight to Heaven. It has been reconstructed several times, but the original plan has been kept. The dome was double; the interior decorated with mosaics and marble. Some of the columns date back to the sixth century.*
[*From* Moslem Architecture *by* G. T. Rivoira. *The Clarendon Press, Oxford, 1918*]

FIGURE 4. *Baptistery of St. John at Poitiers. This is one of the few remaining Merovingian buildings. It is made of brick and stone in the Roman tradition, yet with patterns of stone and brick added to meet the barbarian predilection for decorative richness of surfaces.*

[107a]

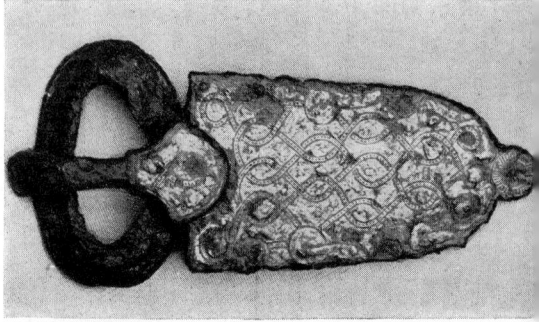

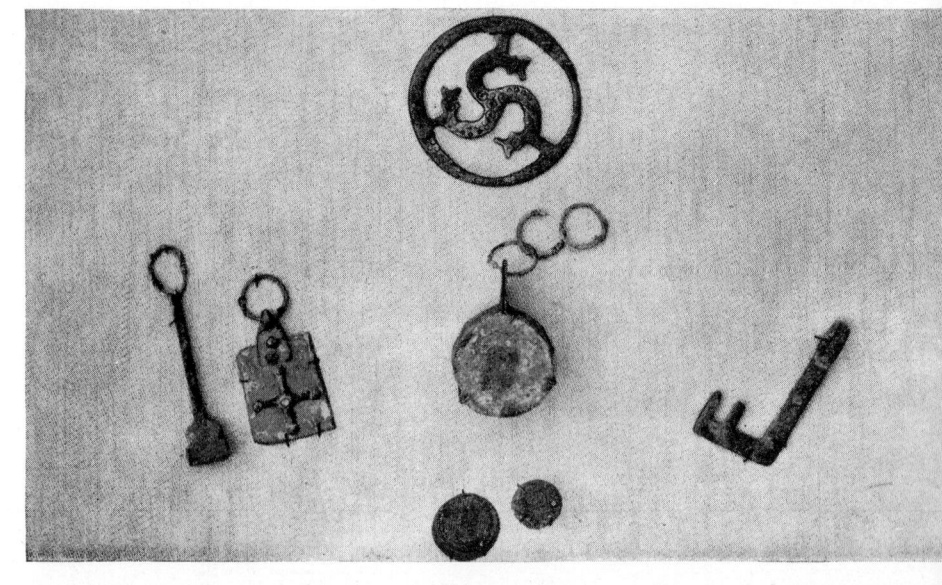

PLATE VI

Seventh Century

FIGURE 1. *Page from* Homilies of St. Augustine. *This manuscript of the* Homilies *was copied and illuminated in the monastery of Luxeuil. It shows how the Irish monks preserved and spread the culture of the Church. The Celt used natural forms, floral and animal, and achieved elaborately interlaced patterns. He had no interest in symmetry, but a very vivid feeling for filling a space with decorative patterns.*

[*Courtesy of the Pierpont Morgan Library, New York*]

FIGURE 2. *Drawing of a stone church in Escomb, Durham, one of the very few English churches that survives from the age of the Synod of Whitby. It represents the type of these churches—a narrow nave and chancel, with small windows. The later church at Bradford on Avon follows the same plan, but the chancel at Escomb is higher. The long windows were opened at a much later period. The stones were brought to the site from some Roman station in the vicinity to construct walls over two feet thick. The church was still being used for regular worship in 1863 when a larger one was erected.*
[*From* The Arts in Early England *by G. Baldwin Brown. John Murray, London, 1903*]

FIGURE 3. *Frankish buckle. This buckle is an excellent example of* niello work. *The design was cut into the metal that was to be ornamented and the lines filled in with a black amalgam. The work is Frankish and the designs show the resemblance of Germanic to Celtic fancy when the former was unaffected by Roman influence.*

[*Courtesy of the Metropolitan Museum of Art, New York*]

FIGURE 4. *Frankish chatelaine with tweezers, amulet, coin purse, coins and key. The custom of carrying a metal chatelaine to which were attached articles of daily use seems to have been fairly common among the Franks. The use of animal forms in decoration was not naturalistic; the animal was fitted into a pattern characteristic of barbarian tradition.*

[*Courtesy of the Metropolitan Museum of Art, New York*]

he was greatly interested since he himself wrote correct—though scarcely inspired—verse. Following the example set by Isidore of Seville, on whom he leaned heavily, he produced a treatise called *De natura rerum*. In this work Bede was able to transmit an enhanced body of classical thought, since he knew the work of the Latin authority Pliny, while Isidore did not. Bede added serious observations of his own, representing the earth as a sphere with a watery heaven about it, and in another treatise, *De temporum ratione,* he expressed original ideas about the relationship between tides and the moon. The innovation for which we are most indebted, perhaps, is Bede's substitution of the method of dating events from the birth of Christ for the elaborate systems of chronology then current.

That Bede accepted miracles as a matter of course in everyday life is evident, not only throughout his many Scriptural commentaries and in his lives of the saints, but also in his most famous work, the *Ecclesiastical History of the English Nation*. Although Bede was quite modern in the way he conscientiously weighed his material and meticulously acknowledged his sources, he did not examine critically his evidence about miracles because he shared the contemporary belief in them. In other ways he was in advance of his times. The title of his history looks ahead, for although the England he knew was made up of many warring states, he still called his book a history of the English nation (*gentis anglorum*), suggesting a community of feeling far ahead of the achievement of political unity.

Although the great bulk of Bede's writings was religious—even the famous history was ecclesiastical—he gave precious glimpses of the secular side of life in scattered references to the progress of the arts. Few of the stone churches which were replacing wooden ones survive for our study, but we are more fortunate in the preservation of the beautiful wayside crosses and of illuminated manuscripts. The splendor of the brilliantly colored Lindisfarne Gospels shows the highest development of the intricate designs that had long been used on brooch and targe, revealing the Celtic contribution of enlaced design and animal form at its best. As models for their portraits of the Evangelists the Lindisfarne artists used the adaptation of pagan types into Christian personages shown in manuscripts which had been brought to England from Italy; the model used for St. Mark has been conjectured to have been a portrait of Cassiodorus. Bede may have seen the Lindisfarne Gospels; he visited Lindisfarne and knew the artist, Eadfrith, by whom he had been asked to write the life of St. Cuthbert, a former abbot of Lindisfarne.

Although Bede's fame as the greatest scholar of his age has outstripped his reputation as a teacher, his influence in education was far-reaching. He is believed to have been the teacher of his close friend Egbert, who became archbishop of York. Bede had visited at York some months before Egbert's consecration as archbishop, and afterward wrote him a long letter dealing with conditions in Northumbria and giving detailed advice on pastoral duties. When Egbert founded his famous cathedral school at York he carried on the tradition of Bede's teaching. And at York was trained the scholarly Alcuin, the English ecclesiastic who became Charlemagne's teacher and librarian, the director of his informal academy, the head of his palace school, and the medium for transmitting the learning of the British Isles to Europe.

Shortly before writing the letter to Egbert, Bede had fallen ill. He continued to work, however, at composition and translation, despite growing weakness, until the hour he died, meeting the expostulations of his brethren with the words, "I will not have my pupils read a falsehood, nor labour therein without profit after my death." As he felt his end drawing near, he sang vernacular verse on the soul leaving the body, and finally asked for the casket which contained his few treasures: some pepper, a few linen napkins, a little frankincense. After he had distributed these among the monks they went away to their duties, leaving him with the boy who was copying for him. Bede made the lad write the final sentence, echoed the boy's "It is finished," and died singing the *Gloria patri*.

When Boniface, the apostle to the Germans, heard about Bede's death, he compared it to the going out of a candle of the church in which the Holy Spirit shone. Bede's learning was without doubt a light which illumined his generation and those that followed: the demand for his writings was inexhaustible, and his appellation the Venerable is probably a tribute to his achievements as well as his piety. His world was one in which no political events of much moment occurred beyond the progress of the Moslems in the East and their defeat by Charles Martel in the West. The redoubtable Charles rises as a great figure because of the heavy blows against the infidel which won him the epithet Martel. Another great contemporary of Bede, Boniface, stands out as the representative of two aspects of monastic activity—missions and social services. Bede represents another aspect, proving the age was not destitute of intellectual interests. The evidence of this is Charlemagne's success during the next generation in securing scholars to lend lustre to his court, scholars drawn from monastery and cathedral schools where young men were studying the classics and their teachers were passing on the tradition of interest in things of the mind. Charlemagne's generation proved the greatness of Bede's; the success of his students is the highest tribute to any teacher.

PART OF CELTIC CROSS AT JEDBURGH
(From *Northumbrian Crosses* by W. G. Collingwood. Faber and Gwyer, London, 1927.)

CHAPTER 7

The World of Charlemagne

[c. 742–814]

~~~~~~~~~~~~~~~~

THE career of Charlemagne, grandson of Charles Martel, so impressed the minds of his own and succeeding generations that he became a legendary figure; in sober chronicle as well as in epic, the deeds of his father and grandfather were attributed to him. His revival of the imperial title in the West came while the tradition of European unity under Roman rule was still a living force; and his portrait, with crown, sceptre, and globe, became the symbol of imperial power for the western world. There were many superficial similarities between the extensive Frankish empire and the old imperial Rome, but the most marked resemblance between Charlemagne and the founders of Roman imperial greatness was in his career as a warrior. He won fame pre-eminently on the battlefield, and with the prestige of military prowess curbed lawless groups and established order. After his death and the disruption of his almost wholly personal empire, western Europe again fell into confusion, and men looked back nostalgically to his era as a period of calm and order. Other circumstances contributed to the creation of the Charlemagne legend, of which not the least important was his own unusual personality; his secretary, Einhard, to whom he was a hero, left a very readable biography of the forceful and agreeable Charles which shows him a winning, and a very human, individual.

Charlemagne's achievements were based solidly on the foundations laid by his ancestors. The Frankish kingdom was saved from potential civil conflict by the death of his brother, shortly after the two inherited the kingdom from their father, Pepin the Short. When Charlemagne, at about the age of 29, became sole ruler of the Franks in 771 he turned at once to the extension of his kingdom's boundaries and, as an integral part of this aggressive policy, to the spreading of the Christian faith. Using, like his predecessors, the assistance of missionaries, he finished the work of converting and bringing under Frankish rule peoples who had never lived within the Roman empire: Thuringians, Frisians, Saxons, Bavarians, Czechs, and Avars.

The various peoples with whom Charlemagne dealt in his conquests showed individual characteristics which were a reflection of their differing environments and cultural contacts. The blue-eyed, fair-haired folk who were the ancestors of all the Germanic peoples of central and western Europe had developed hardy and warlike habits in a severe climate and an inhospitable land. Those who had found homes within the Roman empire had to a greater or less degree adopted late-Roman ways, adapting them to their needs and becoming a settled people, in whose lives war was an interruption rather than a calling. The Thuringians, who dwelt in the forests between the homeland of the Saxons and the upper Danube valley, and the Frisians, who lived along the coasts of modern Holland and Belgium, were not within the Empire, but their customs had been modified by the missionaries Charlemagne's forebears had so sagaciously encouraged. On the other hand, the Saxons along the mouth of the Elbe, who had remained in their homes when their kinsmen left to invade England, sturdily resisted the efforts of missionaries and the attacks of Charlemagne's armies. Thirty-three years were required to subdue them with censer and sword, but those who were left in the end were Christians. Charlemagne made no attempts to overcome the Scandinavians of Denmark, but he conquered the Bavarians on the Danube, and the Lombards in the Po valley, proudly assuming the iron crown of the Lombard kings.

To the east of the regions inhabited by the Germanic peoples conquered by Charlemagne were others, mainly Slavs, who had migrated from the great plains of Russia and Asia. Most of these peoples had words in their speech which show that they had a common origin, though they had developed different ways of life. Charlemagne established a policy of driving back Slav groups who had crossed the Elbe, and he conquered the Slavic Czechs in the mountain-girdled Bohemian plains. Further east, most of the peoples who are to be found there today had settled by the eighth century: Finns from Asia in the upper Baltic region; Letts and Lithuanians in the

The World of Charlemagne [113

forests farther south; the Slavic Poles in the lands to the east of the Saxons; Croats and Serbs in the Balkans. On the lower Danube were the Asiatic Avars, part of whose lands Charlemagne forcibly annexed.

Charlemagne's system for defending his frontiers was to establish marks, or marches, in the border regions, such as the Spanish March, the Danish March, and the East March on the Avar frontier. In the marches the land was taken by the crown and then much of it distributed to nobles and churchmen, always with the obligation of military service. Peasants from the west were encouraged to settle the marches, and thus was inaugurated a return migration of the Germanic peoples from west to east. To facilitate the transfer of fighting men to the frontiers, Charlemagne had roads and bridges repaired, and these were used by merchants as well. Although commerce by sea was largely cut off by Moslem control of the Mediterranean, trade overland with Italy revived with Charlemagne's conquest of the Lombard kingdom. Trade was largely in the hands of Syrian and Jewish merchants since Christian bigotry excluded the Jews from other occupations. Pilgrimages were increasingly popular, but the journey to the Holy Land was expensive, and with the exception of nobles and of peasants who established new settlements in the marches, the population was fairly static and had little contact with non-European civilizations.

The world of Islam, though Christians generally were ignorant of its progress, enjoyed a civilization which far surpassed that of western Europe. Politically the Mohammedans were now divided between two caliphates, one with its capital at Cordova, in Spain, the other at Bagdad. The conquering Arabs had, in the East, adopted the Persian culture, and in the late eighth century under the Caliph Haroun al-Raschid Bagdad was a center of fabulous wealth and considerable learning. Pictures of life under the famous caliph have come down to us in the tales of the *Arabian Nights*. Charlemagne exchanged embassies with Haroun al-Raschid and carried on friendly correspondence, but in the West he attacked the Spanish caliphate and set up the Spanish March south of the Pyrenees to defend the passes into northern Europe. One of Charlemagne's campaigns in Spain became celebrated for a relatively minor incident; as his army was returning northward through the Pyrenees the rearguard was destroyed by the Basques, a Christian people of northern Spain.

Among those killed was the warrior Roland, and in time the campaign became legendary, and formed the basis for one of the greatest medieval epics, the *Song of Roland*.

The relationship between the Frankish kingdom and the papacy under the Carolingians brought about a final emancipation of the popes from the suzerainty of the eastern emperor. The popes, by their continuing acknowledgment of imperial authority, had secured the emperors' recognition of papal primacy in the West. Doctrinal differences occasionally arose but did not cause a serious break until the controversy over images developed; the popes would make no concessions and it soon became evident that the emperors, constantly harried by the Moslems and periodically attacked by the Bulgars in the Balkans, could not protect central Italy from the renewed attacks of the Lombards in the mid eighth century.

At this propitious moment when the popes began to look westward for assistance, Pepin the Short was planning the palace revolution which would make him king instead of mayor of the palace in Neustria. Since the clergy upheld the Scriptural idea that a king was the Lord's anointed, Pepin first secured papal approval for his plan to set aside the currently anointed of the Lord and was anointed king of the Franks in his place. Then when the Lombards threatened Rome the pope appealed to Pepin, who promptly defeated the Lombards and gave to the pope the lands they had seized. This was the Donation of Pepin, which was the basis for the temporal rule of the papacy in central Italy. The policy of aiding the papacy against the Lombards was upheld by Charlemagne's conquest of the Lombard kingdom, and his additional grants of land for the sovereignty of the popes were known as the Donation of Charlemagne. By the Donations of Pepin and Charlemagne the papacy was established as a temporal monarchy in central Italy.

The great services of Pepin and Charlemagne to the papacy were given the highest recognition when Pope Leo III crowned Charlemagne Emperor of the West in the year 800. The immediate inspiration of the action was the assistance rendered to the pope by Charlemagne after a Roman insurrection in which the pope's life had been seriously endangered. After Leo III's reinstatement Charlemagne visited Rome and attended Christmas mass in St. Peter's; it was there that the pope crowned the Frankish ruler emperor. According to Einhard, Charlemagne declared he would never have entered the church that day had he known the pope's intention, but it is not impossible that he wished the title and may have intended to make himself emperor. The pope's assumption of the right to confer the distinction was supported by a famous forgery concocted sometime in the latter half of the eighth century, known as the Donation of Constantine. This was a document by which the Emperor Constantine, after his adoption of Christianity, purportedly gave to the popes, not only spiritual authority over all the other bishops and patriarchs, but also supremacy over all secular powers in the West. The papal claim to superiority over temporal rulers, with the precedent of Charlemagne's reception of the imperial title at the hands of the pope, was to cause a most serious controversy during the succeeding centuries. For his part, Charlemagne as emperor considered himself the successor of Constantine, and thus ruler of the church.

Charlemagne made Aachen (Aix-la-Chapelle), his northern capitol, the scene of his attempts to stage a revival of the glories of ancient Rome. The great palace which he built, with a swimming pool where it was said a hundred men could join him in his favorite exercise, has long ago disappeared, but the chapel, enclosed in later buildings, still survives. The chapel is in the style of a rotunda, decorated with pillars and works of art brought from Italy. There the stately figure of the emperor was to be seen on solemn occasions—tall, heavily-built, dressed in cloth of gold, and wearing a glittering diadem, jewelled boots, and a golden girdle. On ordinary occasions he preferred to go about in the Frankish dress, consisting of a silk-fringed tunic with cross-gartered hose, always girt with a belt which carried a gold- or silver-hilted sword, and wearing a blue cloak that set off his beautiful white hair. Although his neck was too short and thick and he developed a paunch, his bearing was so regal that these defects passed unnoticed. His nose was big, his eyes large and piercing: his expression was good-humored and his manner brisk. Presumably he wore mustaches in the Frankish manner, but no beard. He enjoyed robust health until a few years before his death, and then in illness he was impatient with his doctors and ate what he pleased against their advice. The moral tone of his court was hardly model; he divorced one wife, married three others, and besides his eight legitimate children had six by concubines. He was devoted to all his children, and would not let his daughters marry because he did not wish to part with them.

In order to add greater glory to his court Charlemagne employed the most noted scholars of the day. From England came the greatest, Alcuin, who had been trained in Egbert's cathedral school of York. At Charlemagne's command Alcuin reformed the handwriting then in use, and the books copied in his day were in the so-called Carolingian minuscule, from which comes the small type used in modern books. Other scholars at the Carolingian court were Paul the Deacon, a Lombard who wrote a history of his own people; Theodulf, a Goth; Paulinus of Aquileia; and Peter of Pisa—suggesting a variety of origins that would have done credit to the universality of imperial Rome. There was also a Frank, Einhard, who had been educated at Boniface's monastery in Fulda. Charlemagne employed Einhard on embassies as well as in secretarial duties: the necessity of having trained administrators was one practical reason for assembling at court the best-educated men of the time. Charlemagne's desire to have these scholars teach their successors probably accounts for the establishment of the palace school and for his encouragement of the scholarly activities which have been characterized, with considerable exaggeration, as the Carolingian renaissance.

The best picture of Charlemagne as a ruler is given in his capitularies, or collections of ordinances, which cover a multitude of subjects. These reveal Charlemagne's qualities as an administrator, and the great care he took for details; in the capitulary *De villis,* for example, designed to reform the administration of the royal villas, are long lists of household articles and directions about the preparation of foodstuffs. Like his father and his grandfather, he recognized the value of the church to his administration, and the tone of his capitularies makes clear that he considered his authority over the clergy unquestioned. Provincial administration was in the hands of counts of his own appointment, and he kept track of them by a system of travelling inspectors (*missi dominici*), one lay and one clerical. He reorganized the army in a practical fashion by making the local lords responsible for the levies of fighting men who had to assemble each spring for the current campaign. In fact, it was about the strongholds of the local lords, and about the monasteries, that life throughout the West was centered, for each community became completely self-sufficient in the necessities of existence. The bond between ruler and subject was the oath of allegiance which Charlemagne exacted from every freeman, and the responsibility which he assumed as the fountain of justice for all his people, the protector of the poor and the oppressed.

The world of Charlemagne was a world in which many developments of long-range significance had begun. The church emerged as an independent temporal monarchy under the pope. After the example set by Charlemagne's palace school the patronage of literature and the spread of classical sources was no longer limited to the church. In the field of legislative and administrative activity Charlemagne's capitularies suggest the practice of the next few centuries; he was not a codifier, for the number and variety of the capitularies embodied the principle of different laws for different men according to local custom, locally administered. The effect of Charlemagne's career on the organization of future European states was exceptionally significant. The conquest of Italy and the establishment of the pope as an independent monarch created a background of rivalry between the popes and other temporal rulers which was the bane of Italy to the twentieth century. The consolidation of a huge Frankish kingdom did not have much effect on France, for no radical changes occurred there, but Germanic supremacy in central Europe was assured by Charlemagne's Christianization of that area under the Roman church, and by the check he imposed on the influx of the Slavs. Finally, by his assumption of the imperial title he revived for Europe a noble ideal of unity in the Roman sense—one God, one empire. The collapse of his empire, because it was based on the code of personal loyalty of a recently-primitive people rather than the universal principles of ancient Rome, did not, however, destroy the effectiveness of the ideal. For, in the troubles of the ninth century, Charlemagne's world took on in retrospect the character of an almost legendary golden age.

[THE EIGHTH CENTURY]

Readings

~~~~~~~~~~~~

Bede

THE ECCLESIASTICAL HISTORY
OF THE ENGLISH NATION*

[The temptation is strong to present Bede's account of Augustine's mission (Book I, Chapter 25), of Paulinus at the court of King Edwin (Book II, Chapter 13), of the Synod of Whitby (Book III, Chapter 25), or of Caedmon and his songs (Book IV, Chapter 24), which are all famous passages. Instead, two successive chapters have been chosen, in the portion where Bede was dealing with the events of his own lifetime. Here the factual story of Wilbrord's mission is followed by a story of a resurrection and a heavenly vision equally factual in the eyes of Bede and his contemporaries.]

How the Venerable Swidbert in Britain, and Wilbrord at Rome, were ordained bishops for Frisland. [A.D. 692]

At their first coming into Frisland, as soon as Wilbrord found he had leave given him by the prince to preach, he made haste to Rome, where Pope Sergius then presided over the apostolical see, that he might undertake the desired work of preaching the Gospel to the Gentiles, with his licence and blessing; and hoping to receive of him some relics of the blessed apostles and martyrs of Christ; to the end, that when he destroyed the idols, and erected churches in the nation to which he preached, he might have the relics of saints at hand to put into them, and having deposited them there, might accordingly dedicate those places to the honour of each of the saints whose relics they were. He was also desirous there to learn or to receive from thence many other things which so great a work re-

* Taken from *Everyman's Library;* translated by John Stevens and revised by L. C. Jane; published by E. P. Dutton & Co., Inc., New York.

quired. Having obtained all that he wanted, he returned to preach....

When they who went over had spent some years teaching in Frisland, Pepin, with the consent of them all, sent the venerable Wilbrord to Rome, where Sergius was still pope, desiring that he might be consecrated archbishop over the nation of the Frisons; which was accordingly done, in the year of our Lord's incarnation 696. He was consecrated in the church of the Holy Martyr Cecilia, on her feast-day; the pope gave him the name of Clement, and sent him back to his bishopric, fourteen days after his arrival at Rome.

Pepin gave him a place for his episcopal see, in his famous castle, which in the ancient language of those people is called Wiltaburg, that is, the town of the Wilts; but, in the French tongue, Utrecht. The most reverend prelate having built a church there, and preaching the word of faith far and near, drew many from their errors, and erected several churches and monasteries. For not long after he constituted other bishops in those parts, from among the brethren that either came with him or after him to preach there; some of which are now departed in our Lord; but Wilbrord himself, surnamed Clement, is still living, venerable for old age, having been thirty-six years a bishop, and sighing after the rewards of the heavenly life, after the many spiritual conflicts which he has waged.

[*from Book V, chapter xi*]

Of one among the Northumbrians, who rose from the dead, and related the things which he had seen, some exciting terror and others delight. [A.D. 696]

At this time a memorable miracle, and like to those of former days, was wrought in Britain; for, to the end that the living might be saved from the death of the soul, a certain person, who had been some time dead, rose again to life, and related many remarkable things he had seen; some of which I have thought fit here briefly to take notice of. There was a master of a family in that district of the Northumbrians which is called Cuningham, who led a religious life, as did also all that belonged to him. This man fell sick, and his distemper daily increasing, being brought to extremity, he died in the beginning of the night; but in the morning early, he suddenly came to life again, and sat up, upon which all those that sat about the body weeping, fled away in a great fright, only his wife, who loved him best, though in a great consternation and trembling, remained with him. He, comforting her, said, "Fear not, for I am now truly risen from death, and permitted again to live among men; however, I am not to live hereafter as I was wont, but from henceforward after a very different manner." Then rising immediately, he repaired to the oratory of the little town, and continuing in prayer till day, immediately divided all his substance into three parts; one whereof he gave to his wife, another to his children, and the third, belonging to himself, he instantly distributed among the poor. Not long after, he repaired to the monastery of Melrose, which is almost enclosed by the winding of the river Tweed, and having been shaven, went into a private dwelling, which the abbat had provided, where he continued till the day of his death, in such extraordinary contrition of mind and body, that though his tongue had been silent, his life declared that he had seen many things either to be dreaded or coveted, which others knew nothing of.

Thus he related what he had seen. "He that led me had a shining countenance and a bright garment, and we went on silently, as I thought, towards the north-east. Walking on, we came to a vale of great breadth and depth, but of infinite length; on the left it appeared full of dreadful flames, the other side was no less horrid for violent hail and cold snow flying in all directions; both places were full of men's souls, which seemed by turns to be tossed from one side to the other, as it were by a violent storm; for when the wretches could no longer endure the excess of heat, they leaped into the middle of the cutting cold; and finding no rest there, they leaped back again into the middle of the unquenchable flames. Now whereas an innumerable multitude of deformed spirits were thus alternately tormented far and near, as far as could be seen, without any intermission, I began to think that this perhaps might be hell, of whose intolerable flames I had often heard talk. My guide, who went before me, answered to my thought, saying, "Do not believe so, for this is not the hell you imagine."

When he had conducted me, much frightened with that horrid spectacle, by degrees, to the farther end, on a sudden I saw the place begin to grow dusk and filled with darkness. When I came into it, the darkness, by degrees, grew so thick, that I could see nothing besides it and the shape and garment of him that led me. As we went on through the shades of night, on a sudden there appeared before us frequent globes of black flames, rising as it were out of a great pit, and falling back again into the same. When I had been conducted thither, my leader suddenly vanished, and left me alone in the midst of darkness and this horrid vision, whilst those same globes of fire, without intermission, at one time flew up and at another fell back into the bottom of the abyss; and I observed that all the flames, as they ascended, were full of human souls, which, like sparks flying up with smoke, were sometimes thrown on high, and again, when the vapour of the fire ceased, dropped down into the depth below. Moreover, an insufferable stench came forth with the vapours, and filled all those dark places.

Having stood there a long time in much dread, not knowing what to do, which way to turn, or what end I might expect, on a sudden I heard behind me the noise of a most hideous and wretched lamentation, and at the same time a loud laughing, as of a rude multitude insulting captured enemies. When that noise, growing plainer, came up to me, I observed a gang of evil spirits dragging the howling and lamenting souls of men into the midst of the darkness, whilst they themselves laughed and rejoiced. Among those men, as I could discern, there was one shorn like a clergyman, a layman, and a woman. The evil spirits that dragged them went down into the midst of the burning pit; and as they went down deeper, I could no longer distinguish between the lamentation of the men and the laughing of the devils, yet I still had a confused sound in my ears. In the meantime, some of the dark spirits ascended from that flaming abyss, and running forward, beset me on all sides, and much perplexed me with their glaring eyes and the stinking fire which proceeded from their mouths and nostrils; and threatened to lay hold on me with burning tongs, which they had in their hands, yet they durst not touch me, though they frightened me. Being thus on all sides enclosed with enemies and darkness, and looking about on every side for assistance, there appeared behind me, on the way that I came, as it were, the brightness of a star shining amidst the darkness; which increased by degrees, and came rapidly towards me: when it drew near, all those evil spirits, that sought to carry me away with their tongs, dispersed and fled.

He, whose approach put them to flight, was the same that led me before; who, then turning towards the right, began to lead me, as it were, towards the south-east, and having soon brought me out of the darkness, conducted me into an atmosphere of clear light. While he thus led me in open light, I saw a vast wall before us, the length and height of which, in every direction, seemed to be altogether boundless. I began to wonder why we went up to

PLATE VII
Eighth Century

FIGURE 1. *Page from a psalter, written in England in uncial characters. The Roman capital (maiuscule) and small (minuscule) letters, which were commonly used in inscriptions, do not seem to have been widely used in manuscripts, for the scribe was wont to prefer a cursive hand which could be written rapidly without raising the pen from paper. With the recognition of Christianity, scribes copying the Bible developed the uncial (inch-high) characters which seem to be an adaptation of those used in Greek Bibles at the time. The uncial letter* a *is preserved in modern type.* [*Courtesy of the Pierpont Morgan Library, New York*]

FIGURE 2. *Page from Lindisfarne Gospels. This famous manuscript was created in Lindisfarne Monastery, a Celtic foundation on the shore of the North Sea, in all probability in the lifetime of the Venerable Bede. The perfection of the intricate, purely Celtic design places the book among the supreme achievements of art. The artist had seen manuscripts from Italy and conceded symmetry in pages like the one here reproduced.*
[*From the British Museum*]

FIGURE 3. *Initial page from the Book of Kells, an Irish manuscript. This is an example of the Celtic style untouched by outside influence. In commenting on the unity of this design Charles R. Morey says, "The letter has unity because it lives; its coiling vitality makes symmetry or rhythm unnecessary." (Christian Art, p. 35.) This dynamic force from the north was to provide medieval art with expressiveness of line. The letters are the first three letters in the Greek word for Christ: X P I.*
[*From* English Illumination *by Elfrida Saunders. Harcourt, Brace and Company, Inc., New York*]

FIGURE 4. *Interior of the Mosque of Cordoba, Spain. The chief architectural work of the eighth century was done by Moslem builders. This mosque was erected on the site of Cordoba Cathedral, and the builders used columns with capitals that dated from the first to the seventh centuries. A Moslem place of worship had to have water for ablution, a pulpit or platform from which the Koran was read, a place to pray which showed the direction of Mecca, and a place from which the call to prayer was issued. This last requirement resulted in the minaret.*

PLATE VIII

Eighth Century

FIGURE 1. *Equestrian figure in bronze which is supposed to represent Charlemagne. No completely authenticated portrait has survived. In later ages he was depicted as having a flowing beard, because beards had come into fashion and represented dignity and impressiveness. It is probable that Charlemagne wore mustaches in the Frankish fashion, as in this figure. The horse is possibly of fifteenth century workmanship.*
[*From* Early Lives of Charlemagne, *edited by A. J. Grant. Chatto and Windus, London, 1926*]

FIGURE 2. *Moslem carving in wood, in the Metropolitan Museum of Art. This is an excellent example of the Moslem style of decoration which, like the northern European, eschewed naturalism and got its effects by pattern. Interlacing geometrical patterns fascinated the Arab, and he borrowed them wherever he found them. He liked to ornament every inch of space. In carvings like this, the effect of the pattern was heightened by the contrasts of light and shade. Mohammed decreed literal obedience to the Mosaic injunction not to reproduce animal forms.*
[*Courtesy of the Metropolitan Museum of Art, New York*]

FIGURE 3. *Interior, Chapel of Charlemagne. Charlemagne's desire to revive the glories of ancient Rome led him to have churches erected in the Byzantine manner. For his own chapel he chose, not the basilica, but the central type. The model was probably the Church of St. Vitale at Ravenna, but the design is of greater massiveness. He had ancient Roman columns brought from Italy. The fame of this chapel gave a special name to Charles's new capital of Aix (Aix-la-Chapelle). It survived as the heart of the present cathedral and withstood the bombings of World War II.*

FIGURE 4. *Porch of monastery, Lorsch. The architect of this Carolingian gate-house has adapted the type of tripartite Roman triumphal arch to his purposes. Instead of the three-dimensional articulation of the Arch of Constantine he has created a two-dimensional surface pattern of polychrome stone work to his Northern taste.*

the wall, seeing no door, window, or path through it. When we came to the wall, we were presently, I know not by what means, on the top of it, and within it was a vast and delightful field, so full of fragrant flowers that the odour of its delightful sweetness immediately dispelled the stink of the dark furnace, which had pierced me through and through. So great was the light in this place, that it seemed to exceed the brightness of the day, or the sun in its meridian height. In this field were innumerable assemblies of men in white, and many companies seated together rejoicing. As he led me through the midst of those happy inhabitants, I began to think that this might, perhaps, be the kingdom of heaven, of which I had often heard so much. He answered to my thought, saying, "This is not the kingdom of heaven, as you imagine."

When we had passed those mansions of blessed souls and gone farther on, I discovered before me a much more beautiful light, and therein heard sweet voices of persons singing, and so wonderful a fragrancy proceeded from the place, that the other which I had before thought most delicious, then seemed to me but very indifferent; even as that extraordinary brightness of the flowery field, compared with this, appeared mean and inconsiderable. When I began to hope we should enter that delightful place, my guide on a sudden stood still; and then turning back, led me back by the way we came.

When we returned to those joyful mansions of the souls in white, he said to me, "Do you know what all these things are which you have seen?" I answered, I did not; and then he replied, "That vale you saw so dreadful for consuming flames and cutting cold, is the place in which the souls of those are tried and punished, who, delaying to confess and amend their crimes, at length have recourse to repentance at the point of death, and so depart this life; but nevertheless because they, even at their death, confessed and repented, they shall all be received into the kingdom of heaven at the day of judgment; but many are relieved before the day of judgment, by the prayers, alms, and fasting, of the living, and more especially by masses. That fiery and stinking pit, which you saw, is the mouth of hell, into which whosoever falls shall never be delivered to all eternity. This flowery place, in which you see these most beautiful young people, so bright and merry, is that into which the souls of those are received who depart the body in good works, but who are not so perfect as to deserve to be immediately admitted into the kingdom of heaven; yet they shall all, at the day of judgment, see Christ, and partake of the joys of his kingdom; for whoever are perfect in thought, word and deed, as soon as they depart the body, immediately enter into the kingdom of heaven; in the neighbourhood, whereof that place is, where you heard the sound of sweet singing, with the fragrant odour and bright light. As for you, who are now to return to your body, and live among men again, if you will endeavour nicely to examine your actions, and direct your speech and behaviour in righteousness and simplicity, you shall, after death, have a place or residence among these joyful troops of blessed souls; for when I left you for a while, it was to know how you were to be disposed of." When he had said this to me, I much abhorred returning to my body, being delighted with the sweetness and beauty of the place I beheld, and with the company of those I saw in it. However, I durst not ask him any questions; but in the meantime, on a sudden, I found myself alive among men.

Now these and other things which this man of God saw, he would not relate to slothful persons and such as lived negligently; but only to those who, being terrified with the dread of torments, or delighted with the hopes of heavenly joys, would make use of his words to advance in piety. In the neighbourhood of his cell lived one Hemgils, a monk, eminent in the priesthood, which he honoured by his good works: he is still living, and leading a solitary life in Ireland, supporting his declining age with coarse bread and cold water. He often went to that man, and asking several questions, heard of him all the particulars of what he had seen when separated from his body; by whose relation we also came to the knowledge of those few particulars which we have briefly set down. He also related his visions to King Alfrid, a man most learned in all respects, and was by him so willingly and attentively heard, that at his request he was admitted into the monastery above-mentioned, and received the monastic tonsure; and the said king, when he happened to be in those parts, very often went to hear him. At that time the religious and humble abbat and priest, Ethelwald, presided over the monastery, and now with worthy conduct possesses the episcopal see of the church of Lindisfarne.

He had a more private place of residence assigned him in that monastery, where he might apply himself to the service of his Creator in continual prayer. And as that place lay on the bank of the river, he was wont often to go into the same to do penance in his body, and many times to dip quite under the water, and to continue saying psalms or prayers in the same as long as he could endure it, standing still sometimes up to the middle, and sometimes to the neck in water; and when he went out from thence ashore, he never took off his cold and frozen garments till they grew warm and dry on his body. And when in the winter the half-broken pieces of ice were swimming about him, which he had himself broken, to make room to stand or dip himself in the river, those who beheld it would say, "It is wonderful, brother Drithelm (for so he was called), that you are able to endure such violent cold;" he simply answered, for he was a man of much simplicity and indifferent wit, "I have seen greater cold." And when they said, "It is strange that you will endure such austerity;" he replied, "I have seen more austerity." Thus he continued, through an indefatigable desire of heavenly bliss, to subdue his aged body with daily fasting, till the day of his being called away; and thus he forwarded the salvation of many by his words and example.

[from Book V, chapter xii]

Eginhard

LIFE OF CHARLEMAGNE*

[Eginhard (or Einhard) was a Frank of a well-to-do family who was educated at the monastery which Boniface founded at Fulda. He entered Charlemagne's service when he was about twenty, and for the rest of the great ruler's life acted as minister, councillor, and secretary. The literary model for his biography of the emperor was Suetonius' life of Augustus. For a comparison of the accounts of Charlemagne's attitude toward his coronation see Duncalf and Krey, *Parallel Source Problems*.]

Charles was large and strong, and of lofty stature, though not disproportionately tall (his height is well known to have been seven times the length of his foot); the upper part of his head was round, his eyes very large and animated, nose a little long, hair fair, and face laughing and merry. Thus his appearance was always stately and dignified, whether he was standing or sitting; although his

---

* Reprinted by permission of American Book Company from Eginhard, *Life of Charlemagne*, translated by Samuel Epes Turner.

neck was thick and somewhat short, and his belly rather prominent; but the symmetry of the rest of his body concealed these defects. His gait was firm, his whole carriage manly, and his voice clear, but not so strong as his size led one to expect. His health was excellent, except during the four years preceding his death, when he was subject to frequent fevers; at the last he even limped a little with one foot. Even in those years he consulted rather his own inclinations than the advice of physicians, who were almost hateful to him, because they wanted him to give up roasts, to which he was accustomed, and to eat boiled meat instead. In accordance with the national custom, he took frequent exercise on horseback and in the chase, accomplishments in which scarcely any people in the world can equal the Franks. He enjoyed the exhalations from natural warm springs, and often practised swimming, in which he was such an adept that none could surpass him; and hence it was that he built his palace at Aix-la-Chapelle, and lived there constantly during his latter years until his death. He used not only to invite his sons to his bath, but his nobles and friends, and now and then a troop of his retinue or bodyguard, so that a hundred or more persons sometimes bathed with him.

[*from Chapter XXII*]

He used to wear the national, that is to say, the Frank, dress—next his skin a linen shirt and linen breeches, and above these a tunic fringed with silk; while hose fastened by bands covered his lower limbs, and shoes his feet, and he protected his shoulders and chest in winter by a close-fitting coat of otter or marten skins. Over all he flung a blue cloak, and he always had a sword girt about him, usually one with a gold or silver hilt and belt; he sometimes carried a jewelled sword, but only on great feast-days or at the reception of ambassadors from foreign nations. He despised foreign costumes, however handsome, and never allowed himself to be robed in them, except twice in Rome, when he donned the Roman tunic, chlamys, and shoes; the first time at the request of Pope Hadrian, the second to gratify Leo, Hadrian's successor. On great feast-days he made use of embroidered clothes, and shoes bedecked with precious stones; his cloak was fastened by a golden buckle, and he appeared crowned with a diadem of gold and gems: but on other days his dress varied little from the common dress of the people.

[*from Chapter XXIII*]

Charles was temperate in eating, and particularly so in drinking, for he abominated drunkenness in anybody, much more in himself and those of his household; but he could not easily abstain from food, and often complained that fasts injured his health. He very rarely gave entertainments, only on great feast-days, and then to large numbers of people. His meals ordinarily consisted of four courses, not counting the roast, which his huntsmen used to bring in on the spit; he was more fond of this than of any other dish. While at table, he listened to reading or music. The subjects of the readings were the stories and deeds of olden time: he was fond, too, of St. Augustine's books, and especially of the one entitled "The City of God." He was so moderate in the use of wine and all sorts of drink that he rarely allowed himself more than three cups in the course of a meal. In summer, after the midday meal, he would eat some fruit, drain a single cup, put off his clothes and shoes, just as he did for the night, and rest for two or three hours. He was in the habit of awaking and rising from bed four or five times during the night. While he was dressing and putting on his shoes, he not only gave audience to his friends, but if the Count of the Palace told him of any suit in which his judgment was necessary, he had the parties brought before him forthwith, took cognizance of the case, and gave his decision, just as if he were sitting on the judgment-seat. This was not the only business that he transacted at this time, but he performed any duty of the day whatever, whether he had to attend to the matter himself, or to give commands concerning it to his officers.

[from Chapter XXIV]

Charles had the gift of ready and fluent speech, and could express whatever he had to say with the utmost clearness. He was not satisfied with command of his native language merely, but gave attention to the study of foreign ones, and in particular was such a master of Latin that he could speak it as well as his native tongue; but he could understand Greek better than he could speak it. He was so eloquent, indeed, that he might have passed for a teacher of eloquence. He most zealously cultivated the liberal arts, held those who taught them in great esteem, and conferred great honours upon them. He took lessons in grammar of the deacon Peter of Pisa, at that time an aged man. Another deacon, Albin of Britain, surnamed Alcuin, a man of Saxon extraction, who was the greatest scholar of the day, was his teacher in other branches of learning. The King spent much time and labour with him studying rhetoric, dialectics, and especially astronomy; he learned to reckon, and used to investigate the motions of the heavenly bodies most curiously, with an intelligent scrutiny. He also tried to write, and used to keep tablets and blanks in bed under his pillow, that at leisure hours he might accustom his hand to form the letters; however, as he did not begin his efforts in due season, but late in life, they met with ill success.

[*from Chapter XXV*]

He cherished with the greatest fervour and devotion the principles of the Christian religion, which had been instilled into him from infancy. Hence it was that he built the beautiful basilica at Aix-la-Chapelle, which he adorned with gold and silver and lamps, and with rails and doors of solid brass. He had the columns and marbles for this structure brought from Rome and Ravenna, for he could not find such as were suitable elsewhere. . . . He was at great pains to improve the church reading and psalmody, for he was well skilled in both, although he neither read in public nor sang, except in a low tone and with others.

[*from Chapter XXVI*]

. . . . He cherished the Church of St. Peter the Apostle at Rome above all other holy and sacred places, and heaped its treasury with a vast wealth of gold, silver, and precious stones. He sent great and countless gifts to the popes; and throughout his whole reign the wish that he had nearest at heart was to re-establish the ancient authority of the city of Rome under his care and by his influence, and to defend and protect the Church of St. Peter, and to beautify and enrich it out of his own store above all other churches. Although he held it in such veneration, he only repaired to Rome to pay his vows and make his supplications four times during the whole forty-seven years that he reigned.

[*from Chapter XXVII*]

When he made his last journey thither, he had also other ends in view. The Romans had inflicted many injuries upon the Pontiff Leo, tearing out his eyes and cutting out his tongue, so that he had been compelled to call upon the King for help. Charles accordingly went to Rome, to set in order the affairs of the Church, which were in great confusion, and passed the whole winter there. It was then that he received the titles of Emperor and Augustus, to which he

PLATE IX

Ninth Century

FIGURE 1. *This page from the so-called Vivian Bible of Charles the Bald represents the presentation of the book to the emperor by a deputation of monks from the Abbey of St. Martin of Tours, where it was made. Charles is in the Byzantine costume he is known to have worn on Sundays and holidays. The hand of God directly overhead sheds sanctity upon him and female figures, presumably Francia and Gothia, present crowns. The young men on either side of the king are perhaps his sons Louis and Charles. The central figure below with hands raised is probably Vivian, Abbot of St. Denis. Among the monks behind him the one holding the book is presumably the artist. The welcoming group to the right is made up of ecclesiastics of the court, followed by the count of the palace. The lively, conversational air of these figures strikes a new note in the art of illumination. Charlemagne, in his efforts to revive Christian learning, imported artists as well as scholars, and their influence upon local art produced new schools known today as the Carolingian schools. The Carolingian artists copied or were influenced by early Christian models, rather than by the nonrepresentational Celtic art, but the animals of the top margin recall the stylized beasts of Northern art.*
[*From Bibliothèque nationale, Paris*]

FIGURE 2. *Ship of the Viking age, in the Museum at Oslo. This is one of two such vessels dug up in Norway. Neither was exactly of the type that was used for raiding, but it is possible to tell from their construction what the raiding vessels were like. They are clinker-built, and have keels like modern boats. The rudders were on the right side (steer board, hence starboard). There are holes for oars and arrangements for stepping a mast in the center of the boat. Note the elaborate carving on the bow.*
[*Courtesy of the Metropolitan Museum of Art, New York*]

FIGURE 3. *Beaten gold cover of a manuscript of the Gospels, made in northern France in 875, probably in the monastery of St. Denis. Erigena's translation of Dionysius the Areopagite was in Charles the Bald's library at St. Denis. It has been pointed out that the symbols of the sun and moon above the head of Christ in this cover are arranged according to the unusual description Dionysius gives of the movements of sun and moon on the day of the crucifixion. Moreover, the use of angels in works of art was more frequent after Erigena's translations of Dionysius' work,* The Celestial Hierarchy. *(See A. M. Friend,* Art Studies, *I, 67-75.)*
[*Courtesy of the Pierpont Morgan Library, New York*]

CXLVIII ALLELUIA
CANTATEDNO
CANTICUMNOUUM LAUS
EIUSINECCLESIASCORUM
LAETETURISRAHELINEOQUI
FECITEUM ETFILLISION EX
SULTENTINREGESUO

ALLELUIA
DNOINPOPULOSUO ETEX
ALTABITMANSUETOSIN
SALUTE
EXSULTABUNTSCIINGLORI
A LAETABUNTURINCUBI
LIBUSSUIS

INNATIONIBUS INCRE
PATIONESINPOPULIS
ADALLIGANDOSREGESEORU
INCOMPEDIBUS ETNO
BILESEORUMINMANICIS
FERREIS

PLATE X

Ninth Century

FIGURE 1. *Page from the Utrecht Psalter, illustrating the 149th psalm. The ladies at the top are following the injunction:* "Let them praise his name in the dance; let them sing praises unto him with the timbrel and harp." *The figures in the building on the right are praising the Lord* "with a two-edged sword in their hands." *At the bottom the* "vengeance upon the heathen" *is being carried out duly:* "bind their kings with chains, and their nobles with fetters of iron." *The group of serious thinkers in the shelter at the left of these rueful prisoners is working out the way* "to execute upon them the judgment written." *This manuscript was made at a monastery near Reims by Northern artists. When exposed to the figure drawing of early Christian manuscripts, the skill of men trained in the Northern tradition of exciting linear design lent itself to the dynamic representation of the sharply silhouetted figure in action. Shown to a lesser degree in the Vivian Bible (Plate IX, Fig. 1) this skill reached its climax at Reims in a style which affected the art of all Western Europe in the medieval period.*
[*From* The Utrecht Psalter. *Courtesy of E. T. Dewald, editor. Princeton University Press, Princeton, N. J., 1932*]

FIGURE 2. *Crystal of Lothair. This piece of rock crystal, now in the British Museum, is four and a half inches in diameter. It belonged either to the Emperor Lothair, grandson of Charlemagne, or to the former's son, Lothair II, king of Lorraine. The work was done by artists whose style was similar to that of the men who produced the Utrecht Psalter. The scenes dramatically illustrate the story of Susanna and the Elders in the Apocrypha.* [*British Museum photograph*]

FIGURE 3. *A small building on a hill above Oviedo in Spain. Probably once part of the palace of Ramiro I (843–850), king of Navarre and the Asturias, it is now the Church of Santa Maria de Naranco.*

at first had such an aversion that he declared that he would not have set foot in the Church the day that they were conferred, although it was a great feast-day, if he could have foreseen the design of the Pope. He bore very patiently with the jealousy which the Roman emperors showed upon his assuming these titles, for they took this step very ill; and by dint of frequent embassies and letters, in which he addressed them as brothers, he made their haughtiness yield to his magnanimity, a quality in which he was unquestionably much their superior.

[*from Chapter XXVIII*]

DIADEM OF CHARLEMAGNE

(From *Les Arts de la Moyen Age* by Paul Lacroix. Paris, 1873. Courtesy of New York Public Library.)

PART V

The Ninth Century

CHRONOLOGY

    800 Coronation of Charlemagne emperor in the west
c. 800 Northmen begin to appear in western Europe in force; second great period of Germanic invasions
    804 Subjugation of the Saxons
    814 Death of Charlemagne
    842 Strasbourg oath
    843 Treaty of Verdun
c. 849 Heresy of the Saxon monk Gottschalk
c. 859 Rurik prince of Russia; establishment of Northmen in southern Russia
c. 862 Novgorod established by Northmen; major station in the north on the Russian trading route
    865 First Russian expedition to Constantinople
    871 Alfred the Great king of England
c. 880 Kiev established; became capital of the Russian state
 886–7 Great siege of Paris by Northmen
    893 Tsar Simeon founds a Bulgarian empire

PART V

The Ninth Century

~~~~~~~~~~~~~~~~~~~~~~~~~~~~~~~

THE reign of Charlemagne lasted through the first fourteen years of the ninth century, and his strong rule left an ineffaceable impression. He fulfilled the idea of the anointed king whose person was sacred, who was sworn to protect his people's liberties, who was commander of the kingdom's forces and supreme judge, and who reigned by the grace of God. But Charlemagne had not been able to modify the customs of his age materially; he only regularized them. Without the fortunate circumstances that had made possible undisputed rule by one man during the eighth century the Carolingian empire disintegrated in the ninth. Political decentralization had existed in Charlemagne's time, with much power in the hands of the nobles, though he had exercised a close personal supervision and control through his *missi dominici*. A very significant indication of the personal nature of the Frankish government was that the expenses were met in large measure by the income from the royal demesne, for the Roman system of general taxation for public expenses had collapsed completely. The royal demesne at the beginning of the ninth century was extensive, but badly administered in spite of Charlemagne's attempts at reform; he had also his war booty, which was considerable, and special rights and privileges, which included two-thirds of the fines collected in the royal courts. The system of immunities, however, had greatly lessened the scope of these courts, while it enlarged the power of the nobles.

The immunities were one feature of the social and political institution which had been gradually developing since the fifth century, and became known as feudalism. This was an improvised form of local government in which the status of a man was determined by

[131]

his relation to land; and it grew out of a combination of Germanic and late-Roman customs. Local usage differed, but everywhere the fundamental idea was the same: the noble who received land from a lord and became his vassal gave military service as the principal rent for the land, originally called a benefice but later known as a fief. In the period of disorder when rival barbarian kingdoms had displaced central authority, it became a widespread custom for a small landowner to transfer his land with its peasants to his most powerful neighbor in return for protection. The neighbor in turn gave him back the land to use and enjoy as long as he should fight the invader under the strong man's leadership. To make this contract binding a ceremony was held, in which the former owner (now a vassal) recognized (did homage to) the new owner as his lord, and swore loyalty to him (fealty); the vassal was then invested with the land by the presentation of a symbol, such as a piece of turf.

The contract was considered void if either lord (*seigneur*) or vassal failed in his part of the agreement, and the fief in time became hereditary upon the performance, by each succeeding heir, of the ceremony of homage, fealty, and investiture. Fiefs were divided and subdivided, and other mutual obligations developed; the whole complicated arrangement was a rough and ready government in a period of anarchy. Every lord reserved a part of his fief which was called the domain (demesne) for his own use, and this was cultivated as it had been for centuries. The land was no longer tilled by slaves or *coloni,* but by serfs and villeins, who were attached to the land. They had their own small holdings, for which they paid rent by working on the lord's land and by giving him a specified share of the produce they were able to raise in their remaining time.

The disorders of the ninth century that stimulated the development of feudalism were due in large measure to two factors. One was the breaking up of the Carolingian empire into a number of kingdoms, which revived discord and civil strife among the Franks as each ruler's sons tried to enlist the support of the feudal nobility for his own aggrandizement and made lavish grants of crown land to reward or bribe vassals. The second factor was a new series of Germanic invasions, those made from Scandinavia by the Northmen, or Vikings. To meet this menace lords began to build castles for protection, thus further trenching on royal prerogative, for in theory the kings had been kings because of their monopoly of leadership

The Ninth Century

in war and their assumption of responsibility for defense against invasion. These early feudal castles were made of logs and surrounded by ditches; life in the castles was rude and primitive, for the times were violent. Population dwindled, driven by fear and the famines that followed Viking devastation.

The Vikings were heathen adventurers, keen traders, skilled seamen, and resourceful fighters; the period of their invasions began toward the end of the eighth century and continued through the tenth. Much of our information about them comes from the sagas written in Iceland centuries later, but it can be verified by archaeological and other evidence. Scandinavian society in the invasion period retained some of the features observed by Tacitus among the early Germans, such as the *comitatus,* ready to follow its leader to death in the hope of booty. The leaders were called jarls, and at the other end of the social scale were slaves, called thralls; between the two extremes were lesser nobles and a class of small landholders. The division of estates among the sons meant that the size of holdings tended to decrease beyond the point where subsistence for a family could be provided. Fishing, piracy, and trade, however, were supplementary means of livelihood, for the geography of the Scandinavian lands was such that the sea everywhere offered a ready outlet.

Interest in the sea had stimulated boat-building, and the Vikings had developed one type of vessel useful for carrying a large amount of cargo and passengers, and another type, the long ship, capable of respectable speed. Both types were sailing ships with oars for use when the winds were unfavorable. With the development of kingdoms in all three Scandinavian countries, adventurous nobles as well as small landholders felt the incentive to emigration, instead of the plundering raids which had been a popular pastime for the summer months.

Northmen were seen off the British coast in 786, and in 793 plundered and destroyed the monastery of Lindisfarne. Monasteries and churches provided the best booty, not only because of the vestments and rich altar vessels but because sacred edifices were safe deposit vaults for the treasures of the laity. Viking attacks on the Frisian coast had compelled Charlemagne to do something about his defenses there; he ordered fortifications and ships built, realizing that ships were the only effective answer to the Viking challenge. After his death there remained no central power able to cope with the menace, and throughout the empire local landholders had to meet the invasions with what forces they could muster.

The Viking migrations were in many directions. The Norwegians usually sailed westward and had settled in fairly large numbers in Ireland by 825. They later attacked northern England, settled the islands off the Scottish coast, and toward the end of the century colonized Iceland. The Danes, too, raided England and the Continental coast as far south as Aquitaine. At first these invaders appeared in the spring and sailed home with their booty before cold weather. Later they formed the habit of wintering at the river mouths and, when spring came, sailing up the rivers to attack cities and inland territory. A few Swedes attacked England, but for the most part they ravaged the Baltic lands, seeking furs, and settled as traders in Novgorod, to which they gave its name. These Vikings eventually made their way by the Dnieper River system to the Black Sea; they first attacked Constantinople but later set up trade there, selling the Slavs of Russia whom they captured as slaves.

Northmen, however, were not the only invaders of the ninth century to harry Christian Europe. Since the Moslems controlled the western Mediterranean, they were able to attack coastal cities, and even Rome. From Asia a Mongol group, the Magyars, called Huns because of their resemblance to Attila's destructive hordes, displaced the Avars, and made violent attacks in the West before settling down in the region of the Carpathian basin that perpetuates the epithet. In the Balkans the Bulgars built an empire and periodically warred against the Byzantines, but they accepted Christianity from Constantinople and their great Tsar Simeon, who had been educated to be a monk, established a splendid court in the Greek tradition.

Society in most of Christian Europe in the ninth century was increasingly crude, population tending to center around the isolated strongholds of the feudal nobility. Learning was pursued only in monasteries located far inland, or in Rome, in Constantinople, and for a time at the courts of two leading monarchs—Charles the Bald, king of the Franks, and King Alfred in England. But even in these refuges the shadow of the heresy-hunter limited freedom of philosophical speculation, since knowledge was regarded by the church as subordinate to the faith. It is therefore refreshing to find a figure like John Scotus Erigena in such a world, for he stands out as a bright example of an intellect far in advance of his day, and at a time when the division between the churches of East and West was growing, he was one man of the West who championed the East. In the second half of the century King Alfred in England successfully met the Viking peril and laid the foundation for a united English nation. His establishment of the Danelaw as a place for Viking settlement to divert their energies from conquests in other areas provided a pattern for stemming the invasions of the North men that was later to be followed by the Frankish ruler in Normandy. Alfred also reinforced the tradition begun by Charlemagne under which scholarship was given recognition and encouragement by the wise ruler.

The ninth century was a period of violence, of renewed Germanic migrations, of the break-up of Charlemagne's empire, and of increase in the power of the nobility through the spread of feudalism; but it brought with it some traveling. Perhaps it was a result of the troubled times that pilgrimages to the leading shrines of the Christian faith became increasingly popular. (There was a rather general belief that the invasions of heathen Vikings and infidel Moslems were punishment sent by God for sins which must be expiated.) For the more adventurous in the Christian world, expiation of sins by a pilgrimage not only satisfied the desire to do one's duty, but provided an opportunity to see strange lands and peoples. The Northmen, furthermore, were traders as well as marauders, and their coming gave some stimulus to trade in Europe. Still, only the hardiest could take advantage of the opportunity for pilgrimage or trade to visit new countries; feudalism might free the nobles from the direct control of the kings, but for the great mass of the population it meant a bondage to the land increasingly difficult to break.

DRAWING OF A SHIP, FROM AN ENGLISH
MANUSCRIPT

(From *A Student's History of England* by Samuel R. Gardiner, Longmans Green, London, 1897.)

CHAPTER 8

The World of John Scotus Erigena

[c. 800 – c. 877]

~~~~~~~~~~~~~~~~~~

NOTHING is known of the early life of John Scotus Erigena, but there is no reason to doubt the origin indicated by the double affirmation of his name: "Scot" was the medieval term for Irishman, and "Erin" means Ireland. In some one of the Irish monastic schools he undoubtedly got his thorough education, which included a respectable proficiency in the Greek language, then taught in few Continental schools. As the Norwegians who in Erigena's youth made settlements in Ireland showed the usual Viking zeal in sacking and burning monasteries, Erigena was probably one of the refugees who carried back to the Continent the learning which had been borne from there to Ireland in the fifth century by scholars fleeing the Germanic invasions. By 847 he was living at the court of Charles the Bald, who alone of Charlemagne's grandsons encouraged scholarship.

Charlemagne's empire had passed undivided to Louis the Pious, the only one of his sons who survived him. It was too vast a territory to be governed by one man unless he were of heroic mold, and the worthy Louis emphatically was not such a man, though he was much more learned than his father. Louis, who knew Greek, welcomed some of the Irish refugees at his court and tried to introduce reforms in the Frankish monasteries, which had relaxed the requirements of the Benedictine Rule, but in political affairs he was not able to keep firm control. The members of his own family plagued him, for he made a division of the kingdom among his sons during his lifetime and the land-hungry nobles lined up with one or another of the royal heirs to quarrel over the prospective division of the kingdom.

The World of John Scotus Erigena

On the death of Louis the Pious in 840 two of his sons, Charles the Bald, who was to have the western part of the empire, and Louis the German, who was to have the eastern part, united against their brother Lothair, who was to have the central part and the imperial title. The feudal followers of the new kings were so independent that after one inconclusive battle they required the two kings to take in their presence an oath to each other. The result was the Oath of Strasburg, taken by Charles in German, so that Louis's followers could understand it, and by Louis in French, so that Charles's followers could understand it. The text of this oath, which has survived, shows that the Germans who had settled within the old Roman Empire had adopted enough of the Latin speech to justify the term "Romance" for the new French language, and that the language spoken by the inhabitants of the eastern region resembled modern German.

The year after the taking of the oath at Strasburg a settlement was made at Verdun (843) whereby Charles the Bald reigned in the west, Louis the German in the east, and the eldest, Lothair, was allotted as emperor a middle strip that included the two capitals, Aachen (Aix-la-Chapelle) and Rome. It is significant that the lands in this central strip are today either independent or still sources of conflict between France and Germany, the modern counterparts of the western and eastern parts of Charlemagne's empire. Another settlement at Mersen in 870 wiped out the middle strip temporarily and established France, Germany, and Italy, with Germany's boundary west of the Rhine. The fight for the middle regions soon began.

The most vivid records of this dreary period are the annals of various monasteries, where, upon the margins of the parchment tables for reckoning Easter, monks set down the notable events of the year, as they observed them or as travelers reported them. (Every monastery had its guest house, and monasteries served as centers of hospitality in an age when there were few inns.) These annals record the monotonous tales of incessant warfare among the royal brothers and their successors—the Carolingian rulers of the ninth century unfortunately were usually survived by several sons and the process of division multiplied the number of independent kingdoms. The annals also show how each year, with the spring, the Northmen appeared on the coasts and sailed up the rivers, and how later they began wintering in the valleys. Occasionally among these events appear the records of heresies; in 851 it is told how a Saxon monk, Gottschalk, wrote a book on predestination. Gottschalk was something of a poet, since he wrote songs that have a certain charm, and he was the author of a moral dialogue between Truth and Falsehood which came to be widely used in schools. He was inspired to write his theological treatise by reading the works of St. Augustine. Centuries later another Saxon monk who read St. Augustine (Martin Luther) was to write on predestination with notable results; but Gottschalk was scourged and put in prison, after being obliged to cast his book into the flames.

Gottschalk's conviction had been secured by Hincmar, bishop of Rheims, an energetic prelate who asked John Scotus Erigena to confute the errors of Gottschalk. Erigena was then living at the court of Charles the Bald and was head of the palace school, which Charles maintained as far as possible as his grandfather had done, though with fewer eminent scholars to teach in it. Erigena was a thin, little man with a powerful intellect, a hot temper, and a ready wit. It is related that one evening as he was sitting across the board from the king at supper, Charles asked, "What separates a Scot from a sot?" and Erigena replied instantly, "Only the table."[1] The Scot's response to Gottschalk, however, was a serious matter, since it contained an idea to be condemned as heresy in its turn: Erigena asserted that there was no such thing as evil, for if there were it would have had to be willed by God, and as He was wholly good He could not have willed evil. Erigena made trouble for himself in another ecclesiastical controversy by stating that the elements of the eucharist were not the actual body and blood of Christ but were assimilated spiritually, *"mente, non dente."* The doctrine of the eucharist that he attacked, however, had not yet become dogma.

The theologians spoke scornfully of Erigena's ideas as "Scots' porridge," but the Scot's name is remembered where theirs are forgotten; a profound and original thinker, in his philosophy he was far in advance of his age. Among the works that deeply influenced his thinking in the direction of Neo-Platonism was a copy of the *Celestial Hierarchy* which the Byzantine emperor had sent to Charles the Bald's father and which Charles asked Erigena to translate. The author was the pseudo-Dionysius, a Neo-Platonist of the early sixth

---

[1] *"Quid distat inter sottum et Scottum?"*—*"Mensa tantum."*

century who had claimed to be Dionysius the Areopagite, converted, according to the New Testament account, by St. Paul at Athens. The Areopagite was a personage in whom there was great interest at the French court, for it was believed that he had suffered martyrdom in France, and that he was the founder of the great monastery of St. Denis, near Paris.

Erigena was well acquainted with the works of Augustine and those of some of the Greek fathers, and he had a thorough acquaintance with the Bible. He produced a number of works, some of which have been lost; he probably wrote a commentary on Boethius, and a collection of glosses on Martianus Capella. It was presumably from the latter that he got the idea that Mercury and Venus revolve about the sun, an idea expressed in the work that has won him the reputation of being one of the great metaphysicians of all time: his *De Divisione Naturae*. In this, an effort to reconcile Greek and Christian thinking about the problem of life, Erigena rejected the literal interpretation of the first chapters of Genesis for a symbolic one, and built up a system by which everything came originally from God and would in due time return to Him. Fortunately the book was too profound to be understood by his contemporaries, and escaped condemnation by the authorities until the twelfth century, surviving to affect many generations of thinkers. "Reason cannot be subject to authority, for authority is based on reason," is one statement that marks the witty Irishman as much more modern than his age.

To the reign of Erigena's patron, Charles the Bald, it is possible to trace the creation of some of the important fiefs whose names have become famous in French history. On the eastern frontiers was formed the county of Flanders and the duchy of Burgundy. The region between the Seine and the Garonne was made a duchy which was later to divide into parts as the duchy of Aquitaine and the counties of Champagne and Anjou, but for a long period it was ruled as the march of Neustria by the family of the count of Paris, Robert the Strong, who was destined to found the line of kings that succeeded the Carolingians. Other families exercised practically independent rule in Gascony and Brittany. A similar situation existed in the German kingdom across the Rhine, where the dukes of Saxony, Swabia, Franconia, and Bavaria were more powerful than the king. Feudal lords everywhere, besides receiving the voluntary commendation of lesser lords, forced small landholders to yield their holdings, and there was great suffering among the tillers of the soil induced by change of landlords as well as by the invaders.

The monastic annals record many disastrous events of these sad days for Christendom. The Vikings sailed in to the Mediterranean and devastated the coasts; the Moslems conquered Sicily and attacked some of the cities of Italy, burning a church outside the very walls of Rome and destroying St. Benedict's abbey of Monte Cassino; and in the East they won from the emperor a large part of Asia Minor. The papacy went through a period of eclipse, too, except for the brief career of Nicholas I, who made use of a celebrated forgery known as the False Decretals to support the papal claim to the right of deposing bishops and archbishops—notably in the case of German bishops who had obeyed the German kings rather than the pope. Nicholas also made the Emperor Lothair II take back his wife, and he excommunicated the eastern emperor.

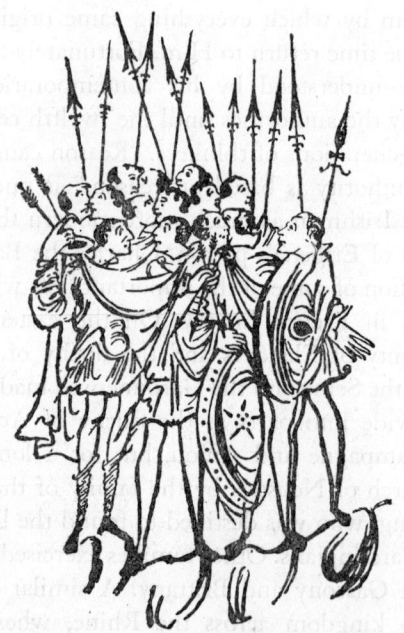

GROUP OF SAXON WARRIORS

(From *A Student's History of England* by Samuel R. Gardiner. Longmans Green, London, 1897.)

The pope asked Charles the Bald to send him Erigena's translation of the pseudo-Dionysius to be examined for possible heresy; this action may have been due to the fact that Erigena had appended to his translation a poem lauding the glories of Constantinople, the patriarch, and the emperor. The papal secretaries, however, seem to have found no evil in Erigena's work, and the papal librarian expressed his wonder at the knowledge of Greek possessed by a man who came from so barbarous a land. The English chronicler William of Malmesbury, who wrote in the twelfth century, tells that after the death of Charles the Bald, King Alfred invited Erigena to England and settled him as teacher in the abbey of Malmesbury, which was an Irish foundation. According to this tale Erigena's students murdered him by stabbing him with their pens. There are certain improbabilities in the story and the weight of modern opinion seems to favor the belief that Erigena lived on undisturbed as the master of Charles the Bald's palace school, and died the same year as his patron.

CHAPTER 9

The World of Alfred

[849–899]

~~~~~~~~~~~~~~~~~~~~~~~~~~~~~~

THE ruthless striking force of the Vikings was quite as destructive in the British Isles during a large part of the ninth century as in the rest of Europe. In British records the Northmen are known as Danes, though some Swedes raided England, and the invaders who wiped out Irish culture were mainly Norwegians. Everywhere their main attack was on churches and monasteries, not because of a hatred for Christianity, but because those places were treasure houses. The principal resistance to the Danes in England was provided by a line of unusually able rulers in the ninth century, the kings of Wessex (one of the many kingdoms set up by the Angles and Saxons). Though there had been no unity among the English kingdoms, first Northumbria and later Mercia occupied a prominent position until the rise of Wessex. Egbert, a king of Wessex in the early ninth century who had fought under Charlemagne, was able to extort admissions of fealty from other English kings and consequently has been called, with some exaggeration, king of all England.

Egbert's son Ethelwulf strove manfully against the Vikings. He shared the contemporary belief that the attacks of these heathen were a judgment of God for the sins of the people; and when after sixteen years of his reign the Northmen continued to assault his kingdom, he sent his four-year-old son Alfred on a pilgrimage to Rome in the hope that prayers at the shrines of St. Peter and St. Paul would placate the Almighty. The Danes did not withdraw, however, so two years later the king gave a tenth of the royal domain to the church and, taking Alfred with him, made the pilgrimage himself, staying in Rome a year. On the way back to

Wessex he paid a visit to Charles the Bald and married the Frankish ruler's daughter Judith. Since the English royal party stayed several months at Charles the Bald's court, Alfred in all probability became acquainted with Erigena; in any case the experiences of these journeys profoundly affected the clever child.

Alfred's three elder brothers followed each other as kings of Essex after their father's death, and all faced Viking raids. During these years important Viking forces were also attacking France, where they worked their way up the Seine, plundering the lands on either side and sacking the Abbey Church of St. Denis near Paris. (One group which made a contract with Charles the Bald to drive another group from the Seine region for a tidy sum, took time out to cross the Channel and attack Winchester, in England.) A Danish army of unparalleled size landed in England in 865, when Alfred's second brother was king. The Danes conquered Northumbria and destroyed the culture which Bede and Alcuin had nourished there, ravaged the kingdom of East Anglia, and brutally murdered its king. Then, with the rest of England at their mercy, they turned on Wessex.

The kingdom of Wessex was divided into shires, each with an efficient army commanded by an official called an ealdorman. One of them gained an initial victory over the Danes, which was soon countered by a defeat of the forces led by the king and Alfred. When Alfred became sole king in 871 he bought a temporary peace during which the Danes, already masters of London, occupied the whole of England north of the Thames. This peace was broken by renewed raids during which Alfred spent some time eluding the invaders; at length he was able to gather sufficient forces to win a decisive battle at Ethandun. He followed up the victory with a statesmanlike peace. He promised not to interfere with the Danes who settled in the Danelaw, a section north and east of London, if they would withdraw from Wessex and accept Christianity. This acceptance of baptism was more or less common among the invaders, and was not always taken seriously, but the Danes of the Danelaw kept to the faith, and as time went on became good Englishmen.

One of the characteristics of the Danes as fighters was their great mobility; it was their habit, upon landing, to seize horses and then make their way on horseback to their chosen destination, where they dismounted to fight. They used the device of the shield wall, assembling the fighting men in a circle and placing edge to edge the great shields which adorned the gunwales of their ships, thus presenting a solid front to the enemy. They were also expert at throwing up burgs (earthworks) when they expected to hold a place, or when they needed a base to take cover in until the swarms of outraged peasants stirred up by their raids had disbanded again.

Alfred, however, showed himself a soldier of genius and was finally able to settle the Danish menace for his own kingdom. He copied the Viking method of building defensive burgs, and apparently adopted their way of getting about on horseback. Furthermore, he reorganized the militia so that part of the freemen were left at all times for the tilling of the soil. As Charlemagne had done, he realized that sea-borne invaders had to be repulsed at sea and by building a new type of vessel capable of performing that office he won the title of founder of the English navy. His fame, like Charlemagne's, was made as a warrior, and, largely through the work of his admiring biographer Asser, an Alfred legend grew up which is more baffling to the historian than the greater Charlemagne legend.

Alfred's achievements in the arts of peace were considerable, but they have often been exaggerated. He was not a great lawmaker: his famous dooms, or statutes, are little more than the recording of the barbarian rules of *wergeld*. He did, however, make reforms in the royal administration; in doing so he found, as had Charlemagne, that he had to restore education in order to have trained officials, for the Danes had done a thorough job of destroying the centers of learning. A century before, Charlemagne had brought the most distinguished of his scholars from England; Alfred had in his turn to import his scholars from the Continent. It is significant that he was interested in providing reading in the vernacular. He himself translated into Anglo-Saxon Gregory the Great's *Pastoral Care,* Boethius's *Consolation of Philosophy,* some of St. Augustine's *Soliloquies,* and Orosius's *Seven Books of History against the Pagans.* He had his scholars translate Gregory's *Dialogues,* and Bede's *Ecclesiastical History*. He also provided for the continuation of historical record by establishing the *Anglo-Saxon Chronicle,* which was carried on from the period of Alfred's campaigns against the Danes half way through the twelfth century.

Although the light of learning lit by Alfred was but a candle, it was brighter than any burning in other Christian lands of the West.

On the death of Charles the Bald in 877 a period of anarchy ensued in the kingdom of the west Franks, and nothing more is heard of the scholarship Erigena had fostered at that court. In 884 Charles the Fat, son of Louis the German, emperor and king of the east Franks, was chosen king of the west Franks and briefly reunited much of Charlemagne's realm. The next year the Vikings attacked Paris, which was successfully defended by Eudes, Count of Paris and Marquis of Neustria. The west Franks deposed Charles for not assisting Eudes, who was elected king in Charles's place by one Frankish faction. Another faction elected Charles the Simple, grandson of Charles the Bald, and the country was torn by civil war—the later Carolingians obviously did not command the respect of the feudal nobility. In Germany the east Franks chose as their king Arnulf, a nephew of Charles the Fat, who fought Northmen and Slavs and was finally made emperor. Amid all the turmoil of war and invasion intellectual life stagnated.

Among the Moslems, however, the situation was very different. All Spain had become Moslem except for a few small Christian kingdoms in the north that alternately fought the Moors and quarrelled among themselves. Cordova was the capital of the Spanish caliphate and Bagdad the capital of the eastern caliphate. Although there were spasmodic struggles with Constantinople and occasional revolts of subject peoples, liberal appropriations were made for research, observatories were built, and libraries were endowed. In the whole Moslem world a new civilization was coming into being; and the ability of the Arabs to infuse new life into the arts of the people they conquered showed itself in architecture, music, design, and especially in the sciences. The Arabs admired Greek science, which was rejected by Christian authorities, and preserved its records besides making developments of their own. (Desert dwellers, they had studied the stars in their courses and had eagerly conned the theoretical astronomy of the Greeks.) They also assimilated Hindu mathematics and contributed to the spread of the basically Hindu features of our modern system of numerical notation. Moslem art was marked by the development of geometric and floral forms into wonderful patterns, to which the skills of Persia and Egypt lent color and life; and as trade with the West gradually revived, these designs on textiles and ceramics profoundly influenced Western art.

The world of Alfred was a world of turmoil in which power

went to those able and willing to grasp it. The foundations of a united England were laid by Alfred's settlement of the Danish menace and by his ordering of the monarchy in Wessex. On the Continent the power of the great feudal lords steadily increased, and families arose which challenged the place of the Carolingians. In the disorders of the day people turned to the consolations offered by the church; and, as it has already been pointed out, the adventuresome turned increasingly to the diversified consolation of pilgrimages.[1] But the routes to religious shrines were used by others besides pilgrims; on them went traders carrying goods, and travelers carrying ideas. The human spirit, expressing itself in curiosity and enterprise, not only survived but was in search of new paths.

[1] The century saw the rise of a new shrine which was to become especially famous—that of Santiago de Compostella, in the Christian kingdom of Castile in Spain, where early in the century were discovered some bones which were believed to be those of St. James and which were consecrated about the time of Alfred's death.

[THE NINTH CENTURY]

Readings

~~~~~~

XANTEN, ST. VAAST, AND FULDA ANNALS *

[The notes of important events of the year, jotted down by monks on the blank pages of the Easter tables, had by the ninth century become more elaborate records. There is no better way of gaining an idea of the confusion, anxiety, and disorders of the period following the death of Charlemagne than by reading extracts from the monastic annals.]

(845) Twice in the canton of Worms there was an earthquake; the first in the night following Palm Sunday, the second in the holy night of Christ's Resurrection. In the same year the heathen broke in upon the Christians at many points, but more than twelve thousand of them were killed by the Frisians. Another party of invaders devastated Gaul; of these more than six hundred men perished. Yet owing to his indolence Charles agreed to give them many thousand pounds of gold and silver if they would leave Gaul, and this they did. Nevertheless the cloisters of most of the saints were destroyed and many of the Christians were led away captive. . . .

(846) According to their custom the Northmen plundered Eastern and Western Frisia and burned the town of Dordrecht, with two other villages, before the eyes of Lothaire, who was then in the castle of Nimwegen, but could not punish the crime. The Northmen, with their boats filled with immense booty, including both men and goods, returned to their own country. . . .

At this same time, as no one can mention or hear without great sadness, the mother of all churches, the basilica of the apostle Peter, was taken and plundered by the Moors, or Saracens, who had already occupied the region of Beneventum. The Saracens, moreover,

---

* Reprinted by permission of Ginn and Company from J. H. Robinson, *Readings in European History* (1904), I, pp. 158ff.

slaughtered all the Christians whom they found outside the walls of Rome, either within or without this church. They also carried men and women away prisoners. They tore down, among many others, the altar of the blessed Peter, and their crimes from day to day bring sorrow to Christians. Pope Sergius departed life this year.

(847) After the death of Sergius no mention of the apostolic see has come in any way to our ears. Rabanus [Maurus], master and abbot of Fulda, was solemnly chosen archbishop as the successor of Bishop Otger, who had died. Moreover the Northmen here and there plundered the Christians and engaged in a battle with the counts Sigir and Liuthar. They continued up the Rhine as far as Dordrecht, and nine miles farther to Meginhard, when they turned back, having taken their booty.

(852) The steel of the heathen glistened; excessive heat; a famine followed. There was not fodder enough for the animals. The pasturage for the swine was more than sufficient.

(853) A great famine in Saxony so that many were forced to live on horse meat.

(854) The Normans, in addition to the very many evils which they were everywhere inflicting upon the Christians, burned the church of St. Martin, bishop of Tours, where his body rests.

John Scotus Erigena

TRANSLATION OF THE *DE COELESTI HIERARCHIA* OF DIONYSIUS THE PSEUDO-AREOPAGITE *

[The Neo-Platonic idea of the transition from the material to the immaterial expressed in this passage became fundamental with John the Scot. It runs through his *De Divisione Naturae,* as the editor, Poole, brings out. Poole's summaries and comment clarify the Scot's words, which are given in quotation marks.]

Every creature, visible or invisible, is a light brought into being by the Father of the lights. . . . This stone or that piece of wood is

* Reprinted by permission of Princeton University Press from the introduction to *Abbot Suger on the Abbey Church of St.-Denis and Its Art Treasures,* Erwin Panofsky, editor (1946).

a light to me. . . . For I perceive that it is good and beautiful; that it exists according to its proper rules of proportion; that it differs in kind and species from other kinds and species; that it is defined by its number, by virtue of which it is "one" thing; that it does not transgress its order; that it seeks its place according to its specific gravity. As I perceive such and similar things in this stone they become lights to me, that is to say, they enlighten me (*me illuminant*). For I begin to think whence the stone is invested with such properties . . . ; and soon, under the guidance of reason, I am led through all things to that cause of all things which endows them with place and order, with number, species and kind, with goodness and beauty and essence, and with all other grants and gifts.

DE DIVISIONE NATURAE*

. . . Sin, he repeats, has no cause because it has no real existence. How then does it arise? . . . Sin is implied in the fact of man's free will. He takes the case of two men looking at a golden vase. There is no evil in the vase, but it may excite in the one feelings only of pleasure and admiration, in the other the passion of covetousness. The one receives the simple impression of a beautiful object; the other colours and deforms it by his own lawless desire. But this desire, this evil, is not indigenous to man's nature; it is the result of the irregular action of his reasonable and free will. The senses are deceived by that which appears to be good, by "false good," and the infection spreads inwardly to the intellect itself. Thus the inner man wherein naturally "dwelleth truth and all good, which is the Word of God, the only-begotten Son of God," becomes corrupt and "sins." But this process does not originate in evil. The bodily sense does not desire a thing because it is evil but because it has the show of goodness. "No vice is found but is the shadow of some virtue." Pride for instance is a perversion of a true sense of power—in good men it takes the form of a love of heavenly excellence and of a contempt of earthly weakness;—and it was from pride that the sin of man began. It was the first exercise of his free will. . . . "For if paradise is human nature formed after the image of God and made equal to the blessedness of the angels, then immediately he [Adam]

---

* From Reginald Lane Poole, *Illustrations of the History of Medieval Thought and Learning* (London, new edition, revised, 1920; reprinted 1932). By permission of The Macmillan Company, publishers.

wished to leave his Creator, he fell from the dignity of his nature. His pride began before he consented to his wife. . . .

"The soul may forget her natural goods, may fail in her striving towards the goal of the inborn virtues of her nature; the natural powers may move, by fault of judgement, towards something which is not their end:" but not for ever. For the universal tendency of things is upward; "and thus from evil is wont to turn good, but in nowise from good evil. . . . The first evil could not be perpetual, but by the necessity of things must reach a certain bound and one day vanish. For if the divine goodness which ever worketh not only in the good but also in the wicked, is eternal and infinite, it follows that its contrary will not be eternal and infinite. . . . Evil therefore will have its consummation and remain not in any nature, since in all the divine nature will work and be manifest. Our nature then is not fixed in evil; . . . it is ever moving, and seeks nought else but the highest good, from which as from a beginning its motion takes its source, and to which it is hastened as to an end." As all things proceed from God, so in God they find their final completion. . . .

John [did not doubt the truth of the Bible, he] sought for the larger meaning concealed within its depths. "For the sense of the divine utterances is manifold and infinite, even as in one and the same feather of the peacock we behold a marvellous and beautiful variety of countless colours." Like principles, as one applied them, might lead to a submissive dependence on the letter, or to amplest freedom of rational enquiry. For in the one writer, reason without the support of authority is weak, in the other it stands firm "fortified by its own virtues, and needs not to be strengthened by any prop of authority."

If we examine more closely the Scot's view of reason it appears that authority is actually related to it as a species to its genus. In both God reveals not himself but the forms in which we can conceive him. The human reason is the dwelling-place of the word of God. . . .

"Intellect . . . and the rest of things that are said to be, are theophanies, [revelations from God], and in theophany really subsist; therefore God is everything that truly is, since he makes all things and is made in all things". . . .

For the mystery of the divine Trinity "passes the endeavours of human reason and even the purest understandings of celestial essences. We infer from the essence of the things that are, that it exists; from the wonderful order of things, that it is wise; from their motion, that it is life. As, saith saint Dionysius the Areopagite, 'The highest and causal essence of all things cannot be signified by any signification of words or names, or of any articulate voice.' For it is neither unity nor trinity, such as can be contemplated by the purest human, by the clearest angelical, understanding. . . . Chiefly for the sake of those who demand a reason for the Christian faith . . . have these symbolical words been religiously discovered and handed down by the holy theologians. . . . Beholding, in so far as they were enlightened by the divine Spirit, the one unspeakable cause of all things, and the one beginning, simple and undivided and universal, they called it Unity; but seeing this unity not in singleness or barrenness, but in a marvellous and fertile multiplicity, they have understood three substances of unity."

. . . This union is revealed in the incarnation, by which the Word of God passed from the region of cause to that of effects, and descended into the sensible world. It was not a temporal act, but the expression of the necessary reciprocity of temporal and eternal, the immanent relation of God and the world. It is the supreme theophany. By it "the light to which no man can approach opened access to every intellectual and reasonable creature. . . . In Him the visible things and the invisible, that is to say, the world of sense and the world of thought, were restored and recalled to unspeakable unity, now in hope, hereafter in fact; now in faith, hereafter in sight; now by inference, hereafter in experience; already effected in the manhood which he assumed, hereafter to be fulfilled in all men without distinction."

. . . If it be otherwise, if there be a sensible world of torments, "then have we laboured in vain, and the sentences of the holy writers which we have alleged will be turned into derision: which God forbid."

. . . The third question involved in John Scotus's view of the return of creation into the Creator concerns the immortality of the individual. He answers it by analogies. The air is still air though it appear to be absorbed into the light of the sun and to be all light. "The voice of man, or of pipe or lyre, loses not its quality when several by just proportion make one harmony in unity among themselves." Nor is it reasonable to suppose that man will subsist in a spiritual state without a body. The body of our present humanity will disappear, but it will be exchanged for the spiritual body inseparable from the idea of man, the body which he had before he entered into the world of matter. The whole man is eternal. "This" therefore "is the end of all things visible and invisible, when all visible things pass into the intellectual, and the intellectual into God, by a marvellous and unspeakable union; but not, as we have often said, by any confusion or destruction of essences or substances". . . .

King Alfred

PREFACE TO THE *DIALOGUES* OF GREGORY THE GREAT *

[These extracts illuminate Alfred's conception of his duty as a king toward the welfare of his subjects, particularly in the field of education. His idea of the function of an editor is arresting.]

I, Alfred, by the grace of Christ dignified with the honour of royalty, have distinctly understood and through the reading of holy books have often heard, that of us to whom God hath given so much eminence of worldly distinction, it is specially required that we from time to time should subdue and bend our minds to the divine and spiritual law, in the midst of this earthly misery. I accordingly sought and requested of my trusty friends that they for me out of pious books about the conversation and miracles of holy men would transcribe the instruction that hereinafter followeth; that I, through this admonition and love being strengthened in my mind, may now and then contemplate the heavenly things in the midst of these earthly troubles. Plainly we can now first hear how the blessed and apostolic man Saint Gregory spake to his deacon whose name was Peter, about the manners and life of holy men for in-

* From G. F. Browne, *King Alfred's Books* (1920). By permission of The Macmillan Company, publishers.

struction and for example to all those who are working the will of God.

PREFACE TO THE *PASTORAL CARE* *

So clean was it fallen away in the Angle race, that there were very few on this side Humber who would know how to render their service in English, or just read off an epistle out of Latin into English; and I ween that not many would be on the other side Humber. So few of them were there that I cannot think of so much as a single one south of Thames when I took to the realm. God Almighty be thanked that we have now any teachers in office. . . . Therefore to me it seemeth better, if it seemeth so to you, that we also some books, those that were most needful are for all men to be acquainted with, that we turn those into the speech which we all can understand; and that ye do as we very easily may with God's help, if we have the requisite peace, that all the youth which now is in England of free men, of those who have the means to be able to go in for it, be set to learning, while they are fit for no other business, until such time as they can thoroughly read English writing: afterwards further instruction may be given in the Latin language to such as are intended for a more advanced education and are to be prepared for higher office. . . .

INTERPOLATIONS IN
THE CONSOLATIONS OF BOETHIUS †

. . . Therefore it is that a man never by his authority attains to virtue and excellence, but by reason of his virtue and excellence he attains to authority and power. No man is better for his power, but for his skill he is good, if he is good, and for his skill he is worthy of power, if he is worthy of it. Study Wisdom then, and, when ye have learned it, condemn it not, for I tell you that by its means ye may without fail attain to power, yea, even though not desiring it. Ye need not take thought for power nor endeavour after it, for if

* From G. F. Browne, *King Alfred's Books* (1920). By permission of The Macmillan Company, publishers.

† Translated by W. J. Sedgefield (1900). By permission of Oxford University Press.

ye are only wise and good it will follow you, even though ye seek it not. Tell me now, O Mind, what is the height of thy desire in wealth and power? Is it not this present life and the perishable wealth that we before spoke of? . . . Since, therefore, every creature shuns its opposite, and strives amain to repel it, what two things can be more opposed than good and evil, which we never find conjoined? Thus, then, thou mayest understand that if the joys of this present life had control over themselves and were good in their own nature they would ever cleave to him who used them for good and not for evil. But when they happen to be good they are so by the goodness of him that uses them for good, and he gets his goodness from God; whereas, if a bad man have them, they are evil by reason of the evil of him that doth evil with them, and through the working of the devil. . . .

[from Chapter XVI]

. . . I desired instruments and materials to carry out the work I was set to do, which was that I should virtuously and fittingly administer the authority committed unto me. Now no man, as thou knowest, can get full play for his natural gifts, nor conduct and administer government, unless he hath fit tools, and the raw material to work upon. By material I mean that which is necessary to the exercise of natural powers; thus a king's raw material and instruments of rule are a well-peopled land, and he must have men of prayer, men of war, and men of work. As thou knowest, without these tools no king may display his special talent. Further, for his materials he must have means of support for the three classes above spoken of, which are his instruments; and these means are land to dwell in, gifts, weapons, meat, ale, clothing, and what else soever the three classes need. Without these means he cannot keep his tools in order, and without these tools he cannot perform any of the tasks entrusted to him . . . . every good gift and every power soon groweth old and is no more heard of, if Wisdom be not in them. Without Wisdom no faculty can be fully brought out, for whatsoever is done unwisely can never be accounted as skill. To be brief, I may say that it has ever been my desire to live honourably while I was alive, and after my death to leave to them that should come after me my memory in good works.

[from Chapter XVII]

TRANSLATION OF
THE SEVEN BOOKS OF OROSIUS
AGAINST THE PAGANS *

[Alfred's most considerable interpolation is an account given by two Northmen of a journey in the Baltic regions. This account was published by Hakluyt in his *Voyages* in 1598, and more recently by Joseph Bosworth in his *Alfred's Geography of Europe by Orosius*. The part given here is the account of the Esthonians.]

Esthonia is very large, and there are many towns, and in every town there is a king. There is also very much honey and fishing. The king and the richest men drink mare's milk, but the poor and the slaves drink mead. There is very much war among them; and there is no ale brewed by the Esthonians, but there is mead enough.

There is also a custom with the Esthonians that when a man is dead, he lies in his house unburnt, with his kindred and friends, for one month, sometimes two; and the king and other men of high rank, so much longer according to their wealth, remain unburnt sometimes half a year; and lie above ground in their houses. All the while the body is within, there must be drinking and sports, to the day on which he is burned.

Then, the same day, when they wish to bear him to the pile, they divide his property which is left after the drinking and sports into five or six parts, sometimes into more, as the amount of his property may be. Then, they lay the largest part of it within one mile from the town, then another, then the third, till it is all laid within the one mile, and the least part shall be nearest the town in which the dead man lies. All the men who have the swiftest horses in the land shall then be assembled, about five or six miles from the property. Then they all run towards the property, and the man who has the swiftest horse comes to the first and largest part, and so each after the other till all is taken: and he takes the least part who runs to the part nearest the town. Then each rides away with the property and may keep it all: and, therefore, swift horses are there uncommonly dear. When his property is thus all spent, they carry him out, and burn him with his weapons and clothes. Most commonly they spend all his wealth, with the long lying of the dead within, and what they lay in the way, which strangers run for and take away.

* From G. F. Browne, *op. cit.*

It is a custom with the Esthonians, that there men of every tribe must be burned; and if any one find a single bone unburnt, they shall make a great atonement. There is also a power among the Esthonians of producing cold; and, therefore, the dead lie there so long and decay not, because they bring the cold upon them.

PREFACE TO THE "BLOOMS" OR *SOLILOQUIES* OF ST. AUGUSTINE *

[There is some question of the authorship of this preface, but whether Alfred wrote it or not, it expresses the spirit of his age.]

Gathered me then staves, and stud-shafts, and lay-shafts, and helves for each of the tools which I could work with, and bow-timbers, and bolt-timbers, for each of the works that I could work, as many as I might bear from the comeliest trees. Neither came I with a burden home, for I did not wish to bring all the wood home, even if I might bear it all. In every tree I saw something which I needed at home, therefore I advise every one who is able, and has many wains, that he guide his steps to the same wood where I cut the stud-shafts; there fetch more for himself, and load his wain with fair rods, that he may wind many a neat wall, and set many a comely house, and build a fair enclosure of them; and thereby may dwell merrily and softly, both winter and summer, so as I now yet have not done. But he who taught me, to whom the wood was pleasing, he may make me to dwell more softly in this temporary cottage on my way while I am in this world, and also in the everlasting home which he has promised us through Saint Augustine and Saint Gregory and Saint Jerome, and through many other holy fathers; as I believe also that for the merits of all those he will both make this way more convenient than it was ere this, and especially enlighten the eyes of my mind so that I may search out the right way to the everlasting home and the everlasting glory, and to the everlasting rest, which is promised us through those holy fathers. Be it so.

It is no wonder that men labour in timber-working, both in the out-leading, and in the building; but every man wishes, after he has built a cottage on his lord's lease and by his help, that he may sometimes rest him therein, and hunt and fowl and fish, and use it

* *Ibid.*

Readings [157

in every way according to the lease, both on sea and land, until the time that he earn book-land of everlasting heritage through his lord's mercy. So may the wealthy giver do, who rules both these temporary cottages and the everlasting homes, may he who shaped both, and wields both, grant me that I be meet for each, both here to be profitable and thither to come.

Augustinus, Bishop of Carthage, wrought two books about his own Mind. The books are called *Soliloquiorum,* that is, of his mind's musing and doubting; how his Reason answered his Mind, when the mind doubted about anything or wished to know anything which it could not before clearly understand.

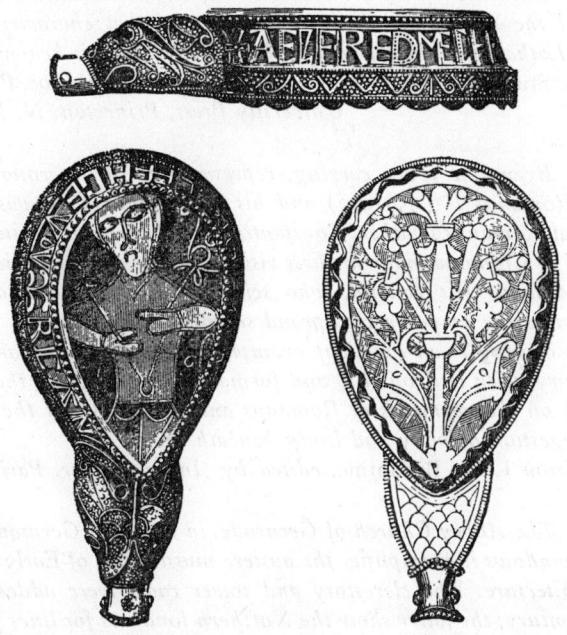

GOLD ORNAMENT, INSCRIBED "ALFRED HAD ME MADE"

(From *A Student's History of England* by Samuel R. Gardiner. Longmans Green, London, 1897.)

PLATE XI
Tenth Century

FIGURE 1. *Ivory carving, representing Christ receiving from Otto I the Cathedral of Magdeburg which he had built. The design has the symmetry of Byzantine work, with Christ "in Majesty," i.e., sitting upon the arc of Heaven, with a group of figures on either side. There are indications of the freer Northern style in the treatment of the faces and the attentive posture of the central figure.*
[*Courtesy of the Metropolitan Museum of Art, New York*]

FIGURE 2. *Illustration from the Stuttgart Psalter. This manuscript is an example of the same enthusiasm for movement that characterizes the Crystal of Lothair and the Utrecht Psalter, but the style is heavier.*
[*From* The Stuttgart Psalter. *Courtesy of E. T. Dewald, editor. Princeton University Press, Princeton, N. J., 1930*]

FIGURE 3. *Byzantine ivory carving, representing Christ crowning the Emperor Romanus II (959–963) and his wife Eudoxia. It was during the reign of Romanus's father, Constantine VII (Porphyrogenitos), that Liudprand of Cremona made his first visit to Constantinople. Nicephoras Phocas, Romanus II's general, who seized power after the death of Romanus, was the emperor Liudprand scornfully described on his later visit. This carving is an excellent example of the Byzantine art of the tenth century, with its frontality and formal symmetry. Note the beautiful pattern on the garments of Romanus and Eudoxia, and the absence of any suggestion of body and limbs beneath them.*
[*From* L'Art Byzantine, *edited by Andre Grabar. Paris, 1938*]

FIGURE 4. *The Abbey Church of Gernrode, in northern Germany. With its heavy windows it exemplifies the austere massiveness of Early Romanesque architecture. The clerestory and tower roofs were added in the eleventh century; the latter show the Northern fondness for lines pointing upward.*

PLATE XII

Tenth Century

FIGURE 1. *David playing on the organ. The pipe organ represented here is presumably like the organs in which Gerbert was so much interested. A somewhat different type is represented in the Utrecht Psalter.*

FIGURE 2. *Ivory plaque of German or Italian workmanship, from a book cover, showing emblems of the Evangelists surrounding an Agnus Dei. The Agnus Dei (lamb of God) was from earliest days a symbol of Christ. The symbols of the Evangelists are also of early origin and each has double significance. St. Matthew is represented by a man, because the gospel of Matthew opens with Christ's descent from David, and because in his incarnation Christ took on the form of a man. St. Mark's symbol is a lion, because his gospel begins: "The voice of one crying in the wilderness," and a lion, besides being one crying in the wilderness, stood for resurrection (it was believed that by roaring it could bring its dead cubs back to life when they had been dead after birth for three days). St. Luke is represented by a calf, because his gospel begins with a sacrifice, and the calf is the sacrificial animal. It stands besides for the crucifixion, also a sacrifice. St. John's symbol is an eagle, because his gospel begins with God (the Word) and the eagle was believed able to gaze directly at the sun. The eagle in his flight also stands for the ascension. From a very early period all these attributes were given wings, and thus the man of Matthew became an angel.*

[*Courtesy of the Metropolitan Museum of Art, New York*]

FIGURES 3 AND 4. *Otto III receiving gifts from Roma, Gallia, Germania, and Sclavonia. These illustrations show the German school of Ottonian art which was definitely influenced by the Byzantine tradition, with its formal arrangements, its frontality, and its use of strong outlines. This influence can be easily explained by the personal ties of the Ottonian house to the Byzantine emperors.*

PART VI

The Tenth Century

CHRONOLOGY

909 Fatimate caliphate established in Egypt
910 Monastery of Cluny founded
919 Henry the Fowler king in Germany
962 Coronation of Emperor Otto I
c. 980 Church introduces Peace of God to restrict destructiveness of feudal warfare
987 Accession of Hugh Capet, ending Carolingian dynasty in France
c. 989 Successful Christian missions in Russia; Prince Vladimir of Kiev converted to Greek Church

PART VI

The Tenth Century

~~~~~~~~~~~~~~~~~

THE tenth was a century marked by the building of states. The disorders typical of the ninth century continued, and strong men took advantage of them to carve out kingdoms for themselves, to settle new lands, or, as vassals, to make trouble for their suzerains. The Saxon house supplanted the Carolingians among the Germans and revived the imperial title (962). This family had considerable success in strengthening its authority against the feudality, cleverly using spiritual lords, even popes, against lay lords. The Carolingian rulers of West Francia gave way to the vigorous house of Capet, descendants of the Count of Paris who had defended Paris against the Northmen in the preceding century.

The Northmen whom Charles the Simple allowed to settle at the mouth of the Seine amalgamated with the French and produced the vigorous and enterprising breed of Normans, whose dukes were among the most turbulent vassals of the French crown. The successors of Alfred overcame the Danes of the Danelaw and became kings of all England. In Scandinavia powerful kingdoms arose. Norwegians who did not wish to submit to the royal power had colonized Iceland in the ninth century; from there they settled Greenland, and from Greenland in the year 1000 Leif Ericson reached America. That same year the kings of Sweden and Denmark, aided by Norwegian nobles, conquered Norway.

In the forests of central Europe the Czech St. Wenceslas and the Pole Mesco laid the foundations respectively of Bohemia and Poland. Since they took their Christianity from Rome, this meant division among the Slavs, most of whom received their Christianity from Constantinople. An astute Magyar duke encouraged the conversion of his subjects by Roman missionaries and paved the way for the kingdom of Hungary. Tsar Simeon of Bulgaria, whose empire had been established at the end of the ninth century, brought his people to their highest point of greatness.

The Scandinavians, who in the ninth century had reached Constantinople, appeared there again with a formidable fleet as the leaders of a motley throng of Slavs. The latter had long exchanged furs, honey, and beeswax with Moslems and Greeks for goods they desired; and the Scandinavian adventurers and traders operating along the Russian river systems had become protectors of the Slavs. Now, after a naval victory over the Byzantines, they negotiated a trade treaty with the empire. Scandinavians, whom the Slavs called *Rus,* built up a Russian principality around the cities of Kiev and Novgorod on the main trade route from the Baltic to the Black Sea, and the acceptance of Christianity from Constantinople meant close cultural ties with the Byzantines. The Byzantine empire had its strong rulers who fought successfully against Bulgars, Moslems, Russians, and their own rebellious subjects.

While these dramatic events were altering the political scene, society continued along the lines already laid. In his translation of Boethius's *Consolation of Philosophy* the English monarch Alfred had set down his own ideas of the kingly office: "a king's raw material and instruments of rule are a well-peopled land, and he must have men of prayer, men of war, and men of work." The main features of feudal society had taken form, and distinctions were clearly marked. At the base were the men of work, the third, or lowest, estate in the feudal hierarchy—nameless thousands who toiled on meagre fare in field and stable and kitchen, or who in the towns were artisans and small tradesmen. They had no hope of rising in the world, except for the occasional gifted lad who rose from altar boy to priest. Once within the order of the men of prayer, by pious agreement called the first estate, such a lad might in due course become a bishop, even the greatest of all bishops, the servant of the servants of God, as the popes in proud humility named themselves. Bishops were great landowners since the lands of the church were being continually increased by gifts of dying men who hoped to save their souls by establishing a lien upon heaven; and, as landlords, the bishops shared the duties of the nobles, the second estate, who were the men of war as well as landholders.

In the disorders which followed the death of Charlemagne, the greater nobles, the magnates, became practically independent. The *missi dominici* of a strong ruler no longer went their rounds. Magnates held court, coined money, levied tolls on roads and bridges, made war upon their neighbors. The old office of duke, done away with by Charlemagne, had been revived by some of the more powerful families, which constantly sought to extend their authority over their neighbors. The dukes believed that bishoprics and abbacies enriched by their own families should be under their authority, or at least that of members of the endowing families who sought careers in the church.

From the feudal point of view the king was only the first of the nobles, *primus inter pares,* but according to popular tradition he was something quite different. He was chosen from a family which either through long custom or popular choice was recognized as royal. This choice by the people, the fact that the monarchy was elective, was never to die out entirely. The symbol survives today in the coronation ceremony of an English king, when he is presented to the people in Westminster Abbey and they shout their acceptance. After it became customary for the church to anoint and crown the king the idea of a sacredness of his person crept in, but did not banish the principle that he was entitled to his crown only as long as he did not go against the law, to which he as well as the meanest of his people was subject. The monarch was chosen to enforce the law, which was the accepted custom of the folk, and if he ceased to do so he was no longer entitled to the people's obedience.

The church shared this idea; but to the church it was not the customary law which the king was bound to enforce, but the law of God and Nature as defined by the church. This idea of the king's being under the law implied the right, even the duty, of laymen to resist the king if he encroached upon their rights as defined by laws. The clergy in their turn maintained the duty of Christians to resist the authority of a king who commanded unchristian behavior. Circumstances, however, made possible the enhancement of royal power. By the tenth century an able and ambitious king did this by stressing now the feudal, now the traditional aspects of his authority. He was king of the folk and also lord of the land. In the period of invasions the tradition of the king as protector of the poor did not die out, but except on the royal domain his relations with the "men of work" were practically non-existent. The power that ruled their destinies was that of their feudal lords, who under all but exceptional kings were a law unto themselves.

The great lords who held directly from the crown (tenants-in-chief) ruled as they chose in their own fiefs, and private wars were the order of the day. Feudalism had developed a complex of reciprocal duties; besides protection the lord owed his vassal justice, and in addition to military service the vassal owed certain money payments in the form of aids or reliefs. Relief was a payment by a vassal's heirs in recognition of the fact that, although his right to inherit was not challenged, his inheritance was a fief from the lord, not a freehold property. Aids were special payments contributed for unusual expenses, such as the knighting of the seigneur's son, the dowry for the marriage of his daughter, the cost of ransom if the lord were captured by an enemy. The vassal must appear when his lord held court, he must entertain his lord with food and lodging (purveyance). The lord had the right of wardship over a minor heir, and of choosing the husband of an heiress. If either party failed to fulfill one of his obligations, the contract was void. If it was the vassal, his fief was forfeit; if it was the lord, his vassal could defy him and retain the fief as his own property if he could defend it. In either case there was war, and it was the men of work who suffered.

The overwhelming majority of the men of work in the ninth and tenth centuries labored on the land; and the common unit of division for working the land and administering the services of the rural populace was the manor. Manors might vary in size according to country and climate, but the fundamental purpose of each was the same; the manor was essentially a self-sufficient economic unit, and was expected to provide enough income over and above the needs of its inhabitants to support a heavily-armored fighting man on horseback. (It is impossible to consider the feudal knight without his horse; footmen might be used as auxiliaries, but the basis of all military tactics from approximately the tenth century was the use, in some form, of heavy cavalry.) The manor was therefore a field of seigneurial exploitation in which the lord exacted revenue and services from the peasantry in return for leaving them in possession of the land. Inasmuch as the lord did the fighting, he was entitled to some recompense, but many of the rights which seigneurs exercised were doubtless originally established by violence and usurpation of former public services unless included in a grant of immunity. Such, for example, would be charges imposed by the lord on those who used roads, bridges, or rivers passing through his estates. Whether the rights were established legitimately or by fraud, they were, however, legally enforceable after a few generations of customary usage.

The services and revenues lords received from peasants can be grouped under four principal headings: redevances, banalities, rights of justice, and prestations. Redevances were payments in money or produce due at fixed times. A head tax was levied, and also a payment for tenure of the peasant's share of the manorial lands; the lord received a portion of the harvest, collected a tax on any transfer of peasant holdings and also for the succession when a peasant holder died. The lord also had certain rights in the matter of commerce and industry, collecting fees on sales of staple commodities such as wheat, salt, or meat, and on the setting up of tables in favorable locations when fairs or markets were held under his jurisdiction. Banalities were essentially monopolies, established by the lord's ban, or proclamation, and enforced under penalty of fine. The peasants were obliged, for example, to use the mill, the oven, and the winepress maintained by the lord, who collected a fee for their use. Wood-cutting, pasture and fishing rights were also procurable for a fee, and the seigneur enjoyed the exclusive right to establish standards of weights and measures. At harvest time the lord enforced a closed season on grain and wine, which gave him an opportunity to dispose of his own part of the produce in a favorable market before it was opened to competition from the peasants.

The rights of justice, which provided the third class of revenue collectible by the lord, were often very lucrative. They were the privilege of levying fines or participation in the product of fines, since shares could be bought or sold in the justice of any given place. There were in general two types of justice: high justice included jurisdiction over all offenses involving fines of 60 sous (in the French terminology) or capital punishment and confiscation of goods, while low justice covered offenses carrying fines up to 60 sous. A seigneur might have the rights to both high and low justice; in the Germanies high justice was frequently limited to the great magnates, and in most areas the scale of fines came to be fixed by contract between the lord and the peasants. An example of types of offense and the accompanying fine is provided in the following scale: for an insult, 4 sous; for striking a blow, 10 sous, and if blood flows, 20; for drawing a cutting weapon against another, 30 sous, and if cutting actually follows, 60. For such offenses as murder, arson, rape, larceny, the punishment was at the discretion of the seigneur, and if the decision was death or banishment it was accompanied by confiscation of property. The lord exacted a fine to exempt a peasant from attendance when a general session to do justice was to be held, levied a tax on privately-settled cases, and had a monopoly of notarial functions.

The theory of justice was unlike the judicial theory of more modern eras because the court was not regarded as a body which sat in the public interest and which was assisted by an agency responsible for initiating prosecution of offenders. The seigneur who held court rendered a service to interested parties, and even in case of a crime took action on the complaint of the victim—or, if he were dead, his relatives. The accuser and the accused were treated equally, both being imprisoned, and if the plaintiff lost his case he paid the fine the defendant would have paid if found guilty. In the case of a criminal caught in the act the procedure was summary, and this led to a frequent resort to methods of pressure, even torture (euphemistically referred to as "the question") in order to extract confession and save the trouble of trial. Punishments were barbarous; the degree of barbarity was determined by the crime: the homicide was beheaded, the thief hanged, the assassin broken on the hurdle and hanged. If a woman incurred capital punishment she was buried alive, a dead criminal received the punishment on his corpse, an effigy was executed if the culprit could not be reached, and an animal that killed a person was hanged or buried alive according to sex.

The fourth type of revenue, prestations, were irregular requisitions of money, produce, or services. The peasants might be called upon to provide entertainment—food and lodging—for a traveling lord and his party. A seigneur also had the privilege of seizing a merchant's goods if he needed them, regardless of willingness to sell, if he gave proper compensation. He might insist on the extension of credit to himself. One form of prestation which eventually became very burdensome to the peasantry was the corvée, which was personal service of some sort—road building, driving a team, cutting wood, or drawing water for the lord's residence.

In France, Germany, and Italy the picture was essentially the same, with only minor differences. When the noble lived in the country there was the village, where the peasants' cottages faced the road leading to the castle, usually built on the highest land. There was the church, whose priest the lord named; the wine or cider press, and the mill, which the lord maintained. There were the fields where the peasants went to labor from dawn to dusk. In the north the peasants drove a communal team of oxen hitched to a heavy plough, and cultivated their own, their lord's, and the priest's strips in two of the three great fields where crops were rotated, one field always fallow. In the south lighter ploughs were used in smaller fields, according to the methods that had survived from Roman days. On the wastelands of the north more sheep grazed, and swine rooted in the ampler woodlands where both peasants and lord had rights. When the word of impending attack came and the peasants with their families and most cherished goods hastily took to the castle court or the forest until all was over, their fundamental activities were halted. If it were harvest time the crops were ruined; in any season the people came back to burned houses and hayricks, bones of slaughtered cattle, devastated fields. When the noble lived in town the town gates were closed; if the case was of two quarrelling town nobles there was fighting in the streets.

The church was the father of the poor, for it supplied what amelioration there was to the peasant's lot. The church saw that he had his rest on Sundays and holidays. The church provided his moments of religious emotion; it gave him what he had of art and music, beyond his own rough songs and dancing. The church even bestirred itself in his behalf against feudal warfare. It had given a religious aspect to knighthood by injecting into the ceremony of making a knight the vigil over arms in a church. In the latter part of the century synods (church assemblies) began to call upon the nobility to take oaths not to use violence against church property or that of the poor and defenseless. This "Peace of God" threatened violators with anathema. It is difficult to conclude how effective this was, but as time went on it developed into more drastic recognition of the rights of non-combatants. The most vital of the church's services were performed by the humble parish priests, usually ignorant men, who administered the sacraments and who allayed social unrest by assuring the peasant and artisan that differences in rank in this world were the inscrutable will of God, but that after the day of judgment all would be changed, and the virtuous peasant would be happy in heaven, while the lord who died unshriven would burn in hell.

Since bishops and abbots were also feudal lords, they tended to become secular in aims and behavior. Many pious monks felt that a reforming movement was due, and eventually such a movement was launched from the Abbey of Cluny, which Duke William of Aquitaine founded in 910. The abbot of Cluny established a novel system of federated monasteries which carried on the work. The Cluniac reformers worked for the abolition of the custom of buying church office (simony), for the celibacy of the clergy, for the abolition of lay investiture to ecclesiastical benefices, and for the abstention of monks from secular activities. The Cluniac reform movement did not affect the papacy, which sank to an unparalleled point of degradation, but it meant the infusion of new life to the monastic system, and provided a wider field for its activities.

In the tenth century population was increasing as a result of greater agricultural production. More land was being brought under cultivation and land was being tilled more effectively. Oxen were more efficiently harnessed, and horses were coming into use since there was more grain produced and two devices had been perfected which were essential for effective traction: iron shoes which enabled them to grip the earth, and a breast collar with traces instead of the yoke, which could not be used on the horse. On the great estates there had developed a complicated network of obligations that peasants owed their lords, roughly comparable in character to the obligations of vassal to suzerain, but infinitely more burdensome. Peasants began slipping away into the forests, where they cleared the land and established forest villages. Landholders perforce began to accept money rents instead of service. Many runaway peasants sought the towns where freedom waited them. Prosperity increased in the towns and commerce revived.

In Germany the century saw a revival in the arts, as a result of the desire of Otto I to maintain a magnificent court, the marriage of his son to a Greek princess, and the tastes of the half-Greek Otto III. The influence of Byzantine craftsmen extended to Denmark and England. There was much activity in cathedral schools and in cloisters such as St. Gall, where classical authors were translated into German.

The struggles of Otto I, king of the east Franks in Germany, with his vassals and with invaders give the best example possible of the problems of a ruler of the tenth century, and the unbelievably complicated personal relationships of the feudal system in politics. Otto recognized the usefulness of the clergy as a foil to the lay lords and established the foundations of the great ecclesiastical states of Germany. By his revival of the imperial title he brought some order into strife-ridden Italy and linked its destinies to that of Germany. The career of Gerbert, the peasant boy of Aquitaine who became pope, provides a conspicuous example of the opportunity offered to a member of the lowest class of feudal society to improve his station through the church, and also of the conduct of a cleric in politics. The program of education which he initiated in France included ideas taken over from the Moslems; it stimulated classical studies, and by its stress on dialectic revived on the one hand the question of the relation of reason to authority and on the other hand prepared the way for later attempts to apply the processes of logic to the conclusions of theology.

BISHOP GIVING A BLESSING

(From *Les Arts de la Moyen Age* by Paul Lacroix. Paris, 1873. Courtesy of New York Public Library.)

CHAPTER 10

The World of Otto I

[912 – 973]

OTTO I is remembered chiefly as the man who restored to currency the title of emperor, which the Romans had made the symbol of world unity. The title of Roman emperor, which had once stood for a united world, then for a united Christendom, was valid under Charlemagne only for France, Germany and Italy. Under Otto it was valid only for Germany and Italy. His authority was not recognized in France. As long as the stock of Charlemagne produced eligible men, the Carolingian remained the acknowledged royal house of the Franks, both east and west. But when that stock failed, recourse was had to other families. The successors of Charlemagne had used his device of the mark as a defense against invaders. In West Francia Charles the Bald recognized Flanders, Neustria, and Burgundy. It was inevitable that the men in charge of these great frontier districts should exercise enormous power, and their families were destined to play important parts in history—witness that of the Neustrian marquis, who was also Count of Paris.

We have seen that when the Emperor Charles the Fat was deposed (887) Eudes, Count of Paris, was chosen by one faction of Frankish nobles as king of the west Franks. He was followed by his son Robert. The Carolingian candidate for kingship of the west Franks, Charles the Simple, made Laon his capital. Charles the Simple followed Alfred's example of stopping the Northmen by allowing a group of them to settle in part of his territory; in 911 he granted the land about the mouth of the Seine to Rolf the Ranger, in the district which became known as Normandy. Rolf's descendants ruled the region as dukes of Normandy and extended their borders. On the death of Charles the Simple, Hugh the Great, son

The World of Otto I   [171

of Robert of Paris, consented to remain the greatest subject in the realm and let the crown go to Charles's young son, Louis d'Outremer (936).

Western Francia, or the kingdom of the West Franks, lay entirely in that part of the old Roman empire where the Germans had always been a minority. The northern part of the middle strip which had been established by the treaty of Verdun in 843 retained the name of Lothair (Lotharingia, later Lorraine) and its eastern boundary reached the Rhine. This was a region from which in Roman days the inhabitants had fled before the Germans, who had settled there in large numbers. Beyond the Rhine, where Latin had never been spoken, was the kingdom of the East Franks. The Carolingians contrived to reign in the eastern kingdom as kings and emperors until 911. Then the great nobles chose Conrad, duke of Franconia, king. After his death they established a new royal house by turning to Henry the Fowler, the Saxon duke (919). Neither Conrad nor Henry assumed the title of emperor. Henry, who has a musical immortality as the king in the Wagnerian opera *Lohengrin*, was a man of energy and ability, and was determined that his descendants should rule as German kings. In the land of the East Franks were four regions where tribal traditions of local independence were strong: in the north his own Saxony, in the south Swabia and Bavaria, and in the center Franconia, the old Frankish land. The Swabian and Bavarian magnates were bitter rivals, ambitious to extend their power over the Alps into Italy. A tradition of royalty clung to the Franconian lands.

Henry the Fowler's first task was to deal with the invaders, a task in which his predecessors had notably failed. He drove the Magyars, or Hungarians, out of Saxony, and established burgs, or fortresses, manned by peasants against them. He captured an outpost of the Slavs in northern Germany and established about it the mark Brandenburg, which was one day to be Prussia. He attacked the Bohemian Slavs in their land so well defended by mountains, and forced their duke to pay him tribute. He met the Danish peril by securing Schleswig and making it into a mark, erecting burgs along the frontier. He made Lorraine a German duchy, and married his daughter to its duke. It has been suggested that he may have borrowed the idea of building burgs from England, where Alfred's son Edward, with his sister's assistance, held off the Vikings and won back the Danelaw. At any rate Henry established close relations with Edward, marrying his heir, Otto, to one of Edward's daughters.

Otto I, who succeeded his father in the year 936, was a high-spirited, generous, vigorous young man of twenty-four who was tall, lean, muscular, and moved quickly but with dignity. His appearance and bearing were impressive; he dressed in the Saxon manner and in his later years his beard reached his waist. He had a cheerful disposition, was loyal and forgiving to rebellious relatives and friends, but could be stern and unyielding, for he knew that if he were to rule as well as reign he must weaken the power of the great German families. He was a shrewd politician and began his reign well. At his coronation in 936 the dukes performed the ceremony of homage and at the coronation feast the dukes of Lorraine, Franconia, Swabia, and Bavaria acted as his chamberlain, his steward, his cup-bearer, and his marshal. They performed their ceremonial tasks and bided their time.

When he began to interfere with them and the inevitable rebellions came, Otto showed that he had plenty of the old Harry in him, putting down the rebels firmly and replacing them with his own kinsmen or trusted supporters. He let these new magnates marry the daughters of the displaced dukes, however, and the old tribal spirit of independence was revived in the next generation. In Franconia he made no new duke, and it became the core of the German kingdom. In another of the rebellions which constantly faced him Otto was saved by a timely diversion, an invasion by the Hungarians. Except on this occasion, the Hungarians were a menace, and so were the Slavs. Otto dealt with the northern Slavs by conquering those between the Elbe and the Oder, and with the Slavs of Bohemia by forcing their duke to become his vassal. He ended the Magyar invasions by defeating them in a great battle on the Lechfeld near Augsburg, a victory which made his name respected throughout Europe. He also forced King Harold Bluetooth of Denmark to become his vassal and to be baptized, along with his wife and his child, Sweyn, who was later to conquer England.

Otto's policy toward the church was to secularize further the great ecclesiastical offices, for he saw the advantage of utilizing the clergy. He interposed in the election of bishops and abbots, but as he always named men of ability there was little or no protest. He had his brother Bruno made archbishop of Cologne, and his son archbishop of Mainz; and both these clerics aided him in organizing a staff of civil servants. This use of churchmen as administrators established the great ecclesiastical principalities which were to give a characteristic tone to German history. Otto also succeeded in getting Magdeburg made an archbishopric, as a center from which the conversion of the Slavs in the north could continue.[1]

The Italian policy of Otto I seems to have been closely linked with his resolution to keep Bavaria and Swabia within bounds, but conditions in the peninsula invited his intervention. The kingship of Italy was periodically in dispute among ambitious feudal lords, the papacy had fallen under the control of the Roman nobility—popes were still elected by the people and clergy of Rome—southern Italy was ruled from Constantinople, and the peninsula was periodically raided by Moslems from Sicily. Otto, who was now a widower, crossed the Alps in 951 and married the widow of the Italian king. Ten years later Pope John XII appealed to him for help and he once more entered Italy and was made king at Pavia; in 962 the pope crowned him emperor. Intrigues of political factions in Rome led to depositions, elections, and restorations of successive popes which Otto I finally stopped by overthrowing the government of the city of Rome and making the pope viceroy. At the same time Otto claimed rights over future papal elections. He remained in Italy for several years to establish his authority throughout the peninsula. He claimed Capua and Benevento as fiefs, and made a treaty with the Byzantine emperor, who gave his step-daughter Theophano as a bride to Otto's son, with the promise of southern Italy and Sicily as dowry. After receiving the bride but not the dowry Otto crossed the Alps for the last time and died in his native Saxony.

Like Charlemagne, Otto I had seen the importance of educating his officials and had entrusted to his brother Bruno the work of establishing a palace school. After Bruno became Archbishop of Cologne he worked diligently for the establishment of cathedral schools for the clergy. Although Otto was not able to surround himself with famous scholars as Charlemagne had done, he employed the Lombard scholar Liudprand of Cremona, who wrote a history of his patron's deeds and a vivid description of Constantinople, where he went on an embassy for Otto. The chief literary figure of

[1] See Plate XI, Fig. 1.

Otto's empire was the nun Hrotswitha of the Abbey of Gandersheim. She praised the emperor in verse and wrote the first Christian dramas, which purported to be written in the style of Terrence, the ancient Latin author of comedies, and which are characterized by skill and humor. Hrotswitha possessed genuine creative powers, and her achievements show that education in her day was not so sterile as it is sometimes represented.

The turbulent world of Otto I, with its frequent rebellions of feudal vassals, must have meant great misery for the tillers of the

A MONK BEING DRIVEN FROM
THE PRESENCE OF A KING

(From *A Student's History of England* by Samuel R. Gardiner. Longmans Green, London, 1897.)

soil. It was a world in which loyalty to the king was less important than the spirit of tribal loyalty in the territories of the great feudal magnates. When Liudprand of Cremona was at Constantinople he spoke slightingly of the Roman tradition and said proudly, "We Lombards, Saxons, Franks, Lotharingians, Bavarians, Swabians, and Burgundians." Otto, on the basis of his father's beginnings, built up a strong government in the Germanies by putting his kinsmen into the great fiefs and by establishing ecclesiastical states. The manner of his revival of the imperial title left for his successors the thorny problem of ruling on both sides of the Alps, but it saved Italy from anarchy at the time. The empire which Otto I established was very unlike Charlemagne's, however; it was organized on a feudal basis, and what control Otto exercised was through members of his family and his adroit exploitation of ecclesiastical administrators. Charlemagne's empire vanished almost at once when he died; that of Otto I, which eventually became known as the Holy Roman Empire of the German Nation, was to last for centuries because it partook of the nature of feudal society. Feudal social organization remained dominant in central Europe throughout the Middle Ages, and the authority of the emperor there was limited by the ambitions of his vassals. In Italy it was limited by urban and papal claims, but on both sides of the Alps the imperial title remained as a symbol of unity.

CHAPTER 11

The World of Gerbert (Silvester II)

[c. 950–1003]

OTTO I had at his court for a short time the greatest European scholar of the tenth century, Gerbert of Aurillac, the French peasant boy who became pope. In the monastery of St. Gerald at Aurillac in Auvergne, near which probably he was born, the lad mastered Latin and grammar under a gifted teacher, the monk Raymond. After Gerbert had become a monk, his unusual talents attracted the attention of a kindly patron who took the young Aquitainian with him into the Spanish mark for further study. Moslem civilization was at its height in Spain, with Moslem architecture flourishing and Cordova a center of scientific study, but Moslem political power had been thrust back somewhat and five Christian principalities had come into being: Leon, Castile, Navarre, Aragon, and Catalonia. Gerbert spent three years in the county of Barcelona, in Catalonia, studying mathematics. During his student years Otto I was carrying on the work of consolidation in Germany.

Gerbert's patron next took him to the papal court at Rome, and the pope recommended him for the post of teacher of mathematics at the court of Otto I, who was then in Italy. This was the year after the betrothal of young Otto II to the Greek princess Theophano, who was supposed to bring southern Italy as her dowry, and Gerbert may have been present at the somewhat delayed wedding. Anxious for further study, Gerbert told the emperor that although he was proficient in the quadrivium, he was deficient in logic and wished to pursue that subject further. Otto accordingly gave him a recommendation to Adalbero, archbishop of Rheims, where there was a famous school. The archbishop of Rheims was the chief prelate of France, but he belonged to an important Lorraine family and Lorraine was a fief of the German crown; consequently, he had close ties with Otto I. A shrewd prelate and a good judge of men, Adalbero soon made Gerbert master of the cathedral school and also employed him as his secretary.

Under the archbishop's patronage Gerbert soon became a famous teacher, gathering a great library of secular as well as ecclesiastical works, and introducing his eager pupils to its contents. One pupil, Richer, left a detailed account of Gerbert's methods; in teaching the trivium (grammar, rhetoric, and logic or dialectic) he made use of the great Latin poets. He also made dialectic tables to give his students practice in debate, and trained them in the methods prescribed by Aristotle, Cicero, and Boethius. In presenting the quadrivium (arithmetic, geometry, astronomy, and music) he introduced novel methods. For arithmetic he devised an improved abacus with Arabic notation; to demonstrate astronomy he constructed spheres for models of the universe; and to make clear the mathematical foundation of music he used the vibrations of strings. He apparently also made experiments with hydraulic power in organs which he built.

The stress which Gerbert put on the use of reason led a teacher at the imperial court to challenge him to debate before Otto II, who had become emperor. In the debate, which lasted all day, Gerbert argued for reason along the lines Erigena had followed, and defended his thesis successfully. In his teaching he emphasized the necessity for churchmen to be learned in the canon law and also to be skilled in the art of speaking, for he was eager that the clergy should be able administrators. In teaching the classical authors he was running counter to one aspect of the reforming movement which had started in the monastery of Cluny and was attracting much attention. The Cluniacs wished to make the clergy less worldly, and forbade the reading of the secular writers Gerbert used extensively. Gerbert was enthusiastic about the Cluniac opposition to simony and marriage of the clergy, but far from following the Cluniac efforts to keep monks in their cloisters he himself practiced politics with great zeal.

After ten years of teaching he was given a post where all his abilities could be exercised: Otto II made him abbot of Bobbio, St. Columban's foundation in Italy, which possessed one of the great libraries of the time. Much of the property of the monastery had been alienated and the monks had departed from the standards of their founder. Gerbert went to work with great energy, but those who had received the monastery property refused to give it up, and the monks were recalcitrant to discipline. On Otto II's death Gerbert abandoned the struggle as hopeless, although he retained his title and continued to buy books for the Bobbio library. He resumed his teaching post at Rheims and with Adalbero worked to defend the interests of the child Otto III against the efforts of Lothair II of the west Franks to win Lorraine from the emperor. They succeeded in gaining the support of the duke of Francia, Hugh Capet, the son of Hugh the Great, and Lorraine remained an imperial fief.

Gerbert's next venture into politics was his most important, for it placed a new dynasty on the Frankish throne. Lothair died in 986 and his son, Louis V, who was the last of the Carolingians to rule in the West, survived him for only fourteen months. The Frankish principle of an elective monarchy had not died out, as the choice of the duke of Francia in 922 had shown. It was customary for the magnates to agree who should be chosen, the archbishop of Rheims then announced the choice, and the crowds in the cathedral shouted their approval before the new king was anointed and crowned. As custom favored election from the reigning family, the logical choice in 987 was the uncle of the late king, Charles, duke of Lorraine. The rival candidate, however, was the greatest magnate in the realm, Hugh Capet, duke of Francia, who was favored by Adalbero and Gerbert. Before the assembly of nobles which met to choose a king, Adalbero delivered an address that turned the trick; as taken down by Richer, one of Gerbert's pupils, it contained all the vote-getting arguments familiar in election speeches to this day.[1] The direct or collateral descendants of Hugh Capet reigned in France until the monarchy was abolished during the French Revolution of 1789, but centuries were to pass before they ruled a united nation. As Richer's account runs: "Hugh was crowned at Noyon . . . as king of the Gauls, the Bretons, the Danes, the Aquitainians, the Goths, the Spaniards, and the Gascons." It is clear that there was no more sense of French unity than of German in the tenth century.

Gerbert had not much time left for teaching and for exercising his passion for the acquisition of books. Two years after the election of Hugh Capet Adalbero died; and after many intrigues over his

---

[1] For Richer's version of this speech, see p. 185.

The World of Gerbert (Silvester II)

successor Gerbert, who was now an adroit politician, was made archbishop of Rheims in 991. He began a vigorous administration but objections were raised against him on the grounds of his obscure birth. He had also defended the French church against papal claims, and when this led to his deposition by the pope, he repaired to the court of Otto III. The brilliant but dreamy young Otto had become emperor at the age of three, and was brought up by his mother, Theophano, a highly-educated Greek princess of unusual ability, who gave him the most thorough education possible. Gerbert's reputation as a man of learning was by now great and he became Otto's tutor, close friend, and adviser. When Otto was crowned emperor at the age of eighteen he proceeded to make Gerbert archbishop of Ravenna (998), and a year later, pope. He was the first Frenchman to hold the office.

Credence was long given by modern historians to the story that as the year 1000 approached there was widespread fear that it would usher in the end of the world. The tale first appeared in the latter part of the fifteenth century and was given wide currency in the eighteenth; modern scholarship has exploded it as a fact, but the legend lingers. The year 999, when Gerbert assumed the tiara, passed like other years. His choice of the name Silvester II as pope, after the first Silvester, who was supposed to have received the Donation of Constantine, forecast Gerbert's intention to co-operate closely with the half Greek and half German emperor in plans to revive the glories of the old Roman empire. Otto made Rome his capital, and believed that the adoption of the elaborate Byzantine court forms would heighten his authority over the turbulent Italians.

Silvester II as pope was ruler of the papal states, including Rome. Italian feudal lords, like magnates as far back as Apollinaris Sidonius, used to maintain town houses. They were townsmen as well as large landholders, and on occasion led their fellow-citizens against the bishop. Rome was full of such nobles, and Silvester II, like his predecessors, had to suffer from these risings. He made a satisfactory compromise as to the Roman government, took the field with an army against a town which defied him, judged cases between quarrelling bishops, confirmed, deposed, and appointed prelates, and generally made a great reputation as an administrator. The story which gained currency in later days that he was in league with the devil may have arisen because of the extraordinary honors to which he had attained by his efforts, or because of the skill with which he met every crisis that he faced. In the face of the general level of ignorance and superstition, such learning as Gerbert's was assumed to denote the presence of magic powers.

One of the great evils of the time was the prelates' habit of leasing church lands to nobles, and thus increasing the nobles' power. As abbot of Bobbio, Silvester had seen what this meant, and he secured the support of the emperor in a policy of checking the flow of church holdings into secular hands. During a campaign against nobles who rose against the new policy Otto fell ill and died (1002). Silvester II did not long survive the young emperor.

The policy of the three Ottos had been a boon for Italy. They put an end to the invasions and initiated a vigorous urban life. Strengthening the power of the bishops and replacing the irresponsible control of nobles by that of competent officials whom they could trust, they ended the scandalous situation in Rome, where rival factions of nobility for years had been making popes and anti-popes. The Ottos did not succeed in acquiring southern Italy, but they kept at bay the Saracens who dominated Sicily and ravaged the Italian seaboard. They brought Byzantine art into the West by their connections with the eastern empire; in a manuscript of German workmanship of the tenth century is a miniature in a new style, blended of German and Byzantine elements, a style which was to appear in Western art for centuries. The picture represents the grandiose idea of Gerbert and Otto III, the union of Europe under the imperial crown: Otto is on his throne, receiving gifts from four queens, labelled *Roma, Gallia, Germania, Sclavonia*.[1]

The idea remained a dream, but the figure of Sclavonia reminds the observer of a change which was real. In Silvester's lifetime the kings of Poland and Hungary received Christianity from Rome. Silvester and Otto III established the churches of the two countries as independent units, and although this curtailed the expansion of German ecclesiastical power, thenceforth both Poles and Magyars had cultural bonds with the West. In the same period the Russians accepted Christianity from Constantinople and, as members of the Greek orthodox church, were to develop an eastern culture. Thus in Slavic Europe a cultural barrier was raised, for whereas the *Sclavonia* of Otto III's and Gerbert's dream looked toward the West and

[1] See Plate XII, Figs. 3, 4.

Rome, the Slavs of Russia began to look toward the Byzantine empire.

Gerbert stands as the greatest man of his time in scholarship and in statesmanship. As a modern historian has said, "everything he said or did had distinction." His political career brings out the feudal disorders that plagued society. He had his part in establishing the Capetian dynasty in France and also in Otto III's endeavor to establish an empire that would be strengthened through papal support and would be enlightened in its administration through ecclesiastical scholarship. Gerbert bridged in some measure the gap between Moslem and Christian learning and passed on to his pupils an interest in the classics of ancient Rome, a skill in argument, and an appreciation of mathematics and logic. His methods were introduced into the school of Laon by one of his pupils and by another into the more famous school of Chartres. His world was externally a world of struggle and violence, but in the monastery and cathedral schools a leaven was at work which was to bring about great progress in learning and lead to the intellectual triumphs of the twelfth and thirteenth centuries.

[THE TENTH CENTURY]

Readings

~~~~~~~~~~~~~~~~~~~~

Liudprand of Cremona

[Liudprand was a witty cleric of Lombard stock, whom Otto I made bishop of Cremona. His works are full of vivid descriptions. The first extract deals with his visit to Constantinople in 949, when Constantine VII was emperor; the second extract is from his long report to Otto I and the empress of his embassy in 968, to propose the marriage of Otto's heir to Theophano, the stepdaughter of the emperor Nicephorus Phocas. The differences between the scholar-emperor, born to the purple (he was called Porphyrogenitos), and the rough soldier-emperor are clearly brought out. Equally clear is the difference in Liudprand's attitude toward each.]

ANTAPODOSIS (TIT-FOR-TAT) *

Three days after I had presented my gifts the emperor summoned me to the palace and personally invited me to dinner with him, after the banquet bestowing a handsome present on myself and my attendants. As the opportunity has occurred to describe the appearance of the emperor's table, particularly on a feast day, and also the entertainments that are given there, I think it best not to pass the matter over in silence but to give an account.

[*from Book VI, chapter VII*]

There is a palace near the Hippodrome looking northwards, wonderfully lofty and beautiful, which is called "Decanneacubita." "The house of the nineteen couches." The reason of its name is obvious: "deca" is Greek for ten, "ennea" for nine, and "cubita" are couches with curved ends; and on the day when Our Lord Jesus Christ was born according to the flesh nineteen covers are always

* From the translation by F. A. Wright (1930). Reprinted by permission of George Routledge & Sons, Ltd.

laid here at the table. The emperor and his guests on this occasion do not sit at dinner, as they usually do, but recline on couches: and everything is served in vessels, not of silver, but of gold. After the solid food fruit is brought on in three golden bowls, which are too heavy for men to lift and come in on carriers covered over with purple cloth. Two of them are put on the table in the following way. Through openings in the ceiling hang three ropes covered with gilded leather and furnished with golden rings. These rings are attached to the handles projecting from the bowls, and with four or five men helping from below, they are swung on to the table by means of a moveable device in the ceiling and removed again in the same fashion. As for the various entertainments I saw there, it would be too long a task to describe them all, and so for the moment I pass them by. One, however, was so remarkable that it will not be out of place to insert an account of it here.

[*from Book VI, chapter VIII*]

A man came in carrying on his head, without using his hands, a wooden pole twenty-four feet or more long, which a foot and a half from the top had a cross piece three feet wide. Then two boys appeared, naked except for loin cloths round their middle, who went up the pole, did various tricks on it, and then came down head first, keeping the pole all the time as steady as though it were rooted in the earth. When one had come down, the other remained on the pole and performed by himself, which filled me with even greater astonishment and admiration. While they were both performing their feat seemed barely possible; for, wonderful as it was, the evenness of their weights kept the pole up which they climbed balanced. But when one remained at the top and kept his balance so accurately that he could both do his tricks and come down again without mishap, I was so bewildered that the emperor himself noticed my astonishment. He therefore called an interpreter, and asked me which seemed the more wonderful, the boy who had moved so carefully that the pole remained firm, or the man who had so deftly balanced it on his head that neither the boys' weight nor their performance had disturbed it in the least. I said that I did not know which I thought *plus merveilleux* that is, more wonderful; and he burst into a loud laugh and said he was in the same case, he did not know either.

[*from Book VI, chapter IX*]

DE LEGATIONE CONSTANTINOPOLITANA (THE EMBASSY TO CONSTANTINOPLE) *

On the seventh of June, the sacred day of Pentecost, I was brought before Nicephorus himself in the palace called Stephana, that is, the Crown Palace. He is a monstrosity of a man, a dwarf, fat-headed and with tiny mole's eyes; disfigured by a short, broad, thick beard half going gray; disgraced by a neck scarcely an inch long; piglike by reason of the big close bristles on his head; in colour an Ethiopian and, as the poet says, "you would not like to meet him in the dark"; a big belly, a lean posterior, very long in the hip considering his short stature, small legs, fair sized heels and feet; dressed in a robe made of fine linen, but old, foul smelling, and discoloured by age; shod with Sicyonian slippers; bold of tongue, a fox by nature, in perjury and falsehood a Ulysses. . . .

[*Chapter III*]

[After Liudprand had explained the purpose of his embassy:]

"It is past seven o'clock," said Nicephorus "and there is a church procession which I must attend. Let us keep to the business before us. We will give you a reply at some convenient season."

[*Chapter VIII*]

I think that I shall have as much pleasure in describing this procession as my masters will have in reading of it. A numerous company of tradesmen and low-born persons, collected on this solemn occasion to welcome and honour Nicephorus, lined the sides of the road, like walls, from the palace to Saint Sophia, tricked out with thin little shields and cheap spears. As an additional scandal, most of the mob assembled in his honour had marched there with bare feet, thinking, I suppose, that thus they would better adorn the sacred procession. His nobles for their part, who with their master passed through the plebeian and barefoot multitude, were dressed in tunics that were too large for them and were also because of their extreme age full of holes. They would have looked better if they had worn their ordinary clothes. There was not a man among them whose grandfather had owned his tunic when it was new. No one except Nicephorus wore any jewels or golden ornaments, and the

---

* *Ibid.*

emperor looked more disgusting than ever in the regalia that had been designed to suit the persons of his ancestors. By your life, sires, dearer to me than my own, one of your nobles' costly robes is worth a hundred or more of these. I was taken to the procession and given a place on a platform near the singers. . . .

[*Chapter IX*]

On this same day he ordered me to be his guest. But as he did not think me worthy to be placed above any of his nobles, I sat fifteenth from him and without a table cloth. Not only did no one of my suite sit at table with me; they did not even set eyes upon the house where I was entertained. At the dinner, which was fairly foul and disgusting, washed down with oil after the fashion of drunkards and moistened also with an exceedingly bad fish liquor, the emperor asked me many questions concerning your power, your dominions and your army. . . .

[*Chapter XI*]

ৡ ৡ ৡ

Richer

ACCOUNT OF THE ELECTION OF HUGH CAPET (987) *

[Not only is this speech entertaining as the perennial electioneering speech, it also succinctly expresses the medieval theory of kingship.]

Meanwhile the nobles of Gaul who had taken the oath came together at the appointed time at Senlis; when they had all taken their places in the assembly, the duke, having made a sign to the archbishop of Rheims, the latter expressed himself as follows: King Louis, of divine memory, left no children; we must therefore take counsel as to the choice of a successor, in order that the country shall not come to ruin through neglect and the lack of a pilot. Our

---

* From J. H. Robinson, *Readings in European History* (1904), I, p. 194. Reprinted by permission of Ginn and Company.

deliberations on this subject were recently postponed, by common consent, in order that each one might here voice the sentiments with which God might inspire him, and that from all these individual opinions a general and collective decision might be reached.

Now that we are once more assembled together, let us endeavor, in all prudence and rectitude, not to sacrifice reason and truth to our personal likes or dislikes. We know that Charles has his partisans, who claim that the throne belongs to him by right of birth. Regarding the question from this point of view, we reply that the throne cannot be acquired by hereditary right. Nor should one be placed upon it who is not distinguished alike by nobility of body and wisdom of mind, and by his good faith and magnanimity. We see in the annals of history rulers of illustrious origin deposed on account of their unworthiness, and replaced by incumbents of equal, or even of inferior, birth.

And what is there to recommend Charles of Lorraine? He is feeble and without honor, faith, or character; he has not blushed to become the servitor of a foreign king [the emperor], nor to take to wife a girl of only knightly rank. How could the great duke bear that a woman belonging to the lowest rank of his vassals should be queen and rule over him? How could he give precedence to a woman, when his equals and even his superiors in birth bend the knee before him and place their hands beneath his feet? If you consider this matter carefully, you will see that Charles' fall has been brought about through his own fault rather than that of others.

Make a choice, therefore, that shall insure the welfare of the state instead of being its ruin. If you wish ill to your country, choose Charles; if you wish to see it prosperous, make Hugh, the glorious duke, king. Do not let yourselves be misled by your sympathy for Charles, nor blinded to the common good by hatred of the duke. For if you blame the good, how can you praise the bad? If you praise the bad, how despise the good? Remember the words of the Scripture: 'Woe unto them that call evil good, and good evil; that put darkness for light, and light for darkness.' Choose the duke, therefore; he is the most illustrious among us all by reason of his exploits, his nobility, and his military following. Not only the state, but every individual interest, will find in him a protector. His great-heartedness will render him a father to you all. Who has ever fled to him for aid and been disappointed? Who that has been left in the lurch by his friends has he ever failed to restore to his rights? . . .

∽ ∽ ∽

Gerbert

LETTERS *

[The Raymond to whom letters 45 and 91 are addressed is Raymond (Ayrardus) of Aurillac, the monastery in Auvergne where Gerbert was educated. Gerbert was an expert letter writer. Here we see his preoccupation with book collecting, and the variety of his interests, intellectual and political. His doubts about his Italian forces are worth noting.]

To Ebrardus Abbot of Tours
(Rheims, c. January, 985)

Since you hold the constant memory of me among things worthy of honor, as I have heard from a great many messengers, and since you bear me great friendship because of our relationship, I think I shall be blest by virtue of your good opinion of me, if only I am the sort of man who, in the judgment of so great a man, is found worthy to be loved. But because I am not the sort of man who, with Panetius, sometimes separates the honorable from the useful, but rather with Tully [Cicero] would add it [the honorable] to everything useful, so I wish this most honorable and sacred friendship may not be without its usefulness to both parties. Since the ways of conduct, and the ways of speaking are not separated by philosophy, I have always added the fondness for speaking well to the fondness for living well, although by itself it may be more excellent to live well than to speak well and, if one be freed from the cares of governing, the former is enough without the latter. But to us, busied in affairs of state, both are necessary. For, speaking suitably for persuasion and restraining the minds of angry persons from violence by smooth speech are both of the greatest usefulness. For this thing

* These letters are published through the courtesy of the translator, Harriet Pratt Lattin. They will appear in her volume of translations of the letters which will be issued in *Records of Civilization,* edited by Austin Lane Evans, and published by the Columbia University Press.

PLATE XIII

Eleventh Century

FIGURE 1. *Page from an English manuscript in the British Museum, which contains illustrations of the metrical version of the Scriptures long attributed to Caedmon. This scene represents the expulsion of Adam and Eve from Paradise. These drawings show clearly the influence of the Utrecht Psalter, which is known to have been taken to England and copied there. An English school of illumination sprang up, characterized by agitated and dynamically outlined figures, frequently with windblown draperies.* [*From the British Museum*]

FIGURE 2. *Landing scene from the Bayeux Tapestry. This famous piece of embroidery—it is not a tapestry—was made long after the events it represents and consequently shows twelfth rather than eleventh century costume. However, as it was apparently made within the lifetime of some of the participants in the Conquest, it is considered a source for those events. Soldiers who participated in the invasion of Normandy from England during World War II are struck by the similarity of the modern invasion barges to Duke William's ships that invaded England from Normandy nearly nine hundred years before.*

FIGURE 3. *Relief from the bronze doors of St. Michael's Church, Hildesheim. Bernwald, bishop of the Saxon city of Hildesheim, was a great admirer of the arts. He studied the carved wooden doors of the Church of Santa Sabrina in Rome and decided to beautify Hildesheim in a similar manner. The bronze doors, made by German workmen, are remarkable both technically and artistically. They depict the fall and salvation of mankind in a realistic manner. The heads of the figures are emphasized by increased projection of the relief. The representation shows the influence of manuscript illustration.*

FIGURE 4. *Church of St. Etienne, Caen (Abbaye aux Hommes), erected by William the Conqueror in the year he invaded England. This church was built in the Romanesque style by Normans. The upper parts of the towers were added in the next century. The division of the west façade into three parts by buttresses, each part having a door, emphasized the division of the interior into nave and side aisles. This arrangement became important in the design of Gothic church façades. The two square towers satisfied the feeling of Northern builders for the appearance of soaring skyward. This vertical feeling was diametrically opposed to the horizontal lines that had been emphasized in Greek and Roman architecture and still dominated in the churches of the Mediterranean region.*

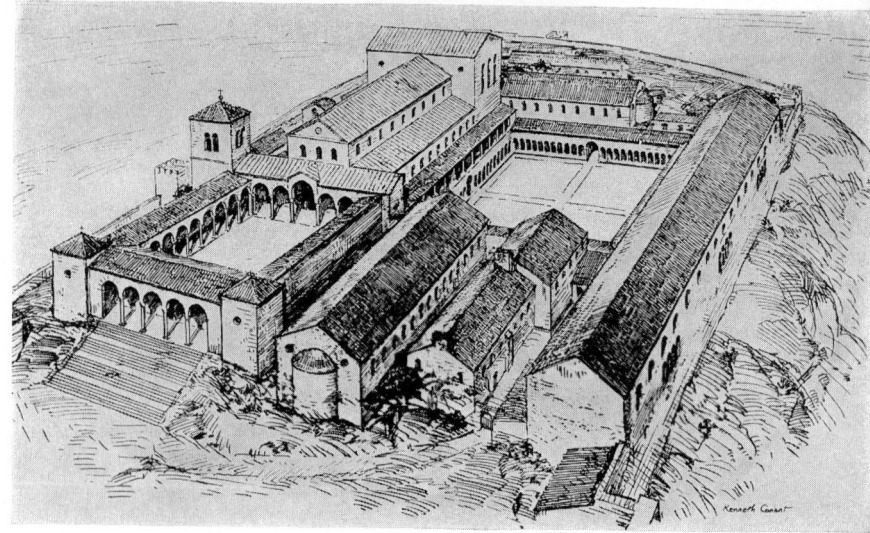

PLATE XIV
Eleventh Century

FIGURE 1. *The Abbey of Cluny, from an eighteenth century engraving. This is the third abbey; it was begun in 1080 and stood until the French Revolution. The ground plan of the church is elaborate, with two transepts and a fully developed eastern end, where chapels surrounding the apse allowed the placing of additional altars at which the mass was celebrated simultaneously.*

FIGURE 2. *Reconstruction of the eleventh century buildings of St. Benedict's ancient foundation of Monte Cassino, which influenced the builder of Cluny. The church was erected between 1066 and 1075, under the direction of an abbot who was inspired by old St. Peter's at Rome. (See Plate II, Fig. 4.) Adjoining the church was the cloister, where the monks walked and where they did work such as copying manuscripts, which demanded a good light. The church-like buildings with apses, adjoining the atrium and the transept, were the refectory and chapter-house. The other buildings were guest-houses, hospital, kitchens, and the other essential offices of a great monastery. Builders from Amalfi were used, and the Saracenic influence is seen in the slightly pointed arches of the colonnades. These pointed arches were copied in Cluny and influenced the development of the Gothic style.*

[From A Brief Commentary on Early Medieval Church Architecture *by* K. J. Conant. *The Johns Hopkins Press, Baltimore, Md., 1942*]

FIGURE 3. *Church of St. Sophia at Novgorod. Russian architecture was inspired by Byzantine, but the bulbous domes pointing skyward were a native development. The domes were symbolical; the central one stood for Christ; those at the corners for the four Evangelists. The beautiful Church of St. Sophia was begun at the time of the Norman Conquest. It was destroyed in the Second World War by the Germans after they occupied Novgorod.*

FIGURE 4. *Apse of Speyer Cathedral. The new Romanesque style produced unified interiors, with pilasters which divided the nave clearly into equal sections, heightening the impression of advance by regular stages to the altar at the east end. The horizontal division was emphasized by arcades, galleries, and windows, and the simple roof-coverings gave way to a stone vault, divided into bays. Vaulting meant heavy walls and piers to bear the added weight, and few windows. Speyer, like other churches in the Rhine Valley, which was the highway into Italy, shows the influence of Lombard builders who tended to greater elaboration than the Normans.*

which must be prepared beforehand I am diligently forming a library. And, just as a short time ago in Rome and in other parts of Italy, in Germany also and in Belgium, I used large sums of money to pay copyists and to acquire copies of authors, permit me to beg that this be done likewise in your locality and through your efforts so that I may be aided by the kindness and zeal of friends who are my compatriots. The writers whom we wish to have copied we shall indicate at the end of the letter. Not unmindful, moreover, of your kindnesses, we shall send parchments to those writing and the necessary funds at your command. Finally, lest we, speaking further, should abuse the laws of letter writing, the reason for so much labor is to acquire a serene disregard of bad fortune. Not nature alone, as appears to many, commands us to this disregard, but a carefully elaborated system of philosophy. Equally in leisure and in work we both teach what we know, and learn what we do not know.

[Letter 44]

To Monk Raymond, G[erbert]
(between December, 984, and March, 985)

By how great love we are bound to you the Latins and foreigners, who are partakers of the fruits of our labor, know. They earnestly desire your presence, since, in fact, it is public knowledge that we, filled with cares, would tarry in a place of study for the sake of no other. For these cares philosophy alone has been found the only remedy. From the study of this, indeed, we have very often received many advantageous things, for instance, in these turbulent times, we have resisted the force of fortune violently raging not only against others but also against us. And, indeed, since this was the condition of the state in Italy that we had to submit shamefully to the yoke of the tyrants, if we professed innocence, or if we attempted to exert our strength, this meant that a following must be secured, camps fortified, thefts, fires and murders made use of, therefore we choose the certain leisure of studies rather than the uncertain business of wars. And, while we follow the footsteps of philosophy, since we do not overtake it, we have not yet curbed all the impulses of a disturbed mind. Now we are turning back to those things which we left. Influenced by the encouragement of our friend Abbot Guarin we are considering now approaching the princes of Spain. However, we are at present turned away from these earlier undertakings by the sacred letters of Lady Theophano, empress ever august, always to be loved, always to be cherished. In such changeableness of things, of sorrow, fear, joy, desire, his son Gerbert particularly asks the opinion of his most trusted father, Gerald, whom these things do not touch, as to what course should be followed.

Farewell. Farewell, father Gerald, farewell, brother Ayrardus, farewell, holy order, my foster-father, and my teacher, may he remember me in his holy prayers and also my father Adalbero, archbishop of Rheims, entirely devoted to him.

[*Letter 45*]

To Raymond Abbot of Aurillac
(January or February, 987)

Bereft of my very illustrious father Gerald, I do not seem to survive as a whole man. But, since you, best beloved, have been made father, agreeably to my wishes, I am reborn anew, a whole man, as son. Not only do I rejoice at your honor, but father Adalbero rejoices, offering himself and his to you from his heart, all the more sincerely, the more you shine with the light of religion and learning. On account of my love for him which he so well merits, I have spent almost three continuous years in Francia. While I endure here the wrath of kings, the disturbances of the people and the disquiet of discordant kingdoms, I am so wearied that I am almost sorry I undertook the care of the pastoral office. But, because my Lady Theophano, empress ever august, orders me to depart with her into Saxony the eighth of the kalends of April [March twenty-fifth], and because I have ordered certain of my monks and soldiers from Italy to assemble there, I do not now know what I shall write for certain about the organs located in Italy, and about sending a monk there who shall learn and practice them, especially since without the presence of my Lady Theophano I dare not rely on the trustworthiness of my soldiers, because they are Italians. Nor am I certain whether I shall lead the army into Italy before autumn, or whether we shall delay in Germany, in order to prepare as many troops as possible against Louis, king of the Franks, unless he shall have quieted down. Events will soon show what sort he is, and what should be thought of him, most disturbing to friends, and not very disturbing to the most baleful enemies. After peace had been established between the leaders and the princes, the most illustrious offspring of Otto, the Caesar, of divine memory, last summer led the legions of soldiers against the Sarmatians, whom they call

Guinidi [Wends] in that language, and there he captured, destroyed and laid waste forty-six well fortified cities by his presence, and by the strength of the soldiers.

Adalbero, archbishop of Rheims, greets you, Ayrardus, and likewise all the associates of the cloister, and I, who am very devoted to you in all things, join him.

Again and again farewell.

[*Letter 91*]

A HOUSE OF THE PERIOD, FROM AN ENGLISH MANUSCRIPT INFLUENCED BY UTRECHT PSALTER

(From *A Student's History of England* by Samuel R. Gardiner. Longmans Green, London, 1897.)

PART VII

The Eleventh Century

~~~~~~~~~~~~~~~~~~~~~~~~~~~~~~

CHRONOLOGY

1000 Christianization of Hungary (Latin Church; coronation of St. Stephen
1013 Sweyn of Denmark conquers all England
1016 Normans in Salerno; beginnings of Norman power in Mediterranean
1031 Fall of the Ommiad caliphate in Spain
1037 First union of Christian kingdoms of Leon and Castile in Spain
1038 Seljuk Turks conquer Persia
c. 1039 Truce of God
1054 Final schism of eastern and western churches
1066 Norman conquest of England begun
1071 Battle of Manzikert; destruction of Byzantine military power by Seljuk Turks
1070–89 Lanfranc archbishop of Canterbury
1073 Hildebrand elected pope Gregory VII
1077 Meeting of Henry IV and Gregory VII at Canossa
1079 Birth of Abelard
1086 Domesday Book
1095 Pope Urban II preaches the first crusade
1098 Cistercian order founded
1099 Crusaders establish the kingdom of Jerusalem

PART VII

The Eleventh Century

~~~~~~

THE combination of feudal anarchy and religious enthusiasm which characterized the tenth century continued throughout the eleventh, and it, too, was a century of piety and violence. The efforts of rulers to control their great vassals and of the popes to control the clergy continued, and the more dramatic events of the century were involved in these endeavors.

Like the eighth and ninth centuries, the eleventh was a period of invasions: not invasions of Christian lands by infidels, but of both infidel and Christian lands by Christians. England was twice invaded: first by the Danish king Sweyn, then by the Norman Duke William. Norman adventurers won Sicily from the Moslems, sacked Rome and invaded the Balkans; the Christian kingdoms in Spain made great headway against the Moors; Moslem islands in the Mediterranean were reconquered. Toward the end of the century the crusading movement was launched by the papacy; by the end of the century the kingdom of Jerusalem was established and much of the Christian territory lost to the Moslems had been regained.

These events fit into a complicated but definite pattern once the relations of Christian groups with each other and with the Moslems are understood. On the Christian side was involved the relation between Byzantium and the West, and in the West was involved the relation between the lay and ecclesiastical functions of the clergy. A spectacular conflict between Pope Gregory VII and the Emperor Henry IV highlighted the controversy over the lay investiture of ecclesiastical officials. The holder of a bishopric, like the holder of a lay fief, owed military service, and his ruler was concerned that the incumbent be a man able to render such service. If an ecclesiasti-

[193

cal office-seeker was willing to pay well for the office, so much the better; and if he were well-educated, he could be useful to the ruler in strengthening royal or imperial administration at the expense of unruly lay vassals.

The Emperor Henry IV's unpopularity among his vassals, due in part to his reliance on ecclesiastical vassals, gave Pope Gregory VII an opportunity to play off vassals against emperor in an effort to reassert papal supremacy over temporal rulers as well as over the western clergy. At the very end of the century the popes, ambitious to enhance their prestige and cement their leadership in the western church, preached the first great crusade, in which Christians were urged to take up arms against the Moslem and recover the Holy Places of Palestine from the infidel.

Disunity and antagonism in the Mohammedan world were important as a background for the inauguration of an invasion of the East from the West, since attack was thereby invited, and the crusading spirit had been building up in Christian Europe throughout the century. Religious and political rivalry combined to divide Islam. The Sunnite Abassid dynasty ruled the Bagdad caliphate, while members of the rival Ommiad dynasty—also Sunnite, however—ruled the Spanish caliphate. Between these two branches of the Mohammedan world a third caliphate had been established in Egypt and Tunis, with a Shiite descendant of the Prophet's daughter Fatima ruling in Cairo. Distracted by the dissension between the three caliphates in the Moslem world, Mohammedans temporarily suspended major attacks on Christian Europe, and Christian powers in a position to do so had an opportunity to attempt an aggressive policy in their turn.

The most formidable military power in the Christian world was still the Byzantine empire. The eastern emperors had been able to maintain a professional standing army in the Roman tradition, but the weaknesses of this military system were that it was costly and that well-trained professional soldiers were not easily replaced on short notice if serious losses occurred. After the seventh and eighth centuries the emperors had concentrated on defensive tactics in the provinces of Asia Minor that faced the Moslem power. The Moslems were unable to subdue the Byzantine forces and conflict with the empire degenerated into border raids. To repulse raids the empire relied on a heavily armed cavalry, which had the advantage of great mobility and was capable of inflicting heavy punishment. Many of the features of armament and tactics among the knights of western Europe originated in the Byzantine East, and for a long time the best large war horses came from there.

In the tenth century the empire resumed the offensive against the Saracens under a series of energetic rulers of a new Macedonian dynasty who took advantage of the increasing evidence of disintegration in the Bagdad caliphate. By reconquering Syria the emperors were in a position to set up a protectorate over the Holy Places of the Near East, which encouraged pilgrims from Christian lands. The fact that the territories of Asia Minor and Syria which the emperors regained from the Moslems had once belonged to the old Roman empire and were held by the Byzantine empire during much of the eleventh century had an important effect on the attitude of the emperors towards the crusaders from the West in the next century.

While the Byzantine empire made inroads on the Mohammedan power in the East, Christian kingdoms in Spain also were making progress against Islam. The Cordovan caliphate had reached its highest point of strength in the tenth century, at a time when the Christian states of Spain were wrangling among themselves and even calling upon their Moslem neighbors for help against each other. The last Ommiad caliph of Spain died in 1031, however, and the eleventh century was a period of disruption in Mohammedan Spain; a number of independent Moslem emirates were established, the emirs in their turn calling upon the Christian kingdoms for aid against other emirs.

The ranks of the Spanish Christians were reinforced in the eleventh century by an influx of the more adventurous knights from northern Europe, particularly France, who sought an outlet for their energies elsewhere when the Peace of God and the Truce of God were established in Christian countries. Introduced by the church and supported by secular authorities, the Truce of God, which reinforced the Peace of God, made warfare illegal between Wednesday's sunset and Monday's sunrise, during Lent, from Christmas to Epiphany and during the planting and harvest seasons. The spread of the Cluniac reform movement further encouraged pilgrimages, already popular; Santiago de Compostella in Spain was one of the leading shrines to which pilgrims were directed, and knights who made the pilgrimage could do additional good deeds by striking a blow at the infidel.

Partly for these reasons the Spanish campaigns against the Moslems in the eleventh century took on some of the characteristics of a holy war, although the motives of the Christian kingdoms, temporarily united in the eleventh century, were primarily political. Taking advantage of the disunity among the Moslems, the Christian kingdoms were uniformly successful in reconquering territory. A significant indication that political aggrandizement rather than religious fanaticism was the dominant factor in the Spanish crusade of the eleventh century was the fact that the victorious Christians allowed the Moslem population of conquered regions to remain.

Some of the important Mediterranean islands, which had served as bases for a steady Mohammedan piracy, were also recovered by Christian powers in the eleventh century. Although Italian towns were among the chief victims of Moslem raids, some of the northern towns, such as Genoa and Pisa, were profiting from their strategic border position in the struggle between the empire and the papacy to build up their independence and their trade. They engaged in a policy of counter-piracy as a protective measure and a means of extending their commercial outlets. Successful punitive expeditions against the Mohammedan island bases meant not only the collection of an indemnity but also the establishment of trading privileges. The most spectacular step in this phase of the weakening of Mohammedan power, however, was the conquest of Sicily by Normans who, as pilgrims passing through the Mediterranean to and from the Holy Land, had discovered the possibilities of plunder. But even this conquest was accomplished in the end because the Moslems in the island were divided and because they were unwilling to call in sufficient help from their co-religionists in north Africa, owing to religious differences with the Cairo caliphate and the fear of being dominated by their African allies if successful.

Once established in Sicily, the Normans began forays into the Byzantine territory of southern Italy. Duke William, the conqueror of England, had set a notable example of what an ambitious feudal magnate could accomplish, and the Normans who were setting up a Sicilian kingdom did not wish to be overshadowed. Norman attacks on Byzantine territory in southern Italy, and later across the Adriatic into the Balkans, were encouraged by the popes in order to distract the Norman freebooters from the church states of central Italy. Furthermore, the permanent schism between the eastern and the western church which began in 1054, made a final division between Roman and Greek Orthodox Christians, and gave the papacy and the Normans of Sicily a common antagonism toward the Byzantine empire. The new aggressive attitude of the popes was in part due to the influence of the Cluniac reform movement. The prestige of the popes had been extremely low during much of the tenth and early eleventh centuries, when they were creatures either of Roman political factions or of the emperors. Although previously the primacy of the bishop of Rome had been generally admitted by a powerful clerical faction in the East, the Greek clergy had become anti-Roman and regarded the pope with contempt. The Norman invasions of Byzantine territory were therefore encouraged by the papacy in the hope of regaining some control over the eastern church.

There were, then, in the eleventh century, many factors of a political nature to pave the way for a resurgence of the West and its attack on the East in the great crusades of the next century, but the crusades would probably not have been possible without the religious enthusiasm of the European population. Christian pilgrimages were an established institution: faith in the healing powers of relics of the saints and the miraculous cures at shrines was undiminished—but the greatest shrines of Christendom were far afield. During most of the eleventh century, however, the three chief centers of pilgrimage—Jerusalem, Rome, Santiago de Compostella—were open to Christians, and the numbers of pilgrims increased. As a pilgrimage was regarded as penance, the pilgrim frequently traveled barefoot and begged his way. In the eleventh century, through widespread interest and the impetus provided by the Cluniac reformers, masses of pilgrims were on the move and had taken to traveling in large bands, partly as a matter of protection.

Against this background of political expansion and religious enthusiasm in Christian Europe a revival of Moslem power in the East occurred in the latter part of the century and once more cut off Jerusalem and the Holy Places from easy access. The declining Bagdad caliphate had taken to employing as mercenaries soldiers from a central Asiatic people known as Turks. Converted to Mohammedanism in the course of their migration through Persia and their service in the caliph's armies, the Turks eventually realized the weakness of the caliphate and set up their own ruler. Establishment of the Seljuk Turkish empire diverted the course of Asiatic migrations, which had formerly gone through southern Russia. The Turks overran Asia Minor, defeating the Byzantine emperor's forces decisively in 1071 at the battle of Manzikert. This battle destroyed the highly trained professional Byzantine army, and the emperors never had an opportunity to recreate a powerful military force but were henceforth dependent on allies. For Asia Minor the significance of the Turkish conquest was the introduction of a nomadic, semi-civilized Asiatic people interested primarily in plunder or pasturage for its flocks in a region which had been largely European in population and economy. The trade, the cities, and the agriculture which had flourished there since ancient Roman times declined, and the region could support only a much-reduced population. Asia Minor, which had been a part of the European world economically, politically, and culturally under Rome and under Constantinople, became Asiatic.

The destruction of the Byzantine military machine was a major disaster for the eastern empire, but the effects were tempered by the energetic conduct of the emperors of the Comnenus family. By recruiting knights from western Europe the emperors were able to save Constantinople from the Turks at the cost of giving up most of Asia Minor. As a counterweight to the Norman threat to Byzantine territory in the Balkans, the emperors made an alliance in 1082 with the Italian city state of Venice. (The Venetians had a strategic position for trade in the Adriatic and their naval support was important to the Byzantine emperor, while in return Venetian merchants received commercial privileges in the empire.) The appeals for aid from the West became a routine matter to the emperors, and it was in response to one such appeal in 1095 that Pope Urban II seized the opportunity to assert papal leadership in the West by preaching a great crusade to recover the Holy Places of the Near East from the infidel Turks. The Byzantine emperor was deluged with assistance.

The century was one of growing prosperity. In the West improved methods of agriculture had greatly increased production and, consequently, population. Agriculture remained the basic industry of Europe, but a profound revolution had taken place. With the light Roman plough of the Mediterranean basin a double plowing, criss-cross, had been required to break up the soil properly. The heavy plough of the Germanic peoples of northern Europe, however, which could accomplish its purpose in a single plowing, in turn made possible the strip-farming system, an essential characteristic of the co-operative cultivation in the manorial system. Another important change was in the use of the three-field rotation, which brought more production from the same area than the two-field system. The two-field rotation was dictated in the south by climatic conditions, since only one planting a year could be made, but it meant that only half of the land produced each year. Three-field rotation in the north was feasible because both a spring and a fall sowing could be made, and two-thirds of the land was in production each year. The result was an increase in the available food supply; more people could be supported, and a general growth in the total of European population took place. This in turn brought about an increase in prosperity—especially in the towns.

The increased wealth and the religious enthusiasm of the century made the building of churches in a new style possible. Magnificent stone edifices in the Romanesque style were designed by skilled architects and the materials were frequently assembled by the voluntary labors of a whole community. Churches were community centers in the fullest sense. To have a finer church than neighboring cities was the ambition of the citizens. The Romanesque style expressed a new spirit which was a fusion of Greek, Roman, and Oriental elements with the genius of the Germanic peoples. Gifted builders developed the basilican church of the sixth century into the Romanesque church which in France, England, Germany, and Italy was essentially the same. These churches had round arches springing from heavy pillars, and were decorated with sculptured figures designed as a part of the architecture. Speyer and Hildesheim, Arles, Caen and Cluny, Winchester and Durham, Pisa and Milan built Romanesque churches. The one great exception was St. Mark's, copied after one of Justinian's churches by Venice, whose spirit was strongly influenced by the East.

The music which filled these Romanesque churches when clergy and people were gathered for service was brought to its perfection in this century. Churchmen since the days of Ambrose had been enriching the Gregorian chant. This music for the human voice,

200] *The Eleventh Century*

purely melodic and without instrumental aid, had developed from Greek and Jewish music into a form which in its ordered and solemn beauty expressed the same spirit as Romanesque architecture.

The papacy's role in the eleventh century was dramatic, because of the conflict with the western emperors in which Gregory VII played so strong a part, and because of the preaching of the first great crusade at the end of the century; but the work of other clerics was in many respects more constructive. The Ottos in the tenth century had revived the state as a going concern in feudal society; but it was left for the clerics of the eleventh century, of whom Lanfranc was the chief, to create the mechanism by which it could function. Lanfranc, whose life extended through the greater part of the century, represents the piety of the age and also the ecclesiastical statesmanship which, in a period of feudal violence, was building the foundations for the later development of national monarchies, and was working passionately for order and restraint in an all too lawless society.

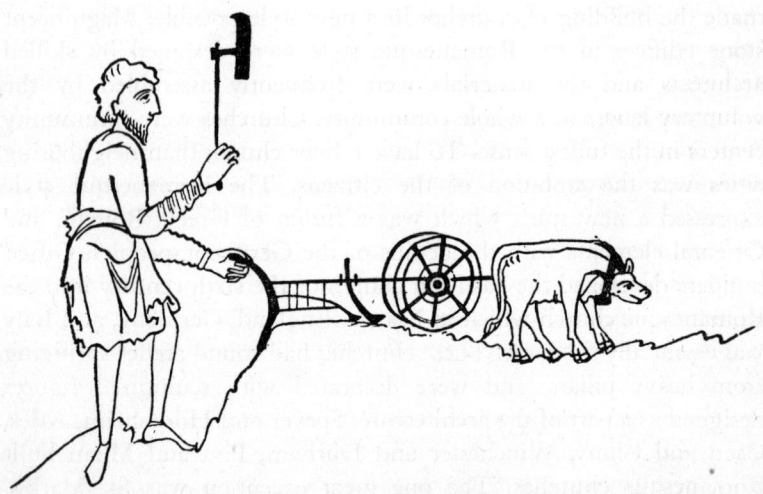

PLOUGHMAN WITH WHEELED PLOW, FROM CADEMON ILLUSTRATION

(From *Archaeologia*, Vol. 24, 1932. Courtesy of New York Public Library.)

CHAPTER 12

The World of Lanfranc

[c. 1005 – 1089]

~~~~~~~~~~~~~~~~~~~~

LANFRANC was born about two years after the death of Pope Silvester II. He was city-born and bred. His birthplace, Pavia, had been the capital of the Lombards and had continued to be important, though it did not rank with Venice, which in the first half of this century became a powerful city state ruled by a doge and dominating the northern Adriatic. The atmosphere in which Lanfranc grew up was that of the renewed urban activity which had been fostered by the Ottos. Pavia had a reputation for legal studies, and Lanfranc's father, who was a judge, gave his son the best education available. Lanfranc may possibly have studied at the law school of Bologna as well as in Pavia. At any rate, he mastered both trivium and quadrivium and gained a reputation as a successful lawyer. On his father's death he went to France and became a teacher at Avranches. Then he took monastic vows at Bec, where he opened a school to which students flocked from all over western Europe. His teaching of dialectics was famous; he was completely orthodox and warned his pupils against those who made of dialectics a tool for misrepresenting the Scriptures.

There was a growing tendency among educated churchmen to use the dialectic method in discussions of doctrine. One subject of widespread interest was the nature of the bread and wine in the Eucharist: did they at the moment of consecration become the actual body and blood of Christ? Gerbert had stressed the Augustinian principle that God gave man reason in order that he could learn the truth; his position was similar to that of John Scotus Erigena. In the school that Gerbert's pupil Fulbert had founded at Chartres the monk Berengar of Tours developed the idea that the body and

[201]

blood of Christ were not in the sacred elements. Fulbert tried to dissuade him, but Berengar persisted; he read Erigena's *De divisione Naturae* and wrote a book on the subject of transubstantiation. Lanfranc was present at a synod held in 1050 when Berengar was tried for his views. Berengar maintained that reason need not bow to authority, at which Lanfranc was shocked and with great eloquence attacked both Berengar's stand on reason and his views on the Eucharist. Berengar was condemned as a heretic and forced to commit his book to the flames. Erigena's treatise, which had so long escaped attention, was condemned at the same time. Lanfranc wrote a confutation of Berengar in which he condemned the use of reason to oppose authority. When he became a prelate he eschewed the use of dialectic as dangerous, but he could not break his long habit of reasoning according to syllogism, and made some of his political decisions by that method of reaching a conclusion.

While Lanfranc was leading the relatively quiet life of a teacher, important changes were taking place in the part of the world where he was to spend his later years. The successors of Alfred had been able to buy off the Vikings temporarily through the payment of tribute, collected by levying the Danegeld, the first direct tax in England. By the end of the tenth century, however, Sweyn, king of Denmark, conquered practically the whole of England. On his death his son Cnut had to fight renewed resistance, but was finally chosen king and made England the capital of his great northern empire, which comprised Norway, Denmark, and England. A devout Christian, he travelled to Rome, paid his respects to the pope, and, as other rulers had done, used the church to civilize his people. (The church of St. Clement Danes on the Strand in modern London occupies the site of the Danish church outside the walls.) In their activities as traders, the Danes established new towns which became commercial centers. Cnut distributed to his jarls large tracts of land, earldoms which provided a new title (earl) for the English nobility. Local institutions he left unchanged; the shire moot, where the bishop presided, aided by the ealdormen and the thanes, continued to administer justice according to ancient custom, on the basis of the evidence of the people concerned. The ancient custom of election of the king by the Witan, or body of wise men, which meant in practice the bishops and great nobles, was continued—and the Witan usually showed its wisdom by choosing the candidate whose accession was most feasible.

Across the Channel, the Northmen who had settled along the mouth of the Seine had adopted the language, customs, and law of the people there, and distinguished themselves as devout Christians, hardy warriors, astute statesmen. The Norman dukes brought feudalism in the duchy of Normandy into unusual order; they divided the lands into knight's fees, the amount of land that would support a single knight fully armed, and thus there could be no question of how many knights' service was due from each vassal. While the king of France had to travel about as Charlemagne had done to consume the produce of his manors, his vassals of Normandy had arranged a system by which they received money payments. Reverent Christians, the Norman dukes yet maintained strict control of the church within their dominions. In fact it was partly as a result of the effort by Norman dukes to standardize and curb the prerogatives of the church that the jury system, which became the most famous of all Norman institutions after its fuller development in England following the Norman conquest, began to evolve.

In Normandy the claims of the church went back to a period before the Viking settlement, and the bishops often asserted rights which conflicted with the interpretation of feudal jurisdiction by the Norman dukes. This was especially true in the matter of various public rights, such as the collection of tolls or market rights, which vassals frequently received along with the grant of a fief. The Norman dukes contended that the immunity of religious foundations did not include these profitable franchise privileges. In the course of controversies with clerics the dukes resorted to holding inquests, or "recognitions," in which the testimony of "old and lawful men" in the community was taken, under oath, to determine the origin of disputed privileges. Originally used to determine the rights of bishops, this sworn inquest was applied to other ecclesiastics, and from application only to financial matters the custom spread to other problems. The procedure was always for the duke to issue a writ ordering an investigation to be held and judgment to be declared on the evidence of those best fitted to represent the collective knowledge of the community: hence the stress on "old and lawful men," whose memories went farthest back toward the origin of practices in dispute, and whose reputations in the community lent confidence in their long experience. Out of this system the familiar modern jury of England and America developed, and although the jury has come to be regarded as the common citizens' paladin against arbitrary governmental power, the original institution was a device to support the king's power against the usurpations of his vassals.

The duke of Normandy in Lanfranc's time was William the Bastard, a stern, fierce, self-willed man of unusual capabilities who was a cousin of Edward the Confessor of England. Edward was the son of the English king whom Cnut had supplanted, for when Cnut died the Danish king's sons were unable to maintain the power he had gained, and Earl Godwin, the most powerful of the English earls, brought back Edward. Edward was half Norman in blood and all Norman in education and sympathies, and he promised Duke William the succession to the English throne. On Edward's death, however, the Witan chose Harold, Earl Godwin's son, as king, and Harold accepted despite the fact that he had sworn not to oppose William.

As soon as Harold became king he was beset with difficulties; the king of Norway attacked him in the north, and Duke William of Normandy prepared to attack from the south. William first submitted his case to Pope Alexander II. One of the pope's most influential advisors was the monk Hildebrand, who knew the Normans well. William's devout vassals were wont to go on pilgrimages to Jerusalem and on their way home they occasionally tarried in ports of southern Italy to take part in the constant forays and raids among Italians, Greeks, and Saracens. Several of these doughty Norman pilgrims received grants of land; the most notable, Robert Guiscard, had been granted Sicily as a fief by an earlier pope. Hildebrand, who had at first opposed these Norman adventurers, came to realize their qualities, and he won the pope to a decision in William's favor on the question of the English throne.

The duke gathered an army of mounted adventurers, landed in England, and in the battle of Hastings (1066) defeated Harold's foot-soldiers, who were weary from a hasty march southward after repulsing the Norwegians. The Witan, overawed by William's army as it marched around London, hastily chose him king. It took him five years to establish his authority throughout the country, and he used his experience of conditions in France to modify English feudalism so that the crown had more control over the nobility than the French king was able to exercise over his subjects. He left other local institutions untouched, and in his census, Domesday Book, he used the old Frankish custom of gathering information by the testimony of neighbors.

In the years before his English adventure William had reorganized and reformed the church in Normandy, putting into office able men from all parts of Europe. He had persuaded the unwilling Lanfranc to become abbot of a monastery that was being established at Caen. In 1070, again protesting, Lanfranc became archbishop of Canterbury, to supervise the reorganization of the English church. Normans were placed in the most important positions, and William used these men, as he did Lanfranc, in the government. One cardinal policy of churchmen in politics was to transfer cases concerning the clergy from the secular courts to ecclesiastical courts. William, probably through Lanfranc's influence, agreed to this policy, which might well have resulted in a strengthening of the papal powers; but William guarded against that possibility by laying down set principles regarding the reception and authority of papal legates in England. Lanfranc's reluctance to accept the important posts William offered him was partly due to the fact that he represented an ancient tendency of the church to attract men out of the world into a life of study and contemplation. He struggled against being drawn into the movement strong rulers of the day were inaugurating to bring the church into the service of the state.

One of Lanfranc's great contemporaries, on the other hand, struggled to bring the state into the service of the church under the leadership of the pope. Three years after Lanfranc became archbishop of Canterbury the monk Hildebrand, a small, pale, weak-voiced man with piercing eyes, became pope as Gregory VII. His years of apprenticeship as papal adviser had qualified him for the position and his remarkable abilities enabled him to carry through far-reaching reforms. He was fully convinced that the church was St. Augustine's City of God, and that the pope as God's vicar had supreme power over the princes of the earth. He demanded that William the Conqueror do homage for England as a fief of the Holy See, but when William refused Gregory did not press the matter. As we have seen, he had a wholesome respect for the Normans, and William's position regarding ecclesiastical courts was definitely a step in the right direction.¹ Gregory then turned toward the German kingdom, whose ruler was less strongly placed.

After Otto III, other descendants of Henry the Fowler were chosen king and crowned emperor for seven generations, and all carried on more or less successfully the Ottonian policies. As a means of Germanizing the Slavs, Otto III's immediate successor, Henry II, founded the archbishopric of Bamberg and built a magnificent church there. Conrad II conciliated the lesser nobility and replaced the clergy in government posts by laymen of mean origin. His son, Henry III, was recognized as overlord by the kings of Bohemia and Hungary, enforced the Cluniac reforms in Germany, and set out to reform the papacy. He deposed three popes and forced the election of several Germans trained in the schools that had been founded by Archbishop Bruno of Cologne. During the papacy of the third of these German-trained popes, Leo IX, a dispute over the claims of Byzantium to rule the church in southern Italy precipitated the final schism between the eastern and western churches.

Henry III put down revolt with a strong hand; but during the minority of his son Henry IV, who was a small child when his father died, the feudality became bold and when he reached manhood he found himself faced with sporadic revolts of his vassals. He was a man of great ability and unbounded ambition, but was inclined to hasty action. He practised simony in the expectation of drawing a large part of his revenues from the filling of church offices, whereupon the Cluniac reformers appealed to Gregory VII. Upon his election as pope, Hildebrand had made clear his intention to establish papal authority. In his *Dictatus* he asserted that the Roman church had never erred and could not err, that the pope was supreme judge, and that only he could call a general council, depose bishops, demand the homage of all rulers, and depose emperors. The German clergy had protested Hildebrand's election, but Henry had given his assent, because at the time he was coping with a revolt in Saxony. A synod at Rome laid down drastic penalties for simony, marriage of the clergy, and lay investiture. It was in accordance with the spirit of an age in which symbolism was supreme that Gregory, instead of directly attacking royal control of the choice of bishops, forbade the symbolic act of investiture by the king with the ring and the staff of episcopal office.

¹ See William's letter and mandate, p. 214.

When called to account for failing to co-operate with the decrees of the Synod of Rome, Henry, who had just quelled the Saxon revolt, caused a German synod to declare that Gregory had been illegally elected, and demanded that he abdicate. Gregory declared Henry deposed and excommunicate, and freed the emperor's subjects from their allegiance. The letters exchanged by the two dignitaries in the course of their quarrel are choice specimens of the vocabulary of vituperation. Gregory, appropriately, was the less violent; he deposed Henry as "a rebel of incredible insolence," but Henry summoned him: "Come down and relinquish the apostolic chair—come down, come down, to be damned through all eternity." The German princes, who had no love for the ambitious Henry, declared they would choose a new king unless he obtained absolution within four months. Henry, in danger of losing his crown, made a rapid journey into Italy to make his peace with Gregory, and at Canossa waylaid the pope, who at the request of the German princes was traveling toward Germany to preside over a synod that would proceed against Henry. The pope was outplayed, and after keeping Henry waiting in suppliant guise three days, gave him absolution. In preventing Gregory from entering Germany Henry won the essential victory, and later in his reign he revenged himself, driving Gregory out of Rome and making a new pope. Gregory called the Normans of Apulia to his aid; led by Robert Guiscard they attacked Rome, expelled Henry, and sacked the city. The scene at Canossa received little attention at the time, but later was used as an example of the power of the church where moral questions were concerned. Since Gregory ended his life in exile, the ascendancy of the popes remained still to be demonstrated, a fact which provided an incentive to his successors to preach the crusades.

While this struggle was going on in Germany, William the Conqueror continued to have chosen as bishops and abbots in England Normans whom he could use as administrators, and made them responsible for military service for their lands. He left Normandy to his eldest son and the crown of England to his second son, William the Red. Lanfranc lived through two years of the reign of this brutal tyrant, who after the archbishop's death kept the See of Canterbury vacant in order to enjoy its revenues.

Lanfranc's was a world struggling for order amid the disorders of feudalism. The conspicuous actors in this struggle towered above him as dramatic figures: Cnut, William I, the Emperor Henry IV, Pope Gregory VII. Each of these men in his own way strove to bring order out of disorder, but their work could not be completed without the services of educated and devoted men able to create an effective government. Lanfranc was such a man. He stood for order and authority in things of the mind as well as in politics, and gave no aid and comfort to the heretic. Ironically enough, however, he passed on the dialetic method his orderly mind loved to men who were to use that method to frame new heresies. The most important work done in his lifetime was William the Conqueror's welding together of Norman and English institutions into an effective government, and in this he had an honorable part. The conflct over investitures waged between Henry IV and Gregory VII dramatized but did not end the conflict inherent in the clergy's position of feudal lordship. Though Lanfranc solved his own problem admirably, rendering to Caesar the things he recognized as Caesar's and unto God what he believed to be of God, it was a purely personal solution. The struggle for supremacy between church and state remained a crucial issue in European society.

[THE ELEVENTH CENTURY]

Readings

A SHIRE-MOOT IN HEREFORDSHIRE (c. 1036) *

[This document shows the composition and functioning of an English court.]

Here is made known in this writing, that a shire-moot sat at Aegelnoth's stone, in the days of King Cnut. There sat Aethelstan, bishop, and Ranig, ealdorman, and Edwin, the ealdorman's son, and Leofwine, Wulfsige's son, and Thurkil White; and Tofig Prud came there on the king's errand; and Bryning, shire-reeve, and Aegelweard of Frome and Leofwine of Frome and Godric of Stoke, and all the thanes in Herefordshire were there. Then came traveling there to the moot Edwin, Eanwen's son, and there raised a claim against his own mother to a portion of land, namely, at Wellington and Coadley. Then asked the bishop, who would answer for his mother. Then answered Thurkil White and said that he would if he knew the claim. Since he did not know the claim, they deputed three thanes from the moot to where she was, which was at Fawley. These were Leofwine of Frome, and Aegelsig the Red, and Winsige Scaegthman. And when they came to her they asked what claim she had to the lands for which her son was suing. Then said she that she had no land that in any way belonged to him, and was bitterly angry with her son. Then she called to her Leoflaed, her kinswoman, Thurkil's wife, and spoke to her as follows, before them all: "Here sits Leoflaed, my kinswoman, to whom I give not only my land, but my gold, and garments, and robes, and all that I own, after my day." And she then said to the thanes: "Do thane-like and well; announce my errand to the moot before all the good men, and tell them to whom I have given my land and all my

* From University of Pennsylvania, *Translations and Reprints*, I, No. 6, *English Constitutional Documents*, edited by Edward Potts Cheyney. Reprinted by permission of The University of Pennsylvania Press.

[209

property; and to my own son never anything, and bid them be witnesses of this." And they then did so, rode to the moot, and declared to all the good men what she had laid upon them. Then Thurkil White stood up in the moot and prayed all the thanes to grant to his wife clean the lands which her kinswoman had given her, and they did so. And Thurkil then rode to St. Aethelbert's monastery, with the leave and witness of all the folk, and caused it to be set in a Christ's book.

[*from Thorpe, Diplomatarium Anglicum, p. 336. Anglo-Saxon*]

ᏕᏕᏕ

William of Malmesbury*

[William of Malmesbury was an English monk who knew both Lanfranc and William the Conqueror. He wrote of them:]

LANFRANC AND WILLIAM THE CONQUEROR

Normans and English, incited by different motives, have written of king William: the former have praised him to excess; extolling to the utmost both his good and his bad actions: while the latter, out of national hatred, have laden their conqueror with undeserved reproach. For my part, as the blood of either people flows in my veins, I shall steer a middle course: where I am certified of his good deeds, I shall openly proclaim them; his bad conduct I shall touch upon lightly and sparingly, though not so as to conceal it; so that neither shall my narrative be condemned as false, nor will I brand that man with ignominious censure, almost the whole of whose actions may reasonably be excused, if not commended. . . .

The Normans, that I may speak of them also, were at that time, and are even now, proudly apparelled, delicate in their food, but not excessive. They are a race inured to war, and can hardly live without it; fierce in rushing against the enemy; and where strength fails of success, ready to use stratagem, or to corrupt by bribery. As I have related, they live in large edifices with economy; envy their equals; wish to excel their superiors; and plunder their subjects,

* From *William of Malmesbury's Chronicle of the Kings of England*, edited by J. A. Giles (1904). Book III. Reprinted by permission of G. Bell & Sons, Ltd.

though they defend them from others; they are faithful to their lords, though a slight offence renders them perfidious. They weigh treachery by its chance of success, and change their sentiments with money. They are, however, the kindest of nations, and they esteem strangers worthy of equal honour with themselves. They also intermarry with their vassals. They revived, by their arrival, the observances of religion, which were everywhere grown lifeless in England. You might see churches rise in every village, and monasteries in the towns and cities, built after a style unknown before; you might behold the country flourishing with renovated rites; so that each wealthy man accounted that day lost to him, which he had neglected to signalize by some magnificent action. . . .

[William] was humble to the servants of God; affable to the obedient; inexorable to the rebellious. He attended the offices of the Christian religion, as much as a secular was able; so that he daily was present at mass, and heard vespers and matins. He built one monastery in England, and another in Normandy; that at Caen first, which he dedicated to St. Stephen, and endowed with suitable estates, and most magnificent presents. There he appointed Lanfranc, afterwards archbishop of Canterbury, abbat: a man worthy to be compared to the ancients, in knowledge, and in religion: of whom it may be truly said, "Cato the third is descended from heaven"; so much had an heavenly savour tinctured his heart and tongue; so much was the whole Western world excited to the knowledge of the liberal arts, by his learning; and so earnestly did the monastic profession labour in the work of religion, either from his example, or authority. No sinister means profited a bishop in those days; nor could an abbat procure advancement by purchase. He who had the best report for undeviating sanctity, was most honoured, and most esteemed both by the king and by the archbishop. . . .

In Kent succeeded Lanfranc, of whom I have before spoken, who was, by the gift of God, as resplendent in England,

> As Lucifer, who bids the stars retire,
> Day's rosy harbinger with purple fire;

so much did the monastic germ sprout by his care, so strongly grew the pontifical power while he survived. The king was observant of his advice in such wise, that he deemed it proper to concede whatever Lanfranc asserted ought to be done. At his instigation also was abolished the infamous custom of those ill-disposed people who used to sell their slaves into Ireland. The credit of this action, I know not exactly whether to attribute to Lanfranc, or to Wulstan bishop of Worcester; who would scarcely have induced the king, reluctant from the profit it produced him, to this measure, had not Lanfranc commended it, and Wulstan, powerful from his sanctity of character, commanded it by episcopal authority. . . .

In the year of our Lord Jesus Christ's incarnation 1072, of the pontificate of pope Alexander the eleventh, and of the reign of William, glorious king of England, and duke of Normandy, the sixth; by the command of the said pope Alexander, and permission of the same king, in presence of himself, his bishops, and abbats, the question was agitated concerning the primacy which Lanfranc, archbishop of Canterbury, claimed in right of his church, over that of York; and concerning the ordination of certain bishops, of which it was not clearly evident, to whom they especially pertained; and at length, after some time it was proved and shown by the distinct authority of various writings, that the church of York ought to be subject to that of Canterbury, and to be obedient to the appointments of its archbishop, as primate of all England, in all such matters as pertained to the Christian religion. . . .

[In another place William cited Lanfranc's answer to the claims of the Archbishop of York. It is a good example of his method of argument. The Archbishop of York is still known as "primate of England" while the Archbishop of Canterbury is "primate of all England." *]

. . . Lanfranc put an end to the discussion, meeting him with this most wary answer: "The view on which you rely needs substantiation in asserting that to Augustine alone was granted the submission of all the bishops of Britain, and even of those who had been consecrated by the Bishop of York. That would have been a very poor and trifling gift bestowed by the pope on his old friend, this new Englishman; especially when the Archbishop of York consecrated none who should be subject to Augustine in his lifetime, as there was no bishop there at all. For indeed the blessed Paulinus, the first prelate of that same city, was sent there, not in the days of Augustine, but of Justus the fourth, archbishop of Canterbury. English history will prove what I say. Knowing this, the supreme

* From *Documents Illustrative of English Church History,* compiled by Henry Gee and William John Hardy (1921), Chapter XIII, "Settlement of the Primacy Dispute." By permission of The Macmillan Company, publishers.

pontiffs have confirmed to the successors of Augustine the submission of all the bishops of England, as the privileges recited show, embellishing the Gregorian scheme, as they call it, with most ornate language, and following it up with generous liberality, the representatives of the same see and patrons of the same policy. Now they hold that all the Churches of the English should borrow the discipline of life from that place from whose fire they caught the flame of faith. For who knows not that the faith of Christ flowed from Kent to York and all the other Churches of England? As for your assertion that St. Gregory could have confirmed, had he wished, to Augustine's successors by word what he had granted to Augustine, it is quite true and beyond denial. But, pray, what prejudice does this give to the see of Canterbury? I will put a parallel case: for when our Lord and Saviour said to St. Peter 'Thou art Peter,' etc., He could have added, had He wished, 'and this same power I grant to thy successors.' As it is, the omission detracts nothing from the reverence due to Peter's successors. Will you oppose these words and cite anything contrary? For indeed it is impressed on the consciences of all Christians that they should fear his successors, even when they threaten, no less than Peter himself, and should gladly acknowledge any kind favour they [the successors] bestow. And so the arrangement of all Church matters is then, and only then, authoritative, if approved by the judgment of Peter's successors. What is the meaning of this but the power of Divine grace passed on through Jesus Christ from St. Peter to his vicars? So in parallel cases, if you understand logic, you will form the same conclusion. Moreover, what holds good in the whole, holds good in the part; what holds good in the greater holds good in the less. The Roman Church is, as it were, the sum of all Churches, and all other Churches are, as it were, its parts. For as in one respect man is the class of his individual members, and yet in each man resides the property of the whole man, so in one way the Roman See is the class and sum of all Churches, and yet in each Church there reigns the entirety of the whole Christian faith: she is greatest of all the Churches, and what holds good in her should hold good in the less, as the power of the first head of any Church continues to his successors unless there be any express and personal exception. Consequently, as Christ said to all the Roman prelates what he said to Peter, so what Gregory said to all the successors of Augustine, he said in Augustine. The result is, that as Canterbury is subject to Rome, because it received the faith thence, so York is subject to Canterbury which sent preachers thither."

William the Conqueror

LETTER TO POPE GREGORY VII [1076 (?)]*

[William's refusal to recognize the pope as his feudal lord is based on precedent. His tone is courteous, but firm. His recognition of the exclusive jurisdiction of ecclesiastical courts over the clergy is given the legal basis of canon law.]

To Gregory, the most noble Shepherd of the Holy Church, William, by the grace of God renowned king of the English, and duke of the Normans, greeting with amity. Hubert, your legate, Holy Father, coming to me in your behalf, bade me to do fealty to you and your successors, and to think better in the matter of the money which my predecessors were wont to send to the Roman Church: the one point I agreed to, the other I did not agree to. I refused to do fealty, nor will I, because neither have I promised it, nor do I find that my predecessors did it to your predecessors. The money for nearly three years, whilst I was in Gaul, has been carelessly collected; but now that I am come back to my kingdom, by God's mercy, what has been collected is sent by the aforesaid legate, and what remains shall be dispatched, when opportunity serves, by the legate of Lanfranc our faithful archbishop. Pray for us, and for the good estate of our realm, for we have loved your predecessors and desire to love you sincerely, and to hear you obediently before all.

[*from Chapter XV*]

MANDATE FOR DIVIDING THE CIVIL AND CHURCH COURTS †

William, by the grace of God king of the English, to R. Bainard, and G. de Magneville, and Peter de Valoines, and all my liege men

---

* From *Documents Illustrative of English Church History,* compiled by Henry Gee and William John Hardy (1921). By permission of The Macmillan Company, publishers.

† *Ibid.*

of Essex, Hertfordshire and Middlesex greeting. Know ye and all my liege men resident in England, that I have by my common council, and by the advice of the archbishops, bishops, abbots and chief men of my realm, determined that the episcopal laws be mended as not having been kept properly nor according to the decrees of the sacred canons throughout the realm of England, even to my own times. Accordingly I command and charge you by royal authority that no bishop nor archdeacon do hereafter hold pleas of

THE CORONATION OF A KING IN THE DAYS OF WILLIAM THE CONQUEROR

(From *A Student's History of England* by Samuel R. Gardiner. Longmans Green, London, 1897.)

episcopal laws in the Hundred, nor bring a cause to the judgment of secular men which concerns the rule of souls. But whoever shall be impleaded by the episcopal laws for any cause or crime, let him come to the place which the bishop shall choose and name for this purpose, and there answer for his cause or crime, and not according to the Hundred but according to the canons and episcopal laws, and let him do right to God and his bishop. But if any one, being lifted up with pride, refuse to come to the bishop's court, let him be summoned three several times, and if by this means, even, he come not to obedience, let the authority and justice of the king or sheriff be exerted; and he who refuses to come to the bishop's judgment shall make good the bishop's law for every summons. This too I absolutely forbid that any sheriff, reeve, or king's minister, or any other layman, do in any wise concern himself with the laws which belong to the bishop, or bring another man to judgment save in the bishop's court. And let judgment be nowhere undergone but in the bishop's see or in that place which the bishop appoints for this purpose.

[*from Chapter XVI*]

PART VIII

The Twelfth Century

PLATE XV

Twelfth Century

FIGURE 1. *Tympanum of the Cathedral of Autun.* The arched space above a church entrance was a convenient place for reminding the entering worshipper of the Day of Judgment. It is worth while to compare these figures with those on the tympanum of the Abbey Church at Vézélay which was completed at about the same time and with the lively figures of the Utrecht Psalter by which they were clearly influenced. In both churches one feels the spirit of the early crusades. About fifteen years after the completion of these sculptures Bernard of Clairvaux preached the second crusade at Vézélay.

FIGURE 2. *Murder of Thomas à Becket, 1170,* from a manuscript in the British Museum. This almost contemporary representation of a historical event shows the dramatic violence of the attack, with the mitre falling from the Archbishop's head. This subject, involving as it did the violation of a holy place as well as the murder of a member of the clergy, became very popular, and was executed in stained glass as well as in illumination. There is a famous example in a window of Chartres Cathedral.
[*Courtesy of the Bettmann Archive, New York*]

FIGURE 3. *Façade of the Abbey Church of St. Denis,* from a drawing made before the restoration of the church in the nineteenth century. As in St. Etienne at Caen (Plate XIII, Fig. 4) the façade reveals the plan of the interior. The rose window shows the beginning of the tendency to dissolve the massiveness of the wall. When Suger carried out the building of his new church he employed builders who experimented boldly with the new principle of a skeleton structure of pointed vaults, piers, and flying buttresses which made it possible to replace large wall-surfaces by windows, thus admitting more light to the interior than was possible in Romanesque churches. By this experiment these builders became pioneers of a new style which sixteenth century admirers of the classical were to call **Gothic** because they thought it barbarous.

PLATE XVI

Twelfth Century

FIGURE 1. *Imperial seal of Frederick I.* The portrait on this seal is probably as close a likeness as we have. The emperor is presented in official guise, enthroned and crowned, holding the imperial symbols—the sceptre and the globe.

FIGURE 2. *Shepherds.* This sculpture in stone from the twelfth century west portal of the Cathedral of Chartres combines the idea of sculpture as strictly subordinate to the architecture and design of which it is a part and a new feeling for the subject. While the treatment is decorative, with a rhythmic repetition of the figures of grazing sheep, the faces of the sly old peasant and the stupid young one are clearly inspired by actual observation.

FIGURE 3. *Aristotle.* One of a series of figures from the same portal of Chartres that represent the liberal arts. Aristotle stands for philosophy. Here we have a figure with stylized treatment of hair, and with the traditional attribute of the scholar—the inkpot. The new realism shows in the concentration of the whole figure on the work in hand.

FIGURE 4. *Nave of Durham Cathedral.* The Normans were great church builders, and they erected in England fine examples of the Romanesque style. Durham is one of the most impressive, since it rises from the steep rock.

CHRONOLOGY

1113 St. Bernard becomes a monk at Citeaux
1115–53 St. Bernard abbot of Clairvaux
1121 Abelard condemned at Soissons
1122 Concordat of Worms; compromise in investiture controversy
c. 1130–54 First gold coined in West since Charlemagne, symbol of trade revival
c. 1136 Geoffrey of Monmouth's *History of the Kings of Britain*
c. 1140 *Nibelungenlied*
1146–47 Insurrection of Arnold of Brescia in Rome
1147 Foundation of Moscow
1147–49 Second Crusade
c. 1145–50 Peter Lombard's *Sentences*
1152 Marriage of Eleanor of Aquitaine and Henry of Anjou (Henry II of England)
1163 Foundation stone of cathedral of Notre Dame in Paris
1170 Murder of Thomas Becket
1176 Defeat of Frederick Barbarossa at Legnano by Lombard League of Italian communes
1180 Philip Augustus king in France
1189 Beginning of the Third Crusade—Philip Augustus, Richard the Lion-hearted, Frederick Barbarossa
1198 Death of Averroës

PART VIII

The Twelfth Century

~~~~~~~~~~~~~~~~~~~~~~~~~~~~~~~~~~~~~

THE twelfth century was one of colonization, of flourishing town life, and of tremendous activity in the field of arts and letters. The skillful architects and artists trained in the process of building and beautifying the Romanesque churches of the eleventh century developed the Gothic style and a sculpture admirably adapted to it. Scholars made translations from Greek authors; and a veritable torrent of Greek works, notably scientific, which had been preserved in Syrian, Hebrew, and Persian versions, poured into Europe from Spain and other Moslem countries.

Europeans discovered that there was greater freedom for the spirit of inquiry under the caliphs than in Europe. Islam did not have within itself any seeds of growth, but in Moslem lands no priestly class dominated the life of a community, intellectually and morally, nor did a powerful church subordinate all knowledge to the purposes of theology. The caliphs promoted study and research along practical lines, with the result that important progress was made in astronomy and in mathematics as an auxiliary science. To the mathematical symbols derived from the Hindus the Arabs added the zero, with its immense simplification in arithmetical processes. Arabs also developed the principles of algebra, and made some progress in trigonometry. Although they used the experimental method, there were limits; their medical practice did not extend to surgery and the study of anatomy, but they did go much further in the use of drugs and curative herbs than their contemporaries in Christian lands. In the course of the century Latin translations of Euclid and of Arabic books on algebra and trigonometry were accessible in Europe; so were Ptolemy's *Almagest* and the *Physics*

[219

of Aristotle. Arabic lore had accelerated the progress of astrology and alchemy toward astronomy and chemistry. Arabic and Jewish medicine was supplementing European "leechdom."

Useful inventions came out of the East: the first windmill known to have been used in Europe, paper mills, and the compass. A very important advance in the art of navigation was the rudder attached to the stern-post instead of used from the side; however, this seems to have been developed independently in the waters of northern Europe. Although the general tendency was to depend upon the authority of the written word, there was some progress in scientific observation and experimentation.

This intellectual activity can be traced to the stimulating force of trade and of the towns, whose prosperity had been increased by commercial activity. The Mediterranean Sea had been the main highway for trade in the Roman world, but in the seventh and eighth centuries it was partly closed by the rise of the Mohammedan empire. The great Carolingian empire had been an inland empire, with little or no naval power, and the coasts had not been successfully defended against either Moslem pirates or Viking raiders. In Charlemagne's time, and after, trade in western Europe had largely been confined to local markets, and the growth of feudalism, with its self-sufficient estates, had promoted the breakdown of everything resembling the former general trading practices. There were no great quantities of produce or goods to market, nor any major urban centers in which to exchange them. There were cities in the feudal period, in the sense that there were relatively large concentrations of people at certain points; but feudal cities were not made up of a separate, non-feudal commercial class, did not depend on trade for their existence, and had no distinct municipal institutions. For the most part feudal cities were political or ecclesiastical capitals, and since the centers of religious administrative units were more important than political capitals in the decentralized feudal system, cities came almost entirely under church rule. To be sure, some cities were fortresses and under the control of secular rulers; but in any case the government was little distinguished from other feudal rule, and the population was largely dependent on food grown in the immediate vicinity.

The eleventh and twelfth centuries, and especially the latter, saw a rapid development of commerce and a consequent revival of cities

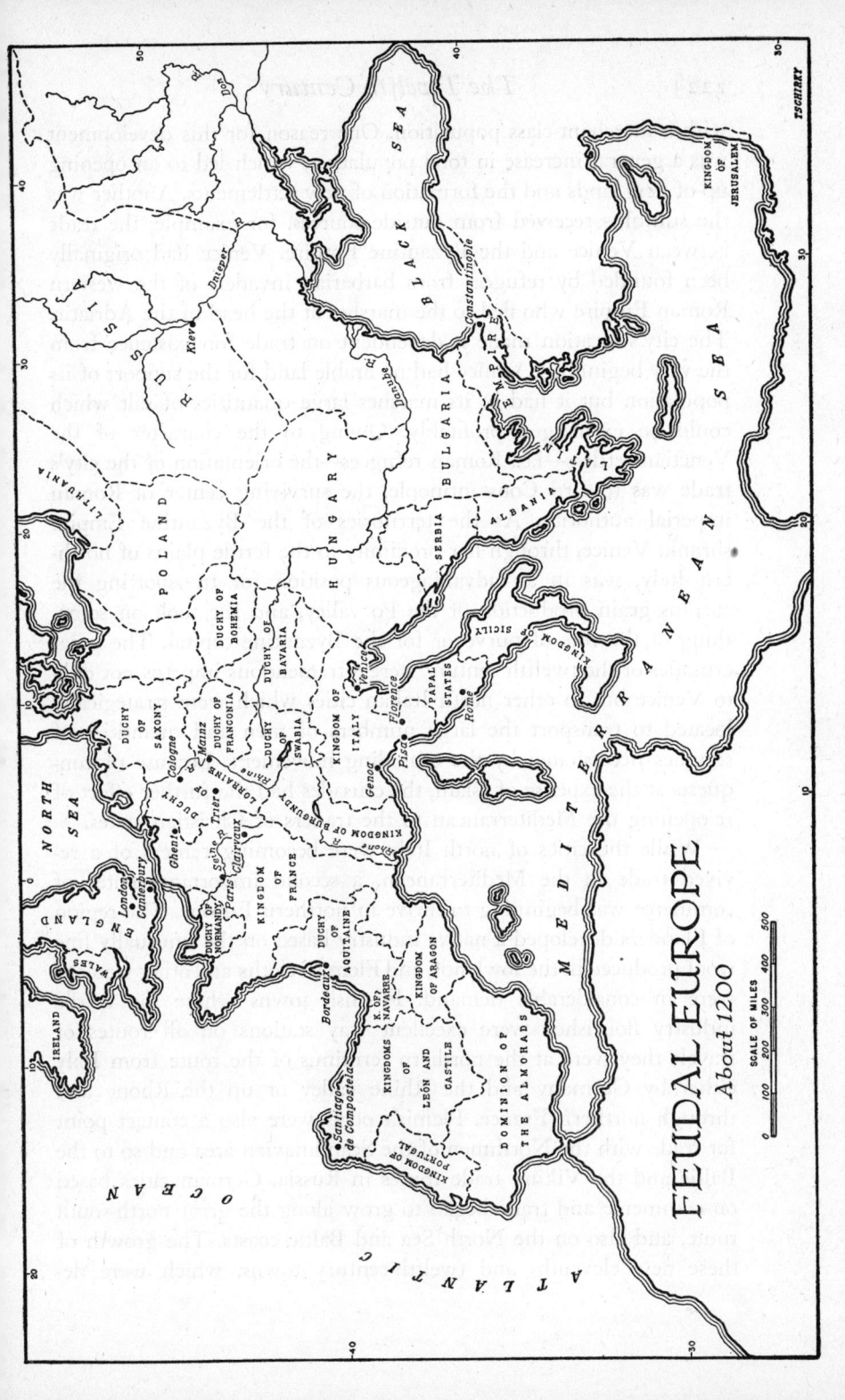

with a merchant-class population. One reason for this development was a general increase in total population, which led to an opening up of new lands and the formation of new settlements. Another was the stimulus received from outside sources, for example, the trade between Venice and the Byzantine Empire. Venice had originally been founded by refugees from barbarian invaders of the western Roman Empire who fled to the marshes at the head of the Adriatic. The city's location made it dependent on trade for existence from the very beginning; Venice had no arable land for the support of its population but it had in its marshes large quantities of salt which could be exchanged profitably. Owing to the character of the Venetian settlers—i.e., Roman refugees—the orientation of the city's trade was toward Constantinople, the surviving center of Roman imperial authority. As the territories of the Byzantine Empire shrank, Venice, through her proximity to the fertile plains of northern Italy, was in an advantageous position for transporting the surplus grain production of the Po valley, and she took on something of the role of purveyor for the Byzantine capital. The great crusades of the twelfth century were a tremendous impetus not only to Venice but to other north Italian cities which were strategically located to transport the large numbers of men and quantities of supplies necessitated by the crusading movement. Because of conquests at the expense of Islam, the crusades had the further effect of re-opening the Mediterranean to the traders of Christian states.

While the cities of north Italy were becoming centers of a revived trade in the Mediterranean, a second important center of commerce was beginning to thrive in northern Europe. The region of Flanders developed a native industry based on the unusually fine wool produced in the lowlands, and Flemish cloths and other woolens were in considerable demand. Flemish towns where the textile industry flourished were excellent way stations on all routes of travel; they were at the northern terminus of the route from Italy either by Germany and the Rhine valley or up the Rhone and through northern France. Flemish ports were also a contact point for trade with the Northmen of the Scandinavian area and so to the Baltic and the Viking trade routes in Russia. German cities based on commerce and trade began to grow along the great north-south route, and also on the North Sea and Baltic coasts. The growth of these new eleventh- and twelfth-century towns, which were dependent on a merchant class distinct from the traditional three estates of feudal society, meant a change in country as well as town life. With the revival of commercial towns a demand was created for agricultural products, for the new towns were not self-sufficient, and the manors which had been operated on a diversified scale to avoid surpluses again found it profitable to produce for a town market.

The origins of the distinctive merchant class that filled the commercial towns of the twelfth and later centuries are in part to be found in the Venetian heritage with which other Europeans came in contact during the crusades. Commercial practices of the ancient world had never died out among the Venetians because of their relationship with Constantinople and the East during the feudal period. In loading for shipment Venetian merchants divided their goods and by thus pooling the risk avoided ruin if a ship were lost. Venetian ships ordinarily sailed in flotillas for increased safety. Successful merchant enterprise required certain co-operative practices, especially for sea commerce, but the same characteristics were essential for the development of a merchant class when overland trade reappeared on the Continent on a large scale. From Genoa, also, merchants borrowed new capitalist techniques.

With the increase of population in the eleventh and twelfth centuries more people became detached from the land, and the adventurous were drawn to the towns as centers of activity and wealth. According to feudal custom a man was a free man if it could not be proved that he had a master, and by maintaining himself in a town for a year and a day a former serf could win his legal freedom. The merchants and free men of the towns were in a peculiar position in a feudal society which was based on personal relationship between lord and vassal. A special law grew up for these traders, and for better protection of their peculiar freedom as well as for control of their conditions of work and profit they began to form associations, or guilds. By organizing, the townsmen were in a position to gain a voice in political affairs, and the growth of municipal institutions distinct from the feudal or ecclesiastical administration of cities took place.

Astute monarchs issued charters giving towns in their kingdoms rights of self-government. The third estate thereby took its first steps toward an emancipation from the control of the aristocracy, both lay and ecclesiastical, through those of the "men of work" who had left the country for the town. The alliance between town and crown was a logical one. The prosperous burgher in his snugly-built town house lived a more comfortable life than the noble in his drafty castle; the townsman had more society, more varied intercourse, in market and guild-hall and tavern. Membership in his guild gave him an importance and self-confidence that he could not have attained as a single individual. In time the town also became a center of intellectual life as the wandering scholar and the merchant brought ideas from one town to another, and often from far countries. Townsmen developed civic pride, and built strong walls for defense. A walled royal town was a useful *pied à terre* for a king whose vassals defied him, and levies of town militia were valuable auxiliaries in a trial of strength against a rebellious vassal.

Although self-governing communes first developed in northern Italy, settlements of traders in northern lands grew into towns under the stimulus of a reviving trade in the twelfth century. Among the ruins of Roman cities and military camps, about monasteries and castles, and at crossroads a town population came into being which welcomed products from far places. In France the Cistercian abbeys, foundations of a new order of the eleventh century, were centers of great activity. The monks themselves toiled and directed lay brothers and others in the development of large tracts of land, which were often procured by draining swamps and building dikes. The Cistercians entered the colonizing movement which was drawing settlers to the north and east, and continued their land-creating there; they did not, however, destroy forests wantonly to obtain farm land, but conserved them carefully. They improved the breeds of cattle, horses, and sheep. In England, where the Norman rulers had curbed civil war and where, consequently, flocks could graze undisturbed, the Cistercians bred sheep with long wool and thus helped England to become a source for wool from which fine cloth could be made.

Cistercians in Flanders developed the cloth industry and imported the wool grown by Cistercians in England. Flemish towns followed their example and grew rich. Cistercians carried French vines to the Rhine region and developed a wine trade. Colonizing feudal lords in the Baltic lands imitated Cistercian methods in the use of dikes and swamp-draining. The prosperity of German lands was further increased by the development of mining. Saxon miners were encouraged to settle in Magyar territory; but generally the Magyar, Czech, and Polish rulers opposed, though they failed to stop, the flocking of the Germans to their lands. It was a great period of prosperity for Hungary, placed as it was on one of the great crusading routes to the Near East. The towns which grew up in these regions were always able to have freer government than towns in the West. Everywhere merchants formed guilds and bargained for rights of self-government with the lords on whose lands the towns stood; later the craftsmen formed guilds of their own, and shared the government of the towns with the merchant guilds.

Trade created a need for a special lay education to train men in computation, and the merchant guilds established schools to teach the rudiments of reading, writing, and arithmetic. This was a radical departure in education, which had been exclusively for clerical personnel, but it did not extend beyond the elementary level. Higher education generally underwent a considerable development during the century along lines already established. The cathedral and monastic schools provided the basis; they had been formed in large part because of the responsibility of bishops or other high ecclesiastical officials for training men to carry on the work of the church. The teaching was ordinarily limited to grammar and scriptural or patristic literature for a selected few under episcopal patronage, but in the twelfth century a number of noted teachers at the great cathedral schools began to attract a variety of students from all over Europe. The school at Chartres was a center for the study of rhetoric, while at Paris dialectics and theology predominated.

Out of the great cathedral schools and the increasing number of students attracted to them by famous teachers, grew the medieval universities. These were essentially universities of men, not of buildings or extra-curricular activities. They continued to be based on the seven liberal arts which had been standard since the time of Boethius. The university proper was simply an organization to conduct examinations and issue teaching licenses to those who had mastered the trivium and quadrivium. Gradually three professional faculties developed in which a learned man might achieve the degree of doctor—divinity, law, and medicine. Guilds of students and teachers were organized at university centers, partly as a matter of convenience for those with common interests, partly for safety, and partly as a means of providing bargaining power to free the members from extortion by the townspeople. Teachers' fees were traditionally low—it had long been regarded as an obligation of the bishop to provide for the welfare of his flock by promoting education—and both students and teachers were perennially worried by the problem of maintenance. Students at the medieval university had clerical privilege and were not subject to the town authorities but had their own discipline; rivalry between town and gown was frequently violent, each regarding the other as fair game.

The methods of all the great cathedral schools and universities were similar. Instruction was based on the study of authority, and since in the beginning there was a scarcity of texts, the teacher dictated from his own manuscript while the students copied it down and learned the material by rote. The multiplication of texts which resulted later made it possible for most students to have copies, whereupon the teacher lectured or made a commentary on the text which the student had before him. The emphasis on authority induced a great command of material, which was demonstrated through a disputation. Examinations, held publicly, required a candidate for a degree to propose a thesis and then defend it in disputation with all comers. Unfortunately one of the consequences of this method was the creation of a spirit of contentiousness, argument for argument's sake, and a desire to win no matter how the material might have to be twisted.

An almost inevitable consequence of the dialectic methods in the disputation was the rise of scholasticism in the medieval universities. The scholastics, or schoolmen, brought philosophy and reason to the support of dogma in an age when the papal monarchy, canon law, organization, and theology of the church were receiving final form. A great problem of scholasticism was what to do when no rational basis existed for some article of faith; and the problem created two points of view, as illustrated by the controversy over universals, or abstractions. The realist point of view was that in a conflict between faith and reason, faith must prevail: one did not seek understanding in order to believe, but believed in order to receive understanding. The opposing nominalist point of view, taken by such a notable teacher as Roscellinus of Compiègne, was that reason must prevail, for nothing is to be believed unless it is first understood. The nominalist, in his mental concepts, proceeded from the particular material object to the universal idea or principle of that object, whereas the realist assumed that the idea came first and then the particular object was created as a reflection of the idea. According to the realist, universals had a real existence entirely apart from human experience with the objects which were the material reflection of the universal. Peter Abelard, although not strictly a nominalist, held the nominalist view of reason, and did much to give it popularity among students.

The language of the universities and of the scholastics was Latin, but in the twelfth century vernacular literature began to appear side by side with the learned tongue. One factor that promoted this was the secular elementary education of the guilds; merchants needed their education for business purposes, not for a study of the Latin literature or ritual of the church. Another factor was the development of a school of lyric poets in the south of France, known as troubadours. The church had not encouraged the idea of romantic love, but in southern France the noble laity were close enough to feel the effect of Saracen culture, and Arab preoccupation with the pleasures of dalliance provided a model. In the north of France a similar group of poets and singers, the trouvères, sang traditional songs of warlike deeds, the *chansons de geste,* perpetuating the Arthurian and Carolingian legends. The *Song of Roland,* one of the greatest of medieval vernacular epics, took written form in this period. Vernacular literature had appeared somewhat earlier in England, with such examples as the *Anglo-Saxon Chronicle* and *Beowulf,* an epic poem. In German the great epic was the *Nibelungenlied,* made up of tales about Theodoric and the invasions of Attila the Hun, but full of mythology and magic; lyric verse appeared in the songs of the minnesingers, who resembled the troubadours of southern France.

The emphasis of the troubadours on the theme of romantic love, which the church had never encouraged, suggests the rather anomalous position occupied by women in the society of the Middle Ages. In theory her status oscillated between the heights and the depths, both with the church and with the aristocracy—the only literate groups. According to some clerical writers women were the cause of all evil because they were daughters of Eve, by whose temptation Adam had fallen from the state of grace and cursed all the sons of man with that original sin; according to other clerical writers women were associated with the salvation of man because of the Virgin Mary, mother of Christ. Indeed the cult of the Virgin reached amazing proportions in the Middle Ages, as is witnessed by the number of great churches named in her honor. The aristocracy also glorified woman, in theory, in the cult of the lady which the chivalric code of the troubadours popularized; on the other hand, women were subjected to men legally in every way. What the peasant classes thought about the exaltation or the subjection of women in society is not recorded, for those classes, like the women themselves, were not articulate.

In practice, the typical woman of any class was a wife and a housewife. Some women remained independent, for there were generally more women than men in the population; if a woman of the upper classes did not marry an earthly husband she frequently took Christ as her bridegroom by entering a nunnery, which was in great measure a class institution, to enter which a dowry was required. Marriage in feudal families was a business affair and the primary consideration was the amount of property, or dowry, that could be given away with the bride; a son or son-in-law was a potential fighting man, and welcome in any family, but no man took the responsibility for adding a female to his household unless she paid her way. The woman of a feudal family who married, however, enjoyed a certain essential equality with the men, for she often had to take over manorial management during her husband's frequent absence on military or other business. A woman's dowry rights were protected by law, and if she were ill-treated she had some bargaining power. (There must have been not a few strong-minded women to justify the medieval wit who said of the fair sex, "God made 'em to match the men.") And if the third estate was composed of the "men of work," the women were no exception. The peasant wife was the replenisher of the estate, and when she was not engaged in that function worked side by side with her husband in the fields.

The dominant role of the clergy in the everyday life of the average individual was established more firmly than ever by the twelfth century with the church's final formulation of the sacramental system. From the dialectic subtleties of the schoolmen evolved an explanation of the transubstantiation of bread and wine of the Eucharist into the body and blood of Christ sufficiently reasonable to secure its adoption as a dogma of the church at the Fourth Lateran Council (1215). The adoption of this dogma meant that the priest, even more than before, was set apart since he, as the language of the time had it, "made God every day." At the same time came the final decision that the sacraments were seven in number; through the administration of the sacraments the church prepared the soul for eternal life, and without them salvation was impossible. By *baptism* the soul was cleansed of the original sin with which all the sons of Adam were born. In *confirmation* the Christian was received into the church as a responsible individual capable of knowing truth from error. If he fell into sin the sacrament of *penance,* after confession before a priest in a truly penitent spirit, restored him to a state of grace and he was fit to receive the *eucharist,* which renewed his communion with God. *Extreme unction* was administered at the point of death to save the soul from the terrors of Hell and to substitute the pains of Purgatory preparatory to salvation. Two sacraments were not universally administered: *marriage,* as a sacrament, was indissoluble if performed correctly, and *ordination* was only for men entering the priesthood. Thus the church marked out the system which guarded frail humanity from birth to death.

Final form was also being given to church organization. In the preceding century the College of Cardinals had been created; the cardinals were the princes of the church, selected by the pope, and charged with one principal function—the election of a successor when a pope died. For the administration of the vast organization of the universal church an elaborate court, or *curia,* grew up at Rome, with important branches to handle papal correspondence (chancery) and finances (*camera*). Wealth from the whole Christian world poured into the papal treasury through the collection of tithes (an income-tax for the benefit of the church) and other revenues. The real pivot of the ecclesiastical administration was the bishop, who was elected by the canons of the cathedral chapter. (In practice, however, the election was often a formality because the bishops were nominated by powerful political rulers.) The bishop directed the church activities in his province, administered church properties, and supervised the parish priests. The latter did the real work of the church among the people, administering the sacraments, and often sharing the hardships and tribulations of the parishioners.

Perhaps the finest monument to the importance which religious interest and the affairs of the church had in the lives of medieval people is provided by the great cathedrals of the eleventh, twelfth, and thirteenth centuries. Technically a cathedral was the bishop's principal church (from Greek *cathedra,* chair) and his official seat. Cathedrals were built as community projects, however, and absorbed the finest talents of all classes of people. The main architectural style of church building until the middle of the twelfth century was that known as Romanesque, which had been evolved from the ancient Roman basilica. The essential Romanesque quality was massiveness; the buildings had thick walls, small windows, semi-circular arches, and barrel-vaulting. Romanesque churches tended to be dark, especially in northern climates which lacked the brilliant southern sunshine under which the style first developed. Mosaics of glass or marble helped relieve the gloom of the interior and provided a part of the pictorial display of religious themes or biblical scenes which helped to make of the cathedrals books in stone for generations that could not read. Symbolism played an important part in cathedral architecture; the principal axis of the building ran east and west, with the altar at the east end. A rough cruciform shape was given to later churches by the addition of transepts on a north-south axis at the point where the nave and choir met. The west front, which was the main entrance, came to have three portals. Many modifications in detail were made on this basic plan, and cathedrals became very complex structures, but the fundamental lines remained.

About the middle of the twelfth century, however, the demand for still finer churches pushed architects to ponder new devices, and led to the rise of the style known as Gothic. It was distinguished from the Romanesque by its delicacy and lightness, effects achieved through the introduction of the pointed arch and ribbed vaulting. Gothic architects were able to concentrate the weight of their vaults at a few points, which made unnecessary the massive walls of the Romanesque style. Heavy piers were needed to support the concentration of weight, but by the addition of flying buttresses these could be raised to great heights without collapsing. The cathedral of Notre Dame in Paris (built 1163-1235) is characteristic of the transition from Romanesque to Gothic, and the cathedral of Chartres, begun a few years before the end of the twelfth century, is one of the best known examples of the new style.

The extent of religious enthusiasm can be seen in the great success of St. Bernard, the man who preserved and made famous the Cistercian order and who upheld the church's standards of life and

The Twelfth Century   [231

faith for every rank of society. St. Bernard made his own the affairs of princes and prelates, directed the decisions of synods, drew up rules for the soldier-monks (the Knights Templar), and preached a crusade. The recruiting in the second and third crusades was very successful, but royal as well as papal prestige profited—the pope made the tactical error of persuading a king to take the cross. The second crusade was a failure, but in the third Philip II (Augustus) of France, Richard I (the Lion-hearted) of England, and Frederick I (Barbarossa) of Germany stole the show, and thenceforth the glory, when there was any, was to go to the rulers who led crusades rather than to the popes who proclaimed them.

Frederick Barbarossa in the twelfth century consciously set out to build up an effective government on Roman principles; his policies toward the towns emphasizes the importance they had achieved,

THE BUILDING OF A CHURCH

(From *A Student's History of England* by Samuel R. Gardiner. Longmans Green, London, 1897.)

and his relations with the papacy form an important chapter in the struggle for primacy between popes and emperors. At the same time in France Louis VI inaugurated a policy of enlarging the royal domain, which Philip II continued with conspicuous success. In England Henry II by scutage (accepting the payment of money in lieu of military service owed by a vassal) weaned many nobles from military preoccupations and provided himself with the funds to pay mercenaries. He further increased the revenues by making royal justice popular and attracting cases to the royal courts, but he failed in his attack upon the special privilege of clerics before the law. All the strong rulers insisted on controlling episcopal nominations, and Frederick I was especially successful in his use of bishops as administrators. It was an age when, as the more astute political minds saw, the church had everything to give that the age was ready for: organizing ability and the power that goes with education. The modern state as a mechanism was created in the twelfth century by churchmen.

CHAPTER 13

The World of St. Bernard of Clairvaux
[1 0 9 1 – 1 1 5 3]

~~~~~~

THE world into which Bernard of Clairvaux was born was the feudal world at its most violent. Papal efforts to free the church from feudal control seemed to have come to nothing, for lay investiture continued and, despite the church's ritual, the knight who was the pure-hearted protector of the weak existed only in song and story. The Truce of God and the Peace of God palliated, but did not eliminate, the evils of feudal warfare. The Byzantine appeal for help in the East against the Turks came at a propitious moment, for it gave the papacy an opportunity, through the crusades, to inaugurate a method of diverting feudal warfare to a new field.

Unorganized crusades had long been popular; French pilgrims to the Spanish shrine of St. James of Compostella aided Spanish Christians against the Moors, Greeks and Normans fought the Saracens in the Mediterranean, and the Guiscards won back Sicily for Christendom. Under the aegis of the papacy Pisa recaptured Sardinia and, together with Genoa, freed the western Mediterranean from Moslem control. Organized crusades were precipitated when the Seljuk Turks, who had secured the Bagdad caliphate and conquered Palestine and Asia Minor, interfered with the access to the Holy Places which Christians had enjoyed under Arab rule. The French pope, Urban II, received an appeal from the Emperor Alexius Comnenus for soldiers to help reconquer Asia Minor, and heard from pilgrims many complaints of Turkish atrocities.

Pope Urban, who had been forced out of Italy because he continued the policy of Gregory VII with regard to simony and investitures, needed to restore his prestige. He was decidedly successful in this when he responded to the appeal of Alexius by proclaim-

[233

ing a holy war for the recovery of Jerusalem. At a council held at Clermont (1095) he appealed to Christian knights to give up fighting one another and to combat the infidel in the name of the Cross, and promised many advantages to crusaders, including plenary indulgences, which meant full release from the pains of Purgatory. Itinerant preachers spread his exhortation, as a wave of enthusiasm swept France, and to some extent affected the chivalry of other countries. Great expeditions, not all of which ever reached their destination, traveled overland to Constantinople and thence with Greek forces through Asia Minor. Several Christian feudal states were set up in Syria by the knights who wore the sign of the Cross, and Jerusalem was taken. According to contemporary accounts the crusaders entered the Holy City with the streets running blood. They proclaimed a kingdom of Jerusalem, and established the military orders of the Knights of St. John of the Hospital and the Knights Templar, to protect Christian shrines against the infidel.

All Christendom was echoing with the dramatic events of the first great crusade, which took place while Bernard was a little boy in Burgundy. He was of noble birth but grew up with the ambition to be a soldier of the Cross in a very different fashion from the crusaders. His delicate physique precluded the career of the feudal warrior, and his relatives urged upon him the life of a scholar, which offered many temptations in the twelfth century.

An intellectual awakening had attended the shift of studies from the cloister to the free atmosphere of the towns, and students wandered from one school to another. In Paris the most famous teacher was the master of the school of Notre Dame, William of Champeaux, and among the students who flocked to hear him was a young Breton nobleman named Peter Abelard. William had introduced the dialectic method, with its use of the syllogism, which had been taught by Gerbert, practiced by Lanfranc, and perfected by Lanfranc's pupil, Anselm of Bec, later of Canterbury. Abelard greatly annoyed William by challenging his statements. In the great controversy over universals, William maintained the realist side: that is, he asserted that a general idea, such as that of the church, had real existence. Abelard had studied with the famous nominalist, Roscellinus, whose position was that a word like *church* was merely a convenient name for an idea and that the only reality was that of its components, such as church buildings, the clergy, the ritual, and so forth. Abelard rejected both these extremes and put forth a compromise theory which has been called conceptualism, to the effect that universals have real existence only in the mind. The importance of this controversy is twofold: it gave the intellectual world practice in thinking and debating, and for the nominalists, who had the better of the debate as time went on, it diverted interest from abstractions to the study of matter, which led to scientific speculation. For the time being, the eloquence of Abelard triumphed, the students deserted the master's lectures for those of Abelard, and William left Paris to accept a bishopric.

Although Bernard, who like Abelard had great literary ability, was tempted by the scholar's life, a sudden mystical experience made him resolve for complete renunciation of the world. With the persuasiveness which was to characterize his whole career he won a group of his young kinsmen to join him. The Cluniac reform had run its course, and a new reformation was due. It began three years after Urban's great speech at Clermont when a Benedictine monk, desirous of living more strictly than the Cluniacs, founded the Cistercian order at Citeaux in a wild and desolate region. Bernard at the age of 22 came there with his band of followers. Two years later he was made abbot of a new Cistercian monastery at Clairvaux in Champagne.

William of Champeaux had become bishop of Chalons-sur-Marne and was called upon to consecrate Bernard as abbot of Clairvaux. Bernard had so weakened himself by fasting and loss of sleep that William was horrified and secured a command from the head of the Cistercian order that Bernard should give himself up to a year of treatment. The regime to which the young man submitted affords a good example of the way monks in that period, forced by their vocation to tend the sick, had developed many of the methods approved by modern therapy. The man assigned to care for Bernard removed him from his cell and placed him in a hut outside the monastery, where he would be in seclusion. There he was kept in bed and fed on herbs and food which experimentation had proved to be strength-giving. This regimen was strictly enforced, and Bernard was able thenceforth to carry on a most strenuous career although he was always delicate. He was of medium height, but his extreme thinness made him appear tall; his hair was pale gold, his beard reddish, his white skin flushed easily, and his eyes were luminous.

Although he had great charm of manner and a nature singularly gentle, he was at the same time fanatically religious and a fiery and eloquent preacher. The Cistercian order was in danger of failure when he entered it, but he imbued it with life. Whereas Gregory VII and Lanfranc in the eleventh century had demonstrated the importance of the secular clergy, Bernard of Clairvaux and the Cistercians in the twelfth century showed what the regular clergy could accomplish. The eager young men who flocked to Clairvaux were sent out to found new monasteries throughout France and in the Netherlands, Germany, and England. Bernard became known as a worker of miracles, his fame as a preacher spread over Europe, and he was in great demand to aid worthy causes.

The abolition of lay investiture was still such a cause, for despite the labors of the Cluniacs it was continuing in England and Germany. William Rufus, after keeping the archbishopric of Canterbury vacant for a long period after Lanfranc's death, finally in the fear of death appointed Anselm of Bec, an Italian pupil of Lanfranc's. Under William's brother and successor Henry I, a bitter quarrel broke out over investiture, and although Anselm was a mild-mannered man, he was firm. In the end a compromise was worked out: the king would give up investiture with ring and staff, and the election would be canonical, that is, by the clergy. The stipulation that it be held in the presence of the king's representative, however, gave an opportunity for pressure in favor of the king's candidate. This agreement provided a model for the settlement of the question in Germany, where Henry V, the rebellious son of Henry IV, continued his father's policy of appointing bishops and quarrelling with the papacy. In 1122, after a protracted struggle, he signed a concordat at Worms on similar terms, but worldly bishops continued to be chosen.

The year before the signing of the Concordat of Worms a heresy case occurred in which a synod at Soissons condemned one of Abelard's books to the flames. After his defeat of William of Champeaux, Abelard had become the most popular teacher in Paris. He seduced and then married his brilliant pupil Heloise, and when her relatives castrated him, he became a monk and she a nun. Abelard continued to teach and wrote a book for his students in which he tried to explain the doctrine of the Trinity on rational grounds; this was the book condemned at Soissons. The church had already begun sanctioning the burning of heretics whose practices were regarded as a menace to society, but it had not yet followed the burning of a dangerous book to the logical conclusion of burning the author along with it. Abelard was merely committed to the custody of the monks of St. Denis, whom he outraged by attacking the story that the Areopagite had founded their abbey.

While Abelard was undergoing these experiences, which he set down in his remarkable *Historia Calamitatum,* Bernard was giving church authorities aid against rulers who practiced simony and lay investiture. In France, Louis VI (the Fat) had been on the throne since 1108, the fifth Capetian ruler in direct succession and the first to make any headway against the power of his vassals. He was also the first of his house to adopt a consistent policy of strenghening the royal power by using the townsmen's support, for he issued charters to towns and to groups of men who would settle on waste lands. He used the *bourgeoisie* (townsmen) and lesser clergy in administrative office, in order to break the power of the great nobles who at the beginning of his reign controlled the *curia regis* (the king's council). The most useful of his clerical officers was Suger, who had been his tutor and whom he made abbot of St. Denis, for, thanks to Suger, Louis remained in Bernard's good books by making appointments of which the papacy approved.

Louis was also the inaugurator of an astute policy of organizing and extending the royal domain: by this a fief, on falling vacant, was added to the royal domain and administered by royal officials, and hence meant one less vassal to give trouble. The eyes of Louis were especially on the fiefs held by the English crown. William the Conqueror's third son Henry, who succeeded William Rufus in 1100, proceeded to conquer Normandy, declared his daughter Matilda his heir, and married her to Count Geoffrey of Anjou. The son of this marriage would in due course become both king of England and lord of the French fiefs of Normandy, Anjou, Maine, and Touraine. Louis VI threw out an anchor to windward by marrying his own heir to Eleanor, the granddaughter of the troubadour duke of Aquitaine, thus hoping to annex a large part of southern France. (Incidentally, Eleanor brought to the French court men of letters who popularized the new lyric poetry.) Louis VII, when he succeeded his father, came to take his wife's advice rather than that of his able counsellor, Suger. Even with Suger at his elbow, when

Louis began to nominate bishops he was no match for Bernard, who used the ambition of secular lords to defeat the king's bid for ecclesiastical control.

In 1128 Bernard attended the Synod of Troyes, which recognized the most famous of the military orders which sprang from the Crusades, the Knights Templar. Later he took them to task for worldliness; still later he drafted rules for them. Two years after the Synod of Troyes he championed the cause of Pope Innocent II, whom the Normans of Sicily had driven from Rome in favor of an anti-pope. Innocent came to France for help; and though Bernard secured the support of the French king and of Henry I of England for the pope's cause, he had greater difficulty with the emperor. In Germany Henry IV's policy of replacing his great vassals by unknown men had borne its natural fruit, for these men founded great families in their turn. Henry had made a Hohenstaufen (or Waibling, from the name of one of their seats) duke of Swabia, and a Guelf (or Welf) duke of Bavaria. These two families continued the long rivalry of Swabia and Bavaria, and also came to be associated with the political conflict between emperors and popes, the former being Henry's designated heirs. After the death of Henry V, who had been as anti-clerical as his father, the archbishops of Mainz and Cologne succeeded in securing the election of the strongly-clerical Lothair II, duke of Saxony and father-in-law of the Welf duke. Then began the long rivalry of Welf and Waibling (Guelf and Ghibelline), factions respectively papal and imperial, by which the empire, and especially Italy, were riven.

Lothair hesitated for a long time before recognizing Innocent II, but Bernard finally prevailed and Lothair accompanied Innocent to Italy with an army, sworn to establish the pope in Rome. Lothair's vassal, Conrad of Hohenstaufen, and Roger Guiscard of Sicily, however, supported the anti-pope, and all of Bernard's eloquence and ingenuity were required to end the schism. Finally Innocent was installed, and he crowned Lothair emperor at Rome (1133). The pope gave the emperor as a fief the lands of the Countess Matilda of Tuscany, where the scene at Canossa had taken place, and these proved to be a valuable foothold for an emperor with Italian ambitions.

That popes should give fiefs like other feudal lords was a commonplace, but papal control of the city of Rome was periodically challenged by Roman nobles and populace, and Innocent II had his troubles. His position was complicated by the exhortations of a certain Arnold of Brescia, who in violent terms attacked the papacy's worldliness and bureaucracy and the whole theory of its temporal power. The agitation for communes—strong at the time in northern Italy, where the commercial stimulus of the crusades was widely felt—spread to Rome, and a commune was set up there which Arnold defended and served. Bernard, who did not hesitate to rebuke popes for worldliness in his letters to them, had already marked out Arnold as a dangerous agitator; public agitation was another matter, and he persecuted the Roman leader relentlessly.

Bernard's methods did not depend on force; for example, he believed heretics should be confronted with argument, and he was an unyielding opponent of the brutalities against the Jews which were an accompaniment to the Crusades. But he did not believe heresy should flourish unchecked, and he was much troubled by the renewed fame of Abelard, now an abbot and again a renowned teacher. Bernard wrote: "In France we have a monk without rule, a prelate without care, an abbot without discipline; we have Peter Abelard disputing with boys, conversing with women. . . . In the streets and thoroughfares the Catholic faith is discussed. Men dispute over the childbearing of the Virgin, the sacrament of the altar, the incomprehensible mystery of the Trinity. . . ." He wrote far and wide to this effect, and Abelard, believing offense was the best defense, demanded to be allowed to confront Bernard at the Council of Sens held probably in 1140. The meeting took place and Bernard began his attack, but Abelard, apparently realizing that the assembly would yield to the fiery eloquence of the most famous preacher of the day, declared that he appealed to Rome, and left the assembly. The difference between the two monks was summed up by Bernard himself in a letter to Pope Innocent: "He defines faith as being opinion . . . faith is not an opinion, but a certitude." Thus the mystic condemned the rationalist.

Bernard was indefatigable in attacking anything connected with religion which seemed to him to smack of luxury or worldliness, even the magnificent churches that were being built. Although Suger rebuilt the Abbey of St. Denis in the new Gothic fashion, the favorite style was still the Romanesque, whose great round arches and heavy pillars were very impressive, though the small windows in the thick walls kept the interiors dark. In a highly stylized sculpture subordinated to the architecture, sermons in stone for the instruction of the faithful were put in the porches and over the doors. There an attenuated Christ sat in judgment, souls were weighed in the balance, and the damned were tortured by the devil's auxiliaries —medieval folk were early schooled to see cruelty under approved auspices. The great Cluniac monasteries were built in this style, and Bernard deplored their size and denounced the sculpture as worldly and a sinful waste, as he also reproached the Cluniac monks for the softness of their lives. He wrote letters of reproach, counsel, and adjuration to great and lowly, to pope, king, and emperor. Everywhere his letters were received with respectful attention; every assembly he addressed yielded to his eloquence. He took a great deal of care with a letter to Pope Eugenius III, warning him of the dangers to the papal office inherent in the growing practice of appeals to papal courts, a practice encouraged on account of the revenue entailed.

Eugenius, on his part, made use of Bernard's eloquence for the preaching of the second crusade in 1145. The feudal kingdom of Jerusalem was the most important of the Christian states that had been set up in Palestine as a result of the first crusade. Jerusalem made treaties with the great Italian trading cities and gave them special privileges, including that of tax-free commerce; thenceforth for the most part crusaders and well-to-do pilgrims traveled by sea, to the vast enrichment of Venice and Genoa. Intercourse with the Moslems led to imitation of their ways of life, and these new contacts meant an influx of goods and ideas into Europe. The Moslems, on their side, naturally planned reconquest of their lands; in 1144 they captured the principality of Edessa, and other states of the crusaders were threatened. Pope Eugenius III, who had been a Cistercian and a pupil of Bernard, had, like Urban II, ideas of increasing papal prestige and believed another crusade was in order. He persuaded Louis VII of France—who had a guilty conscience because he had been responsible for the burning of a church full of people —that it was the king's duty to lead the crusade, and he appointed Bernard to preach it. Bernard succeeded in convincing the emperor that the latter should divide the leadership with Louis. The emperor was Conrad III, a Hohenstaufen successor of the Welf Lothair II, and he spent his entire reign in civil warfare, with the ill-starred second crusade as its only interlude.

Bernard preached the crusade in many French and German cities and evoked intense enthusiasm. The expedition was a complete failure, however, and when the survivors came straggling back Bernard experienced unpopularity for the first time in his career and was violently attacked. He was unmoved, however, believing the failure to be the inscrutable will of God.

The second crusade had, in the end, an important result: Louis VII obtained a papal annulment of his marriage. His wife, Eleanor of Aquitaine, had insisted upon accompanying her husband to the East and had aroused his jealousy by her flirtatious behavior. It was the culmination of years of disillusionment, for she had also failed to produce an heir for him. Her hand was immediately sought by Henry Plantagenet, son of Matilda, the heiress of the English king, Henry I; and the great duchy of Aquitaine passed out of French control. Since her father's death in 1135 Matilda had been fighting for the succession against Stephen of Blois, the son of William the Conqueror's daughter, and England had lapsed into anarchy. A compromise was reached in 1153, the year of the death of Pope Eugenius III, who had proclaimed the second crusade, and of St. Bernard, who had preached it. According to the treaty of Wallingford, Stephen was to be king, but on his death the crown was to go to Matilda's son Henry. When, in the following year, Henry II and his wife Eleanor arrived in an England torn by civil war, they

SEAL OF ST. BERNARD

(From *Life and Works of Saint Bernard* translated by Samuel J. Eales. Burns, Oates, and Washbroune, Ltd., London.)

brought with them an interest in letters that was to create an intellectual revival once order was restored.

The world of St. Bernard of Clairvaux was a world in which urban life was playing an increasing part. In this atmosphere criticism flourished, and took the form of a questioning of existing institutions and prevailing beliefs. The atmosphere engendered by crowds favors the preacher who appeals to emotions, and by this Bernard profited. His childhood memories of the excitement attending the first crusade lent fire to his preaching of the second, and though the crusade failed, the spirit of the crusades was still in the ascendant. From one point of view mundane figures such as Louis VI and Louis VII in France, Henry I in England and Henry V in Germany, busy at putting their royal houses in order, made little show against St. Bernard, going about his Father's business. On the other hand, their continued employment of trained clerical administrators, Henry I's use of itinerant justices, Henry V's negotiation of the Concordat of Worms, meant important steps toward bridling the power of the feudal lord.

CHAPTER 14

The World of Frederick Barbarossa

[1123–1190]

~~~~~~~~~~~~~~~~~~~~~~~~~~~

DURING the years that Frederick Barbarossa was preparing himself for the role of a Roman emperor, the anarchy of England under Stephen (1135-54) was showing what happened to a feudal kingdom without an effective ruler. The France of Louis VI and Louis VII was not in much better case, although the former had taken steps in the right direction by adding vacant fiefs to the royal domain and by replacing great nobles in office with men of lower rank. Both he and his son easily fell under the sway of any more energetic character to whose influence he was exposed. On the other hand, in the German lands the tradition of Otto I's rule was still strong after almost two centuries, and although the conditions Frederick faced were as chaotic as those which had confronted Otto, he was as resolved as Otto had been to rule as well as reign. Frederick was a handsome, impressive figure, with golden hair and much personal magnetism. He had been given an excellent education, was well-read in history, and knew his classical authors. Although the empire as revived by Otto had not been universal, great prestige attached to the title, and the limits of imperial authority were indefinite; therefore Frederick had a high opinion of what might be the scope of his power.

Frederick had the good fortune to be both Welf and Waibling; his mother was a Welf, and Henry the Lion of Saxony was his cousin. As heir of the Hohenstaufen emperor, Conrad III, Frederick was elected German king without hesitation. Like his uncle, he watched with complacency the extension of German territory by certain of his vassals, who crusaded against the heathen Slavs, extended their possessions beyond the Elbe, pushed back the Danes

[243

in Holstein, and colonized these conquered lands with peasants brought from Germany. They laid the framework of German power in the Baltic, recovered Mecklenburg, founded Lubeck, and opened trade with the Scandinavians, whom they encouraged to settle. Henry the Lion was the chief of these enterprising magnates, and Frederick recognized him as practically independent in the lands beyond the Elbe, but twenty years later, when Henry refused to follow the emperor into Italy, Frederick confiscated his lands and broke up the great Saxon duchy. Frederick also acquired the county of Burgundy by marrying its heiress, and other lands he bought from Welf lords.

Frederick planned to establish his power on the basis of Roman law and Roman tradition. He employed Roman lawyers, declared his empire the Holy Roman Empire, and revived the title of Caesar for his son. His reign saw the inauguration of the custom that the election of an emperor should be by a body of electoral princes, composed of the chief magnates of Germany. His policy toward the church was to put into every vacant benefice a bishop whom he could depend upon to support the emperor rather than the pope, for he saw in papal power a threat to imperial power. He strengthened the allegiance of these bishops by endowing them with greater authority.

It is illuminating to compare Frederick's policy with that of his contemporary, Henry II of England. Henry was a powerfully-built man with a short neck, piercing eyes, and a red face. Full of nervous energy, he was always dashing about; even in church he talked or scribbled or looked at pictures. With his enormous inheritance and acquisitions by marriage he was a threat to the French crown, for he held more than half of France in fief. His rule in England coincided almost exactly with Frederick's as emperor; he became king two years after Frederick's accession and died the year before him. As English king he destroyed the castles that had been illegally built during the anarchy of Stephen's reign. He replenished the treasury through reforms in taxation and in the courts. He also revived his grandfather's custom of sending out itinerant justices, and he made royal justice popular and lucrative by extending the ancient system of sworn witnesses which William the Conqueror used for compiling Domesday Book. From this developed grand juries and trial juries as we know them. The law administered in the royal courts was the common law, based upon the custom of the people but consonant with the principles of Roman law, as one of Henry's judges demonstrated. Henry dealt with his lay vassals through a reorganization of the militia into a force that could be used against them at need. He allowed the substitution of money payments for military service (scutage), and with the money hired professional soldiers, thus encouraging his vassals to cultivate the arts of peace.

Henry II hoped to solve the problem of the power of the spiritual lords with the help of his friend and chancellor, Thomas Becket, whom he made archbishop of Canterbury. Becket, however, as archbishop became the defender of the clergy against the king. When Henry appealed to ancient custom in an attempt to prevent criminous clergy from getting off with nominal punishment because all who could read were considered clergy and tried in ecclesiastical courts, Becket defied him. Because Henry did not control the famous Angevin temper in the quarrel that ensued, Becket was murdered by the king's over-eager followers, who took some of Henry's words too literally. After the murder Henry was obliged to give up his efforts to reform clerical justice, Becket became a saint in popular opinion, and the Canterbury pilgrimages began, while "benefit of clergy" continued to plague English courts until modern times. In order to avoid the outburst of popular indignation that followed the murder, Henry crossed to Ireland and forced the Irish to admit his overlordship, but they failed to understand what the feudal oath meant, and the foundation was laid for centuries of conflict with their English suzerains. Henry also made the Scottish ruler his vassal.

In the task of strengthening the royal power Frederick I was less successful than Henry II but more successful than Louis VII, his French contemporary. In the course of his reign he succeeded to a large extent in breaking up the great fiefs and creating a Germany of small principalities, archbishoprics, and free cities. In Germany he favored the towns as a part of his attempt to weaken the authority of the great feudal lords. In Italy, however, he followed a very different policy, especially in the Po valley. Many of the towns there had set up their own governments and entrusted to a chief magistrate, called a consul, the rights which bishops and nobles had formerly exercised. These rights, called *regalia,* the emperor regarded as legally his, as did also the popes, who claimed to have received the *regalia* from the emperor Constantine. The English pope Adrian IV gave Frederick an opportunity to intervene in Italy by appealing for aid against William, the Norman king of Sicily. Frederick, on his arrival in Rome, demanded coronation as emperor, but the pope refused to go through the ceremony until Frederick, after bitter expostulations, consented to hold the pope's bridle and stirrup. Adrian had expelled Arnold of Brescia and he had been turned over to the secular arm as a heretic. Frederick had him executed, but left the pope to settle his own affairs with William. Adrian secured recognition of papal overlordship from William, but Frederick later registered a more substantial gain by betrothing his son to the Sicilian heiress, as Otto II had done two centuries before.

After his imperial coronation Frederick held a diet at Roncaglia, where he set forth his claims to the *regalia*. Since the Italian towns refused to recognize his claims, the emperor resorted to force, and the struggle lasted for many years with varying fortunes. In the fifth of Frederick's six expeditions into northern Italy the league of Lombard towns won a great victory over the imperial troops at Legnano, which was the first serious defeat of feudal horsemen by foot soldiers. The emperor was finally obliged to yield the towns their *regalia,* but the consuls were to become his vassals and the citizens to swear fealty.

In the course of Frederick's Italian campaigns he also carried on a struggle with the papacy, maintaining a series of anti-popes. Peace was finally made on terms of practical equality, but Frederick retained Matilda's lands in Tuscany which gave him a strategic foothold in central Italy. The great bulwark of papal prestige was the preaching of the crusades. A third crusade was proclaimed in 1188 and Frederick thought to outshine the pope by heading it. In England, Henry II was struggling against his rebellious sons. In France, young Philip II had been king since his father's death in 1180. Philip had shrewdly made an alliance with Henry and secured the English king's help in putting down a revolt of the French magnates, but when Henry's son Richard rebelled against his father, Philip joined him against Henry in 1189. Henry died during the campaign and Richard succeeded him. Not to be outdone by the emperor, Richard took the cross and Philip II did likewise. These two monarchs journeyed to the East by sea, but Frederick took the overland route and was drowned while fording a stream.

The World of Frederick Barbarossa

Frederick's personality took hold upon the imaginations of the German people and he became a figure of legend. In later years many stories told of his grandson Frederick II crystallized around the first Frederick's name. The story of "der alte Barbarossa," sleeping through the centuries in a cave in the mountains, with his sword in his lap and his red beard grown to his feet, ready to come to life when Germany was in danger, was told hopefully by many Germans as fortune turned against them in World War I, as it had been in other periods of great crisis.

In the world of Frederick I, with kings leading the holy war abroad and extending the king's peace at home, there was the chance that the national state might one day put in a claim for the people's attention. The extension of the king's peace, originally confined to the king's court, made its most notable progress in the work of Henry II of England. Progress in the same direction in France was apparently in some degree due to imitation of Henry II's methods; Philip II extended the king's peace to the royal domain in France by his *baillis*, who combined the functions of the English sheriffs and itinerant justices. The world of Frederick I was much like that of St. Bernard—but it had no great mentor constantly concerned with keeping people's eyes turned heavenward.

[THE TWELFTH CENTURY]

Readings

Urban II

SPEECH AT THE COUNCIL OF CLERMONT (NOVEMBER 26, 1095) *

[There are several versions of this famous speech. This one gives most succinctly the various motives to which the pope appealed.]

Since, oh sons of God, you have promised the Lord more earnestly than heretofore to maintain peace in your midst and faithfully to sustain the laws of the church, there remains for you, newly fortified by the correction of the Lord, to show the strength of your integrity in a certain other duty, which is not less your concern than the Lord's. For you must carry succor to your brethren dwelling in the East, and needing your aid, which they have so often demanded. For the Turks, a Persian people, have attacked them, as many of you know, and have advanced into the territory of Romania as far as that part of the Mediterranean which is called the Arm of St. George;[1] and occupying more and more the lands of those Christians, have already seven times conquered them in battle, have killed and captured many, have destroyed the churches and devastated the kingdom of God. If you permit them to remain for a time unmolested, they will extend their sway more widely over many faithful servants of the Lord.

Wherefore, I pray and exhort, nay not I, but the Lord prays and exhorts you, as heralds of Christ, by frequent exhortation, to urge men of all ranks, knights and foot-soldiers, rich and poor, to hasten

---

* From University of Pennsylvania, *Translations and Reprints*, I, No. 2. Reprinted by permission of The University of Pennsylvania Press.

[1] The Hellespont.

to exterminate this vile race from the lands of our brethren, and to bear timely aid to the worshippers of Christ. I speak to those who are present, I proclaim it to the absent, but Christ commands. Moreover, the sins of those who set out thither, if they lose their lives on the journey, by land or sea, or in fighting against the heathen, shall be remitted in that hour; this I grant to all who go, through the power of God vested in me.

Oh, what a disgrace if a race so despised, degenerate, and slave of the demons, should thus conquer a people fortified with faith in omnipotent God and resplendent with the name of Christ! Oh, how many reproaches will be heaped upon you by the Lord Himself if you do not aid those who like yourselves are counted of the Christian faith! Let those who have formerly been accustomed to contend wickedly in private warfare against the faithful, fight against the infidel and bring to a victorious end the war which ought long since to have been begun. Let those who have hitherto been robbers now become soldiers of Christ. Let those who have formerly contended against their brothers and relatives now fight as they ought against the barbarians. Let those who have formerly been mercenaries at low wages, now gain eternal rewards. Let those who have been striving to the detriment both of body and soul, now labor for a two-fold reward. What shall I add? On this side will be the sorrowful and poor, on the other the joyful and the rich; here the enemies of the Lord, there His friends. Let not those who are going delay their journey, but having arranged their affairs and collected the money necessary for their expenses, when the winter ends and the spring comes, let them with alacrity start on their journey under the guidance of the Lord.

Abbot Suger (1081-1151)*

[John Scotus Erigena's translation of Dionysius the Areopagite was in the Abbey of St. Denis. It was apparently from this translation that Abbot Suger derived the idea of the connection between the material and the immaterial which we have seen in Erigena's work, and which appears both in the inscription and in the abbot's book.]

POEM ON THE DOORS OF THE CENTRAL WEST PORTAL

Whoever thou art, if thou seekest to extol the glory of these doors,
Marvel not at the gold and the expense but at the craftsmanship of the work.
Bright is the noble work; but, being nobly bright, the work
Should brighten the minds so that they may travel, through the true lights,
To the True Light where Christ is the true door.
In what manner it be inherent in this world the golden door defines:
The dull mind rises to truth through that which is material
And, in seeing this light, is resurrected from its former submersion.

THE BOOK OF SUGER, ABBOT OF ST.-DENIS ON WHAT WAS DONE UNDER HIS ADMINISTRATION

Of the Golden Crucifix

We searched around everywhere by ourselves and by our agents for an abundance of precious pearls and gems, preparing as precious a supply of gold and gems for so important an embellishment as we could find, and convoked the most experienced artists from diverse parts. . . . One merry but notable miracle which the Lord granted us in this connection we do not wish to pass over in silence. For when I was in difficulty for want of gems and could not sufficiently provide myself with more (for their scarcity makes them very expensive): then, lo and behold, [monks] from three abbeys of two Orders—that is, from Cîteaux and another abbey of the same Order,

---

* From *Abbot Suger on the Abbey Church of St.-Denis and Its Art Treasures,* edited, translated and annotated by Erwin Panofsky (1946). Reprinted by permission of Princeton University Press, publishers.

and from Fontevrault—entered our little chamber adjacent to the church and offered us for sale an abundance of gems such as we had not hoped to find in ten years, hyacinths, sapphires, rubies, emeralds, topazes. Their owners had obtained them from Count Thibaut for alms; and he in turn had received them, through the hands of his brother Stephen, King of England, from the treasures of his uncle, the late King Henry, who had amassed them throughout his life in wonderful vessels. We, however, freed from the worry of searching for gems, thanked God and gave four hundred pounds for the lot though they were worth much more. . . .

[*from Chapter XXXII*]

Thus, when—out of my delight in the beauty of the house of God—the loveliness of the many-colored gems has called me away from external cares, and worthy meditation has induced me to reflect, transferring that which is material to that which is immaterial, on the diversity of the sacred virtues: then it seems to me that I see myself dwelling, as it were, in some strange region of the universe which neither exists entirely in the slime of the earth nor entirely in the purity of Heaven; and that, by the grace of God, I can be transported from this inferior to that higher world in an anagogical manner. . . . To me, I confess, one thing has always seemed pre-eminently fitting: that every costlier or costliest thing should serve, first and foremost, for the administration of the Holy Eucharist. *If* golden pouring vessels, golden vials, golden little mortars used to serve, by the word of God or the command of the Prophet, to collect the *blood of goats or calves or the red heifer*: *how much more* must golden vessels, precious stones, and whatever is most valued among all created things, be laid out, with continual reverence and full devotion, for the reception of the *blood of Christ!* Surely neither we nor our possessions suffice for this service. If, by a new creation, our substance were re-formed from that of the holy Cherubim and Seraphim, it would still offer an insufficient and unworthy service for so great and so ineffable a victim; and yet we have so great a propitiation for our sins. . . .

[*from Chapter XXXIII*]

St. Bernard of Clairvaux

LETTERS*

[The letter to Suger shows that St. Bernard was lavish of praise when he felt it was deserved. On the other hand nowhere is it possible to find sterner condemnation of the mingling of lay and clerical functions in the higher ranks of the clergy in the feudal age. The letter to Louis is a good example of plain speaking to royalty.]

To Suger, Abbot of S. Denis

A piece of good news has reached our district; it cannot fail to do great good to whomsoever it shall have come. For who that fear God, hearing what great things He has done for your soul, do not rejoice and wonder at the great and sudden change wrought by the Right Hand of the Most High. Everywhere your courage is praised in the Lord; the gentle hear of it and are glad, and even those who do not know you, but have only heard of you, what you were and what you are now, wonder and glorify God in you. . . .

But who made you aspire to this degree of perfection? I confess that though I earnestly desired to hear such things of you, I never hoped to see it come to pass. Who would have believed that you would reach, so to speak, by one sudden bound, the practice of the highest virtues, and approach the most exalted merit? Thus we learn not to measure by the narrow proportions of our faith and hope the infinite pity of God, which does what It will and works upon whom It will, lightening the burden which It imposes upon us, and hastening the work of our salvation. What then? the zeal of good people blamed your errors at least, if not those of your brethren: it was against your excesses more than theirs that they were moved with indignation; and if your brothers in religion groaned in secret, it was less against your entire community than against you; it was only against you that they brought their accusation. You corrected your faults, and their criticisms had no longer an object; your conversion at once stilled the tumult of accusation. The one and only thing with which we were scandalized was the luxury, the pride, the pomp, which followed you everywhere. At length you laid down

---

* From *Life and Works of Saint Bernard*, translated by S. F. Eales (London, n.d.). Burns and Oates, Ltd.

your pride, you put off your splendid dress, and the universal indignation ceased at once. . . .

That spot so noble by its antiquity and the royal favour, was made to serve the convenience of worldly business, and to be a meeting-place for the royal troops. They used to render to Caesar the things which were Caesar's promptly and fully; but not with equal fidelity did they render the things of God to God. I speak what I have heard, not what I have seen: the very cloister itself of your monastery was frequently, they say, crowded with soldiers, occupied with the transaction of business, resounding with noise and quarrels, and sometimes even accessible even to women.

. . . Now, the house of God ceases to open to people of the world, there is no access to sacred precincts for the curious; no gossip about trifling things with the idle; the chatter of boys and girls is no longer heard. The holy place is open and accessible only to the children of Christ, of whom it is said: "Behold I and the children whom the Lord hath given me" (Isaiah viii, 18). It is reserved for the praises of God and the performance of sacred vows with due care and reverence. . . .

In our time two new and detestable abuses have arisen in the Church, of which one (permit me to say it) was no stranger to you when you lived in forgetfulness of the duties of your profession; but this, thanks to God, has been amended to His glory, to your everlasting gain, to our joy and an example to all. . . .

For whose heart is not indignant, and whose tongue does not murmur either openly or secretly to see a deacon equally serving God and Mammon, against the precept of the Gospel heaping up ecclesiastical dignities, so that he seems not to be inferior to Bishops, yet so mixed up in military offices that he is preferred even to Dukes. What monster is this, that being a clerk, and wishing at the same time to appear a soldier, is neither? It is equally an abuse that a deacon should serve at the table of the King, and that the server of the King should minister at the altar during the holy mysteries. Is it not a wonder, or rather a scandal, to see the same person clothed in armour march at the head of armed soldiery, and vested in alb and stole read the Gospel in the midst of the Church; at one time give the signal for battle with the trumpet, and at another convey the orders of the Bishop to the people. . . ?

[*from Letter 78 (1127)*]

To Louis the Younger, King of the French

If the whole world were to conjure me to join it in some enterprise against your royal Majesty, I should still through fear of God not dare lightly to offend a King ordained by Him. Nor am I ignorant who it is that has said, "Whosoever resisteth the power resisteth the ordinance of God" (Rom. xiii. 2). Nor yet do I forget how contrary is lying to the Christian calling and still more so to my profession. I say the truth, I lie not; what was done at Langres in the matter of our Prior was contrary to my expectation and my intention and that of the Bishops. . . . The staff of my weakness has been taken from me, the light of mine eyes removed from me, my right arm cut off. All these waves and storms have gone over me. Wrath has swallowed me up, and on no side do I see any way to escape. When I fly from burdens, then I have them placed upon me to my great discomfort. I feel that it is hard for me to kick against the pricks. It would perhaps have been more tolerable for a willing horse than for one that is restive and obstinate. For if there were any strength in me, would it not be easier for me to bear these burdens on my own shoulders than on those of others?

But I yield to Him that disposeth otherwise, to contend with whom in wisdom or strength is neither prudent nor possible for either me or the King. He is, indeed, terrible among the kings of the earth. It is a terrible thing to fall into the hands of the living God, even for you, O King. How grieved have I been to hear things of you so contrary to the fair promise of your early days! How much more bitter will be the grief of the Church, after having tasted first of such great joys, if, which God forbid, she shall chance to be deprived of her pleasant hope of protection under the shield of your good disposition, which up to the present has been held over her. . . .

[*from Letter (1138)*]

Frederick I

LETTERS
To Pope Eugene III, announcing his election, 1152*

[In this letter to Eugenius III Frederick states clearly his belief that empire and papacy were co-equal powers. The account of the occasion when he yielded precedence to Adrian IV comes from the Vatican archives. The letter to Leopold was written the year before his death, after he had embarked upon the third crusade.]

To his most beloved father in Christ, Eugene, pope of the holy Roman church, Frederick, by the grace of God king of the Romans, Augustus, [sends] filial love and reverence.

. . . Following the custom of the Roman emperors, we have sent to you as ambassadors, Eberhard, venerable bishop of Bamberg, Hillo, bishop elect of Trier, and Adam, abbot of Eberach, to notify you of our election and of the condition of the church and the realm.

After the death of Conrad, king of the Romans, all the princes of the kingdom came together at Frankfurt, and on the day of their assembling elected us king. The princes displayed complete harmony in this election and the people received it with the greatest approval and delight. Five days later, just after the middle of Lent, we were anointed at Aachen by your beloved sons, the archbishop of Cologne, and other venerable bishops, and were raised to the throne with their solemn benediction. And now that we have been invested with the royal authority and dignity by the homage of the secular princes and the benediction of the bishops, we intend to assume the royal character, as set forth in our coronation oath; namely, to love and honor the pope, to defend the holy Roman church and all ecclesiastical persons, to maintain peace and order, and to protect the widows and the fatherless and all the people committed to our care. God has established two powers by which this world should be ruled, the papacy and the empire; therefore we are prepared to obey the priests of Christ, in order that, through our zeal, the word of God may prevail during our time, and that no one may disobey with impunity the laws of the holy fathers or the decrees of the councils, and that the church may enjoy her ancient honor and dignity and the empire be restored to its former strength. We know

* From Oliver J. Thatcher and Edgar Holmes McNeal, *A Source Book for Mediaeval History* (1905). Reprinted by permission of Charles Scribner's Sons.

that you were greatly distressed at the death of our uncle and predecessor Conrad, but we assure you, beloved father, that we have succeeded him not only in the kingdom, but also in the love which he bore you. We undertake his work of defending the holy Roman church, and we intend to carry on the plans which he made for the honor and liberty of the apostolic see. Your enemies shall be our enemies, and those that hate you shall suffer our displeasure.

To Leopold of Austria (Adrianople, November 1189) *

Frederic, by the grace of God, emperor and always august, to his beloved kinsman Leopold, duke of Austria,—greeting and all good wishes.

We thought we ought to tell you, because of your love for us, that our brother, the emperor of Constantinople, although he ought to have been bound by brotherly love, has from the very first violated all the oaths which are known to have been sworn by his chancellor at Nuremberg, in the presence of the princes of the empire, in regard to our security on the march, and markets and exchanges. Moreover, he has seized and ignominiously thrown into prison our ambassadors, the bishop of Münster, count Rupert and Markward, our chamberlain, together with all their attendants, whom we had sent to confirm the peace and to arrange for our peaceful march on this expedition of the quickening cross. At length, however, after long negotiations, grievously delaying our march until the dangerous winter season, he has sent back to our excellency the aforesaid ambassadors on the feast of St. Simon and St. Jude, as if matters had been satisfactorily arranged, and he has again promised us good markets, the usual exchanges and an abundance of vessels.

Truly, because the burnt child dreads the fire, we can in the future have no confidence in the words and oaths of the Greeks. In order to avoid the stormy winter season, we propose to stay until spring at Philippopolis and Adrianople, and to cross over to Constantinople in the favorable season. Therefore, although we rejoice in a well-equipped army, yet we must seek divine succour in our prayers. For these reasons we ask and desire of your love, that in your prayers and pious devotions you commend us and the whole army of the crusaders to God. In addition we ask of your prudence to see that the letters which we send to the pope reach him through

---

* From University of Pennsylvania, *Translations and Reprints*, I, no. 4. Reprinted by permission of The University of Pennsylvania Press.

your aid and exertions, because you can arrange this more successfully than anyone else.

THE STIRRUP EPISODE, 1155*

The king [Frederick] advanced with his army to the neighborhood of Sutri and encamped in Campo Grasso. The pope, however, came to Nepi, and on the day after his arrival was met there by many of the German princes and a great concourse of clergy and laymen, and conducted with his bishops and cardinals to the tent of the king. But when the cardinals who came with the pope saw that the king did not come forward to act as the esquire of the pope [i.e., to hold his stirrup while he dismounted], they were greatly disturbed and

* Thatcher and McNeal, *op. cit.*

TWELFTH CENTURY SHIP, FROM A MANUSCRIPT
IN THE BRITISH MUSEUM

(From *A Student's History of England* by Samuel R. Gardiner. Longmans Green, London, 1897.)

terrified, and retreated to Civita Castellana, leaving the pope before the tent of the king. And the pope, distressed and uncertain what he should do, sadly dismounted and sat down on the seat which had been prepared for him. Then the king prostrated himself before the pope, kissing his feet and presenting himself for the kiss of peace. But the pope said: "You have refused to pay me the due and accustomed honor which your predecessors, the orthodox emperors, have always paid to my predecessors, the Roman popes, out of reverence for the apostles, Peter and Paul; therefore I will not give you the kiss of peace until you have made satisfaction." The king, however, replied that he was not under obligations to perform the service. The whole of the following day was spent in the discussion of this point, the army in the meantime remaining there. And after the testimony of the older princes had been taken, especially of those who had been present at the meeting of king Lothar and pope Innocent (II), and the ancient practice had been determined, the princes and the royal court decided that the king ought to act as the esquire of the pope and hold his stirrup, out of reverence for the apostles, Peter and Paul. On the next day the camp of the king was moved to the territory of Nepi, on the shores of lake Janula, and there king Frederick, in accordance with the decision of the princes, advanced to meet the pope, who was approaching by another way. And when the pope came within about a stone's throw from the emperor, the emperor dismounted and proceeded on foot to meet the pope, and there in the sight of his army he acted as the pope's esquire, holding his stirrup for him to dismount. Then the pope gave him the kiss of peace.

PART IX

The Thirteenth Century

CHRONOLOGY

c. 1200 Philip Augustus grants a charter to the University of Paris
1204 Sack of Constantinople by Fourth Crusaders
1209 Foundation of Franciscan order
1215 Magna Carta
1216 Death of Innocent III
1217 Foundation of Dominican order
c. 1220 Death of Wolfram von Eschenbach, German minnesinger
1227 Death of Genghis Khan
1242 Victory of Alexander Nevsky of Russia over Teutonic Knights
1258 Provisions of Oxford
1265 Simon de Montfort's Parliament
—— Simon de Montfort killed at battle of Evesham
1267 Roger Bacon's *Opus Majus*
1261-9 *Summa Theologiae* of St. Thomas Aquinas
1270 Genoese sailors rediscover Canaries
1273 Election of Rudolph, first Hapsburg Emperor
1282 Sicilian Vespers
1291 End of Latin kingdom of Jerusalem
—— Confederation of three forest cantons; beginning of Switzerland
1294 Dante's *Vita Nuova*
1295 Edward I's Model Parliament
1296 Boniface VIII's bull *Clericis laicos*

PART IX

The Thirteenth Century

~~~~~~~~~~~~~~~~~~~~~~~~~

THE thirteenth century marked a turning point. Certain institutions reached their full development and began to decline, while others, which have developed fully only in our day, had their beginnings. Feudalism reached its height; the feudal lord in his well-fortified stone castle dominated society. Except in England he exercised many of the attributes of sovereignty, coining money, holding court, establishing markets, and levying tolls on roads and bridges. His peasants worked his domain and paid for the compulsory use of his mill, bakehouse, brewhouse, and winepress. He had lucrative rights over his vassals, and on occasion he even defied his king. He was to retain power and prestige for centuries, but before the thirteenth century closed rulers had less need of him. The efficiency of the central government was increased by Louis IX in France, Edward I in England, and Frederick II in Sicily. In several kingdoms the rise of the third estate was recognized by the summoning of its representatives to the great council of the realm. The possession of money was becoming more important than the possession of land. The success of the Genoese cross-bowmen against the feudal army at the battle of Bouvines reinforced the warning of Legnano that warfare was not to continue the affair of the feudality alone.

The papacy reached its height in the thirteenth century. Innocent III made the proudest monarchs bow to his will, received eight rulers as vassals,[1] and for a few years was acknowledged head of the Eastern church. A great new monastic movement was devoted to papal service. St. Thomas Aquinas gave a formulation to the Chris-

[1] The rulers of England, Denmark, Poland, Hungary, Bulgaria, Serbia, Portugal, and Aragon.

tian faith which is still authoritative for the Roman communion. Gothic churches of a beauty not before known expressed the devotion of the faithful. Yet in the last decade of the century Boniface VIII met defeats at the hands of Philip the Fair and Edward I. When the fourth crusade, at the beginning of the century, turned into a commercial enterprise against Constantinople, and the Albigensian crusade was launched against heretics in southern France, it became evident that the ardor which put Christendom in arms against the East in the name of the faith had waned. Louis IX, with all his sainthood, could not revive it. Society was turning secular.

These changes were not unconnected with the intellectual and social stimulus that resulted from contact with the Moslem world. This influence had long been at work, but its effects, cumulative in this century, gave a definite character to the period. The contact between Christian and Moslem in Spain, in Sicily, and in Syria during the period of the Christian feudal kingdoms there, produced in each group a certain toleration for the faith of the other. Commercial contacts between Europe and the East had even more notable consequences, however, than the intermingling of peoples. Such products new to Europeans in the field of textiles as cotton, muslin (Mosul), and damask (Damascus), were introduced. New trade routes were exploited, and more advanced techniques of navigation were widely spread through contact with Byzantine, Moslem, and Italian practices—larger vessels, use of instruments like the compass and the astrolabe, and better maps. Adventurous merchants were able to penetrate Asia even beyond Syria; the Venetians, through their contacts with Constantinople, were led to the Black Sea, into Russia, and so across central Asia to the Far East. It is also noteworthy that Genoese sailors, apparently trying to outflank the Mohammedan control of the middle routes to the East, rediscovered the Canary Islands about 1270.

Commerce and the crusades stimulated the return of money and credit to the economic system of Europe in general; during the earlier feudal age it had been based to an important degree on barter. Gold was used in coinage again. (The ducats minted in the duchy of Apulia in the middle of the twelfth century are supposed to have been the first gold coins struck in western Europe since the time of Charlemagne.) Credit was practically a necessity during the crusades to meet the needs of pilgrims or crusaders who found it at best inconvenient and usually dangerous to carry any large sums of money with them. The order of the Knights Templar, with chapter houses in many parts of the European and Mediterranean world, employed banking practices, accepting deposits at one branch and advancing on credit from another. The trade empires built by Italian city states during the crusading era used the same methods.

The social character of western Europe changed greatly during this period. The number of freemen who could swell the ranks of the merchant class and town population was increased by a process of serf emancipation, sometimes as a pious act by a noble crusader uncertain of the fate in store for him, sometimes by sale in order to raise capital to finance a crusade. For many people of western Europe the new opportunities opened by commerce and the crusades meant a freedom from the agricultural existence to which they had been bound. The gain in the free class was accompanied by a corresponding decline among the feudal nobility, who lost financial resources in the expenses of the crusades, as many were forced to surrender property rights or feudal dues. This feature of the period, together with the inevitable casualties in the male population of noble families, was particularly advantageous for the kings who were trying to build up monarchical power in a feudal society.

The new power of the townsmen was increasing year by year, both in England and on the Continent. The feudal lords held their authority as long as land was the chief source of wealth, and little money was in circulation. Papal claims to power had been facilitated by the effectiveness of papal taxation, which drew off much of the money in existence. By the thirteenth century, when the towns had become centers of trade, money was to be found there, and the nobles, when they needed funds to outfit themselves for the crusades, borrowed it from the townspeople and gave concessions in exchange.

While their feudal lords were away in the East, towns grew prosperous. Craft guilds had come into existence, established on sound social principles, and were replacing the merchant guilds. The craft guilds maintained high standards of craftsmanship, established ceiling prices, forbade cornering the market and other unethical practices, provided death benefits, and cared for widows and orphans. A poor man by himself was nothing; as a member of his guild he was a figure in society, for he might take part in a mystery play with others of his guild, and he could point proudly to the window his guild had placed in the new cathedral. Cathedrals in earlier days were usually built where it suited the bishop's convenience—accessible to his palace, which was frequently on the citadel. With the growth of the townsmen's importance they came to be built in the market place, where the citizens gathered.

The thirteenth-century cathedrals, in the new Gothic style developed in northern France, were beautiful structures. Romanesque churches had been comparatively dark; in the Gothic churches the walls, no longer needed for support of the roof, more and more were simply frames for gloriously colored glass. The whole structure gave the impression of unity, through multiplicity. The music that rang from the choir through the soaring nave was a music that expressed a similar spirit. Polyphony, or counterpoint (which had probably originated in the singing of the Celts and Germans, among whom an instrument accompanied the voice) had also come into use in the church, where the principal part came to be accompanied by another sung several tones below, and then by three or four voices an octave apart. In the thirteenth century rounds were sung commonly by the people, and the tune of the farmers, "Sumer is icumen in," was supplied with religious words. In France the motet was developed.

While Frenchmen were building Rheims Cathedral and Englishmen Salisbury, the Moors of Granada built their Alhambra. Religion was an impelling force, but the static character of Islam prevented it from becoming a force for progress.

The secular nature of Saracen culture began to have its counterpart in the trends of thirteenth century European society. The Gothic cathedral in the market place was confronted by the guildhall. The guilds of teachers and of students which were organizing into universities became centers of learning where laymen like the great Italian poet Dante studied with no intention of becoming priests. The universities also served as centers for a new study of Aristotle, based on works of which the West had been ignorant but which were introduced to it in the thirteenth century from the Islamic world through the translations of Averroës. The learned and original Robert Grosseteste and his pupil Roger Bacon, English university men both, went so far as to proclaim experiment the way to the attainment of knowledge. Although West had learned much from East during the period of the crusades, after the thirteenth century the West overtook and outstripped both Byzantine and Mohammedan culture.

The fourth crusade gave Venice control of the trade of Constantinople, but later in the century the Greeks overthrew the Latin kingdom with the help of Genoa, which thenceforth shared control of the eastern trade. A great new power arose in Asia, the Mongol empire of the mighty warrior, Genghis Khan, whose forces overran eastern Europe and ruled Russia for the next two hundred years. The Venetian merchant, Marco Polo, traveled across Asia to the court of the Great Khan in China, and his account of what he saw there was to influence men's imaginations in the following centuries.

It is difficult to place inventions into an exact period, but we know that spectacles came into use in Italy in the latter part of the thirteenth century. Mechanical clocks were used. The spinning wheel, long known in India, did much to develop the flourishing cloth industry in Europe. Elaborate looms, known in China, began to be common in Europe.

Up to a point the Christian church followed the movement of its people toward secular preoccupations. Innocent, unable to prevent the diversion of the crusades to secular purposes, settled for temporary control of the Eastern church. Later popes definitely utilized the remnants of the crusading spirit to further purely secular ends —especially against the Hohenstaufen, employing money raised originally for holy war against Islam. It came to be suspected that the papacy regarded crusades as a matter of expediency and as a justification for taxes. There was also some breakdown in the discipline by which the church maintained its authority in everyday life. The administration of the sacrament of penance was a strong weapon, but its effectiveness was vitiated by the system of indulgences—that is, a remission of penance, which had been granted occasionally for acts of unusual piety. During the crusades the popes promised plenary indulgence for the noteworthy good deed the crusader performed by fighting the infidel. Abuse developed over release from the vow taken by every crusader, when for some cause it became impossible to fulfill. To avoid excommunication for failure to keep the vow, a material contribution to the holy cause could be substituted. When releases thus became vendible, the papacy had actually acquired a new source of revenue which later came to be used for any papal need, not simply for war against infidels. The popes indirectly aided the work of secularization by providing a new stimulus to learning. The Franciscan order was turned from its pursuit of poverty to become a bulwark of the papacy and leader in the cause of learning. Following the Dominicans, Franciscans became professors in the universities.

Three men typify thirteenth century tendencies. Innocent III brought the authority of the church to its height. Frederick II waged the medieval battle between empire and papacy; in his Sicilian kingdom he inaugurated a modern state. Dante was the new figure: the educated layman. He was a modern in his use of the vernacular, which throughout Europe was coming into its own. Everywhere

CHINESE DRAWING OF THE THIRTEENTH CENTURY SHOWING LOOM

(By permission from *History of Mechanical Inventions* by Abbott Payson Usher, copyrighted, 1929, by McGraw-Hill Book Co., Inc.)

the *fabliaux,* short stories of the life of the people, and moralized stories of animals like "Reynard the Fox" were within the common speech. The morality plays sanctioned by the church were in the vernacular. Jean de Meung wrote the *Romance of the Rose;* Villehardouin, the *Conquest of Constantinople;* and de Joinville, his *Life of Louis IX,* in the vernacular. Dante wrote his learned works in Latin, but put his great poem, *The Divine Comedy,* in the Tuscan dialect for all to read. In subject and treatment, however, the poem is entirely medieval. Dante shows the sun, moon, and planets revolving about the earth as a center, providing abodes of bliss graduated to the desert of souls who had won salvation. Toiling up the mountain of Purgatory, those destined for salvation expiate their sins in order of their heinousness. In the bowels of the earth the damned suffer torments proportionate to their degree of guilt. Moving from one level to another, the poet voices accepted moral judgments, placing sinful popes in Hell, and mourning over the failure of the emperor to give reality to the ancient vision of a united Christendom where, under the aegis of the universal power of the Roman Empire, peace would unite the peoples under law. Progressing from one crystalline sphere to another, Dante witnessed the increasing bliss of those whose lives on earth approached perfection more nearly, until beyond the seventh heaven lay the empyrean, the abode of celestial beings. Thus the astronomy of Ptolemy was made to fit into the divine vision.

CHAPTER 15

The World of Innocent III
[1161–1216]

~~~~~~~~~~~~~~~~~~

POPE INNOCENT III was born eight years after the death of St. Bernard. He was eleven when Thomas Becket was murdered in his cathedral at Canterbury, and he was about twenty when in the city of Assisi was born the child whose fame was to grow until he was recognized as one of the greatest of the saints—St. Francis. When Innocent was 29 he was made a cardinal, and just a year later Richard Coeur de Lion and Philip Augustus were in Sicily making their stormy way toward the Holy Land in the third crusade. At the age of 37 Innocent was made pope (1198). He was a nobleman of mixed German and Italian blood, a small man, of dignified bearing, thoroughly trained in theology and law; and he took up the office of Vicar of Christ with the firm purpose of vindicating its supremacy. He chose for the text of his consecration sermon: "For to me it is said in the Prophets, I have this day set thee over the nations and over the kingdoms." A born diplomat and a shrewd observer of men, he looked cannily over the nations and the kingdoms.

What Innocent saw was a welter of discord. Of the secular rulers the most formidable was Philip II (Augustus) of France, who had built walls about the city of Paris and made it a more comfortable place of residence, and whose eyes were fixed firmly on the royal domain, in spite of his participation, reluctantly, in the third crusade. Philip reformed the administration, installing trained royal officials known as *baillis,* and he planned for a wider domain to which these reforms should be extended. The obvious additions were the fiefs held by Richard of England, since the danger that England might swallow up France was real at the end of the twelfth century.

Richard I, the so-called troubadour king, had spent his youth in Aquitaine and had always a minstrel or two in tow, but he was primarily a soldier. He had gone with enthusiasm on the third crusade. Philip II went along because French public opinion expected it, but quarrelled with Richard, sought the first opportunity to return to France, and began intrigues with Richard's brother John. Richard negotiated a truce with the Saracen leader Saladin, deserted his army, and returned homeward in disguise—only to be taken prisoner and held for ransom by Barbarossa's successor, Henry VI. The English raised the heavy ransom Henry demanded, and Richard on his release forced Philip to return the lands he had seized with John's complicity. Innocent III caught Philip at a disadvantage and excommunicated him for having put away his wife, a Danish princess. Not daring to face public disfavor, Philip yielded and restored her to her rights.

When Richard died, Philip recognized John as heir although John's young nephew, Arthur, had a better claim. Within a few years John failed to appear at a feudal court held by Philip to be tried for an offense against another of Philip's vassals, and as this was a breach of the feudal contract, John's fiefs were declared forfeit. Within the year John offended his French vassals by having Arthur murdered, and he failed to prevent Philip from taking over Normandy and the Angevin lands. John was able, however, to succeed to his mother's fiefs of Aquitaine and Gascony.

Innocent had his way clear with John, who was one of the ablest of the Angevins but was unprincipled and unlucky, since John set every class of his subjects against him by his rapacity. He substituted his own nominee for the archbishop elected by the monks of Canterbury, and when both appeared at Rome claiming the *pallium,* the strip of wool which designated the office, Innocent chose instead an able Englishman named Stephen Langton. John refused to accept him and Innocent proceeded to lay England under an interdict, which meant deprivation of the sacraments. As this did not bring John to terms, he was first excommunicated and then deposed, and when Innocent invited Philip to enforce the deposition, the French king, nothing loth, prepared to invade England. John hastily accepted Langton and went far beyond the pope's demands, for he declared England was a papal fief—a shrewd bit of diplomacy which guaranteed him papal support.

In the meanwhile the Emperor Henry VI's marriage to the heiress of Sicily had fulfilled its purpose. A son was born, a second Frederick, who on the death of his father became king of Sicily, which included southern Italy up to the borders of the papal states. Between Sicily and the imperial lands to the north, the papal states were caught like a nut in a nutcracker. Innocent knew well, through the troubles of his predecessors, what dangers this power of the Hohenstaufen constituted for the papacy; and consequently he set aside the claims of his young ward, Henry's son Frederick, in favor of the Guelf candidate, Otto of Brunswick, grandson of Henry II of England. Although Otto made great promises before his coronation, as emperor he repudiated them, and Innocent during the quarrel decided to encourage young Frederick to take over the crown after all. Philip II sided with Frederick, and John, hoping to win back his lost French fiefs, supported Otto, who also had on his side a number of Philip's vassals. But Frederick's supporters won the battle of Bouvines in 1214, and John had to face rising discontent at home.

The great vassals in England were dissatisfied with John's demands for aids and in 1215, led by the Archbishop Stephen Langton, whom he had distrusted, they rose against him. He was forced to accept the famous Magna Carta, which recognized the rights of the feudal nobility. John's submission to Innocent III now stood him in good stead, for the pope declared Magna Carta void, but the barons fought the decision, and John's sudden death brought the quarrel to an end. Magna Carta was confirmed by later kings, and through a too literal interpretation of some of its provisions it became in a later day an instrument for securing the liberties of the citizen. It was for the most part a feudal document and actually a check on feudalism since it defined, and thus limited, the extent of a feudal lord's power over his vassals. It was of constitutional importance because it revived the ancient principle that the king was subject to the law. The success of the barons was an acknowledgment of their right to use force against a king who broke the law.

Venice was the most important of the Italian cities and its prosperity rested upon its Eastern trade. The Venetians developed a grudge against the cities the Normans had established in southern Italy and Sicily because they were rivals in trade and had the power to close the entrance to the Adriatic. When a Hohenstaufen at-

The World of Innocent III

tempted to squeeze the papal states in central Italy, the pope could always look for help to Venice and other cities of northern Italy which had adopted the policy of opposition to the emperor fostered by the Lombard League.

The crusading movement had been launched by the papacy and had given the popes prestige at first, but later the glory had been stolen by the monarchs. Innocent determined to win it back, and early in his pontificate issued a call to a fourth crusade. The wily Venetians succeeded in diverting the crusaders to the conquest of Constantinople, and set up a Latin kingdom which lasted until 1261. Innocent expressed annoyance at the turn the crusade had taken, but was placated when he was asked to nominate the patriarch of Constantinople. He then preached a Crusade for the conversion of the heathen in the Baltic region, and gave still another turn to the crusading movement by launching a crusade against heretics.

Heretics were actually regarded as worse than heathen since they had once known the true faith and departed from it. Heresy had increased with the development of towns, where life provided many secular interests and the critical spirit flourished. Heresies usually took either the form of criticism of the clergy for departing from the simplicity of the gospel or that of doctrinal aberration. The heresy of Peter Waldo of Lyons belonged to the first class; he concluded that God meant men to guide their lives by the Scriptures, and he formed a society whose members translated and expounded the Bible, turning their backs upon priests and organized religion. The second form of heresy was most conspicuously represented in Innocent's day by the Albigenses, or Cathari, whose beliefs led them to social irregularities and whose ideas had spread through the most prosperous regions of southern France. Innocent's crusade was a crusade against these two groups; the Waldenses were driven into the Alps, where they survived, while Philip II cynically allowed some of his vassals to be advance agents for the royal domain by joining the fight against the Albigenses. Led by Simon de Montfort, the French nobles began the liquidation of the Albigenses, who, before the end of the reign of Philip's successor, had been exterminated; and the lands of the feudal rulers of southern France were escheated to the French crown.

Although Simon de Montfort deterred Innocent from preaching a crusade against the Moors in Spain, the pope interfered with the rulers of the Christian kingdoms which were slowly pushing the Moors southward. He forced the king of Aragon to recognize him as overlord, the king of Leon to put away his wife, and the king of Portugal to pay him tribute. He was so successful in imposing his will upon the king of Poland that the prince of Bulgaria deemed it advantageous to declare himself the pope's vassal.

Innocent's power was at its height when, in 1215, the year of Magna Carta, he called the fourth great council to assemble in the ancient church of St. John of the Lateran. At this council, which was attended by the representatives of princes as well as by the clergy, Innocent decreed the use of a special tribunal, the Holy Office, or Inquisition, for the suppression of heretics. He declared that the duty of all Christians was to confess and take communion at least once a year. He provided for reorganization of the hierarchy and the election of future popes by a two-third's majority of the College of Cardinals. Frederick II, and not Otto IV, was proclaimed the lawful emperor, and Raymond of Toulouse, who had protected the Albigenses, was to be deposed in favor of his conqueror, Simon de Montfort, who was to hold Toulouse as a papal fief. Regulations were devised to set aside the Jews as a subordinate people; measures were taken for setting the clergy apart from the laity and for freeing them from taxation. Transubstantiation was made a dogma. Triumphant in all his policies, Innocent then proclaimed a new crusade, but did not live to launch it, for he died in the next year.

Innocent III was to go down in history as the pope who most completely realized the ideal of papal supremacy. Perhaps his most important single achievement was his diversion to the papal service of a movement which was the negation of his majestic claims. On Innocent's accession to the papacy Francis of Assisi was a boy of sixteen, enjoying with other sons of prosperous merchants the pursuits of carefree youth. Suddenly he had a conviction of sin, gave away all that he had, and started to live a life devoted to the love and service of all created things. By practicing the gospel of Christ literally Francis hoped to confound the heretic, convert the heathen, and regenerate the earth. The brethren of the order which he formed were to labor for their food and to live a wandering life, barefoot and clad in a brown robe girded by a rope. The possibilities of the Franciscan brotherhood as a valuable weapon were perceived by Innocent, but to Francis's request for recognition he gave only lim-

The World of Innocent III [273

ited approval, seeing in the stress on poverty a reproach to recognized custom which might be dangerous. Thus not until the Franciscans had modified the aims of the friars was their order to receive full commendation; a literal following of the Sermon on the Mount could scarcely appeal to the majestic lord of all the earth.

Innocent's task was to maintain the unity of the church—to scrutinize and chastise heresy. Heresy was always ready to break out, either as a criticism of the worldliness of the clergy in comparison with the simplicity of Christ, or as a questioning of the Church's doctrine in the light of Scripture or the Fathers. Francis's stress on poverty might well develop into the former type of heresy, despite the fact that to him "holy poverty" was a confutation of heresy. Innocent's world was an age which saw a succession of important scholars; the great Arab Averroës died the year of Innocent's accession to the papacy, and Robert Grosseteste belonged to Innocent's

A BISHOP ORDAINING A PRIEST, FROM A MANUSCRIPT MADE EARLY IN INNOCENT'S LIFETIME

(From *A Student's History of England* by Samuel R. Gardiner. Longmans Green, London, 1897.)

generation. By Innocent's crusade against the Albigenses, the Spanish St. Dominic was inspired to found his Order of Preachers to work for the conversion of the heretic and the heathen. Dominicans were the most important rivals of the Franciscans, and at the beginning reflected the difference between the two founders. Dominic and Innocent had much in common in matters of the faith, for both were well-educated men, but when it came to religion pure and undefiled both the triumphant pope and the learned preacher had to yield to St. Francis of Assisi.

CHAPTER 16

The World of Frederick II

[1194–1250]

~~~~~~

THE marriage of Frederick Barbarossa's son to the heiress of the kingdom of Sicily had far-reaching results. Some historians hold that Frederick II, the issue of the marriage, as ruler of the southern kingdom brought the modern world of predominantly secular interests into being. Growing up among the ruins of ancient Greece and Rome, surrounded by influences that stemmed from Byzantium and from the Moors, he developed an outlook on life less completely overshadowed by the church than that of his contemporaries.

In contrast, Louis IX, the grandson of Philip Augustus, was a king who so successfully typified the ideal of a Christian ruler that he was canonized by the church. France during his reign was the Middle Ages at its height. In Paris the schools of Abelard's day had developed into a guild of teachers chartered as the University of Paris, and its faculty of theology, under the leadership of the Dominican Albertus Magnus, was busy building on the basis of the prevailing interpretation of Aristotle a harmonious system of doctrine. Vincent of Beauvais was writing a compendium of human knowledge. Outside the precincts where divinity reigned, vernacular literature was finding its footing in Goliardic songs, in Villehardouin's *Conquest of Constantinople,* and in Jean de Meung's completion of the *Romaunt de la Rose.* Leonin, the choirmaster of Notre Dame, and his successor, Perotin, had used the new polyphonic music in elaborate compositions in which the organ, supporting boys' and men's voices, filled with swelling chords the lofty naves of the churches. The finest of these churches was Chartres, dedicated in the new fashion to the Virgin, not to a saint or archangel, like earlier fanes.

While the troubadours had developed an elaborate code of honor and of service to a chosen lady and had thereby brought into society a civilizing force, the church, fearful of the idealization of physical passion, strove to substitute for devotion to an earthly woman the adoration of the Mother of God. Churches in increasing numbers were being dedicated to Our Lady. In churches and cathedrals otherwise dedicated, Lady chapels appeared in the place of honor behind the high altar. To the mystery and miracle plays popular among the people were added new plays about miracles the Virgin wrought for sinners who called upon her name. Educated in the best learning of the day and in the code of chivalry and a devout servant of the church, Louis IX, when he attained his majority, dedicated himself to the recovery of the Holy Places and set out on a crusade against the sultan of Egypt, who controlled them.

In England another boy king, John's son Henry III, grew up a pious prince, though no paladin. His first guardian twice reissued Magna Carta, with modifications, and the second bowed to papal mandates and began a policy of allowing the pope to provide Italian incumbents for English benefices. When Henry took over the government he continued to do this and he also put into office the relatives of his French wife. These policies aroused much criticism and in time produced revolt and civil war.

Meanwhile the German princeling, Frederick II, grew up in Sicily under Greek and Moslem tutors, a resolute though sickly man, with the curiosity of a modern scientist and unlimited ambition. His whole career was given over to struggle. We have seen how the battle of Bouvines, which sealed the loss of King John's French fiefs, secured for Frederick the imperial crown under Innocent III's patronage. Frederick was crowned at Rome in 1220 by Innocent's successor, Honorius III. Before his coronation as emperor he had persuaded the Germans to choose his son Henry as king, but to do so had been obliged to extend the powers of the ecclesiastical princes. These powers included the control of all the towns in ecclesiastical lands, and as a result the great archbishoprics, Mainz, Trier, and Cologne, became practically independent states.

Like his grandfather and many of his successors, Frederick had an eye for German expansion eastward. German crusaders had formed a military order, known as the Teutonic Knights, which a Polish duke invited to aid him in the conversion of the Prussians.

Frederick confirmed the grants given them, and they proceeded, along with their missionary labors, to carve out a principality for themselves along the Baltic which effectively cut Poland off from the sea.

Frederick II renewed the claims the first Frederick had made on the north Italian towns and proceeded to enforce them in a series of campaigns, during which one pope after another joined his enemies. This was to be expected in view of Frederick's possession of Sicily. His aim was to build up a system of strong government in both his northern and his southern kingdoms, and the ruler of the papal states in the middle was unlikely to be enthusiastic. Frederick had put a weapon into the papal hands when, apparently yielding to impulse, he took the Cross during his coronation ceremony. He was excommunicated for not fulfilling his vow to go on a crusade, and was excommunicated a second time for starting to fulfill it while excommunicate. When he finally secured by treaty instead of conquest the end his crusade had in view, he was excommunicated a third time for dealing with the unbeliever, and a crusade was declared against his Sicilian lands.

In the intervals of Frederick's struggles with the papacy, he established in his Sicilian realm the strong government which is his greatest claim to fame. The modern idea of a state supported by an efficient system of taxation, and giving its citizens protection and justice in an orderly fashion, was only slowly developing in England and France out of the conflict between crown and feudal lords. In Sicily both Greek and Mohammedan influences pointed toward such a state, and to a considerable extent Frederick succeeded in establishing one there. There was nothing feudal in his system of administration and taxation. His methods were the same as those by which twentieth century dictators consolidated their power: restriction on the freedom of the citizen, government control of trade, religious persecution, and a special police without sympathy for human suffering.

At his Sicilian court Frederick surrounded himself with men of learning, regardless of creed. Brought up among Moslems and Greeks, Frederick II saw the best points of the Mohammedan faith; one of the most bitter accusations hurled against him by the papacy was that he declared that Christ, Moses, and Mohammed were all imposters. He had an extensive menagerie, and set down the results of his observations of birds in his well known treatise on falconry. Much useful research in the sciences was carried on directly by him or under his patronage. He revived the old school of medicine at Salerno, and set the fashion of royal charters for universities by creating a university at Naples.

The world of Frederick II was a world which he amazed and shocked, for he was too modern to be understood and esteemed. The ideal figure of the age was Louis IX of France, the perfect champion, the embodiment of chivalry, the knight who was pure in heart and protected the weak. Louis's reign was so genuinely one of devotion to high principles that his assumption that he was delegated by God to rule his people was accepted by his subjects as a true conception of the monarchy, and enabled his successors to exercise arbitrary power when they did not, like St. Louis, have the people's welfare at heart. Frederick's checkered career ended somewhat ignominiously. He had left Germany in the hands of his son, who proved unfaithful to the trust and whom he threw into prison. After finally securing the election of a pope whom he thought he could trust, he found himself again the object of papal hostility and began the conquest of the papal states. He died in the middle of this campaign. Although his son Conrad IV lived four years longer, effective Hohenstaufen rule ended with the death of Frederick II, whom men called *Stupor Mundi*.

BATTLE SCENE, FROM A MANUSCRIPT IN THE BRITISH MUSEUM

(From *A Student's History of England* by Samuel R. Gardiner. Longmans Green, London, 1897.)

CHAPTER 17

The World of Dante

[1265–1321]

~~~~~~~~~~~~~~~~~~~~~~~~~~~~~~~

WHILE in France and England the royal power was being extended at the expense of the feudal lords, and in Germany feudalism reigned triumphant despite the efforts of the Hohenstaufen to strengthen imperial power, Italy was developing along quite different lines. In the centre of the peninsula the popes dominated a chain of states which stretched from the Mediterranean to the Adriatic. South of the papal states, dukes of Anjou and princes of the Spanish house of Aragon claimed the lands where Frederick II had built up a well-governed realm, for the dynasty of the Hohenstaufen came to an end with his ill-fated grandson Conradin (1268). In Italy the feudal lords had long since given up their isolated castles and gone to live within the walls of the towns, where their interests became identical with those of the townsmen. Each town claimed the surrounding territory upon which it was dependent for food, and sought to enlarge this territory at the expense of its neighbors.

Of these city states the republic of Venice, enriched by trade with the East, was the most powerful. Its chief rival was Genoa, which had grown rich by carrying crusaders to the Holy Land and by building up a prosperous return trade. Milan, dominating the Lombard plain, acted as middleman in the commerce between the East and the countries north of the Alps. The prosperity of Florence had a double base: Florentine cloth-makers had won a great reputation for turning rough fabrics into beautiful brocades and damasks, and Florentine bankers did the greater part of the banking for the popes, spreading their activities to all cities of Europe. Other cities copied the methods of these leading city states on a smaller scale, and in all of them local politics followed the old pattern, made in Germany,

PLATE XVII

Thirteenth Century

FIGURE 1. *Gold Augustal of Frederick II, with portrait head and eagle. This is undoubtedly a likeness of the young emperor. There is a figure in his treatise on falconry which presumably represents Frederick, but it gives little indication of his personality.*
[*Courtesy of the American Numismatic Society*]

FIGURE 2. *Nave of Chartres Cathedral. This, one of the most impressive of the Gothic naves, illustrates the idea that Gothic architecture resembles a forest vista. The soaring lines satisfied the instinct of Northern people and the details of leaves and flowers bursting forth at points where the lines changed direction heighten the impression of growth and change.*

FIGURE 3. *Apse of Reims Cathedral, the scene of the coronation of French kings. Reims was begun in 1211 and finished with great rapidity. As Gothic churches grew larger the principle of support by thrust and counterthrust demanded the extension of the supporting base and a complex system of flying buttresses was devised. The effect was one of airy beauty. At Reims the traditional three portals are ornamented by lacelike carving which completely screens the walls. The Gothic builder, as C. R. Morey has pointed out, combined realism with mysticism. He wanted light but when he attained it through virtual elimination of the walls by the use of large windows, he filled the windows with stained glass which transformed the natural light into what seemed the light divine.*

FIGURE 4. *Cloth Hall, Ypres. The building of the huge guild hall of the weavers of Ghent went on through the whole of the thirteenth century, and the dedication took place only in 1304. The size of the building is emphasized by the town hall at the end of the Cloth Hall, which was built in the decorated Gothic style, in the fourteenth century. The Cloth Hall was one of the historic glories of Ypres until the first World War when it was completely wrecked by German artillery.*

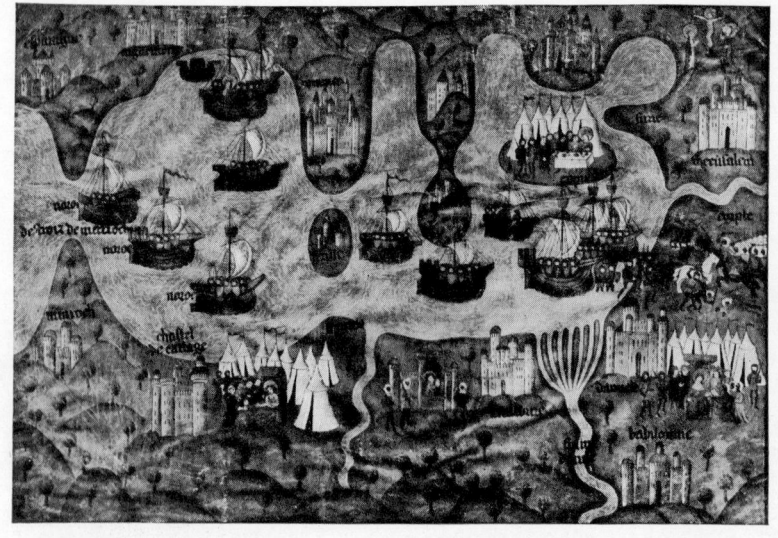

PLATE XVIII

Thirteenth Century

FIGURE 1. *Portrait of Dante as a young man. This fresco, painted by Giotto in the chapel of the Palazzo del Podestà in Florence, was hidden by whitewash until 1840. When it was brought to light an Englishman and an Italian succeeded in making drawings of Dante's head before it was irreparably damaged by unskillful repainting. This is the Italian's drawing. A nail had been driven through the eye in the fresco and the resulting hole appears in the white spots of the drawing. This head is probably the only surviving portrait made during Dante's lifetime. The Dante here is the Dante of the* Vita Nuova, *the young poet.*
[*Alinari photograph*]

FIGURE 2. *Sculptured figures from the west façade of Amiens Cathedral, representing the Presentation of Jesus in the Temple. These sculptures show the idealized realism and the greater individualism of high Gothic art. The stylized hair and garments and stiff posture which formerly made such figures a part of the architectural design has disappeared. The Virgin is a lovely young woman who stands with dignity on her own feet. Although she is still attached to the façade, she is not an integral part of it.*

FIGURE 3. *A unique map of the Mediterranean region. This map was made after the canonization of Louis IX, to show his crusades.*
[*Courtesy of the Metropolitan Museum of Art, New York*]

of rivalry between Guelf and Ghibelline—papal party versus imperial party.

Sons of prosperous merchants in the great commercial cities were able, if it suited their fancy, to pursue an education with no thought of vocational aim, and thus appeared the phenomenon which was to help build the modern world—the educated layman. The Florentine Dante Alighieri was one of these, a man of extraordinary mental powers, who became the greatest scholar of his time. It is not known, however, where he was educated. His native city had no university and was not to have one for another hundred years. There were, however, many well known intellectual centers: in Italy the universities of Bologna and Padua, already famous for law, Salerno, for medicine, and Frederick II's new university at Naples. In France Montpellier and Toulouse were popular. But the renown of the University of Paris was greatest of all; there Thomas Aquinas (d. 1274), the great Dominican pupil of Albertus Magnus, had worked out his *Summa Theologiae*. The *Summa* was a philosophical system in which the *Metaphysics* of Aristotle, recovered from the Arabs and prohibited to Paris students at the beginning of the century, was harmonized with Christian doctrine and thenceforth prescribed instead of proscribed. Dante knew the *Summa* thoroughly, and he learned all that Albertus Magnus and Roger Bacon had known of natural science. Brunetto Latini, a Florentine who was a great student of classical antiquity and an advocate of popular learning, we know was one of his teachers. With Dante, though, scholarship was not an end; he was first of all a poet. Unfortunately, however, he was also a politician, and in 1302 was banished from Florence with others of his party and spent the rest of his life in exile.

Two years before Dante left Florence, Pope Boniface VIII held a jubilee in Rome (1300); its success encouraged the pope's exalted idea of the papal office. Boniface, like Gregory VII and Innocent III, put forth claim to the right of popes to control and even depose princes. The chief opponents of the pope's claim were two princes who had been systematically and efficiently consolidating monarchy in their respective countries: Edward I of England, and Philip IV (the Fair) of France. Edward I had been able to learn in the reign of his pious father, Henry III, the dangers that follow the misuse of royal power. The English were attached to their ancient common law, and kings who failed to respect the rights believed to be embodied in the "good old laws of Edward the Confessor" were likely to have trouble on their hands.

After the death of Frederick II the pope offered the crown of Sicily to Henry, who was subservient to the papacy, and he accepted it for his younger son. He raised money for the conquest of the island without regard to the limitations of his powers. The king was unpopular and all classes backed a movement to apply the principle that the king was under the law. The barons invoked the provisions of Magna Carta. By the Provisions of Oxford, drawn up in 1258, the barons compelled the king to reaffirm Magna Carta, dismiss foreign favorites, oppose heavy papal taxation, and submit to the supervision of a committee of the Great Council. The king did not keep his agreement, and for a brief period Edward was drawn into the struggle against his father. In the civil war that broke out, the leadership of the rebels was assumed by Simon de Montfort, a younger son of the leader of the Albigensian crusade. The end of the wars came with Simon's defeat and death at the battle of Evesham (1265).

Edward I's accession marked the emergence of a prince who was wholly English in training and sympathy. One of the chief grievances against Henry III had been his favor to foreign prelates appointed by the pope to English benefices. Edward resolved that papal provisions should cease and that the growing power of canon law should be checked. He restricted the jurisdiction of the ecclesiastical courts and levied heavy taxes on the clergy to pay the expenses of his foreign wars. Boniface VIII issued the famous bull *Clericis Laicos* (1296) which threatened with excommunication kings who taxed the clergy without papal consent. Edward's response was to outlaw clergy who refused to pay such taxes. Philip IV of France, who had also embarked on a policy of taxing his clergy to help pay for his wars, prohibited the export of all money from France. Boniface thereupon was forced to withdraw his bull. Another papal grievance was Edward's statute which forbade grants of land to the church without the king's consent. By this statute and another which forbade further subinfeudation, Edward secured greater control of the English landholding system. The wars upon which he expended vast sums were fought to protect his lands in France and to make himself ruler of Wales and Scotland. His proclamation of his son as the Prince of Wales provided the sentiment for Welsh loyalty which developed in the course of the next hundred years. Two wars were fought in Scotland, and although Edward did not succeed in subduing the Scots he carried off the famous stone of Scone for the English coronation chair.

During the barons' war Simon de Montfort had summoned to the great council, which was beginning to be called parliament, two knights from each shire and two burgesses from each borough to sit with the feudal magnates. Edward followed this plan when in 1295 he called the parliament which became the model for succeeding parliaments. Edward's model parliament consisted of four houses, which later were to be reduced to two: the feudal magnates both lay and ecclesiastical, representatives of the lower clergy, knights from the shires, and burgesses from the towns. He quoted the Roman law, "What touches all should be approved by all." With the growth of the towns, their wealth could not be disregarded by a monarch who needed funds, and the presence of their representatives was expected to guarantee the townsfolk's payment of the taxes voted. Assemblies of this sort were not uniquely English; Frederick II had called them in Sicily, and they were to be found in the Spanish kingdoms, in France, Germany, and Bohemia. In 1302 Philip IV of France convened such an assembly for the purpose of demonstrating that his subjects were solidly behind him in his quarrel with Boniface VIII over taxation of the clergy.

The discord between Philip IV and Boniface VIII broke out again after Philip tried a French bishop in a secular court. A notable exchange of abusive letters followed and Boniface finally issued the bull *Unam sanctam,* in which he claimed that "it is altogether necessary to salvation for every human creature to be subject to the Roman pontiff." Under the threat of excommunication, Philip sent agents to seize the pope at Anagni, (1303) and they used insulting behavior toward him. The aged pope died under the strain of his treatment, and Philip secured the election of a Frenchman. The French pope made the city of Avignon in southern France the official papal residence, and thus in 1305, three years after Dante's exile, began the so-called Babylonian captivity of the papacy, which lasted for 73 years. By their patronage of art the popes made Avignon a center of artistic activity. The new Flemish painting in oils, to which Burgundian dukes were giving their patronage, and a new French school of art were also encouraged by the Avignon popes.

While the popes were enjoying life in Avignon, Dante was eating out his heart in exile and writing the series of works which are so remarkable a summation of the medieval mind. He was one of the writers who believed in the future of the Italian language, and although he wrote his scholarly books in Latin, his poetry was in the vernacular, and this contributed greatly toward making his native Tuscan the predominant dialect of Italy. The prose and poetry of his *Vita Nuova* dealt with romantic love; the great poem of his maturity, *The Divine Comedy,* was written to draw men's thoughts toward the attainment of salvation in the ways prescribed by the church. In it is to be found the final synthesis of traditional thought and faith. As a scholar who remained a layman, and a poet who used the vernacular for his great poem so that all could read it, Dante was a modern. He was a man of his age in the subject of the poem and its treatment; he showed the life after death as his age conceived it, in a universe as his world accepted it from the second-century Greek Ptolemy. It had met the tests of the best astronomical observation then possible, and been checked by scripture as expounded by the Fathers of the Church. Dante's doctrine was the orthodox doctrine which Thomas Aquinas had built upon the authority of the medievalized Aristotle.

Whereas in his great epic Dante showed his views of the theology of the day, in his *De Monarchia* he set forth the political theory that the events through which he lived had developed. He put his faith in the Ghibelline solution for Italy's ills: an emperor who could unite the land under beneficent rule. After the breakdown of imperial power with the death of the last Hohenstaufen emperor no generally recognized emperor had existed for a score of years. When Dante was a boy the Great Interregnum, as this period was called, had come to an end with the election of the head of an unknown Alsatian family, Rudolph of Hapsburg, to the imperial title. Rudolph's chief preoccupation was the establishment of his family as a great landed power; when his vassal, the king of Bohemia, failed to meet his feudal obligations, Rudolph declared his fiefs forfeit and annexed them, thereby obtaining the Austrian lands the house of Hapsburg was to rule until the end of World War I. Rudolph gave up imperial claims in southern Italy, and under his successor three Alpine cantons revolted and formed the Swiss confederacy. In 1308, however, a Luxemburger, Henry VII, became emperor and, hoping to revive imperial power in Italy, crossed the Alps, took several towns, and was crowned at Rome. Dante hailed him as the promised savior of Italy, but the expedition meant only continued civil and ecclesiastical strife.

While Dante recorded the spirit and achievement of the world in which he had grown up, a friend of his youth, the painter Giotto, was starting a new movement in art which stemmed from the return to naturalism and simplicity of St. Francis of Assisi. The only authentic portrait of Dante as a young man was painted by Giotto, who knew him well. A master of the formalism and allegory in which Byzantine tradition had long imprisoned painting, Giotto mingled with it a movement and drama which gave his paintings realism. Already in the days of Frederick II a sculptor who found in a late Roman sarcophagus the inspiration to follow nature more realistically had settled in Pisa, whence he received the name Niccolo Pisano. Giotto may, or may not, have been influenced by the work of Niccolo and his nephew Giovanni; he was definitely inspired by the gentle Francis, who had preached to the birds and called fire and water his sisters.

Dante's world saw the defiance by the English and French kings of the claims of Pope Boniface VIII. It saw the transfer of the papal seat to Avignon, and the renewal of the imperial title by a new dynasty in the person of Rudolf of Hapsburg. It saw Edward I renew and vindicate the claim of Henry II to rule throughout the British Isles. The summoning of the third estate to the great council of the realm in several countries shows that in power, though not in prestige, the moneyed class was overtaking the landed class.

[THE THIRTEENTH CENTURY]

Readings

Innocent III

ANSWER CONCERNING THE INTERDICT (1208) *

[This is an official statement of just what could be expected by the population of a country that was laid under an interdict.]

Innocent the bishop, &c., to the Bishops of London, Ely, and Worcester, greeting and apostolic blessing. We reply to your inquiries, that whereas by reason of the interdict new chrism cannot be consecrated on Maundy Thursday, old must be used in the baptism of infants, and, if necessity demand, oil must be mixed by hand of the bishop or else priest, with the chrism, that it fail not. And although the viaticum seem to be meet on the repentance of the dying, yet, if it cannot be had, we who read it believe that the principle holds good in this case, 'believe and thou hast eaten,' when actual need, and not contempt of religion, excludes the sacrament, and the actual need is expected soon to cease. Let neither gospel nor church hours be observed in the accustomed place, nor any other, though the people assemble in the same. Let religious men, whose monasteries people have been wont to visit for the sake of prayer, admit pilgrims inside the church for prayer, not by the greater door, but by a more secret place. Let church doors remain shut save at the chief festival of the church, when the parishioners and others may be admitted for prayer into the church with open doors. Let baptism be celebrated in the usual manner with old chrism and oil inside the church with shut doors, no lay person being admitted save the godparents; and if need demand, new oil must be mixed. Penance is

* From *Documents Illustrative of English Church History,* compiled by Henry Gee and W. J. Hardy (1921), No. XXIV. By permission of the Macmillan Company, publishers.

[285

to be inflicted as well on the whole as the sick; for in the midst of life we are in death. Those who have confessed in a suit, or have been convicted of some crime, are to be sent to the bishop or his penitentiary, and, if need be, are to be forced to this by church censure. Priests may say their own hours and prayers in private. Priests may on Sunday bless water in the churchyard and sprinkle it; and can make and distribute the bread when blessed, and announce feasts and fasts and preach a sermon to the people. A woman after childbirth may come to church, and perform her purification outside the church walls. Priests shall visit the sick, and hear confessions, and let them perform the commendation of souls in the accustomed manner, but they shall not follow the corpses of the dead, because they will not have church burial. Priests shall, on the day of the Passion, place the cross outside the church, without ceremony, so that the parishioners may adore it with the customary devotion.

St. Francis of Assisi

CANTICLE OF THE SUN *

[This is the most famous of St. Francis's utterances. The reader has no difficulty in understanding the spell he cast on his generation, and the spirit which quickened art. In his will St. Francis answered the criticisms that were being made of his movement, and stated his aims and methods with simplicity and clarity.]

O most high, almighty, good Lord God, to thee belong praise, glory, honor, and all blessing!

Praised be my Lord God with all his creatures, and specially our brother the sun, who brings us the day, and who brings us the light; fair is he and shines with a very great splendor: O Lord, he signifies to us thee!

Praised be my Lord for our sister the moon, and for the stars, the which he has set clear and lovely in heaven.

Praised be my Lord for our brother the wind, and for air and

---

* From Matthew Arnold, *Essays in Criticism* (1883, 1929). By permission of The Macmillan Company, publishers.

cloud, calms and all weather by the which thou upholdest life in all creatures.

Praised be my Lord for our sister water, who is very serviceable unto us, and humble, and precious, and clean.

Praised be my Lord for our brother fire, through whom thou givest us light in the darkness; and he is bright and pleasant, and very mighty, and strong.

Praised be my Lord for our mother the earth, the which doth sustain us and keep us, and bringeth forth divers fruits, and flowers of many colors and grass.

Praised be my Lord for all those who pardon one another for his love's sake, and who endure weakness and tribulation; blessed are they who peaceably shall endure; for thou, O most Highest, shalt give them a crown.

Praised be my Lord for our sister, the death of the body, from whom no man escapeth. Woe to him who dieth in mortal sin. Blessed are they who are found walking by thy most holy will, for the second death shall have no power to do them harm.

Praise ye and bless the Lord, and give thanks unto him and serve him with great humility.

WILL *

See in what manner God gave it to me, to me, Brother Francis, to begin to do penitence; when I lived in sin, it was very painful to me to see lepers, but God himself led me into their midst, and I remained here a little while. When I left them, that which had seemed to me bitter had become sweet and easy.

A little while after I had quitted the world, and God gave me such a faith in his churches that I would kneel down with simplicity and I would say: "We adore thee, Lord Jesus Christ, here and in all thy churches which are in the world, and we bless thee that by thy holy cross thou hast ransomed the world."

Besides, the Lord gave me and still gives me so great a faith in priests who live according to the form of the holy Roman Church, because of their sacerdotal character, that even if they persecuted me I would have recourse to them. And even if I had all the wisdom of Solomon, if I should find poor secular priests, I would not preach

* From Paul Sabatier, *Life of St. Francis of Assisi* (1926). By permission of Charles Scribner's Sons, publishers.

in their parishes without their consent. I desire to respect them like all the others, to love them and honor them as my lords. I will not consider their sins, for in them I see the Son of God and they are my lords. I do this because here below I see nothing, I perceive nothing corporally of the most high Son of God, if not his most holy Body and Blood, which they receive and they alone distribute to others. I desire above all things to honor and venerate all these most holy mysteries and to keep them precious. Whenever I find the sacred names of Jesus or his words in indecent places, I desire to take them away, and I pray that others take them away and put them in some decent place. We ought to honor and revere all the theologians and those who preach the most holy word of God, as dispensing to us spirit and life.

When the Lord gave me some brothers no one showed me what I ought to do, but the most High himself revealed to me that I ought to live according to the model of the holy gospel. I caused a short and simple formula to be written, and the lord pope confirmed it for me.

Those who presented themselves to observe this kind of life distributed all that they might have to the poor. They contented themselves with a tunic, patched within and without, with the cord and breeches, and we desired to have nothing more.

The clerks said the office like other clerks, and the laymen *Pater noster*.

We loved to live in poor and abandoned churches, and we were ignorant and submissive to all. I worked with my hands and would continue to do, and I will also that all other friars work at some honorable trade. Let those who have none learn one, not for the purpose of receiving the price of their toil, but for their good example and to flee idleness. And when they do not give us the price of the work, let us resort to the table of the Lord, begging our bread from door to door. The Lord revealed to me the salutation which we ought to give: "God give you peace!"

Let the Brothers take great care not to receive churches, habitations, and all that men build for them, except as all is in accordance with the holy poverty which we have vowed in the Rule, and let them not receive hospitality in them except as strangers and pilgrims. . . .

Frederick II

MATTHEW PARIS'S ENGLISH HISTORY *

[Matthew Paris was an English monk who wrote a history of England which included a great deal of important information concerning Continental history also, and many documents. This letter of Frederick II contains contemporary impressions of the Mongol conquests.]

Frederick, emperor, &c., to the king of England, greeting.—
We cannot be silent on a matter which concerns not only the Roman empire, whose office it is to propagate the Gospel, but also all the kingdoms of the world that practise Christian worship, and threatens general destruction to the whole of Christianity: we therefore hasten to bring it to your knowledge, although the true facts of the matter have but lately come to ours. Some time since a people of a barbarous race and mode of life called (from what place or origin I know not) Tartars, has lately emerged from the regions of the south, where it had long lain hid, burnt up by the sun of the torrid zone, and, thence marching towards the northern parts, took forcible possession of the country there, and remaining for a time, multiplied like locusts, and has now come forth, not without the premeditated judgment of God, but not, I hope, reserved to these latter times for the ruin of the whole of Christianity. . . . We have, however, by some means or other, been forewarned of and foreseen all these events, and have by letters and messengers frequently requested of your majesty, as well as other Christian princes, and earnestly advised and entreated of you, to allow unanimity, affection, and peace, to flourish among those who hold supreme authority; to settle all dissensions, which frequently bring harm on the commonwealth of Christ; and to rise with alacrity, and unanimously to oppose those lately emerged savages, inasmuch as weapons foreseen are less apt to wound; that so the common enemies of us all may not have cause to rejoice, in furtherance of their progress, that discord is shooting forth amongst the Christian chiefs. . . . We have, therefore, turned our attention to both matters; and, with the help of God's providence, will apply our strength and industry to avert the scandal to the Church caused on one side by our enemies at home, and on the other, by these

* Translated by J. A. Giles (1852), Volume I. Reprinted by permission of G. Bell & Sons, Ltd.

savages; we have, therefore, expressly sent our beloved son Conrad, and other chiefs of our empire, with a strong force, to meet and check the attacks and violence of these barbarians. And we most sincerely adjure your majesty, in the name of the Lord Jesus Christ, the author of our Christian faith, with the most careful solicitude, and by prudent deliberation, to take precautions for the protection of yourself and your kingdom, which may God keep in a state of prosperity, and to prepare as soon as possible a complete force of brave knights and soldiers, and a good supply of arms; and this we beg of you, by the blood of Christ shed for us, and by the ties of relationship, by which we are connected. And let them prepare themselves to fight bravely and prudently in conjunction with us, for the freedom of Christianity; so that by a union of our forces against these enemies, who are now purposing to enter the boundaries of Germany, which is, as it were, the door of Christendom, the victory may be gained, to the honour and renown of the Lord of Hosts; and may it please your majesty, not to pass these matters by unnoticed, or to delay giving your attention to them. . . .

༄ ༄ ༄

Salimbene

CHRONICLE *

[Salimbene was a Franciscan friar, a native of Parma (1221–88), from whose *Autobiography,* as quoted by Mr. Coulton, the following extracts are taken. His description of Frederick's personal characteristics, and of his scientific experiments, form the principal basis of the accounts given by modern historians of this extraordinary personage. The sketch of St. Louis, and of the feast he offered the monks, is full of interesting detail. These samples show that the *Autobiography* as a whole is well worth reading for a picture of the thirteenth century.]

The Emperor Frederick II

Of faith in God he had none; he was crafty, wily, avaricious, lustful, malicious, wrathful; and yet a gallant man at times, when he would show his kindness or courtesy; full of solace, jocund, delightful, fertile in devices. He knew to read, write, and sing, and to

---

* From G. G. Coulton, *From St. Francis to Dante* (1907).

make songs and music. He was a comely man, and well-formed, but of middle stature. I have seen him, and once I loved him, for on my behalf he wrote to Brother Elias, Minister-General of the Friars Minor, to send me back to my father. Moreover, he knew to speak with many and varied tongues, and, to be brief, if he had been rightly Catholic, and had loved God and His Church, he would have had few emperors his equals in the world.

Frederick's Experiment with Children

Bidding foster-mothers and nurses to suckle and bathe and wash the children, but in no wise to prattle or speak with them; for he would have learnt whether they would speak the Hebrew language (which had been the first), or Greek, or Latin, or Arabic, or perchance the tongue of their parents of whom they had been born. But he laboured in vain, for the children could not live without clappings of the hands, and gestures, and gladness of countenance, and blandishments. . . . When he saw the Holy Land, (which God had so oft-times commended as a land flowing with milk and honey and most excellent above all lands,) it pleased him not, and he said that if the God of the Jews had seen *his* lands of Terra di Lavoro, Calabria, Sicily, and Apulia, then He would not so have commended the land which He promised to the Jews. But Ecclesiasticus saith: "Speak nothing rashly, nor let thy heart be swift to utter thy speech before God: for God is in the heaven, and thou upon earth; wherefore let thy words be few." Take an example of that clerk who uttered against God such words as should not have been said: wherefore he was smitten forthwith by a thunderbolt from heaven, and fell dead. His fourth excess was that he oft-times sent one Nicholas against his will to the bottom of the Faro, and oft-times he returned thence; and, wishing to know in sooth whether he had indeed gone down to the bottom and returned thence, he threw in his golden cup where he thought the depth was greatest. So Nicholas plunged and found it and brought it back, whereat the Emperor marvelled. But when he would have sent him again, he said: "Send me not thither, I pray you; for the sea is so troubled in the depth that, if ye send me, I shall never return." Nevertheless the Emperor sent him; so there he perished and never returned: for in those sea-depths are great fishes at times of tempests, and rocks and many wrecks of ships, as he himself reported. He might have said to Frederick in Jonah's words "Thou hast cast me into the deep, in the heart of the sea, and the flood encompassed me about; all thy whirlpools and waves went over me." ... Moreover, Frederick had likewise other excesses and curiosities and cursed ways and incredulities, whereof I have written some in another chronicle: as of the man whom he shut up alive in a cask until he died therein, wishing thereby to show that the soul perished utterly, as if he might say the word of Isaiah "Let us eat and drink, for to-morrow we die." For he was an Epicurean; wherefore, partly of himself and partly through his wise men, he sought out all that he could find in Holy Scripture which might make for the proof that there was no other life after death, as for instance "Thou shalt destroy them, and not build them up": and again "Their sepulchres shall be their houses for ever" [also Ps. xxxviii. 14, Ecclus. xlviii. 12, Ps. cvi. 5, Eccl. iii. 19–22,] and many such, which Solomon said in Ecclesiastes in the person of carnal folk: ... Sixthly, he fed two men most excellently at dinner, one of whom he sent forthwith to sleep, and the other to hunt; and that same evening he caused them to be disembowelled in his presence, wishing to know which had digested the better: and it was judged by the physicians in favour of him who had slept. Seventhly and lastly, being one day in his palace, he asked of Michael Scot the astrologer how far he was from the sky, and Michael having answered as it seemed to him, the Emperor took him to other parts of his kingdom as if for a journey of pleasure, and kept him there several months, bidding meanwhile his architects and carpenters secretly to lower the whole of his palace hall. Many days afterwards, standing in that same palace with Michael, he asked of him, as if by the way, whether he were indeed so far from the sky as he had before said. Whereupon he made his calculations, and made answer that certainly either the sky had been raised or the earth lowered; and then the Emperor knew that he spake truth. ... He was wont at times to make mocking harangues before his court in his own palace, speaking for example after the fashion of the Cremonese ambassadors, who were sent to him by their fellow-citizens; one of whom would begin by praising the other with manifold words of commendation, saying "This lord [my fellow] is noble, wise, rich, and powerful": and so after commending each other the ambassadors would at last come to their proper business. Moreover, he would suffer patiently the scoffings and mockings and revilings of jesters, and often feign that he heard not. For one day, after the destruction of Victoria by the men of Parma, he smote his hand on the hump of a certain jester, saying "My Lord Dallio, when shall this box be opened?" To whom the other answered, " 'Tis odds if it be ever opened now, for I lost the key in Victoria." The Emperor, hearing how this jester recalled his own sorrow and shame, groaned and said, with the Psalmist, "I was troubled, and I spoke not." If any had spoken such a jest against Ezzelino da Romano, he would without doubt have let him be blinded or hanged. Again, another time he suffered patiently that Villano da Ferro mocked him at the siege of Berceto; for the Emperor asked him how men named the mangonels and catapults which were there, and Villano gave him for their names certain mocking words, namely *"sbegna"* and *"sbegnoino."* But the Emperor did but smile and turn away.... One day, when he was excommunicated by Pope Gregory IX and had come to certain parts where was the Patriarch of Aquileia, the Lord Berthold, whom I have seen and known, a comely man and uncle to St. Elizabeth of Hungary,—then the Emperor sent word to him to come and hear Mass with him. But the Patriarch, knowing all this, called his barber and caused himself to be bled before he had seen the Emperor's messenger; then he sat down and began to dine, and sent word to the Emperor that he could not go and hear Mass with him, since he had been bled and was set down to meat. So the Emperor sent a second time, bidding him come forthwith, all impediments notwithstanding: whereupon, willing to redeem his vexation, he humbly obeyed, and came and heard Mass with him.

King Louis IX

Now the King was spare and slender, somewhat lean, and of a proper height, having the face of an angel, and mien full of grace. And he came to our Church, not in regal pomp, but in a pilgrim's habit, with the staff and the scrip of his pilgrimage hanging at his neck, which was an excellent adornment for the shoulders of a king. And he came not on horseback, but on foot; and his blood-brethren, who were three counts, (whereof the eldest was named Robert, and the youngest Charles, who did afterwards many great deeds most worthy of praise), followed him in the same humble guise, so that they might have said in truth that word of the prophet "Woe to them that go down to Egypt for help, trusting in horses, and putting their confidence in chariots, because they are many, and in horsemen, because they are very strong: and have not trusted in the holy One of Israel, and have not sought after the Lord." Nor did the King care for a train of nobles, but rather for the prayers and suffrages of the poor; and therefore he fulfilled that which

Ecclesiasticus teacheth "Make thyself affable to the congregation of the poor." In truth he might rather be called a monk in devotion of heart, than a knight in weapons of war. . . .

. . . Moreover, the King took upon himself all that day's cost, and ate together with us in the refectory; and with us sat down to meat the King's three brethren, and the Cardinal, and the Minister-General, and Brother Rigaud, Archbishop of Rouen, and the Minister-Provincial of France, and the Custodes and Definitores, and the Discreti, and all who were of the capitular body, and the Brethren our guests, whom we call "foreigners." . . . This then was our fare that day: first, cherries, then most excellent white bread; and choice wine, worthy of the King's royal state, was placed in abundance before us; and, after the wont of the French, many invited even the unwilling and compelled them to drink. After that we had fresh beans boiled in milk, fishes and crabs, eel-pasties, rice cooked with milk of almonds and cinnamon powder, eels baked with most excellent sauce, tarts and junkets, [or curd-cheeses] and all the fruits of the season in abundance and comely array. And all these were laid on the table in courtly fashion, and busily ministered to us. . . .

Dante

DE VULGARI ELOQUENTIA *

[Dante the Florentine patriot and Dante the citizen of the world are agreeably commingled in this bit of self-examination.]

. . . But we, to whom the world is our native country, just as the sea is to the fish, though we drank of Arno before our teeth appeared, and though we love Florence so dearly that for the love we bore her we are wrongfully suffering exile—we rest the shoulders of our judgment on reason rather than on feeling. And although as regards our own pleasure or sensuous comfort there exists no more agreeable place in the world than Florence, still, when we turn over the volumes both of poets and other writers in which the world is

---

* Translated by G. Ferrers Howell, Book I, Chap. VI; from *A Translation of the Latin Works of Dante* (The Temple Classics, 1940). Reprinted by permission of J. M. Dent and Sons, Ltd.

generally and particularly described, and take account within ourselves of the various situations of the places of the world and their arrangement with respect to the two poles and to the equator, our deliberate and firm opinion is that there are many countries and cities both nobler and more delightful than Tuscany and Florence of which we are a native and a citizen, and also that a great many nations and races use a speech both more agreeable and more serviceable than the Italians do. . . .

THE DIVINE COMEDY: INFERNO *

[*The Divine Comedy* deals with the fate of souls after death. In the first book, the Inferno, Dante, under the guidance of the poet Virgil, visits the nine circles where those who sinned beyond redemption were suffering. In the second circle he saw whirled about by contrary winds souls which had yielded to the temptation of forbidden love. Dido was one of these, and a famous pair, Francesca da Rimini and her lover Paolo.]

"O living creature, gracious and benign! that goest through the black air, visiting us who stained the earth with blood. If the King of the Universe were our friend, we would pray him for thy peace; seeing that thou hast pity of our perverse misfortune. Of that which it pleases thee to hear and to speak, we will hear and speak with you, whilst the wind, as now, is silent.

"The town where I was born, sits on the shore, where Po descends to rest with his attendant *streams*. Love, which is quickly caught in gentle heart, took him with the fair body of which I was bereft; and the manner still afflicts me. Love, which to no loved one permits excuse from loving, took me so strongly with delight in him, that, as thou seest, even now it leaves me not. Love led us to one death. Caïna waits for him who quenched our life." These words from them were offered to us.

After I had heard those wounded souls, I bowed my face, and held it low until the poet said to me: "What art thou thinking of?"

When I answered, I began: "Ah me! what sweet thoughts, what longing led them to the woful pass!"

Then I turned again to them; and I spoke, and began: "Francesca, thy torments make me weep with grief and pity. But tell me:

* From *Dante's Divine Comedy: The Inferno*, translated by John A. Carlyle (New York, 1867). By permission of Harper & Brothers.

in the time of the sweet sighs, by what and how love granted you to know the dubious desires!"

And she to me: *"There is* no greater pain than to recall a happy time in wretchedness; and this thy teacher knows. But if thou hast such desire to learn the first root of our love, I will do like one who weeps and tells,

"One day, for pastime, we read of Lancelot, how love constrained him. We were alone, and without all suspicion. Several times that reading urged our eyes to meet, and changed the color of our faces; but one moment alone it was that overcame us. When we read how the fond smile was kissed by such a lover, he, who shall never be divided from me, kissed my mouth all trembling: The book, and he who wrote, was a Galeotto. That day we read in it no farther."

[*from Canto V, lines 73–138*]

[In the third chasm of the eighth circle those who practiced simony were being punished. They were placed head downwards in holes of the rock, and flames played upon the soles of their feet. Dante finds that the sufferer who showed the greatest agony was Pope Nicholas III. He had occupied his position of chief sufferer among popes who were simoniacs for twenty years. He prophesies that his successor would be Boniface VIII, who quarreled with Philip the Fair, who would yield in turn to Clement V when Clement would hold that unhappy distinction. Clement V was the French pope who transferred the papacy to Avignon.]

. . . "Art thou there already standing, Boniface? Art thou there already standing? By several years the writ has lied to me. Art thou so quickly sated with that wealth, for which thou didst not fear to seize the comely Lady by deceit, and then make havoc of her?"

I became like those who stand as if bemocked, not comprehending what is answered to them, and unable to reply. Then Virgil said: "Say to him quickly, 'I am not he, I am not he whom thou thinkest.'"

And I replied as was enjoined me. Whereat the spirit quite wrenched his feet; Thereafter, sighing and with voice of weeping, he said to me: "Then what askest thou of me? If to know who I am concerneth thee so much, that thou hast therefore passed the bank, learn that I was clothed with the Great Mantle; and verily I was a son of the She-bear, so eager to advance the Whelps, that I pursed wealth above, and here myself. Beneath my head are dragged the others who preceded me in simony, cowering within the fissure [s] of the stone. I too shall fall down thither, when he comes for whom I took thee when I put the sudden question. But longer is the time already, that I have baked my feet and stood inverted thus, than he shall stand planted with glowing feet: for after him, from westward, there shall come a lawless Shepherd, of uglier deeds, fit to cover him and me. A new Jason will it be, of whom we read in Maccabees; and as to that *high priest* his king was pliant; so to this shall be he who governs France."

I know not if here I was too hardy, for I answered him in this strain: "Ah! Now tell me how much treasure our Lord required of St. Peter, before he put the keys into his keeping? Surely he demanded naught but 'Follow me!' Nor did Peter, nor the others, ask of Matthias gold or silver, when he was chosen for the office which the guilty soul had lost. Therefore stay thou *here,* for thou art justly punished; and keep well the ill-got money, which against Charles made thee be bold. . . ."

[*from Canto XIX, lines 52-99*]

THE DIVINE COMEDY: PURGATORIO *

[In the *Purgatorio,* where souls destined ultimately for Heaven were purged of sin, Dante falls into talk with a Venetian nobleman, not long dead, who bewails the degeneracy of the times. Dante asks him if this degeneracy is due to the influence of the planets, or to men themselves. The Venetian replies sadly:]

Ye who are living refer every cause up to the heavens alone, even as if they swept all with them of necessity. Were it thus, Freewill in you would be destroyed, and it were not just to have joy for good and mourning for evil. The heavens set your impulses in motion; I say not all, but suppose I said it, a light is given you to know good and evil, and Freewill, which, if it endure the strain in its first battlings with the heavens, at length gains the whole victory, if it be well nurtured. Ye lie subject, in your freedom, to a greater power and to a better nature; and that creates in you *mind* which the heavens have not in their charge. Therefore, if the world to-day goeth astray, in you is the cause, in you be it sought, and I now will be a true scout to thee therein. From his hands who fondly loves her ere she is in being, there issues, after the fashion of a little child that sports, now weeping, now laughing, the simple, tender soul, who knoweth naught save that, sprung from a joyous maker, willingly she turneth

---

* Taken from *Temple Classics,* translated by Thomas Okey, published by E. P. Dutton & Co., Inc., New York.

298] *The Thirteenth Century*

to that which delights her. First she tastes the savour of a trifling good; there she is beguiled and runneth after it, if guide or curb turn not her love aside. Wherefore 'twas needful to put law as a curb, needful to have a ruler who might discern at least the tower of the true city.

[*from Canto XVI, lines 67–96*]

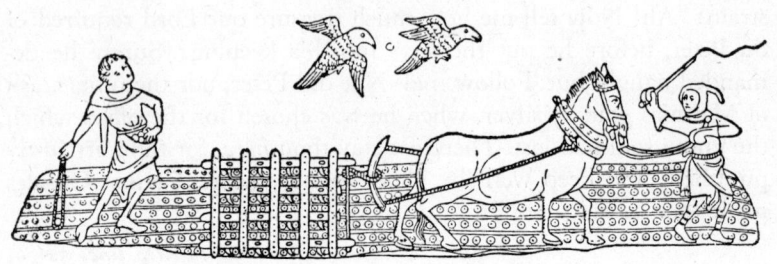

DRAWING FROM THE LUTTRELL PSALTER, SHOW-
ING HARROWING WITH A HORSE WEARING A
PADDED COLLAR

(From *A Student's History of England* by Samuel R. Gardiner. Longmans Green, London, 1897.)

PART X

The Fourteenth Century

CHRONOLOGY

- 1302 First Estates General of France
- 1307–21 Dante's *Divina Commedia*
- 1309 Seat of papacy transferred to Avignon
- 1314 Battle of Bannockburn; Scot independence of England confirmed
- 1324 *Defensor Pacis* of Marsilio of Padua and John of Jandun
- 1331 Coronation of Stephen Dushan, creator of the Serbian Empire
- 1340 Battle of Sluys, giving English naval supremacy at beginning of Hundred Years' War
- 1346 Battle of Crecy; feudal heavy cavalry defeated by longbow
- 1347 Prague University established
- 1348–50 Black Death
- c. 1350 Boccaccio's *Decameron*
- 1356 Turks begin to settle in Europe, crossing from Asia Minor
- 1356–58 Etienne Marcel and revolt of French Estates General
- 1371 Sir John Mandeville's *Travels*
- 1378 Beginning of the Great Schism
- c. 1380–82 English Bible
- 1381 Peasants' Revolt in England
- 1385 Heidelberg University founded
- 1389 Battle of Kossovo; subjection of Serbs
- 1396 Chrysoloras teaching Greek in Northern Italy

PART X

The Fourteenth Century

~~~~~~~~~~~~~~~~~~~~~~~~~~

THE fourteenth century was a period of movement, innovations, and inventions. This was partly cloaked by the rise of chivalry which had been growing for centuries and reached its height at this time. Chivalry accented the international character of feudalism. In its origins it had owed much to the efforts of the church to idealize the knight as the servant of God, the protector of the weak. It was indebted also to the Arab code of behavior with which westerners came in touch on the Spanish border and during the crusades. At its core were the feudal virtues: valor, prowess, loyalty, open-heartedness. With the aid of the minstrels the ladies developed the code of courtly love. According to the code, a knight's prowess was increased by devotion to a lady. In order to win her approval he must be proficient in the courtly arts. The *Book of the Knight of La Tour Landry* and the *Chronicles* of Froissart give some idea of the fourteenth century behavior patterns. By that time the brutal exercise of the tournament had become a spectacle where the ladies watched their knights, in heavy armor, trying with blunted weapons to unhorse each other. Courtly love and the idealization of women had already provoked the church to a counter movement in the cult of the Virgin. With the waning importance of the knight in war the mock combat of the tournament became his serious occupation. As a landed proprietor, with peasants at his disposal, he had a solid base for his prestige. Its demise was slow, and the chivalric code was to rule polite society for centuries, to be studied eagerly by even the townsmen's sons who were not to the manor born but who were coming of age as the heirs to the landed proprietor's dominant position in society.

Townsmen were continuing to make history. Even before the thirteenth century, leagues of cities, such as the Lombard League in Italy, had been in existence mainly for political purposes. In the fourteenth century the Hanseatic League, a union of German towns along the North Sea and Baltic trade lanes, virtually controlled the trade of the north. The Order of Teutonic Knights, which had profited by the German colonization and town-building in the Baltic area in the conquest of the Prussians, encouraged the colonization of Poland and Lithuania. This German invasion was opposed by the Polish king, who was a town-builder himself and had established the new capital of Cracow. He lost Pomerania to the Teutonic Knights, but his successor formed an alliance with the Grand-Duke of Lithuania. He encouraged the activities of the Jews and founded the University of Cracow. He was succeeded by a cadet of the house of Anjou, who although he increased the power of the nobles, was also a patron of the townsmen. The opposition of the Poles and Lithuanians finally resulted in Poland's winning West Prussia, with Danzig, its great Baltic port. German colonization was successful in Bohemia, which came under rulers of German blood, and important town populations grew up. The second German king, who was also emperor, founded the University of Prague.

In eastern Europe the city of Moscow became important when the princes of the Moscow region were able to impress their importance on their Mongol overlords and even defeat them on the field of battle. In Hungary Louis the Great, a member of the Angevin house, encouraged cities and trade. Louis won Dalmatia from Venice and had considerable success in the Balkans, but was beaten in Serbia by the national hero, Stephen Dushan. The Serbians had developed an interesting culture on the Greek model. Stephen created a great Serbian empire and planned to succeed the Byzantine emperors, but after his death the Serbs were defeated by the newest invaders of southeastern Europe, the Ottoman Turks, on the field of Kossovo (1389) and Serbia became a vassal state. The tradition of this great age and leader remained as the kernel about which the spirit of Serbian nationality was to grow in later centuries.

National consciousness in England and France was developing as a result of the Hundred Years' War between the two countries, which began toward the middle of the fourteenth century. England in the days of John had adopted the English language to replace

French as fashionable speech, and as the century went on English soldiers led to battle by an English king longed for familiar food and talk in an alien land. At the same time soil trodden by plundering invaders became sacred to the French. New vernacular literatures enhanced these national sentiments. In German lands the imperial title lapsed, and local loyalties developed in the cities, but the homogeneous nature of the German population provided a common fund of tastes and traditions, and these were kept alive by the minnesingers and meistersingers. As the Germans pushed eastward, the Slav with his strange habits was the foreign danger, the opponent in their search for new homes. Common opposition to the Slav stimulated a feeling of German solidarity.

In Italy city loyalties had never disappeared, and they became more intense with urban rivalries and struggles for the intervening countryside among the city-states. The tradition of descent from the ancient Romans provided a rallying point for Italian nationality but the tradition expressed itself chiefly in the field of arts and letters. The demand of the sons of rich merchants for reading matter which dealt with this world rather than the next was supplied in the vernacular by Boccaccio's *Decameron;* for the learned, in the works of classical authors. It became fashionable to ape the ancient Romans' tastes and hobbies, and a few specimens of ancient sculpture provided inspiration for artists. The subject matter of art on the whole was still religious, but potent forces in society were aiding secular interests in the field of faith. A new movement in secular music, known as *ars nova,* became popular in Italy, France, and the Netherlands, providing settings for Dante's and Petrarch's sonnets and the stories of Boccaccio. It was polyphonic, included elaborate instrumental accompaniment, and its spirit was romantic.

The fourteenth century was also notable for inventions. In general there was evident a quickening in the tempo of European life which was the fruit of many generations of progress in developing the medieval counterpart of modern science and technology. The significance of many inventions or new devices introduced from far places piecemeal during the feudal ages becomes evident only over long periods. Devices already in use—such as mechanical clocks and looms—were perfected. When windmills and watermills were adapted to the principle of the crank in changing one type of action to another, non-human power development took further great

304] *The Fourteenth Century*

strides. Modern mechanical genius has built on the same foundations. The agricultural revolution of the Middle Ages was completed in the fourteenth century, and the European population level became more or less stationary until the next great agricultural revolution beginning in the eighteenth century.

Certain revolutionary social forces were also at work during the fourteenth century. The papacy at Anagni was fallen from the high estate to which Innocent III had raised it, and at Avignon it fell still further. In the last quarter of the century the rivalry over the papal office which led to the division known as the Great Schism gave papal prestige a yet more resounding blow. In an age when townsmen were feeling their importance and peasants had more bargaining power as a result of the terrible loss of life during the Black Death (1348–50), the Avignon popes, with an improved machinery for collection, increased their financial demands. A population irked by the tax Peter's Pence and by papal provisions furnished an excellent breeding ground for heresy; and John Wycliffe started a movement in England whose repercussions are still heard.

DRAWING OF THE FOURTEENTH CENTURY, SHOWING QUILLING WHEEL FOR WINDING A BOBBIN

(By permission from *History of Mechanical Inventions* by Abbott Payson Usher, copyright, 1929, by McGraw-Hill Book Co., Inc.)

CHAPTER 18

The World of John Wycliffe
[c. 1330–1384]

~~~~~~~~~~~~~~~~

JOHN WYCLIFFE, a Yorkshireman, was born some nine years after Dante's death. About the early part of his life there is controversy; that he first studied and then taught at Oxford is certain. He may have been a member of the Parliament of 1366 which refused to pay the tribute money due the papacy as a consequence of King John's homage and fealty to Innocent III. The men and women of his world were those of whom his contemporary, Geoffrey Chaucer, has given a vivid picture in the prologue to his *Canterbury Tales*. The prototype of Chaucer's "Clerk of Oxenford" rubbed shoulders in Oxford lanes with the young men Wycliffe trained year after year to go out as "poor preachers" and carry the gospel to all parts of England, where the decay of preaching had left men ignorant of the faith. Wycliffe himself had many of the qualities of Chaucer's parish priest; he was, however, more fiery than meek. He had a pleasant wit and a firm determination to stand fast against abuses prevalent among the clergy and against what he believed to be false doctrine. When he was still a boy, his sovereign became involved in the great struggle with France which was to absorb much of English energies for several generations and has come to be known as the Hundred Years' War.

This war was as inevitable as most wars appear to be in retrospect. Significant for the history of Europe in the fourteenth century are the facts that both English and French monarchies had simultaneously achieved a rather high degree of order and stability under strong monarchs, and that their territories were contiguous. The successors of Philip the Fair were becoming aware of the possibilities of the natural frontiers of France. Blocking expansion toward one

[305

of them—the Pyrenees—was Aquitaine, held as a fief by the king of England, an embarrassingly powerful vassal. The profitable trade which the English enjoyed with southern France through the port of Bordeaux was a constant source of irritation and jealousy on the part of the French. The English, on the other hand, were no more pleased that their strong sovereign was a vassal of the French crown.

While the question of Aquitaine was a long-standing cause of the conflict between the two monarchies which had been going on sporadically since King John lost Normandy, the immediate occasion of the war was the problem of Flanders. The Flemish weavers in the prosperous lowland towns were the principal purchasers of English wool. Discrimination against English merchants and wool by the count of Flanders led to an uprising of the Flemings in which the count was expelled. The count of Flanders was a vassal of the king of France, and when the latter attempted to reinstate him the Flemish rebels appealed to the English. The Avignon papacy, usually sensitive to the desires of the French kings, imposed a fine on the Flemish merchants unless they should receive their lawful ruler peaceably. Thereupon Edward III of England was persuaded to put forward his claim to be the lawful ruler of France in order to release his Flemish friends from the papal charge of rebellion.

Edward's claim to the throne of France was purely a diplomatic move; rivalry over fishing grounds had long existed between French and English sailors in the English Channel and the North Sea and actual hostilities had broken out. When Edward III quartered the lilies of France on his shield and set out to conquer his inheritance, he was reviving a very doubtful right. His father Edward II had married a daughter of Philip the Fair of France. Philip's three sons ruled successively and all died without direct male heirs, leaving the French the choice of accepting descent through a female or shifting to a collateral branch of the royal family and choosing Philip of Valois, a nephew of Philip the Fair. Philip of Valois was selected, and Edward III recognized him as king of France and did homage for his French fiefs. When the Flemish revolt gave him the opportunity, Edward changed his mind and argued his claim to the French throne through Philip the Fair's daughter. When the French king assembled a fleet to sweep the English sailors from the disputed seas, Edward caught the French fleet in the harbor of Sluys and destroyed it (1340). The English king thus had the initial advantage of control of the seas, and prepared to invade France.

Edward could count on the support of every important class in England. The clergy were resentful of the influence the French were presumed to have over the papacy at Avignon, the merchants wished their trade with Flanders and Aquitaine secured, the yeomen (small landowners) profited from having the Flemish market open to English wool, and the feudal knights and barons looked forward to a fine field for adventure and ransom-collecting. Edward furthermore had the rudiments of a royal and national army, thanks to his predecessors' foresighted policy of commuting feudal military service to money payment, and it was an army equipped with a distinctively English weapon—the longbow. The English had been experimenting with the longbow against the Welsh and the Scots and developed suitable tactics to go with it. Archery was a national pastime in England, and the English yeoman was the master of his weapon through practice from boyhood. The longbow had a range of about three hundred yards, and could pierce armor at one hundred; it had a tremendous advantage over the crossbow as a missile weapon because of the rapid fire that could be maintained. The successful tactics developed by the English required close co-ordination between knights and archers; the former were dismounted and placed in the center to invite the charge of the feudal cavalry, with the yeoman along the flanks to pour their deadly hail of arrows into the advancing enemy ranks.

The English invaders won a spectacular success when Edward met a French force at the battle of Crecy (1346). The havoc wrought by the longbow was almost incredible; French losses ran into many thousands, including several hundred knights, while the English casualties numbered two or three score. The celebrated French chronicler, Froissart, a devout admirer of chivalry, records the success of the longbow at Crecy, tells how the English went on to capture the port of Calais, and then relates the second and equally overwhelming success of the longbow at Poitiers, when the capture of the French king paved the way for the treaty of Brétigny in 1360. Edward was granted full sovereignty over his French possessions.

Less picturesque records than Froissart's chronicle tell of the devastating effects of the Black Death, the epidemic of bubonic plague which ravaged Europe in 1348–50, killing more than a third of the population in England, ruining the nascent cloth industry, and producing a labor shortage which led workers to demand higher wages. Parliament enacted a price control and maximum wage act (Statute of Laborers), but it proved unenforceable, and landowners began to enclose their fields for sheep-raising, which required fewer laborers.

The Black Death in Italy was described in a well known book. Readers of Boccaccio will remember that he represents the gallants and ladies of his *Decameron* meeting in a church of Florence and going thence to the country to while away their time with storytelling while the Black Death raged in Florence. The *Decameron* belonged to the movement to use the vernacular which Dante started when he wrote *The Divine Comedy* in the Tuscan dialect. Boccaccio's friend, Petrarch, who was a lad of seventeen when Dante died, contributed to the movement poetry in the sonnet form. Petrarch, however, developed an interest in Latin literature which he shared with Boccaccio, and both men came to regard their work in the vernacular as much less important than the revival of the Roman cult of *humanitas,* that is, admiration of the literature of the Greeks, and collection of their writings, works of art, gems, and coins. Petrarch wrote letters to dead authors in a Latin he hoped was Ciceronian, and fired his followers with enthusiasm for finding manuscripts of Greek and Latin authors that lay neglected in monastery libraries. Chaucer, journeying to Italy, seems to have met Petrarch; the Englishman borrowed Petrarch's poetical devices and Boccaccio's diverting stories, but the movement of humanism was not transferred to England for many years.

The intellectual life of the English proceeded along traditional lines. At Oxford, where the Franciscans were leaders in scholarship, the inquisitive Roger Bacon was followed in Wycliffe's time by the invincible debater, William of Occam, a nominalist. William of Occam declared the church was a man-made institution; that the pope could err and should be corrected by laymen. He went further and denounced the whole doctrine of an ordered universe of which the papacy for centuries had been the recognized guardian. He denounced the wealth and corruption of the clergy.

The second Avignon pope, John XXII, got into a quarrel with the Franciscans, and some of them, including William of Occam, sought refuge at the court of the Emperor, Louis the Bavarian, who had refused to recognize the election of John. Refugee scholars were utilized to write attacks upon papal claims. The most famous pamphlet to issue from the group was Marsiglio of Padua's *Defensor Pacis,* which revived the classical theory that the original source of governmental power is the people who delegate it to a ruler and may withdraw it. Marsiglio claimed that authority in the church resided in the people and was exercised through general councils, and that the pope was chosen by the clergy as their head for ecclesiastical purposes only and had no temporal power. A number of years later arguments to the same end, though based on different premises, were uttered by Wycliffe in his crowded lecture room in Oxford and were applauded.

English society in the latter half of the fourteenth century had been profoundly changed by the war. Wages had risen, war profits had enriched the class that provided war materials and goods formerly imported from France, and the fighters had profited by ransoms and pillage. A strong anti-clerical spirit was growing, for the popes as Frenchmen were under suspicion, the Avignon popes had greatly increased the efficiency of papal machinery for attracting money, and papal provisions (nominations) of Frenchmen to English benefices were a growing grievance. Prosperity created a secular atmosphere, and attacks on the Curia were popular. In 1351 parliament passed the Statute of Provisors, to prevent appointment of foreign clerics to English sees, and two years later, the Statute of Praemunire, to prohibit ecclesiastical appeals out of the kingdom. Within a few years an English poem, *Piers the Plowman,* expressed the grievances of the peasants against both state and church, and agitators went about the land preaching social equality.

Similar conditions existed in France, where the Black Death had been as calamitous as in England and Italy. John II, a king who was the ideal of chivalric behavior but a great waster of public funds, faced a revolt of the merchants of Paris led by its richest citizen, Etienne Marcel, in 1355. The king was forced to promise that he would levy no new demands for money without consulting the Estates of the Realm and that he would allow them to direct the expenditure of the money. The following year Edward III's son, the Black Prince, defeated John at Poitiers and took him and his sons prisoner. During the king's imprisonment Etienne Marcel attempted

PLATE XIX

Fourteenth Century

FIGURE 1. *Portion of a page from a manuscript of Wycliffe's Bible, in the New York Public Library. The archaic English can be understood today. This manuscript was produced in the lifetime of men who knew Wycliffe.*
[*From the Wycliffe Bible. Courtesy of the New York Public Library*]

FIGURE 2. *Devotional image carved from wood, representing Christ and St. John. This is a sample of fourteenth century German art which expresses the mysticism that spread in Germany after the Black Death. The group is isolated from the dramatic scene of the Last Supper and brought close to the individual, who can, in a mystical way, identify himself with John and share the bliss of resting on Christ's bosom.*

FIGURE 3. *Marienburg Castle in Prussia, the stronghold of the Teutonic knights. This was one of the most elaborate and formidable of the German castles. The building to the left of the round towers is the castle of the Grand Master; the large building to the right is the High Castle, part of which dates back to the thirteenth century. The castle withstood a number of sieges, including one by the Poles in 1410.*

FIGURE 4. *Cathedral of Palma, on the island of Majorca. Most of the Gothic churches of Spain were designed by Frenchmen, but a Catalan who was a native of Majorca designed several which were definitely Spanish in character. Besides the Cathedral of Palma he built the cathedrals of Barcelona and Gerona, and the Church of Santa Maria del Mar in Barcelona. They are all remarkable for daring height and breadth of nave, and for austere simplicity of structure.*
[*From* The Cathedral of Palma de Mallorca: An Architectural Study *by Ralph Adams Cram. The Medieval Academy of America, Cambridge, Mass.*]

PLATE XX

Fourteenth Century

FIGURE 1. *The careful recording of a historical event: a banquet given in 1377 by Charles V of France (the Wise) to his uncle, the Emperor Charles IV, and the emperor's eldest son, Wenceslas, king of the Romans. The Archbishop of Reims sits at the left, then the emperor, the French king, Wenceslas, and two ecclesiastics. The chronicle tells how, between courses, a curtain was drawn aside and a boat appeared, moved along as if sailed by two men inside. At the bow were twelve crusaders, and in the stern Peter the Hermit. Then a curtain at the other end of the table was drawn back, disclosing the wall of Jerusalem, with a muezzin calling the devout to prayer, and Saracen forces at the top. The crusaders leaped from the ship and proceeded to erect scaling ladders and fight with the Saracens. This scene from the first crusade was chosen because Charles the Wise was planning to urge the emperor to proclaim a new crusade. The artist has followed customary usage and represented the crusaders in the dress and equipment of his own century.*

[*From a manuscript in Bibliothèque nationale, Paris*]

FIGURE 2. *Ivory relief in the Metropolitan Museum of Art showing a tournament. Note the courtly realism of the scene at a time when court life showed extreme elaboration; the costume of the ladies; the equipment of the jousters.*

[*Courtesy of the Metropolitan Museum of Art, New York*]

to establish a parliamentary rule in France by the Estates General, but his reforms were too radical and pushed too fast. The prestige of the monarchy was strong, and Marcel's reliance on the support of the Parisian mob led to his assassination by his more conservative wealthy colleagues. Ransom raising and war taxation added to the burdens of the people already hard-pressed by pillage and the losses of the Black Death, and caused a peasant rebellion (Jacquerie).

Shortly after the English claims to Calais and southwestern France were recognized in the treaty of Brétigny, the duchy of Burgundy reverted to the French crown, but instead of being added to the royal domain it was granted to one of the king's sons. His marriage to the heiress of the count of Flanders made Burgundy a formidable fief for the king of France, and later marriages added lands in the Low Countries (Netherlands) to the Burgundian holdings. Charles V (The Wise) succeeded his father as king of France in 1364 and shrewdly regained financial control from the Estates General. Besides strengthening the administration he reorganized the army and navy. He had not the physique to be a fighter and he lacked any fine chivalric notions. His lack of chivalric nonsense was shared by Bertrand du Guesclin, whom Charles made Constable (commander-in-chief). Much military progress was made under Bertrand by the use of guerilla tactics against the English, and as the French navy was able to cut off English supplies, the English forces were driven out of France, except for a few ports on the English Channel.

During the last decades of the fourteenth century activity in the Hundred Years' War lagged; more pressing affairs created a distraction. In 1377 Edward III died, and his neurotic grandson Richard II became king; and since Richard was not of age, his uncle, John of Gaunt, Duke of Lancaster, governed in his name, with the assistance of parliament. In 1380 Charles VI succeeded his father as king of France, and as he was subject to fits of insanity, France was ruled by his uncles, under whom the country fell into disorder that led to civil war. When an Avignon pope who had gone to Rome on a visit died there the papacy entered a period of crisis. The Romans elected an Italian to succeed him, but the cardinals at Avignon elected another French pope; and as each pope had supporters, the Great Schism was created which lasted into the next century. With two men claiming to be pope, Christendom was in evil case.

The subject of papal provisions was frequently discussed in England; Wycliffe lectured in Oxford and preached in London against the temporal power of the clergy and violently denounced the Great Schism. Wycliffe's ideas were politically useful to John of Gaunt, who protected the preacher when the clerical party the duke opposed brought Wycliffe to trial for preaching the ideas of Marsiglio of Padua and other opponents of the papacy. The trial came to nothing, and Wycliffe's ideas progressed from one position to another in the direction of heresy. At this time he began sending out his poor priests to preach the faith, and embarked upon his translation of the Bible. John of Gaunt was not troubled about Wycliffe's idea that priests were not necessary to mediate between the individual and God, but when Wycliffe began to deny that the sacraments were essential and to question transubstantiation, the duke withdrew his support.

Wycliffe was again cited for trial as a heretic in 1381, the year of the Peasants' Revolt. There had been extensive emancipation of the peasants in England from feudal dues because the lords had found paid free labor more efficient. Unable, however, to keep wages down following the Black Death, the nobles tried to compel the peasants to go back to performing services for their holdings instead of paying money as rent. Since commutation of services for money payments had been going on for generations, wide dissatisfaction ensued. Enactment of a poll tax was another grievance, and peasants began rioting and attacking castles in order to burn the old records. A formidable number marched on London, but the young king tricked the leaders into submission and hanged them; the remaining peasants dispersed to their homes, where the nobles were permitted to wreak a bloody vengeance. Wycliffe's poor preachers, known as the Lollards, were accused of having helped stir up the rising. His trial led to his withdrawal to his parish, but no further action was taken against him, and he died in peace at Lutterworth. His ideas had spread among all classes, and were carried into Bohemia by some of the Czechs who had come to England for the marriage of Anne of Bohemia to King Richard II. There they were to work a ferment in the mind of a Czech professor, John Huss, who became a notable martyr in the next century. College professors now and then make history.

The world of Wycliffe was one in which many currents of

thought were abroad. Wycliffe's fellow-countryman, Geoffrey Chaucer, some ten years his junior, enriched English style and left unforgettable pictures of the life of the people of the fourteenth century. Petrarch and Boccaccio had inaugurated a classical revival in Italy before they died, a few years before Wycliffe's first attack upon papal provisions (c. 1376). The Great Schism of the papacy left a legacy of trouble to plague Christians in the next century and encouraged heretics. For the most part the fourteenth century bequeathed problems of destruction to the fifteenth, for much of the Hundred Years' War remained to be fought. A constructive feature in England, however, was the custom, which became permanent during the Hundred Years' War, of summoning knights and burgesses to attend the Great Council of the Realm. They developed the habit of deliberating together, apart from the bishops and peers, and a parliament of two houses was beginning to form rules and establish precedents which gave it an important place in English life.

[THE FOURTEENTH CENTURY]

Readings

John Wycliffe

BULL OF POPE GREGORY XI, AGAINST JOHN WYCLIFFE *

[This bull admirably illustrates the attitude of the papacy toward heresy. Note that the tares are not to be allowed to grow along with the wheat until the harvest. The connection made between Wycliffe's ideas and those of the *Defensor Pacis* is significant. Wycliffe's answer to the summons of a later pope shows his dauntless spirit.]

Gregory, bishop, servant of the servants of God, to his beloved sons the chancellor and University of Oxford, in the diocese of Lincoln, grace and apostolic benediction.

We are compelled to wonder and grieve that you, who, in consideration of the favors and privileges conceded to your university of Oxford by the apostolic see, and on account of your familiarity with the Scriptures, in whose sea you navigate, by the gift of God, with auspicious oar, you, who ought to be, as it were, warriors and champions of the orthodox faith, without which there is no salvation of souls,—that you through a certain sloth and neglect allow tares to spring up amidst the pure wheat in the fields of your glorious university aforesaid; and what is still more pernicious, even continue to grow to maturity. And you are quite careless, as has been lately reported to us, as to the extirpation of these tares; with no little clouding of a bright name, danger to your souls, contempt of the Roman church, and injury to the faith above mentioned. And what pains us the more is that this increase of the tares aforesaid is known in Rome before the remedy of extirpation has been

* From University of Pennsylvania, *Translations and Reprints*, II, No. 5. Reprinted by permission of The University of Pennsylvania Press.

[313]

applied in England where they sprang up. By the insinuation of many, if they are indeed worthy of belief, deploring it deeply, it has come to our ears that John de Wycliffe, rector of the church of Lutterworth, in the diocese of Lincoln, Professor of the Sacred Scriptures, (would that he were not also Master of Errors,) has fallen into such a detestable madness that he does not hesitate to dogmatize and publicly preach, or rather vomit forth from the recesses of his breast certain propositions and conclusions which are erroneous and false. He has cast himself also into the depravity of preaching heretical dogmas which strive to subvert and weaken the state of the whole church and even secular polity, some of which doctrines, in changed terms, it is true, seem to express the perverse opinions and unlearned learning of Marsilio of Padua of cursed memory, and of John of Jandun, whose book is extant, rejected and cursed by our predecessor, Pope John XXII, of happy memory. This he has done in the kingdom of England, lately glorious in its power and in the abundance of its resources, but more glorious still in the glistening piety of its faith, and in the distinction of its sacred learning; producing also many men illustrious for their exact knowledge of the holy Scriptures, mature in the gravity of their character, conspicuous in devotion, defenders of the catholic church. He has polluted certain of the faithful of Christ by besprinkling them with these doctrines, and led them away from the right paths of the aforesaid faith to the brink of perdition.

Wherefore, since we are not willing, nay, indeed, ought not to be willing, that so deadly a pestilence should continue to exist with our connivance, a pestilence which, if it is not opposed in its beginnings, and torn out by the roots in its entirety, will be reached too late by medicines when it has infected very many with its contagion; we command your university with strict admonition, by the apostolic authority, in virtue of your sacred obedience, and under penalty of the deprivation of all the favors, indulgences, and privileges granted to you and your university by the said see, for the future not to permit to be asserted or set forth to any extent whatever, the opinions, conclusions, and propositions which are in variance with good morals and faith, even when those setting them forth strive to defend them under a certain fanciful wresting of words or of terms. Moreover, you are on our authority to arrest the said John, or cause him to be arrested and to send him under a trustworthy guard to our venerable brother, the Archbishop of Canterbury, and the Bishop of London, or to one of them.

Besides, if there should be, which God forbid, in your university, subject to your jurisdiction, opponents stained with these errors, and if they should obstinately persist in them, proceed vigorously and earnestly to a similar arrest and removal of them, and otherwise as shall seem good to you. Be vigilant to repair your negligence which you have hitherto shown in the premises, and so obtain our gratitude and favor, and that of the said see, besides the honor and reward of the divine recompense.

Given at Rome, at Santa Maria Maggiore, on the 31st of May, the sixth year of our pontificate. [1377]

WYCLIFFE'S REPLY TO THE SUMMONS OF POPE URBAN VI TO APPEAR IN ROME, 1384*

I have joy fully to tell what I hold, to all true men that believe and especially to the Pope; for I suppose that if my faith be rightful and given of God, the Pope will gladly confirm it; and if my faith be error, the Pope will wisely amend it.

I suppose over this that the gospel of Christ be heart of the corps of God's law; for I believe that Jesus Christ, that gave in his own person this gospel, is very God and very man, and by this heart passes all other laws.

I suppose over this that the Pope be most obliged to the keeping of the gospel among all men that live here; for the Pope is highest vicar that Christ has here in earth. For moreness of Christ's vicar is not measured by worldly moreness, but by this, that this vicar follows more Christ by virtuous living; for thus teacheth the gospel, that this is the sentence of Christ.

And of this gospel I take as believe, that Christ for time that he walked here, was most poor man of all, both in spirit and in having; for Christ says that he had nought for to rest his head on. And Paul says that he was made needy for our love. And more poor might no man be, neither bodily nor in spirit. And thus Christ put from him all manner of worldly lordship. For the gospel of John telleth that when they would have made Christ king, he fled and hid him from them, for he would none such worldly highness.

And over this I take it as believe, that no man should follow the Pope, nor no saint that is now in heaven, but in as much as he

---

* From University of Pennsylvania, *Translations and Reprints*, II, No. 5. Reprinted by permission of The University of Pennsylvania Press.

follows Christ. For John and James erred when they coveted worldly highness; and Peter and Paul sinned also when they denied and blasphemed in Christ; but men should not follow them in this, for then they went from Jesus Christ. And this I take as wholesome counsel, that the Pope leave his worldly lordship to worldly lords, as Christ gave them,—and move speedily all his clerks to do so. For thus did Christ, and taught thus his disciples, till the fiend had blinded this world. And it seems to some men that clerks that dwell lastingly in this error against God's law, and flee to follow Christ in this, been open heretics, and their fautors been partners.

And if I err in this sentence, I will meekly be amended, yea, by the death, if it be skilful, for that I hope were good to me. And if I might travel in mine own person, I would with good will go to the Pope. But God has needed me to the contrary, and taught me more obedience to God than to men. And I suppose of our Pope that he will not be Antichrist, and reverse Christ in this working, to the contrary of Christ's will; for if he summon against reason, by him or by any of his, and pursue this unskilful summoning, he is an open Antichrist. And merciful intent excused not Peter, that Christ should not clepe him Satan; so blind intent and wicked

COAT OF ARMS OF EDWARD III

(From *A Student's History of England* by Samuel R. Gardiner. Longmans Green, London, 1897.)

counsel excuses not the Pope here; but if he ask of true priests that they travel more than they may, he is not excused by reason of God, that he should not be Antichrist. For our belief teaches us that our blessed God suffers us not to be tempted more than we may; how should a man ask such service? And therefore pray we to God for our pope Urban the sixth, that his old holy intent be not quenched by his enemies. And Christ, that may not lie, says that the enemies of a man been especially his home family; and this is sooth of men and fiends.

PART XI

The Fifteenth Century

CHRONOLOGY

1400 Death of Chaucer
1405 Death of Timur the Lame
1410 Battle of Tannenberg; military power of Teutonic Knights broken
1414 Council of Constance
1415 Execution of John Huss
1438 Pragmatic Sanction of Bourges
1440 Lorenzo Valla demonstrates the forgery of the Donation of Constantine
c. 1441 Thomas à Kempis's *Imitation of Christ*
c. 1450 Printing developed in the Germanies
1453 Fall of Constantinople to the Turks
1454 Beginning of Wars of Roses—dynastic and civil conflict in England
1455 Gutenberg's printed Bible
1476 Setting up of Caxton's press in England
1480 Ivan III of Russia ends Tartar suzerainty
1485 Bosworth Field and establishment of Tudors in England; Caxton's edition of Malory's *Morte d'Arthur*
1486-8 Portuguese sailors round the Cape of Good Hope
1492 Fall of Granada; Columbus' first voyage to the Indies

PART XI

The Fifteenth Century

~~~~~~

THE fifteenth was emphatically the townsman's century. The rigid framework of the three estates was giving way: and a member of the third estate, if he were a merchant and sufficiently rich, might play the part of a great noble. The noble had justified his dominance by his defense of the people, but the triumph of the archer in the Hundred Year's War had·invalidated his claim. When in the course of the fifteenth century artillery could batter down the feudal stronghold, where formerly a noble's peasants could find refuge, his social value was gone. His ability to survive now depended upon his firm hold on the land and those who tilled it. Kings, henceforth dependent on mercenary troops in war rather than feudal levies, turned to those who had money for funds to pay soldiers. In earlier days the Jews, barred from trade, had monopolized money-lending, as the church forbade Christians to accept interest. Ways had been devised of circumventing the ban, however, and in fifteenth-century Italy banking on a large scale was being carried on by prominent families grown rich in trade. Jacques Coeur introduced the custom into France.

The great prosperity of the Italian city states focused attention on Italy. These city states inaugurated a political device of great importance and of special interest today. Weary of the warfare caused by interurban rivalries, Italian towns began forming leagues in the interest of peace on a federative principle. With the French invasions of Italy which began at the end of the fifteenth century they became organizations of defense. The rulers of England, France, and Spain were not slow to borrow this idea of leagues which, adorned by high-sounding phrases, such as Holy League, might be used to further aims of national aggrandizement.

The municipal institutions of the medieval city state had, by the fifteenth century, undergone a considerable transformation. Originally the town population of the commercial cities had been made up of free men, that is, men free from the personal dependence that characterized the three primary classes of feudal society. This freedom from feudal intrusions had been maintained in the towns, frequently by royal charter, but by the fifteenth century changes within urban society were producing tyranny. With the great increase of wealth in the towns, a natural differentiation among the citizens occurred: at the top was a very small group of extremely wealthy men, merchants or bankers or both; next was the middle class whose members made up the craft guilds and managed small scale industries or retail trade; and at the bottom was the increasing class of wage earners who worked for the other two groups. The government of cities tended toward oligarchy because the wealthiest class, which generally was composed of the most enterprising and most influential members of the population, took the lead in winning charters of independence and self-government for the communes. Since the prosperity of the wealthy class depended on a vast expansion of commerce, efforts were made to break down the monopolistic guild system, and this led the guilds to demand, and frequently obtain, a share in the government. The wage earners resorted to the organization of guilds of their own and demanded a share of political power; there was no individual representation in the self-governing communes of the middle ages, but only representation through a corporation. In the long run the wage earners never succeeded in winning any permanent place in the government beside their richer fellows. This was demonstrated in the fate of such uprisings as the Peasants' Revolt in England, the Jacquerie in France, and numerous revolts in the towns of Flanders and Germany about the same period.

Two trends were at work in urban political life: a recognition of the value of capable leadership by an oligarchy of the wealthy, and an insistence on the democratic principle of individual rights. In any but the most primitive self-government a delegation of rights or powers is necessary to create a functioning organization. The townsmen as a whole, represented through their guilds, were the source of

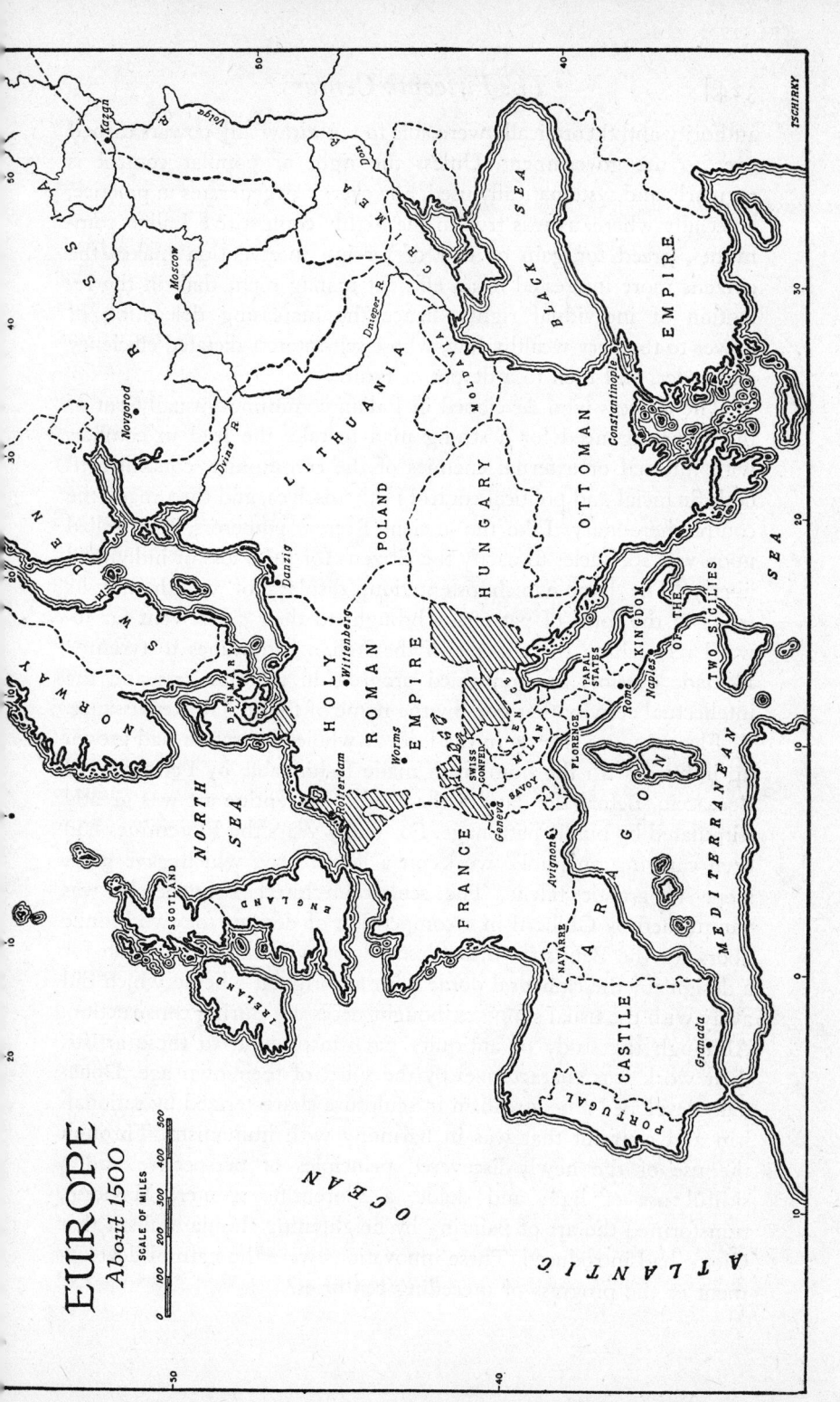

authority and theoretically were able to withdraw any powers turned over to the government. Unless the right of popular control is regularly and systematically used, however, it degenerates in practice, especially where, as was true in the highly competitive Italian communes, greed for gain or fear of foreign intervention makes the citizens more interested in an efficient management than in the retention of individual rights—hence the increasing delegation of power to the very wealthy few, whose self-interest dictated efficiency and order, and then to a despot or tyrant.

The despots who developed in Italian communes, usually out of the recurring need for a strong man to take the lead in conflicts with internal or external enemies of the community, concentrated both financial and political control in themselves, and then made the control hereditary. Like the ancient Roman emperors, they relied upon vast spectacles to pacify the citizens for their loss of individual liberty. The fame which ostentatious displays of wealth and its fruits in the form of patronage brought to their cities went far toward reconciling the citizens of the Italian communes to tyranny. It made possible the continued progress in the fine arts and the intellectual activity that goes by the name of the Italian Renaissance.

Florence was already in the lead. A whole generation had grown up imbued with the humanism made fashionable by Petrarch and Boccaccio. Before the days of the Medici Florentine art was greatly stimulated by public patronage. For many years the Florentines had been carrying on public works in a lavish way, which gave great scope to artistic talent. The sculptor-architect Brunelleschi was vanquished by Ghiberti in a competition of designs for two bronze doors for the Baptistry. Brunelleschi later won the competition for a design for the cathedral dome with an original scheme which did away with the usual supports thought necessary during construction. Although the study of antiquity gave inspiration to these artists, their work was characterizel by the spirit of their own age. Donatello developed a new realism in sculpture characterized by rationalism and restraint that was in harmony with humanism. Through the use of the newly-discovered principles of perspective and a skilful use of light and shade, a Florentine painter, Masaccio, transformed the art of painting by heightening the naturalism that Giotto had introduced. These innovations were the natural development of the progress of preceding centuries.

The Fifteenth Century   [325

Flemish towns contributed to painting the technique of oil as a medium, and methods developed in the art of illumination; the dukes of Burgundy and other magnates, including the Avignon popes, aided these developments by their patronage. From Flanders came also elaborations of music comparable in spirit to the flamboyant Gothic of the new town architecture. In German cities as well as in the Netherlands municipal pride expressed itself in the founding of universities, to which the wandering scholars who flocked to Italy brought back new fashions in learning. Among the Germans there was much progress in metallurgy and the mechanical arts; the high point was the perfection of the art of printing from movable types. Block printing had long been known and from it developed the arts of wood engraving and, later, copperplate engraving.

Leonardo da Vinci, whose career extended into the sixteenth century, exemplified the combination of the thinker capable of dealing with abstractions and the practical inventor. He stated the problems of dynamics and made progress in statics; at the same time, using his creative imagination, he made a wide range of inventions. It is impossible to say whether all the drawings in his notebooks were of original inventions; it is probable that some, perhaps many, represented devices already in use. Some, like his flyer for spindles, were capable of immediate practical application; others needed perfecting.

On the other side of the picture an increased preoccupation with the devil and his angels produced the revolting excesses of the witch persecutions. The special interest in diabolism at this time has been variously explained as an aftermath of the Black Death, or consequences of the disputations of the schoolmen, or an extension of the repression of heresy. Attempts have been made to prove that the witch persecutions were caused by actual survivals of ancient fertility rites, but the weight of evidence indicates that those who actually practiced witchcraft or sorcery did so for profit or with the hope of injuring their enemies, and that many of the victims were either sufferers from psychic disorders or innocent persons who confessed to escape further torture. The outbreak of persecutions followed the church councils summoned in the first part of the fifteenth century in the hope of ending the Great Schism. The period of church councils, or conciliar movement, was marked by discussions about the relative powers of pope and council—discussions in which arguments were brought forth that were of transcendent importance and which are of great interest today, because the question was one of sovereignty. The councils tried to establish the principle that the authority of a representative assembly of the church was above the undivided authority of the pope. The failure of the movement led to the Reformation and the papacy as it exists today.

With the ending of the schism the popes took control, dropped the reform program of the conciliar movement, but pushed heresy hunting by the Inquisition, which was put into the hands of the Dominicans. As witches were considered heretics, the Inquisition was also entrusted with the prosecution of witchcraft. A papal bull directed attention to witchcraft, and two inquisitors published the *Malleus Maleficarum,* which provided a formula for trials which made the conviction of an accused person a foregone conclusion. In city after city neighbor accused neighbor, and thousands of men, women, boys, and girls under torture confessed the practice, incriminated others, and were burned at the stake. The madness died down only after accusations spread to the magistrate who enforced the penalties. Witchcraft trials continued, sporadically, into the seventeenth century, spreading even to America.

It has been suggested that the activities of the Inquisition may explain the failure of fifteenth-century thinkers to make more progress in investigating natural phenomena. The fifteenth was a barren century in the field of pure science; it did, however, produce tools which were to promote scientific progress in the next hundred years. Mathematics began to come into its own with the rise of large-scale business. Urban life created a demand for a more exact measurement of time, and watches and clocks were perfected. Other forms of measurement were developed in connection with seafaring and had speedy results. The cheapness of water transport had led the Venetians and Genoese to trade with England and Flanders by sea, sending fleets that coasted along Spain and France. Charts, worked out from observation and soundings, laid the foundations of accurate map-making. The map-maker Toscanelli measured the height of the sun. The compass, which had long been known, was fitted to enable a helmsman to keep his course. Charts, compass, and other devices made it possible to sail a straight course in cloudy weather out of sight of land. Atlantic island groups—the Canaries, the Ma-

The Fifteenth Century

deiras, and the Azores—were occupied and became outposts of European expansion. After the Ottoman Turks in the East occupied the regions where the trade-routes lay, and became masters of Constantinople, the prices of Oriental goods increased. It was inevitable that the Western nations should look for new routes to the fabulous sources of wealth in the East, and before the century ended a Genoese seaman had found for the Spanish rulers the continent that barred the way via the West, and Portuguese seamen had reached the East by sailing south around Africa.

Two notable townsmen faithfully reflect the chief trends of the fifteenth century. The French merchant Jacques Coeur, who helped to introduce into his country large scale banking and merchant enterprise on the Italian model, illustrated the emancipation of the enterprising townsman and the importance of trade with the East. Lorenzo dei Medici, scion of a family of merchant princes, a patron of humanists and artists, a collector of books, and a writer of songs, lived his life in Florence during some of the most colorful days of the Italian Renaissance.

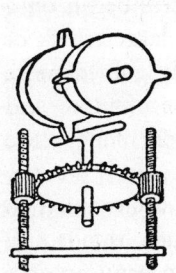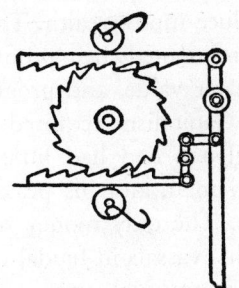

LEONARDO DA VINCI'S DEVICES FOR WHEEL AND PINIONS, SWINGING AND ROTARY MOTION, AND GEARS

(By permission from *History of Mechanical Inventions* by Abbott Payson Usher, copyright, 1929, by McGraw-Hill Book Co., Inc.)

CHAPTER 19

The World of Jacques Coeur

[c. 1395–1456]

~~~~~~~~~~~~~~~~~~~~~~~~~~~~~~~~~~~~~

JACQUES COEUR was a French merchant who was born about ten years after Wycliffe's peaceful death at Lutterworth. His extraordinary career demonstrates the social and economic changes that brought in the modern world, for the transformation of society which had been slowly preparing for some centuries was accomplished by the last half of the fifteenth century. The change was wrought by the accelerated development of capitalism, which is best defined as the use of wealth to produce more wealth. The process began on a wide scale when traders reinvested their profits in a larger stock of goods or in goods of greater value, and progressively gained more profits for reinvestment. Capitalism required the use of more and more money. The feudal age had had little use for money; the landed man was the rich man, and his peasants provided for the greater part of his needs. The only money he was accustomed to handle was that paid by his vassals in feudal dues, such as aids and reliefs. When he needed an unusual sum, on such an occasion as a crusade, he was forced to borrow it from the merchants in the towns. Here more and more wealth was accumulated as the demand for the rich goods from the East developed and as property increased in value; and in the towns the amount of money in circulation increased enormously. Guild halls were built in the new Flamboyant Gothic style, which threw off the restraint of the thirteenth-century Gothic, and towns redoubled their rivalry in the building of churches and cathedrals which would testify to their prosperity.

The cities which first showed the effects of this new prosperity were in Italy. Venice had maintained its trade with Constantinople. Florence, which had grown rich through the finishing of fine cloth, minted a new gold coin, the florin, which became a widely used standard of value because the Florentines never debased their coinage as kings were wont to do. In Florence and Venice and in the Lombard towns the art of banking developed extensively and great banking families rose to prominence. Jacques Coeur was the first Frenchman to see the possibilities of combining banking and trade. The son of a merchant, he established direct French trade with the Levant and amassed an enormous fortune. He owned silver, lead, and copper mines, a silk factory, and a paper mill; he had great fleets on the seas and agents everywhere. He loaned money to governments, more often than not for war purposes—wars had become expensive because of the use of mercenary troops.

The feudal army had never been an effective one because its members were free to return home when their brief terms of service expired. By the fourteenth century its effectiveness had been further diminished by the growing tendency to concentrate on the capture of conspicuous enemies who could be held for ransom, as is made clear in the pages of the admiring Froissart. As has been pointed out, the longbow of the English yeoman sealed the doom of the feudal fighting-man. Gunpowder, although at first used largely to frighten horses, was soon to batter down feudal strongholds. The victorious armies of the future were to be mercenary armies paid from the royal purse, captained by seasoned adventurers, and living at the expense of the inhabitants of invaded countries.

Since the Hundred Years' War was fought on French soil, it was the French peasants who suffered, but in both France and England the merchant class profited. In fact, the war was so profitable that its renewal under Henry V of England, after internal English political difficulties had been overcome, was very popular. During the regency of John of Gaunt for King Richard II, concessions to parliamentary consultation in the government had been made. When Richard later tried to disregard parliament and rule according to his own whims it deposed him and made his cousin, John of Gaunt's son Henry, king of England (1399). Since parliament a century earlier had deposed Edward II also, the double precedent enhanced its prestige, and both Henry V and Henry VI allowed it to increase its power because they owed to it their possession of the crown. Because of the exigencies of the war parliament had, during the fourteenth century, secured general acceptance of its right of impeachment and the principle that no new taxes were to be levied without parliamentary consent. Under Henry IV and Henry V it became customary to vote taxes on the last day of a session, making redress of grievances precede the granting of supply. This was the weapon that eventually gave the English parliament an importance attained by no other medieval estates.

Henry V (1414-1422), a born fighter, took advantage of French internal difficulties to renew the Hundred Years' War. Sporadic civil war in France had resulted from the attempts of the chief relatives of the mad Charles VI to secure control of the king's person and therewith of the royal government. The two chief factions were the Burgundians and the Armagnacs, but something more than family rivalry was involved in the conflict, because the former to a certain extent represented the interests of town industry in northern France and Flanders and the latter the predominantly agricultural interests of the south. The renewed English invasion of northern France was followed by the overwhelming defeat of the French at Agincourt, and a few years later the treaty of Troyes (1420) was concluded between the English and the Burgundian faction, disinheriting Charles VI's son as illegitimate and making Henry V heir to the kingdom of France. Henry V's infant son succeeded him as Henry VI in 1422, and when Charles VI died that same year Henry VI was proclaimed king of France as well.

The French south of the Loire, however, where English troops had not penetrated, recognized Charles VI's son as Charles VII (1422). The powerful duke of Burgundy continued to support the English, and Charles VII made no effort to secure his throne until he was forced to it by a rising tide of French patriotism symbolized by a young peasant girl, Joan of Arc. During her brief career (1428-31) the French army was led to victory and Charles VII's coronation celebrated at Rheims. Once the French king's crown was secure, he allowed Joan to be captured by the Burgundians, who turned her over to the English, by whom she was tried for witchcraft before an ecclesiastical court and burned at the stake. Roused from his lethargy, Charles won over the duke of Burgundy and organized a standing army to take the place of the feudal levies. He made Jacques Coeur master of the mint, put him in charge of the royal expenditures, and permitted him to make far-reaching financial reforms. Charles sent him on several embassies, and borrowed huge

The World of Jacques Coeur [331

sums to pay the expenses of a series of campaigns by which the English were finally driven from France. It was largely by the French artillery, against which the much vaunted English longbow was at a disadvantage, that the English were expelled from all France but Calais.

While the resources of France and England were being expended in warfare, the fruits of centuries of intellectual and artistic activity continued to be garnered in the city-states of Italy. Petrarch's disciples made humanism the intellectual fashion of the day. They were called to the courts of despots who saw a new way of enhancing their prestige, and through the influence of humanists rulers made collections of ancient works of art, coins, gems, and books. Pope Nicholas V was one of the patrons of learning. Among his proteges was Lorenzo Valla, who had exposed as a forgery the Donation of Constantine, basis of proud papal claims—a feat of scholarship which led the humanist pope Nicholas V to employ him to seek for manuscripts. Some of the Italian despots employed humanists to teach their children, and a new kind of education based on the old Greek idea of training the body as well as the mind was developed. New universities devoted to humanistic studies were founded, and to them came noted teachers. The study of Greek was accelerated by the arrival at Florence in 1396 of Manuel Chrysoloras who taught there several years and placed Greek studies on a firm foundation in Italy.

It was inevitable that this new movement should be carried beyond the Alps through the medium of wandering scholars. Unconscious preparations were being made in Germany; a movement of mysticism which had been started by a contemporary of Dante, Meister Eckhardt, took the form of educational organizations, such as the Friends of God and the Brethren of the Common Lot. They maintained schools where simple piety was taught and also a better Latin than was then current. Many students trained in these schools were prepared to take up humanistic studies. When they traveled to Italy and fell under the spell of the humanists they were more likely than not to be attracted to the circle of a celebrated Florentine, Pico della Mirandola, who thought Hebrew as worthy of study as the other ancient tongues. The success of German workmen experimenting with block books led after a long period of preparation to the perfection of the art of printing from movable types.

Thus the method of perpetuating corrected versions of classical texts came into use concurrently with the development of scientific literary criticism by the humanists. More important still, the diffusion of ideas more widely than ever before was now possible.

Corresponding progress was being made in the fine arts. Medieval architects had recognized the favors of princes by placing their sculptured effigies along with those of saints on the façades of churches, but the figures were identified by traditional heraldic devices and made subordinate to the architecture. Then with the appearance of rich merchant donors without coats-of-arms came the demand for likenesses, and sculptors began to give their work more realistic treatment, which meant success for naturalistic sculpture. It also meant, especially in the Netherlands, the adaptation of the methods of the miniaturist to painting in a larger scale and in a new oil medium which the Flemings developed. The popes at Avignon and the dukes of Burgundy imported these artists to adorn not only churches but dwellings, and rich merchants followed suit, having their portraits painted for their descendants. In Italy, where the Gothic had not been greatly favored, architects were developing along the lines of the basilica vast churches encrusted with particolored marble. They introduced variety into the fortress-palaces of the great Italian families, decorating them with designs, some of Eastern origin, some drawn from the study of long-neglected Roman remains. Roman sarcophagi inspired naturalistic sculpture, and Giotto's introduction of action into painting flowered in the magnificent compositions of Masaccio, which in turn were to inspire Leonardo da Vinci and Michelangelo.

Humanism was spread incidentally by the church councils that were called to put an end to the Great Schism. The conciliar movement was furthered by an emperor of the house of Luxemburg, who wished to maintain unity in Christendom in face of the advance of the Ottoman Turks. In 1347, the year before the Black Death, Charles of Luxemburg had become the Emperor Charles IV. His mother was heiress of Bohemia, and his interests were more Czech than German; he was the founder of the University of Prague. It was Charles IV who had issued the Golden Bull of 1356, which put imperial elections firmly into the hands of seven electors: the archbishops of Mainz, Trier and Cologne, the count palatine of the

Rhine, the duke of Saxony, the margrave of Brandenburg and the king of Bohemia.

Charles was succeeded by his son Wenzel, who was followed, after a period of rival emperors, by Sigismund of Luxemburg, king of Bohemia and Hungary (1410). Sigismund was determined to end the Great Schism. The cardinals of Avignon and Rome had agreed to call a council at Pisa (1409), but this council merely complicated matters by electing a third pope. He died the next year and the council chose another, John XXIII, a totally worldly man whom Sigismund forced to call a council at Constance (1414-18). This assembled with three avowed purposes: to end the Schism, to reform the church, and to extirpate heresy. The great heretic of the day was the Czech, John Huss, who preached Wycliffe's doctrines with some additions of his own and who had come to the council on a safe-conduct from the Emperor Sigismund. The council, however, burned Huss and his follower, Jerome of Prague, and performed the futile gesture of ordering Wycliffe's body dug up and burnt. The burning of Jerome is described in a letter of Poggio Bracciolini, a papal secretary, who characterizes Jerome's demeanor as like that of an ancient Roman. Poggio was a leading humanist and spent much of his time while at the council rummaging for ancient manuscripts in the libraries of the monasteries around the Lake of Constance.

Before proceeding to the work of reformation the council elected Pope Martin V, who promptly dissolved the council and failed to carry out his pledge of reform measures. His successor, Eugenius IV, called the Council of Basel and endeavored unsuccessfully to dissolve it when it opened negotiations with the followers of Huss, who had begun a national Bohemian movement that was both religious and political on the basis of Huss's teachings. Seceders from the Council of Basel (1431-49) sat in the Council of Ferrara-Florence (1438-45), which tried to reunite the Eastern and Western churches. Many Greek scholars from Constantinople came to attend this council, and when the Ottoman Turks took Constantinople its treasures of Greek scholarship had already in large measure been transferred to the West.

The triumphant advance of the nomad Ottoman Turks, who planned to win the Balkans, ruined the Levant trade in which

Jacques Coeur had been active. In the year of the fall of Constantinople (1453) the English port of Bordeaux fell to the French forces to whose equipment Jacques Coeur had made important contributions. The Hundred Years' War was over; not an Englishman remained on French soil, except at Calais, which the English kept until the next century. Two years before, Coeur had been accused by spiteful tongues of having poisoned the king's mistress, Agnes Sorel. He was arrested on Charles's order, stripped of his honors and his fortune, and cast into prison. He escaped, however, to Rome, where Nicholas V took him into the papal service. The next pope put him

LARGE SHIP AND SMALL BOAT OF THE
FIFTEENTH CENTURY

(From *A Student's History of England* by Samuel R. Gardiner. Longmans Green, London, 1897.)

in command of a fleet sent to relieve the island of Rhodes, which Turks were besieging, but he fell ill and died on the way. The house he had built at Bourges stands today as a witness of the magnificence to which it was possible for a bourgeois to attain by the middle of the fifteenth century, in a world where commerce was coming into its own and class lines were re-forming.

CHAPTER 20

The World of Lorenzo the Magnificent
[1441 – 1492]

ALTHOUGH in fifteenth-century France a great capitalist could exercise power and influence, the nobles still called the tune. In Italy, too, nobles had made themselves the rulers of many of the city states, but Florence, the cradle of humanism, the home of the Italian Renaissance, retained republican forms. The term merchant-prince applies fittingly to the heads of the great banking and trading family of Medici, who had no noble blood in their veins but whose descendants sat upon some of the greatest thrones of Europe.

Cosimo (d. 1464), the grandfather of Lorenzo dei Medici, held no office but was virtually dictator of Florence. He made an alliance with Naples, and helped a soldier of fortune named Francesco Sforza win the lordship of neighboring Milan from the Visconti family, believing that by doing so he was winning security for his own city. Greatly interested in humanism, especially in Greek studies, Cosimo established the famous Platonic Academy which met in his villa in the hills above Florence and kept a light burning before the bust of Plato. He educated a promising boy, Marsiglio Ficino, so that when he grew up he could translate the works of Plato into Latin. He was the friend and patron of Donatello, the sculptor. Donatello in sculpture and Masaccio in painting tried to express harmoniously the spirit of humanism and the conflicting tendencies of the age. Masaccio made skillful use of the contrasts of light and shade and the newly-discovered principle of perspective, and had great influence on the artists who followed him. Rationalism characterized the work of Masaccio and that of the sculptors Ghiberti and Luca della Robbia, as well as the early work of Donatello; but later a mystical or romantic spirit showed itself in the work of such painters as Botticelli and Ghirlandaio, and the sculptor Verrocchio. Although Ghiberti and Brunelleschi, the sculptor-architect, were aided by the study of antiquity, their work was characterized by the spirit of their own age.

Cosimo's grandson Lorenzo was born fifteen years before the death of Jacques Coeur and three years after the Council of Ferrara-Florence assembled. He grew up a leader in the varied, joyous life of the city, an enthusiastic humanist, and also a writer of gay songs in the vernacular. When, in 1478, he succeeded to the unofficial dictatorship of Florence, he gave the citizens pageants more elaborate than they had ever seen and became a patron of the arts. He also built up a reputation as a diplomat. Anxious to keep peace in the Italian peninsula, he renewed his grandfather's alliances with the powerful states in the north and south, Milan and Naples, which, however, were balanced by an alliance between Venice and the papacy.

The keynote of the history of Naples is the struggle between the French house of Anjou and a cadet branch of the Spanish house of Aragon. Both had claimed Sicily and Naples since the thirteenth century, but Alfonso of Aragon ruled Naples and Sicily from 1435 to 1458. He won fame as the patron of humanists and of the Academy of Naples, instituting many reforms and leaving a rich and prosperous kingdom to his illegitimate son Ferrante. Milan had been ruled since 1277 by the Visconti, who had extended their control over much of northern Italy. They were patrons of the arts; and when Francesco Sforza drove them out with Cosimo's aid, he too, as duke of Milan, made his court a center for artists and humanists.

The other leading powers in Italy were the papacy and Venice. Ever since the end of the Schism the popes had concentrated more and more upon building up their power in the papal states, and their interests as territorial princes frequently overshadowed their preoccupation with matters ecclesiastical. Among those who were patrons of the humanists and of art was Nicholas V, who established the Vatican Library and began the rebuilding of St. Peter's in Rome. Venice's dominance in the Mediterranean had been destroyed by the advance of the Ottoman Turks, who succeeded in capturing Constantinople in 1453. This misfortune did not, however, prevent the Venetians from extending their power in northern Italy at the expense of Milan. The Venetians did not adopt humanism until later, but the Venetian printing press of Aldus Manutius turned out fine editions of the classics.

Although the conflicting ambitions of these city states had kept the peninsula in a turmoil for centuries, the Medici policy of a strong alliance among the three strategically placed states of Milan, Florence, and Naples might have won peace had not their jealousies brought in the foreigner at the end of the century. Conditions north of the Alps were making the invasion of Italy not only possible but probable. The means were at hand. The end of the Hundred Years' War left two professional armies without occupation.

The English soldiers sold their swords to rival claimants of the throne, descendants of the dukes of Lancaster and York. Three years before Cosimo dei Medici died, the Lancastrian Henry VI was deposed and the Yorkist Edward IV put in his place. After Edward's death, his brother had Edward's two sons put to death and reigned briefly as Richard III. In 1485 Henry Tudor defeated him at Bosworth Field and was crowned as Henry VII. His royal blood came through his mother, a Lancastrian; his father belonged to a Welsh family with traditions of thrift and other middle-class qualities which were new to English rulers. Henry's marriage to Elizabeth of York united Yorkists and Lancastrians and the country again saw peace and prosperity.

In France there was no disputed succession to break up a seasoned army. Charles VII kept his together as a regularly paid force. He died the year Henry VI was deposed in England and was succeeded by his son, Louis XI. Louis, an exceedingly unpleasant person but as able as he was unpleasant, made the army more efficient than ever and set out to break the power of the French nobles. He was largely successful. His powerful vassals, the dukes of Burgundy, had almost established Burgundy as a kingdom, but Louis rendered them powerless through a combination of cleverness and luck. Duke Philip the Good of Burgundy, a great patron of the arts, was succeeded in 1467 by his son Charles the Bold. Edward IV of England promptly married his daughter to Charles, but Louis foiled this intrigue through the aid of the Swiss. These hardy Alpine dwellers, who had long since made themselves virtually independent of their Hapsburg overlords, were skillful fighters and defeated Charles' cavalry in a series of battles, in the last of which Duke Charles himself was slain. Louis then added the duchy of Burgundy to the royal domain.

Duke Charles had married his heiress, Mary, to Maximilian, heir of the Hapsburg territories, and their son Philip inherited the rest of the vast Burgundian lands. A partial compensation was secured by Louis when he married his son, who was to succeed him as Charles VIII, to Anne of Brittany, and thus added to the royal domain the last of the great French fiefs.

Absorbed by his struggles with Burgundy, Louis did not realize that, with the increase of wealth and the consequently enhanced demand for the products of the Far East, the future lay with those states which faced the Atlantic. The buying public in those countries found themselves paying enormous prices for Eastern goods, brought by stages across the deserts of the East to the Black Sea or the Levant. Handled by Byzantine or Italian merchants and bought in Italian cities by traders from beyond the Alps, these goods were sold at fantastic prices in France and England. Marco Polo's description of China and other widely circulated tales of travelers made known how cheap were spices and other products of the East in the lands of their origin. It is not strange that venturesome souls conceived the idea of reaching the Indies by sailing across the Atlantic to reap fabulous profits through buying cheap and selling dear. The stories told by hardy seamen of Bristol and other western ports—tales of islands in the Atlantic which would serve as stepping-stones—made such projects seem feasible, especially as Ptolemy's computation of the size of the globe made it a third less than the actual size.

Spain had for centuries been a land of perpetual crusade against the Moor. One by one, Christian kingdoms had been founded at the expense of the Moslem state. These kingdoms tended to merge, and the marriage of Ferdinand, king of Aragon, to Isabella, the heiress of Castile, united the greater part of the Iberian peninsula. In 1492, the year when Lorenzo dei Medici died, Granada fell, the last Moorish stronghold in Spain. The crusade against the Moor was at an end, and Queen Isabella had time to grant an interview in her camp before the fallen stronghold to an Italian sailor named Columbus, who engaged her in the new crusade, a crusade to carry the cross to the lands beyond the western sea. The success of Columbus's timely interview had momentous consequences: Spanish expansion was diverted from Africa, its logical path, to America.

Portugal, the remaining crusading kingdom of the Iberian peninsula, had been founded in the twelfth century by returning cru-

PLATE XXI

Fifteenth Century

FIGURE 1. *House of Jacques Coeur, Bourges. The house is a palace in the Flamboyant Gothic style. The adaptation of the late Gothic in its decorative richness to the purpose of domestic architecture for a wealthy merchant, is nowhere better illustrated than in this building.*

FIGURE 2. *Illustration from the so-called Nuremberg Chronicle. The book was published by Anton Koberger in 1493. It is supposed to be a history of the world, and begins with the creation. A few blank pages at the end are provided for recording events after 1493. The Nuremberg Chronicle is one of the most famous of the books that were printed before 1500; these books are known as incunabula. The work is profusely illustrated, but one woodcut is made to do manifold duty; although the one above is labeled Paris it appears elsewhere repeatedly to represent other maritime cities. The vessel is typical of the period. A similar one was in a stained glass window in Jacques Coeur's house.*

[*Courtesy of the Pierpont Morgan Library, New York*]

FIGURE 3. *Louis IV (d'Outremer) presenting the child-duke of Normandy, Richard the Fearless, to the citizens of Rouen, who had revolted. This is a fifteenth century record of tenth century history. According to the chroniclers, the people of Rouen revolted because they feared King Louis was going to kidnap Duke Richard, and they were pacified only when the boy was placed in their hands. This illustration is from a copy of the Chronicles made for the magistrates of Rouen. The artist, according to custom, used the costume and accessories of his own time which correspond in their dramatic quality to the flamboyant style of late Gothic architecture. He shows the exaggerated pointed shoes, many-folded headdress, and long gowns of the period, and gives an idea of fifteenth century Rouen. Note the complete sheet armor, the elaborate helmets, and the newly improved pike.*

[*From a manuscript in the Bibliothèque nationale, Paris*]

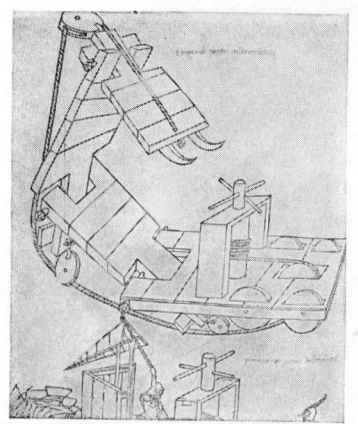

PLATE XXII

Fifteenth Century

FIGURE 1. *Detail from Ghirlandaio's painting of St. Francis receiving his charter, showing Lorenzo dei Medici standing between two members of the Sassetti family. The realism which characterizes the art of the early Renaissance unshrinkingly reproduces the jutting jaw and flattened nose of the young despot. There is no doubt that we are looking at the Lorenzo his fellow citizens met in Florentine streets, churches, and palaces.* [*Courtesy of the Metropolitan Museum of Art, New York*]

FIGURE 2. *Drawing showing devices for lifting a drawbridge, from Robertus Volterius,* De Re Militaribus, *Venice, 1472. This book is an example of the way the perfecting of printing and engraving on wood accelerated the process of invention by making possible the wide circulation of details of inventions already in use.*
[*Courtesy of the Metropolitan Museum of Art, New York*]

FIGURE 3. *Equestrian statue of the* condottiere Gattemelata, *by Donatello. This was the first large equestrian statue cast in bronze since the latter days of the Roman empire in the west. The artist of the early Renaissance has created a figure that appeals to reason through the clear and static balance of horse and rider. The statue has the restrained, ordered authority of a classical work. It is more than the portrait of an individual* condottiere. *It is the type of ruthless, professional military man, ready to make or unmake the fortunes of a sovereign state.*

FIGURE 4. *Detail from a set of tapestries in the Metropolitan Museum of Art in New York that represent the sacraments. This is a good example of the usefulness of tapestry as a historical record of costume. Fifteenth century costume had a tendency to go to extremes. The towering headdresses of women, whether of the two-horned or cornucopia model, and the men's caps made like a modern toboggan cap drawn out to inordinate lengths and wrapped around the head in fold after fold are shown here to perfection. Tapestries played an important part in the draughty halls of medieval castles, which were still the residences of the nobility.*
[*Courtesy of the Metropolitan Museum of Art, New York*]

saders. For years before the historic interview between Isabella and Columbus, Prince Henry the Navigator, the brother of the king of Portugal, had been sending expeditions along the coast of Africa, partly to explore and partly to spread Christianity among the natives. These expeditions sailed farther and farther south until in 1487 the Cape of Good Hope was rounded and it became evident that Ptolemy had been wrong in believing the Indian Ocean to be a closed sea. Columbus' brother Bartholomew and perhaps Christopher himself had gained experience on these Portuguese voyages. When Christopher Columbus sought aid from the Portuguese king for his project of reaching the Indies by sailing west, that sovereign was too hopeful of results from the southern route to give ear to the project. So it was under the auspices of Castile that Columbus' little fleet sailed westward to the Bahamas and on October 12, 1492, landed on the island of San Salvador, which he supposed to be Cathay, the land of the Great Khan. In 1453 the humanist pope Nicholas V had granted to the crown of Portugal exclusive rights of navigation and discovery "south and east" of an imaginary line drawn west of the Azores. When Columbus returned and reported his discovery, the Spanish pope Alexander VI consented to grant to the Spanish sovereigns similar rights to the west of this line.

In the famous year 1492 Lorenzo dei Medici lay dying in Florence. He was visited by a Dominican friar named Savonarola, who disapproved of the vanities so dear to Lorenzo, and who was to meet death himself six years later as a result of his defiance of Alexander VI. The world on which Lorenzo's eyes closed was not the old world centered by the Mediterranean. This sea was no longer the sole approach to the distant region whence came spices and rich goods, and whence came also the alien peoples of whom the latest arrivals had been the Ottoman Turks. The menace of the mysterious ocean had been successfully challenged and the global world had swung into man's ken.

[THE FIFTEENTH CENTURY]

Readings

~~~~~~~~~~~~~~~

Jacques Coeur

COMPLAINT OF CHARLES VII *

[Mr. Kerr prints two letters of Coeur which are interesting, but not so illuminating for the details of the Levant trade as the documents from which extracts are given below. The descriptions of his dress were elicited in an effort to ascertain whether he had ever assumed clerical garb. Comparison with the plates will aid in forming a picture of the man.]

Charles, by the grace of God, King of France, let all present and to come know: We have received the humble application of Jean de Village, native of our said city of Bourges, stating that he might have been about fifteen years old, a youth living in the said city of Bourges when, because he had a great desire to advance himself in the business of merchandising, and that the late Jacques Coeur, who then was of good and great authority under us, carried on a very great merchantry both on land and sea, the said suppliant found means of entering the service of Jacques Coeur; who, after he was with him a certain while, because of the confidence which he had in the said suppliant, gave him his niece to wife and advanced him strongly, and gave him some important charges in his affairs, and especially at sea, in the conduct and guidance of his galleys; on which the said de Village, the suppliant, has trafficked in the business of merchandising for the space of from ten to twelve years, and commanded the said galleys, and in so doing has traded with the Moors, Turks, and other foreign nations, both in the countries of the Levant, Barbary, Myour, the Ponant and elsewhere, without permission or license from us; in making which voyages,

---

* From Albert Boardman Kerr, *Jacques Coeur, Merchant Prince of the Middle Ages* (1927). Reprinted by permission of Charles Scribner's Sons, publishers.

[341

this suppliant, on several occasions, has carried on his galleys and withdrawn from our said kingdom and transported into the said foreign lands a great quantity of alloyed silver, both minted and in the form of plate, and among other things, in a voyage which he made to the Levant, when he was at Rhodes, he delivered to Bernard de Vaux and Lazarin d'Andrea, of Montpellier, a certain quantity or sum of solid silver, which he had in his said galley—he did not remember clearly the amount—to be minted, and which silver was minted in the said place of Rhodes by the said de Vaux and Lazarin, with nine or ten pence of alloy, or thereabouts, and was by them marked with a silversmith's mark in the establishment where the said silver was coined; which mark, on his advice, was that of a clover-leaf. And this [coin] he transported to Alexandria, there to sell it and spend it, as was done; and has on his said galleys passed along other merchandise, and also a number of Moorish, Turkish, and other foreign personages, when they travelled from one country to the other.

And also the said suppliant, Village, made a voyage to the Levant during which he went to Cairo and had an audience with the Sultan and delivered to him letters from us, which the said Jacques Coeur, his master, had handed him, and by the order of his said master, presented to the said Sultan as gifts from us, a small *jazeran* of mail, a steel cross-bow, four small jacks of steel for bending the cross-bow, equipped with their quivers, six battle-axes, six fancy arms, and a small cup of enamelled gold and silver; to receive in return from the said Sultan certain foreign objects and garments of his country to be carried back to us, which was done and we were presented with them in our said city of Bourges. . . .

LETTER OF THE SULTAN TO CHARLES VII*

The Grand Sultan sends thee this letter to assure thee that good friendship and accord reign between us. Thy letter we have seen and read, and believe that thou dost wish us well, as we do thee.

Thy ambassador, a man of honor, a gentleman, whom thou callest Jean de Village, has come to our Sublime Porte, and has presented thy letter together with the presents thou hast sent me, and I have received them; and what thou hast written that thou desirest of me, that have I done. Accordingly I have made a peace

---
* *Ibid.*

with all thy merchants for all my countries and seaports, as thy ambassador has requested of me.

The said ambassador came in great state and has taken his presents in great love and pleasure for the love of thee.

That which thou hast desired, is decreed and done; I have commanded all the lords of my dominions, and especially the Lord of Alexandria, that good-fellowship be shown to all the merchants of thy land, and to all others having liberty therein, and that honor and pleasure be done unto them; and when the consul of thy country is come, he shall have high favor amongst the other consuls.

And I have ordained that good-fellowship shall be extended to the pilgrims of thy country, who go to Jerusalem and Saint Catherine; for the said ambassador has also begged this of me, and nothing shall be taken of them but what is customary to pay to other sultans; they shall be despoiled by none, nor injury of any sort done to them. And all that the said ambassador has asked for the pilgrims, and all other things, have I done for thy love, and thy ambassador departs from our Sublime Porte with his answers. And I have clothed him in a robe of state according to custom, in honor of thee, which I have given him, having told the said ambassador that I consent that a consul shall be sent from thee to reside in my dominions in order that peace may be between us.

I send thee a present by the said ambassador, to wit, a balm made from our holy vine; a beautiful leopard; three porcelain bowls from Sinan;[1] two large platters of open-work porcelain, two bouquets of porcelain, a wash-basin and *lavoir-es-mains* of finely wrought porcelain; a jar of fine green ginger; one of almond kernels; a jar of green pepper, some almonds, and fifty pounds of our fine bamouget; and a quintal of fine sugar.

God lead thee to salvation, Charles, King of France.

DESCRIPTION OF COEUR'S DRESS [*]

With regard to his habit, I have seen him in the past wear one without a collar, the sleeves of the doublet being striped with red against a black background. During his visit to Normandy, I have seen him wear a hat covered with velvet with large silk folds on top; long-pointed laced shoes. I have also seen him wear generally

---

[1] China
[*] *Ibid.*

a short robe, reaching half-way to the knees, gathered at the shoulders and open at the sleeves, red or green-and-gray shoes, and robes of all colors, several of them being without a collar, in the style that gentlemen of the court are wont to attire themselves.

I have seen Jacques Coeur wear a large hat of scarlet brocade and a robe without a collar, reaching half-way to his knees, gathered at the sleeves, heavily bordered with sable and slashed at the sides. This was in 1447, 1448, and the years following. I have never seen Jacques Coeur wear a long robe except during the past year, two months before his arrest, in the month of May, 1451. Then I saw him wear, at Montpellier, a long robe, I do not recall of what color, trimmed with vair; I have seen him wear hose of scarlet and other colors and long-pointed laced shoes. . . .

Lorenzo dei Medici

CARNIVAL SONG: *TRIUMPH OF BACCHUS* *

[The author of the light-hearted Carnival song seems another person from the anxious father giving worldly-wise advice to the son who was to rise to the papacy as Leo X.]

> Fair is youth and void of sorrow;
>   But it hourly flies away.—
> Youths and maids, enjoy to-day;
> Nought ye know about to-morrow.

> This is Bacchus and the bright
>   Ariadne, lovers true!
> They, in flying time's despite,
>   Each with each find pleasure new;
> These their Nymphs, and all their crew
>   Keep perpetual holiday.—
> Youths and maids, enjoy to-day;
> Nought ye know about to-morrow. . . .

> See this load behind them plodding
>   On the ass, Silenus he,

---

* From J. A. Symonds, *Renaissance in Italy*, vol. 4 (1921). Reprinted by permission of Charles Scribner's Sons, publishers.

Old and drunken, merry, nodding,
  Full of years and jollity;
Though he goes so swayingly,
  Yet he laughs and quaffs alway,—
  Youths and maids, enjoy to-day;
Nought ye know about to-morrow.

. . . .

Midas treads a wearier measure;
  All he touches turns to gold:
If there be no taste of pleasure,
  What's the use of wealth untold?
What's the joy his fingers hold,
  When he's forced to thirst for aye?—
  Youths and maids, enjoy to-day;
Nought ye know about to-morrow.

Listen well to what we're saying;
  Of to-morrow have no care!
Young and old together playing,
  Boys and girls, be blithe as air!
Every sorry thought forswear!
  Keep perpetual holiday.—
  Youths and maids, enjoy to-day;
Nought ye know about to-morrow. . . .

LETTER *

To his son Giovanni, who had been made a cardinal at the age of fourteen

You, and all of us who are interested in your welfare, ought to esteem ourselves highly favored by Providence, not only for the many honours and benefits bestowed upon our house, but more particularly for having conferred upon us, in your person, the greatest dignity we have ever enjoyed. This favor, in itself so important, is rendered still more so by the circumstances with which it is accompanied and especially by the consideration of your youth and of our situation in the world. The first that I would therefore sug-

* From Roscoe's *Life of Lorenzo de' Medici* in *A Literary Source-Book of the Italian Renaissance,* by Merrick Whitcomb (1898). Reprinted by permission of The University of Pennsylvania Press.

gest to you is that you ought to be grateful to God, and continually to recollect that it is not through your merits, your prudence, or your solicitude, that this event has taken place, but through his favour, which you can only repay by a pious, chaste and exemplary life; and that your obligations to the performance of these duties are so much the greater, as in your early years you have given some reasonable expectations that your riper age may produce such fruits. . . .

I well know, that as you are now to reside at Rome, that sink of all iniquity, the difficulty of conducting yourself by these admonitions will be increased. The influence of example is itself prevalent; but you will probably meet with those who will particularly endeavor to corrupt and incite you to vice; because, as you may yourself perceive, your early attainment to so great a dignity is not observed without envy, and those who could not prevent your receiving that honour will secretly endeavor to diminish it, by inducing you to forfeit the good estimation of the public; thereby precipitating you into that gulf into which they had themselves fallen; in which attempt, the consideration of your youth will give them a confidence of success. . . . Avoid, however, as you would Scylla or Charybdis, the imputation of hypocrisy; guard against all ostentation, either in your conduct or your discourse; affect not austerity, nor even appear too serious. This advice, you will, I hope, in time understand and practice better than I can express it. . . .

You are now devoted to God and the church: on which account you ought to aim at being a good ecclesiastic, and to shew that you prefer the honor and state of the church and of the apostolic see to every other consideration. Nor, while you keep this in view, will it be difficult for you to favour your family and your native place. On the contrary, you should be the link to bind this city closer to the church, and our family with the city; and although it be impossible to foresee what accidents may happen, yet I doubt not but this may be done with equal advantage to all; observing, however, that you are always to prefer the interests of the church.

You are not only the youngest cardinal in the college, but the youngest person that ever was raised to that rank; and you ought therefore to be the most vigilant and unassuming, not giving others occasion to wait for you, either in the chapel, the consistory or upon deputations. You will soon get a sufficient insight into the manners of your brethren. With those of less respectable character converse not with too much intimacy; not merely on account of the circumstance in itself, but for the sake of public opinion. Converse on general topics with all. On public occasions let your equipage and address be rather below than above mediocrity. A handsome house and a well-ordered family will be preferable to a great retinue and a splendid residence. Endeavor to live with regularity, and gradually to bring your expenses within those bounds which in a new establishment cannot perhaps be expected. Silk and jewels are not suitable for persons in your station. Your taste will be better shewn in the acquisition of a few elegant remains of antiquity, or in the collecting of handsome books, and by your attendants being learned

ILLUSTRATION FROM A MEDICAL BOOK
Regimen Sanitatis zu Deutsch, Augsburg, 1482

and well-bred rather than numerous. Invite others to your house oftener than you receive invitations. Practise neither too frequently. Let your own food be plain, and take sufficient exercise, for those who wear your habit are soon liable, without great caution, to contract infirmities. The station of a cardinal is not less secure than elevated; on which account those who arrive at it too frequently become negligent; conceiving their object is attained and that they can preserve it with little trouble. This idea is often injurious to the life and character of those who entertain it. Be attentive therefore to your conduct, and confide in others too little rather than too much. . . . With respect to your speaking in the consistory, it will be most becoming for you at present to refer the matters in debate to the judgment of his holiness, alleging as a reason your own youth and inexperience. You will probably be desired to intercede for the favours of the pope on particular occasions. Be cautious, however, that you trouble him not too often; for his temper leads him to be most liberal to those who weary him least with their solicitations. This you must observe, lest you should give him offence, remembering also at times to converse with him on more agreeable topics; and if you should be obliged to request some kindness from him, let it be done with that modesty and humility which are so pleasing to his disposition. Farewell.

PART XII

The Sixteenth Century

CHRONOLOGY

1509 Erasmus's *Praise of Folly*
1517 Luther's 95 theses
—— Machiavelli's *The Prince*
1521 Diet of Worms; Luther under the ban of the Empire
1529 Siege of Vienna by the Turks
1530 Confession of Augsburg
1535 Act of Supremacy; Henry VIII head of the English church
1536 Calvin's *Institutes of the Christian Religion*
1534 Society of Jesus founded
1543 Death of Copernicus
1545–63 Council of Trent
1555 Peace of Augsburg
1572 Massacre of St. Bartholomew
1584 Assassination of William the Silent
1588 Defeat of the Spanish Armada
1594 Henry IV in Paris; first Bourbon king of France
1598 Edict of Nantes

PART XII

The Sixteenth Century

~~~~~~~~~~~~~~~~~~~~~~~~~~

IN THE sixteenth century men stopped looking back toward a golden age, and began to look forward. The world had taken on new aspects. Imagination was stimulated by the mere knowledge of the existence of new lands beyond the sea and of peoples who lived in a widely different stage of culture from that of Europe. The printing presses had brought the ideas of the Greeks and Romans into currency and put forth travelers' tales, attacks on dogma, and a wealth of new poetry, plays, and romances. The printing presses were to lead toward a break in the universal church, which had been one of the noblest ideals of the Middle Ages, while the discoveries of new lands made possible the preponderance of Spain, which affected nearly all the leading states of Europe.

The spirit which characterized the Italian Renaissance had made its way north of the Alps by the beginning of the sixteenth century, but it suffered a change. Where the Italian humanists had for the most part kept their interests free from religious speculation, the humanists north of the Alps moved in the direction of heresy, through concentration on Christian rather than pagan antiquity, and through broader criticism of the church. The great northern humanists never left the church, but by their efforts toward reform within it they prepared the ground for the leaders who did. The general criticism of the church, given wide diffusion through the printing press, came at a time when papal prestige was low as a result of the worldly conduct of the Renaissance popes in the role of petty Italian despots. There were also undeniable abuses in the church administration which irked large classes of people: the sale of indulgences to raise money for the temporal needs of the papacy was a notable example, but not the only one. Apparently among the clergy there was a larger number of unsuitable persons than formerly; it has been suggested that the church had never fully recovered from the tremendous destruction of the Black Death, after which the need to replenish the hierarchy rapidly had resulted in a lowering of standards.

The wealth of the middle or bourgeois class made possible the patronage under which humanism flourished, and education was becoming widely diffused among laymen. The printing press made the problem of heresy no longer an affair restricted largely to the clerical world. When the Saxon monk Martin Luther in the sixteenth century raised the question of predestination, as the Saxon monk Gottschalk had done in the ninth century, the heresy could not be dealt with so simply as was that of Gottschalk—by burning a book. Moreover, the usefulness of heresy as a political weapon against the church was recognized by astute princes and nobles in Germany, where the power and wealth of ecclesiastical states was still very evident. The national monarchies in England and France had succeeded in establishing a considerable degree of control over the clergy in their lands and church wealth. All over Europe, but notably in Germany, princes looked hungrily at the church lands—fully one-third of the best lands in Christendom. Fanned by secular greed as well as religious conviction, the heresy of the Saxon monk spread until the breach with the universal church became final by the middle of the century.

The latter half of the century was filled with warfare which wore the cloak of religion, much of it under the auspices of Spain. The conflict between secular and religious interest is well illustrated in the Spanish conquest of the overseas empire which was known as the "Indies." Spanish exploration and colonization bore many of the aspects of a crusade, and the crown was consistently solicitous for the welfare and the conversion of the native populations in the conquest. But many of those by whom the actual conquest was accomplished appear to have been dominated by motives of self-interest and personal gain. From the outset the Indies were treated as the personal estate of the crown and systematically exploited to provide the greatest possible revenue. With the flood of precious metals that poured into Spain her rulers were able to undertake an aggressive policy in Europe which would have been entirely beyond their means without the resources of the new world. Charles V and Philip II, who ruled Spain through most of the century, were sincere champions of the ancient faith and willing secular tools in the church's effort to recover the ground lost in the religious revolt begun by Martin Luther.

In the end it was the Spanish efforts to maintain two empires, the one American and the other European, which lost Spain the preponderance she held in the sixteenth century. European Spain was neither populous enough nor rich enough in natural resources to support one empire except by skillful and progressive management. Much of the finest Spanish talent, however, went to the Indies, where the opportunities were great, and this further impoverished the mother country. Spanish imperialism in Europe provoked powerful antagonists, one after another, until Spain's enemies succeeded in wresting from her the control of the seas, thereby making the maintenance of her American empire hazardous and expensive. Without the wealth of the Indies Spanish imperialism could not be supported; but as a consequence of Spanish policy the Indies became spoils of war, and inroads on the Spanish monopoly in the Americas were made particularly by the English and later by the French.

The sixteenth was the century of opportunity for the lands which faced the Atlantic. The Italian city states were forced from the center of the stage and Italy became a pawn in a game between the new national states. France for the most part in this century missed the trans-Atlantic opportunities, first because of the French crown's preoccupation with Italian conquest, later because of civil wars. Portugal waxed fat on its Asiatic trade, but from 1580 to 1640 she was under the control of the Spanish crown and much of her overseas trading empire was absorbed by the Dutch during their revolt for independence from the Spanish monarch.

Efforts were made by European states to counter the preponderance that Spain had won with American gold and silver. In the late fifteenth century the leading city states of the Italian peninsula had formed leagues to prevent the preponderance of any single state, and the policy was fairly successful. This maintenance of a balance of power—a strategy initiated by Cardinal Wolsey, Henry VIII's minister—was imitated in the sixteenth century by the leading nation states. It was to become a favorite method of British statesmanship.

Imposing rulers, like Henry VIII and Francis I, and later Philip

II and Elizabeth, advanced the growth of nationalism in the sixteenth century. These figures emerged because the policies of their predecessors had drawn into their royal treasuries the revenues which had formerly gone to the feudal lords. The knell of feudalism had sounded. The chivalry which Spenser made the setting of Elizabeth in his *Faerie Queen* had the stiffness of age upon it, and the system was bowed out by the Spaniard, Cervantes, in his great novel, *Don Quixote*.

The rise in prices due to the influx of gold and silver from America added to the impoverishment of the feudal lords and peasants, and ruined the small tradespeople in the towns. The class which profited was the merchant class. The most striking example of middle-class prosperity was given by England, which profited to the full by the new opportunities because of a social revolution which brought importance to the middle class. Rich merchants bought monastery lands and became country gentlemen when King Henry VIII broke with the Roman church and confiscated monastic holdings. Many received titles and became nobles. With practical sense these English landowners saw the advantages of the wool trade and enclosed their fields for sheepwalks, producing a problem of unemployment in the rural population at a time when the doles of the monasteries were at an end. This new leisure class invested in the chartered merchant companies which reached out into Russia and the Far East. English merchants sold goods to Spain and infringed on Spain's colonial monopoly in America. The royal house of Tudor was a family which had middle-class traits, and all the Tudors had an understanding of middle-class psychology. Increased wealth provided a background for unprecedented intellectual activity in England at a time when the Inquisition was at work stamping out freedom of thought in Spain and Italy. The fifteenth-century ferment of ideas from Italy which had been cherished by Humphrey, Duke of Gloucester, the century before, could not flourish in the atmosphere of war, but the sixteenth century saw the Italianate Englishman decorating the scene. The early printing presses in England poured out books in English, and English literature flourished and produced a large group of men of letters, with Shakespeare as their chief.

The peace which Elizabeth maintained for her people during the greater part of her reign provided an excellent soil for the flour-

The Sixteenth Century [355

ishing of letters. It was otherwise with France. The genius of Rabelais poured forth the rollicking tales of Gargantua and Pantagruel, with their unveiled attacks upon asceticism, hypocrisy, and bigotry, but the literature of the last half of the century ran to political pamphleteering. However, the thoughtful essays of Montaigne, like those of Francis Bacon in England, inaugurated a new form of prose writing. In Italy humanism had lost its appeal, but Renaissance painting was at its height. Raphael made his great compositions for the Vatican and painted his exquisite Madonnas. Leonardo painted his Last Supper. Titian brought the rich coloring of the Venetian school to its height; Michelangelo painted the ceiling of the Sistine Chapel and executed his brooding and majestic sculptures. His designs for the new St. Peter's showed him to be the greatest architect of his day.

The development of music printing accelerated the progress of music. In Rome Palestrina composed music in a noble religious style that matched the spirit of Raphael's madonnas and that still dominates the music of the Roman Catholic Church. A new form of church music rose in Germany among the Reformation churches following Luther's example of using old hymn tunes and folk songs in the chorale for congregational singing.

The great scientific achievement of the century was the Copernican theory, but it attracted little attention at the time. The bombastic Paracelsus made some advances in medicine. The pendulum clock was invented, and Leonardo's ideas inspired a number of improvements in mechanics.

Rational methods of thought led to ideas which endeavored to check the barbarities of persecution. The physician John Weyer protested against the witch trials, demonstrating that the accused were at worst in need of physicians; and Reginald Scot argued against the very existence of witchcraft.

The striking personality of Erasmus of Rotterdam, one of the greatest figures of the humanist movement in the north, provides a convenient bridge between the fifteenth and sixteenth centuries. He represents the scholarly achievement of Italian humanism and suggests the critical spirit which was to lead others, though not himself, to break with the church. One of the leading organizers of the new churches of the Reformation was the Frenchman John Calvin, whose legalistic mind built up a system of theology that was remorselessly logical but scarcely heart-warming. In the latter half of the century many of the leading currents of the period were drawn together in the reign of Queen Elizabeth of England. Elizabeth Tudor represented much that was most characteristic of the age, and most characteristic of Englishmen in an age when they were preparing for an important role in the European scene. She had some learning, was an enlightened patron of arts and literature, and was an excellent businesswoman as manager of the royal properties. The English church had broken with Rome, but at Elizabeth's insistence it had kept many aspects of the faith that had comforted Europe for so many centuries. England successfully resisted the crushing efforts of Spain at the height of power, and under Elizabeth's leadership began the fight for naval supremacy and a share in overseas trade and empire which was to have such fruitful results in later centuries.

FRONTISPIECE BY ALBRECHT DURER

(From *The Life of the Virgin Mary*, 1511.)

CHAPTER 21

The World of Erasmus

[1469–1536]

～～～～～～～～～～～～～～～～～～～～～～～～

DESIDERIUS ERASMUS of Rotterdam was a cosmopolitan in an age of growing nationalism. In the republic of letters, of which he was acknowledged head, Englishmen, Frenchmen, Poles, and Germans spoke and wrote Latin. This was no longer the flexible Latin of the Middle Ages but a pseudo-classical Latin—the Latin taught them by an earlier generation who had crossed the Alps and sat at the feet of Italian humanists. These travelers were very likely to seek out Pico della Mirandola, who believed the Hebrew tongue was as worthy of study as the Greek. From the newly invented printing presses were pouring the new editions of Greek and Latin classics which were read and discussed in all the cities of Europe. Erasmus, a frail little man with a lively wit and a bad digestion, braved the indifferent food and the insect pests of public inns in order to visit Italy, and later dwelt happily in England in the home of Sir Thomas More on the banks of the Thames.

The old international bonds still held—all western Europe bowed to the behests of the Roman pontiff, and the knightly code of manners as set down by Baldassare Castiglione in the *Book of the Courtier* was sedulously aped by merchants' sons from London to Naples. But other forces were at work. The Hundred Years' War had stirred up hatred between the English and the French and developed in them devotion to their kings as national leaders. These kings, finding feudal arrangements insufficient, created more efficient agencies for gathering in their subjects' wealth, with which they hired professional soldiers for their new standing armies and enlarged the number of officials in their administrative systems. Henry VIII of England had at his disposal the wealth gathered by his father, who, like all the Tudors, was extraordinarily grasping. Louis XI left a similar hoard to Charles VIII in France, who squandered much of it; but the new system raised more for his successors. Ferdinand and Isabella organized Castile and Aragon on similar lines. Maximilian I had efficient tax gatherers in the Hapsburg territories and in the Burgundian lands his wife had brought him—the pickings were especially rich in Flanders, Brabant, and the Dutch cities. He strove to increase the imperial power by reforming the creaking machinery of the empire, but to little avail.

To the eastward, the Kings of Bohemia, Poland, and Hungary had done little toward establishing their power over their vassals because the kingship was elective and the nobles bargained for privileges. Since the late fourteenth century the Polish crown had been worn by the family of Jagello, who brought the grand duchy of Lithuania under Polish sovereignty. The Jagellons fought the Teutonic Knights for a Polish outlet to the sea and were successful, three years before Erasmus' birth, in breaking the Order's political power on the Baltic.

Still further east, there had emerged from the struggles of Slavs and nomads on the plains of Russia the principality of Moscow. Moscow was strategically located to serve as the nucleus of a Russian state that could be expanded by driving back the Tatar horde which had swept over Russia in the thirteenth century. This principality had its headquarters well within the forest zone, thus giving the inhabitants refuge from the Tatar horsemen who carried all before them on the open steppes to the south. It occupied an area between the headwaters of the four principal river systems of European Russia, and these great rivers not only served as highways for expansion but gave Moscow a controlling interest in the development of trade. Feudalism in Russia, however, was on the rise, not declining as it was in western Europe, because in the slow reconquest of European Russia from the Tatars the frontiers had to be kept in a constant state of military defense. A military nobility, with a dependent peasant population, was created in much the same way as in western Europe after Charlemagne.

Of all the powers in Europe, France was the one whose ruler, with a united people behind him, had the funds for an aggressive policy at the beginning of the sixteenth century. Italy, divided as it was into hostile units, was a promising field for aggression, and Charles VIII yielded to temptation. He had inherited the claim of the duke of Anjou to the kingdom of Naples. The Emperor Maximilian I, who had married his son to the daughter of Ferdinand and Isabella regardless of her occasional fits of insanity, had through his grandson Charles, the fruit of that union, common interests with the house of Aragon. Ferdinand and Maximilian watched with great interest as Charles VIII swept through Italy. The Dominican friar Savonarola, who had won authority over the people of Florence by his eloquence in denouncing from the pulpit their worldliness and devotion to the new forms of art, welcomed the French king as God's scourge for the vices of the citizens. Charles VIII drove the Medici from Florence, and proceeding south, conquered the Aragonese king of Naples. Then Maximilian joined with Ferdinand, Pope Alexander VI, Venice, and Milan, and drove the French invader ignominiously from the peninsula. The only lasting result of the campaign was the carrying into France of loot which converted the French to the new movement in the arts.

Louis XII, Charles VIII's successor, claimed Milan as well as Naples, and although he managed to conquer both, was forced to relinquish his southern conquest. He joined Maximilian, Ferdinand, and the warlike Pope Julius II in the League of Cambrai against Venice. Julius with great astuteness, however, made a private peace with the Venetians and formed a Holy League to drive the French from Italy. Ferdinand and Maximilian then came over to this league, and even the new English king, Henry VIII, was persuaded to spend on the venture some of the treasure his father the seventh Henry had thriftily laid away. The league against France triumphed, but the next French king, Francis I, allying himself with Venice in his turn, entered Italy with an enormous army, won a smashing victory at Marignano against a new coalition, and occupied Milan (1515).

The confused maneuvers of the French invasions of Italy were the events over which Erasmus brooded when he wrote his famous treatise against war, *The Compleynt of Peace*. These leagues and counter leagues, these wars and plottings, were also watched and adjudged by a disappointed Italian politician named Niccolo Machiavelli, who came to conclusions quite different from those of Erasmus. In his native Florence he had played an important part, travelling on diplomatic missions from one Italian state to another, and even to Spain and more distant lands. He studied the policies of Ferdinand of Aragon, of Louis XI and his successors, and of the leading Italian despots. Driven into exile as Dante had been, he thought much about these matters of politics and compared modern deeds and policies with those of the great figures of antiquity whom he had been brought up to admire. Hoping to get back into politics himself, he welcomed the return of the Medici to Florence at the behest of the Holy League in 1514. Books of advice to rulers were fashionable and he made such a book, extracting suitable passages from his unfinished work on the whole field of politics. Machiavelli's book of advice was dedicated to Lorenzo dei Medici, the grandson of Il Magnifico, whose brooding figure Michelangelo placed on the Medici tomb. Thus came into existence *The Prince,* the famous handbook which set the amoral tone of the principles followed by despots from Francis I to Mussolini and Hitler.

Soon after the publication of *The Prince* another handbook for princes appeared which was to have repercussions in the political field, though its subject was primarily religious and its author a Saxon monk and university professor. His name was Martin Luther and the book was the *Address to the Christian Nobility of the German Nation.* Luther was the son of a German miner, and as a child he knew the simple piety that pervaded many laborers' homes at the end of the fifteenth century. While attending the University of Erfurt he suddenly relinquished his studies, entered a monastery of Augustinian Eremites, and strove through monkish practices to gain assurance that his soul would be saved. He became a priest and a professor in the University of Wittenberg, where, after much study of the Bible and of the works of St. Augustine, he began to question first the usages and then the doctrines of the church. Beginning with criticism of the way indulgences were being peddled in a neighboring city, Luther posted on the door of his church at Wittenberg for public debate a list of 95 theses concerning indulgences. His continued criticism of doctrine led to his being excommunicated as a heretic and declared an outlaw by an imperial diet at Worms. His assertion of the right of every man to find in the scriptures his guide to life was ultimately to lead to the doctrine of the freedom of the individual, for by emphasizing faith rather than good works as a means to salvation he dispensed with the authoritarian mediation of the church. His *Address to the Christian Nobility of the German Nation,* however, which recognized the authority of a ruler over the church in his dominions, led to the doctrine that rulers could compel the faith of their subjects, and to the foundation of national, territorial churches.

When Erasmus heard of Luther's attack upon the abuses of the church he was filled with enthusiasm. He himself had been a pupil in one of the schools of the Brethren of the Common Life and had fallen under the influence of the earlier German humanists. He had put his Greek to the work of issuing a new edition of the New Testament with a Latin translation. He had eagerly taken part in the movement to remedy the abuses of the church by ridicule and to bring about a reformation through education. Called to England to lecture, he had joined the English group which was working toward this end under the leadership of John Colet, Dean of St. Paul's. It was in conversations with one of the group, Sir Thomas More, that Erasmus conceived the idea of his satiric poem, the *Encomium Moriae* (*The Praise of Folly*), the title of which was a punning tribute to his English friend. To these humanists Luther's attack on indulgences seemed that of a co-worker, and Erasmus entered upon a friendly correspondence with him. When Luther was cast out of the church Erasmus, however, drew back, foreseeing that the quarrel about points of dogma would mean the end of his campaign to reform the church without splitting it into factions. He denounced Luther, remained faithful to the church, and lived to see his fears confirmed and the promising humanist movement in Germany at an end.

Luther kept much of the ancient faith. He took over the Old Testament with its eye for an eye, its Satan, its witchcraft, its sun and moon standing still at Joshua's command; he retained infant baptism. On the other hand, his doctrine of justification by faith alone took away the mediation of the priest. He modified transubstantiation, recognized civil marriage, and rejected monasticism, celibacy of the clergy, and invocation of the saints. Finally, by his rejection of the canon law and of papal authority he created a breach that could not easily be healed. His stress on the right and duty of all Christians to read the Scriptures meant not alone the translation of the Bible whereby he made his dialect the language of his countrymen, but popular education; state education for all citizens is a heritage of Lutheranism.

Erasmus recognized quite as well as Luther the necessity for many reforms, but he hoped to achieve results through the enlightenment of education alone, without a direct break with the universal church. His was a less stormy personality; a man of wit, intelligence, and character, he was primarily a scholar. All these attributes are suggested in the portrait by Holbein, one of many artists of Germany and the Netherlands whose work, fortunately, was not affected by their choice between Lutheranism and the ancient faith. The tolerance of the scholarly Erasmus, however, was not exhibited by the later religious reformers—especially in the case of one of the great organizers of the new faith, John Calvin.

SIEGE OF BOULOGNE BY HENRY VIII

(From *A Student's History of England* by Samuel R. Gardiner. Longmans Green, London, 1897.)

CHAPTER 22

The World of John Calvin

[1509–1564]

~~~~~~

JOHN CALVIN was an eight-year old French boy when Luther began his revolt by posting on the door of the church at Wittenberg his attack on the peddling of indulgences. The French scholar Jacques Lefèvre d'Etaples, a little man with a crooked smile, had preceded Luther in criticizing the doctrines of the church. A group of humanists formed around Lefèvre, and Calvin, who was then a serious, single-minded student of the law, attached himself to this group. One member of the group was confessor to Marguerite d'Angoulême, sister of Francis I and later Queen of Navarre. In the beginning Francis I played with the idea of a reform in France similar to that in Germany, where one of the reasons for the success of Luther was his recognition of the right of the German princes to take over the lands of the church and divert their revenues from Rome. After Francis succeeded in making a concordat with the pope which gave the French king virtual control of the church in France, this powerful argument for joining the revolt made no appeal to him, and the excesses of some French Lutherans finally decided him in favor of orthodoxy. Francis I began persecuting those who had adopted the ideas of the reformers, but Marguerite protected the group to which Calvin belonged and the king's shifts of politics gave some respite to the persecuted.

Political troubles gave relief to the Lutherans in Germany also. When Maximilian I died in 1519, the three young sovereigns—Francis I of France, Henry VIII of England, and Maximilian's grandson Charles—were candidates for the imperial crown, and Charles was elected. His hereditary domains touched those of Francis I at several points; and they both had Italian claims; con-

[363

sequently they engaged in a series of wars. It was at the first diet of Charles V, which was held at Worms in 1521, that the monk Luther was outlawed for his beliefs. Charles, who was a serious young man of 21, took an oath to devote his life and energies to stamping out this heresy, but he had to hurry away to put down a revolt in Spain and during the rest of his reign he was constantly calling diets to raise troops for his campaigns. As he could not afford to do without the troops of the Lutheran princes of Germany, he was forced to compromise with Lutheranism until it grew too strong to be eradicated. In his first war against Francis I, Charles' army defeated the French forces at Pavia (1525) and made the king a prisoner. Pope Clement VII, however, absolved Francis from an oath he had taken in order to regain his freedom, and hostilities recommenced. The pope joined Francis's League of Cognac against Charles, who took Milan and in 1527 sent troops to Rome against the pope. Benvenuto Cellini in his *Memoirs* describes the siege and the success of the imperial troops; the Lutherans among them took pleasure in sacking the city and defiling the altars of its churches. The war was ended by the Treaty of Cambrai (1529), called the Ladies' Peace because it was negotiated by Charles's aunt and Francis's mother.

In the meantime the German peasants, encouraged by some of Luther's ideas, revolted against their lords in an effort to remove some of their social and economic burdens. Luther, who feared to lose the support of the princes for his movement, sided with the lords against the peasants and even approved the cruel methods the lords used in suppressing them. In 1529 the emperor felt free to proceed against the Lutherans, and the formal protest of the Lutheran princes against a resolution of the Diet gave them the name of Protestant. As a measure of defense these princes formed the Schmalkaldic League with some of the imperial cities. Before long, however, Charles had to have troops again, this time to defend Vienna against the Turks, and he was obliged to revoke his measures against the Lutherans. Luther kept peace among the factions of German princes until his death in 1546, but that same year the Schmalkaldic war broke out between the Lutheran princes and those who remained faithful to the pope.

In 1545 Pope Paul III had summoned a general council of the church at Trent for the purpose of ending the schism if possible and of carrying on a reform within the church. The Protestants refused to attend, as preliminary negotiations had not succeeded in reaching any compromise over the question of the sacraments. The Council of Trent proceeded to restate, without any concessions, the doctrines attacked by Luther, but it took measures for preventing the recurrence of the scandals in clerical life which had long been criticized even by the faithful. It prepared a program for winning back the lands lost to the reformers, reorganized the Inquisition, and arranged for an Index of forbidden books. In 1555, at the Diet of Augsburg, religious peace was established in Germany on the basis of the right of each Lutheran and Catholic prince to force his faith upon his subjects (*cujus regio ejus religio*). Thenceforth the German states were aligned in two hostile camps.

Not all of the Protestants, however, were Lutherans. A Swiss, Ulrich Zwingli, had established in many of the Swiss cantons a faith which pronounced the Eucharist merely a commemorative meal. Groups both in Germany and Switzerland carried the ideas of Luther to their logical conclusion by insisting upon a literal following of the scriptures. Some of these groups declared infant baptism unscriptural; others were pacifists; the leaders of still others set themselves up as patriarchs and in imitation of Old Testament figures practiced polygamy. All these groups believed churches to be voluntary societies over which government had no control. On this basis they refused to pay tithes and denounced religious persecution. They scandalized Catholics and Lutherans alike, and were stigmatized as Anabaptists, although not all of them rejected infant baptism. Because of their definition of a church, they all believed in religious liberty, and it is along the lines they laid down that the idea of the separation of church and state has developed.

Francis I attempted to justify his persecution of the Lutherans by declaring that he was merely suppressing Anabaptists. John Calvin thereupon published a little book, *The Institutes of the Christian Religion,* in the preface of which he took Francis to task. The *Institutes* stated the religious faith which Calvin had developed, and this book became the textbook of Calvin's followers. Invited to direct the reform movement in the Swiss city of Geneva, Calvin by his influence made it a city of refuge for the persecuted Protestants of France, to which refugees from other countries flocked later. He established at Geneva a society of the elect, that is, of individuals who believed they were predestined for salvation and ought therefore to live strictly as they thought the elect should live. Those who wanted to be considered members of the elect society conformed; those who did not voluntarily practice the code of the elect were kept in order by severe laws so that they might not disgrace the community. Calvin took life very seriously, especially his role of protecting Geneva from what he considered blasphemy. When a learned Spanish physician named Michael Servetus was passing through the city, Calvin had him arrested and burned at the stake because Servetus questioned the divinity of Christ.

The English Reformation took a course entirely its own. Henry VIII had married his brother's widow Catharine, the daughter of Ferdinand and Isabella. Catharine was older than he was, and when she was middle-aged and he still young his eyes strayed to one of her ladies in waiting, Anne Boleyn. He decided that Catharine's failure to bear him a son was the judgment of God upon him for having married his deceased brother's wife, and asked the pope to set aside a predecessor's dispensation which had permitted the marriage. This would have offended Catharine's nephew, Charles V, who at the time was all powerful in Italy. The pope refused, and Henry then persuaded the English parliament to pass a series of acts which separated the English church from Rome and made the king "supreme head" of the church in England. His old friend and chancellor, Sir Thomas More, author of the *Utopia,* refused to put the seal on the act and was beheaded. Meanwhile Henry had secretly married Anne Boleyn and had secured from the court of the Archbishop of Canterbury a decision that his marriage with Catharine was illegal and that Anne was legally his wife.

The following year the great English monasteries were dissolved, and the members of parliament who had complaisantly made Henry head of the church were able to purchase confiscated lands from the crown. These new gentry built themselves country houses in the new style of stone-faced brick, facing south, with great windows to admit the sparse English sunshine. The model had already been set in the great palace of Hampton Court, built by Cardinal Wolsey, Henry VIII's ambitious but unsuccessful agent in the negotiations with the pope over Catharine. With the development of the Tudor country house, the day of the moated feudal castle was over.

Anne bore Henry a daughter Elizabeth, but no son. Jane Seymour, the third of his six wives, bore him a son, who succeeded him as Edward VI. Henry had made a few changes in the church, mostly organizational, but he died in the belief that he was still a good Catholic. Edward's mother had been Protestant and the boy had been stuffed with theology from his cradle. He encouraged his guardians to carry through a reform on Protestant lines, and Cranmer, the archbishop of Canterbury, compiled the *Book of Common Prayer,* which was a masterly translation of the book of the mass, with the addition of some prayers of the early church. Edward, a sickly lad, died after a few years, and his older sister Mary, Catharine's daughter, came to the throne with the fixed idea of restoring the church to the Roman obedience. Cranmer and other bishops who refused to change were burned at the stake, and those who did not aspire to a martyr's death escaped to the Continent. These Marian exiles settled along the Rhine and in Geneva and became accustomed to the simple forms of Calvinist worship. Mary married Philip II of Spain, the son of Charles V, but Philip remained in England only long enough to see the restoration of papal authority accomplished.

When Charles V abdicated in 1556, Philip II was the most powerful ruler in Europe. Although the Hapsburg lands in Germany and the imperial crown went to his brother Ferdinand I, Philip was king of Spain, Lord of the Low Countries, Milan and Naples, and in addition ruled the so-called "Indies." Spanish adventurers had conquered Mexico and Peru, and from the new world vast amounts of gold and silver came into the royal coffers. Philip was a fervent Catholic and worked to restore Roman supremacy wherever possible. He stamped out the promising Protestant movement in Spain, endeavored to do so in the Netherlands, and was the chief single agent of the papacy in carrying out the work of counter reformation. The papacy had another superb weapon in the Society of Jesus, which was founded and placed at the service of the popes by the Spaniard, Ignatius Loyola. The Jesuits, with their splendid organization and military discipline, were put in charge of the program of the Council of Trent and were recognized throughout Christendom as the pope's army and his agency for spreading the gospel among the heathen.

In 1543, two years before the Council of Trent assembled, a book was published which was to have a profound effect upon humanity. It embodied the results of a long chain of reasoning. Throughout the medieval period men had been studying the heavens for purposes of astrology since casting horoscopes was then, as it is today, a way of making a living. The theories of the ancients, made easy of access by the printing press, frequently corroborated the observations of the more scientifically-minded of these men who desired to know the secrets of the heavens. In some of the Italian universities there was a strong movement away from the geocentric astronomy of Ptolemy toward the heliocentric idea held by some of the earlier Greeks. The Polish astronomer Copernicus studied mathematics at the University of Cracow, canon law and astronomy at Bologna, and medicine at Padua. In Bologna and Padua he became interested in this movement toward the science of the ancients, and when he went back to Poland he practiced medicine and studied the skies. He corresponded with other astronomers, who encouraged him to publish his views. On his deathbed he was shown a printed copy of the book, *Revolutions of the Celestial Bodies,* which he had written to demonstrate that the earth is not the center of the universe but that it and the other planets revolve about the sun. His editor had written a preface in which it was stated that the idea was put forward merely as an hypothesis, and it was consequently many years before much attention was given to the book.

WITCHES ON THEIR WAY TO A SABBATH

(Illustrations from Ulrich Molitor, *Hexen Meystereye,* 1545.)

In Calvin's lifetime the menace to Christendom from the Ottoman Turks increased. They had appeared in Asia Minor at the end of the thirteenth century, were first brought into Europe to fight the battles of the Byzantine emperor, and then established themselves at the expense of the empire. They fought the various Balkan rulers and alternately fought and made treaties with the republic of Venice. Their successful siege of Constantinople in 1453 made them a recognized European power. They began a new era of conquest with the accession of Suleiman I in 1520, for they captured Belgrade in 1521, occupied a large part of Hungary between 1526 and 1528, and laid siege to Vienna in 1529. (It was because of the necessity of raising troops to meet this peril that the Lutherans got one of their earlier breathing-spells from Charles V.) Repulsed at Vienna, the Turks took to the sea and in the course of time were able to dominate the African coast and ravage the coast of Spain. Francis I, during one of his wars with Charles V, took advantage of the menace the Turks represented to the emperor by making an alliance with Suleiman. Suleiman died two years after Calvin, leaving a great empire to threaten a divided Christendom.

PLATE XXIII

Sixteenth Century

FIGURE 1. *Portrait of Erasmus by Hans Holbein, the younger. Without arbitrarily interpreting the character of his sitter, Holbein grasps his personality merely by the objective recording of his physiognomy. This is only one of a number of portraits he painted of Erasmus. Both men were, for a long time, fellow-citizens of the Swiss city of Basel.*
[*From* Holbein *by Hans Reinhardt. The Hyperion Press, New York, 1938*]

FIGURE 2. *This recently discovered portrait of Calvin shows no effort on the artist's part to tone down what he saw. This is the Calvin who made Geneva a citadel of righteousness, and who was proud of the inflexibility with which he brought Servetus to his death. It is the Calvin of the* Institutes of the Christian Religion.
[*From* Concerning Heretics *by Robert H. Bainton. Columbia University Press, New York, 1935*]

FIGURE 3. *Illustration from* Der Weiss König, *a book devoted to the achievements of Emperor Maximilian I. The paraphernalia of sixteenth century warfare, as well as the ceremonial outfit of rider and steed, are convincingly portrayed.*
[*Courtesy of the Pierpont Morgan Library, New York*]

FIGURE 4. *Hampton Court Palace. This palace on the Thames, fifteen miles above London, was built by Cardinal Wolsey, Henry VIII's minister. It is an excellent example of Tudor architecture, with its large windows and many twisted chimneys. The use of brick instead of stone gave a warmth of color very pleasant in the English landscape, and a snugness the stone castle never knew. Hampton Court became the favorite country residence of English kings. Elizabeth enjoyed riding on horseback from Westminster to Hampton Court, where she spent a great deal of her time. One wing of the palace was rebuilt in the classical style in the reign of William III (1689–1702).*

PLATE XXIV

Sixteenth Century

FIGURE 1. *Portrait, by an unknown artist, of Queen Elizabeth as a young woman. The extraordinary physical handicaps under which women of the upper class functioned in the sixteenth century are brought out by this presentation of the tightly corseted queen, with ruff, farthingale, multiplicity of petticoats.*
[*Courtesy of the Metropolitan Museum of Art, New York*]

FIGURE 2. *Tomb of the Medici by Michelangelo. The restless and unresolved tensions of Michelangelo's later work reveal his belief that the struggle of the soul to escape from the body is made in vain. The artist felt the insecurity of mankind in a world where the Reformation had challenged the dominant role of the Catholic Church.*

FIGURE 3. *Engraving from* De Re Metallica, *Basel, 1561, showing machinery for removing water from a mine. This book is a treatise on mining, lavishly illustrated, and was a great aid to invention. The bucket system for raising water goes back to the ancient Egyptians, but these representations of the exact shapes of the parts, the best that had been evolved by the sixteenth century, provided material for the inventive mind.*

FIGURE 4. *Spring, engraved by Peter Breughel the elder. Breughel was the painter who brought the common man into art. He reveled in representations of peasants at work and at play, and his treatment is filled with sympathy for the worker. Here the contrast between the laborers and the stiff mistress who directs them is filled with meaning.*
[*Courtesy of the Metropolitan Museum of Art, New York*]

CHAPTER 23

The World of Elizabeth of England

[1533–1603]

QUEEN ELIZABETH of England, the daughter of Henry VIII and Anne Boleyn, had her father's astuteness and her mother's vanity. The greatest problem which she faced at her accession was that of the church. Her half-sister Mary, the daughter of Catharine of Aragon, had returned to the church the monastery lands which remained in the hands of the crown, and she had wished to force the return of the rest, but even her Catholic advisers had persuaded her that this was not expedient at the time. Since it was clear that those who had bought church lands would not feel secure under the continuance of the Catholic regime, this was probably a determining factor in Elizabeth's decision to return to her father's policy. She called herself governor, not head, of the church, and until her excommunication by the pope she kept open the possibility of conciliation with Rome. The exiled clergy were restored to their livings, but they came back wishing to purify the English church of what they had learned from the Calvinists to consider popish abuses. Elizabeth, however, liked candles on altars and surplices on the clergy, and she disapproved of these "Puritans" as they came to be called.

Elizabeth gave titles and favors to men who amused and flattered her, but shrewdly chose able men as ministers. She seldom allowed her favorites to meddle in state affairs. She delighted in having a magnificent court, with pageants and spectacles in the Italian fashion which had penetrated somewhat slowly into England, but she was parsimonious and as far as possible got her wealthy subjects to pay for these splendors. She hated the expense of wars, but made the mistake of going into the first of the French wars in the hope of

The World of Elizabeth of England [371

regaining Calais. Thereafter she used her shrewd matrimonial diplomacy to preserve English peace. She kept French princelings dangling as suitors while, if it seemed desirable, she gave a little secret aid to the Huguenots, as the French Protestants were called. She was severe to her parliaments when they reminded her that it was her duty to produce an heir, and solemnly gave ear to proposals from one country or another. She gave England peace for 30 years by her astuteness, and in that period the English people won the prosperity which enabled them to bear the expenses of the war with Spain which won them the supremacy of the seas.

The Catholics, who regarded Elizabeth as illegitimate, considered Mary Stuart, Queen of Scotland, the rightful ruler of England. Elizabeth's grandfather, Henry VII, had married his daughter Margaret to the king of Scotland, and the son of this marriage, James V, continued a traditional alliance with France by marrying Mary, daughter of the powerful duke of Guise. Their daughter Mary Stuart was married to the short-lived French king, Francis II, and on his death returned to rule Scotland. John Knox, a follower of Calvin, had reformed the Scottish church, and Mary's struggles with its magnates finally drove her to seek refuge with Elizabeth, who kept her a prisoner for many years.

When England broke with Rome there was no further reason to refrain from challenging the monopoly of the seas awarded by the papacy to Spain and Portugal. A sailor named Cabot had reached the mainland of North America in the reign of Henry VII, and by virtue of this voyage, which had been made under the English flag, the English now laid claim to the Atlantic seaboard. Efforts of individuals to establish colonies there failed because no private person could command sufficient wealth to sustain such a colony until it could fend for itself. The only possible way of success was through government assistance. Elizabeth would never face the expense of direct control, as Spain was doing, but she did encourage the formation of companies of merchants for exploiting overseas trade. She gave a charter to a group of merchants who established a stock company for trading with Muscovy, and another to a group who formed an East India Company, which sent vessels around the Cape of Good Hope to challenge the monopoly of Portugal in the Spice Islands. The Muscovy company established connections with Ivan the Terrible, the first of the princes of Moscow to take the title of tsar, and he joined the company of Elizabeth's rejected suitors.

The chartered company method was to succeed as a colonizing device in America under Elizabeth's successor. In the meanwhile, hardy English seamen descended upon the African coast and captured negroes, whom they took to the Spanish colonies and sold as slaves. Others by carrying much-desired goods to these Spanish colonies further infringed upon the monopoly of trade which Spain zealously guarded. These and other exploits ultimately brought to an end the peace which Elizabeth had given her subjects while her Continental neighbors were at war.

The almost constant warfare of France under Francis I had continued until 1559 under his son Henry II. Nearly half a century of civil war followed—fought under the cloak of religion but due also to the efforts of political factions to control the crown. Henry II had married Catherine de Medici, the great-granddaughter of Lorenzo the Magnificent. After Henry's death (1559) she had the problem of supervising the reigns of her three young sons, Francis II, Charles IX, and Henry III. The Catholic house of Guise and the Protestant house of Bourbon were rivals for the favor of these sickly lads, and the religious zeal of their followers gave them the excuse for civil war. Catherine was persuaded by her wise Chancellor, Michel de l'Hôpital, to try the experiment of religious toleration, but when this failed she was induced by the Guises to sanction the bloody method of assassination and murder. The massacre of St. Bartholomew (1572), in which such a leading Protestant as Admiral Coligny perished, for centuries provided the Protestants with talking points against the church of Rome. Only the military triumph of the Bourbon claimant to the throne after the death of the last of Catherine's sons (1589) put an end to the struggle. The Protestant Henry of Navarre (Bourbon) declared Paris worth a mass, and as the Catholic Henry IV he gave the Protestants a guaranteed toleration by the Edict of Nantes (1598).

In the meantime, Philip II of Spain had built at Madrid his palace, the Escorial, had reaped the glory of a great naval victory over the Turks at Lepanto (1571), and had become king of Portugal (1580). In 1567 he awakened a hornet's nest by endeavoring to establish new taxation and to root out Protestantism in the Netherlands. Both the Catholic regions in the southwest—the Belgium of today—and the Protestant provinces in the northeast—the Holland of today—revolted against this interference with cherished privileges. The former were finally placated, but the Dutch fought on. Elizabeth gave them a little surreptitious help, though not enough to embroil her with Spain. Philip II, however, enraged by the depredations of the English seamen in the Spanish colonial trade, which were always disavowed but really encouraged by Elizabeth, decided when Elizabeth finally executed Mary Stuart (1587) on suspicion of being implicated in an assassination plot, to finish off England first and put down the Dutch afterwards. In 1588 he sent against England a great Armada which had been assembled at colossal expense. Some of the unwieldy Spanish galleons were defeated by the ill-equipped English in their more easily maneuvered vessels, and the remainder were dispersed by a storm and most of them wrecked. Philip II had no resources left with which to cope with the Protestant Netherlands; they were thenceforth independent in fact, although Spain refused to recognize this until 1648.

In the course of the French and Dutch wars, certain important political theories were evolved. The Huguenots got from Calvin a guarded recognition of the right of rebellion. Two Scots, George Buchanan and John Knox, claimed rebellion as an unqualified right. A Catholic jurist, Jean Bodin, elaborated the doctrine of state sovereignty, which was to become one of the main bulwarks of nationalism. He believed the king should exercise sovereignty uncontrolled, but a Spanish Jesuit, Juan de Mariana, believed ultimate sovereignty rested with the people, and maintained the right of subjects to assassinate a ruler of the wrong faith. William the Silent, the great leader of the Dutch revolt, was disposed of in this way, and a series of attempts were made upon the life of Elizabeth (one of these plots had driven her to execute Mary, Queen of Scots).

The war with Spain crystallized English national feeling about the person of Elizabeth and strengthened the anti-Catholic bias which had been caused by the activities of the Jesuits and the wide reading of Foxe's *Book of Martyrs*. The Catholic Irish, who had never been treated wisely by the English, rebelled in Elizabeth's last years and were put down with great severity.

The dissolution of the English monasteries had left the poor uncared for, and the situation was met by the enactment of the first poor law, which enforced labor upon the physically fit and provided for parish funds to care for the weak and ill. The Poor Law of 1601 remained in force until well into the nineteenth century.

In England, where all children of a lord except the eldest son were commoners, there was no such fixed line to cut nobles off from the rest of society as on the Continent. All who were able to buy land and live in the country without working became gentry, and freely intermarried. The hands of rich merchants' daughters were sought by great nobles for their sons. Society in the days of Elizabeth is depicted in all the plays of Shakespeare, whatever their setting and story. The period is frequently characterized as the English Renaissance, for Italian influence in manners and in the arts was strong. In music it is the only period in which the English have distinguished themselves; the Italian madrigal was transformed into something wholly English. All stringed instruments then known, whether of the violin or the newly-invented keyboard type, were in great demand, and both men and women became accomplished performers. The singing of part songs was the evening amusement of families of the middle as well as the upper classes. The spirit of the age was the spirit of adventure and movement that had been awakened by the discovery of the new world. Richard Eden translated for his compatriots the stories from other tongues that told of the lands overseas awaiting settlement, and his work was followed by the collections of travelers' tales by Hakluyt and Purchas.

In Elizabeth's last days there was an increased tendency in parliament, especially on the part of members of the Puritan party, to criticize her arbitrary ways. Under Elizabeth a new phase of constitutional history began. The English parliament had come of age. It had built up precedents for centuries. In the upper house, or House of Lords, sat the Lords Temporal: dukes, earls, and barons; and the Lords Spiritual: the Archbishops of Canterbury and York, and all the bishops. This house was the highest court in the realm: all peers were entitled to be tried there. It had once been the sole legislative body; until the days of the Lancastrian kings the House of Commons merely petitioned that laws they desired be enacted. Since then the two houses shared legislative functions; and the House of Commons, made up of two knights from each shire and two burgesses from each ancient borough, had a certain advantage, for it won the right to initiate grants of money. On the theory that such humble persons might be overawed by royal majesty and thus forced to action they would not take of their own initiative the sovereign did not enter the hall where the Commons met, but summoned them to the Lords' house when he had anything to communicate. (On such occasions they stood huddled behind a bar set up at the end.) The members of the Royal Council, or ministers of the crown, had seats in the house befitting the station of each, and were useful in transmitting the sovereign's wishes informally, and sounding out the mood of the members.

In the early part of her reign Elizabeth was periodically infuriated by the insistence of parliament that she marry and secure the succession. Later the Puritans were troubled by the menace of "popery," and the burghers, as business men whose interests were affected, protested against Elizabeth's policy of granting monopolies to her favorites. The modern phrase "Tudor despotism" is as applicable to Elizabeth as to all the Tudors. Tudor despotism was skillfully applied: the Tudors got their way, but they got it usually through parliament, not in spite of it. Parliament contributed the supply of money for the sovereign's needs; and it was best to keep it in good humor. But if there was need, Elizabeth—like all the Tudors—was ready to overawe parliament when it did not grant the royal desires as her ministers transmitted them: she would appear before them or summon them before her and give them a good tongue-lashing. These occasions grew more frequent in her later days; but remembering her age and her services to her country, parliament decided to let the old lady die in peace, and reserved its attacks for her successor.

[THE SIXTEENTH CENTURY]

Readings

~~~~~~~~~~~~~~~~~

Erasmus

LETTERS

To Faustus Andrelinus (England, 1499) *

[The first letter shows the side of Erasmus which endeared him to his friends. The letters to Luther and Pace are most illuminating for his attitude toward the Reformation and its probable effect on the literary movement which was his solution for the evils of the time. He is frank about his constitutional inability to be cast in the role of martyr.]

Heavens, what do I hear? Is our Scopus really turned all at once from poet to soldier, and handling deadly weapons instead of books? How much better was it when he did battle with Delius the Volscian, as he called himself, and what a triumph awaited him, if he had slain that champion!

We too have made progress in England. The Erasmus you once knew is now become almost a sportsman, no bad rider, a courtier of some practice, bows with politeness, smiles with grace, and all this in spite of himself. If you are wise, you too will fly over here. Why should a man with a nose like yours grow to old age with nothing but French filth about him? But you will say your gout detains you. The devil take your gout, if he will only leave *you!* Nevertheless, did you but know the blessings of Britain, you would clap wings to your feet, and run hither; and if the gout stopped you, would wish yourself a Daedalus.

To take one attraction out of many; there are nymphs here with divine features, so gentle and kind, that you may well prefer them to your Camenae. Besides, there is a fashion which cannot be

---

* From F. M. Nichols, *The Epistles of Erasmus* (1901), I. Reprinted by permission of J. B. B. Nichols.

commended enough. Wherever you go, you are received on all hands with kisses; when you take leave, you are dismissed with kisses. If you go back, your salutes are returned to you. When a visit is paid, the first act of hospitality is a kiss, and when guests depart, the same entertainment is repeated; wherever a meeting takes place there is kissing in abundance; in fact, whatever way you turn, you are never without it. Oh Faustus, if you had once tasted how sweet and fragrant those kisses are, you would indeed wish to be a traveller, not for ten years, like Solon, but for your whole life, in England.

The rest of my story we will laugh over together, for I hope to see you before long. Farewell.

To Martin Luther (Louvain, May 30, 1519) *

My dearest brother in Christ,—Your letter, in which you show no less your truly Christian spirit than your great abilities, was extremely acceptable to me. I have no words to tell you what a sensation your writings have caused here. It is impossible to eradicate from people's minds the utterly false suspicion that I have had a hand in them, and that I am the ringleader of this "faction," as they call it. Some thought an opportunity had been given them for extinguishing literature, for which they cherish the most deadly hatred, because they are afraid it will cloud the *majesty* of their divinity, which many of them prize before Christianity; and at the same time destroying myself because they fancy I have some influence in promoting the cause of learning. . . .

You have friends in England, and among them men of the greatest eminence, who think most highly of your writings. Even here there are some who favour you, and one of these is a man of distinction. For myself, I am keeping such powers as I have to help the cause of the revival of letters. And more, I think, is gained by politeness and moderation than by violence. It was thus that Christ won the world to obedience to His authority. It was thus that Paul abrogated the Jewish law, putting an allegorical interpretation on its enactments. It is more expedient to declaim against those who abuse the Pope's authority than against the Popes themselves; and the same thing may be said of kings. Instead of holding the universities in contempt, we ought rather to endeavour to recall them

* From Robert Blackley Drummond, *Erasmus, His Life and Character as Shown in His Correspondence and Works* (1873), II, chapter XIII. Reprinted by permission of John Murray.

to more sober studies; and regarding opinions which are too generally received to be rooted all at once from people's minds, it is better to reason upon them with close and convincing arguments than to deal in dogmatic assertions. The violent wranglings in which some persons delight we can afford to despise, and it is useless attempting to answer them. . . .

To Richard Pace (Brussels, July 5, 1521) *

. . . I fear the Dominicans and some of the divines will use their victory intemperately, especially against me, and have found in Jerome Aleander an instrument most admirably adapted to this purpose. This man is mad enough naturally, without any one to instigate him; but, as it is, he has instigators who might drive even the most moderate to madness. The most virulent pamphlets are flying about on all sides, and Aleander ascribes them all to me, though I was ignorant of the existence of many of them before I heard of them from him. Luther has acknowledged his own books in the presence of the Emperor, and yet the "Babylonian Captivity," which is one of them, is ascribed to me. A prolific author indeed I must be, seeing that I was able to write so many pamphlets, while meantime I was emending the text of the New Testament with the utmost labour, and editing the works of Augustine, not to speak of other studies. May I be lost if in all Luther's works there is a single syllable of mine, or if any calumnious book was ever published of which I was the author; on the contrary, I do all I can to deter others. Now, however, they are adopting a new course, and asserting that Luther has borrowed some of his doctrines from my works, as if he had not borrowed more from Paul's Epistles. I now, at last, see clearly that it was the policy of the Germans to implicate me whether I would or not in Luther's business; a most impolitic piece of policy indeed, for nothing would sooner have alienated me from them. Or what aid could I have given to Luther if I had associated myself with him in his danger? The only result would have been that two must perish instead of one. I can never sufficiently wonder at the violent spirit he has displayed in his writings, by which he has certainly brought immense odium on all the friends of polite literature. Many indeed of his doctrines and exhortations are excellent, and I wish he had not vitiated the good in his writings by intolerable faults. If, however, he had always written in the most

* *Ibid.*

reverent spirit, still, I had no inclination to risk my life for the truth. It is not everybody who has strength for martyrdom, and I am afraid that if any outbreak should take place I should imitate St. Peter. When the Popes and the Emperors decree what is right, I obey, which is the course of true piety; but when they command what is wrong, I submit, and that is the safe course. I think also that good men are justified in acting thus if there is no hope of success. They are again trying to fix on me the authorship of the book on Julius, so determined are they to leave nothing untried to injure both myself and the cause of letters, which they cannot bear to see prospering. . . .

John Calvin

INSTITUTES *

[Calvin's concept of predestination is expressed more clearly in his own words than in any elucidation of them. His political ideas, which were so influential through the activities of the Presbyterians in Scotland, the Huguenots in France, and the Puritans in England and America, should be read as he expressed them himself before one plunges into modern expositions of their importance.]

Predestination

If it be evidently the result of the Divine will, that salvation is freely offered to some, and others are prevented from attaining it,—this immediately gives rise to important and difficult questions, which are incapable of any other explication, than by the establishment of pious minds in what ought to be received concerning election and predestination—a question, in the opinion of many, full of perplexity; for they consider nothing more unreasonable, than that, of the common mass of mankind, some should be predestinated to salvation, and others to destruction. . . . We shall never be clearly convinced as we ought to be, that our salvation flows from the fountain of God's free mercy, till we are acquainted with his eternal

---

* From *A Compend of the Institutes of the Christian Religion* by John Calvin, edited by Hugh Thomson Kerr, Jr. Copyright, 1939, by the Board of Christian Education of the Presbyterian Church in the United States of America, and used by their permission.

election, which illustrates the grace of God by this comparison, that he adopts not all promiscuously to the hope of salvation, but gives to some what he refuses to others. . . .

[*from III, xxi, 1*]

. . . Predestination we call the eternal decree of God, by which he has determined in himself, what he would have to become of every individual of mankind. For they are not all created with a similar destiny; but eternal life is foreordained for some, and eternal damnation for others. Every man, therefore, being created for one or the other of these ends, we say, he is predestinated either to life or to death. This God has not only testified in particular persons, but has given a specimen of it in the whole posterity of Abraham. . . .

[*from III, xxi, 5*]

In conformity . . . to the clear doctrine of the Scripture, we assert, that by an eternal and immutable counsel, God has once for all determined, both whom he would admit to salvation, and whom he would condemn to destruction. We affirm that this counsel, as far as concerns the elect, is founded on his gratuitous mercy, totally irrespective of human merit; but that to those whom he devotes to condemnation, the gate of life is closed by a just and irreprehensible, but incomprehensible, judgment. In the elect, we consider calling as an evidence of election, and justification as another token of its manifestation, till they arrive in glory, which constitutes its completion. As God seals his elect by vocation and justification, so by excluding the reprobate from the knowledge of his name and the sanctification of his Spirit, he affords an indication of the judgment that awaits them. . . .

[*from III, xxi, 7*]

Government

The exercise of civil polity . . . is equally as necessary to mankind as bread and water, light and air, and far more excellent. For it not only tends to secure the accommodations arising from all these things, that men may breathe, eat, drink, and be sustained in life, though it comprehends all these things while it causes them to live together, yet, I say, this is not its only tendency; its objects also are, that idolatry, sacrileges against the name of God, blasphemies against his truth, and other offences against religion, may not openly appear and be disseminated among the people; that the public tranquillity may not be disturbed; that every person may enjoy his property without molestation; that men may transact their business together without fraud or injustice; that integrity and modesty may be cultivated among them; in short, that there may be a public form of religion among Christians, and that humanity may be maintained among men. Nor let any one think it strange that I now refer to human polity the charge of the due maintenance of religion, which I may appear to have placed beyond the jurisdiction of men. For I do not allow men to make laws respecting religion and the worship of God now, any more than I did before; though I approve of civil government, which provides that the true religion which is contained in the law of God, be not violated, and polluted by public blasphemies, with impunity. But the perspicuity of order will assist the readers to attain a clearer understanding of what sentiments ought to be entertained respecting the whole system of civil administration, if we enter on a discussion of each branch of it. These are three: The magistrate, who is the guardian and conservator of the laws: The laws, according to which he governs: The people, who are governed by the laws, and obey the magistrate. . . .

[*from IV, xx, 3*]

. . . The forms of civil government are considered to be of three kinds: Monarchy, which is the dominion of one person, whether called a king, or a duke, or any other title; Aristocracy, or the dominion of the principal persons of a nation; and Democracy, or popular government, in which the power resides in the people at large. It is true that the transition is easy from monarchy to despotism; it is not much more difficult from aristocracy to oligarchy, or the faction of a few; but it is most easy of all from democracy to sedition. Indeed, if these three forms of government, which are stated by philosophers, be considered in themselves, I shall by no means deny, that either aristocracy, or a mixture of aristocracy and democracy, far excels all others; and that indeed not of itself, but because it very rarely happens that kings regulate themselves so that their will is never at variance with justice and rectitude; or, in the next place, that they are endued with such penetration and prudence, as in all cases to discover what is best. The vice or imperfection of men therefore renders it safer and more tolerable for the government to be in the hands of many, that they may afford each other mutual assistance and admonition, and that if any one arrogate to himself more than is right, the many may act as censors and masters to restrain his ambition. . . .

[*from* IV, xx, 8]

Now, as it is sometimes necessary for kings and nations to take up arms for the infliction of such public vengeance, the same reason will lead us to infer the lawfulness of wars which are undertaken for this end. . . . It is the dictate both of natural equity, and of the nature of the office, therefore, that princes are armed, not only to restrain the crimes of private individuals by judicial punishments, but also to defend the territories committed to their charge by going to war against any hostile aggression; and the Holy Spirit, in many passages of Scripture, declares such wars to be lawful. . . .

[*from* IV, xx, 11]

The first duty of subjects towards their magistrates is to entertain the most honourable sentiments of their function, which they know to be a jurisdiction delegated to them from God, and on that account to esteem and reverence them as God's ministers and vicegerents. . . .

[*from* IV, xx, 22]

Hence follows another duty, that, with minds disposed to honour and reverence magistrates, subjects approve their obedience to them, in submitting to their edicts, in paying taxes, in discharging public duties, and bearing burdens which relate to the common defence, and in fulfilling all their other commands. . . . Under this obedience I also include the moderation which private persons ought to prescribe to themselves in relation to public affairs, that they do not, without being called upon, intermeddle with affairs of state, or rashly intrude themselves into the office of magistrates, or undertake any thing of a public nature. If there be any thing in the public administration which requires to be corrected, let them not raise any tumults, or take the business into their own hands, which ought to be all bound in this respect, but let them refer it to the cognizance of the magistrate, who is alone authorized to regulate the concerns of the public. I mean, that they ought to attempt nothing without being commanded; for when they have the command of a governor, then they also are invested with public authority. . . .

[*from* IV, xx, 23]

But, if we direct our attention to the word of God, it will carry us much further; even to submit to the government, not only of those princes who discharge their duty to us with becoming integrity and fidelity, but of all who possess the sovereignty, even though they perform none of the duties of their function. For, though the Lord testifies that the magistrate is an eminent gift of his liberality to preserve the safety of men, and prescribes to magistrates themselves the extent of their duty, yet he at the same time declares, that whatever be their characters, they have their government only from him; that those who govern for the public good are true specimens and mirrors of his beneficence; and that those who rule in an unjust and tyrannical manner are raised up by him to punish the iniquity of the people; that all equally possess that sacred majesty with which he has invested legitimate authority. . . .

[*from IV, xx, 25*]

. . . If we are inhumanly harassed by a cruel prince; if we are rapaciously plundered by an avaricious or luxurious one; if we are neglected by an indolent one; or if we are persecuted, on account of piety, by an impious and sacrilegious one,—let us first call to mind our transgressions against God, which he undoubtedly chastises by these scourges. Thus our impatience will be restrained by humility. Let us, in the next place, consider that it is not our province to remedy these evils, and that nothing remains for us, but to implore the aid of the Lord, in whose hand are the hearts of kings and the revolutions of kingdoms. It is "God" who "standeth in the congregation of the mighty," and "judgeth among the gods." . . .

[*from IV, xx, 29*]

But in the obedience which we have shown to be due to the authority of governors, it is always necessary to make one exception, and that is entitled to our first attention,—that it do not seduce us from obedience to him, to whose will the desires of all kings ought to be subject, to whose decrees all their commands ought to yield, to whose majesty all their sceptres ought to submit. . . . If they command any thing against him, it ought not to have the least attention; nor, in this case, ought we to pay any regard to all that dignity attached to magistrates; to which no injury is done when it is subjected to the unrivalled and supreme power of God.

[*from IV, xx, 32*]

Queen Elizabeth of England

LETTERS*

To William Cecil, Lord Burghley (May 8, 1583)

[When he had threatened to resign from the Council Elizabeth dispatched to him this letter, which under its playful manner conveyed to him a stern reminder of his duty.]

Sir Spirit,

I doubt I do nickname you for those of your kind, they say, have no sense. But I have lately seen an *ecce signum,* that if an ass kick you, you feel it too soon. I will recant you from being spirit, if ever I perceive that you disdain not such a feeling. Serve God, fear the King, and be a good fellow to the rest. Let never care appear in you for such a rumour, but let them well know that you desire the righting of such wrong by making known their error, than you to be so silly a soul as to forshow what you ought to do, or not freely deliver what you think meetest, and pass of no man so much, as not to regard her trust who putteth it in you.

God bless you, and long may you last,

Omnino E. R.

To Robert Dudley, Earl of Leicester (February 10, 1586)

[Leicester was Elizabeth's favorite, and, presuming on her fondness for him he accepted the governorship of the Netherlands without asking for the Queen's permission. He received this sharp reproof.]

How contemptuously we conceive ourself to have been used by you, you shall by this bearer understand, whom we have expressly sent unto you to charge you withal. We could never have imagined had we not seen it fall out in experience that a man raised up by ourself and extraordinarily favoured by us above any other subject of this land, would have in so contemptible a sort broken our commandment, in a cause that so greatly toucheth us in honour; whereof, although you have showed yourself to make but little accompt, in most undutiful a sort, you may not therefore think that

---

* From *The Letters of Queen Elizabeth,* edited by G. B. Harrison (1935), Chapters III and IV. Reprinted by permission of Cassell & Company.

we have so little care of the reparation thereof as we mind to pass so great a wrong in silence unredressed: and, therefore, our express pleasure and commandment is, that all delays and excuses laid apart, you do presently, upon the duty of your allegiance, obey and fulfil whatsoever the bearer hereof shall direct you to do in our name: whereof fail you not, as you will answer the contrary at your uttermost peril.

To James the Sixth, King of Scotland (August, 1588)

[After the defeat of the Armada Elizabeth took no chances but dispatched the following warning to her kinsman in the North. Her jubilance about the great victory contrasts sharply with her anxiety about what James might do.]

Now may appear, my dear Brother, how malice conjoined with might strivest to make a shameful end to a villainous beginning, for, by God's singular favour, having their fleet well beaten in our Narrow Seas, and pressing with all violence, to achieve some watering place, to continue their pretended invasion, the winds have carried them to your coasts, where I doubt not they shall receive small succour and less welcome; unless those Lords that, so traitors like, would belie their own Prince, and promise another King relief in your name, be suffered to live at liberty, to dishonour you, peril you, and advance some other (which God forbid you suffer them live to do). Therefore I send you this gentleman, a rare young man and a wise, to declare unto you my full opinion in this great cause, as one that never will abuse you to serve my own turn; nor will you do aught that myself would not perform if I were in your place. You may assure yourself that, for my part, I doubt no whit but that all this tyrannical, proud and brainsick attempt will be the beginning, though not the end, of the ruin of that King, that, most unkingly, even in the midst of treating peace, begins this wrongful war. He hath procured my greatest glory that meant my sorest wrack, and hath so dimmed the light of his sunshine, that who hath a will to obtain shame, let them keep his forces company. But for all this, for your self sake, let not the friends of Spain be suffered to yield them force; for though I fear not in the end the sequel, yet if, by leaving them unhelped, you may increase the English hearts unto you, you shall not do the worst deed for your behalf; for if aught should be done, your excuse will play the *boiteux;* if you make not sure work with the likely men to do it. Look well unto it, I beseech you. . . .

SPEECH PROROGUING THE PARLIAMENT, 1586*

[In this speech Elizabeth makes clear her attitude toward Puritans as well as toward Catholics, and her conception of her functions in relation to the Church of England. She does not conceal her pride in her reputation as a learned lady.]

The royal assent being given to 30 public and 13 private Acts, her Majesty, in person, made the following Speech to both Houses of parl:

"My Lords and ye of the Lower House; My silence must not injure the owner so much, as to suppose a substitute sufficient to render you the thanks that my heart yieldeth you, not so much for the safe keeping of my life, for which your care appears so manifest, as for the neglecting your private future peril, not regarding other way than my present state.—No prince herein, I confess, can be surer tied or faster bound than I am with the link of your good-will, and can for that but yield a heart and a head to seek forever all your best; yet one matter toucheth me so near, as I may not over-skip, Religion, the ground on which all other matters ought to take root, and being corrupted, may marr all the tree. And that there be some fault-finders with the Order of the Clergy, which so may make a slander to myself and the Church, whose over-ruler God hath made me; whose negligence cannot be excused, if any schisms or errors heretical were suffered. Thus much I must say, that some faults and negligences may grow and be, as in all other great charges it happeneth, and what vocation without? All which if you my Lords of the Clergy do not amend, I mean to depose you. Look ye therefore well to your charges. This may be amended without heedless or open exclamations. I am supposed to have many studies, but most philosophical. I must yield this to be true, that I suppose few (that be no professors) have read more. And I need not tell you, that I am so simple that I understand not, nor so forgetful that I remember not; and yet amidst my many volumes, I hope God's Book hath not been my seldomest lectures, in which we find that which by reason (for my part) we ought to believe; that seeing so great wickedness and greeves in the world in which we live, but as wayfaring pilgrims, we must suppose that God would never have made us but for a better place, and of more comfort than we find here. I know no creature that breatheth, whose life

---

* From Cobbett's *Parliamentary History of England*. Reprinted by permission of Longmans Green & Co. Limited.

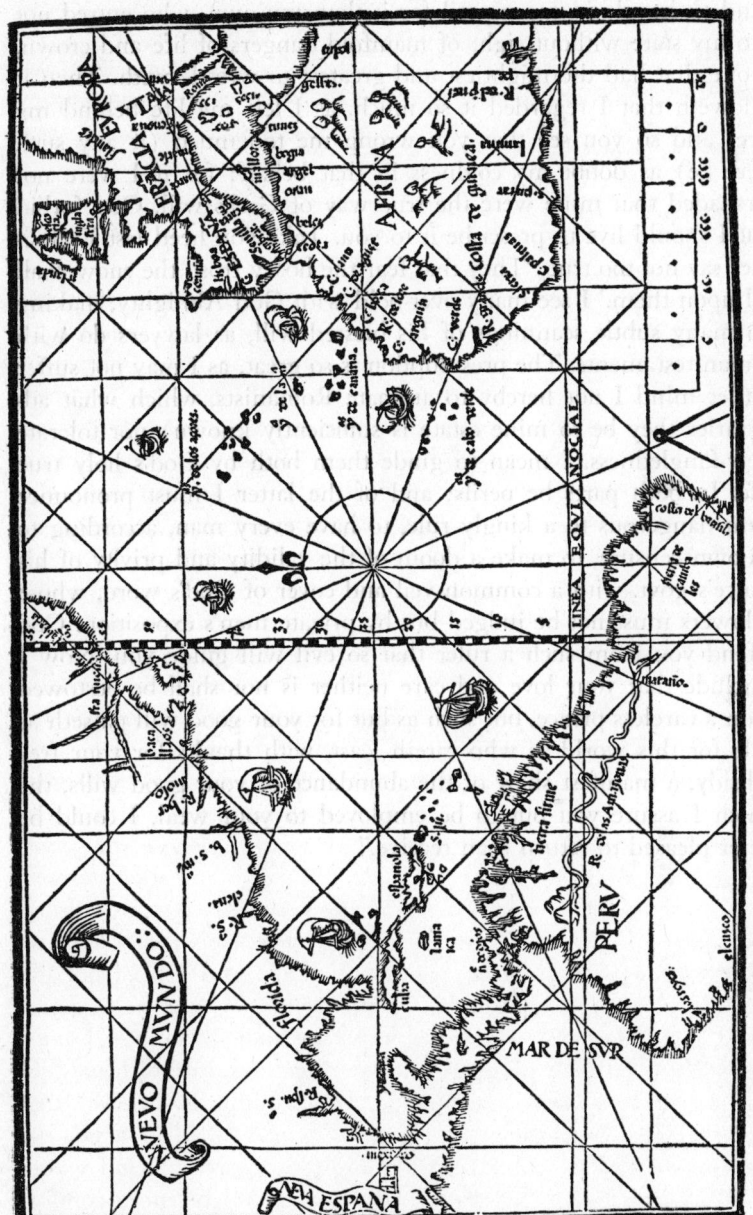

MAP OF THE WORLD FROM PEDRO DE MEDINA'S "ARTE DE NAVIGAR," VALLADOLID, 1545

standeth hourly in more peril for it than my own, who entred not into my state without sight of manifold dangers of life and crown, as one that had the mightiest and greatest to wrestle with. Then it followeth that I regarded it so much, as I left my life behind my care; and so you see that you wrong me too much (if any such there be) as doubt my coldness in that behalf; for if I were not persuaded that mine were the true way of God's will, God forbid that I should live to prescribe it to you. Take you heed lest Ecclesiastes say not too true, 'They that fear the hoary frost, the snow shall fall upon them.' I see many over-bold with God Almighty, making too many subtle scannings of his blessed will, as lawyers do with human testaments. The presumption is so great, as I may not suffer it (yet mind I not hereby to animate Romanists, which what adversaries they be to mine estate is sufficiently known) nor tolerate New-fangledness. I mean to guide them both by God's holy true rule. In both parts be perils; and of the latter I must pronounce them dangerous to a kingly rule, to have every man, according to his own censure, to make a doom of the validity and privity of his prince's govt. with a common veil and cover of God's word, whose followers must not be judged but by private men's exposition. God defend you from such a ruler that so evil will guide you. Now I conclude that your love and care neither is nor shall be bestowed upon a careless prince, but such as but for your good will passeth as little for this world as who careth least, with thanks for your free Subsidy, a manifest shew of the abundance of your good wills, the which I assure you but to be employed to your weal, I could be better pleased to return than receive."

PART XIII

The Seventeenth Century

CHRONOLOGY

1603 Accession of James I in England; beginning of Stuarts
1605 Gunpowder Plot
1609 Publication of Kepler's principal work on Copernican astronomy
1610 Assassination of Henry IV
1618 Revolt in Bohemia, beginning of Thirty Years' War
1620 Bacon's *Novum Organum*
1632 Galileo's dialogues on Copernicus
1635 French Academy founded
1640 Convention of the Long Parliament
1648 Peace of Westphalia
1649 Execution of Charles I of England
1660 Stuart Restoration
1661 Beginning of personal rule of Louis XIV of France
1679 Habeas Corpus Act in England
1682 Declaration of the Gallican Clergy
1683 Siege of Vienna; last great Turkish invasion
1685 Revocation of the Edict of Nantes
1687 Newton's *Principia*
1689 Bill of Rights; William and Mary reign in England
1690 Locke's *Essay on Human Understanding*

PART XIII

The Seventeenth Century

THE manifold activities of the sixteenth century, which extended the interests of Europeans into every field of thought and action, carried over into the seventeenth. They were most spectacular in the field of science, and nowhere was the international character of human society more evident than in the interchange of ideas among the great minds of that age. The scientists of the seventeenth century were the spiritual descendants of the tolerant Erasmus, though they lived in a world of bigotry inherited from the religious struggle and of the narrow dynastic ambition of Bourbons, Stuarts, and Habsburgs.

Of the many men of science and letters of the seventeenth century, which has been aptly styled the century of genius, perhaps none illustrates better than Galileo the complexities created by changing ideas in a world where the thinking of the average man and woman was still dominated by ancient beliefs and institutions. A Florentine, passionately attached to his birthplace, Galileo was a citizen of one of the hundreds of minute political entities which harked back to feudal decentralization in politics. Yet he, as much as any scientist, drew upon the work of others in many parts of Europe and had an international reputation; intellectually speaking, he was a citizen of the universe. The universality of the European world in the Middle Ages (represented by the concept of the Empire and that of the universal Christian church) had yielded to the national feeling that was furthered by the rise of national monarchies and by the Protestant Reformation. But the idea of universality persisted in the realm of science, where ideas were the heritage of all men and where national boundaries were unknown.

Scientific inquiry had never come to a standstill. The discussions of the Schoolmen had frequently been on subjects fundamentally scientific, and much scientific information had come from the Arabs. Despite the Church's disapproval, human bodies were dissected long before the new movement in art led men like Leonardo da Vinci and Michelangelo to study anatomy. Leonardo penetrated deep into the investigation of human organs, and the Fleming, Vesalius, published his book on the human body the same year that Copernicus's *De Revolutionibus Orbium Celestium* appeared (1543). The work of the humanists and the discovery of printing had put the scientific speculations of the ancients more fully at the disposal of investigators, and the printing press rapidly disseminated new ideas. The remarkable scientific experiments and inventions of Leonardo were never printed, but his notebooks were widely circulated and inspired further discoveries. (Palissy, the potter, who made geological studies, was one of the men who saw the notebooks.) Unlike the Schoolmen, however, investigators were becoming more interested in the question "how" than the question "why," and there was a practical turn to the curiosity of men like Leonardo. Sir Francis Bacon was the great popularizer of the idea that science could make men's lives easier.

The Pole, Copernicus, used the basic procedure of the modern scientist: he made observations on the basis of an hypothesis, and fitted the final statement of his hypothesis to the results of his observations. There had been medieval scholars who used observation and experiment, but they followed the example of Greek observers, who gave philosophical reasons for their conclusions. Copernicus went astray when he accepted one of these philosophical notions: that the planets moved in circles because a circle is the most perfect motion; but in the seventeenth century this was corrected by the German, Kepler, who used the records of the Danish Tycho Brahe's observations, as well as recently-improved instruments. He was able to show that the movement of the planets was elliptical, and to establish the mathematical laws of planetary motion. Much of the rapid progress of modern science has been due to scientists' command of instruments of precision and to the policy according to which they make public the steps by which they reach their conclusions. The academies for the advancement of knowledge formed by the learned men of the seventeenth century were important in this

The Seventeenth Century

pooling of experiments, and the universities were fundamental. For example, the Englishman Harvey was studying medicine in Padua when the Florentine Galileo was conducting his informal academy there in connection with his lectures. Combining Galileo's physics with Vesalius's anatomy, Harvey worked out his theory of the circulation of the blood.

Galileo developed modern dynamics by the experimental method, as the Greeks had done, generalizing his observations mathematically. With the analytical geometry worked out by Descartes, a Frenchman, the Englishman Newton developed the calculus. Leibnitz, a German and one of the most universal geniuses of his age, also developed the calculus independently. With the calculus, Galileo's laws of motion, and the law of gravitation, Newton was able to prove that Kepler's laws were correct. The measurements of the Abbé Picard and the work of the Dutchman, Huygens, and others enabled Newton to work out the Newtonian physics.

Galileo formulated an hypothesis about atmospheric pressure. His compatriot, Torricelli, demonstrated it mathematically; the Frenchman, Pascal, and the Irishman, Boyle, developed the idea further and devised machines which were the predecessors of the steam engine. Newton, Descartes, Huygens, and Roemer made investigations that led to the discovery that light could be measured. It became clear that with the calculus it was possible to measure motion, and theoretic proof of experiments in heat and electricity became possible. The capstone was set upon the work of Galileo by Newton.

The new political development of centralized territorial monarchy affected science, in that rulers found that it reflected credit on them to patronize scientists. They employed astronomers to cast their horoscopes in the manner of astrologers and Louis XIV deflected men of science from their cogitations to work out systems of water pumps feeding fountains and so forth.

In the arts, too, both the church revolution and the new monarchy were influential. The Jesuits gave their patronage to baroque architecture, which by a dramatic effect of movement and strong contrasts of light and shade appealed to the emotions and stimulated religious feeling. In music the Protestant churches developed the choral prelude. The fusion of drama and music in the new form of opera was not unconnected with the patronage of royal courts. In the construction of Versailles and its park, Louis XIV set new architectural standards. The fashions in clothes which he set allowed a range of behavior all the way from dignity to pomposity, and his designers produced the first really comfortable chairs in history.

The century saw fruitful developments in the field of political thought. The controversies about the state and about the right of rebellion which grew out of the religious wars in France had produced theories which were used in the English civil wars. During those wars the idea of universal manhood suffrage was debated; Milton in his *Areopagitica* set forth the basic arguments for freedom of expression. Thomas Hobbes's defense of arbitrary power in his *Leviathan* was countered by John Locke's *Treatise of Civil Government,* which justified the revolution of 1688 and provided arguments in the eighteenth century for the American and French Revolutions. Harrington's doctrine of the separation of the powers was to be transported to France and to America in the eighteenth century, but his attack upon the accumulation of great wealth without proportionate labor was to escape attention for a longer time.

One of the most far-reaching changes in the political scene during the seventeenth century was the consolidation of the national state as we know it today. While in England the authority of the crown was tempered by parliamentary oligarchy, on the Continent the idea of the king who ruled by divine right flourished and the absolute monarchy achieved the centralized state of which feudalism had been a political negation. The absolute monarchy of the seventeenth and eighteenth centuries was a political reaction against the practical decentralization of the Middle Ages. Many of the characteristics of feudal behavior, transferred to larger scale, and many important social and economic traits of the feudal period survived in the new national state.

Some of the characteristics which we ascribe to modern nations are more intelligible when we remember that the personification we unconsciously apply to the state had a real basis in the seventeenth and eighteenth centuries. The modern phrase "France's honor" has no meaning. At the beginning of the seventeenth century it had, for France's honor was the honor of Henry IV, her king, whose personal estate or fief under God the kingdom of France was. The medieval conception of the king as the first among equals was disappearing as the result of the persistent aggrandizement of the royal domain by marriage, inheritance, escheat, or outright aggression against other great feudal magnates. The territorial building-up of the great states of Europe was accomplished as an expansion of personal estates. They were not fully nations in the modern sense until the great French Revolution injected the idea of fraternity and changed men's thinking about themselves as units in the state from a vertical to a horizontal plane.

The consolidation of royal power in the centralized territorial state of the seventeenth and eighteenth centuries did not mean the end of the almost incessant warfare of feudal society. The anarchy was simply lifted to a higher plane; the dynasties which ruled the great European states had the family pride and family honor which might be expected, for they were feudal families with vastly improved resources for waging war. Although commercial factors had a rapidly rising importance, it is none the less true that the most fruitful cause of wars in the period of the absolute monarchy was dynastic rivalry. Dominated by feudal trends of political thinking, kings worked for personal and dynastic aggrandizement like any feudal lord. The evil effects of this policy during the period of the absolute monarchy are only now becoming fully apparent. So thoroughly were the attributes of the feudal lord associated with the dynastic states of the seventeenth and eighteenth century that when the dynasties disappeared and only the nation remained, men still attributed to the nation the personal characteristics of the feudal lords by whom they had been governed. Hence, wherever among modern nations European continental thinking on the subject of nationalism is dominant, it is considered the honorable thing for nations to fight rather than arbitrate, and the accepted thing for them to aggrandize themselves at the expense of other, temporarily weaker, nations.

The development of the absolute monarchy was tempered in this century by the great prestige and tenacity of medieval institutions. The Roman Catholic Church, feudalism, and the Holy Roman Empire had each contributed to the concept of universality in the Christian world. By the seventeenth century the institutions remained, but the concept of universality they represented had suffered heavy blows. The unhealed breach of the Protestant Reformation was a dangerous threat to the dominant position in society of the church as an organization, but the church was still an absolutely indispensable part of men's thinking and living. It was representatives of the church who were close to the ordinary man or woman in this life, and who alone could offer any real hope or consolation about the next. It was the church which walked with the individual at every step of the road, caring for him when he was sick or penniless, and monopolizing the ceremonies attendant upon the three great moments of existence—birth, marriage, and death. The material poverty of the bulk of the European population, dominantly agricultural and culturally depressed, politically and economically repressed by the small privileged ruling class, left it very little to look forward to in this life. The key to the next life was the church, whether Catholic or Protestant, through the sacraments or through clerical assistance. Therefore the church retained a powerful hold upon the imagination of the rank and file, and consequently was powerfully supported by the increasingly secular ruling class in perpetuation of the traditional league between throne and altar which was sanctified by centuries of custom.

When a scientist with international renown, like Galileo, publicly supported a new conception in which the earth's inhabitants were not the centre of the universe, church leaders saw a mortal threat to the church's position as the leading institution of human society. The church had always taught that man was the final step in creation and that the universe was perfect and unchanging. It was for this reason that the church's great powers of censorship were directed toward the suppression of many new scientific ideas and that Galileo was persecuted. The state supported the church in this endeavor, for any weakening of such a potent ally would ultimately weaken the state when the two were mutually dependent. Even in the Protestant countries, the concept of government and church as mutually dependent allies prevailed, and the church officially played a dominant role in the life of the society. Toleration, in any modern sense, was ignored in the seventeenth century; not to support the officially established church, whether Catholic or Protestant, was a civil crime.

Although national boundaries raised no barriers to intellectual progress, the growth of strong monarchies produced political problems. The absolutism of the French monarchy under Louis XIV made him both the envy and the model of other rulers. In the latter half of the century *le roi soleil*—Louis selected the sun as an emblem —blazed in the European sky at his zenith. Consciously at times, unwittingly at others, he set the pace for Europe, in all fields from fashion to war. As a symbol of national greatness he had no peers in his lifetime, and some aspects of his or his ministers' policies dominated the century after his death. In the latter part of the seventeenth century the chartered company was put into service by the English and the French as an instrument of colonization, and this led ultimately to war. Louis XIV embarked upon the French struggle for the Rhine Valley that still plagues the world. His aggressive policy and the genius of his generals laid the foundation for the militarism that has not ceased to grow. The menace to England of a strong power in possession of the Netherlands became a preoccupation of British foreign policy. The foundations were laid for two new and powerful states, Russia and Prussia. Yet despite all the growing nationalism and political upheaval of which Louis XIV was so symbolic and so salient a cause, the peaceful work of Galileo and Newton probably did more to make the modern world what it is than any war ever fought. In short, the seventeenth century saw the beginnings of the headaches as well as the scientific progress of the modern world.

ENGRAVING BY THE FRENCH ARTIST JACQUES CALLOT (1592-1635)

CHAPTER 24

The World of Galileo

[1564–1642]

~~~~~~~~~~~~~~~~~~~~~~~~~~~~~~~~~~~~

GALILEO GALILEI was born in Pisa the year that Calvin and Michelangelo died. He was a gifted lad, interested in music and painting much to the disappointment of his careworn father, an impoverished noble, and his shrewish mother, whose diabolical temper made the family life a harrowing experience. During much of his life Galileo was hounded by his family, by lack of finances, by the Church, and sometimes by all together. He came naturally by his tastes and his innovating spirit. His father was proficient in mathematics and was a skillful performer on the lute; he wrote in an original vein on music, and contributed to the development of the new musical form, the opera, which expressed in music the same spirit which in painting, sculpture, and architecture is known as the baroque. The artistic background of Galileo's life was this rich, emotional, varied style in the arts, which Michelangelo had forecast in his later works.

Galileo's early education was in the hands of the Jesuits, who gave him sound training in the classics and possibly awakened his curiosity in scientific matters. Many currents of thought were in the air in Italy as in all of Europe. The settlement of the new world meant travelers' tales of primitive peoples and strange animals and plants which disturbed the old system of a universe settled and known; the ideas of Copernicus and the star-gazers were in circulation; magical arts were practiced, and astrology was fashionable. No wonder the Holy Office (the Inquisition) was busy hunting down heretics.

Galileo's father wanted him to become a cloth-maker, as he had to be self-supporting, but the lad spent his time making mechanical toys, painting, and playing on the lute, and he was sent to study medicine at the University. At the University of Pisa, as at all universities, the medievalized Aristotle dominated scientific study. Although Aristotle used the method of observation and experiment, he was wont to generalize on the basis of intuitive thinking, and come to a conclusion on the basis of what seemed right and fitting, sometimes without sufficient tests. Peter Ramus and others had fought his influence in the preceding century. Leonardo da Vinci attacked the Aristotelian appeal to authority and insisted on mathematical proof.

As a student at Pisa Galileo annoyed his teachers by following a principle of his father's: refusing to accept statements not accompanied by reasonable proof. While still studying medicine he devised an instrument by which the swing of a pendulum could be used for taking a patient's pulse. He gave up his medical studies and devoted himself to physical investigations. His success won him the professorship of mathematics in the University of Pisa, where he made many experiments, the most famous of them with bodies in motion. Thinkers in the seventeenth century were more interested in the answer to the question "how" than to the question "why." Aristotle had been interested in the question why a moving body stopped. Since according to observation a body moves if force is applied to it, intuitive thinking suggests the answer that it stops when the force is no longer applied to it. Galileo, thinking speculatively that objects might continue to move indefinitely if not interfered with, analyzed an instance of motion, such as a ball rolling down an incline, to find the mathematical principle involved, worked it out mathematically, and then made further tests, until he was satisfied that his hypothesis was correct. This has been the method of scientists from that day to this.

Galileo was attacked for his criticism of Aristotle, and obliged to give up his post. In 1592 he was appointed professor of mathematics at the University of Padua. Padua was in Venetian territory. The Venetian republic was carrying on a struggle to limit papal authority in its dominions, and a certain academic freedom reigned. Galileo became famous throughout Europe—he made a number of enemies because of his caustic language in controversy. He was responsible for many inventions, for most of which others got the credit. When on a visit to Venice, he heard of a Dutch toy which made far-off objects appear near; he thought over the idea and invented the telescope. This was in 1609, and in the following year he published important discoveries in the heavens that his invention enabled him to make. He had read and pondered the neglected treatise of the astronomer Copernicus; another astronomer, the Dane Tycho Brahe, had made important discoveries but rejected Copernicus's theory, though Tycho's pupil, Kepler, who inherited his records, accepted it. Kepler got into trouble with the authorities in the University of Tübingen for this, but some liberal-minded Jesuits protected him.

Another convert to the Copernican system was the philosopher, Giordano Bruno, who fell into the hands of the Inquisition and was executed in 1600. The belief in the heliocentric theory was only one of a number of eccentric ideas he held, and his fate did not deter Galileo from accepting and openly espousing Copernicus's ideas. Unfortunately this was after he had left Padua, where the powerful influence of Venice would have protected him. In 1610 he went to Florence as the philosopher and mathematician of the Grand Duke of Tuscany. After a good deal of controversy the Inquisition declared that the belief that the sun was the centre of the world and immovable was contrary to Scripture and therefore heretical, and that the belief that the earth moved was erroneous. Galileo was told at the order of Pope Pius V that he should renounce these opinions and should not teach or defend them. Galileo is supposed to have agreed.

The action was disapproved by some of the clergy, among them by a cardinal who later became Pope Urban VIII, but it was generally held consistent with the Church's duty to stamp out heresy. Religious toleration as understood today did not exist; the only notable exceptions to the intolerance of the age existed in the United Netherlands and in France. In the cities of the Netherlands, which were centres of industry and commerce, a stern Calvinism was professed, but the need for workers was so great that there was a tacit recognition that the faith of a worker would not be inquired into if he did not call attention to it. The rigid censorship of the press, which suppressed both political and religious heresy in the monarchies, was not allowed to interfere with the thriving publishing business in Dutch cities.

Toleration in France was limited but explicit. When Henry of Navarre eventually became King Henry IV of France he accepted Catholicism, which was the religion of the majority of his subjects.

Brought up as a Protestant and strongly supported by French Protestants while contesting the succession to the French throne, Henry was too fair and too statesmanlike to embark on the course of persecution which some of his new advisers advocated. To protect the Protestant minority against the superior force of their Catholic opponents and to give Protestants a legal standing, Henry had issued the Edict of Nantes in 1598, which gave Protestants both freedom of worship in certain designated areas which were recognized as Protestant and also the right to fortify and garrison certain key Protestant towns to guarantee the freedom of worship. By this measure Henry hoped to keep the support of both Catholic and Protestant in his kingdom. The Edict both limited the area of Protestant activity and gave it royal protection. It should be noted, however, that this semi-toleration of the Huguenots, as the French Protestants were called, was unwillingly accepted by the Catholic community, and that within the Protestant zones the Huguenots were equally intolerant of Catholics. Henry's religious settlement, however, at least ended the murderous religio-civil wars that had plagued France in the latter half of the sixteenth century.

A contributing factor to the disorders of that period had been the rivalries of the great French feudal nobles and their efforts to dominate a series of weak kings. Henry was a strong king, and set out to impose the king's peace on the second estate as well as the first. In this he made only a beginning before his career was cut off by his assassination in 1610, the year Galileo left Padua for Florence. Henry's efforts, however, pointed the way to the later development of monarchical absolutism. Under Henry was inaugurated the system of ennobling wealthy members of the bourgeoisie, which had far-reaching consequences. The system provided the king with badly needed funds, but tended to create a division in the privileged second estate because the new nobility were rewarded for administrative service rather than military—hence their designation as nobility of the robe, whereas the older nobility were the nobility of the sword. The newer nobles were sometimes socially snubbed by the more ancient branch. Finally, Henry's system had the effect of buying off the potential leaders of the voiceless, uneducated, amorphous third estate.

The policy of strengthening the crown and weakening or subordinating other elements of French society was ably furthered by

Cardinal Richelieu, the principal minister of King Louis XIII after the regency which followed Henry's death. Although he was a high official of the Roman Catholic Church, Richelieu devoted himself wholeheartedly to fostering the absolute authority of the crown in France. One of his first steps was to undo part of the work of Henry IV's religious settlement. The Edict of Nantes had in a sense created a state within a state by allowing fortifications and garrisons. It gave one group in the kingdom the means with which to resist the royal authority should a crisis arise when the loyalty of the Huguenots to the crown might weaken. Richelieu therefore compelled the Huguenots to disband their garrisons and destroy their fortifications, and he employed the royal army when the great Huguenot fortress town of La Rochelle resisted the decree. The cardinal did not, however, revoke the Edict of Nantes, which remained to give legal basis to the toleration of Protestant worship in France for another half-century.

Richelieu made an equally determined drive against the power of the French nobility to resist the authority of the king. Many of the great nobles—with their vast estates, fortified castles, and armies of private retainers—could effectively challenge the crown in time of crisis by shutting themselves up on their own domains. The cardinal decreed the abolition of the right of livery (the maintenance of armed followers who wore the private uniform of the nobleman) and ordered the destruction of all fortified places not essential to the defense of the frontiers. There was opposition and conspiracy on the part of the nobles, which Richelieu either circumvented by cleverly exploiting the jealousies of the nobility or which he crushed by ruthless and arbitrary force. Acting consistently on the principle that any measure was justifiable which was in the interest of the state, he laid the foundation for the complete domination of France by the king under Louis XIV by undermining the support of the potential forces of resistance.

The foundations of French prosperity were laid during these years. Henry IV with the aid of his minister Sully had reformed the administration, built roads and canals, established the silk industry, and encouraged agriculture. Verrazano and Cartier, sent by Francis I, had established claims to America, and in Henry's reign Quebec was founded. Cardinal Richelieu carried on Henry's enlightened policies. He saw the advantages of expansion overseas and encouraged exploration there. Settlements were made in the West Indies and expanded by the Company of the Isles of America. The Company of the Hundred Associates was established to colonize continental America. Given internal peace, France was ready to profit from these advantages; the strong government for which all classes yearned was to be provided by Louis XIV.

In German lands the compromise of Augsburg failed to be satisfactory partly because it made no provision for Calvinism, chiefly because its stipulations against the secularization of church lands were not observed. This angered the Catholic princes who had won back from the Lutherans almost the whole of southern Germany. War broke out in 1618 when the Bohemians refused to accept the rule of the Catholic Ferdinand of Hapsburg. The Bohemian Protestants elected in his place Frederick, the Elector Palatine, who had married a daughter of James I of England, the son of Mary Stuart. A Catholic League drove out Frederick and gave a large part of the Palatinate to Catholic Bavaria. King Christian of Denmark then led the Protestant armies, but was defeated and sued for peace. Later the king of Sweden, Gustavus Adolphus, whose grandfather had made Sweden a Lutheran state, entered the war. He won two brilliant victories, but was killed in 1632.

That same year Galileo published his *Dialogue on the Two Principal Systems of the Universe*. Urban VIII, who had disapproved the action of the Inquisition in 1616, was now on the papal throne; Galileo had demonstrated to him his *Il Saggiatore,* a witty work which explicitly disclaimed the Copernican theory, but ridiculed the use of authority to suppress the results of observation. He had argued the Copernican theory before the pope himself and had been benevolently treated. He therefore rashly concluded that official opinion was sufficiently modified to allow the publication of a veiled defense. In the *Dialogue* the defender of the Ptolemaic theory was plainly outmatched by the champion of Copernicus. Galileo had been too optimistic. He was denounced to the Inquisition and was summoned to Rome to stand trial. The *Dialogue* was placed on the Index of Prohibited Books, and he was forced to abjure the Copernican theory. He was sentenced to prison, but after a time was allowed to return to Florence, where he lived in merely technical captivity, and was free to continue his scientific research. He was over 70, and before long became totally blind, but he worked indomitably at the task of bringing together all his work in what he had made the science of mechanics. One day he was visited by a young Englishman, John Milton, who, when he, too, was a blind old man, was to write in *Paradise Lost* an exposition of the Copernican theory.

England, upon the death of Elizabeth, had been brought under the rule of a new family, the house of Stuart, when James I, Elizabeth's cousin, who had been king of Scotland sixteen years, came to the English throne in 1603. Chartered companies had taken over the business of founding colonies overseas, which were too expensive to succeed as individual enterprise, and in 1607 the Virginia Company made the first permanent settlement in America and named it Jamestown in honor of the king. James I had been brought up under the stern guidance of Presbyterian pastors, one of whom called him to his face "God's silly vassal," and had come to believe that Presbyterianism "agreed with monarchy as God with the Devil." In answer to a book by the Scot, George Buchanan, which maintained the right of subjects to resist oppressive rulers, James published a treatise in which he proved to his own satisfaction that kings ruled by divine right. He was very stiff with English Puritans. The Puritans were horrified when he refused to go to the aid of his Protestant son-in-law at the beginning of the Thirty Years' War. They were still more horrified when he tried to marry his son Charles to the Spanish Infanta and, when this failed, betrothed him to the daughter of Henry IV. They were Calvinists and approved the decision of the Dutch, in the Synod of Dort, that Arminius, who believed it possible that all men might be saved, was a blasphemer.

English merchants lived comfortably in the days of James I. Following the ways of nobles they built great houses. English architects had developed a rich variation of the Tudor style in the type called Jacobean after the king, and clever English cabinet-makers carved elaborate mantel-pieces and designed heavy furniture to match for these houses which were being built in town as well as in the country.

Puritan merchants kept an attentive eye upon the king, who was interfering with the business which produced their wealth by giving monopolies to favorites as Elizabeth had done. They saw little to approve of in James except his action in promoting a new English version of the Bible. Puritan merchants and gentry were sending their sons to the universities, especially to Christ Church College in

Cambridge. Thither went Oliver Cromwell, the son of a country gentleman, and John Milton, a London youth who wrote verses. It had become fashionable to make a tour on the Continent upon leaving the university. By the time Milton was ready to make his tour James had been succeeded by his son, Charles I (1625-49).

Milton's visit was in 1638, the year when Galileo had discreetly arranged with the printing house of Elzevir in Amsterdam to issue his *Dialogue of the New Sciences* as if he had not authorized it. In this book he set a model for all the scientific work that was to follow him. He divorced philosophy from science and dispensed with the musty philosophical terminolgy. He demonstrated the modern method of speculative thinking checked by observation. He formulated the law of falling bodies and set forth the principles which were to be applied in the pendulum clock and the microscope. He showed his understanding of the laws of motion which were to be formulated by his great successor, Newton.

John Milton returned to England, where trouble was brewing for Charles I and his popish queen. The Puritans wanted church ritual simplified, and the business men wanted economy in government. In those days nobody understood that the vast amounts of American gold and silver which Charles V and Philip II had scattered over Europe had brought about inflation. The Stuart kings would not have been able to manage with the sums that had sufficed Elizabeth, even if they had been as thrifty as she. Charles, moreover, felt it his duty to maintain the established ritual of the church and backed Laud, the Archbishop of Canterbury, in his campaign to banish the Puritan usages which had crept into many churches.

The Anabaptist idea of the separation of church and state had spread to England, and congregations of Separatists had sprung up, especially in the eastern counties. Their refusal to pay tithes led to persecution. One congregation from Scrooby in Norfolk migrated to Holland and later in the English ship *Mayflower* to America. As time went on, large numbers of Puritans migrated to Massachusetts Bay because of their unwillingness to submit to what they considered a popish ritual. There they set up a state church which persecuted non-Puritans. Puritans both in England and America held to the Calvinistic disapproval of games and sports, regarded celebration of Christmas as popery, and made the whole of Sunday a day of worship on which not even a hot meal was prepared. They stressed also that part of the fourth commandment which said, "Six days shalt thou labor," and to them work was a virtue and idleness a sin. They opposed the trunk hose, earrings, plumes, and slashed doublets that were the mode, and wore plain garments in protest.

Thus the English people whether middle-class, gentry, or noble divided sharply. One group continued in the gay habits of the old "merrie England," dancing on the green when church was over on Sunday. The other began and ended the day with Bible reading and prayer, and kept the Sabbath solemnly with long sermons and much reading of the Bible and Foxe's *Book of Martyrs,* which told of the execution of Protestants in Mary's reign. The beautiful cadences of the English translation of the Bible that had been made by the order of James I had its effect upon English speech and letters, and Foxe's *Book of Martyrs* nourished hatred of the Roman Catholics.

Especially in the towns Puritanism flourished, and a large proportion of the borough members of parliament were Puritan merchants. They eagerly continued the parliamentary opposition to the exercise of arbitrary power by the crown to which James I had yielded whenever the pressure became extreme. Charles, however, was more obstinate than his father, and finally the refusal of parliament to vote supplies until grievances had been met led him to try to rule without parliament. The parliament which met at his accession, instead of making the usual grant of customs revenue for his whole reign, showed its lack of confidence in the new monarch by making it for one year only. He had just married Henrietta Maria, the daughter of Henry IV of France, and this marriage vastly displeased the Puritans. His second parliament was still more critical than the first, and refused to transact business until he set free two of its leaders whom he had imprisoned. His foreign policy was unpopular, he raised money by arbitrary methods, and his third parliament refused to make him money grants until he had assented to the Petition of Right, which opposed his arbitrary acts. Finally Charles ruled eleven years without summoning parliament, and raised money by reviving ancient methods and selling monopolies. Parliamentary leaders, however, kept in touch with each other by holding meetings of colonial and other companies. They had in the years of opposition perfected parliamentary procedure and learned the advantages of the committee system. They were ready to function smoothly when the king should be forced to summon a new parliament. The time came in 1640, when the rebellion of the Scots (induced by Charles's attempt to coerce them into using the Book of Common Prayer) forced him to raise funds. The struggles reopened in 1640 and in 1642 led to the outbreak of civil war.

In 1642 the Great Elector of Brandenburg, who was to lay the foundation of modern Prussia, had been at the head of the state for two years. Louis XIII was enjoying the last year of his carefree reign, and Cardinal Richelieu, who had assumed the royal cares, died. In Florence Galileo breathed his last, and in England Isaac Newton was born.

MONUMENTAL BRASS OF AN ENGLISH KNIGHT
AND HIS LADY, ABOUT 1630

(From *A Student's History of England* by Samuel R. Gardiner. Longmans Green, London, 1897.)

CHAPTER 25

The World of Isaac Newton

[1642 – 1727]

~~~~~~~~~~~~~~~~~~~~~~~~

IN THE year of Galileo's death there was born in England a yeoman's son who was to bring together the results of his predecessors' work and build on the foundations laid by Galileo and his predecessors the structure of modern physics. Isaac Newton's childhood was passed in a world at war, for his country was split by the struggle between an absolutist king and a belligerently recalcitrant parliament. In the war, which began in the year of his birth, the royal forces were victorious at first; but the tide was turned by the military genius of Oliver Cromwell, a Puritan gentleman who had never seen an army until he was called to lead one in the field. He sat upon the court of justice which sentenced Charles I to death (1649), and brought about the submission of Scotland and Ireland.

In 1654 Newton, a twelve-year-old boy, was sent to a grammar school, where he called attention to himself by making windmills and water clocks. The Commonwealth which had been set up in place of the monarchy had just been overthrown and Cromwell was made Lord Protector of England, Scotland, and Ireland. Some of the men who raised him to power had wished to make him king, but he refused the title. Cromwell was a leading Puritan and belonged to the Independent Party, a group which believed neither in the old Episcopal organization of the Anglican Church nor the Presbyterianism of the Scots, but in Congregationalism, a form of separatism which promoted a much broader toleration in religious affairs because of its organization of individual church units.

Cromwell made England respected all over Europe. He sent to the West Indies an expedition which seized the Spanish island of Jamaica, although England was at peace with Spain. That nation was beginning to decline because of its dependence on the precious metals from America and its failure to build up the industries formerly carried on by the Moors. Its colonial empire was at the mercy of any ambitious power. The idea of colonies as a source of wealth and prestige was toyed with both in France and England. The English merchants of the Commonwealth had enacted a navigation act to regulate colonial trade for their own advantage even before Cromwell seized Jamaica. After the death of Cromwell and a period of anarchy, in 1660 Charles I's son was summoned back from exile as Charles II. Soon the new king had another navigation act enacted. He extended to the colonies his policy, which was unsuccessful at home, of direct control by the crown. As he had no money, he rewarded the men who had brought him back to England by grants of land in America, and thus introduced a proprietary system in Carolina, Pennsylvania, and Maryland. Thus, while Newton was extending the empire of the mind, his compatriots were extending the empire of commerce.

The French settlements in Canada languished without much government support in these years of expanding English colonial activity, but at the same time France was becoming the leading power in Europe. Henry IV's policy of developing French industries was continued and amplified. In the minority of Louis XIV Cardinal Mazarin, by the same means, was able to make the young king master of untold riches. Louis XIV became king in the year that followed Newton's birth. Five years later the Thirty Years' War was brought to an end by the treaties of Westphalia (1648).

Although the immediate cause and the early stages of this Thirty Years' War, which had begun in 1618, had a religious emphasis, the conflict had other implications. In part it was a civil war in the Germanies to prevent the extension of imperial control by the Hapsburg emperors at the expense of the independent rights of the other German states large and small. Spain became involved because her Hapsburg rulers were bound by family ties to the interests of their Austrian cousins. The ties were stronger because, since the English conquest of Spain on the seas, the principal supply route over which reinforcements were sent to Spanish forces in the Netherlands was by way of northern Italy, Austria, and the Rhine valley. Ultimately Spanish control of the Netherlands helped provoke open French intervention. Richelieu, whose aim was to establish French hegemony in Europe, brought France in on the side of the Protestants, though he was a cardinal of the Roman Catholic Church. The last phase of the war was a dynastic struggle between the Bourbons and the Hapsburgs and did not end until the resources of both sides were exhausted and the German lands were laid waste in a devastation from which they did not recover for a century and a half. German national unification was even longer delayed, for the creation of a strong centralized monarchy under Hapsburg leadership was made impossible.

The treaties of Westphalia established the boundaries of European states that remained virtually unchanged until 1713. Richelieu's shrewdness had brought France into the war on the side of the Protestants in 1635 after the Swedish intervention had failed to destroy Hapsburg power across the Rhine. His policy was justified when France was rewarded in 1648 by extensive grants in Alsace, on the west bank of the Rhine, which was to become a bone of contention between France and Germany in the nineteenth and twentieth centuries. Sweden's acquisitions of German territory gave her a voice in the Diet of the empire. Frederick William, the Great Elector of Brandenburg who held East Prussia as a fief from the king of Poland, received lands which strengthened the position of the house of Hohenzollern. Switzerland and the United Netherlands were declared independent of the Empire. The principle that each ruler could control the religion of his subjects was reaffirmed for the German states and extended to include the Calvinists. The religious differences, the practical independence of the princes, and the economic ruin of the country put off all prospect of a united Germany for more than two centuries. Both Catholic and Protestant armies had lived upon and wrecked the land, and the population was greatly reduced. The horrors of the struggle led a Frenchman, Crucé, to write *The New Cynée,* proposing the abolition of armies and the establishment of a world court. About the same time a Dutchman, Hugo Grotius, wrote a book that endeavored to set legal limits to the excesses of war. This book, *On the Law of Peace and War,* marked the beginning of modern international law.

The treaties of Westphalia were completed five years after the accession of the boy Louis XIV to the throne of France (1643-1715). The work of Richelieu was carried on by another churchman, Cardinal Mazarin. He was, however, handicapped in his dealings

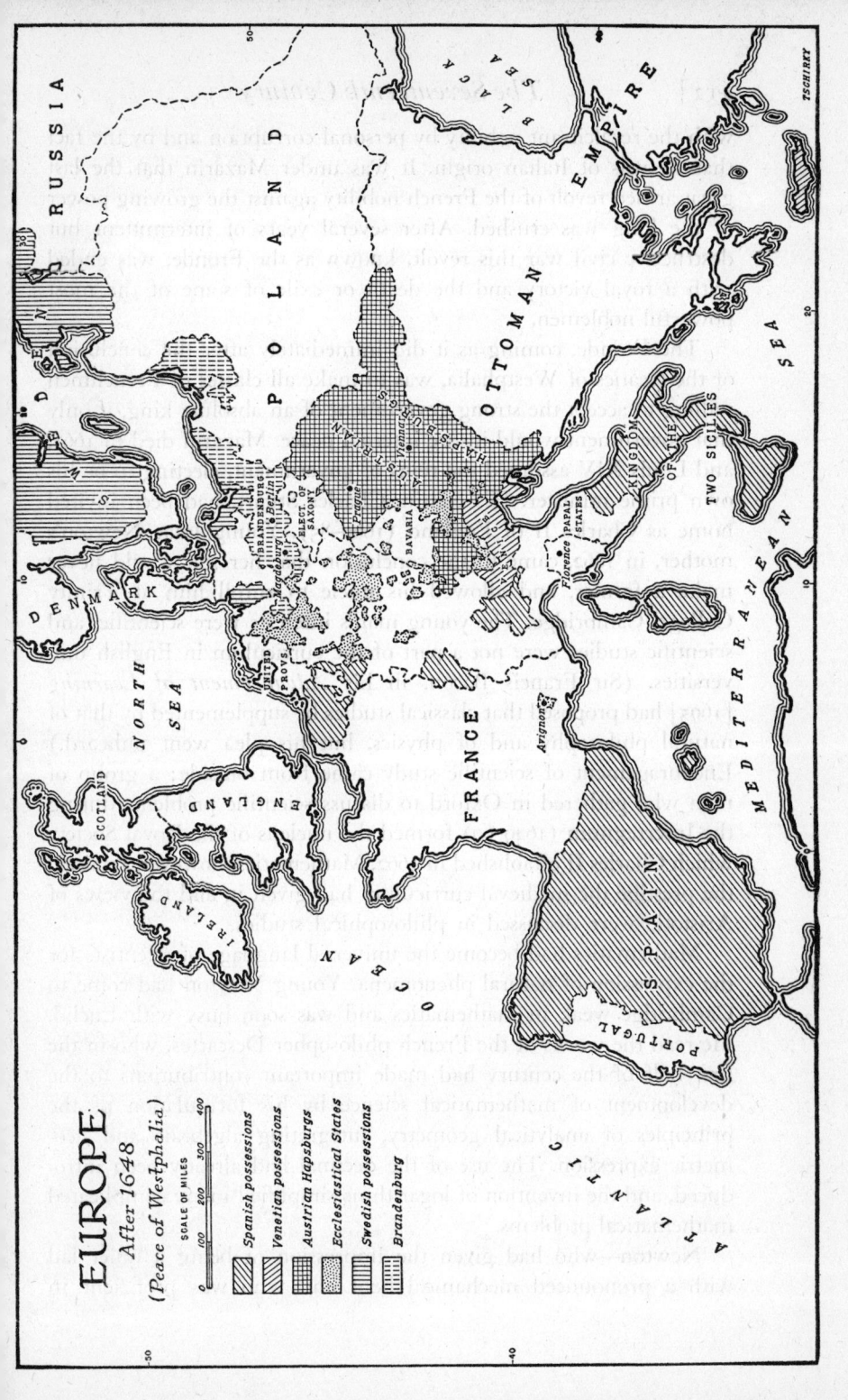

with the recalcitrant nobility by personal corruption and by the fact that he was of Italian origin. It was under Mazarin that the last great armed revolt of the French nobility against the growing power of the king was crushed. After several years of intermittent but destructive civil war this revolt, known as the Fronde, was ended with a royal victory and the death or exile of some of the most powerful noblemen.

The Fronde, coming as it did immediately after the conclusion of the treaties of Westphalia, was to make all classes of Frenchmen willing to accept the strong government of an absolute king, if only that government would insure internal peace. Mazarin died in 1661, and Louis XIV assumed the reins of government, electing to be his own prime minister. His cousin, Charles Stuart, had been invited home as Charles II of England (1660–85). Young Isaac Newton's mother, in 1662, came to the conclusion that her son would never make a farmer, and allowed his uncle to enroll him at Trinity College, Cambridge. The young man's interests were scientific, and scientific studies were not a part of the curriculum in English universities. (Sir Francis Bacon, in his *Advancement of Learning* [1605] had proposed that classical studies be supplemented by that of natural philosophy and of physics, but his plea went unheard.) Encouragement of scientific study came from outside: a group of men who gathered in Oxford to discuss scientific problems during the Interregnum (1649–60) formed the nucleus of the Royal Society which Charles II established in 1662. Mathematics, however, retained the prestige the medieval curriculum had given it, and the views of Aristotle were discussed in philosophical studies.

Mathematics had become the universal language of scientists for the expression of natural phenomena. Young Newton had come to Cambridge weak in mathematics and was soon busy with Euclid. He read the works of the French philosopher Descartes, who in the first half of the century had made important contributions to the development of mathematical science by his formulation of the principles of analytical geometry, integrating algebraic and geometric expression. The use of the decimal had already been introduced, and the invention of logarithms simplified many complicated mathematical problems.

Newton—who had given the impression of being a quiet lad with a pronounced mechanical bent and who was proficient in drawing, observant of natural phenomena, and inclined to lose himself in thought—had attained full intellectual maturity (1665). Meditating upon the ideas of Descartes and other mathematical innovators, he invented the calculus, which made possible the application of algebraic forms to problems of time and motion that had been insoluble by the older forms of mathematical science. Newton was fascinated by color, and as a result of his experiments in optics he discovered the spectrum. He studied the ideas of Galileo and Kepler and planetary motion. The principle of gravitation as a force which attracted bodies to the earth was generally accepted. Newton, however, decided that gravitation was a universal force which governed all matter, and with his new tool, the calculus, he worked out the laws according to which the force of gravity functioned. All these great discoveries were made between 1665 and 1667, a period in which he was at home much of the time on account of the plague. Recognizing the need of much verification, he kept his discoveries to himself for many years, working out details and proofs. As a Fellow of his college and after 1669 as professor of mathematics, he was able to develop his ideas at leisure. In addition he made practical inventions, such as the reflecting telescope. In 1672 he became a Fellow of the Royal Society.

This society, as well as the *Académie des Sciences* which Louis XIV established in imitation, was supposed to further practical inventions. Louis was especially assiduous in impelling French scientists in this direction. Science and technology thus progressed hand in hand, while the business of politics went on.

Under Louis XIV the absolutism of royal power became so firmly established that through most of the eighteenth century the French monarchy was able to maintain its pre-eminent position in Continental affairs, despite growing internal discontent and often incompetent or weak leadership. Louis XIV continued to weaken the nobility along the lines set by his predecessors. To compensate the nobles for their loss of political power he gave them a monopoly of military and social privilege. He realized the impressiveness of lavish expenditures. He wanted to get away from the Paris mob, with which as a boy during the Fronde he had come into all too intimate contact, so he built himself a palace outside Paris at Versailles, which he deliberately chose as the site. There was no water there, but he had it pumped out in such quantities that he could keep a vast system of fountains playing night and day. The palace itself was built on a scale that dwarfed human beings; and the pompous little king, his height increased by high-heeled shoes, lived there in lavish splendor. He required the principal noble families to live in attendance upon the king's person at all times, and supplied lavish amusements to make their new life palatable. Obliged to ruin themselves at court and to get out of touch with the people upon whom they depended for funds, the French nobility, unlike the English, were prevented by custom from recouping themselves by investing in stock companies. Thus uprooted from the source of their old power —their great feudal estates in the provinces—the nobility henceforth were limited largely to military affairs in winning renown. For this they had ample opportunity in the many wars of the period.

In one respect the seventeeth-century degradation of the French nobility, though necessary to consolidate the royal power and end the anarchy which rivalry between the nobility and the crown produced, was unfortunate. A justification for the existence of the nobility as a privileged class under the feudal system was that it rendered important service to the rest of the population and provided real leadership. Although it no longer served the people of France in the old way, the old privileges were retained. Louis XIV continued to rely on the nobility of the robe for administrative work, perpetuating the cleavage within the second estate which further weakened the nobility as a class and had a critical effect on the solidarity of the conservative classes when the old régime was threatened by rising reform forces at the end of the eighteenth century.

Domination of the nobility was necessary if the king were to be absolute. The king would not actually have full control, however, unless he also dominated the clergy and the third estate, the bourgeoisie. Since the bourgeoisie was legally unprivileged, though numerically large, that class was not difficult to manage in most circumstances. Only a minority had wealth and education, and so the third estate was unable to secure any voice in public affairs. It might have done so had the clergy or the nobility provided leadership, or had the wealthy members of the class taken the initiative. The latter failed to do so, partly for lack of opportunity, for the only representative body in France where bourgeois leaders might have been heard as spokesmen for their class was the Estates General, made up of delegates from each of the three orders of society sitting separately. The French kings were able, after 1614, to dispense with the calling of this body, and ruled without formal consultation of the three estates. The wealthy bourgeoisie also failed to serve as the spokesmen for the third estate partly for lack of incentive; having wealth and usually education, they differed from the members of the first two estates only in lack of privilege, and even this they occasionally received through ennoblement for administrative service to the crown or through marriages with impoverished members of the nobility. In a sense, the potential leaders of the third estate were systematically bought off by the crown or the aristocracy. The king could count on the loyalty of the great bourgeoisie because they were wholly dependent upon him for their privileges.

To insure complete absolutism for the crown, only the domination of the clergy remained; and this Louis accomplished in the course of his long reign. The problem of royal control of the first estate was complicated by the fact that the church was an international organization and in certain important institutional matters not subject to national authority. The first step in securing the so-called liberties of the Gallican church had been taken in the Pragmatic Sanction of Bourges in 1438, and the second in Francis I's Concordat of Bologna (1516). Louis's personal rule had existed only a few years before he became involved in a major controversy with the pope over affairs of the Roman Catholic Church in France. Louis asserted the right of the king to collect the revenues from all vacant benefices in his kingdom. There was precedent for this only in some districts, not in all, and the pope refused to admit Louis's claims. In order to make good the king's claims, a number of the leading clergy were persuaded to draw up the Declaration of the Gallican Clergy (1682), which advanced the argument that the Catholic Church in France was subject to the king, not the pope, in purely organizational matters. This also the pope denied.

In this controversy it was essential for Louis to prove that regardless of whatever purely temporal disputes he might have with the Holy Father, he was still a good Catholic. Personally he was sincere, even bigoted, and a combination of expediency and conviction largely explains his treatment of the two main dissident religious groups in France. One was the Huguenots, who still enjoyed the legal protection of the Edict of Nantes. There had been some persecution of French Protestants during most of Louis XIV's reign, but not until the years 1680–85, when the controversy with the pope was at its height, was an intensive program of forced conversion put into effect. So successful was this program in either converting Protestants or compelling them to emigrate that by 1685 Louis's advisers persuaded him that Protestantism had been virtually exterminated and the Edict of Nantes was no longer necessary. Accordingly it was revoked and Protestants were deprived of legal protection in France. The emigration of Huguenots was a loss to France because they were the skilled tradesmen of towns of the south and west, who took their skills with them to enrich other countries, some of them France's enemies. For all practical purposes France became a Catholic country and has so remained.

Louis was no less zealous in the repression of heresy within the Catholic Church. The followers of Jansen (a bishop of the Low Countries who professed to find in the writings of St. Augustine a doctrine of salvation by faith that was similar to Protestant ideas) were regarded as heretics by more orthodox members of the church, and especially by the Jesuits. The Jansenists accused the Jesuits of condoning too low a standard of morality in the laity, and they established schools which challenged Jesuit methods of education. The Jansenists claimed to be good members of the church; and during part of the period of Louis XIV's quarrel with the papacy they were allowed some degree of toleration, for they supported the king and the idea of the Gallican Church, whereas the Jesuits were the chief supporters of ultramontane principles. The Jansenist views, however, were condemned, in spite of the efforts of Pascal in his *Provincial Letters,* and the Jansenists were all finally driven into exile.

When Innocent XI, the pope with whom Louis developed his most serious quarrel, died, Louis modified his intransigence and a compromise was reached with the papacy. The Declaration of the Gallican Clergy was withdrawn, the right of the king of France to administer vacant bishoprics and to nominate bishops for French sees was reaffirmed. Thus the crown could retain the support of the first estate by naming only those men who would be loyal to the king, and in practice thereafter the higher French clergy were always taken from members of the French nobility. Louis's dominance of the clergy provided the basis for a split in one of the privileged classes which was to become important at a crucial period at the end of the eighteenth century. The monopoly of the higher positions among the clergy which members of the nobility enjoyed deprived members of the third estate of opportunities to advance. As a consequence, at the end of the eighteenth century many members of the first estate, although belonging to a privileged class, sympathized with the third estate from which they came and with whom they worked, while the higher clergy were linked with the nobility. Nevertheless, by the end of his reign Louis XIV held in France an untrammeled absolutism: there appeared to be religious uniformity, the nobles were subservient, and the bourgeoisie were as yet voiceless.

While Louis XIV was building in France an absolutism attained by no other ruler in Europe, some of his great ministers were putting into effect programs and innovations which helped build up France as a great European nation—programs which, like Louis's absolutism, became models for other states to follow. Among Louis's great servants Louvois, minister of war, had a high place. Louvois helped lay the foundation for modern armies. Before his time relatively few regiments were maintained at full strength in time of peace. It was customary for the king to sell commissions in the army; the officer raised his own troops, and had an allowance from the royal treasury according to the number of men on the muster-rolls. This system led to delays, untrained or poorly trained troops, and widespread corruption. Padded muster-rolls enriched the holders of commissions, put a heavy drain on the treasury, and also gave a misleading appearance of military strength. Artillery was in a primitive stage of development; cannon, especially siege cannon, were privately owned and leased for campaign purposes. All fighting was seasonal: in the autumn most of the troops were sent home for the winter to support themselves, and were called up again for the spring campaign. During campaigns armies lived on the country, whether friendly or enemy territory.

Louvois by systematic and rigorous inspection maintained regiments at their reported strength—one of his inspector generals, Martinet, has left his name as a symbol of strict discipline. Not only did he maintain a large standing army, but he encouraged the development of new weapons. To offset the advantage of cavalry in the field the pike had been developed: well-trained pikemen could keep cavalry at bay. The musket, however, destroyed a great deal of the effectiveness of the pikeman. But for a long time firearms were of limited effectiveness: muskets were muzzle-loading, and took so long to reload and were so cumbersome to fire that a determined charge, provided the attackers could withstand the first volley, usually routed the musketeers. During the latter part of the seventeenth century the bayonet was developed to combine the offensive and defensive qualities of the musket and the pike. The modern infantryman capable of attacking or of defending himself even in close combat was thus derived, and remains today the real basis of tactics. Whatever ancillary branches have been developed in military institutions, the infantryman on the ground still holds the key to any position and must be dislodged.

Another military development of the reign of Louis XIV was the perfection of siege warfare by the celebrated French engineer, Vauban. His trench system and use of artillery made it possible for the French to attack successfully any fortification then existing. The great fortified towns and forts of Europe had no longer to be starved out but could be assaulted in brief sieges. In an effort to find defenses against his own system of siege warfare, Vauban developed the star redoubt and the sunken fortification. In order to penetrate the sunken fortification the mortar and bomb were developed in the eighteenth century. By then most of the ideas of modern warfare had been developed, and it was only necessary to improve and perfect the weapons already designed.

The military establishment maintained by Louvois cost money, and to provide it was largely the work of another of Louis XIV's great ministers, Colbert. Recognizing the possibility of war, Colbert developed the mercantile system even more fully than it was developed in England. Mercantilism was a method of increasing a country's wealth by commerce, and was an adoption by the national state of the system practiced by the medieval towns to secure the necessities of life for the townsmen. The towns had regulated the provision of foodstuffs and the raw materials for industry in sufficient amounts at prices the citizens were able to pay. This meant price regulation, the limitation of persons admitted to the different trades, the number of men a tradesman was allowed to employ, and the exclusion of foreigners from the privileges of the town. As the national state developed, rulers took over these practices, recognizing that the state, like the town, was prosperous in proportion to the prosperity of its citizens, and that from the citizens must come the wealth necessary to support the machinery of the state, the manpower to form armies and man fleets, and workers to make or provide their equipment. One of the mercantilist theories was that a nation gets rich if more gold and silver comes into the country than goes out. The accumulation of specie was also essential to provide a well-lined war chest to cover the ruinous demands for cash in military campaigns. Far-seeing rulers like Henry I of France and Elizabeth of England consequently interested themselves in furthering the prosperity of their subjects, and they used mercantilist methods. It is Colbert, however, with whom the idea of mercantilism is most frequently connected. His specific services to France were establishment and support of such enterprises as the Gobelin tapestry works, general encouragement of industry, building of roads and canals, reforms in finance and justice, and creation of a navy and merchant marine. He tried to interest Louis XIV in the colonies on the St. Lawrence with only temporary success, but adventurers extended French rule through the Mississippi valley to the Gulf of Mexico.

The program of Louvois offered Louis the opportunity for pre-eminence in Europe through military aggrandizement. Colbert's program offered him a pre-eminence in Europe no less real but based on peaceful methods and the economic dominance of the Continent. With Louis's dynastic inheritance the choice was inevitable, and the efficacy of Louvois's war machine was tested in a series of great dynastic wars. The underlying cause of all Louis's wars was a desire to weaken the great rival dynasty of Europe, the Hapsburgs, and to substitute a Bourbon for a Hapsburg hegemony in Continental affairs. France was left with a legacy which has had a dominant effect on foreign policy ever since: the idea of the balance of power—which has worked sometimes to the advantage, sometimes to the detriment of French policy—and the idea of the natural frontiers of France—the Rhine, the Alps, the Pyrenees—which is still a cardinal point in French policy. This meant acquiring the Spanish Netherlands and the Free County of Burgundy from Spain and Lorraine and Savoy from their respective dukes, not to mention a part of the United Netherlands.

Louis's first war, the War of the Devolution, began in 1667. Claiming that his wife, Maria Theresa, had inherited part of the

Spanish Netherlands, he occupied it. The Dutch, seeing their security threatened, succeeded in allying the English and Swedes against him, and he had to be content for the time with twelve fortified towns in Flanders. In 1670, however, he persuaded Charles II of England to desert the Triple Alliance and join him in a war against the Dutch. In 1672 Louis invaded Holland, but the Dutch opened their dikes and blocked his invasion. Other nations joined the war, and he made peace in 1678, returning to the Dutch the lands he had seized from them, but keeping Franche Comté, which he had taken from Spain.

Charles II got into trouble with his parliament over his agreement with the French king and the unsuccessful naval war with the Dutch which followed. He had spent his youth as a fugitive and an exile, and he was determined not to travel again. He wished to live as an absolute monarch like his French cousin, but found strong opposition in his parliaments, which kept him short of funds. Consequently he made peace with the Dutch, but secretly agreed not to defend them against Louis, and lived until 1685 as a pensioner of the French king. On Charles's death, his brother succeeded to the throne as James II, but his Roman Catholicism and his arbitrary behavior led a group of influential men to offer the crown to his cousin William, Prince of Orange, and William's wife Mary (daughter of James II). William was a patriotic Dutchman and accepted the offer in order to bring England into the struggle against Louis XIV. The English welcomed him, James fled, and the Bloodless Revolution of 1688 was accomplished after William had signed a Declaration of Rights, which was enacted by parliament as a Bill of Rights and which guaranteed the English people parliamentary rule and a Protestant succession. The Bill of Rights was the culmination of the series of seventeenth-century measures by which parliamentary rather than royal supremacy was fixed in England. By compelling acceptance of the Bill of Rights parliament was securing recognition of parliament's right to establish *conditions* under which the king might reign. When during William and Mary's reign and that of Anne, who followed, parliament also undertook to declare *who* might reign, parliamentary supremacy was fully accomplished. The philosopher John Locke set down his theory of government in justification of the revolution and the principle it embodied.

A year before the revolution of 1688 a still more important revolution was precipitated by the appearance of Newton's *Principia*.

At last the lonely thinker was ready to back up his great discoveries with ample proof. In the *Principia* he formulated the fundamental principles of mechanics in his three laws of motion. He explained the calculus and applied the law of universal gravitation. The *Principia* represented twenty years of abstract thinking. When he had finished it he was ready for a vacation. Turning to politics, he joined the opposition to James II and was chosen to represent the University of Cambridge in the parliament that offered the crown to William of Orange. William made him Warden of the Mint in 1696 and Master three years later.

After 1678 Louis XIV continued his acts of agression until his enemies formed a coalition called the League of Augsburg. William took England into the war of the League of Augsburg in 1689. The war spread to the American colonies, where it was known as King William's War; commercial and colonial rivalry supplemented European dynastic conflicts. In the peace settlement Louis was allowed to keep Alsace. His next venture was the War of the Spanish Succession (1702-13), which lasted into the reign of James II's daughter Anne and was known in America as Queen Anne's War. It was in effect a world war: it drew in most of the European states, and ended with the Treaty of Utrecht (1713-14), another significant event in modern history.

By its terms Louis's grandson was made king of Spain as Philip V. England got from France Newfoundland, Nova Scotia, and the Hudson's Bay region. From Spain she got Gibraltar, Minorca, and the right to supply Spain's colonies with slaves. Austria received the Spanish Netherlands, and the Duke of Savoy became king of Sicily (which he later exchanged for Sardinia). Frederick William, the Elector of Brandenburg, was recognized as king in Prussia. He began laying the foundations of the great military power Prussia was to display under Frederick II in the eighteenth century. Frederick William had seen the effects of the Thirty Years' War and learned from the foreign interventions that the best protection for a German state in the future would be such a strong military establishment that other powers would hesitate to intervene. He began a policy which was ably continued by his successors: rigid economy to provide a war chest, and maintenance of a large army.

In the last years of the century western Europe was reminded of a great power arising in eastern Europe. Peter the Great, the Russian tsar (1689-1725), began the economic development which was to give his country the resources for playing the role of a great power in Europe and for a growing military influence. Reports of progress in science and the great military and naval successes in the wars of England and Spain woke a spirit of emulation in the breast of this almost oriental potentate. He carried on a great campaign and won Russia an outlet to unfrozen water by his capture of Azov in 1696. The following year he visited France, England, and Holland. He worked in Dutch ship yards and investigated Western ways of life, which he then introduced into Russia by forcible means. Although the Black Sea outlet was subsequently lost in Peter's reign, Baltic provinces were won in a long war with Sweden. Peter shifted attention to the Baltic area, building his capital there. He put into practice mercantilist principles by developing a favorable trade in naval stores, timber, and grain. New industries were established for textile, metal, and munition manufacture. Though privately managed, they were in a sense government financed and were operated by unpaid, forced, or servile labor. The army and navy were the principal consumers, and Russia remained overwhelmingly agricultural and almost wholly feudal.

By the early part of the eighteenth century Great Britain and France had emerged as leading powers in the European scene. The rise of a strong parliamentary régime, representing the landed aristocracy and great merchant classes, coupled with the fact that Great Britain was a leading power in the resistance against Louis XIV's aggrandizement and had emerged from the War of the Spanish Succession a strong colonial power, made her a major factor in European affairs. In William's reign her financial position was firmly established by the funding of the public debt and the establishment of the Bank of England, and in Anne's reign the personal union of England and Scotland became the parliamentary union of the two countries as Great Britain under the Union Jack (1707). The consolidation and expansion of France under Louis XIV and the great military prowess of the French had established France as the leading Continental nation. The rise of these two powers was accompanied by a decline in the powers which had previously dominated the European scene, a trend which was to continue through the century. Austria, Spain, and Turkey showed signs of weakness. Austria had been buttressed by her allies first at the expense of the Turks and later, in the War of the Spanish Succession, at the expense of Spain.

For all Louis XIV's grandiose schemes to establish a Bourbon hegemony in Europe, France and Spain were the losers in the War of the Spanish Succession. A Bourbon sat on the throne of Spain, but both France and Spain were exhausted, France had suffered colonial losses, had not reached her natural frontiers, and the Spanish possessions had not been kept intact. Further, Louis XIV left France, upon his death in 1715, with a heritage of debt and economic decline which complicated the problems of the French monarchy throughout the eighteenth century and ultimately provided the immediate cause for the outbreak of the Revolution of 1789.

Louis XIV was a person of limited intelligence but immense shrewdness who succeeded in impressing himself upon his contemporaries as a very great man. The princes of the German states strove to reproduce in little the grandeur of his court. The elaborate architecture and furniture he approved were copied everywhere, and he set the style in costume. Molière, Corneille, and Racine, whose literary works were produced under his patronage, made his name illustrious, and he condescended to encourage science by founding an academy as Charles II had done in England. Louis had been 72 years a king when he died in 1715.

Across the English Channel Queen Anne had died the year before, leaving no heirs. According to act of Parliament the crown went to her nearest Protestant relative, the elector of Hanover. George I took a friendly interest in Newton, who had been knighted by Queen Anne, and who as Master of the Mint and President of the Royal Society was a person of some importance. Newton was also in the public eye because of the controversies which his ideas created. A modest man personally, he was a fierce champion of his ideas, and often became embroiled with other scientists, but the net result of his controversies was the wider spread of new ideas. One of his most noted controversies was with Leibnitz. Newton was one of the greatest mathematical geniuses of all time, but he valued mathematics only as a tool, and put off making known his discovery of the calculus until Leibnitz had published the result of his own investigation.

When Newton died, in 1727, he received a public funeral befitting a king, and that was as it should be. The seventeenth century had abounded in scientists and philosophers: Galileo in Italy, Descartes and Pascal in France, Hobbes and Newton in England, Leibnitz in Germany. Louis XIV's dominion extended only over the Frenchmen of his time; the dominion of the scientists extended over the minds of all men for many succeeding generations and created the kind of society in which an absolute monarch claiming to rule by divine right is an anachronism. In truth the achievement of this period which dwarfs others into insignificance was Newton's *Principia*, his most celebrated publication, wherein he detailed the principles of a physical system which explained the universe in a fashion satisfactory to reason. The Newtonian theory is still the basis of calculations in many fields of physics. Einstein has demonstrated that a new theory is needed in some fields, but for the generations that followed the Newtonian system provided a new point of departure in both science and social thinking.

[THE SEVENTEENTH CENTURY]

Readings

Galileo

THE SIDERIAL MESSENGER (1610)*

[Nothing could be more straightforward and clear than Galileo's account of his construction of the telescope. Very different is his presentation of the heliocentric theory, where the censure of the church was to be feared. The then popular method of the dialogue made it possible to present all sides, without championing any. Galileo in the person of Salviatus most effectively propounds the Copernican arguments, and leaves the defense of the Ptolemaic system to an obviously less skillful protagonist.]

The Telescope

About ten months ago a report reached my ears that a Dutchman had constructed a telescope, by the aid of which visible objects although at a great distance from the eye of the observer were seen distinctly as if near; and some proofs of its most wonderful performances were reported which some gave credence to but others contradicted. A few days after, I received confirmation of the report in a letter written from Paris by a noble Frenchman, Jacques Badovere, which finally determined me to give myself up first to inquire into the principle of the telescope, and then to consider the means by which I might compass the invention of a similar instrument, which after a little while I succeeded in doing through deep study of the theory of Refraction; and I prepared a tube, at first of lead, in the ends of which I fitted two glass lenses, both plane on one side, but on the other side one spherically convex and the other concave. Then bringing my eye to the concave lens I saw objects satisfactorily large and near, for they appeared one-third of the

---

* Translated by E. S. Carlos (1830). Reprinted by permission from Shapley and Howarth, *A Source Book in Astronomy* (McGraw-Hill Book Company, Inc., 1929).

distance off and nine times larger than when they are seen with the natural eye alone. I shortly afterwards constructed another telescope with more nicety, which magnified objects more than sixty times. At length, by sparing neither labour nor expense, I succeeded in constructing for myself an instrument so superior that objects seen through it appear magnified nearly a thousand times, and more than thirty times nearer than if viewed by the natural powers of sight alone.

First Telescopic Observations

It would be altogether a waste of time to enumerate the number and importance of the benefits which this instrument may be expected to confer when used by land or sea. But without paying attention to its use for terrestrial objects I betook myself to observations of the heavenly bodies; and first of all I viewed the Moon as near as if it was scarcely two semidiameters of the Earth distant. After the Moon I frequently observed other heavenly bodies, both fixed stars and planets, with incredible delight; and when I saw their very great number I began to consider about a method by which I might be able to measure their distances apart, and at length I found one. . . .

SYSTEM OF THE WORLD (Salisbury, 1661) *

There was published some years since in Rome a salutiferous Edict that, for the obviating of the dangerous Scandals of the present Age, imposed a seasonable Silence upon the Pythagorean Opinion of the Mobility of the Earth. There want not such as unadvisedly affirm that the Decree was not the production of a sober Scrutiny, but of an ill informed Passion; and one may hear some mutter that Consultors altogether ignorant of Astronomical Observations ought not to clip the Wings of Speculative Wits with rash Prohibitions. My zeale cannot keep silence when I hear these inconsiderate complaints. I thought fit, as being thoroughly acquainted with that prudent Determination, to appear openly upon the Theatre of the World as a Witness of the naked Truth. I was at that time in Rome; and had not only the audiences, but applauds of the most Eminent Prelates of that Court; nor was that Decree Published without Previous Notice given me thereof. Therefore, it is my resolution in the

* *Ibid.*

present case to give Foreign Nations to see that this point is as well understood in Italy, and particularly in Rome, as Transalpine Diligence can imagine it to be: and collecting together all the proper Speculations that concern the Copernican Systeme, to let them know that the notice of all preceded the Censure of the Roman Court; and that there proceed from this Climate not only Doctrines for the health of the Soul, but also ingenious Discoveries for the recreating of the Mind. . . .

We shall treat of three principal heads. First I will endeavor to show that all Experiments that can be made upon the Earth are insufficient means to conclude its Mobility, but are indifferently applicable to the Earth moveable or immoveable: and I hope that on this occasion we shall discover many observable passages unknown to the Ancients. Secondly, we will examine the Cœlestiall Phœnomena that make for the Copernican Hypothesis, as if it were to prove absolutely victorious; adding by the way certain new observations which yet serve only for the Astronomical Facility, not for Natural Necessity. In the third place I will propose an ingenuous Fancy. I remember that I have said many years since that the unknown Probleme of the Tide might receive some light, admitting the Earth's Motion. This Position of mine passing from one to another had found charitable Fathers that adopted it for the issue of their own wit. Now because no stranger may ever appear that defending himself with our armes, shall charge us with want of caution in so principal an Accident, I have thought good to lay down those probabilities that would render it credible, admitting that the Earth did move. I hope that by these Considerations the World will come to know, that if other Nations have Navigated more than we, we have not studied less than they; and that our returning to assert the Earth's Stability, and to take the contrary only for a Mathematical Capriccio, proceeds not from inadvertency of what others have thought thereof, but (had we no other inducements) from those Reasons that Piety, Religion, the Knowledge of the Divine Omnipotency, and consciousness of the incapacity of man's Understanding dictate unto us. . . .

SALVIATUS   In the *Ptolomaick Hypothesis* there are diseases, and in the *Copernican* their cures. And first will not all the Sects of *Phylosophers* account it a great inconvenience, that a body naturally moveable in circumgyration, should move irregularly upon its own Centre, and regularly upon another point? And yet there are such deformed motions as these in the *Ptolomaean* Hypothesis, but in the *Coper-

nican all move evenly about their own Centres. In the *Ptolomaick*, it is necessary to assign to the Cælestial bodies contrary motions, and to make them all to move from East to West, and at the same time from West to East; but in the *Copernican*, all the Cælestial revolutions are towards one onely way, from West to East. But what shall we say of the apparent motion of the Planets, so irregular that they not only go one while swift, and another while slow, but sometimes wholly cease to move; and then after a long time return back again? To salve which appearances *Ptolomie* introduceth very great *Epicicles*, accommodating them one by one to each Planet, with some rules of incongruous motions which are all with one single motion of the Earth taken away. And would not you, *Simplicius*, call it a great absurditie, if in the *Ptolomaick* Hypothesis, in which the particular Planets have their peculiar Orbs assigned them one above another, one must be frequently forced to say that *Mars*, constituted above the Sphaere of the Sun, doth so descend that, breaking the Solar Orb, it goeth under it, and approacheth nearer to the Earth than to the Body of the Sun, and by and by immeasurably ascendeth above the same? And yet this and other exorbitancies are remedied by the sole and single annual motion of the Earth. . . .

Sir Isaac Newton

PRINCIPIA *

[The lucidity of Newton's style appears in his statement of the laws of motion. His remarks on the orbits of the planets show how his discovery of these laws simplified the demonstration of the Copernican system.]

Axioms, or Laws of Motion

Law I: *Every body perseveres in its state of rest, or of uniform motion in a right line, unless it is compelled to change that state by force impressed thereon.*

Projectiles persevere in their motions, so far as they are not retarded by the resistance of the air, or impelled downwards by the force of gravity. A top, whose parts by their cohesion are perpetually

---

* Third edition, 1726, translated by Andrew Motte (1729). Reprinted by permission from Shapley and Howarth, *A Source Book in Astronomy* (McGraw-Hill Book Company, Inc., 1929).

drawn aside from rectilinear motions, does not cease its rotation, otherwise than as it is retarded by the air. The greater bodies of the planets and comets, meeting with less resistance in more free spaces, preserve their motions both progressive and circular for a much longer time.

Law II: *The alteration of motion is ever proportional to the motive force impressed; and is made in the direction of the right line in which that force is impressed.*

If any force generates a motion, a double force will generate double the motion, a triple force triple the motion, whether that force be impressed altogether and at once, or gradually and successively. And this motion (being always directed the same way with the generating force), if the body moved before, is added to or subducted from the former motion, according as they directly conspire with or are directly contrary to each other; or obliquely joined, when they are oblique, so as to produce a new motion compounded from the determination of both.

Law III. *To every action there is always opposed an equal reaction: or the mutual actions of two bodies upon each other are always equal, and directed to contrary parts.*

Whatever draws or presses another is as much drawn or pressed by that other. If you press a stone with your finger, the finger is also pressed by the stone. If a horse draws a stone tied to a rope, the horse (if I may so say) will be equally drawn back towards the stone: for the distended rope, by the same endeavour to relax or unbend itself, will draw the horse as much towards the stone, as it does the stone towards the horse, and will obstruct the progress of the one as much as it advances that of the other. If a body impinge upon another, and by its force change the motion of the other, that body also (because of the equality of the mutual pressure) will undergo an equal change, in its own motion, towards the contrary part. The changes made by these actions are equal, not in the velocities but in the motions of bodies; that is to say, if the bodies are not hindered by any other impediments. For, because the motions are equally changed, the changes of the velocities made towards contrary parts are reciprocally proportional to the bodies. This law takes place also in attractions, as will be proved in the next scholium. . . .

Lastly, if it universally appears, by experiments and astronomical observations, that all bodies about the earth gravitate towards the earth, and that in proportion to the quantity of matter which they severally contain; that the moon likewise, according to the quantity of its matter, gravitates towards the earth; that, on the other hand, our sea gravitates towards the moon; and all the planets mutually one towards another; and the comets in like manner towards the sun; we must, in consequence of this rule, universally allow that all bodies whatsoever are endowed with a principle of mutual gravitation. For the argument from the appearances concludes with more force for the universal gravitation of all bodies than for their impenetrability; of which, among those in the celestial regions, we have no experiments, nor any manner of observation. Not that I affirm gravity to be essential to bodies: by their *vis insita* I mean nothing but their *vis inertiæ*. This is immutable. Their gravity is diminished as they recede from the earth. . . .

Concerning the Orbits in the Planetary System

Because the fixed stars are quiescent, one in respect of another, we may consider the sun, earth, and planets, as one system of bodies carried hither and thither by various motions among themselves; and the common centre of gravity of all will either be quiescent, or move uniformly forward in a right line: in which case, the whole system will likewise move uniformly forward in right lines. But this is a hypothesis hardly to be admitted; and, therefore, setting it aside, that common centre will be quiescent: and from it the sun is never far removed. The common centre of gravity of the sun and Jupiter falls on the surface of the sun; and though all the planets were placed towards the same parts from the sun with Jupiter the common centre of the sun and all of them would scarcely recede twice as far from the sun's centre; and, therefore, though the sun, according to the various situations of the planets, is variously agitated, and always wandering to and fro with a slow motion of libration, yet it never recedes one entire diameter of its own body from the quiescent centre of the whole system. But from the weights of the sun and planets above determined, and the situation of all among themselves, their common centre of gravity may be found; and, this being given, the sun's place to any supposed time may be obtained.

About the sun thus librated the other planets are revolved in elliptic orbits, and, by radii drawn to the sun, describe areas nearly proportional to the times. If the sun was quiescent, and the other planets did not act mutually, one upon another, their orbits would be elliptic, and the areas exactly proportional to the times. But the actions of the planets among themselves, compared with the actions of the sun on the planets, are of no moment, and produce no sensible errors. . . . And, therefore, astronomers are not far from the truth, when they reckon the sun's centre the common focus of all the planetary orbits. . . .

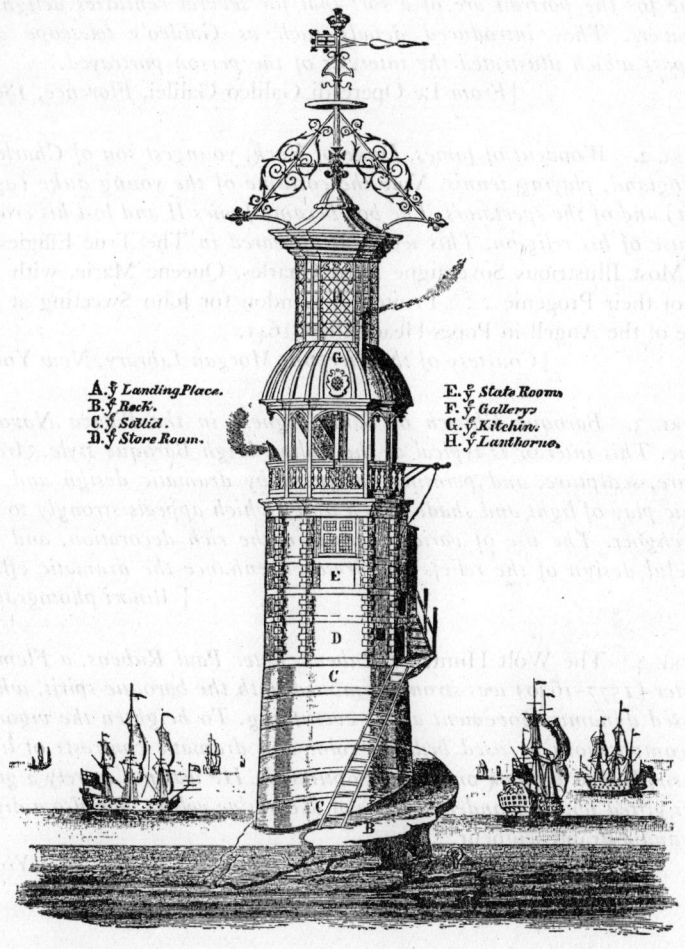

ENGRAVING OF THE FIRST EDDYSTONE
LIGHTHOUSE

(From *A Student's History of England* by Samuel R. Gardiner. Longmans Green, London, 1897.)

PLATE XXV

Seventeenth Century

FIGURE 1. *Engraved portrait of Galileo, first used as frontispiece in his Letters on the Sun Spots, 1613. He is shown at the age of forty-nine, when he was at the height of his powers. The decorations which make a frame for the portrait are of a sort that for several centuries delighted engravers. They introduced details such as Galileo's telescope and compass which illustrated the interests of the person portrayed.*
[From Le Opere di Galileo Galilei, *Florence, 1895*]

FIGURE 2. *Woodcut of James, Duke of York, youngest son of Charles I of England, playing tennis. Note the costume of the young duke (aged eight) and of the spectators. The boy became James II and lost his crown because of his religion. This woodcut appeared in* The True Effigies of our Most Illustrious Soveraigne Lord Charles, Queene Marie, with the rest of their Progenie . . . Printed at London for John Sweeting at the signe of the Angell in Popes-Head Alley, 1641.
[*Courtesy of the Pierpont Morgan Library, New York*]

FIGURE 3. *Baroque Church of Santa Agnese in the Piazza Navona, Rome. This interior is typical of the Italian High Baroque style. Architecture, sculpture, and painting are fused by dramatic design and dynamic play of light and shade into a unity which appeals strongly to the churchgoer. The use of varied marble in the rich decoration, and the forceful design of the reliefs and frescoes, enhance the dramatic effect.*
[*Alinari photograph*]

FIGURE 4. The Wolf Hunt, *by Rubens. Peter Paul Rubens, a Flemish painter (1577–1640) was strongly imbued with the baroque spirit, which stressed dynamic movement above everything. To heighten the vigor of his compositions he used brilliant color and dramatic contrasts of light and shade. His outlook on life was optimistic. He was not merely a great artist gifted with a wonderful sense of decorative values, but also a diplomat and a* grand seigneur.
[*Courtesy of the Metropolitan Museum of Art, New York*]

PLATE XXVI

Seventeenth Century

FIGURE 1. *Portrait of Isaac Newton. From a drawing in india ink made about 1691, when his career as a Member of Parliament was over, and he was on the eve of a nervous breakdown.*
[*From Sir Isaac Newton's* Mathematical Principles. *University of California Press, Berkeley, 1934*]

FIGURE 2. *Engraving by the Dutch artist Adrien van Ostade (1610–1685) made in 1653. The Dutch artists of the seventeenth century loved to represent life among the lowly and the humble, who found their rightful place in the young republic and its art, as they were unable to do in that part of the Netherlands that was still ruled by Spain.*
[*Courtesy of the Metropolitan Museum of Art, New York*]

FIGURE 3. *Engraving by the Dutch artist, Wenceslas Hollar, showing ships of the Dutch East India Company. The trade with the Dutch colonies in the East Indies was one phase of the enormous commerce which made Amsterdam one of the busiest ports of Europe.*
[*Courtesy of the Metropolitan Museum of Art, New York*]

FIGURE 4. *Engraving by a Swiss or South German artist, Abraham von Werdt, showing the interior of a printing shop. Here it is possible to study the tools of the printing craft in the Netherlands, which was one of the great centers of the publishing trade. This engraving appeared as an illustration in the* Orbis Pictus *of Comenius, 1658.*
[*Courtesy of the Metropolitan Museum of Art, New York*]

PART XIV

The Eighteenth Century

CHRONOLOGY

1701 War of the Spanish Succession
1709 Defeat of Charles XII of Sweden by the Russians in the Great Northern War
1713 Peace of Utrecht, ending War of the Spanish Succession
1714 Accession of George I in England
1715 Death of Louis XIV
1723 Montesquieu's *Persian Letters,* beginning of *philosophe* movement in France
1732 *Poor Richard's Almanac* of Benjamin Franklin
1740 Frederick the Great king of Prussia; beginning of the War of the Austrian Succession
1748 Montesquieu's *Esprit des Lois*
1751 First volume of Diderot's *Encyclopédie*
1763 End of Seven Years' War; England acquires bulk of French overseas empire
1768 Watts' steam engine, Arkwright's spinning jenny
1773 Pugachev peasant rebellion in Russia
1776 Adam Smith's *Wealth of Nations*
—— Beginning of American War of Independence
1783 Peace of Paris; England acknowledges American independence
1789 Beginning of great French Revolution
1792 Outbreak of French Revolutionary Wars
—— Fall of the French monarchy
1799 *Coup d'état* of Brumaire; Napoleon Bonaparte becomes First Consul in France

PART XIV

The Eighteenth Century

~~~~~~~~~~~~~~~~~~~~~~

THE eighteenth century saw an enormous increase in the wealth of the world. This increase came in great measure from the industrial utilization of inventions based upon the scientific discoveries of the seventeenth century; and it was helped by the importation into Europe of the products of other parts of the globe. England had the lead in these changes, and amassed the wealth with which she financed the Napoleonic wars; France lagged behind because of the out-moded system of government from which she was unable to free herself. By the early eighteenth century Great Britain and France had emerged as leading powers in the European scene. The rise of a strong parliamentary régime, representing the landed aristocracy and great merchant classes, coupled with the fact that England was a leading power in the resistance against Louis XIV's aggrandizement and emerged from the War of the Spanish Succession a colonial power, made Great Britain a major factor in European affairs.

Germany was still suffering from the economic results of the Thirty Years' War. With money wrung from a miserable peasantry, her princelings, however, continued to ape the magnificence of the French court. They were able to hire the great musical geniuses of the age—Bach, Mozart, Beethoven—to give glory to their courts, and one of them could boast of an intellectual giant, the cosmopolitan Goethe. On the Continent as a whole the old order prevailed in monarchies ranging from that of Poland—which suffered under a nobility able by a single negative vote to stifle any progress and which was wiped off the map—to that of Russia—which shared

[435

with Prussia the honor of emerging in the course of the century from an unimportant country to the rank of a great power.

The most advanced state politically was England. The coming in of the Hanoverian line had meant the growth of cabinet government and the development of the theory of ministerial responsibility, for George I and George II left everything to their ministers. The attempts of George III to exercise authority facilitated the revolt of the American colonies, and the periodical fits of insanity of his later years restored ministerial control in the days of the French Revolution. England's writers and artists have ably pictured social conditions there. Addison, Steele, Fielding, and Goldsmith give us the gambling, hard-drinking nobility, the ignorant Tory squires, and glimpses of sordid poverty in country and town. The satirist Hogarth depicts the last; Gainsborough and Raeburn the more presentable aspects of the gentry. These Englishmen took for granted their parliamentary form of government with a king who reigned but did not rule, and they were amazed when their cousins in America used the arguments of Locke to justify their own claims to responsible government.

The arguments of Locke were based upon the Newtonian physics. Newton's system had provided a new basis for scientific progress; applied to the social field, it gave a direction for speculation which was eagerly seized by the men of the so-called Enlightenment. Natural law was invoked in the cause of individual liberty, constitutional government, and religious toleration. These ideas were promulgated by a group of men known as the *philosophes*—for the most part Frenchmen who had as a background for their ideas the social inequalities of French society, its barbarous penal system, and the shackles which censorship placed on the press.

Although each philosopher had his special hobby, all believed that even as Newton had discovered the laws which governed motion it was possible to discover the laws that should govern society, and that benevolent rulers could revise legal systems to conform with their principles. Locke had built upon the Newtonian physics a theory of man which postulated equality and freedom of the individual, and envisaged a government whose chief end was to secure him in the possession of his rights, his property, and his religion. The *philosophes* were not always original thinkers nor profound theorists; they were intellectual journalists who were conscious of the evils in their society and popularized a program of reform to remedy those evils. The program they evolved provided the framework for the major political and social development of European society until the present century.

One characteristic common to the *philosophes* was their belief in rationalism. The rise of rationalism was the result of a long process of breaking away from old authority that culminated in the eighteenth century with the substitution of reason for established authority as a criterion of truth. Several factors had led to a gradual decline in respect for old authority. The two great authorities had been the church and state, both of which had been undermined by the scholarly investigations of the Renaissance and the Reformation. The splitting of orthodoxies which occurred during the Protestant Reformation, the rise of science and the deism which accompanied it, all weakened the authority of institutions which claimed an authority based on unalterable divine revelation. The state's authority also was weakened by the rise of classes and the struggles between crown and aristocracy, or crown and church. Since a practical working union between church and state had long existed, a threat to the authority of either weakened both.

Not only was the old authority weakened, but a new method of acquiring knowledge was being developed. John Locke's argument for the acquisition of all knowledge through experience provided a substitute for revelation. Though mostly developed in England, rationalism was transferred to France through the Huguenots, many of whom migrated to England but retained contact with France, through the spread of clubs and cafés where new ideas could be discussed or introduced by travelers, and through contacts of the *philosophes* with England. After his three-years' sojourn in England, Voltaire, one of the greatest of the *philosophes,* made Locke's theories and the practical workings of the English system well-known among the French. Others visited or lived in England for varying periods. Even had there not been the contact with England, the reforming French *philosophes* might have been produced by conditions in France. There had been a few aristocratic reformers in the period of Louis XIV. The royal government after Louis XIV was often incompetent, and weakness at the center in the highly centralized and cumbersome French administration led to chaos in the provinces. Growing inefficiency, perennial bankruptcy, extravagance and corruption, inability to tackle reform by attacking privilege, evils of the tax system, and legal confusion—all were evident to serious students of conditions in France and were sufficient incentive to reformers even without the added influence of English ideas.

The program of the reformers called for certain modifications in the existing structure of government and society in order to make the actual law in harmony with what they regarded as the "higher law." This was the law of nature; what was natural, what was reasonable, should be the foundation for organized government. The reformers were not always in agreement on what changes should be made in government. Some followed the ideas of Montesquieu based on historical development and an attempt to temper absolutism by restoring some authority to the aristocracy, as the representatives of the people. Montesquieu was impressed with the English constitution and advocated the separation of governmental powers into three distinct branches—executive, legislative, and judicial. Many followed the idea of contract, of which Rousseau became the most famous exponent. The theory of contract was based on the supposition that before civilized society was organized man existed in a state of nature. In order to insure respect for the natural rights of all, man tacitly contracted with his fellow man to organize a government. By this contract it was the duty of man to obey his government while it fulfilled the function for which it was established, but to change it when it abused those natural rights. In this theory there was logically the conception of popular sovereignty—the people being ultimately the source of governmental authority—a direct contradiction of divine right and royal sovereignty.

The chief natural rights were property, liberty, and equality, and by far the greatest emphasis was placed on property. It was generally believed that property owners, having the greatest interest in the maintenance of law and order because that affected the security of their property, should constitute the base of government. Possession of landed property should be made a qualification for voting or participating in a government based on popular sovereignty. The idea of liberty was generally construed as freedom in the sense of modern civil liberties—freedom of speech, press, assembly, and religion. Under the old régime censorship of expression and an effort to curtail freedom of thought was maintained through the agency of the church, sustained by the state. When eighteenth-century reformers spoke of equality, they meant the abolition of class privileges and equal treatment for all before the law.

In their economic ideas the *philosophes* foreshadowed the nineteenth century development of *laissez-faire*. Many of them believed in free trade, partly perhaps as a reaction against the restrictions of the mercantile system, which had apparently done no better for France than produce bankruptcy. Some believed in taxation according to ability to pay, a radical idea dangerous to the privilege and tax-exempt position of the clergy and nobility, who, although they were a very small percentage of the population, controlled nearly half the wealth of France. In their attack upon the authority of the church and their criticism of it as an institution—because of its censorship and its isolation of wealth—the *philosophes* were endangering the many humanitarian services the church was able to perform only because of its great wealth. Thus they helped to develop the idea of lay philanthropy. Other reforms which the *philosophes* advocated through a humanitarian interest in the society around them were the correction of many barbarous abuses in the legal system which were relics of the Middle Ages. The reform of the wretched prison conditions and treatment was a cardinal point in their program. They also campaigned for the abolition of inhuman punishments, such as branding and mutilation, and for the abolition of serfdom and slavery. The most important single reform, perhaps, was to call attention to the necessity for the codification of the laws, for there were literally hundreds of legal codes in existence in different parts of the kingdom, contradictory and obsolete.

Under the absolutism of the old régime there was no way for the *philosophes* to accomplish these reforms except through educating people. Education, however, was private and a monopoly of the clergy, which to the *philosophes* simply meant the perpetuation of the superstition and prejudice of which they accused the church. It was to be expected then that, with their faith in individual human reason, they should feel it was necessary only for people to know for them to improve the conditions of society. To secure an educated populace, which through reason could accomplish an indefinite improvement of the condition of mankind, the *philosophes* advocated universal, compulsory, free, secular education. This was impractical for many reasons under the old régime, one important consideration being the tremendous expense, a decisive factor for a government facing bankruptcy.

The program of the *philosophes* might also be given a trial, of course, if the rulers could be influenced by the ideas of reform. In a desire for the wide promulgation of political, industrial, and scientific knowledge Denis Diderot designed a great encyclopedia. The first volume appeared in 1751 and the *Encyclopédie* became the great medium for spreading the new ideas of the Enlightenment. Article after article underlined the political backwardness of France, where the king was absolute ruler, where clergy and nobles were practically exempt from taxation, and where the administrative system prevented the fruits of the Enlightenment from coming to full development.

The success of the American Revolution swelled the stream of ideas which the men of the Enlightenment based upon the English system that Locke had defended. The grievances of the French third estate arose from the burden laid upon them by the system of privilege. The refusal of the privileged classes to yield precipitated the struggle, and the wars of the French Revolution spread the ideas of liberty, freedom, and equality across Europe. The Revolution also put at the service of militarism the idea of the nation in arms, which made warfare possible on a scale that could not be attempted as long as soldiers were mere mercenaries.

Great Britain was able to finance the wars against the French Revolution because of her economic development in the eighteenth century. In wealth and commerce she forged ahead because of improvements in cotton manufacture. Thomas Newcomen's invention of the steam engine (1705) solved the problem of power, but the improvements of James Watt (1764) were needed before it was generally used. The successive inventions of the spinning jenny, water frame, mule, and power loom increased remarkably the ease and rapidity of the process of making cotton cloth. Parallel developments were going on in the silk industry in France, but the market for silk was more limited than that for cotton, and English maritime supremacy gave her a practical monopoly.

England had certain other advantages. With the advent of steam for power England had coal for fuel; English capital was available for commercial enterprise; and a great increase in the enclosure movement forced the agricultural population to seek employment in the factories, in such numbers that wages could be kept low. To justify the tender-minded on this last point she had the *laissez-faire* policy which grew from the same root as the equalitarian ideas of the French Revolution.

ENGRAVING MADE IN 1717 SHOWING A STEAM PUMP USED IN MINES

(From *A Student's History of England* by Samuel R. Gardiner. Longmans Green, London, 1897.)

CHAPTER 26

The World of Benjamin Franklin

[1706–1790]

THREE revolutions went on in Franklin's lifetime, and he had his part in each of them. They were all essentially middle-class movements. The so-called Industrial Revolution, which had for several hundred years been increasing the amount of wealth in the world, made its most spectacular gains in this century. This economic revolution meant a shift of political power to the middle class, of which the first fruits were the American and French Revolutions.

When Benjamin Franklin, a young man of about nineteen, arrived in England in December, 1724, he walked through streets of stone-faced brick houses such as he had left in Boston and Philadelphia. He saw the masterpieces of Sir Christopher Wren which had inspired the builders of churches in those cities. He mingled with crowds of apprentices, artisans, and small tradesmen such as he knew at home. When he was admitted to a coffee house he heard the same talk of far-off ventures as made up the chat of well-to-do men who had patronized him in Philadelphia as a promising young fellow. He saw the influence of the gazettes and the Royal Society, and became acquainted with the borrowing of books from bookshops. He probably heard some of the much-discussed operas and oratorios of the Saxon composer, Haendel. Of the authors of the much-copied *Spectator* Steele was still alive. Franklin was eager to catch a glimpse of the great Sir Isaac Newton, but the old man appeared in public very little. It was easier to get a view of George I and of the shrewd Robert Walpole who managed the government for his sovereign. George I knew no English and was bored at meetings of ministers in his private room, or cabinet, where he could communicate with them only in Latin. He was glad to leave them with Walpole, and the king's cabinet gave its name to the little group of ministers who ran England in the king's name.

Franklin worked hard at the printing trade and enjoyed himself in various ways, but after a year and a half he decided to return to America. He left London a month too early to see a lean-faced, keen-eyed Frenchman called Voltaire, who came over to study the ideas of Newton and the philosophy of John Locke. Returning to Philadelphia in the year of George II's accession (1727), Franklin set up his Junto and his newspaper and planned his public library. He could explain to his fellow clubmen the wisdom of Walpole's peace policy. When in 1739 Walpole was forced into the war of Jenkins' Ear with Spain, Franklin could make it plain how it was through the influence of the trading interest in parliament, which approved breaking into Spain's colonial monopoly. Americans knew that it was the French who were now the rivals of the British for colonies and commerce, and that it was wise, when a year later Frederick of Prussia stole Silesia from Maria Theresa of Austria, to go into the War of the Austrian Succession (1740-48) on the side opposite the French.

The emperor who died in 1740 had bargained with his contemporaries to get them to agree that they would allow his daughter Maria Theresa to become Queen of Bohemia and Hungary and archduchess of Austria after his death. But other claimants appeared, and the general war that ensued lasted eight years. In America it was known as King George's War. Since Frederick II of Prussia retained Silesia after the war, a bitter enmity remained which broke out into the Seven Years' War in 1756. The Americans had been fighting the French and Indian War a year when their hostilities became official, as England became engaged in the French and Indian War that was to be called the Seven Years' War. The war in Europe was due to the aggressive policies of Frederick II, which Austria, France, Russia, and Sweden feared—and with reason. By backing Frederick and providing him with funds, the English under the skillful direction of William Pitt were able to win from France her dominions in America and India. Franklin was in England again during this war and contributed to the final settlement; his pamphlet urged that England demand from France not Guadeloupe, which the sugar merchants wanted, but Canada.

Franklin had prospered greatly in business since his first visit to

England. He had been an editor and publisher and postmaster of Philadelphia. He had invented the Franklin stove, experimented with electricity, and drawn up his plan for a union of the colonies. During the war he helped the ill-fated General Braddock by setting up a system for transporting military stores, and later saw actual military service. When he went to England it was as agent for Pennsylvania. He was now well known as a leading American and as a scientist who had been honored by the Royal Society. He was showered with honors, and associated with the leading thinkers of the day. In 1761 George III came to the throne, and Franklin witnessed his coronation, returning to America the following year.

The Treaty of Paris which was signed in 1763 made young George III the titular head of a great empire. He had been brought up to believe he should be a king in fact as well as in name, and he developed the policy of building up a party of his own in parliament. This party, "the king's friends," proved useful when he found himself annoyed by the attacks of John Wilkes, who held the new ideas about individual freedom.

Meanwhile Franklin came again to England on a mission from Pennsylvania, which was restive under its proprietary government. His opinion was asked from time to time in the period when ministers of the young George III, seeking for new means of revenue to pay for the war, began reading the dispatches of colonial governors and realized that the acts passed to restrict American trade and manufacturers to channels profitable to England had never been enforced to any extent and were constantly evaded in a vast smuggling trade. Franklin had repeatedly recorded his opposition to the restrictive policy. On the other hand, he had long been an outspoken advocate of British imperialism, seeing America as the great outpost of Empire.

He advised against the decision to make the Americans help pay for their own defense by the proceeds of a Stamp Act. When the Americans resisted on the ground that the tax was a direct one, the ministers put through some indirect taxes, to which the Americans objected that they had no representation in parliament. George III was an obstinate man, and when he began to use force, the Americans began to talk of independence—and the American Revolution was on. Franklin sailed for home in time to help advise his compatriots and to become one of the signers of the Declaration of Independence.

Franklin's political philosophy, like that of Thomas Jefferson and the Englishman Thomas Paine, was based on the philosophy of John Locke. It was natural that he should belong to the Enlightenment, whose political side had a solid basis in Locke's theories and their embodiment in English institutions. It was also natural that the rulers of Continental countries, who had adopted French as a court language and copied French manners and arts, should be converted to some aspects of the Enlightenment. Several despotic rulers were so impressed that they sought to temper their despotism by reform.

The most conspicuous of these enlightened despots was Frederick II of Prussia, generally known as Frederick the Great. The rise of Prussia is a tale of the improbable, when its small, poor, underpopulated area is considered. That Prussia became and remained a great power in Europe was due to a series of able Hohenzollern rulers who consistently maintained a complete mobilization of Prussian resources. Efficient organization and unprecedented social discipline made possible a regularly balanced budget—a miracle by eighteenth century standards—although the cost was high. Perhaps 40 percent of peasant earnings went to the state, and in addition the peasants owed feudal dues. This helps to explain the continued poverty of the people.

Prussia's aggrandizement began in the seventeenth century. Frederick William, the elector of Brandenburg who entered the Thirty Years' War, laid the foundations of the great military power Prussia displayed under Frederick II in the eighteenth century. Frederick William learned from the foreign interventions of the war that the best protection for a German state in the future would be a military establishment so strong that other powers would hesitate to intervene. He followed the policy of rigid economy in order to save up a war chest, and he maintained a large standing army. His successors ably continued these policies.

The prestige of the house of Hohenzollern was greatly enhanced in 1701 when the successor of the Great Elector, with the emperor's permission, assumed the title of King in Prussia. He followed his father's example of maintaining a large standing army. The government was administered by an elaborate bureaucracy. When Frederick the Great came to the throne in 1740 the system inaugurated by the Great Elector was fairly stabilized and the treasury was full. He was therefore able to play his spectacular part in European affairs.

Frederick the Great was a hardworking man. He alone formulated policy, while his cabinet ministers carried out orders, most of which they received by letter. The Prussian bureaucracy was highly centralized, under military discipline, and with a precise system of accountability. The civil service was selected on the merit system, another novelty for the eighteenth century; but because of the royal distrust of civil servants the officials were hardly more than slaves of the state, without legal rights and subject to imprisonment without trial. Poverty forced men into the service of the state, but the social position they attained was a compensating factor. Prestige came not from wealth but from connection with the army and the civil service.

Frederick was keenly interested in letters and the arts. It was for him that Bach, the greatest musician of the day, wrote his Brandenburg concertos. Voltaire became Frederick's guest. Pursuing the Hohenzollern policy of maintaining a great standing army, the king needed to encourage the growth of population in his dominions. He subsidized immigration, supported agriculture, improved trade and industry, carried on public works. He enacted judicial reforms and organized education.

Another despot who tried to justify despotism by Enlightenment was Catherine II of Russia. Like Prussia, Russia was a power which emerged from relative obscurity in the eighteenth century. The immediate ancestor of the modern Russian state was the Grand Duchy of Muscovy, whose princes had taken the title "tsar" in the sixteenth century. As heads of the most powerful Russian state the rulers of Moscow took the lead in defending the Russians against the Tatars, and they steadily expanded their territory at the expense of both Asiatic and European neighbors. The ablest of them saw that their future lay to the west rather than the east. We have seen how the Tsar Ivan made Queen Elizabeth an offer of marriage, and how Peter the Great in the seventeenth century tried to turn his subjects westward.

The basis of the new Russia created by the expansion of Muscovy, was the idea of the service state. The great vassals of the tsar owed him service, and the tsar repaid them in land, usually conquered land. The population was fixed to the soil in order to give it value through labor, and this gave rise to the system of peasant serfdom. Originally the grantees did not acquire title to the land, but it was still vested in the tsar; they had the use of it and were obliged to render the tsar certain services, such as the collection of taxes, administration of justice, and maintenance of police. Since the reign of Peter the Great Russia had made enough economic progress to render the primitive method of payment by land grant no longer necessary, and the tsars had sufficient resources to pay their nobles in money. The Tsarina Elizabeth (1741-62) alleviated the service obligations of the nobles and allowed them a monopoly of inhabited estates. The nobles were still regarded as local governmental authorities, but the concept of private property right in the land rapidly developed. Estates became hereditary and could be alienated by the possessors.

The administration of the Russian autocracy was characterized by an elaborate bureaucracy, with detailed regulations for which there were in the beginning no trained bureaucrats. In the numerous bureaus with their hierarchical division of regions, provinces, and local manorial lords, there was graft, bribery, and corruption. The practice in the public prosecutor's office of using informers and an organized system of espionage in an effort to check corruption was demoralizing and only added to the opportunities for graft and blackmail. The seriousness of the faults in the administration are suggested by the fact that probably only a third of the income collected ever reached the central treasury. It should be said, however, that most of the officials were woefully underpaid and were simply supplementing their incomes to raise them to at least a subsistence level.

Private property among the nobility was in sharp conflict with peasant custom. The peasants lived in village communities and had no individual property rights; certain tracts of land were allotted for village use, and the village community divided these lands according to need. The principal peasant obligation was the capitation tax, and the lands of the villages were periodically redistributed in accordance with changing individual needs. Among the peasants therefore the idea of public law and the use of land for support was developed—a primitive communism that became deeply rooted in Russian society. The peasant existed as a member of an organized village community. Because of the local administrative functions of the estate owner he owed obedience to a master upon whose estate his village was located. To insure tax collection it was necessary under the system for every peasant to have a master. In the eighteenth century the nobility won legal independence and wealth through such measures as those of the Tsarina Elizabeth, and gradually ceased to participate in the central administration. The tendency was toward provincial and local authority, which was more useful for the promotion of special local interests.

In 1762 Elizabeth was succeeded by her son who was assassinated that same year; his widow, a German princess of extraordinary vigor and resourcefulness, succeeded as Catherine II (1762-96). Like Frederick the Great, she was a patron of *philosophes*. She made a magnificent but ineffective gesture toward reforming the laws and ameliorating the condition of the serfs; she took steps for the encouragement of industry and commerce. She was more persistent, however, in co-operating with Frederick II and the Empress Maria Theresa to annex Polish territory in 1772. Maria Theresa wept—but took more than half of Galicia. When Prussia and Russia were satisfied for the time being, Poland had lost a quarter of her territory and a fifth of her population.

Maria Theresa's son, the Emperor Joseph II, was the most consistent reformer among the enlightened despots; but his haste in making changes, the lack of a middle class to cope with the ignorance of the peasantry, and the cupidity of the nobility annulled most of his reforms. Charles III of Spain and Gustavus III of Sweden were enthusiastic proponents of Enlightenment, and in Denmark and Portugal able ministers brought about reforms in the name of the monarch.

In countries where the middle class was impotent or non-existent enlightened despotism came to nothing. Some reforms, like the abolition of torture, remained here and there, but the chief effects were in showing the existence of abuses and suggesting the possibility of correction. Striking examples of what a politically emancipated middle class could accomplish existed in England and America. It was the English middle class that had secured England's prosperity. In the English parliament and in colonial assemblies overseas the middle class had been vocal and effective. It was the American middle class that carried through the American Revolution. In

France, it was to the middle class that most of the *philosophes* belonged.

Louis XVI of France, who came to the throne in 1774, was not clever enough to be a successful enlightened despot, but he made an effort at the beginning of his reign. France was one of the richest nations in Europe yet it was on the verge of bankruptcy. One recipe for averting bankruptcy was offered by a group of theorists who called themselves Physiocrats. They believed that land was the only source of wealth and that all taxes should be based upon land. They also believed that all government controls over trade should be removed; that if freed from the tight controls of mercantilism trade would naturally prosper. This theory of freedom of trade, under the name of *laissez faire,* was advocated by a Scot named Adam Smith, in a book called *Wealth of Nations,* published in 1776. One of the French Physiocrats was Turgot, and Louis XVI made him finance minister, but his efforts came to nothing. Louis himself freed the serfs on the royal estates, and declared that he was going to do something for all peasants. In his announcement, which was read in every parish, he reminded the peasantry of their burdens under the system he was planning to rectify. The French peasants were relatively well off in comparison with the peasants of other European countries, but this reminder made them sorry for themselves. The money borrowed for agricultural reforms still further burdened the finances, and at every point the nobles and higher clergy opposed the reforming measures and all proposals for freeing trade.

Among the *philosophes* Benjamin Franklin had an important place. He shared and effectively circulated their ideas. In the movement that led to the American Revolution he firmly promulgated the political doctrines that were derived from Locke. The Continental Congress sent him to France in 1776 to persuade the government to strike at their ancient enemy, England, by helping its rebellious colonists. He was a favorite with the ladies, a patriarchal example of the "natural man" from the American wilderness, an eager talker about the rights of man, and a distributor of copies of the constitutions of American states, with their bills of rights, which embodied some of the leading items on the *philosophes'* agenda. The aid which he helped persuade the French government to give was of inestimable value to the Americans, but put another heavy burden on the French treasury.

Franklin remained in France until the end of the war, and as one of the commissioners to negotiate peace with Great Britain he formulated the terms which made the basis of the final treaty. He seized every opportunity to witness "philosophical experiments" and after watching a balloon transport passengers across the Seine speculated on the possibility that, if airborne soldiers could be dropped in warring countries to wreak damage, perhaps the time was come when rulers could be convinced of the follies of war. In 1785 he left France for America and sat as a member of the Constitutional Convention. In the country which he left, the nobles were engaged in the struggle to save their privileges. In 1788 men of the middle class began to use the political ideas of the Enlightenment as the basis of a concerted movement to force governmental reform.

In the reform program of the *philosophes* can be found the seeds of some of the most characteristic aspects of nineteenth-century development: popular government, civil liberty and toleration, equal treatment before the law, separation of church and state, and general public education. By the last quarter of the eighteenth century the French bourgeoisie had widely adopted these ideas and had worked out a reform program based upon them. There remained only the necessity for an opportunity to put the program into practice. That opportunity came in 1789 when the king, in a desperate effort to help solve the serious financial crisis facing the government, was persuaded to call the Estates General, which had not assembled since 1614. The Estates General was the nearest thing to a representative body that France possessed and it provided the springboard for reform and revolution.

While financial disaster was the immediate cause of the French Revolution there were other remote causes. There was no co-ordination of the beneficiaries of the old régime, and there was no coherence within groups of beneficiaries. During most of the eighteenth century there had been a three-cornered fight between the king, the aristocracy, and the middle class to win the support of the people. Even the *parlements* of France, whose functions were practically those of law courts and that represented the views of the nobility of the robe, had come to the point of suggesting the Estates General as the logical body to bring about constitutional change some years before the king actually convoked them. The Estates General which the king and the privileged orders had in mind was the traditional body organized in three separate houses, by order; each of the three feudal classes of society having approximately equal representation. In any such body the privileged classes ran little risk of losing their position, because they outvoted the third estate by two houses to one.

The Estates General which actually met in May, 1789, embodied significant changes. The most important was the double representation allowed to the third estate. This concession itself was meaningless unless the representatives of all three orders were allowed to meet together as one house, and the question of organization—whether by head or by order—was the first major issue to arise. The king directed that the members assemble by order, but the third estate declared itself the National Assembly and summoned the other estates to join them. A gradually increasing number of liberal nobles and lesser clergy did so. One morning the Assembly found its usual place of meeting locked, and the members flocked into an adjoining tennis court and took an oath not to adjourn until they had drawn up a constitution for France. The king finally consented to allow the organization by head, which gave the third estate an equal chance with the two privileged estates in voting. When the king began to collect troops around Versailles, where the National Assembly met, the members of the third estate feared that he intended to coerce them, and radical leaders in nearby Paris roused mob spirit to defend the National Assembly. The result was the taking of the Bastille on July 14, 1789.

The seizure of the Bastille marked the introduction of violence, particularly Parisian mob violence, into the mechanics of reform efforts. The king publicly accepted the idea of revolution, thereby yielding to the demonstration of popular force; and force having once succeeded in exacting concession from the king, there was in the future a constant temptation to use force to break any deadlock on controversial issues. Soon after the storming of the Bastille the first émigrés left France and began the work of counter-revolution from abroad, thereby increasing the probability that the revolution in France would become involved with European-wide forces.

The attack on the Bastille helped to set off a series of spontaneous peasant uprisings in the summer of 1789. News of these outbreaks effected a voluntary relinquishing of feudal rights on the part of the privileged classes in the National Assembly. A Declaration of the Rights of Man and the Citizen was drawn up, providing a program upon which the constitution makers could base their work. Censorship was lifted, a popular press sprang up, and a long public debate over the proposed new constitution began.

To meet the financial crisis the National Assembly nationalized the church lands, which were valued in 1791 at about the amount of the national debt. Against the security of the former church lands *assignats* were issued to provide the revolutionary government with funds. The *assignats* were originally interest-bearing notes to be used in the purchase of church lands; it was the intention of the revolutionary leaders to distribute the benefits of the nationalized lands more widely among the people and increase the size of the property owning class. However, the continued need for funds to meet the great expenses of the revolutionary reforms, and then of the war, led to the creation of a simple fiat currency and resulted in serious inflation. As it nationalized church lands the government took over the institutional functions of the church. Clergy were to become salaried civil servants. Though this measure helped to meet a serious financial problem and actually did result in a broadening of the landowning base of French society, it alienated many people from the revolution. The pope condemned the revolution, and many clergy joined the forces of counter-revolution.

The most important work of the National Assembly consisted of a series of reforms which became permanently fixed in French life. Legal equality was established; privilege was abolished in tax matters, popular control of the budget was instituted, and the tax system was simplified and reorganized; a beginning was made on a system of universal public education; the antiquated administrative organization was overhauled and a redivision of the kingdom made into *departements,* which have remained the unit of provincial administration ever since.

Franklin followed with great interest the news of the events of the Revolution. He was practically an invalid during the last two years of his life. He lived into the presidency of Washington, and died peacefully on April 17, 1790. When the news reached France, Mirabeau rose to propose that the National Assembly wear mourning for three days as homage "both to the rights of man and to the philosopher who has most contributed to extend their sway over the whole earth."

By 1791, the Assembly had hammered out a constitutional monarchy and France seemed to be pulling abreast of the England of 1688. Although in June, 1791, the king and his family attempted to flee Paris, whither they and the National Assembly had been moved in order to be better "protected" by the populace, he was brought back and agreed to accept the constitution. When the National Assembly disbanded, having with misguided patriotism provided that none of the members would sit in the next elected legislative body, it might have seemed as though the revolution were over.

THE BRITISH HOUSE OF COMMONS, SITTING
IN 1741-42

(From *A Student's History of England* by Samuel R. Gardiner. Longmans Green, London, 1897.)

CHAPTER 27

The World of Napoleon Bonaparte
[1769–1821]

~~~~~~~~~~~~~~~~

THE Enlightenment was based on reason and science; it produced the idea of progress and precipitated the quarrel of the Ancients and the Moderns. Its failure to provide for the emotions left a need which was filled in various ways. Methodism satisfied the English middle class; a more widespread need was met by romanticism. Coleridge, Shelley, and Wordsworth in England, Goethe and Schiller in Germany appealed to the mystic in man. The Enlightenment had done little for the arts beyond encouraging the taste for classical architecture. What romanticism could do was shown by the Revolutionary painter David, who gave the French a romanticized classicism, and by the English landscape and portrait school. The realism of Hogarth was a protest against romanticism. Romanticism aided music, but an individual genius like Beethoven carried his art to farther fields. The Romantics were intense idealists and important contributors to the French Revolution.

Napoleon Bonaparte, who spread the ideas of the Revolution across Europe, had his practical side, but he was incurably romantic. He was a Corsican and started out as a Corsican patriot. Patriotism was one form of romanticism. His formative years were passed in a primitive society where the family was of supreme importance, and his family loyalty was always strong. Corsica passed to France in the year of his birth, so that he was technically French. A short, gaunt, sallow youth, sulky and moody, a dreamer, he was trained in French schools to be an artillery officer, and was performing his military duties as a subaltern during the early phases of the revolution.

The new constitution which Louis XVI agreed to try in 1791

provided for middle-class domination. The king had only a suspensive veto, but he was allowed considerable latitude in appointments. Although equality before the law was insured to all citizens, only property holders could vote or sit in the one-chamber legislature. In social and economic respects, also, the Revolution favored the middle class. The old guilds and monopolies were done away with, and the bourgeoisie had free rein for their economic enterprise. Titles were abolished, and the clergy, like the nobility, ceased to be a socially-privileged class. Since the two classes of society which had been superior to the bourgeoisie were abolished, the middle-class group became the leading element in French society.

When the National Assembly was succeeded by the Legislative Assembly in 1791 the only important parts of the old régime left in France were the monarchy and the bureaucracy. To overthrow the king and set up a republic in France was the hope of many, and it was the main purpose of the new radical party known as the Girondins, who took their name from the region in southwestern France where some of their important leaders originated. By the spring of 1792 the increasing activity of émigrés outside the borders of the kingdom led to serious international tension, and for differing reasons virtually all parties favored war against the rulers of Austria and Prussia, who had made an alliance. The king hoped that in a struggle in which the French were beaten his triumphant brother-in-law, the Emperor, would bring help and restore him to his former absolute position. The Girondins hoped to catch the king in treasonable correspondence with his émigré friends and thus to discredit him and bring about his downfall. The Girondins would then win prestige and power by saving the country in a successful war. A declaration of war against Austria and Prussia in April of 1792 was easily secured on the ground that they were harboring the enemies of France.

The Austrian and Prussian forces slowly but steadily invaded France, and their successes aroused unrest in Paris. Radicals like Robespierre, Danton, and Marat, leaders of the Jacobin club, which met in a former Jacobin convent, plotted an insurrection to overthrow the monarchy and seize control. On August 10, by a successful organization of popular violence, the king was seized, and the constitutional monarchy overthrown. A new constitutional convention was called for September, 1792, and the efforts of the revolutionary leaders were directed at stemming the tide of the foreign invasion. On the eve of the meeting of the Convention, at the battle of Valmy, the French were successful and by halting the invasion secured a temporary breathing spell to set about the reorganization of the government.

The Convention chosen to give France a new constitution took the reins and ruled France for the next three years. It was a body which had no constitutional or popular limitations, and was free to act as it chose so long as it could convince the people of France of its patriotism and its success. Having overthrown executive tyranny in France first by limiting and then by abolishing the monarchy, the French were now to experience another extreme, for the Convention developed a legislative tyranny. All branches of government—legislative, executive, judicial—were combined under the control of one body. Executive functions were carried out by a Committee of Public Safety, made up of Convention members and responsible to the Convention. The Convention also set up as an emergency measure to ensure the successful prosecution of the war and to protect the revolutionary government, a special court called the Revolutionary Tribunal. Because of its summary powers, speedy procedure, and the frequency with which it sent people to the guillotine, the period when the Revolutionary Tribunal functioned most vigorously (September, 1793–July 27, 1794) was known as the Terror. The great problems before the Convention were the question of the deposed king, the foreign war, and the new constitution.

Each of the main problems served as an issue in the contest for control by the two leading factions in the Convention—the Girondins and the Jacobins. Both parties were small minorities but were effectively organized and had a program of action; they were able to swing with them the majority of the delegates of the Convention through their intense patriotism and ruthless defense of the revolutionary government. The Girondins were primarily federalists and were interested in securing the political revolution in France. The Jacobins favored a highly centralized republic since their chief support came from the lower and working classes of the cities, especially Paris. War conditions helped the Jacobins, for many centralizing measures were necessary for successful prosecution of the war; and the Girondins were compelled to accept measures of which they did not approve. By the summer of 1793 the Jacobins had won control of the Convention and expelled their opponents; the king had been executed and the Jacobin dictatorship established which was to make the name as hated and feared in the Europe of 1794 as the name Bolshevik became in twentieth century Europe.

Under the Jacobin leadership the war was converted into a successful offensive campaign, and the Convention issued several propaganda decrees in an effort to undermine the strength of France's enemies. Nearly every important country of Europe had joined in the war against France after the death of Louis XVI, and the propaganda decrees promised to help oppressed peoples everywhere to throw off the yoke of the old régime. The French Revolution, which had arisen out of internal problems in France, thus became a European crusade to change a system of society and make the revolution safe at home by destroying the forces of tyranny and privilege elsewhere. Under the pretext of liberating those lands from their oppressors, French armies occupied Belgium and the Netherlands, and extended the territory of France to the natural frontiers dreamed of by Louis XIV. The success of the French armies was due to the skillful organization by the Jacobins of all the resources of the country for war purposes, their introduction of the *levée en masse* (the predecessor of modern universal conscription), and their ruthless use of the Terror to maintain revolutionary fervor.

At home the Jacobins introduced social and economic reforms such as maximum price and minimum wage laws to benefit the proletarian groups by which they were supported, and they established a new calendar and the cult of Reason. These were all swept away, but when the Convention adjourned, its work done, it had notable achievements to its credit: it had abolished the remains of feudalism, begun the codification of the laws, abolished slavery in the colonies, reformed education, finance, and local government, and established religious freedom. Factional strife among the Jacobin leaders, however, led to their downfall, and a period of reaction followed in the last days of the Convention. The extreme measures of the Jacobin dictatorship were withdrawn, the Revolutionary Tribunal was suppressed, and control reverted to that middle class group which was primarily interested in maintaining itself in political power. In view of the foreign success a general peace might well have been concluded, but the leaders feared the impact of several hundred thousand unemployed soldiers, mostly of Jacobin sympathy, returning to Paris. Popular feeling spread against the self-seekers of the Convention, however, and they were compelled at last to write the long postponed constitution which they had been summoned to prepare.

The constitution they evolved was that of the Directory (1795). It was a step in the effort of the revolutionary period to evolve a political answer to two evils—executive tyranny as demonstrated by the absolute monarchy, and legislative tyranny as demonstrated by the Convention. Accordingly it provided for a complete separation of powers. The property franchise was restored, but the unpopularity of the Convention in 1795 pretty well assured the acceptance of the constitution. Executive power was given to a group of five Directors, who had no veto power over the legislature. To avoid tyranny the multiple executive was matched in the legislative branch by the provision for two chambers to act as checks on each other. In practice the Directory turned out to be about as unpopular as the Convention was during its last year. The Directory attempted to restore government credit (the paper money having declined to the vanishing point): it introduced a regular budget, made efforts to improve collection of taxes, and reestablished indirect taxes. It alienated large parts of the middle class and after a few years found itself increasingly dependent upon military success abroad for its prestige; this prestige came to rest largely on the victories of one of its generals, Napoleon Bonaparte.

Bonaparte's rise to prominence had been very rapid. He had commanded the troops which suppressed a rebellion against the setting up of the Directory in 1795, was rewarded by being sent to Italy to take charge of the campaign there, and promptly stole the show. He brought the Austrian emperor to bay and forced him to recognize the Rhine as the frontier of France. After rearranging northern Italy in republics according to the French style of the moment, Napoleon returned to France in the wake of huge quantities of Italian loot. He was hailed as a hero. For his next assignment he was sent against England, which he considered France's chief enemy.

The English East India Company was now returning fabulous profits to its stockholders. By utilizing a series of mechanical inventions Great Britain had progressed to the factory system, where the employer owned the machines and controlled the lives of the workers. Although the system was producing vast social changes, it was making England enormously rich, and she could afford to be paymaster of the forces fighting France. Bonaparte proposed to attack India, England's more obvious source of wealth, and he struck first by way of Egypt. Defeated by the English Admiral Nelson's use of sea power, Bonaparte returned to France, helped engineer a *coup d'état* which established a government headed by three consuls, and as First Consul became the real ruler of France. He had himself made consul for life in 1802, and finally, in 1804, Emperor of the French, Napoleon I.

Napoleon's European policy was the most spectacular aspect of his career, but much more lasting and of permanent importance was his consolidation of the gains of the Revolution inside France. By far the most significant was his completion of the codification of the laws of France in a series of five codes known collectively as the *Code Napoléon*. The civil code dealt with relations between individuals and between individuals and the state in matters of property and political behavior. The code of civil procedure dealt with the procedure of the courts in civil cases. The commercial code was an expansion of the civil code, particularly in matters pertaining to business. The code of criminal instruction dealt with the relationship of the courts to individuals in criminal cases, and the penal code dealt with the punishment for criminal violations. The system of courts was also reorganized, and the centralized hierarchy of lower and higher courts established which, with minor changes, has lasted along with the *Code Napoléon* to the present day.

Although the codes of Napoleon contained some of the features of the old régime, they were the greatest single achievement of the Revolutionary period. All unwritten feudal vestiges were abolished. Equality before the law became permanent in the written, systematized code. The relationship of individuals to each other, to landlords, to tax collectors—where there had been great abuses under the old régime—was fixed by written code, before which all persons had the same right. Thus the codes perpetuated the chief victories of the Revolution. In regard to family, labor, and the position of women, however, the Napoleonic codes were reactionary. The father was restored to his position as head of the family, and the wife could not enter contracts without her husband's consent. The complete freedom of testamentary disposition established by the Revolution was compromised; the idea of community property had to be respected, insuring some share, fixed by law, for all members of the family. This was in part designed to break down large landholdings, and in this it was successful. Labor and employer organizations were both prohibited—the old régime had permitted employers but not workmen to form combinations; and workmen were obliged to carry passports which certified honorable discharge from the last employment.

The legal codification was a measure of internal policy, but it affected all Europe, for wherever the conquering French armies penetrated they introduced the salient features of the Revolutionary reforms. Therefore much of Napoleon's work, though accomplished inside France, was European in scope. His religious settlement had similar importance. Personally Napoleon did not care about religion as long as people were good subjects, but he did notice (if he did not borrow the idea from eighteenth century reformers) that religion was useful in making people better citizens. By making peace with the church Napoleon hoped to win an ally. The Concordat with the papacy signed in 1801 was considered by some as a retraction of one of the most important reforms of the Revolution, the separation of church and state. The church of France was reestablished, Catholicism was proclaimed as the religion of the majority of the people, and the state assumed the expenses of the church. The state received the right to nominate priests, bishops, and archbishops—although nominations still had to be ratified by the pope. All claims of the church to church property confiscated during the Revolution were renounced by the papacy. In determining administrative procedure the bishops of France, not the pope, were the highest authority, and the pope was recognized as supreme only in doctrine. Napoleon later allowed the regular orders, abolished under the Revolution, to return—first the teaching orders and later the convents. Even the educational system was permitted by Napoleon to come largely under the control of the church. By the Concordat Napoleon fixed on France the problem of clericalism until 1905, when separation of church and state was again attempted. In his dealings with the papacy, both in political and religious matters, Napoleon practically dictated, and probably no single set of events in modern history did so much to weaken the prestige of the papacy as the treatment accorded it by Napoleon.

Under the empire the church gradually gained control of the educational system, and this meant both the growth of private schools for the new imperial nobility to the detriment of the public educational system and the disappearance of the free, compulsory, universal, lay education principle of the Revolution. Napoleon came to the problem of education so late in his career that the church had already secured its position. The public system he set up was inadequate in primary instruction, to the advantage of the private schools, which were either émigré organizations or run by religious orders. Primary education was not compulsory under the empire. Napoleon's attitude toward education, like his attitude toward the church, was determined by his desire to make good citizens.

His European policy was influenced by several factors. He extended the Revolution, as it seemed probable that the overthrow of the old régime in France could never be final while the old régime existed in the rest of Europe. Napoleon had inherited from the Revolution the natural frontiers desired by Louis XIV, and he attempted to protect them by creating beyond them buffer states under his control. Also, for the security of France, he attempted to diminish the authority of Austria and weaken any other big power that he could defeat. Eventually he undertook to control the entire sea-coast of Europe in order, by his Continental System, to diminish the power of England by ruining her trade. Through all his European adventures, however, he felt that military victory was the fundamental support of his personal prestige.

To halt the progress of Napoleon's encroachment one coalition after another was formed against him, always sparked by the English. The great English admiral, Nelson, shattered Napoleon's navy at Trafalgar in 1805, and from then on Napoleon was compelled to limit his campaigns to continental Europe. He humiliated the Prussians, and gave a large part of Prussian territory to Saxony; he brought the Holy Roman Empire to an end, leaving the emperor to rule Austria and erecting a Confederation of the Rhine subservient to himself. The more important princes in the Confederation he made kings, and he distributed the free cities and ecclesiastical states among the princes, until instead of 300 German states only 30 were left.

The states of the Confederation were induced to adopt constitutions like that of France: with the *Code Napoléon* or a code modelled

PLATE XXVII

Eighteenth Century

FIGURE 1. *Bust of Benjamin Franklin by the French sculptor Jean Antoine Houdon (1740–1828). The work of Houdon shows extreme naturalism and makes surfaces and textures convincing to the eye. The realism of such a head provides a valuable historical record, and Houdon, who modeled most of the public characters of his day, has left many such records.* [*Courtesy of the Metropolitan Museum of Art, New York*]

FIGURE 2. *Lacquered Chippendale secretary, now in Metropolitan Museum of Art, in New York. Furniture in the style made popular by the English furniture-maker Thomas Chippendale was transported in sailing ships to China, where is was lacquered and decorated with chinoiseries. The effect upon English taste of the trade with the East was very striking. Similar examples could be given of the influence on French and Dutch taste.*
[*Courtesy of the Metropolitan Museum of Art, New York*]

FIGURE 3. *Company in a Park by Jean Antoine Watteau (1684–1721), a French painter of Flemish origin to whom tuberculosis gave a curious verve. He painted the gay life of the French aristocrats of the early part of the eighteenth century, their elegance and their insouciance, but his work has an undertone of slight melancholy, as if he were aware that the artificiality of this life could not last much longer.*

PLATE XXVIII

Eighteenth Century

FIGURE 1. *Unfinished portrait of Napoleon, by Jacques Louis David (1748–1825). Napoleon, then first consul, recognized the ability of David and on his return from Italy came to his studio and asked to be painted. David began the work but the first consul never found time for another sitting. The artist has caught the young Napoleon's dramatic sense of himself as an actor in great events.*

FIGURE 2. *Sans Souci, one of three palaces of Frederick the Great at Potsdam. He took an active part in the designing of these palaces. Sans Souci shows the baroque merging into the more delicate rococo.*

FIGURE 3. The Oath of the Tennis Court. *This picture by David shows his conception of his role as the recorder of historical events in the grand manner with which he wished to glorify the civic virtues of the republic. The picture helped David win election to the Convention, of which he became president.*

[461b]

upon it, liberties of the subject, abolition of privilege, and emancipation of Jews. There were many liberals in the former free cities who welcomed these reforms and who cherished the idea of a new Germany. In ecclesiastical states the bishops, no longer political princes, devoted themselves to the spread of their respective faiths. In Prussia and Austria the old order survived. Napoleon made Polish Prussia the Grand Duchy of Warsaw and would have wiped Prussia from the map had the tsar not intervened.

Napoleon had induced the tsar to make peace and to promise aid in the destruction of English commerce. This he proposed to do by closing Continental ports to British goods; England responded with a naval blockade of continental proportions; and both countries systematically interfered with neutral commerce. In his efforts to enforce his system Napoleon outraged the pride of the Spanish people by making his brother Joseph their king. The English utilized this disaffection by sending an army under Wellington, which with Spanish co-operation administered to Napoleon's armies their first defeats. Encouraged by these, the Austrian emperor tried another war, but was defeated and forced to make an alliance and cement it by the gift of his daughter, who produced an heir for Napoleon. On the ground that the pope was not supporting the blockade, the Papal States were annexed. Even in Spain in 1810–11 Napoleon was partially successful; and again on the pretext that the blockade against England was being violated in 1812, he turned against Russia, the only place left to conquer.

In explaining Napoleon's military successes it must be remembered that he had had excellent training as a general and that he inherited from the Revolution an army of patriots, not mercenaries. The Revolutionary armies were not highly drilled as the old professional armies had been, but they did things with zest. Napoleon also inherited from the Revolution a remarkable set of officers and an organization able to carry out complicated plans of campaign. Pre-Revolutionary armies had acted independently by each unit; Carnot, the great Jacobin organizer, developed a semaphore telegraph, instituted integrated campaigns, and was always able to operate on internal lines. Napoleon received from the Revolution the idea of the nation-in-arms, with the entire manpower at the disposal of the government. He and his generals were also able to handle numbers. He depended in large part on great numbers of cavalry and artillery, and used many old methods but more expertly than his predecessors or contemporaries. He also emphasized speed and movement. He always had centralized control over all the armies on his side, in contrast to his opponents, who in many cases neutralized each other's moves.

Toward the end of the Napoleonic period, however, the role of Napoleonic armies and that of his enemies was partially reversed. The Napoleonic armies were becoming professionalized by about 1809 and at this period the Continental powers opposed to him began to recruit patriot armies. One of the reasons for Napoleon's eventual failure was that his selected and trained officers carried out details and could not, ordinarily, produce plans of their own for a campaign. Napoleon followed as far as possible a policy of making war pay for itself, both by plunder and by indemnity. The legacy of the Napoleonic era which has done as much damage in people's thinking about war as any other is the belief that war can be made to pay as it did in Napoleon's time.

Napoleon's invasion of Russia proved to be a major catastrophe. The Russians retreated before Napoleon's unprecedentedly large armies, practicing a scorched-earth policy. Although Napoleon took Moscow, the tsar would not make terms; and in the end the French retreated, vanquished by impossibly long communication lines, lack of supplies, and the merciless Russian weather. Harried the length of its retreat by the Russian cavalry, only the melancholy remnants of an army returned.

Moreover, in Napoleon's absence, Prussia had been transformed. A disgruntled knight named Stein, whom Napoleon had lent to Frederick William III, persuaded that monarch that if he aroused his people's devotion to the crown by a series of reforms Prussia could be made into the centre of a movement for a free Germany. The Prussian landholders, the Junkers, persuaded the king to dismiss Stein and pursue instead a Prussian policy. Serfdom was abolished, but in the process the Junkers got the land into their own hands, and all but the rich peasants under their control even more firmly than before. Hardenberg, a former associate of Stein, strengthened the government, and Prussians were taught that they had obligations to the state. Scharnhorst and Gneisenau reorganized the army, under terms of universal military service. All Prussians were to be militarized, and a new system of education was to have the inculcation of the military spirit as its main purpose. An athletic poet, Jahn, got up gymnastic societies which drilled and paraded. In the new University of Berlin a patriotic movement had started under the leadership of the philosopher Fichte, who taught the glorification of the state. The Prussian state was to lead in the liberation of Germany, according to Fichte's idea.

Prussia was able to fight again, but the coalition against Napoleon in 1813 probably had less national enthusiasm behind it than has usually been supposed. The opportunity to attack a beaten general seemed heaven-sent. Returning to France, Napoleon had to raise a new army to fight Russia, Austria, and Prussia, who announced that their quarrel was not with the French people but with Napoleon, who had misled them. He was defeated at Leipzig in October, 1813. France was invaded, Paris taken, and the emperor forced to abdicate. He was allowed to retire to the island of Elba, and the Bourbons were invited back to Paris. A congress assembled at Vienna to remake the map of Europe. Some of the leading states were represented by their rulers, but the ablest man there was Prince Metternich, the Austrian delegate. Metternich had watched the French Revolution with disgust, and to him its boasted liberties were anathema. As ambassador to France he had helped Napoleon to marry an Austrian grand-duchess; when Napoleon failed in Russia, Metternich, not nationalist enthusiasm, had been the architect of the coalition against him. He was now to be the architect of a new Europe.

The deliberations of the Congress of Vienna were interrupted by the news that Napoleon had returned to France and again was raising an army. He was finally defeated at Waterloo (June, 1815) and sent as a prisoner to the island of St. Helena in the South Atlantic.

The arrangements made at Vienna lasted, with minor changes, until the end of World War I. Not only the matter but the manner of the settlement is worthy of study. France as the vanquished nation was not expected to have any influence, but its gifted representative, Talleyrand, declared that it was the sacred duty of the Congress to replace legitimate monarchs on their thrones. France, he maintained, had suffered as much as any nation at the hands of Napoleon, and deserved the return of the Bourbons and the restoration of their original patrimony. The idea appealed to the tsar and

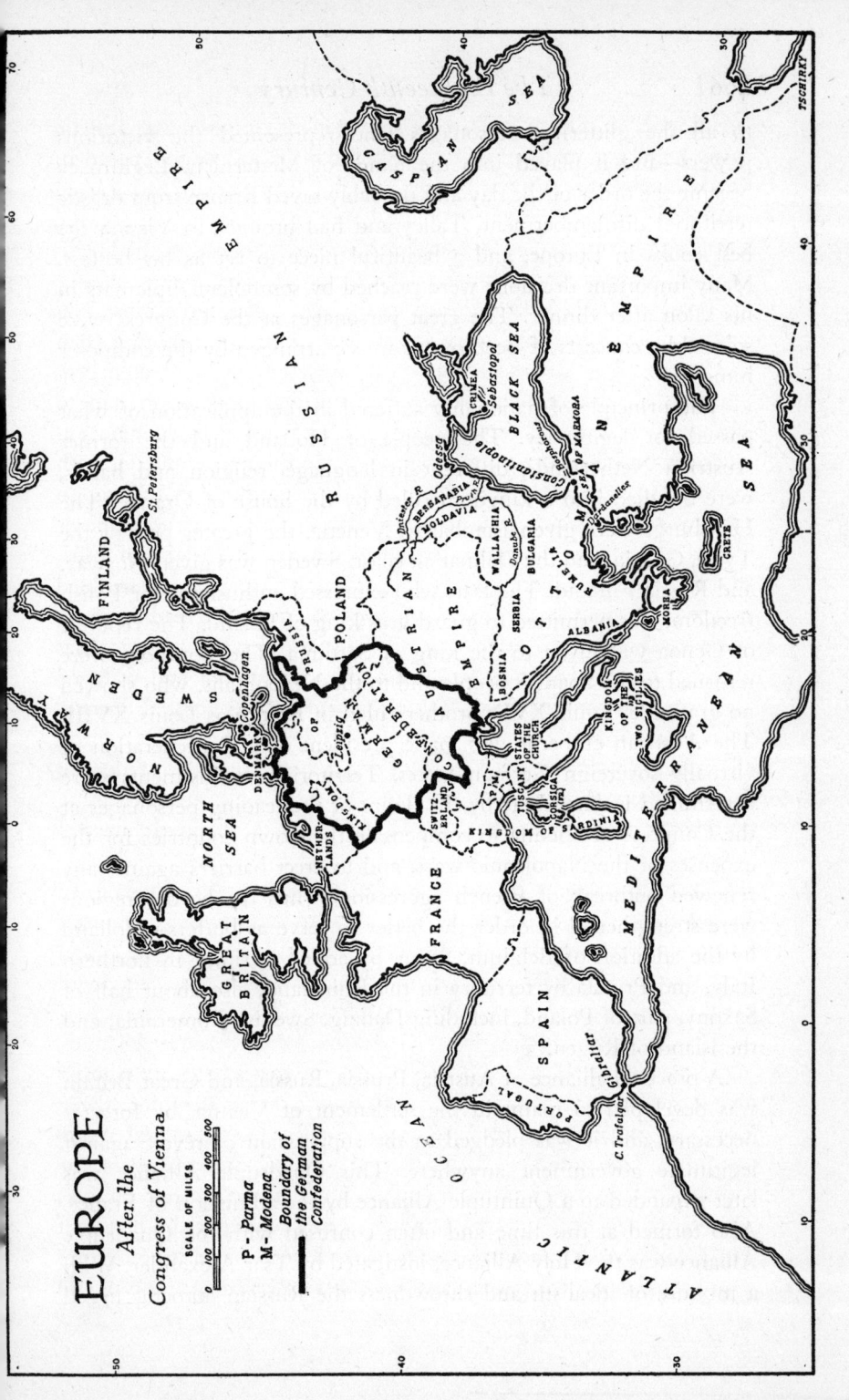

to all the glittering personages who represented the victorious powers—and it played into the hands of Metternich. Legitimacy became the order of the day and probably saved France from drastic territorial dismemberment. Talleyrand had brought to Vienna the best cooks in Europe, and a beautiful niece to act as his hostess. Many important decisions were reached by somnolent diplomats in his salon after dinner. The great personages at the Congress were solaced by concerts of Beethoven's music arranged by the composer himself.

The principle of nationality suffered in the application of what passed for legitimacy. The people of Holland and the former Austrian Netherlands, different in language, religion and habits, were bundled into a kingdom ruled by the house of Orange. The Hapsburgs were given Lombardy, Venetia, the greater part of the Tyrol, Galicia, and the Dalmatian coast. Sweden was given Norway, and Russia Finland. The tsar, who expressed enthusiasm for Polish freedom, was permitted to guard it as king of Poland. The republic of Genoa was given to the king of Sardinia. The Bourbons were returned to the Spanish people and to the Neapolitans, who showed no gratitude. Louis XVI's brother ruled in France as Louis XVIII. The Austrian emperor was made president of a Confederation of virtually sovereign German States. Territorial readjustments were determined in large part by the desire of the leading personages at the Congress of Vienna to compensate their own countries for the expenses of the Napoleonic wars, and to erect barriers against any renewed outbreak of French aggression. Thus the border regions were strengthened in order the better to serve as buffers—Holland by the addition of Belgium, Savoy by added territory in northern Italy, and Prussia by territory in the Rhineland, also about half of Saxony, part of Poland, including Danzig, Swedish Pomerania, and the island of Rügen.

A practical alliance of Austria, Prussia, Russia, and Great Britain was developed to maintain the settlement of Vienna, by force if necessary, and it was pledged to the suppression of revolt against legitimate government anywhere. This Quadruple Alliance was later expanded to a Quintuple Alliance by the admission of France. Also formed at this time and often confused with the Quadruple Alliance was the Holy Alliance, instigated by Tsar Alexander. With a mixture of idealism and shrewdness the Russian autocrat urged the establishment of an international organization to keep the peace, and proposed a covenant among rulers whereby they would all govern in accordance with the moral principles of Christianity. Although the Holy Alliance—which had no specific organization or function—was characterized as "a piece of sublime mysticism and nonsense" by the British Foreign Minister, Castlereagh, practically every ruler of Europe signed Alexander's declaration.

Signs that revolutionary ideas had survived were not long in appearing, and the great powers of Europe held congresses to meet the threat. For a time they succeeded in suppressing revolts, delegating one of their number to police duty in the threatened country; but shortly the Quintuple Alliance foundered because of divergent interests among the powers. Great Britain withdrew from participation in Continental affairs, and by her commanding position on the seas prevented any scheme for the restoration of Spanish sovereignty over the revolting American empire. This failure to preserve the principle of legitimacy adopted at Vienna was dictated by the hope of securing the trade of independent former Spanish colonies, and this expectation was fully justified by events. Indeed Napoleon might have smiled grimly if on his deathbed at St. Helena he could have been apprised of the troubles that awaited his conquerors.

The attempt to govern Europe by congresses proved futile, but it is useful to contemplate the revolution in international thinking which the Congress of Vienna implied. By providing for future congresses the statesmen at Vienna gave recognition to the fact that the affairs of one or more of the European nations were a concern to all. Because the welfare of the community of European nations depended upon the good relations of any of its members, collective attention to affairs of international interest was important. No longer could nations afford to ignore such internal phenomena as the French Revolution, since they could affect all Europe. Furthermore, the Congress of Vienna and the several congresses which followed introduced the idea of legalizing changes in international status by community action. This provided a direct contrast with eighteenth-century practice, in which unadulterated force governed international relations and settlements were made directly between belligerents regardless of the rights or interests of other powers. Force was still applied by the congresses, but by and with the assent of the "concert" of European powers. When France intervened in

Spain to suppress revolt against the king, or Austria invaded Naples to restore the Neapolitan tyrant, the action was authorized in advance by a congress of powers. Later in the century congresses served a different function, that of registering, approving, or modifying a forcible change already accomplished. To one or the other of these principles can be attributed the famous international congresses of the nineteenth century—Vienna, Verona, Aix-la-Chapelle, Laibach, Troppau, Paris, Berlin.

The congress principle represented a groping for some kind of standard, some legality in relations between states, such as characterizes relations between individuals within states. There are two contrasting methods, both with historical example in European national development, of securing such a standard—gradually, by precedent and tradition as with England, or more speedily, by setting up a fixed code as with France. The congresses by their actions set precedent for collective, orderly action to accomplish necessary change and promote two fundamental premises in European society —maintenance of the balance of power, and insistence that governmental changes be legitimate and constitutional rather than revolutionary.

[THE EIGHTEENTH CENTURY]

Readings

~~~~~~~~~~

Benjamin Franklin

LETTERS AND PAPERS*

[Fundamental ideas of the Enlightenment appear in these extracts from Franklin's correspondence. The principle that people should have a voice in their own government appears in the first letter. In the second, written to the famous Physiocrat who was an ancestor of the American Dupont family, he shows his sympathy with the ideas of the Physiocrats. The letter to Dr. Babcock expresses sentiments that would have profoundly shocked the noble ladies who in later years made much of Franklin in France.]

To Lord Kames (London, April 11, 1767)

... I am fully persuaded with you, that a *Consolidating Union,* by a fair and equal representation of all the parts of this empire in Parliament, is the only firm basis on which its political grandeur and prosperity can be founded. Ireland once wished it, but now rejects it. The time has been, when the colonies might have been pleased with it: they are now *indifferent* about it; and if it is much longer delayed, they too will *refuse* it. ...

Upon the whole, I have lived so great a part of my life in Britain, and have formed so many friendships in it, that I love it, and sincerely wish it prosperity; and therefore wish to see that Union, on which alone I think it can be secured and established. As to America, the advantages of such a union to her are not so apparent. She may suffer at present under the arbitrary power of this country; she may suffer for a while in a separation from it; but these are temporary evils that she will outgrow. Scotland and Ireland are

---

* From *The Writings of Benjamin Franklin,* edited by Albert Henry Smyth (1907), Vols. V and X. Reprinted by permission of The Macmillan Company, publishers.

differently circumstanced. Confined by the sea, they can scarcely increase in numbers, wealth and strength, so as to overbalance England. But America, an immense territory, favoured by Nature with all advantages of climate, soil, great navigable rivers, and lakes, &c. must become a great country, populous and mighty; and will, in a less time than is generally conceived, be able to shake off any shackles that may be imposed on her, and perhaps place them on the imposers. In the mean time, every act of oppression will sour their tempers, lessen greatly, if not annihilate the profits of your commerce with them, and hasten their final revolt; for the seeds of liberty are universally found there, and nothing can eradicate them. And yet, there remains among that people, so much respect, veneration and affection for Britain, that, if cultivated prudently, with kind usage, and tenderness for their privileges, they might be easily governed still for ages, without force, or any considerable expence. But I do not see here a sufficient quantity of the wisdom, that is necessary to produce such a conduct, and I lament the want of it. . . .

To Du Pont de Nemours (London, July 28, 1768)

. . . . I am sorry to find that that wisdom which sees the welfare of the parts in the prosperity of the whole, seems yet not to be known in this country. . . . We are so far from conceiving that what is best for mankind, or even for Europe in general, may be best for us, that we are even studying to establish and extend a separate interest of Britain, to the prejudice of even Ireland and our colonies. . . . It is from your philosophy only that the maxims of a contrary and more happy conduct are to be drawn, which I therefore sincerely wish may grow and increase till it becomes the governing philosophy of the human species, as it must be that of superior beings in better worlds. . . .

To Dr. Joshua Babcock (London, Jan. 13, 1772)

. . . . I have lately made a Tour thro' Ireland and Scotland. In those Countries a small Part of the Society are Landlords, great Noblemen, and Gentlemen, extreamly opulent, living in the highest Affluence and Magnificence: The Bulk of the People Tenants, extreamly poor, living in the most sordid Wretchedness, in dirty Hovels of Mud and Straw, and cloathed only in Rags.

I thought often of the Happiness of New England, where every

Man is a Freeholder, has a Vote in publick Affairs, lives in a tidy, warm House, has plenty of good Food and Fewel, with whole cloaths from Head to Foot, the Manufacture perhaps of his own Family. Long may they continue in this Situation! But if they should ever envy the Trade of these Countries, I can put them in a Way to obtain a Share of it. Let them with three fourths of the People of Ireland live the Year round on Potatoes and Buttermilk, without Shirts, then may their Merchants export Beef, Butter, and Linnen. Let them, with the Generality of the Common People of Scotland, go Barefoot, then may they make large Exports in Shoes and Stockings: And if they will be content to wear Rags, like the Spinners and Weavers of England, they may make Cloths and Stuffs for all Parts of the World.

Farther, if my Countrymen should ever wish for the honour of having among them a gentry enormously wealthy, let them sell their Farms & pay rack'd Rents; the Scale of the Landlords will rise as that of the Tenants is depress'd, who will soon become poor, tattered, dirty, and abject in Spirit. Had I never been in the American Colonies, but was to form my Judgment of Civil Society by what I have lately seen, I should never advise a Nation of Savages to admit of Civilization: For I assure you, that, in the Possession & Enjoyment of the various Comforts of Life, compar'd to these People every Indian is a Gentleman: And the Effect of this kind of Civil Society seems only to be, the depressing Multitudes below the Savage State that a few may be rais'd above it. My best Wishes attend you and yours, being ever, with great Esteem, Dear Sir, etc.
B. [Franklin]

QUERIES AND REMARKS RESPECTING ALTERATIONS IN THE CONSTITUTION OF PENNSYLVANIA
(Published in the Federal Gazette, November 3, 1789)

[On a proposal for a legislature of two houses, of equal power, the upper elected by a property franchise.]

Several Questions may arise upon this Proposition. 1st. What is the Proportion of Freemen possessing Lands and Houses of one thousand Pounds' value, compared to that of Freemen whose Possessions are inferior? Are they as one to ten? Are they even as one to twenty? I should doubt whether they are as one to fifty. If this

minority is to chuse a Body expressly to controul that which is to be chosen by the great Majority of the Freemen, what have this great Majority done to forfeit so great a Portion of their Right in Elections? Why is this Power of Controul, contrary to the spirit of all Democracies, to be vested in a Minority, instead of a Majority?
... Suppose one of our Indian Nations should now agree to form a civil Society; each Individual would bring into the Stock of the Society little more Property than his Gun and his Blanket, for at present he has no other. We know, that, when one of them has attempted to keep a few Swine, he has not been able to maintain a Property in them, his neighbours thinking they have a Right to kill and eat them whenever they want Provision, it being one of their Maxims that hunting is free for all; the accumulation therefore of Property in such a Society, and its Security to Individuals in every Society, must be an Effect of the Protection afforded to it by the joint Strength of the Society, in the Execution of its Laws. Private Property therefore is a Creature of Society, and is subject to the Calls of that Society, whenever its Necessities shall require it, even to its last Farthing; its Contributions therefore to the public Exigencies are not to be considered as conferring a Benefit on the Publick, entitling the Contributors to the Distinctions of Honour and Power, but as the Return of an Obligation previously received, or the Payment of a just Debt. The Combinations of Civil Society are not like those of a Set of Merchants, who club their Property in different Proportions for Building and Freighting a Ship, and may therefore have some Right to vote in the Disposition of the Voyage in a greater or less Degree according to their respective Contributions; but the important ends of Civil Society, and the personal Securities of Life and Liberty, these remain the same in every Member of the society; and the poorest continues to have an equal Claim to them with the most opulent, whatever Difference Time, Chance, or Industry may occasion in their Circumstances. ...

To David Hartley (Philadelphia, December 4, 1789)

.... The Convulsions in France are attended with some disagreeable Circumstances; but if by the Struggle she obtains and secures for the Nation its future Liberty, and a good Constitution, a few Years' Enjoyment of those Blessings will amply repair all the Damages their Acquisition may have occasioned. God grant, that not only the Love of Liberty, but a thorough Knowledge of the Rights of Man, may pervade all the Nations of the Earth, so that a Philosopher may set his Foot anywhere on its Surface, and say, "This is my Country." . . .

∽ ∽ ∽

Napoleon Bonaparte

LETTERS *

To M. Naudin

[Written July 27, 1791 when the young Bonaparte was a lieutenant of artillery. These sentiments were no longer held by the writer when he was himself in the possession of sovereign power.]

. . . . Will there be war? The question has been asked for months past. I have always said, no. Tell me what you think of my reasons.

Europe is divided between those sovereigns who rule over men, and those who rule over cattle or horses. The former thoroughly understand the Revolution. They are terrified of it. They would willingly make pecuniary sacrifices to destroy it. But they will never dare raise the mask, for fear the flame may set their own houses on fire. That is the history of England, Holland, etc.

As for the sovereigns who rule over horses, they cannot grasp the Constitution: they despise it. They think this chaos of incoherent ideas spells the ruin of France. Judging from what they say, you would suppose our brave patriots are going to cut each other's throats, purge the earth with their blood from the crimes committed against kings, and end by bowing their heads lower than ever beneath the mitred despot, the cloistered *fakir,* and (above all) the brigand whose weapon is a deed-box. Such sovereigns will make no move. They are waiting for the outbreak of civil war, which, according to themselves and their dull ministers, is sure to come. . . .

---

* These extracts are all taken from a collection of 300 documents chosen as characteristic out of 41,000 by J. M. Thompson and published under the title *Napoleon Self-Revealed* (1934). Reprinted by permission of Houghton Mifflin Company.

To Citizen Oriani, the Astronomer (Milan, May 24, 1796)

[Written after Napoleon's conquest of Italy. His interest in the arts and sciences was politic as well as enlightened. He knew the value of such patronage in enhancing the prestige of a ruler.]

Science, which dignifies the mind of men, and Art, which beautifies life, and transmits its great achievements to posterity, ought to be specially honoured by every free government. Every man of genius, every office-holder in the Republic of letters, in whatever country he may have been born, is a French citizen.

Learned men in Milan used not to enjoy the consideration they deserved. Hidden in their laboratories, they thought themselves happy if kings and priests did them no harm. It is not so to-day. In Italy thought has become free. There is no more inquisition, no more intolerance, no more tyranny. I invite all learned men to meet together, and to tell me what methods should be adopted, or what needs supplied, in order to give the sciences and the fine arts a new life and a new existence. Any of them who care to visit France will meet with a distinguished reception by the Government. The French people sets a higher value upon the acquisition of a learned mathematician, a famous painter, or the distinguished exponent of any branch of study, than upon that of the richest and most populous city in the world.

Pray express these sentiments for me to the distinguished men of learning resident at Milan.

To the Inspectors of the Conservatoire de Musique at Paris (Headquarters, Milan, July 26, 1797)

I have received your letter of the 16th messidor, with the accompanying memorandum. There are persons busy, at this very moment, in the different cities of Italy, copying and arranging all the music you ask for.

Let me assure you that I shall take the greatest trouble to see that your intentions are fulfilled, and that the Conservatoire is enriched with any musical treasures it may lack.

Of all the Fine Arts, music is that which most influences the passions, and that, therefore, which a legislator should do most to encourage. A few bars of moral music, composed by a master hand, cannot fail to affect the feelings, and have much more influence than a well-written book about morality, which convinces our reason without altering our habits.

Note for the Minister of Public Worship
(Paris, February 12, 1806)

[Written the second year after Napoleon became emperor. The remarks on Russia in the letter that follows are not without interest today.]

Considering how necessary it is to give a religious sanction to solemn occasions, whilst at the same time diminishing the number of festivals which distract people from their work, two feasts may be suggested:—

(1) On August 15th, the Feast of St. Napoléon, which would celebrate at the same time the Emperor's birthday, and the ratification of the Concordat; with this festival could be associated acts of thanksgiving for the prosperity of the Empire; and one could try to give the procession, which would still take place on this day, a character tending to efface its old associations.

(2) On the first Sunday following the day corresponding to the 11th frimaire one could commemorate both the success of the Grand Army and the occasion of the Coronation; and one of the clergy could preach a sermon making special mention of local citizens who fell in the battle of Austerlitz.

To Talleyrand (St. Cloud, June 9, 1806)

.... (6) My ambassador must always be on the look-out for opportunities to put Russia out of favour. He must depreciate the strength of her army, and the courage of her troops, whenever and in whatever way he can. He must adopt a distant attitude towards the Russian legation—show it little attention, and treat it with disdain rather than condescension. Whatever the relations of Russia and France elsewhere, the French legation at Constantinople must be on cool terms with the Russian. On the other hand, once peace is made, it can be friendly with Austria, Prussia, and England.

(7) All our negotiations ought to aim at these points: (1) closing the Bosphorus against the Russians, and prohibiting the passage of their vessels from the Mediterranean to the Black Sea, whether they are armed or unarmed (for it is an utter fraud to close the ports of a warship and call it a troopship); (2) forbidding any Greek to sail under the Russian flag; (3) fortifying or arming every position

against the Russians; (4) subduing the Georgians, and re-establishing the absolute rule of the Porte over Moldavia and Wallachia.

(8) I don't want to partition the empire of Constantinople: even if I were offered a three-quarters share, I should refuse to do so. I want to strengthen and consolidate this great empire, and to use it, as it is, against Russia.

To Fouché, Minister of Police (Finkenstein, April 4, 1807)
[Napoleon's appreciation of the power of the press was thoroughly modern.]

Most of the papers are badly conducted. It may be difficult to remedy this. All the same, I should like you to see that they never talk about the interests of the new dynasty, which they treat rather as though they were a party affair. That dingy publication, the *French Courrier,* can insult the *Empire Journal* as much as it likes; but they mustn't bring *me* into the business. . . . I have no wish to start the charge of *lèse-majesté* again: I attach no importance to these gutter-press debates. But I won't let any paper speak of the Bourbons, or of the present dynasty, as the *Courrier* does. Can't it defend its case without bringing in the government? A man can be as atheistical as Lalande, as religious as Portalis, or as famous a philosopher as Regnaud, without being any less a supporter of the government, and a good Frenchman. Then why in the world should we allow the papers to go and tell these men that they are bad citizens? . . .

The first time this paper mentions the Bourbons, or my interests, suppress it. . . .

To his brother Joseph (Rheims, March 14, 1814)
[Compare this letter with the one written in 1791 by the young lieutenant of artillery.]

I have received your letter of March 12. I am sorry you told the Duke of Conegliano what I wrote to you. I don't like all this tittle-tattle. If it were part of my plan to put the Duke elsewhere, all the prattlers in Paris would not prevent my doing so. The National Guard in Paris is part of the French people, and I will be master *everywhere* in France, as long as I have a breath in my body. Your character is quite different from mine. You like flattering people, and falling in with their ideas: I like people to please me, and to fall in with mine. I am master to-day, every bit as much as at Austerlitz. Don't let anyone flatter the National Guard. Refuse to allow Regnaud, or anyone else, to become its advocate. I suppose they *do* admit that there is a difference between the times of Lafayette, when the people was sovereign, and the present moment, when I am? I have decreed that 12 battalions of the mass levy are to be raised in Paris. This measure must not be held up on any pretext whatsoever. I am writing to the Ministers of Home Affairs and Police to the same effect. If the people once see us doing what they like, instead of what is good for them, they will obviously imagine that they are the sovereign, and will have a very poor opinion of those who govern them.

MEDAL ISSUED BY NAPOLEON TO COMMEMORATE THE INVASION OF ENGLAND WHICH HE PLANNED IN 1804

(From *A Student's History of England* by Samuel R. Gardiner. Longmans Green, London, 1897.)

PART XV

The Nineteenth Century

CHRONOLOGY

1804 Civil Code of Napoleon
1814 Congress of Vienna assembles
1815 Battle of Waterloo
1830 Revolutionary movement; bourgeois control in France confirmed
1832 First Reform Bill in England
1837 First telegraph
1847 Marx and Engels's *Communist Manifesto*
1848 Widespread revolutionary movements for constitutional reform
1856 Congress of Paris
1857 Indian Mutiny
1859 Darwin's *Origin of Species*
1861–63 Emancipation of serfs in Russia by Alexander II
1866 Marx' *Capital*
1871 Formation of German Empire
1878 Congress of Berlin
1882 Formation of Triple Alliance
1894 Franco-Russian Alliance
1899 Marconi sends wireless messages across English Channel

PART XV

The Nineteenth Century

~~~~~~~~~~~~~~~~~~~~~~~~~~~~~~

THE nineteenth century was a period of great scientific and technological progress, but thought in social and economic fields lagged behind material advance. Improved mathematics, precision tools, and the publication of results of research meant rapid developments in science which were applied to the control of man's environment. Technological improvements brought increased wealth, wealth brought increased population, and developments in the field of medicine cut down the incidence of disease and prolonged life. Existence became easier and pleasanter in many ways for whole communities, but the conditions of life for workers in the industrial system produced grave social maladjustments.

It was in England during the first three-quarters of the nineteenth century that the Industrial Revolution made its most spectacular progress. The machines, the factories, the tools, and the products were the most impressive outward manifestations of the Industrial Revolution and the industrial society it produced. The heavy-metal industries were basic. The age of iron and steel was built up by the quantity production which developed, mainly in England, late in the eighteenth century and early in the nineteenth. Comparatively small quantities of cast iron had long been used for tools and hardware. Structural use of cast iron had been made in the 1770's, tremendously increasing the amount needed. This was followed by its use in canal boats in the 1790's and then, as a fireproofing measure, in mills shortly after the turn of the century. Simultaneously arched bridges using cast-iron girders were being constructed, and by the end of the first quarter of the nineteenth century the practical limits of cast-iron structural development were approached.

[481

During the middle third of the century wrought iron replaced cast iron, a development forced by the demands of shipbuilding and railroad construction, for which cast iron was unsatisfactory. The use of wrought iron meant not only economy of material but doubling its application. The growth and expansion of the iron industry in Great Britain was phenomenal, owing to huge home consumption and a large export market because of her leadership in the building up of the basic heavy industry. After the middle third of the century, when large-scale steel processes were invented, steel in many instances replaced earlier products. Then the lead began to shift from Great Britain to Germany and the United States since Britain's resources were not so well adapted to steel production. The unification and expansion of the United States and Germany made competition possible; they had the large-scale ore deposits which steel manufacturing processes demanded. Great Britain was forced to import supplementary ores from Sweden and Spain, and a gradual decline in British iron exports set in. She, however, retained in large measure the great world carrying trade which she had built.

Railroad and locomotive development provided impetus for the inauguration of an age of iron and steel, and the story is now generally familiar. Increased demands for coal and the expansion of mines led to the necessity for devices capable of hauling large loads. This was met by rails, wagons to move on them, and finally machine power to pull them. The first successful commercial railroads were built to move coal from mines to ports. After the development of steam locomotive power came steamships of iron construction. The building of steamships necessitated the establishment of coaling stations; the location of coaling stations powerfully influenced steamship lines and trade. Britain attained pre-eminence in the coal-carrying trade, exporting coal and supplying the distant coaling stations; her ships on the return voyages brought the heavier foods and raw materials produced in the world's colonial areas. The development of iron ship construction was partly due to a decline of the European supply of wood, the rising cost of ship construction, and the increasing demand for carrying space. Iron ship construction eventually reduced the cost of shipbuilding below that of American-built wooden ships, increased available shipbuilding materials, and enlarged carrying capacity.

The factory system was one major cause of social changes, but perhaps equally important were the modifications of the transport system effected by railroad and steamship. The practical limit to the size of wooden shipping was between four and five thousand tons. Iron ships could be built many times larger, and their size affected the distribution of shipping, bringing it more and more into ports suitable to large vessels. Great concentrations of population were difficult to maintain in the days before such carriers as the railroad and the steamship came into use, but with the new techniques in transport the balance between urban and rural areas was upset. In the industrial society that supplanted the agrarian, fuel for the machines was more important, relatively, than food for men. Machines could be located near their sources of power, and food brought from distant areas to the men that worked the machines. Population became increasingly concentrated around the machines, destroying the rural village and market town which had existed because of the need for proximity to the food-producing areas, and building up that noteworthy feature of modern industrial society, the predominantly urban settlement.

Thus the so-called Industrial Revolution caused sweeping social changes. Labor was transferred from the home to the factory, from the country to the city. Child labor, long hours, slum conditions due to overcrowding resulted. The British government in the first third of the century did nothing to cope with these evils. Adam Smith in his *Wealth of Nations* had formulated a strong criticism of government regulation of commerce and industry. On this basis English thinkers built the *laissez-faire* school of economic thought, which held that any legislation in the field would be harmful. However, although *laissez-faire* decried all legislation to remedy working conditions, it was not used to favor the repeal of laws which prevented the formation of labor unions.

Adam Smith believed that freeing trade from all shackles would result in a great increase of wealth. He warned, however, against the danger of allowing the amassing of large fortunes without due service rendered, and urged the importance of an adequate system for the distribution of wealth. These two ideas went practically unnoticed until Karl Marx formulated his social theories. But since Marx's system called for the overthrow of capitalism it was generally considered subversive, and well-disposed persons who saw the need of reform preferred to advocate liberalism.

Nineteenth century liberalism developed out of the Enlightenment; it was rational and cosmopolitan, emphasized common humanity and the rights of man, and stressed individualism. It went hand-in-hand with humanitarianism, another product of the Enlightenment. In the eighteenth century, only a small minority had protested the horrors of criminal law, gruesome executions, and slavery. Nineteenth century generations took those protests as self-evident truths. Adopted by religious groups, humanitarian concepts led to agitation for prison reform, abolition of slavery, and restriction of the death penalty. The influence on practical politics is evident in the concrete results achieved; slavery had been swept away by France in the Revolution, the English halted the slave trade in 1807-08, and finally abolished slavery (with compensation) in 1833-34. Since these measures were to a certain extent economically hurtful, they were justified on the grounds of compassion for the suffering of human beings without regard to their race, religion, or social condition; these were fundamental ideas of liberalism. These sentiments were also, in some measure, the cause of political hostility toward the Turkish Empire, in which the liberal recognition of the dignity of man did not prevail.

Although its origins were different, humanitarianism had much in common with romanticism, which was a reaction against the Enlightenment. Romanticism was characterized by a revival of interest in the past and an emphasis on nature—not the theoretical "nature" of the eighteenth-century *philosophes,* but nature as expressed in the heart: sentiment, feelings of sympathy, and interest in the individual. It expressed humanitarianism and individualism in the broadest sense, a love of men, a belief in the innate nobility of man, and indignation at social injustice. There was even something of mysticism, with imagination, simplicity of vision, and single-minded following of ideals, and thus a complete break was made from the rationalism of the eighteenth century.

In England romanticism was voiced by the poets Coleridge, Keats, and Shelley; in Germany, by Goethe and Lessing. Goethe pointed out that rationalism in its neglect of emotion failed to consider an important part of experience; Kant supplied a rational basis for Goethe's appeal to experience. A group of German philosophers, including Hegel, used romanticism in developing the idea of the duty of conserving existing institutions, such as the state, sacrificing if necessary the interests of the individual to those of the state. *Étatism* (statism) and nationalism were justified along these lines.

Humanitarianism linked liberalism and romanticism, and the nationalism quickened by romanticism was reinforced by the nationalism which Napoleon's ruthlessness had evoked. Nationalism flourished widely: it triumphed in Germany and Italy; in Germany and France it allied itself with militarism. Ireland seethed with nationalism, and Irish efforts for self-government worried English statesmen throughout the century.

In England, liberalism was the point of departure for the utilitarianism of James Mill, for cosmopolitanism, and for the idea of progress. This idea had in the eighteenth century given impetus to the evolutionary idea, with which men's minds had played since the days of the Greeks. St. Augustine, John Scotus Erigena, and Giordano Bruno had expressed it; later philosophers from Descartes to Goethe held evolutionary views. A basis was provided for these views by observation; Francis Bacon had pointed out varieties in animals and plants, and in the eighteenth century Linnaeus and Buffon worked to classify plants and animals into *genera* and *species*. On the basis of this preliminary work the Frenchman, Lamarck, at the beginning of the nineteenth century, developed a theory of the mutability of species, and in 1859 Darwin showed the possibility of evolution through the struggle for existence.

The application of the evolutionary idea to the social field raised new problems. It provided arguments for war. Increasing population in the industrial countries made possible armies on an unprecedented scale. The application of modern science to devising new instruments of warfare made war more destructive, and efforts were made at international conferences to limit its incidence and deadly possibilities. At the same time colonial and commercial rivalries increased the likelihood of wars. The exploitation of colonial populations became a problem for the tender-minded.

Imperialism was an expression of nationalism, but its basis was economic. It was an extension of the forces which had brought the Germans into the Roman empire and many of their descendants eastward into the lands of the Slavs. Even Americans were affected; they took the Philippines when there was no more cheap land in the West. For industrial countries to have sources of raw materials and markets for manufactured goods under the flag came to seem a national need and a legitimate goal. France and Great Britain in the eighteenth century had tested the value of native troops, and as France was a country where population had ceased increasing this seemed an important fact. Colonies as a source of cheap labor appeared more and more desirable as the trades-union movement progressed.

We have seen how the doctrine of *laissez-faire* kept back improvement in the condition of workers in the early part of the century. As the workers began to organize, they were able to secure legislation in their interest wherever they attained political power. To the liberals this seemed the solution of the workers' problem. The strike was a wasteful device, but by its means the condition of workers in organized trades was greatly improved. Unfortunately wage increases won after strikes did not prove permanently satisfactory; as industrialization spread to more countries, business crises and depressions became more frequent. Competing industrialism raised both internal and international problems. Competing industrialism is a useful term to cover not only the rivalry of industrial nations but the competition within a country of investors and employers for profits, of consumers for goods they can afford to buy, of workers for wages. What was the role of the state toward these interests of its citizens? What was the worker's share of the product of his long, monotonous hours at the machines, hours which were more and more monotonous as the machines grew more complicated?

The answer of Karl Marx to this question was not widely accepted, but a partial adoption of his ideas led to the development of various brands of socialism. The anarchists had their answer also, and they proceeded to seek their end by means of bombs. A confusion between the anarchists and the communists, however, led the public mind to connect bombs and communism, and to some extent this confusion was extended to socialism; it was clear that all three groups were dissatisfied with the existing order. The socialist formula was public control of the means of production. The individualism which was exhibiting its powers in the amazing industrial progress of the century firmly opposed the idea of government interference in industry, although imperialism was in itself a recognition of the value of government aid in securing fields for industry's expansion.

The Nineteenth Century [487

The influence of industry upon the arts was clearly marked. The classicism of the early part of the century expressed itself in architecture chiefly in lifeless copying; and this copying continued, running the gamut of Gothic, Renaissance, and eclectic styles; but experiments were being made in the use of materials such as iron which in time were to be utilized in a new architecture. These experiments were made notably in constructing vast halls to house the international exhibitions which displayed the marvelous advances in industry and the lack of originality in art. In furniture the classicism of the Empire and Regency gave way to the products of the machine. The jig-saw exhausted its possibilities in producing ugly objects, and until the end of the century people enjoyed living in rooms crowded with heavy furniture, their tables and cabinets cluttered with small objects.

The development of photography opposed a new kind of realism to the prevailing realism in painting, which, however, continued to please the public. Painters dissatisfied with realism were in revolt in the latter part of the century. Turner and, later, Corot sought expression in romantic landscapes; Whistler found inspiration in the art of the Japanese. Finally the impressionists abandoned realism and started a movement which had its importance for the twentieth century. In sculpture Rodin pioneered in emphasizing the material with which the artist worked.

In music the work of establishing the form of the sonata and the concerto and the symphony continued. The spirit of romanticism found expression in the compositions of Beethoven, Schubert, Mendelssohn, and others. Italian and French composers wrote tuneful operas. Much ado was made over the musical dramas of Richard Wagner, who considered himself a daring innovator but whose music was essentially in the harmonic tradition of the eighteenth century. Wagner, however, helped give direction to the spirit of German nationalism by his use of German legends.

The great scientific achievement of the century was that of Darwin, but there were others of great importance. The foundations of geology and experimental psychology were laid; progress was made in the use of anaesthetics and in the control of germs; the principles of heredity were laid down in the Mendelian law, the theory of the conservation of energy was put forward, and the X-ray was discovered. In technology the perfecting of machine tools for making interchangeable parts made possible the rapid manufacture of labor-saving inventions. The production of power was transformed by the development of the turbine and the dynamo; the internal combustion engine was perfected, and the first Diesel engine produced. The lag lay in the perfection of social techniques for fitting man into the world he had produced.

THE FIRST ENGLISH STEAM ENGINE USED FOR A PASSENGER TRAIN, DEVISED BY GEORGE STEPHENSON AND IN OPERATION IN 1825

(From *A Student's History of England* by Samuel R. Gardiner. Longmans Green, London, 1897.)

CHAPTER 28

The World of Charles Darwin

[1809–1882]

CHARLES DARWIN'S ancestors were yeomen. His maternal grandfather, Josiah Wedgwood, one of the early industrialists, won for Staffordshire pottery the reputation it still enjoys. Charles's paternal grandfather, Erasmus Darwin, a physician, enjoyed talking with James Watt, who improved the steam engine, and corresponding with Benjamin Franklin. He believed that nature was not unchanging and expressed the idea of evolution in pedestrian verse. His grandson was born into an England which was financing the war against Napoleon with the money earned by the new industrialism. He was a little boy in those days of the Regency, when George III was living out his last days in impotent insanity. After the victory at Waterloo had disposed of Napoleon, the post-war depression led to agitation by the working class. William Cobbett tried to educate workingmen by Franklin's methods of newspapers and association. Cobbett, socially-minded and a freethinker, did not fit comfortably into the English society of the day, which was permeated with evangelicalism and definitely class-conscious. Miss Hannah More wrote pious screeds which exhorted the workers to be contented in the lot to which God had called them. That lot included an increased price for bread, and the obstinate workers persisted in agitation for repeal of the Corn Laws, which had been passed to protect the English grain grower.

Public opinion turned against the workers as they resorted to violence, and approved repressive legislation; but while working-class agitation at home seemed dangerous, agitation for constitutional government abroad was another matter. English opinion was not unfavorable toward the revolutionary movements which swept

[489

across the Continent in the 20's, 30's, and 40's. Especially did English merchants deplore the aid suggested by the Quintuple Alliance to the Spanish effort to recover the revolted colonies which had opened their trade to the world. Canning's proposal of a protest evoked the American Monroe Doctrine. Although the Alliance abandoned concerted action, French troops helped put down the revolt in Spain, and Austrian troops performed the same service in Naples. Student agitation in German universities was held in check by Metternich's Carlsbad decrees which abrogated academic freedom. The only successful revolution of the 20's was that of the Greeks. Most Britons gave it tacit approval as a national movement of Christians against Turks, and romantic enthusiasts for liberty like Byron gave active aid.

A more successful wave of revolutions occurred in the 30's, when the French exchanged the reactionary Charles X for the bourgeois royalty of Louis Philippe. The Belgians freed themselves from their union with the Dutch at the price of accepting a German king. A revolt of the Poles against the tsar, however, was put down. In England the middle class had long been agitating for parliamentary reform to secure a better distribution of votes in the House of Commons, where seats for deserted boroughs were sold by large landowners while populous cities went unrepresented. In agitation for reform the aid of the laboring class was accepted. When a reform act was passed in 1832 this aid was rewarded by laws affording some protection, but not the vote, to factory workers.

The signal for the third wave of revolutions, those of 1848, came, like the second, from France. None of the many factions thoroughly approved of the government of Louis Philippe. The industrialization of the country had led to the spread of socialism. In 1848 the phrase was the "right to work." Opinion stopped short of the idea of the dictatorship of the proletariat, advocated in Marx and Engels's *Communist Manifesto* of that year. The Paris mob took over a middle-class movement for extension of the suffrage, and the second republic was proclaimed. Its motto was liberty, equality, fraternity. Louis Napoleon, a nephew of Napoleon I, was elected first president by manhood suffrage, and less than four years later by a military *coup d'état* he made himself emperor as Napoleon III.

The news of the French revolt caused a rising in Vienna and the flight of Metternich, the arch-priest of reaction. Czechs and

Hungarians rose, but the Hapsburg princes triumphed; a constitution was granted, however, and the peasants were emancipated. The nationalist movement was still alive in Germany. The German Confederation was ineffective, but an economic bond had been established under the leadership of Prussia in the form of a customs union (*Zollverein*). By 1844 it included most of the German states, but not Austria. It was a useful device for furthering the interests of Prussia, which was ruled by a romantic, Frederick William IV. When his subjects revolted in 1848, he made concessions and allowed a group of liberals from a number of German states to meet in Frankfort. They had been elected by universal manhood suffrage, and planned a strong federal government for Germany. He gave Prussia a constitution which lasted until 1918, but when the Frankfort parliament drew up a liberal constitution for a united Germany and proposed to make him emperor he refused. A promising opportunity to unite Germany under a truly liberal constitution was lost because a man who prided himself on ruling by divine right would not accept an imperial crown from a liberal assembly. After an abortive attempt at a union which would include Austria, the old Confederation was revived. A national movement in Italy had been kept alive since 1830 by the liberal Mazzini. In 1848 the country was swept from north to south by a wave of unsuccessful revolutions. Thus, except in France, the revolutions of 1848 failed. Many proscribed leaders found a welcome in the United States.

England escaped the violence of revolutionary struggle because the powerful middle class was enjoying its prosperity and was able to further it by political means. The employing class, desiring cheap food for the workers and utilizing the arguments of Cobden and Bright, forced the repeal of restrictions on the import of grain. This opened the road to a complete free trade policy. Steam had come into use on the sea as well as in the factory; a new development of chartered colonies was extending the British Empire; the British navy was enforcing peace and acquiring coaling stations on all the seas of the world. There was labor unrest and the Chartists in 1839 demanded universal manhood suffrage and other forms of political equality, but the movement collapsed by 1848.

Charles Darwin all his life shared the views of the comfortable class in which he was born, and his scientific work conformed to its traditions of order and moderation. As a boy he had more than

PLATE XXIX

Nineteenth Century

FIGURE 1. *Charles Darwin, photographed about 1854, when he was forty-five years old. This was the year when he finished a work on barnacles, which he had been preparing since 1846. It provided important evidence for his Origin of Species, which was beginning to take shape in his mind.*
[*From* More Letters of Charles Darwin *by Francis Darwin. D. Appleton-Century Co., Inc., New York, 1903*]

FIGURE 2. *Detail from* Liberty Leading the People, *painted by Eugene Delacroix (1798–1863) to commemorate the July rising of 1830. Delacroix was one of the great Romantic painters, and was especially interested in recording contemporary historical scenes that had dramatic quality.*

FIGURE 3. The Uprising *by Honore Daumier (1808–1879). This is a historical record of the revolution of 1848, which Daumier witnessed. More practical minded than Delacroix, Daumier does not subordinate citizens fighting for their liberty to a personification as Delacroix did.*
[*Courtesy of the Phillips Memorial Gallery, Washington, D.C.*]

FIGURE 4. *Engraving of the Crystal Palace, one of the early experiments in the skeleton framework of iron and glass whose functional construction is identical with its design. When a competition was announced for a temporary structure to house the first large-scale international exhibition, which was held in London in 1851, the winning plans were submitted not by an architect, but by a gardener who had constructed large greenhouses. The building occupied eighteen acres in Hyde Park. It was twice as wide as St. Paul's Cathedral and four times as long, and was built of iron piers and girders supporting walls of glass. In order to save some fine old elm trees a transept 108 feet high was incorporated. After the exposition the building was re-erected in a suburb where it was used for exhibition purposes for many years. The success of the experiment meant a wide use of iron construction, and when steel was substituted for iron the modern skyscraper became possible.*
[*From* Space, Time, and Architecture *by Sigfried Giedion. Harvard University Press, Cambridge, Mass., 1941*]

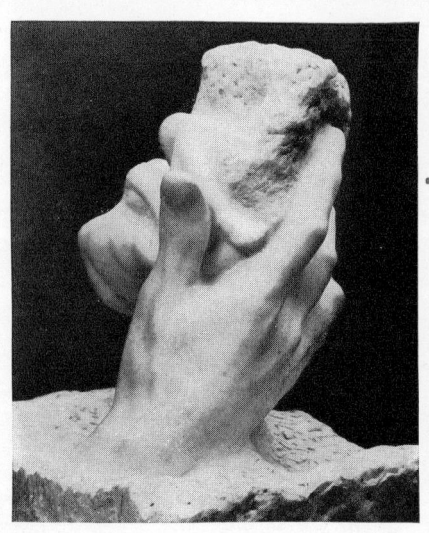

PLATE XXX

Nineteenth Century

FIGURE 1. *Photograph of Jean Jaurès. In his biography of Juarès, J. Hampdon Jackson quotes what Romain Rolland said about him: "I see his full face calm and happy, like that of a kindly, bearded ogre; his small eyes bright and smiling, eyes as quick to follow the flight of an idea as to observe human nature. I see him pacing up and down the platform, walking with heavy steps like a bear, his hands crossed behind his back, turning sharply to hurl at the crowd, in his level metallic voice, words like the call of a trumpet which reached the farthest seats in the vast amphitheater and went straight to the heart, making the soul of the whole multitude stir in one united emotion."*
[*From* Outlook, *vol. 107, August 15, 1914*]

FIGURE 2. *The Hand of God by Auguste Rodin (1849–1917). Rodin was very much concerned with expressive subjects and was inventive in finding them. He was able to make the whole body express emotion. His approach to sculpture was that of a painter insofar as he treated the surfaces of marble in such a way that the light softens the forms, getting his effect in the impressionists' manner.*
[*Courtesy of the Metropolitan Museum of Art, New York*]

FIGURE 3. *Le Port d'Honfleur by Claude Monet (1840–1926). Monet was a leader in the impressionist movement, which transformed painting as completely as Rodin transformed sculpture. Instead of representing forms he studied the fugitive effects of light, and secured the effect of shimmering luminosity of sunlight by putting primary colors in juxtaposition on the canvas instead of first mixing them on a palette.*
[*From Arnhold Collection, Berlin*]

FIGURE 4. *Paris Opera House. This building, erected between 1861 and 1874, covers three acres of ground. The architect followed the usage which had prevailed for over a century: the reproduction of an established historical style. He chose the rococo, with its profusion of classical detail. Rich material, gilding, paintings, and enormous sculptured groups form the profuse decoration. Employing the new techniques and materials that had come into use, the architect solved successfully the problem of providing under the same roof facilities for the proper presentation of the opera, with accommodations for orchestra, cast, and scenery, and opportunities for large crowds to promenade, eat, and drink between the acts. The building occupies one of the finest sites in Paris and was one of the most admired structures of its day.*

the usual interest in making collections, and after his university career, at the age of 22, he accepted an invitation to go as naturalist on a scientific expedition which made soundings and observations on the coast of South America. He took along with him the just-published book of Sir Charles Lyell which made clear that the natural world had in the course of ages undergone many changes. When he reached England again at the end of five years he had notebooks filled with observations that recorded changes in plant and animal life. He decided to spend the rest of his life in scientific research, and he did so, although his work was greatly impeded by serious ill health. He was obliged to live a life of seclusion, but he followed world events with interest.

A kindly man, he sympathized with the North in the American war between the states, because of his objections to Negro slavery. He was ready to subscribe to the prosecution of an English civil servant who had been brutal to the Negroes in an English colony. Yet he was an ardent supporter of British imperialism. When he was tired he enjoyed lying on the sofa in his crowded Victorian living room while his wife read him a novel of Jane Austen. He kept Mark Twain's works by his bedside and found delight in Tennyson's poetry.

His studies led him to believe that species were not immutable, but that new species came into being through the survival in the struggle for existence of those best fitted to survive. Lamarck's theory of evolution had been based on the idea of adaptation to environment. Darwin was confirmed in his theory of struggle by reading Malthus' book on population. He was still getting evidence for his theory when another scientist, Alfred Wallace, sent him observations that had led him, independently, to arrive at similar conclusions. Darwin published these notes together with evidence that he held these ideas before Wallace. He went to work upon his *Origin of Species,* which was published in 1859. There was much excitement in the learned world, and a violent controversy arose. Huxley in England and Haeckel in Germany were Darwin's most eloquent defenders, but he went on with the amassing of further proof. The bitter controversy among theologians has its own history, but the effect upon scientific research put the name of Darwin alongside that of Galileo and Newton. To their conceptions of the reign of law in the universe, Darwin added the principle of a constantly changing universe, a living universe instead of a machine. That view remains the basis of scientific thought, though details have been modified by later research.

Although scientists disputed and clergymen held forth in the violent controversy over the *Origin of Species,* English society as a whole was more interested in prosperity than in evolution. The prosperous classes aligned themselves behind government policies that would further British trade. They looked askance at the tsar, who was beginning to show an interest in the Mediterranean where the British navy reigned supreme. A quarrel with Turkey over the Holy Places in Palestine led to a Russo-Turkish war in 1853. Pursuing each its particular end, the governments of England, France, and Sardinia went into the Crimean War on the Turkish side. The Russians were defeated in a war marked by costly mismanagement on both sides, and the tsar was forced to postpone his plans. To keep the Turks in Constantinople and thereby forbid the Russians access to the eastern Mediterranean became a fixed British policy.

To extend British trade in the Far East Great Britain had already fought an Opium War with China and gained Hong Kong (1842); by a second war in 1856 she forced further concessions from China. Disraeli secured English control of the Suez Canal, which was completed in 1869. He persuaded Queen Victoria to accept the crown as Empress of India. It was in Disraeli's conservative administration that a second reform bill (1867) enfranchised the British industrial worker, but the series of social reforms that followed were presided over by the Liberal prime minister, Gladstone, who also struggled with the Irish question.

In Italy the misrule of the Hapsburgs kept alive the nationalist sentiment fostered by Mazzini's Young Italy movement. Leadership in Italian affairs was claimed by the house of Savoy. As king of Sardinia, Victor Emmanuel II ruled Savoy, Piedmont, and Genoa; but to Cavour, his able minister, belongs the chief credit for the unification of Italy. He brought Sardinia into the Crimean War and engineered an alliance with France. Provoking a war with Austria, he won Lombardy but had to cede Savoy and Nice to Napoleon III in return for his aid. Four of Austria's satellite states joined Sardinia. An Italian adventurer, Garibaldi, was persuaded in 1860 to unite the successful uprising he had led with the larger movement and Sicily and Naples were added to the expanding state. A year later Victor

Emmanuel was proclaimed king of Italy over the protest of Pius IX, who finally declared himself a prisoner in the Vatican. (His successors followed his example until 1929.) Victor Emmanuel ruled Italy under a fairly liberal constitution. The chief problems were the poverty of the country and the differing interests of the industrial north and the agricultural south.

Prussia was to be the unifying force of Germany, as Sardinia had been for Italy. Prussia under the Hohenzollerns was the leading German state economically as well as politically; a well-coordinated system of education had made the Prussians one of the most literate peoples in Europe; the large landholders, the Junkers, were hard-headed, hard-working men who exercised an influence that was out of proportion to their numbers. Otto von Bismarck, a Junker who became chancellor in 1861, the year that the American Civil War broke out, believed that by a policy of "Blood and Iron" he could unite Germany under Prussian leadership. He transformed the Junkers into a military caste, officers of a huge conscript army, perfectly trained and equipped. He decided not to include Austria in his union, for the Hapsburgs would refuse to yield first place to the Hohenzollerns and they had so many non-German subjects that they could not concentrate on purely German interests. Determined to show the Prussians what a well-trained army could accomplish, he persuaded Austria to joint intervention in a dispute between Denmark and her dependencies, Schleswig and Holstein. In the ensuing war the two provinces were seized. He then picked a quarrel with Austria and drew the new king of Italy into the war by promising him Venetia. Prussia won the Seven Weeks' War, and Francis Joseph, the Austrian emperor, was forced to agree that the German states in the north be organized into the North German Confederation. The young emperor allayed discontent in his own dominions by reorganizing them in two parts, each with its parliament and administration. This, the Dual Monarchy, he ruled as Emperor of Austria and King of Hungary.

Bismarck organized the North German Confederation and proceeded to form military alliances with south German states. He decided that a war in which Prussian armies would lead German states to victory would be a powerful unifying force, and that the volatile and ambitious Napoleon III would be a suitable victim. Napoleon allowed himself to be tricked into a declaration of war, and the German armies rapidly defeated the French and captured the emperor. In January, 1871, a German empire was proclaimed at Versailles, with the king of Prussia as its emperor. A revolutionary commune in Paris was overthrown by the provisional government that had negotiated the armistice, and the Third French Republic was established. It was forced to cede Alsace and part of Lorraine and agree to an enormous indemnity. The money was rapidly paid, and the recovery of the lost provinces was thenceforth considered the sacred duty of all Frenchmen.

Nationalism was not confined to western and central Europe. During the first three-quarters of the nineteenth century it developed to a striking degree among the peoples of the Balkan peninsula. This mountainous region, a crossroads between Europe and Asia, contained one of the most confused intermixtures of peoples to be found in Europe: indigenous peoples like the Albanians, the Vlachs, and the Greeks were mingled with invaders such as the Serbs, Bulgarians, and Turks. At the beginning of the nineteenth century the whole of the Balkan peninsula was part of the empire of the Ottoman Turks, a decadent theocracy organized on the basis of creed. The Balkan peoples, who were largely Christian, were subjected to discrimination and oppression, often brutal, by their Moslem overlords. Among the Christian subject peoples the Greek Orthodox Church held a privileged position because it was used as the instrument for governing all Christians. The distinction accorded the Greeks in the empire, who also represented a trading element which grew wealthy and influential in Constantinople, helped to foster among them a feeling of separateness and superiority. A renaissance of Greek language and culture in the early nineteenth century had further contributed to the national feeling of the Greeks, who in the 20's began the revolt which led through massacre and counter-massacre to European intervention and the establishment of an independent Greece.

The independence won by the Greeks was imitated by other Balkan peoples. The Serbs, who lived in one of the most inaccessible parts of the mountainous peninsula and the most remote from Constantinople, were perforce allowed considerable local self-government. Increasing resentment at measures imposed upon them by the Turks led the Serbs, under the patriotic leadership first of Karageorge and then of Milosh Obrenovich, to revolt and secure an autonomous status. The assassination of Karageorge led to a blood feud between the Karageorgevich and Obrenovich families which troubled the country throughout the century. The autonomy of Romania was won through the persistent intervention of Russia to secure a protectorate over the principalities of the lower Danube; Turkish concessions were granted, often under compulsion. Nationalism in Romania developed after autonomy was secured and was an outgrowth of resentment against Russian rather than Turkish control. As they were freed of Turkish restrictions and given an opportunity to revive their native culture and language, patriotic Romanians realized that they had only shifted from a Turkish to a Russian yoke. Romanian independence and unification were not realized until after the Crimean War.

The last of the Balkan peoples to feel the rise of nationalist spirit were the Bulgars, whose native Slav culture had been nearly obliterated by the efforts of the Greek Church to Hellenize them. As in the case of Romania, Russia compelled the Turks to take steps which led to the resurrection and growth of the native culture and fostered a nationalistic revival among her fellow Slavs. A Bulgarian National Church was created in 1870 which soon rivaled the Greek Church in the number of its adherents in the eastern Balkans. Since the Turks made national groupings according to religious affiliation, the struggle between the Bulgarian and the Greek churches gave a tremendous impetus to nationalism; the rivalry was not over religion, but over culture and national control.

In 1875 the first of a series of revolts against Turkish rule broke out among Serbs in the Turkish province of Bosnia; it was followed by an uprising of the Bulgarians, which was bloodily repressed. Taking advantage of the anti-Turkish sentiment in Europe, Russia declared war on Turkey, hoping to gain her long-desired outlet to the Mediterranean via Constantinople, and soon defeated the Sultan's forces. The treaty which Russia imposed on Turkey created a large independent Bulgarian state embracing all the territory dominated by the Bulgarian National Church. Big Bulgaria quite dwarfed the other Balkan states and included a good many non-Bulgarian peoples. The powers of Europe, led by England and Austria, who were jealous of the expansion of Russian influence in the Balkans, intervened and at the Congress of Berlin in 1878 compelled a revision of the Russian settlement.

The great powers rearranged the map of the Balkans without regard for the interests or desires of the Balkan peoples and attempted to satisfy their own jealousies by adding to the areas under their influence. Russia was robbed of the fruits of military victory, and future trouble was sown by the fact that all the Balkan states whose independence Turkey recognized in 1878 could claim territory still held by the Turks on the basis that it was inhabited by peoples of their nationality. Although there was an independent Greece, Serbia, Romania, and Bulgaria, many people of Greek, Serb, Romanian, and Bulgar language and culture remained under Turkish rule. Their revolts and the efforts of the dissatisfied national states in the Balkans to expand were to cause constant embarrassment for the great powers in the years following the Congress of Berlin.

The year 1871 saw not only the proclamation of the German empire, but an event curiously linked with its fate: the publication of Darwin's *Descent of Man*. Darwin had continued to work at the gathering of evidence for his theory, and from time to time published it in a volume. In the *Descent of Man,* as the title indicates, he concentrated upon evidence of man's evolution from the higher primates. The book revived the theological controversy and led to the transfer of the idea of evolution to fields where its application led to unscientific results.

It was not realized that the workings of evolution are too slow to be perceived in the brief period of recorded history, and Darwin's ideas were used to predicate progress in social and political fields. The socially-minded worked and hoped for the speedy perfecting of human relations; the politically-minded began investigating which race was best fitted to survive. The continued exploitation of colored peoples by the white seeemd clearly a part of nature's plan, for white dominance was assuredly the result of the fitness of the white race to survive. Of the white race those destined to inherit the earth must be the group best fitted to succeed on the battlefield.

The idea of white superiority fitted admirably into the growing vogue of imperialism. As population increased, land hunger grew. Possessions where emigrants could find new homes under their own flag seemed eminently desirable. Many flourishing industries needed raw materials which could be obtained only overseas. With competition growing, it was still possible to keep prices up if colonial markets were open. Labor was cheap in colonies, and it was the duty of the white man to extend his influence to backward peoples. British backs were the ones that were most generally bent under the white man's burden, but France was spreading her dominions in Africa, and the Dutch reaped vast prosperity from their plantations in the East Indies. The king of the Belgians secured international approval of his so-called Free State in the Congo. The prestige value of colonies was great, and the Italian and German governments, coming into existence when the best pickings were gone, hurried to the feast.

In the 80's, industrial prosperity, increased proportionally with improvements in communications, was rapidly transforming society. Railroads and telegraph made more efficient the methods of increasing wealth in peace and destroying it in war. Thinkers evolved different philosophical methods of reconciling religion and science. Yet new movements had begun. In the year of Darwin's death Oscar Wilde delivered a series of lectures on the new aesthetics, and the London public listened for the first time to Wagner's *Ring of the Nibelungs*. The same year English forces put down a native movement in Egypt, Italy established the colony of Eritrea, and the Germans organized a colonial society to prepare the way for the active entrance of Germany into the world scramble for markets.

ENGRAVING OF EARLY STEAMBOAT, 1813

(From *A Student's History of England* by Samuel R. Gardiner. Longmans Green, London, 1897.)

CHAPTER 29

The World of Jean Jaurès
[1859–1914]

~~~~~~~~~~~~~~~~~~~~~~~~~~~~~~~~~~

JEAN JAURÈS grew up in a troubled France when the Second Empire was moving towards its fall and the Third French Republic was struggling to establish itself in the face of clerical and royalist opposition. He came of the upper bourgeoisie, but spent his boyhood on a farm and knew from actual experience the problems of the land-owner and the peasant. He was given the education of a scholar, and to the end of his life read Greek authors in the original for pleasure. In his native province he saw the effects of large-scale industry upon workers, and decided to go into politics to fight the great employers. He served in the Chamber of Deputies between 1885 and 1889 at a time of serious domestic and foreign crisis, and then retired to teach and write on history and philosophy. He became interested in socialism and again went into politics, serving in the Chamber of Deputies, except for a short interval, from 1893 until his death. He became one of the principal leaders in the Socialist Party, whose strength in the Chamber steadily increased in the years before the outbreak of the great war in 1914.

Socialism had spread from England to other countries as they became industrialized. There were many brands of socialism, however, and not all socialists accepted the theory of the German Karl Marx that the original form of social organization was communism and that, when conditions were right, capitalism would disappear, communism would be re-established, and the state would wither and die.

To Jaurès socialism meant the collective ownership of the means of production, which would, he believed, prevent too great inequality in the distribution of wealth and give every individual the oppor-

[499

tunity to develop the best that was in him. The most notable achievement of the nineteenth century was the enormous increase of material wealth due to the application of rapidly developing scientific knowledge to industry. Machine production made life easier in hundreds of ways for all classes of the population. The socialists, however, continued to insist that under capitalism the rich would grow richer and the poor poorer. To this the nineteenth century liberals did not agree. They believed in representative government based on a wide franchise and the maintenance of individual freedom of religion, speech, and the press. Liberals worked for legislation to protect exploited groups and believed in the march of progress toward a world where in due time the advantages of wealth would flow down to all in ample measure.

The idealism of the German philosopher Kant had an important part in the development of liberalism. Jaurès, who had started out as a liberal, lectured on Kant to his students at the University of Toulouse. His socialism resulted from a wide range of reading, beginning with another German philosopher, Fichte, and ending with Karl Marx. The systems of Kant and Fichte, however, had different effects upon German thought. Germans accepted the Kantian theory of absolute submission of the individual to the state, and rejected with him the premise of consent of the governed. They accepted Fichte's development of the ideas of Kant into the worship of the state, which entailed the sacrifice of the interests of the individual to whatever was believed to be the interest of the state. This idea fitted neatly into the nationalism which dated back to Napoleon's invasion.

Compulsory military service was accepted as a necessity in the face of France's public plan for revenge for the war of 1870. Most of the officers of the German army were members of the landed aristocracy and full of autocratic ideas. The German emperor was also King of Prussia, and the régime that had its center in Berlin was an authoritative one. Germans became accustomed to strong government and to the dominance of a military caste.

Although to the French people militarism was distasteful and strong government abhorrent, within the French army the officers developed a spirit of caste modeled upon that of the Germans. Jaurès won the first widespread recognition of his leadership when he insisted that the government investigate the Dreyfus case, in which the nation took sides between the prestige of the army and justice to an individual.

During the period between 1871 and 1914, when the principal causes of World War I were crystallizing, the leading European industrial powers offered interesting parallels and contrasts. In Great Britain a strong executive based on a parliamentary majority governed moderately and progressively. The two-party political system usually provided the government with solidly-organized party support for its measures. Labor organizations, after costly failures to win concessions by direct means, went into politics and were able, in the first decade of the twentieth century, to increase their parliamentary representation. By 1914 an elaborate program of workingmen's reforms had been achieved by legislative means and the prediction of Karl Marx that the working class would gradually take over the reins of government seemed plausible.

Although the Third French Republic by no means presented the picture of stability evident across the Channel, it continued to survive. The parliamentary system in France was on a multi-party basis, elaborate coalitions of small parties being necessary to achieve a parliamentary majority. The efficient centralized bureaucracy which dated from Napoleon's time compensated for the weakness of the executive and its apparent instability, and there was a surprising continuity in French administration despite frequent shifts at the top. The workingmen in France made slower and less satisfactory progress than their counterparts in England. In France, too, direct action was attempted unsuccessfully, and labor went into politics. The working class remained divided until World War I, however, on the merits of direct action or parliamentary representation. Though many socialist deputies sat in the Chamber of Deputies, their leaders usually preferred not to participate in coalition cabinets and be forced to accept responsibility for measures they did not approve.

The federation of German states which had become the German Empire was autocratically governed under a constitution which gave it many of the trappings of parliamentary rule. Here again, as generally on the Continent, the multi-party political system was in vogue, and parliamentary majorities were coalitions of many factions. The real power was exercised by the chancellor, an official appointed by the emperor and responsible only to him. Though the chancellor usually found it expedient to cultivate a majority following in the Reichstag, he remained independent. Under William II a policy of concession to the demands of the socialist and working class groups was followed. The government voluntarily adopted measures of social security for the laborer until Germany in the early twentieth century had the most advanced social legislation in the world, but nonetheless socialist political strength steadily increased. In 1914 the Social Democrats were the largest party in the Reichstag.

The most notorious exception to the pattern of parliamentary government was Russia, which remained an autocracy with a privileged aristocracy and a semi-feudal social organization. The aristocracy dominated the governmental agencies and bureaucracy, which were steeped in graft and corruption. The Russian Orthodox Church, with a hereditary clergy that was ignorant and corrupt, was dependent upon the state. Autocracy, orthodoxy, and nationalism were the keystones of tsarist policy, and in conjunction with the third of these a program of Russification was imposed on the subject nationalities of the empire. Perhaps the worst sufferers in this policy were the Jews. Nearly 60 per cent of Europe's Jews were subjects of the tsar, in whose realm they were confined to a region known as the Pale, forbidden to buy or lease agricultural land, denied participation in the professions or the bureaucracy, and restricted in educational possibilities. Pogroms at periodic intervals increased their misery under a régime whose avowed purpose was to force a third of their number into exile, convert another third to Christianity, and exterminate the rest.

The most ancient of surviving Continental monarchies was the empire of the Hapsburgs, organized in 1867 into the Dual Monarchy of Austria-Hungary. It was a league of unwilling nations, which incessant conflict between centripetal and centrifugal forces threatened with dissolution. One force that held it together was the dynasty; Francis Joseph, tutuored under Metternich, outlived his age and emphasized militarization, Catholicism, and autocracy until his death in 1916. Other centripetal forces were the aristocracy, the Roman Catholic Church, the bureaucracy, the free trade unity of the empire, socialism, and capitalism. The last was largely represented by Jews and this provided economic foundation for German anti-Semitism. Against these forces was arrayed the spirit of nationalism, which in the end was powerful enough to overcome the combined centripetal forces. The conflict of nationalities had two aspects: the resistance of other nationalities to the German-Magyar hegemony, and the struggle between the Germans and Magyars themselves. Although the Germans were the largest national unit in Austria, they formed a minority of the whole population; the Magyars represented a majority in Hungary, but the combined German and Magyar population was less than the total of other nationalities. When the World War I put too heavy a strain on the creaking structure the Hapsburg monarchy disintegrated, with Czechs, Poles, Jugoslavs, Romanians, and Italians, each following their national bent.

The spirit of nationalism was also strong in the Balkans by 1870. The great powers exploited Balkan nationalism to their own advantage and to the detriment of the Turkish empire. Not only in the Balkans, but all over the world, modern imperialism, which was an expression of nineteenth century nationalism, spread the marks of European industrialism. The rivalries in international trade, the result of rapid industrial development after 1870, produced a scramble to partition the backward and defenseless regions of Asia and build great colonial empires for the profit of the exploiting nation.

Jaurès, from the time of his re-entry into public life in 1893, never ceased to fulminate eloquently against imperialism. He regarded it as the most deplorable result of capitalism, which by underpaying the worker restricted consumption at home and then sought an outlet for goods in markets obtained by force and corruption. He thought that corruption invariably accompanied imperialism and that money spent in colonial enterprises should have been used at home to improve the condition of the people. His arguments fell on deaf ears. French capitalism sought markets abroad and the markets when opportunity offered were brought under the French flag.

Easily the greatest of the colonial empires was that of Great Britain. Parts of the British Empire were self-governing dominions: Canada, Australia, New Zealand, and the Union of South Africa were in temperate zones, ruled by whites and, except for the Union of South Africa, definitely colonized by people of British origin. The dominions depended on Great Britain in matters of defense, and were bound to the Empire by economic ties. The Empire included crown colonies, ruled under the direct supervision of the Colonial Office in London which appointed governors and civil officials; protectorates, where native states had their foreign and some of their domestic affairs controlled by the British government; and spheres of influence, where native states were more or less controlled by British commercial interests. Quite a different matter was India, where a relatively small group of Europeans in an efficiently organized administrative system ruled the destinies of a huge native population. Autocratic but benevolent, the district officers, who were chosen by civil service examination, enforced laws, administered justice, and collected taxes; and the India Office drew the finest of British talent. The basic difficulties in the Indian administration came from extreme overcrowding, racial mixture (India was the crucible of Asiatic peoples), and wide differences in physical characteristics, language, religion, and state of civilization. Few Indians were literate, a large percentage never learned English, and the whole population was riven by an elaborate caste system. India was an inchoate 3000-year old civilization upon which the British attempted to impose Western laws, education, and technology.

Although Great Britain began the long and difficult process of organizing an educational system and instituting medical and social reform, progress was extremely slow. Materially there was much advance; internal conflict was eliminated, preventive medicine and modern hygiene lowered the death rate (adding to the problem of overcrowding), and India became an important center of industry in the Far East. Much of the profit from the material advancement went to the British who supplied the capital, lack of which has hampered native industry. The value of India to Britain has been immense as a reservoir of raw material and a market for manufactures. India absorbed a tremendous amount of British investment capital, and so since imports always exceeded exports to India the crucial position of India in imperial economy was evident. British rule has benefited India in that it provided centralized government and internal peace, but the natives were not westernized and their economic progress benefited not them but the British.

In the race for colonies most of the continent of Africa was absorbed in a few decades. Great Britain and France were the leaders, though Germany, Belgium, Portugal, and Italy all acquired African territory. On the whole, up to the First World War the

African natives were not thought capable of Western skills and were not given much progressive treatment. Imperial rivalry in the Far East was confronted with much more advanced civilization. In China the policy of the Open Door, which consisted of bolstering the decadent Chinese government and exacting from it special treatment for all foreigners, was due to the United States and was adopted after European imperial powers had often been on the verge of war. Japan, the one Oriental nation which successfully resisted European colonial exploitation, was watched with interest because apparently the Japanese had determined to cast off their backward habits. Japanese students appeared all over the Western world to learn modern methods of business and manufacture. Japan built herself a navy of modern vessels and fought a successful war against the obsolescent vessels of Russia, demonstrating that white men were not invincible (1904). The British, suspicious of Russia, applauded, and as time went on Japan was allowed to bully the Chinese, who, however, had their eyes opened by the Japanese victory. The small number of Chinese in American and European universities increased. A political genius, Sun Yat-Sen, set on foot a movement to give China constitutional government, and revolution broke out in 1911. Sun Yat-Sen became the first president of China when the monarchy was overthrown, but he resigned in favor of Yuan Shik-k'ai in order to prevent factional strife. During World War I, however, China became the scene of civil war which was chronic and sapped the strength of the modernizing movement.

At the end of the nineteenth century British, Russian, and French imperialism conflicted. Britain and France were Mediterranean and African powers, and the clash occurred in Egypt. British and Russian interests conflicted in Persia. Both with Russian and French imperialism, the British conflict concerned strategic points on the route to India.

Although imperialism was the fashion of the day, which even the United States adopted when it took over the Philippines, there were in all the imperialist countries wide-spread protests against it, to which Socialists like Jaurès contributed their arguments. The question whether imperialism pays can easily be answered: it does not pay so far as the taxpayer is concerned; heavy expenditures have been necessary to acquire and maintain colonies. The Italian dependencies in Africa were a complete liability; and even Germany, whose colonial organization was remarkably efficient, had an unfavorable balance between trade and colonial expense. The French had long wars with insurgents in their colonies, and British administrative and military costs were high. Imperialism does, however, pay individuals and corporations. French and British industry have depended heavily on exports to colonies. Individuals, rather than nations, exploit colonial raw materials. Colonies are not dependable sources of raw materials, especially as communications may break down in wartime, and colonies have made no modern nation an autarchy, for other nations rather than dependencies have been the source of essential commodities. Colonies were also a failure as absorbers of surplus population at the period when imperialism was at its height. Of the nearly twenty million emigrants from Europe after 1890 fewer than 3% went to colonial dependencies of the countries they left and even in the case of the British Empire, where conditions were most favorable, half the emigrants from Britain came to the United States compared to a third to British Dominions.

The force that prevailed over all the arguments against imperialism was national pride, for prestige went with colonies, and the opportunity to look down the nose at subject peoples. Racial prejudices were whipped up in this connection. Nonsense about a supposed "yellow peril" swept the West. A theory of racial supremacy couched in pseudo-scientific terms had wide acceptance, especially in Germany. A Frenchman named Gobineau believed that the part of the white race which was the favored child of evolution was the so-called Aryan or Nordic strain, and that of the Aryans the fittest to survive were the Germanic peoples. The Germans, who had already been helped along the path of complacency by the ideas of Fichte and Hegel, gladly accepted this idea. Students had for years been flocking from other countries to German universities, where new methods of scientific investigation and historical study had been developed. German technical publications were read everywhere. German industrialists were consulted by the industrialists of England and America. The German way of life apparently would be welcomed everywhere and the future of the world lay in German hands.

During the two decades that followed the establishment of the German Empire, Germany dominated the diplomatic scene and Bismarck maintained a European hegemony that embraced every important European state except France. Bismarck was not unmindful of the general mistrust with which Germany was regarded after the Franco-Prussian War, and determined to keep the peace because his country had accomplished all that could be accomplished by military means. Bismarck's system of diplomacy was based on certain fundamental postulates, and the involved and apparently confusing series of alliances he concluded with other powers can easily be understood by keeping those postulates in mind. Germany was nearly surrounded by three great powers—Russia, Austria-Hungary, and France. A combination of the three against Germany would be fatal, and a combination of any two made Bismarck too dependent on the third. France, according to Bismarck's reasoning, was a permanent enemy and could not be expected to forgive the seizure of Alsace-Lorraine. He concluded, therefore, that he must keep close to both Austria and Russia, and isolate France. To that end he schemed and planned, making secret defensive alliances with any country that was willing. The most permanent of these alliances was the Triple Alliance of Germany-Austria-Italy, and it became the cornerstone of German policy. Owing to the rivalry of Austria and Russia in the Balkans it was not possible to keep them allied, but Bismarck did maintain an alliance between Germany and Russia until his fall in 1890.

After two decades of diplomatic isolation in Europe, France by 1890 was desperately eager to find some ally on the Continent. During those decades two parties had contended in French foreign policy, the one insisting upon making the recovery of Alsace-Lorraine and European prestige the keystone of French policy, the other urging the abandonment of European quarrels and a concentration on colonial expansion. When the successors of Bismarck in Germany failed to heed his warnings and allowed relations with Russia to lapse, the isolation of both France and Russia led logically to alliance, which was cemented in 1894. The Franco-Russian Alliance, like the Triple Alliance, was allegedly defensive, but both had the dangerous provision that if one country mobilized the others would.

Mobilization, under the system of universal service maintained by all Continental powers, was regarded as the last step before war and meant putting armies on a war footing, calling up reserves, and preparing for whatever campaign the general staff had planned. One of the weaknesses of the general staff technique was that, in order to handle the large numbers of the modern army and assemble reserves rapidly and effectively, detailed plans had to be made in advance for transporting the men and equipment, and this could not be done unless it were known what country was the enemy. As all plans for general mobilization had to be directed toward a war with some specified country, a general mobilization of five major powers was a risky business: with five great armies concentrating on frontiers, incidents which might lead to hostilities were inevitable. Most military authorities agreed that, once set in motion, the armies of reserves were difficult to stop and that mobilization meant war. This meant that Europe was in a state of unstable equilibrium. A diplomatic crisis might mean war if the stage of mobilization was reached, for national policy must be maintained; and jockeying of rival powers kept war as a last measure of national policy.

The conclusion of the Franco-Russian alliance, making a line-up among European powers as it did of three against two, gave new importance to the position of England. Through most of the nineteenth century Great Britain had retained a "splendid isolation." Increasing colonial rivalries and near-escapes from war with both France and Russia, however, finally led England to end her isolation. British overtures to Germany were refused. Commercial competition, continued German colonial expansion, and the German policy of economic imperialism in Turkey through the Bagdad Railway estranged her from Great Britain. Ultimately, in the face of a new threat in the form of German naval rivalry, Britain and France settled their problems and came to an understanding (1904). A few years later Great Britain and Russia were able to compose their most pressing differences, and the Franco-Russian Alliance was expanded to a Triple Entente. The turn of the century, therefore, had been decisive in the diplomatic background of the World War.

Bismarck's principle of Continental hegemony to keep the peace had been abandoned. Bismarck's postulates had been ignored by later German statesmen; and in place of the Bismarck system, which had always been so heavily weighted that the weaker side of the balance could never challenge, there had grown up an even balance among the six greatest European powers. In fact, the Triple Alliance was not so strong as it seemed: there was rivalry and jealousy between Italy and Austria over Balkan affairs, the Triple Alliance had a provision that it was never to operate against Great Britain because of Italian vulnerability in the face of English sea power, and Italy had even made secret commitments with France. An even balance of power increases rather than lessens the risk of war because either side, defeated in diplomacy, may resort to military measures in the hope of reversing the position. Several times war almost broke out over jealousies about affairs of the Turkish empire, in the Balkans, and in North Africa.

Russia was the power most directly interested in the Balkans because of her desire for an outlet to the ocean via Constantinople. Religious and nationalist fanaticism was played up—many of the Balkan Christians were of the orthodox faith, as was Russia, and many were Slav. Austria was the first challenger of Russian encroachment in the Balkans and claimed an older right of interference as the medieval champion of Christendom against the Turks. The Hapsburg monarchy also had Slav elements, which created a problem in relationships with the independent Slav states of the peninsula. After the completion of German and Italian unification, Austria was denied further westward expansion and the Balkan peninsula was the most logical field left. The interest of Great Britain was not territorial, but the Turkish Empire held a strategic position on the all-important British "lifeline" to India. Britain wanted to be the strongest Mediterranean power and to checkmate Russian encroachment by maintaining the integrity of the moribund Turkish Empire, which was no threat to British supremacy. Until after the turn of the century German interest in the Balkans was negligible, and it became a major force only when the construction of the Berlin-to-Bagdad Railway opened a land route to the Near East by which German and Austrian industry could compete with that of the British and French, who dominated the sea trade. In this situation Italy, dreaming of the days of Venetian trade supremacy, put in a claim to the eastern Adriatic littoral in order to strengthen her sea power.

The decade of 1904–14 was a period of numerous crises; the specter of war rose and dissolved again so often that many people and especially important statesmen decried the recurrent war scares: they were sure that the balance of power so nicely regulated by the Triple Alliance and the Triple Entente would prevent war. In the face of the solidarity of the alliance systems, one side would always back down. In 1905, and again in 1911, serious difficulties arose over

French economic penetration in Morocco. The real trouble was created by the rivalries of German and French commercial interests which the governments of each country used to stir up nationalist feeling, hoping to improve their positions in the diplomatic bargaining which went on behind the scenes. In the Moroccan crises, France emerged victorious, but at a terrible cost in public sentiment. Jaurès strongly opposed anything but peaceful penetration of Morocco, and when Germany precipitated the first crisis in 1905 his influence was great in preventing the failure of the Algeciras conferences which confirmed Moroccan independence.

In 1911 the German government sent a gunboat to Agadir, producing another crisis which ended with France assuming a protectorate over Morocco, except for a Spanish zone in the north. Germany was placated by a slice of the French Congo. Italy, not to be left out, seized Tripoli and the Dodecanese Islands. In 1908 and in 1912–13 crises developed in the Balkans over Austrian and Russian designs for expansion. Here also, a general European war was averted, but the Austrian victories in the annexation of Bosnia in 1908 and the curbing of Serbia in 1913 inflamed public opinion in the rival countries. As a consequence of the even score for each alliance system that resulted from these crises, both systems had determined not to retreat in the next. Given such a state of mind, and with the professional diplomats of all powers firm in their decision, the next serious international incident was bound to produce a general European war if the alliances remained solid. This does not necessarily mean that the professional diplomats in the pre-war world wanted war; but they felt that alliances to ensure getting their way must be maintained even at the expense of peace.

The Balkan crises of the pre-war decade provide one of the important keys to the outbreak of the war. It was a Turkish nationalist revival in 1906 which persuaded the European powers that they must seize what territory they wanted from the Turkish Empire before a rejuvenation of the "sick man of Europe" enabled Turkey to hold what was hers. Accordingly Austria annexed the adjacent provinces of Bosnia and Herzegovina, which she had administered for incompetent Turkey since the Congress of Berlin. This annexation infuriated Russia, which got no compensating advantage, and enraged Serbia. The inhabitants of Bosnia were Serbs, and Serbia had intended eventually to secure Bosnia for herself and with it an

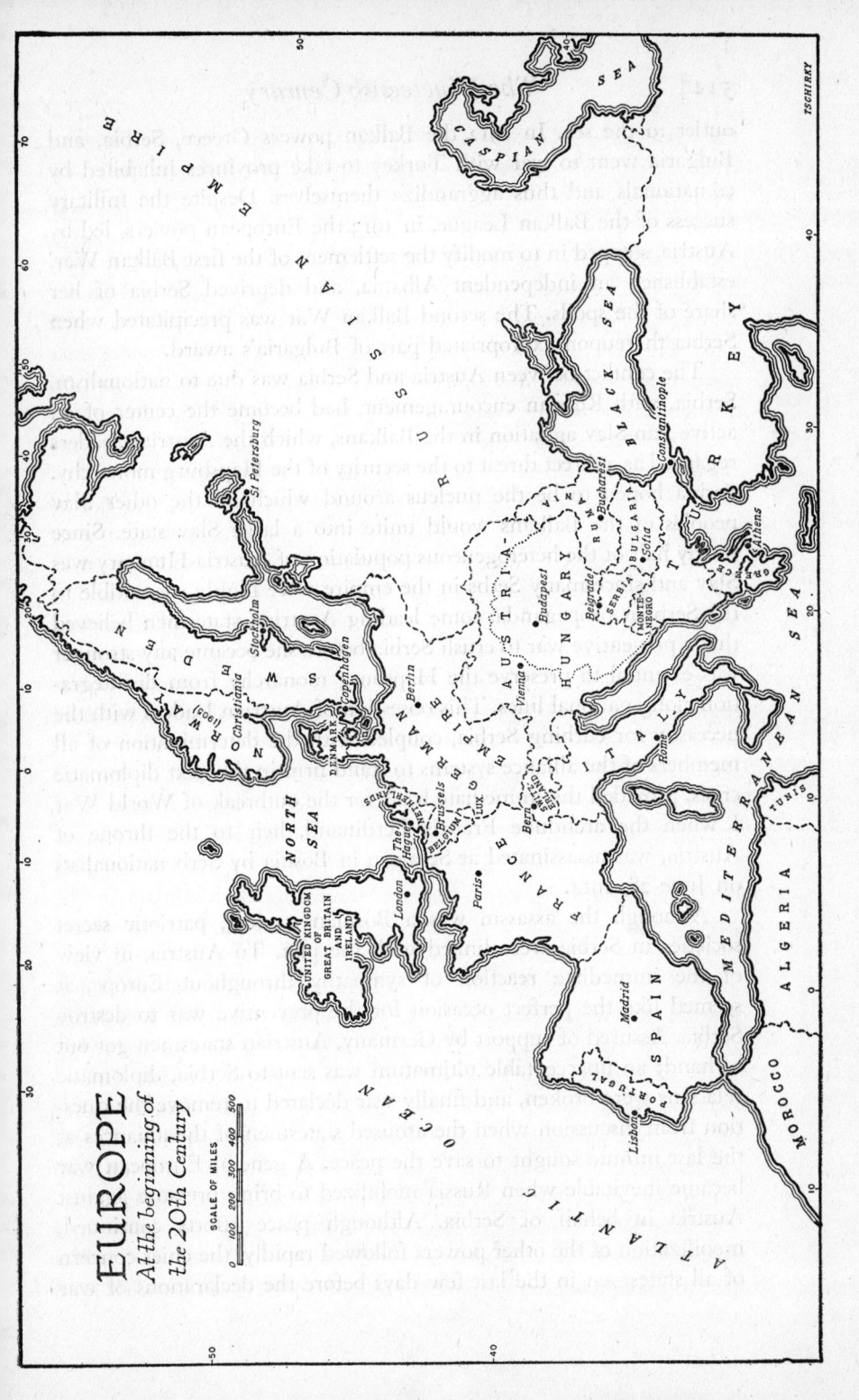

outlet to the sea. In 1912 the Balkan powers Greece, Serbia, and Bulgaria went to war with Turkey to take provinces inhabited by co-nationals and thus aggrandize themselves. Despite the military success of the Balkan League, in 1913 the European powers, led by Austria, stepped in to modify the settlement of the first Balkan War, established an independent Albania, and deprived Serbia of her share of the spoils. The second Balkan War was precipitated when Serbia thereupon expropriated part of Bulgaria's award.

The conflict between Austria and Serbia was due to nationalism. Serbia, with Russian encouragement, had become the center of an active Pan-Slav agitation in the Balkans, which the Austrian leaders regarded as a direct threat to the security of the Hapsburg monarchy. Serbia hoped to be the nucleus around which all the other Slav peoples of the Balkans would unite into a large Slav state. Since nearly half of the heterogeneous population of Austria-Hungary was Slav and since many Serbs in the empire were highly susceptible to the Serbian propaganda, some leading Austrian statesmen believed that a preventive war to crush Serbia before she became any stronger was essential to preserve the Hapsburg monarchy from disintegration along national lines. This obsession of Austrian leaders with the necessity for curbing Serbia, coupled with the determination of all members of the alliance systems to stand firm in the next diplomatic crisis, provided the immediate basis for the outbreak of World War I when the archduke Francis Ferdinand, heir to the throne of Austria, was assassinated at Serajevo in Bosnia by Serb nationalists on June 28, 1914.

Although the assassin was a Bosnian student, patriotic secret societies in Serbia were linked with the plot. To Austria, in view of the immediate reaction of sympathy throughout Europe, it seemed like the perfect occasion for the preventive war to destroy Serbia. Assured of support by Germany, Austrian statesmen got out of hand; an unacceptable ultimatum was sent to Serbia, diplomatic relations were broken, and finally war declared to remove the question from discussion when the aroused statesmen of the alliances at the last minute sought to save the peace. A general European war became inevitable when Russia mobilized to bring pressure against Austria in behalf of Serbia. Although peace efforts continued, mobilization of the other powers followed rapidly, the chief concern of all statesmen in the last few days before the declarations of war being to get their countries into the war as innocently as possible. So successfully was this done that the rank and file of the population on both sides rallied to the support of their governments in the sincere conviction that they were the victims of brutal aggression. The Italian government alone did not enter the war at once, announcing that the Triple Alliance did not bind her in a war of aggression. After much bargaining Italy came in against Germany in 1915.

The entrance of Great Britain was a serious blow to Germany, with whom she had no quarrel in 1914. The British had a secret naval commitment to defend the northern coasts of France in the event of German attack, and the German invasion of Belgium en route to France, contrary to international guarantee of Belgian neutrality, provided an excellent issue to rally British public opinion to the war. Part of the evil here came from the institution of the general staff. The nightmare of the German general staff was the possibility of a war on two fronts against Russia and France. In view of the long period of time required for Russian mobilization and because of the alliance between Russia and France, the German general staff planned in the event of war with Russia to attack and defeat France first in a matter of a few weeks and then turn to face the Russians alone by the time mobilization there was completed. Thus though there was no real grievance against France in the summer of 1914, the Russian mobilization forced the German army to provoke war with France in order to utilize its elaborately worked-out plans of campaign. At the last minute the military men got out of control and took precedence over the civil authorities; hypersensitive under the responsibility for the security of their countries, they insisted on taking belligerent measures which nullified the last-minute efforts of the statesmen to keep the peace and which made all proposals seem insincere.

The underlying causes of the war were clearly national illusions and jealousies, colonial rivalries, competing industrialism, and staggering armaments which made every nation believe it was prepared for war and which simply added to the frightfulness of the war when it came. But the immediate cause was largely the result of a system of alliances that made fine distinctions between offensive and defensive wars. That question did not arise in any country in the final crisis. The balance of power and not aggression was the welding issue that held allies together. Convinced of the defensive nature of its action, every people went to war for its allies.

Jaurès had by 1914 become an important figure in international socialism, and a leader in its organ, the Second International. Under German pressure he had abandoned the policy of strategic cooperation with other French parties. He was a firm believer in international Socialist solidarity, and defended it in his newspaper, *L'Humanité*. When the war danger appeared inevitable he tried to persuade the International to declare a general strike against war. On July 31, the eve of the German declaration of war against Russia, when the preliminaries of French mobilization were already under way, he was assassinated by a nationalist fanatic who feared that socialist internationalism and pacificism would create disunity for France in her hour of peril. The fanatic was wrong: socialists in every nation sacrificed their principles for the defense of their fatherland against aggression.

[THE NINETEENTH CENTURY]

Readings

Charles Darwin

AUTOBIOGRAPHY *

[This matter-of-fact account of the steps by which Darwin came to his important conclusions and the circumstances under which he gave the results to the world is free from technical jargon.]

From September 1854 I devoted my whole time to arranging my huge pile of notes, to observing, and to experimenting in relation to the transmutation of species. During the voyage of the *Beagle* I had been deeply impressed by discovering in the Pampean formation great fossil animals covered with armour like that on the existing armadillos; secondly, by the manner in which closely allied animals replace one another in proceeding southwards over the Continent; and thirdly, by the South American character of most of the productions of the Galapagos archipelago, and more especially by the manner in which they differ slightly on each island of the group; none of the islands appearing to be very ancient in a geological sense.

It was evident that such facts as these, as well as many others, could only be explained on the supposition that species gradually become modified; and the subject haunted me. But it was equally evident that neither the action of the surrounding conditions, nor the will of the organisms (especially in the case of plants) could account for the innumerable cases in which organisms of every kind are beautifully adapted to their habits of life—for instance, a woodpecker or a tree-frog to climb trees, or a seed for dispersal by hooks

* From *Charles Darwin, His Life Told in an Autobiographical Chapter and in a Selected Series of His Published Letters,* edited by his son, Francis Darwin (1893). Reprinted by permission of D. Appleton-Century Company, Inc.

[515

or plumes. I had always been much struck by such adaptations, and until these could be explained it seemed to me almost useless to endeavour to prove by indirect evidence that species have been modified.

After my return to England it appeared to me that by following the example of Lyell in Geology, and by collecting all facts which bore in any way on the variation of animals and plants under domestication and nature, some light might perhaps be thrown on the whole subject. My first note-book was opened in July 1837. I worked on true Baconian principles, and without any theory collected facts on a wholesale scale, more especially with respect to domesticated productions by printed enquiries, by conversation with skilful breeders and gardeners, and by extensive reading. When I see the list of books of all kinds which I read and abstracted, including whole series of Journals and Transactions, I am surprised at my industry. I soon perceived that selection was the keystone of man's success in making useful races of animals and plants. But how selection could be applied to organisms living in a state of nature remained for some time a mystery to me.

In October 1838, that is, fifteen months after I had begun my systematic enquiry, I happened to read for amusement Malthus on *Population,* and being well prepared to appreciate the struggle for existence which everywhere goes on from long-continued observation of the habits of animals and plants, it at once struck me that under these circumstances favourable variations would tend to be preserved and unfavourable ones to be destroyed. The result of this would be the formation of new species. Here, then, I had at last got a theory by which to work; but I was so anxious to avoid prejudice, that I determined not for some time to write even the briefest sketch of it. In June 1842 I first allowed myself the satisfaction of writing a very brief abstract of my theory in pencil in 35 pages; and this was enlarged during the summer of 1844 into one of 230 pages, which I had fairly copied out and still possess.

But at that time I overlooked one problem of great importance; and it is astonishing to me, except on the principle of Columbus and his egg, how I could have overlooked it and its solution. This problem is the tendency in organic beings descended from the same stock to diverge in character as they become modified. That they have diverged greatly is obvious from the manner in which species of all kinds can be classed under genera, genera under families, families under sub-orders, and so forth; and I can remember the very spot in the road, whilst in my carriage, when to my joy the solution occurred to me; and this was long after I had come to Down. The solution, as I believe, is that the modified offspring of all dominant and increasing forms tend to become adapted to many and highly diversified places in the economy of nature.

In September 1858 I set to work by the strong advice of Lyell and Hooker to prepare a volume on the transmutation of species, but was often interrupted by ill-health, . . . I abstracted the MS. begun on a much larger scale in 1856, and completed the volume on the same reduced scale. It cost me thirteen months and ten days' hard labour. It was published under the title of the *Origin of Species*, in November 1859. Though considerably added to and corrected in the later editions, it has remained substantially the same book.

It is no doubt the chief work of my life. . . .

Early in 1856 Lyell advised me to write out my views pretty fully, and I began at once to do so on a scale three or four times as extensive as that which was afterwards followed in my *Origin of Species;* yet it was only an abstract of the materials which I had collected, and I got through about half the work on this scale. But my plans were overthrown, for early in the summer of 1858 Mr. Wallace, who was then in the Malay archipelago, sent me an essay *On the Tendency of Varieties to depart indefinitely from the Original Type;* and this essay contained exactly the same theory as mine. Mr. Wallace expressed the wish that if I thought well of his essay, I should send it to Lyell for perusal.

The circumstances under which I consented at the request of Lyell and Hooker to allow of an abstract from my MS., together with a letter to Asa Gray, dated September 5, 1857, to be published at the same time with Wallace's Essay, are given in the *Journal of the Proceedings of the Linnean Society,* 1858, p. 45. I was at first very unwilling to consent, as I thought Mr. Wallace might consider my doing so unjustifiable, for I did not then know how generous and noble was his disposition. The extract from my MS. and the letter to Asa Gray had neither been intended for publication, and were badly written. Mr. Wallace's essay, on the other hand, was admirably expressed and quite clear. Nevertheless, our joint productions excited very little attention, and the only published notice of them which I can remember was by Professor Haughton of Dublin, whose verdict was that all that was new in them was false, and what was true was old. . . .

Jean Jaurès

WRITINGS *

[Jaurès, a scholar as well as dreamer, was able to sketch the Socialist ideal in a way which would not shock and alienate the ordinary reader.]

I was walking the other evening in the country, and talking with a young friend who had just graduated among the first of his class at the École Polytechnique after having done very good work in literature, and who is as broad-minded as he is keen. . . .

"Yes," I said to him, "the thing that angers me in our present society is not only the physical suffering that might be mitigated by another régime, but the moral suffering that is brought by a state of warfare and monstrous inequality.

"To labour should be a natural function and a joy; often it is nothing more than servitude and suffering. It ought to be the war waged by all mankind united against inanimate things, against the fatalities of nature and the difficulties of life; it is the war of man with man. Men spend their days struggling to take from one another the joys of life by fraud, by the arts of bitter greed, the oppression of the weak, and all the violent methods of unlimited competition. Even among those who are called happy there are few who are really happy, because the brutal conditions of life hold them in their grip; they hardly have the right to be just and kind under pain of ruin. In the universal warfare, some are the slaves of their fortune as others are the slaves of their poverty. Yes, above and below, our present social order produces nothing but slaves, because those men are not free who have neither the time nor the strength to follow the noblest instincts of their minds and their souls.

"And if you look at the lower grades, what poverty you see, I don't say in the means of life, but in life itself! Look at the millions of labourers; they work in the factories and in the workshops, yet they have no right whatever in those factories and workshops; they can be turned out to-morrow. Neither have they any right over the machine they tend, no share of ownership in the immense tool that humanity has bit by bit created for itself; they are strangers in the

---

* From "Moonlight," Chapter XVI in *Studies in Socialism*, by Jean Jaurès, translated by Mildred Minturn (1906). Reprinted by permission of G. P. Putnam's Sons.

organised power of the world; they are almost strangers in the civilisation of the world.

"In the mines, the canals, the railroads, the ports, the prodigious applications of steam and electricity and all the great enterprises that develop the power and the pride of man, they have no part, no part at all, except that of inert instruments. They have no seat in the councils that decide on new undertakings and direct them; these are entirely in the hands of a limited class which knows all the joys of intellectual activity and hardy initiative, just as it possesses all the pleasures of wealth, and which would be happy if it were permitted to man to be happy apart from human solidarity. There are millions of labourers who are reduced to an inert and mechanical existence. And, terrifying as the idea is, if to-morrow machines could be substituted for them, nothing would be changed in human existence.

"When, on the contrary, Socialism has triumphed, when conditions of peace have succeeded to conditions of combat, when all men have their share of property in the immense human capital, and their share of initiative and of the exercise of free-will in the immense human activity, then all men will know the fulness of pride and joy; and they will feel that they are co-operators in the universal civilisation, even if their immediate contribution is only the humblest manual labour; and this labour, more noble and more fraternal in character, will be so regulated that the labourers shall always reserve for themselves some leisure hours for reflection and for a cultivation of the sense of life.

"They will have a better understanding of the hidden meaning of life, whose mysterious aim is the harmony of all consciences, of all forces, and of all liberties. They will understand history better and will love it, because it will be their history, since they are the heirs of the whole human race. Finally, they will understand the universe better; because when they see conscience and spirit triumphing in humanity, they will be quick to feel that this universe which has given birth to humanity cannot be fundamentally brutal and blind, that there is spirit everywhere, soul everywhere, and that the universe itself is simply an immense confused aspiration toward order, beauty, freedom, and goodness. Their point of view will be changed; they will look with new eyes not only at their brother men, but at the earth and the sky, rocks and trees, animals, flowers, and stars. . . .

"Well and good," answered my young engineer, "but why don't you simply talk about social progress; why do you bring in Socialism? Social progress is a real thing, whereas Socialism is nothing but a word. It is the name of a small, but very vehement or rather violent sect, which is, moreover, divided against itself: it is not a serious force making for progress. . . .

"As a matter of fact, all the elements of the problem exist already in our present society and the solution is indicated or even roughly sketched in: the solution of the social problem is wholly comprised in political liberty, the development of popular education, and the right of labour to organise. Well, political liberty exists, education, and an education always more advanced, is becoming more and more diffused in the labour world, and the workers have the right to organise.

"When they are better educated they will begin by taking part through their imagination and their intelligence in all great human undertakings, and when their personal subjective value has been increased in this way, it will react of its own accord on the social régime by an irresistible action from within outward. . . .

". . . There will be reforms, great reforms even, but they will come to pass without having been given a name, and they will not trouble the calm life of the nation any more than the dropping of ripe fruit troubles the still autumn days. Humanity will raise itself insensibly toward fraternal justice, just as the earth that bears us rises with a silent motion in the starry spaces."

"My dear fellow, I can hardly wait to answer you, I have so many things to say."

"No, no; don't answer me to-night, only look and listen. While we are dreaming of the future and arguing, everything that lives, everything that exists is giving itself up to the joy of the passing moment, to the instant sweetness of the serene night. . . . Come, let the universe be; it contains joy for all. It is Socialistic after its own fashion."

PART XVI

The Twentieth Century

PLATE XXXI

Twentieth Century

FIGURE 1. Lenin addressing the crowds that assembled for the funeral of a comrade. [Courtesy of Sovfoto, New York]

FIGURE 2. Harvesting wheat in the north Caucasus. The most modern agricultural machinery is used on the great collective farms of Russia. When such machinery was first introduced it went to pieces rapidly because of ignorance of its use and care, but today mechanics are better trained, and the resulting production is enormous.
[Courtesy of Sovfoto, New York]

FIGURE 3. Bird in Flight by the Roumanian sculptor Constantin Brancusi (1876–   ). The widespread feeling of modern artists that the old forms of representation have been exhausted and that new forms must be invented has expressed itself in many ways. Brancusi creates an abstract and seemingly weightless form from bronze and stresses the beauty of the material by a high polish. Through purely abstract means of design he gives the suggestion of the movement, symmetry, and smoothness of a bird in flight.
[Collection of the Museum of Modern Art, New York]

FIGURE 4. Country house near Paris, designed by the French architect, Le Corbusier, in 1928. The leading tenet of modern architecture in the 1920's was functionalism, and this house illustrates the term excellently. The geometric shapes express the construction and function of the building. It is to be lived in; therefore windows play a large part, light and air being the chief requisites after shelter. The roof is flat, since in the neighborhood of Paris there are neither heavy snow storms nor excessive rain. There is no extraneous decoration to hide or enrich the purity of design.

PLATE XXXII

Twentieth Century

FIGURE 1. Tube Shelter Perspective *by Henry Moore. The London subway popularly called the Tube is very deep, and was used as an air raid shelter during World War II. There could be no more effective historical record of what modern methods of warfare did to civilians than this drawing by the English sculptor Henry Moore. The deep vista of the tube with people huddled along the curving walls enhances the expressiveness of his subject.*
[*Courtesy of Sir Eric Gregory, owner of the drawing*]

FIGURE 2. *The cyclotron is the device perfected for the purpose of atomic fission. It represents the most revolutionary development of modern science.*
[*Courtesy of Black Star Publishing Company, Inc., New York*]

FIGURE 3. *The signing of the Charter of the United Nations, June 1945. The first signatory, the representative of China, is seated at the table, while other representatives stand by, against a background of flags.*
[*Courtesy of the Press Association, Inc., New York*]

CHRONOLOGY

1901   Death of Queen Victoria of England
1907   Formation of Triple Entente
1908   Austrian annexation of Bosnia
1911   Moroccan Crisis
——   Parliament Act in Great Britain
1912–13   Balkan Wars
1914   Assassination of the Archduke Franz Ferdinand at Sarajevo; outbreak of the World War
1917   Great Russian Revolution (Bolshevik)
1918   General armistice
1919   Paris Peace Conference; Treaty of Versailles
1922   Rise of Mussolini in Italy
1931   Statute of Westminster
——   Japanese seizure of Manchuria
1933   Hitler becomes Chancellor of Germany
1935   Italian invasion of Ethiopia
1936   Beginning of Spanish Civil War
1938   Munich settlement and partition of Czechoslovakia
1939   German invasion of Poland; general European war
1941   German invasion of Russia; entry of United States into the war
1945   Surrender of Germany and Japan, ending world conflict

PART XVI

The Twentieth Century

~~~~~~

IN THE twentieth century the discovery of atomic fission has profoundly altered the outlook for humanity and should force a reexamination of the problems inherited from the past. World War II sprang from the same underlying causes as its predecessor of 1914, and these causes still survive as potential causes of yet another world war. They are national illusions and jealousies, colonial rivalries, competing industrialism, and staggering armaments.

The nineteenth century had inherited from the French Revolution a faith in liberty, equality, and fraternity, but each of those watchwords had a meaning derived from conceptions of society in a preindustrial world. In 1914 faith in democracy existed in a world where individualism was triumphant; political liberty and legal equality were the fruits of the French Revolution which offered every individual in the nineteenth century the right to stand on his own feet and go as far as he liked. There was another side, also, to the bequest of the French Revolution: the idea of fraternity was usually restricted to national boundaries; there was a persistent assumption that revolution was the most successful means of getting changes and achieving ideals; there was the fatal confidence that war paid, as illustrated by the practice of imposing indemnities upon the conquered and by the progress of the movements for national unification. Finally there was the democratization of war, with universal conscription in peacetime and the building up of immense classes of reserves, which inevitably carried with it the militarization of democracy.

Upon a European world which cherished the ideal of democracy, feasible in an agrarian society where the individual with proper freedoms could be self-sufficient, nineteenth-century industrial society was grafted. City civilization and increased population forced the development of a collective society where individuals were mutually dependent. Life became increasingly monotonous for workers at the machines. Tremendous inequality existed while former ideals were retained unmodified; the old association between wealth and political power persisted. In the new industrial society wealth meant money and machines. Machines and money meant political power, and between 1870 and 1914 Jaurès and his contemporaries saw the beginning of a struggle to break the power of capitalist groups as the French Revolution had broken the power of the landed aristocracy. The men who had taken the place of the old aristocracy made concessions, partly to keep their positions, partly because of the traditions of liberalism and humanitarianism. Their successors in the twentieth century were less amenable to these traditions, but the workers had the advantage of the union and the strike.

All industrial nations were vexed by certain aspects of modern society: the recurrence of business crises; the conflict between employer and labor; and the problem of poverty, intensified at intervals by the increase in unemployment, when industry thought it was overproducing and shut down factories. Occasional economists occupied themselves with the problem of distribution in a world which modern science had enabled to produce enough wealth to feed and clothe all its inhabitants. According to the followers of Karl Marx these problems could be solved only by the abolition of the capitalist system; and the fear of communism became an obsession with conservatives, many of whom inclined to look with favor on any system, such as fascism, which professed to put the state at the service of the *status quo*. To some, even war did not seem an unmixed evil since in wartime governments became profitable customers of industry.

Scientific advance remained international. In view of international organizations in every field of science and in every field of intellectual and social activity, optimists at the opening of the twentieth century told each other they were living in a world too civilized to make war on a large scale. Pessimists, on the other hand, subscribed to current attacks upon the doctrine of progress, and to theories of the rise and fall of civilizations.

Nationalism reached new heights. The Irish revived the ancient Gaelic as their national tongue. Denmark and Sweden supplied examples of the way countries with limited resources and no colonies could attain by co-operation and industry a prosperity shared by every class of the population, but these were ignored. Trade rivalries and colonial ambitions swelled the rising tide of nationalism. Special sore spots were cherished, such as France's determination to recover Alsace—a determination influenced by the relative location of iron and steel deposits in the Rhine region. Austria-Hungary was prosperous because it lay in an economic unit, the great valley of the Danube, but Czechs and Magyars cherished national aspirations. Russia, which had trailed along a century behind western Europe, was still an absolute monarchy that exiled political reformers to Siberia. Russia's policy in the Balkans was looked on with suspicion by Austria-Hungary. British and German trade rivalry outside Europe was intense; German dissatisfaction with her colonial empire and suspicion of French expansion in Africa were strong.

World War I demonstrated that the results of modern warfare are ruinous for both sides. The demonstration was not immediately clear; an illusion of security existed because of the League of Nations. Fears of Soviet Russia, a sense of guilt about certain aspects of the Versailles Treaty, and complacency about the stock market diverted attention from the re-arming of Germany. The German industrialists were leaders in fostering international cartels, for they used them to restrict production by other nations of materials vital for war, while under cover they reestablished their own war industries. Equally unnoticed was the decay of the French political structure.

Signs of the times could be seen in the arts. In painting, the impressionism of the nineteenth century resulted in the growth of various schools that worked at the problem of further analyzing the visual process. Interesting methods of expression were found, but what was expressed was usually frustration and despair. Similar experiments were made in literature and in music; discords were analyzed in search for new harmonies.

On the other hand, development was extraordinary in the field of science. The Newtonian physics was profoundly altered by the work of Einstein. The discovery of X-rays in the last year of the nineteenth century led to the discovery of radium. Investigation of the structure of the atom and study of electrons pointed the way to atomic fission. Progress in medicine and surgery made life easier, and results of study in genetics were applied to plant and animal husbandry. The swift development of the airplane after the flight of the Wright brothers in 1903, improvements in telephone and telegraph, in the automobile and other means of transportation brought all parts of the world closer physically even while politically they drifted apart.

An important trend of the first quarter of the century was the political enfranchisement of women. Finland enfranchised women in 1906, Norway in 1913, Denmark in 1915. In England and the United States in the nineteenth century woman suffrage agitation had led to little more than hilarity among legislators. During World War I, however, the need for women to replace men in industry enhanced their importance, and in a number of countries they were given the vote by 1922.[1] In Soviet Russia women not only voted, but worked in heavy industry beside the men and served on the battlefront. In France and Italy women were given the vote only after World War II.

The prophecy that the women's votes would be conservative was ungrounded. The tendency in most European countries has been away from monarchy and toward republican forms. The retention of the monarchy in Great Britain is frequently attributed to conservatism, but is probably largely due to the usefulness of the crown as a unifying force in the British Commonwealth of nations.

World War II demolished the myth of German superiority. It demonstrated that states of very different political organization could work harmoniously to a common end and solve successfully the problems of supply and distribution, health control, and unemployment. Whether this knowledge will be applied to the solution of peace-time problems is still an unanswered question. The discovery of atomic fission has made possible the further transformation of the material world and the extension of man's power over his environment in ways that stagger the imagination. Since atomic power was first used in war, and may be used again in a world divided between two social and economic systems, fear will rule the world until the secret of the atomic bomb has passed from national to international control.

As atomic fission is the greatest scientific achievement of the first half of the twentieth century, the greatest political achievement

---

[1] Netherlands, Austria, 1917; Great Britain, Germany, 1918; United States, Hungary, 1920; Poland, Sweden, Czechoslovakia, 1921; Irish Free State, 1922.

is the practical application of the idea of world unity. The League of Nations failed for many reasons; the structure of the United Nations is in certain respects better than that of the League, and it has much wider support. It has the machinery for dealing with national illusions and jealousies, colonial rivalries, and competing industrialism. It could banish all need for staggering armaments.

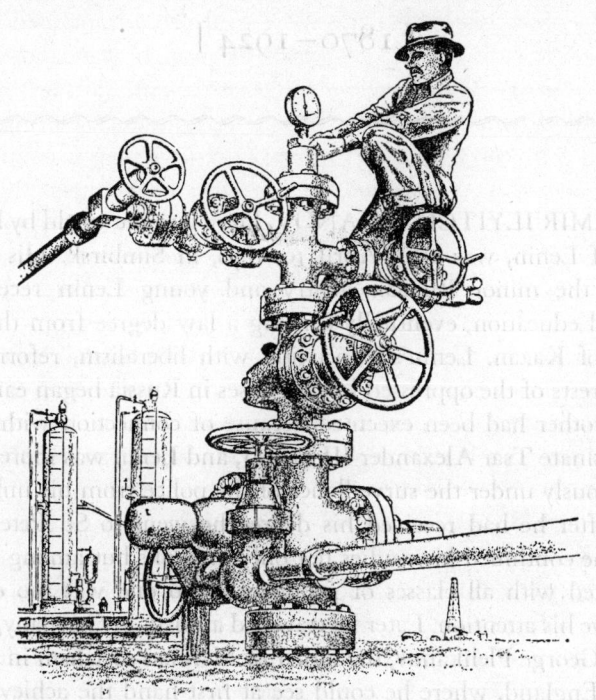

THE "CHRISTMAS TREE" WHICH REGULATES
THE FLOW OF OIL FROM A WELL

(Drawn by Jack Housez. From *This Fascinating Oil Business* by Max W. Bell, copyright 1940, used by special permission of the Publishers, The Bobbs-Merrill Company.)

CHAPTER 30

The World of Nikolai Lenin

[1870–1924]

~~~~~~~~~~~~~~~~

VLADIMIR ILYITCH ULIANOV, known to the world by his pen name of Lenin, was born April 10, 1870, in Simbirsk. His family was of the minor Russian gentry and young Lenin received a standard education, eventually earning a law degree from the University of Kazan. Lenin's association with liberalism, reform, and the interests of the oppressed lower classes in Russia began early. An older brother had been executed because of connection with a plot to assassinate Tsar Alexander III (1891), and Lenin was more or less continuously under the surveillance of the police from his university days. After he had received his degree he went to St. Petersburg, where he continued his studies not only in books but among people. He talked with all classes of people, and no one was too obscure to receive his attention. Later he travelled abroad, in Germany, where he met George Plehkanov, the father of Marxian socialism in Russia, and in England, where he could see at first hand the achievements of the most advanced industrial nation in Europe.

The Russian world into which Lenin was born was a European anachronism characterized by autocracy, orthodoxy, and nationalism. There was no more legitimate development in Russian history than the autocracy of the Russian state. First defense against the Tatars, then feudal disorders, and later the continuous expansion of the Russian state called for strong rule. Peter the Great, Elizabeth, and Catherine the Great further consolidated the autocratic system by their leadership in Russian imperial expansion. In the nineteenth century, when industrialization began to come to backward Russia and her economic strength improved, the pressure for the expansion with which the tsars were so closely associated was intensified. Russia had few good ports, and the autocracy fought against the other imperial powers of the world for outlets to the open seas in the Near, Middle, and Far East.

Probably the single most important achievement of the autocracy in the nineteenth century was the emancipation of the serfs, in the decade before Lenin was born. Emancipation had become a practical necessity: serfdom was not only an unprogressive institution which shamed the more enlightened Russians of all classes and the humanitarian instincts of the nineteenth century generally, but it also threatened upheaval from below if there was not reform from above. In the reign of Nicholas I (1825-55) there were some 550 separate peasant rebellions. There was no general organization or leadership, but the fact that these peasant uprisings were spontaneous had unmistakable significance. By a series of imperial decrees (1861-63), Alexander II emancipated the serfs. The terms of the emancipation, however, did not bring about a full solution of the problem of peasant unrest; in fact, the conditions of the emancipation were a primary cause of the growth of the political discontent and economic distress which led to the revolution of 1905 in Russia. The peasants received legal freedom and were given about half the land; the landowning aristocracy received compensation. The amount of land was not adequate for the peasants' needs, and the land was not given outright; the peasants were compelled to reimburse the state for its compensation of the nobility by long-term payments, which kept the peasants in an economic servitude that often made their legal freedom seem a dead letter. The land, furthermore, was not given to individuals but to the village community; it was re-divided as numbers increased, and the old unprogressive communal peasant cultivation continued. The land-owning nobility were deprived of a labor supply and were dissatisfied at the higher cost of free labor. In general no class was wholly content, but the emancipation was a courageous attack on some of the evils of serfdom, and did make possible a mobile and free labor supply which could provide the basis for an industrial working class and the beginnings of a belated industrial revolution. Alexander also instituted rural *zemstvos* and municipal dumas—i.e., local councils which provided training in self-government by allowing a certain jurisdiction over local social services of a non-political character—but they were constantly watched for political activity. Under the Russian autocracy political activity was a governmental monopoly.

Nationalism was a logical outgrowth of the Russian autocracy, for the tsars tried to establish uniformity as the empire expanded to include non-Russian peoples. When Russia was expanding eastward or southward it was at the expense of Asiatic or infidel peoples whom the Russians might legitimately regard as culturally inferior. In westward expansion Russia encountered cultural superiority but political decadence. In either case the conquest produced subject peoples with Russian overlords, and there was an effort to Russify non-Russian groups, in which the Poles and the Jews were probably the worst sufferers. The position of the Russian Orthodox Church was also in a sense the logical outgrowth of autocracy and a passion for uniformity. Russian Christianity came from Constantinople, with its Byzantine tradition of the subordination of church to state as an administrative branch. Again the chief sufferers were the Jews, and the Poles, who were Roman Catholic. Religious intolerance and forcible Russification meant legal disabilities on religious and racial grounds.

Unsuccessful foreign wars have more than once aroused Russia to meet the need of change. The Crimean War, a major military and diplomatic disaster for Russia, prompted several fundamental and far-reaching reforms which produced a revolution in Russian economy by 1900. The emancipation of the serfs provided a pool of labor for industrial development. By the nineties, a sound program of financing and a stable currency had been established, which encouraged foreign investment and made available a reservoir of capital for industrial expansion. A program of tariffs to protect the new industry and encourage foreign capital followed, and with the era of railroad construction in the last years of the nineteenth century the industrial revolution might be said to have arrived. But the social changes incident to industrialization produced the usual result—political discontent and economic distress. The conscious relating of these two factors, according to the Russian historian and liberal political leader Paul Milyukov, brought a revolutionary situation. The occasion for revolution was provided by the unsuccessful war with Japan in 1904–05.

The aggravated political discontent and economic distress which led to revolutionary action can be traced in part to a policy of maintaining autocracy. Autocracy was supported by such semi-feudal groups as the nobility and clergy, but these groups were increasingly in conflict with the new social forces that came with industrialization, the small but growing middle class and proletariat. There were still legal class divisions, despite the emancipation of the serfs, but there was no provision for new classes like the industrial wage-earner and laborer. Many of the Russian industries, including railroads, were government owned or controlled, and working conditions were bad. Strikes were prohibited, and workers forbidden to organize. Ruthless exploitation of labor was permitted as an inducement to foreign capital. Since strikes were illegal, any strike had a political aspect, and the strike leaders began to relate their grievances against employers to a grievance against the government.

As political organization was illegal, the two important parties before the revolution of 1905 were of necessity underground groups. One was the Socialist Revolutionary, or SR Party, which operated chiefly among the peasants with a program of propaganda and terrorism. As a socialist party it advocated the abolition of private property and the formation of federations of industrial and agricultural communes. The second group was the Russian Workmen's Social Democratic, or SD Party, which operated mainly among the laboring class, with a Marxian socialist program basically similar to that of other European social democratic workers' parties. The essential principle of the Marxian socialist program was for the industrial wage-earning proletariat to assume control of the means and instruments of production, thereby abolishing private ownership and eliminating the exploitation of man by man which according to Marx characterized the capitalist system. After 1903 the Russian SD Party was split into two factions, known as Bolshevik and Menshevik from the Russian words for "more" and "less." The Bolsheviks wanted to limit group membership to professional revolutionaries and operate on a revolutionary program which included the peasants; the Mensheviks limited their aims to arousing the bourgeoisie. While the Bolsheviks emphasized strict party discipline, non-cooperation with other socialist or non-socialist parties, and a violent social revolution, the Mensheviks favored political action and believed a democratic government was a necessary step before social revolution. The leader of the Bolsheviks was Lenin, who had actively entered political activity when he returned from his travels in Germany and England, editing a radical journal and writing revolutionary pamphlets. In 1895 his work earned him the usual reward of the Russian professional revolutionary—arrest by the secret police, which was the tsarist weapon to combat political activity, a sojourn in prison, and exile to Siberia. In 1900 he left Siberia for Switzerland.

The growing discontent could not break the strength of the entrenched autocracy until a new factor arose in 1904 in the shape of the war with Japan. Russian expansion eastward and the completion of the trans-Siberian railroad had been followed by the exploitation of Manchuria and an effort to erect a sphere of influence in China. The Japanese war, which broke out without formal declaration over disputed concessions in Korea, was not unwelcome to the government because it believed that a victorious war might help in handling the critical internal problems of the empire. The conscious liberal and radical opposition saw no vital interest at stake in a capitalists' quarrel over timber lands in Korea and positively wanted a defeat to discredit the autocracy and perhaps bring about reform at home.

The revolution of 1905 grew out of a petition for constitutional government. January 22, 1905, was called "Bloody Sunday" after the guards at the tsar's palace fired into an orderly and unarmed body of petitioners. This event shook the faith of the common people in the tsar. An increasing number of strikes culminated, after the ignominious end of the Japanese war, in a successful general strike in St. Petersburg in October, 1905. To meet the demand for a constitutional assembly, democratically elected by equal, universal suffrage and direct, secret ballot, the tsar issued the famous October Manifesto (October 30, 1905), which promised civil liberties and an elective body with full legislative powers. Autocracy in Russia seemed legally dead; Lenin returned to Russia in November and took an active part in politics.

In practice there was no substantial change in the old governmental system after the 1905 revolution because there was still autocracy and there were reprisals to liquidate revolutionary activity. The tsar retained an absolute veto, the ministers remained solely responsible to the tsar, and the duma could not initiate amendments to the constitution. The first duma proposed a radical solution of the land problem favorable to the peasants, and the tsar dissolved it after about two months of debate (1906). A second duma was elected and met early in 1907; it was dissolved because of conflict over the budget and the land question. The tsar then arbitrarily changed the election law so that it insured a conservative upper-class majority, and the third duma, elected in 1907, proved able to work with the government. Since a fourth duma, elected in 1912, lasted until the revolution of 1917, the duma institution survived as a project politically educational but without real power. The workmen's political movement of 1905 was broken, and from then until World War I the principal radical leaders lived abroad. Lenin returned to Switzerland.

Although the policy of the government from 1905 to the outbreak of the war was reactionary, the period was not one of stagnation. The chief figure in the government after 1906 was Stolypin, prime minister until his assassination in 1911. He tried to remove agricultural unrest by making the purchase of state lands easier and by subsidizing migration to Siberia so as to encourage private peasant land holdings outside the village commune. Stolypin also secured legislation designed to break up the communal system of land tenure because he regarded it as a brake on peasant initiative. This policy he hoped would liquidate the economic revolution by inspiring a respect for private property and creating a peasant class of individual proprietors. Stolypin hoped to win the peasantry to the support of the tsar; propertyless men are seldom as ready to support a government as property owners. The economic position of Russia was definitely improved in the last years before 1914, partly as a result of a certain amount of stirring up from the Japanese war and the Stolypin land policy, partly because of a series of excellent crops and a large influx of foreign capital. The economic progress should not, however, be exaggerated. Russia was still at least 75% agrarian, with agriculture far and away the most important industry, and Stolypin's land program had affected only about 10% of the land and the peasant population. In the whole empire, with about 170,000,000 people, only some 6,000,000 could be classed as industrial proletariat, the class with which Lenin and other Marxian socialists were chiefly concerned.

When Russia entered the war in 1914 most classes supported the move with patriotic fervor. Liberal opinion considered the war to be in the national interest, not imperialistic, but in behalf of a long-standing policy of Russian participation in the solution of

Balkan problems. Imperial Germany was regarded as support for the reactionary element in the Russian government, and France as support for constitutional development, hence the French alliance was popular with Russian progressives. The moderate socialists, Mensheviks and SRs, went nationalist and supported the war. The Bolsheviks openly opposed it as imperialistic, and those in exile, Lenin particularly, appealed to the peoples of all belligerent powers to convert it into civil wars between workers and their exploiters. Little attention was paid to the appeal at the time. The national minorities in Russia supported the war, hoping for liberation through the influence of Russia's allies, England and France. The Russian general staff mobilized in the belief that they could meet the Germans better then than later.

The events of the war condemned the elaborate military preparations that had been made for it on both sides. The numbers of troops involved were far and away greater than those of any previous armies. In armaments emphasis was placed on weight and size, rather than mobility. Yet with all the bulk of equipment and masses of men the theory of waging war was to adopt a very rapid offensive. The test of the military men came when the initial campaigns for which they had carefully prepared failed and they proved incapable of successful improvisation. After the opening campaigns manoeuvre and surprise were almost nil, weight and manpower were universally relied upon, and the defensive proved stronger than the offensive. There was less economy of manpower than in any war in history, and the tactics throughout were prodigal of human life.

The opening German campaign in the West came within an ace of a decisive defeat of the French. Once disrupted, the opposing armies dug in with an intricate series of trench lines that extended from the English Channel to the Swiss frontier, and the stalemated character of the war remained essentially unchanged until the armistice. New weapons were tried from time to time—the military aeroplane, poison gas, and the tank—but the tactics were the billy-goat-butting technique of mass attack in an effort to create a break-through and regain mobility behind the enemy lines. The dream of a break-through was never realized; use of the aeroplane did not extend much beyond reconnaissance and strafing; and though poison gas nearly demoralized the defenders upon whom it was first used, it lost its effectiveness after the element of surprise was eliminated. The tank, when first tried, was so ineptly used that its effectiveness was diminished by giving the enemy time to prepare a defense.

On the eastern front the German and Austrian armies were more successful, though they did not succeed in driving Russia from the war until two great revolutions had completely overthrown the tsarist régime. The Russian army was very badly equipped and plagued with the perennial curse of Russian military effort—inadequate transportation facilities. Troops often had to go into battle without weapons and face the murderous enemy fire, depending on retrieving the guns of their fallen comrades as they advanced. Russian artillery was hopelessly outranged by the German.

The Russian autocracy during the war years proved utterly incapable of capitalizing on the patriotism evoked by the war or of assuming forceful leadership in a vigorous war effort. Public initiative was restricted since the autocracy saw the specter of revolution everywhere and was obsessed with the fear that any public organization might become political. The bureaucracy's failure showed up the more in the restriction of public initiative; there were extensive military disasters. Under army pressure, public organization behind the war effort was reluctantly permitted from 1915 to 1916, and the army was more successful, thanks to the effort on the home front for more efficiency. Then, in the summer of 1916 the government returned to restrictive measures, and at the same time there was increasing economic distress from shortage of supplies and consumer goods. Public organization, which had demonstrated its efficiency, was suppressed; all ministers who favored public organization or co-operation with the duma were dismissed. By autumn the military front had collapsed. The prime minister, who wanted peace, was accused of trying to promote revolution by provocatory measures. There was, however, no preparation for revolution; even the radicals admitted that they had no organization for it. Food shortage developed in the cities, owing to poor distribution and the breakdown of transportation.

At the beginning of March, 1917, bread riots broke out spontaneously in the capital, but regiments brought out to maintain order went over to the crowds. General rioting then developed and the workmen joined in. The street fighting and overcoming of the police by the soldiers and workmen in March did not constitute a formal revolution. To create a political revolution the leaders of the duma, unrepresentative as it was, set up a committee to take charge of the situation and attempt to restore order. The tsar was forced to abdicate. The Socialists of the duma set out to organize soviets of workmen and soldier deputies in order to control the riotous elements. All the initial action took place in the capital; the army sat down to wait developments.

The new government, the provisional revolutionary government, was primarily the triumph of the liberal movement, brought to a head by the soldiers and workmen. Its program emphasized its liberal character to gain support. There was general amnesty, and many radical leaders returned to Russia—Lenin arrived in April, 1917. The death penalty which under the tsarist régime had been used almost exclusively for political offenders was abolished; civil liberties were established; all restrictions because of religion, social class or nationality were abolished; and soldiers were given equal rights with other citizens. It was understood that the provisional government stood for vigorous prosecution of the war. It disclaimed competence on the subject of land reform, deferring the question until a constituent assembly could be elected on a basis of universal, direct, secret suffrage. In the name of revolutionary democracy the Petrograd [1] Soviet undertook the role of watchdog, and as the Soviet sometimes acted independently there were actually two governments existing side by side from the beginning of the March revolution. By June, 1917, soviets had been set up in all the cities on the model of the Petrograd Soviet.

Revolutions tend to develop from moderation to violence. Many complications ruined the first, or March, revolution: the foreign situation, the fact that the provisional government was committed to the war and the people cried for peace, the complete economic breakdown that occurred when an offensive was attempted, and the lack of co-operation between political factions. The factions had co-operated to secure the revolution but could not work together for constructive purposes. The leaders of the provisional government had oratory but not statesmanship to carry them between the two extremes, reactionary and radical. They could not check the growing anarchy and dissolution of local government.

[1] The name of the capital was changed from St. Petersburg to Petrograd at the beginning of the war, as being more Russian and less German. After the capital had been moved to Moscow, Petrograd became Leningrad.

The Bolshevik party, under the leadership of Lenin, was the best organized of the socialist parties. Lenin had broken with the evolutionary socialists and believed Marx's doctrine to be revolutionary, advocating a violent revolution by the workingmen to overthrow the rulers. Unlike the brilliant Menshevik, Leon Trotsky, Lenin thought the revolution would not be spontaneous. He believed in a small select Communist party over and above the masses which led them and worked for them. He thought that the Communist group, once in control, should organize a temporary dictatorship for the benefit of the working class. Lenin defined government as the organization of one class of society to exploit another class, and he therefore wanted his transitional dictatorship of the proletariat to exploit the bourgeoisie. Once the ultimate ideal of classless society had been achieved by the elimination of the non-proletarian classes, he believed government in the old sense would cease to exist and communism would have arrived.

In 1917 Lenin opposed the war and did not advocate a peaceful procedure in the revolution; he offered no compromise with the bourgeois provisional government. To the end of July the Bolsheviks were able to take advantage of the freedom of speech, press, and assembly. Then, following an abortive uprising, the provisional government headed by Kerensky ordered the suppression of Bolshevik papers and the arrest of Lenin and Trotsky. Lenin went into hiding but continued to direct propaganda for the revolution. The Bolsheviks, anticipating that the constituent assembly when elected would be 85% peasant, advocated the immediate turning over of the land to the peasants since the constituent assembly was bound to vote the measure anyhow. The peasants began the redistribution of the land, illegally but in a more or less orderly fashion. The news reached the soldiers and they started home to participate. Whether the Bolshevik propaganda was responsible for the land seizure and desertion, or whether the Bolsheviks simply formulated the popular demands better than any other party, the provisional government was failing. The March revolution had failed to solve the political and economic problems of the war, during war, by democratic methods, on the basis of class co-operation. The revolutionary intelligentsia succeeded in the social revolution which followed.

An All-Russian Soviet Congress was scheduled to meet November 7, 1917, in Petrograd, and at Lenin's insistence the Bolsheviks made active preparations for an armed uprising. By October, 1917, the Bolsheviks had secured a majority in the Petrograd Soviet. Constant replacing of delegates had made this possible. Trotsky, the president of the Soviet, joined the Bolsheviks and supported Lenin. On the eve of the meeting of the congress the Bolsheviks, having won over the Petrograd garrison, arrested all the members of the provisional government except Kerensky, who escaped, and seized the key financial, military, and governmental centers. It was then announced that the provisional government was overthrown and a Council of Peoples Commissars (made up of the Bolshevik leaders) would exercise control until the constituent assembly met. Faced with an accomplished fact, the Congress of Soviets endorsed the move. The group of extreme radicals which thus secured control retained it.

The dominant figure in the group was Lenin, who at Trotsky's insistence became president of the new council. Lenin was a utopian fanatic who believed in ruthless action and class war. Reproached once with reports that coercion seemed necessary to accomplish the people's program, he replied: "Yes, comrade, coercion is necessary, and it is much better to recognize it frankly than to hide one's head under one's wing and pretend that everything is all right." He was an effective orator who had grown adept with words in the long period of his underground agitation. He had bulldog tenacity, no sentiment, and an unbounded faith in the power of the masses for destruction. He had a complete conviction of ultimate success, a raging hate against exploiters, and a master's touch in the psychology of advertisement. His sound sense of timing and the simplicity of the demands of the Russian scene are both excellently illustrated in the slogans with which he won popular support before the coup d'état of November: *immediate* conclusion of a general peace; *immediate* confiscation of the landed estates without compensation; *immediate* possession and operation of factories by the workers; *immediate* substitution of soviets for the duma.

In order to retain power, the little group of Bolshevik leaders was forced to a rapid return to tsarist measures of repression. A political police, the *cheka*,[2] was used to terrorize all opposition, and

---

[2] The name, like so many words in Soviet terminology, is derived from the initial letters or syllables of the Russian. The political police has undergone several reorganizations; for a time it was known as the GPU; then as the NKVD; at present as the MVD.

even against Social Democrats. When the constituent assembly was finally permitted to meet at the beginning of February, 1918, its SR majority was given an ultimatum to accept the Bolshevik revolution. Upon its refusal to accept the ultimatum the assembly was forcibly dissolved by Trotsky and Lenin. A decree abolishing landlord-ownership of land kept the peasants busy seizing the land while the Bolsheviks consolidated their power over the workmen and the cities and at the same time ruined the heart of the counter-revolutionary groups, the landholding aristocracy. Passive resistance took the form of sabotage and refusal to work. The banks were nationalized, so that people would not have resources with which to live without working; and other aspects of Russian economy were nationalized at a fairly rapid pace in an effort to combat lack of co-operation with government. By ruthless suppression the Bolsheviks secured control of the cities without immediate civil war.

The Bolshevik appeal to the peoples and governments of belligerents to make peace—without annexations or contributions—was answered only by the Germans. Germany made full use of the Russian collapse, and Trotsky, the negotiator, refused to sign the severe peace terms she offered. As there was no Russian army, the government could not fight; and Lenin urged that peace must be signed since the preservation of the revolution demanded that one of the dangers it faced be removed. Peace was signed on the German terms, which meant the loss of Finland, the Baltic provinces, Poland, the Ukraine, and part of the Caucasus. By this treaty, signed at Brest-Litovsk, March 15, 1918, Russia lost 25% of her prewar territory and 44% of her population.

The Allies had welcomed the first revolution, hopeful that it would mean a more effective prosecution of the war. The Bolshevik revolution and the Brest-Litovsk treaty affected the war adversely since it enabled the Central Powers to concentrate on the western front. Military aid was imperative. A great asset of the Allies was the blockade of Germany that their command of the sea had made possible. The Germans had proclaimed a blockade of the British Isles and tried to enforce it by unrestricted use of the submarine. At first as a result of American protest they modified their methods, but at the beginning of 1917 they renewed unrestricted submarine warfare in the hope of forcing Britain out of the war. The United States thereupon entered the war on the side of the Allies. Both

Great Britain and Germany had invaded neutral rights in the course of the war, but the unrestricted submarine campaign was costing American lives whereas British search and seizure had injured only pocketbooks. The German submarine nearly won the war. By the end of 1917, however, the Allies were launching ships faster than the Germans could sink them, and although the losses had been high, the submarine menace was overcome.

The entrance of the United States into the war brought into prominence one of the most important weapons in modern warfare —propaganda. Propaganda in wartime has several purposes—to make the enemy appear iniquitous, usually by means of atrocity stories; to whitewash one's own cause by identifying it with religion and by exalting one's own heroes; and to undermine enemy morale. In the early stages of the war the aims of the belligerents were imperialist and greedy. The allied powers had made secret partition treaties. In 1917 Wilson came into the war, wanting no territory, fighting on foreign soil in a war not obviously defensive, and having to rationalize his position. He launched the legend of the holy war, the crusade for civilization, a war to end war and make the world safe for democracy. The Russian revolutions, ending tsardom, were a fortuitous circumstance. Wilson was completely sincere, and had to be, for his propaganda was for himself as well as others. It kept people favoring the war, undermined German morale, paved the way for the collapse of the German and Austrian empires, and gave a moral basis for the peace.

Before the American expeditionary force had greatly affected the fighting front, Wilson proclaimed fourteen points essential to a peace with the German people, carefully distinguished from their government. Among these points was the principle of self-determination for all nationalities. This helped to deprive the national groups in the Hapsburg monarchy of an incentive to fight for the preservation of the empire and contributed materially to the disintegration of Austria-Hungary into its component national parts. It was broadly hinted in Allied propaganda that the imperial German government was unsatisfactory; when German generals in the late summer of 1918 announced they could no longer hope to win the war and when peace proposals indicated the government's weakness, Emperor William II was induced to abdicate and an armistice was concluded.

There was no Talleyrand among the German delegates to the

Paris Peace Conference in 1919, and the German delegates were not even admitted to the peace table until the Treaty of Versailles was ready for their signatures. The representatives of France and England succeeded in getting into the treaty most, but not all, of the provisions of their secret treaties. President Wilson concentrated on the insertion into the treaty of his plan for a League of Nations which would, he hoped, revise those terms of the treaty which were inequitable. The Allied Powers had decided that Austria-Hungary must be dismembered, that German territory should be reduced, and that a line of buffer states should be erected between the central powers and Russia to immunize them from the spread of Bolshevism, which was the terror of western statesmen. This plan fitted in with the Wilsonian principle of the self-determination of peoples. Poland was made an independent state, with a strip of territory reaching to the sea and dividing East Prussia from the rest of Germany. The Czechs were given their ancient kingdom of Bohemia, to which were added Moravia and Slovakia—an arrangement which departed from the principle of self-determination in the case of the two latter regions but did create a state well-placed for economic development and for defense against a possible recrudescence of German aggression. Hungary was made independent, and a group of Serbs, Croats, and Slovenes was created as the kingdom of Yugoslavia to carry the line of "Succession States" to the Mediterranean. Italy, which was not given the eastern Adriatic littoral she had expected, regarded the Austrian Tyrol as an insufficient reward for her services. Austria was reduced to a small territory around Vienna. The German colonies were parcelled out to the powers chiefly interested, not as outright possessions but according to an ingenious scheme of mandates under the League of Nations.

The treaty contained an avowal which the German delegates signed under protest that Germany had been solely responsible for the war. On the basis of this avowal Germany was to pay an indemnity, not fixed but on a sliding scale which was to rise as the Germans showed signs of recovery. The complete abolition of German armaments was decreed, with general disarmament to follow. Strong isolationist sentiment in the United States and partisan political tactics made it impossible for Wilson to secure American ratification of the Versailles Treaty because of its inclusion of the League of Nations as an integral part. Finally the United States made a treaty in which it ratified all the provisions of the treaty except the international organization clauses, thus endorsing all the bad points and ignoring the most constructive. Without the United States as a member, and with Germany and Russia excluded, the League of Nations was dominated by Great Britain and France. The English desired German recovery because the Germans had been their best customers; the French dreaded it because with good reason they feared a renewal of German aggression. France had been led to believe that England and the United States would guarantee assistance in such a case. When it became evident that the belief was mistaken, France became implacable against Germany, and a few years after the war, when Germany failed to make the reparation payments due, took advantage of the opportunity to occupy the German industrial districts of the Rhineland.

War industry had brought wealth to many, and it was not at first obvious that the enormous expenditures of the war were threatening to ruin the victorious as well as the vanquished nations. The United States had become a creditor nation, but her legislators, not realizing that a creditor nation must accept goods and services in payment of debts, raised tariffs instead of lowering them. In Europe the succession states put up tariff walls, and international trade was disrupted in an area which had a natural economic unity. In short, the exclusiveness of nationalism was transferred to the field of economy. The wartime and brief post-war prosperity of the United States was followed by a serious depression which affected the whole world; in all industrial countries except Russia there was unemployment and unrest, and the well-to-do feared a communist revolution.

The Russian revolution of March, 1917, had been moderate, but the Bolshevik revolution was something different. The fear of communism among conservative and property-owning people was partly the result of the excesses of the Bolsheviks and partly of the theoretical basis of their activities. There was haziness about much of the theory, but that it envisaged the disappearance of capitalism was generally recognized. After March, 1918, there was open civil war in Russia and Siberia between the Bolsheviks and other Russian groups, usually headed by tsarist officers. Always an allied expeditionary force came to the aid of the anti-Bolsheviks. The expressed aim of these forces was to prevent the acquisition by Germans of war supplies sent by the Allies to Russia; a real motive of foreign intervention was undoubtedly fear of the new régime. The effect of the intervention, however, was to consolidate the Bolsheviks and put the country behind them against those who supported the foreigners, who were English, Americans, Czechs, Poles, and Japanese.

The peasantry supported the Bolsheviks because the counter-revolutionary forces attempted to restore landlord ownership of land. None of the counter-revolutionary movements attempted to restore tsarism. The exigencies of the situation forced the Bolsheviks to adopt, apparently faster than they had intended, a highly centralized government. In September, 1918, in response to SR individual terror, the Bolsheviks decreed mass terror; groups were executed, even members of the group who had not actually taken part in the act of opposition in question. Mass terror was intended to break the spirit of opposition groups and classes. The three years of civil war, with fighting, mass terror, and destruction of property, cost Russia as much as her participation in the World War. The intervention and the civil war made it possible for the Bolsheviks to justify the extreme measures used, both with the peasants and with their own followers. As a consequence they were safe at home, but there was no world revolution, as the leaders had expected and hoped.

The first Soviet constitution, in 1918, established the Russian Socialist Federated Soviet Republic. It set up class institutions with indirect election; and since the government was a proletarian dictatorship, representation was weighted in favor of the workers. The name of the party was changed to Russian Communist Party (Bolshevik) in order to dissociate it from all other Socialist groups and parties. The government was designed to have a broad democratic base with the executive committees at the top, but in practice the executive committees were appointed from above. There was not the division of executive and legislative power characteristic of western European and American constitutional development. Institutions which could not be sovietized were abolished, except the church, which was rigidly separated from the state, education, and all social services. Toleration was extended to all non-Orthodox sects but they were allowed to maintain only places of worship. Institutions which were sovietized were eventually given government functions. In the winter of 1923–24 the Union of Socialist Soviet Republics (USSR) was formed. In theory, it was voluntary. The largest unit was the RSFSR, and the most important organizations in the USSR were not federal but centralized—the party, soviets, army, trade unions, and so on.

The period from 1918 to 1921 is known as the period of war communism. The expression was used after 1921 to explain the failure of the economic policy of those years. The leaders insisted that war communism was not the real economic policy of their party but a policy dictated by circumstances, that the events of the civil war and intervention had forced the leaders to go faster and further than was originally intended. The policy under war communism was drastic, and it was an utter failure. A state monopoly of trade, food production, and supply was instituted as a weapon to combat opposition. The land was nationalized but granted to the peasants for use. Since the state owned the land it determined what was the surplus yield, claimed it, and subjected the peasants to requisitioning. In retaliation the peasants refused to sow more than enough for their own immediate needs, and by the spring of 1921 only one half of the prewar acreage was in cultivation. Under centralized control all products, raw materials, consumers' goods—in short all results of economic activity—were rationed and the rationing system was used to discriminate against opposition groups.

Since the state distribution system did not meet the minimum needs of even those highest on the rationing system, peasant smuggling developed widely. Efficient management and labor discipline were not promoted in large manufacturing units by the workman control the Bolsheviks had instituted. By the end of 1920 there was a marked decrease in the number of workers and production declined to about 15% of the prewar figure. A tremendous currency inflation—designed to break the middle class—made accounting impossible. By 1921 all raw materials and even the reserves of equipment inherited from the tsarist régime were used up. It was asserted by the leaders that socialism (i.e., in the Marxian sense of proletarian control and exploitation of the means and instruments of production) could not be established without the resources of a more industrialized country than backward Russia. The failure on the economic front was becoming a political threat because of the wide discontent, for the action of the workmen and peasants was discrediting the revolution.

With characteristic courage Lenin announced that the government had gone too fast, and made a strategic retreat. Gradually the

New Economic Policy (NEP, 1921–28) was developed, marking a distinct period of the revolution. Requisitioning was abolished, and a fixed tax in kind was applied, announced in advance of the sowing. The surplus was to be under the complete control of the peasants for free disposal. In 1923 the payment in kind was changed to payment in money, and a stable currency was established. Land was held individually and could be rented for limited periods; labor could be hired for cultivation, but sale or mortgage of land was prohibited. The smaller industries were denationalized by leasing to individual owners, to be operated for individual profit. The new capitalistic class thus formed was, however, deprived of political rights and was considered a hostile economic force. The Nepmen were tolerated but not trusted. The government retained considerable control of raw materials and machinery, while large-scale industry, mines, oil wells, and power developments remained state enterprises and were not denationalized. Control of the commanding heights, as Lenin said, enabled the proletarian state to encourage or discourage individual efforts and to keep the people on the road toward socialism. Since the basic aim of the NEP was to get production going again, the state had to be careful in the application of measures of repression. The state also retained the monopoly of foreign trade. The NEP

AUTOMOBILE OF 1912

(Copyright by the Locomobile Club of America. Bridgeport, Connecticut, 1911.)

accomplished its purpose—the resumption of economic processes—
and by 1927 Russia had nearly reached the level of production that
had prevailed in 1913.

Lenin died early in 1924, after many months of partial incapacitation following a stroke. There is an old Russian saying: "The greatest tsar must be put to bed with a shovel at last." To the great mass of Russians Lenin was the symbol of Holy Russia, as the tsar had been. He was the greatest of the tsars, for he had given the people their land, and to every one of them he had given a hope of a better world. They did not put him to bed with a shovel, but his embalmed body was placed in the Red Square in Moscow so that Russians could always look at the man who had given them the land and the vision.

CHAPTER 31

The World of Winston Churchill
[1874 –

~~~~~~~~~~~~~~~~~~~~~~~~~~~~~~~~~~

WINSTON LEONARD SPENCER CHURCHILL, the son of an English father and an American mother, was born on November 30, 1874. His paternal ancestry was distinguished; his father, Lord Randolph Churchill, was a younger son of the seventh duke of Marlborough and a brilliant Conservative Party figure in Parliament. His most famous ancestor was John Churchill, created duke of Marlborough for his spectacular services against the French aggrandizement of Louis XIV in the War of the Spanish Succession. Winston Churchill belonged to that world of great English families which had a powerful voice in the management of the British Empire in the nineteenth century even after a series of reform bills had begun to chip away the political entrenchment of the landed and moneyed aristocracy. Educated at Harrow and Sandhurst, he had the traditional English public school training for a political and army career, and spent brief periods in actual field service.

From the outset Winston Churchill's career was linked with the fate of Britain as an empire. His earliest prominence came as an author of books on his experiences in India, the great proving ground of British talent in the nineteenth century, and as a correspondent in the Boer War in South Africa. First elected to Parliament in 1900 as a Conservative, after a few years he joined the Liberal Party and as under-secretary for colonies was a brilliant champion of the policy that led to the organization of the Union of South Africa. He was also an active supporter of the Liberal Party's program of social legislation to benefit English workingmen in the years before World War I. In 1911, Asquith, the Liberal prime minister, put Churchill in the cabinet office responsible for naval affairs, where he made a

[547

considerable contribution to the reorganization of British naval command in preparation for the war that began in 1914. Churchill always retained a nineteenth century conviction of the importance of the navy as a paladin of empire.

Churchill's direction of naval affairs in the early period of the World War involved him in another major legacy of nineteenth century British foreign policy—the ancient problem of Turkey at the Straits, the Russian outlet to the sea. The Dardanelles campaign of 1915, a daring gamble to beat a supply path to southern Russia through the aggressive use of naval power, was Churchill's conception. The failure of that campaign was a contributing factor in the fall of the Liberal government of which Churchill was a member. During the middle part of the war Churchill saw military service in France and was then recalled to political office in the government of Lloyd George, where he held various cabinet offices until 1922. As secretary for war Churchill directed the active military intervention against the Bolsheviks in Russia. During the period of his brief retirement from 1922–24 Churchill changed once again to the Conservative Party and upon his return to Parliament was given cabinet rank in the Conservative government.

The problems of eastern and southeastern Europe, with which Churchill was so closely associated in his first great war leadership, justly occupy a crucial position in the twentieth century world between the wars of 1914 and 1939. If the Balkans were the tinderbox of Europe in 1914, the same region, extended to the Baltic in 1939 and to the eastern Mediterranean in 1948, may still be so regarded. Yet for a brief decade and a half following the armistice of 1918 there was evidence to give hope that for the first time in more than a century some measure of peace and progress might be achieved in southeastern Europe. The war and its aftermath brought about the final liquidation of the Turkish Empire, which had been both a brake upon modernization in southeastern Europe, and a recurrent battleground for the imperialism of France, Great Britain, Russia, and Austria-Hungary.

Although the Turks in 1919 had seemed to be the most completely defeated of the Central Powers and their satellites, the Turks were the only victims who successfully defied Allied dictation in the final peace settlement. A Turkish nationalist movement similar to the nationalist self-determination movement of the Balkan peoples had been developing under the leadership of the group known as the Young Turks whose movement received considerable stimulus after Turkey's defeat in the war. This combination of circumstances was utilized by Mustapha Kemal Pasha to achieve the completely successful Kemalist revolution. Under his leadership the Turks resolved to fight the Treaty of Sèvres (although it had been accepted by the sultan and the Constantinople officials) because it embodied the imperialistic aims of the great powers and reduced Turkey to economic dependence on these powers. The British and French—victors falling out over other spoils—could not agree on a plan of intervention, while the Greeks and Italians were on the verge of war over the division of former Turkish islands in the Aegean. The Turks played up the jealousies of the powers and when the Greeks made a military effort to impose the Treaty of Sèvres they had to make it alone. Although they were at first successful, Mustapha Kemal eventually succeeded in driving them completely out of Asia Minor. The Turkish leader was an able, veteran officer who had put together an organization with something to fight for, operating on its home grounds.

By 1921 the Turks had concluded a French alliance and then a treaty with Italy. In both cases they made economic concessions in return for relinquishment of the terms of the Treaty of Sèvres. The peak of the Turkish diplomatic success was a treaty with bolshevist Russia; the two powers made an offensive and defensive alliance and declared their solidarity against European imperialism. The price the Turks paid was the cession of most of Armenia to Russia, but in the end the Treaty of Sèvres was submitted to revision and in 1923 the Treaty of Lausanne was signed. Turkey received the whole of Asia Minor, kept a part of the province of Thrace in Europe, eliminated all restrictions on her sovereignty at Constantinople, and canceled all of the reparations payments. The minority question between Greece and Turkey was eased by the provision of an exchange of population. The bitter hostility between the two peoples was so ameliorated by this arrangement that by the 1930s the two countries were actually in alliance. The new Turkey emerged as a sovereign state, except for the neutralization and demilitarization of the Straits. By 1936 even that restriction was abandoned in the Montreux Straits Convention.

The Treaty of Lausanne was probably the fairest of the post-war treaties. It was a negotiated, not a dictated, treaty. That this was possible was due largely to the elimination of the Hapsburg monarchy and tsarist Russia during the war, together with the temporary collapse of the German Empire and the preoccupation of France and Great Britain with other major problems. It would be hard to overemphasize the importance of these factors for an understanding of the reason Turkey (as well as the Balkan states) was allowed the unusual opportunity of working out her own destiny—in stark contrast to nineteenth century and pre-1914 practice among the great powers.

In the new Turkey legislative and executive powers were united under a unicameral Grand National Assembly, indirectly elected on the basis of universal manhood and womanhood suffrage. Executive authority was delegated to a president of the republic, elected by the assembly for four-year terms, and a cabinet chosen by the president which was theoretically responsible to the assembly. The Republican People's Party had all the delegates to the Grand National Assembly except some score of independent delegates, permitted for criticism of detail, not policy. Party discipline was insisted upon, following a program set at a quadrennial congress of the party, and the party filled practically all administrative posts. Beyond these features the Republican People's Party did not have the paraphernalia of single-party systems in other totalitarian states. Since Turkey's population is 70 per cent peasant the simple structure of the government seemed desirable while the enormous task of educating and secularizing a backward people accustomed to theocratic rule was attempted. The ideal of Mustapha Kemal, which was achieved in most essentials, was a new Turkey which would be independent—and Turkish.

During the immediate post-war decade the unhappy Balkan states enjoyed a temporary respite from the extremes of European great power diplomacy. The strategic significance of the Balkans with respect to the Danube valley and the Straits remained unchanged, and the economic significance of the Balkans as raw materials suppliers still invited exploitation by industrial countries. The intruding Ottoman, tsarist Russia, and Hapsburg empires, however, were gone. The resulting vacuum permitted the development of peasant parties in the several Balkan states, which before 1914 had been under the control of more or less foreign-supported class governments of a semireactionary character. Under the lead of such great peasant party spokesmen as Stambulisky in Bulgaria or Radich in Yugoslavia there was increasing recognition of the value of federation to promote progress in individual states. Unusual success in steps toward Balkan union between 1930 and 1934, unfortunately was followed by a recrudescence of great power pressure in the Balkan peninsula. Following the establishment of the Hitler régime in Germany, the old imperfectly submerged nationalistic rivalries of the Balkan states were revived in the general European jockeying between revisionist and *status quo* countries. In the scramble for diplomatic position in the thirties the Balkan countries were caught again between the aggressive imperialism of Germany and Italy on the one hand, and the eastern Mediterranean interests of France, Great Britain, and the Soviet Union on the other. As was the case before 1914, the prospect of effective Balkan union in the interest of the Balkan peoples pleased no combination of great powers.

Imperial Britain probably faced the most acute problems of any of the powers whose conflicting interests met in that troubled zone of Europe which extends deep into the eastern Mediterranean. The British Empire-Commonwealth emerged from World War I more extensive and, on the surface, more powerful than before. The best traditions of British imperialism suggested that the empire was held in trust—witness the freedom to be allowed to self-governing dominions—but in large sectors there seemed to be no adequate policy that would lead to an early liquidation of the trust. This criticism was increasingly made with respect to Palestine and India. Palestine offers an excellent example of a political problem that proved incapable of settlement on the basis of justice to the people directly concerned in the area. It is a practical impossibility today to disregard the emotional interest of Jews and Arabs outside Palestine. It is equally impossible to ignore the pressure of power politics in any area close to a strategic waterway like the Suez Canal, or close to the great oil reserves of the Arabian-inhabited Near East. In the case of India Britain faced probably the greatest single imperial problem of the world. The power of imperialism to arouse nationalism—so well demonstrated in the nineteenth century—was even more strikingly evidenced by India, which had none whatsoever, but developed between 1919 and 1939 a notable nationalist movement. The failure of Britain to solve the problem of trusteeship in Palestine and India before 1939 along nineteenth century lines of colonial development meant that at the conclusion of the next great war she was forced to accept an extremist solution.

The efforts of southeastern Europe, the Near and Middle East, to throw off the leading strings of European imperialism constituted only one facet of post-1919 nationalism. The states of Europe increasingly resorted to economic nationalism as a substitute for the more or less self-regulating system of international trade destroyed by the war. Paced by the United States of America, which enjoyed an unprecedented position in international finance and trade as a consequence of the war, one nation after another raised formidable barriers to the flow of trade with its neighbors. The desire for national self-sufficiency, carried to its logical extreme, helped to prevent the general economic recovery upon which the prosperity of all depended and contributed to the vast economic depression of the early 1930s. Mass unemployment, and its accompanying political unrest, confronted hard-pressed governments everywhere with the unsolved problem of social justice and demands for still further intervention of the state in economic life.

The international repercussions of internal policy began to become even more clear after the creation of the Hitler government in Germany in 1933. The resurgence of Germany pointed up certain internal factors in Great Britain and France, and helped to bring about a change in the Soviet Union's policy of internal warfare against its own subjects. On the whole the Soviet Union was neglected in western European plans for the containment of Germany, due in no small part to the unwillingness of such groups as the Conservative Party in Great Britain to co-operate with bolshevism. As a result France became the kingpin in anti-German systems.

From the standpoint of demographic and economic potential France was a fatally weak kingpin. France had been the main sufferer as respects manpower from the war of 1914–18. With a static birth rate, a vast empire necessitating heavy defensive obligations, and the biological losses of the war still uncompensated by 1939, France might well be expected to hesitate before making sacrifices that could mean her annihilation as a force in Europe. Everything else being equal, a nation of forty million could not afford to fight one of seventy million, whose industrial output was superior. France had traditionally maintained a close balance between agricultural and industrial production in her economy. In the past this diversity had contributed to quick French recovery from the ravages of war, but it also meant that French industry was based to a greater degree on a home market and quality products than that of Germany or Great Britain and was therefore less adaptable to the requirements of modern industrial war. French governments consistently tended to check emigration from land to city, instead of directing a further exodus from the land to raise industrial production and lower the burden on agricultural production of high cost small-unit farming.

Indeed, few governments of Europe had met head-on the fact of a large proletariat, which had grown slowly with the industrialism that most great powers encouraged. Progressive broadening of franchise and the entrance of labor into politics had not been sufficient. The old basis of government, which had been protection of the security of property, did not meet the needs of the proletariat, which was interested in the security of wages. The approach to work of the proletariat generally was collective and not individual. Yet the free trade-union movement which developed step by step with the growth of the proletariat in many ways served as a bulwark of existing liberal governmental institutions. Wherever trade unions were allowed freedom to contract with employers and could arbitrate without interference they were part of the traditional democratic and even capitalist pattern of society which was the condition of their existence. Labor in politics before 1914 had led to the development of socialist parties as important elements in every major parliamentary system and had produced valuable social legislation for the benefit of working people. This progress was interrupted by the war, hampered partly by lack of incentive in the prosperity of reconstruction or by economic necessity during the great depression of the latter twenties and the thirties.

In those parts of Europe where the government had directly faced the problem of a proletariat and the issue of social justice raised by industrialism, the solution was not enviable. The Soviet answer was nationalization, but this example of emphasis on collective economic security was accompanied by such open disregard for individual political or intellectual freedom that it found no important imitators before 1939. In Germany and Italy government authority imposed compulsory settlement of disputes and eliminated industrial war between management and labor. The temptation to accept compulsory arbitration as a solution to the problem of industry-labor relations was tempting, but the consequences again were unattractive. When a democratic government attempts to coerce large groups in the population it runs serious risk of demonstrating its weakness or of being compelled to resort to undemocratic means. Neither Germany nor Italy succeeded in solving the problem of social justice by compulsory arbitration without losing what other western European countries and the United States generally understand democracy to mean.

The dilemma of how to recognize the new forces at work in twentieth century industrial society without losing long-established values of representative democratic governmental process, individual liberty, and human dignity was unresolved when the European world went to war in 1939. Perhaps not the least tragedy of that between-wars period was the paucity of young leaders in Europe. Most of the potential leaders of that generation fell in the carnage of 1914-18. And so when Great Britain faced her most desperate crisis of the twentieth century in the new world war of 1939 it was an old leader, Winston Churchill, to whom she turned and who led his fellow countrymen through the conflict.

Winston Churchill was an old leader in the sense that he represented a dead world whose ghost still walked abroad. He stood for a nineteenth century conception of privilege in society and government at home, and privilege in imperial exploitation of colonial areas abroad which was more and more an anachronism. Yet he was utterly unconscious of being out of place, and paradoxically that magnificent arrogance from the past probably saved the cause of Great Britain in the war when her continental allies had all fallen in 1940. It could never have occurred to Winston Churchill that there might not always be an England, as he knew England. During a great war growing out of old evils, when England struggled for survival, Winston Churchill became the spokesman and the symbol of victory for all that was greatest in the tradition of England. He was an essential link with the glorious old order while the war lasted—but expendable when the time came to attack the problems of a new peace and a new society at the war's end.

CHAPTER 32

Our World

~~~~~~~~~~~~~~~~~~~

THE general peace established at Versailles in 1919 and confirmed by supplementary treaties lasted only twenty years. One reason why peace did not last longer was the spread of nationalism. In the so-called Succession States nationalism expressed itself in tariff barriers —a ruinous policy for peoples living in a natural economic unit like the Danube valley. Nationalism also expressed itself in the harsh treatment of minorities, giving them grievances that could be exploited by other nations. Czechoslovakia, the most prosperous Succession State, had a very heterogeneous assortment of minorities, but on the whole governed them wisely. Even the Germans in Czechoslovakia, who stubbornly retained their own national customs, were prosperous and satisfied until alienated by propaganda from Germany. Like the Czechs, the Poles set up a republic; and encouraged by the recognition of their historic claims to an outlet to the sea (Gdynia), they proceeded to occupy other old possessions and got into trouble with their neighbors, Lithuania and Russia. The Baltic states—Lithuania, Latvia, and Estonia—turned their backs on Soviet Russia. In Hungary the Magyars set up a communist government that was soon replaced by a reactionary one, favored by the great powers under the delusion that the Magyars might otherwise accept the domination of Soviet Russia. In the Balkans the Serbs controlled the Yugoslav government, and were opposed at every turn by the Croats and Slovenes. Added to all this nationalistic lack of harmony within the small nations of Europe was increasing friction among the larger victorious nations. Soldiers who had returned home to America, England, and France were scornful of the achievements and habits of their late comrades-in-arms. Germany was not immune to this nationalist reaction. Since the Allied armies had not entered German territory until after the armistice, it was easy for nationalist leaders to persuade the people that they had not suffered military defeat. Accordingly there was general support for the Junker military caste as they began secretly to re-form the army. The well-meaning men who ran the republican government at Weimar did not have the courage to oppose the Junkers nor to halt their covert rearming of Germany. Later they proved equally helpless before the great industrialists whose mines and factories were busy with rearmament. Nationalism was spreading rapidly to the Orient too. Young men trained in European or American universities went back to their native lands full of enthusiasm for leading their people to a better and more independent way of life.

In Russia a new generation was growing up, trained to regard the new Russia as the best of all possible worlds, but the rest of the world, except for some neighboring countries, long remained aloof. Following Lenin's death bitter factional strife broke out in the party. In 1926 the opposition, in which Trotsky was the leading figure, was expelled from the party and then exiled from Russia. Joseph Stalin (1878–) emerged with the upper hand, and the party was—and is—kept orthodox and fanatical by the same iron discipline Lenin had insisted upon from the beginning. There are periodic purges in the party for disciplinary purposes; usually expulsion from the party is sufficient, though the purge of 1937 was one of blood, with numerous executions. Although world revolution as a policy was discarded after Lenin's death and Trotsky's expulsion, technically the revolution is still in progress; the goal of a classless, communist society has not yet been achieved and the present socialist régime is regarded as a transitional stage.

Although Lenin died midway of the NEP, the third phase of the Soviet economic policy that began in 1928 was not inconsistent with his theory and practice. The dispute within the party that had come to a head in 1926 and resulted in Stalin's triumph was in part a controversy over tactics. In 1928 it became obvious that there could not be more production without either more capitalism or more socialism and economic planning. Therefore the NEP, which Lenin had always regarded as only a half withdrawal, had reached the end of its usefulness. It could not increase production without some coordination of effort in either a socialist or capitalist way. It was decided to resume the socialist offensive, both for political and economic reasons; capitalism might become strong enough to turn into a political danger. Therefore a commission to integrate Russian life in a socialist scheme by gigantic planning was set up and the period of the five-year plans began.

The primary emphasis in the first five-year plan was on heavy industry. This emphasis was necessary for a twofold reason: economically, expansion and new construction were fundamental to the further industrialization of Russia; politically, it was imperative to increase the numerical weight of the proletariat in the population as a whole. In order to collectivize agriculture and thus bring the peasants into the socialist scheme, there was class war in a literal sense. Force was used to bring the peasants—and their belongings—into collectives; control over the collectives after formation was maintained by keeping agricultural equipment in state-operated stations. Machinery was loaned, not actually turned over, to the collectives. By 1932, 64% of peasants were in collectives—three times the figure set by the first five-year plan. The speed at which the process was carried out had been tremendous, but production had not increased according to the plan. In fact production was reduced, and there was famine in 1933, but from a political standpoint the socialization of agriculture had been necessary. Industry could not be maintained on a socialist basis while agriculture was on an individualist basis.

A fundamental paradox that helps explain the inconsistencies of bolshevik Russia was that the leaders were trying to achieve a utopia of classless society by means of ruthless, repressive dictatorship; it involved much suffering, but it was a noble ideal and no defeatism was permitted. In many ways Russia seemed democratic; there was wide suffrage, though certain classes were disenfranchised, but those were mainly liquidated by 1936. There was remarkable equality of men and women and of subject non-Russian nationalities. No private wealth was permitted to corrupt government. On the other hand in many ways Russia was not democratic. There was over-representation to workers at the expense of the peasants until 1936; there existed an extremely powerful executive and the Communist Party—the name was adopted by the Bolsheviks in 1919—was the only legal political party. It formulated the policy and had all the real power since its leaders were the executive. Despite interesting social and economic experiments, Russia was a totalitarian state with strong tyranny. The Communist Party was kept orthodox, and fanatical, by an iron hand and periodic purges. The practicability of the world revolution was discarded and Stalin made socialism a nationalist affair, wishing to make Russia the shining example when the rest of the world got around to the inevitable revolution.

Economic policy in Russia has experienced three phases: a period of war communism (1918–21), which was drastic and an utter failure; the New Economic Policy (1921–28), when a partial return to capitalistic organization was encouraged in order to get production under way again; and the era of the five-year plans after 1928, when the socialist offensive was resumed.

The desire to become independent of the West—never fully realized—made possible some spectacular achievements in heavy industry during the first five-year plan. The achievements of the plan, however, came at a very high cost in living standards, which became noticeably and progressively worse. Consequently under the second five-year plan consumer goods were emphasized and there was a considerable easing up of pressure, economically and politically. The Stalin constitution of 1936 equalized the representation for workers and peasants, and created no disenfranchised classes. An increasing differentiation of wages did not exactly produce a new class because the standard of living had to be extended on earnings, not on unearned increment from privately owned property or investments. In the middle of 1936 production began to decline and pressure was reasserted. At the end of the second five-year plan the international situation was so threatening that the chief emphasis on the production front was war equipment.

The resumption of the socialist offensive which the five-year plans indicated did not bring a resumption of the socialist offensive in other countries. Stalin insisted on holding to the decision that socialism could be built in one country regardless of the rest of the world. The building material was not of the best. Russia, backward, not industrially-minded, did not fit the program of the revolution. There was too much Russia and there were too few industrial workers; considering the European opposition there was too much Europe for the experiment. But the declaration of the constitution of 1936 that the Soviet Union was a socialist state is supported by the fact that in 1939 there was 98% or more state ownership or collectivization of the means or instruments of production. There was no private ownership. There are still two classes because of the difference in the relationship of the workman and the peasant to production. The workman is a wage earner, the peasant is a member of a collective group. The basic differences have been eliminated and the peasant is considered closer to the proletarian state under the collectivization of agriculture. The right to work is guaranteed, so there is no unemployment, but work is also an obligation, and recalcitrant groups are put to forced labor.

In Italy, which also fell into turbulence and anarchy at the end of the war, deliverance for workers and capitalists alike was promised by Benito Mussolini, a former Socialist who formed a party pledged to revive the glories of ancient Rome. Taking their name from the *fasces,* an axe bound with rods which had been the emblem of Roman jurisdiction, the Fascists began by attacking Communists and Socialists. After the so-called "March to Rome" in 1922, Mussolini received the office of premier from the king and proceeded to organize a dictatorship under the form of a corporate state, where all were to sacrifice their individual interests for the common good. Opposition was put down by the most bestial means, of which the administration of large doses of castor oil was typical. Mussolini pleased Catholics by making an agreement with the pope, delighted archaeologists by ordering the Rome of the Caesars dug up and restored, and dazzled the younger generation by telling them that the future was in the hands of youth who were ready for war. He impressed tourists by cleaning up cities and policing them by pairs of boys in neat military dress, he saw that trains ran on time, and he openly planned for war as the highest destiny of mankind.

These sentiments struck a discordant note among discussions of disarmament in a world where peace was to be assured by the League of Nations. In the Covenant of the League the member states promised to protect one another's territory and independence, to reduce armaments, to submit disputes to peaceful examination, and in no case to go to war until three months after decision; members undertook to break commercial and financial dealings with violators; members authorized the Council of the League to recommend military measures for backing up economic sanctions. The League had an Assembly, in which all states were equally represented; a Council, in which the great powers had a privileged position by their permanent seats; and a Secretariat that provided expert investigation and publicity. To encourage the peaceful settlement of international disputes a Permanent Court of International Justice (World Court) was set up, and to improve social conditions and help regulate labor relations an International Labor Office was established. By means of the various international organizations much effective work was done during the first decade after the war in the study of problems of international concern, mainly in non-political fields. Politically, the League was able to settle difficulties between small states, but demonstrated a fatal weakness in dealing with great powers or their proteges. The United States steadfastly refused to join the League, but Germany was admitted in 1926, and even Russia in 1934.

Unfortunately at the beginning of the nineteen-thirties an economic depression of world-wide scope enervated the leading nations upon which the success of the League depended. Partly an aftermath of the tremendous economic disruption created by World War I, and aggravated by widespread economic nationalism, conditions of economic depression helped give rise to internal movements in several countries which subsequently developed into international aggression. The economic and commercial rivalry before the war in 1914 had found some outlet in the occupation of backward regions of the world not claimed by more progressive powers. Such areas no longer existed, and when national rivalries were spurred by economic distress in the thirties European powers were forced to vent their spleen on one another. Disarmament conferences bogged down in national jealousies. The United States, where the usual post-war overturn put a brake on Wilsonian policies, produced the Kellogg-Briand Pact (1927) whereby ultimately 53 nations pledged themselves not to employ war as an instrument of national policy, but doubts were currently voiced that this was more than the expression of a pious hope.

Great prosperity had been enjoyed by American business and manufacturing interests both before and during the war, and this cushioned for a time the effects of the enormous destruction of wealth in the war. In other countries widespread suffering, insecurity, and unrest were expressed by strikes and unemployment. A bellicose régime already existed in Italy in the form of Mussolini's dictatorship, and Italy's dissatisfaction with her share of spoils in World War I continued to rankle while economic conditions grew progressively worse. In Germany, another nation dissatisfied with the results of World War I and suffering from its economic consequences, the militant Nazi dictatorship of Adolph Hitler came into existence.

The immediate causes were the weakness of the Weimar republic, in spite of its model democratic constitution and the good intentions of its members, and a financial situation so acute that it was impossible for any ministry to tackle the financial burden and keep a majority in the legislature. The nationalists were few in numbers but represented influential army and industrial groups. At the opposite extreme, growing stronger through the depression, were the communists, whose weakness was that they were not nationalist. Hitler, who had been a corporal in World War I, used one disaffected group after another, raised a private army of thugs from flotsam and jetsam cast up by the war, and by promising all things to all men won considerable popular support. Intriguing with industrialists and nationalists who wanted to use him to crush socialism and communism, he became Chancellor of Germany in January, 1933. He reorganized the government on the fascist model, launched a program of anti-Semitism and intensely nationalist propaganda, and finally secured the fanatical support of the German people after carrying out the murder of hundreds of his own supporters. In the face of Hitler's militarist pronouncements, the members of the League rapidly lost all remaining interest in disarmament. Within a few years he had withdrawn Germany from the League of Nations, unilaterally denounced the disarmament clauses of the Versailles Treaty, and reoccupied the Rhineland.

The German withdrawal from the League had not been the first major defection. In 1931 a Japanese nationalist and militarist clique which had won control of the government from a liberal party inaugurated a notable series of acts of aggression by seizing Manchuria. Japan renamed the captured Chinese province Manchukuo and erected a puppet government there. China appealed for League action, but although the United States offered co-operation the British and French governments prevented anything beyond verbal condemnation, and Japan withdrew from the League. This failure to act against undisguised aggression set a bad precedent at an unfortunate moment. Italy and Germany, owing to internal unrest, were finding it increasingly important to distract popular interest with foreign adventures. The patent unwillingness of the so-called satiated powers—Great Britain and France—to take effective measures to stop aggression gave encouragement to the two fascist dictators of Europe.

The challenge to the League which offered the best opportunity for the collective security organization to show its power to halt aggression came in the Italian invasion of Ethiopia (1935). The time was opportune for Mussolini's exploit since France was undergoing a German scare and Laval, in charge of French foreign policy, was absorbed in the problem of security against German aggression. Laval and Mussolini privately agreed that France was to condone the Italian imperialist venture in Africa in return for Italian support against Hitler. The British position at this time was ambiguous; public opinion backed the League of Nations and collective efforts to preserve the peace, while the Conservative Party leadership which controlled the government wished to avoid taking any action carrying a risk of war. The only common denominator was the universal desire in Britain to avoid war. British prosperity depended upon a flourishing world trade and the avoidance of any disruption of world economic exchange. The lessons of World War I appeared self-evident to the English; as victors, they had suffered quite as heavily as the vanquished and were only in the middle thirties beginning to recover fully the commanding position in world trade which they had enjoyed before 1914. War was a folly which might easily destroy overnight not only renewed prosperity but the political dominance of the Conservative Party under whose auspices that prosperity was being achieved.

When Italy, after months of procrastinating negotiations which allowed full opportunity for military preparation, actually invaded Ethiopia, the League met and after a short delay declared economic sanctions in effect against the aggressor. One important item was omitted from the initial declaration—oil, without which the heavily mechanized Italian campaign would have been impossible. But Mussolini with most convincing bluster asserted that the imposition of oil sanctions would mean war. It was apparent that in a Mediterranean war the bulk of the responsibility for action would fall upon the British, the leading naval power. Although the British might reasonably expect a victorious war against a country so vulnerable to sea power as Italy, even small losses might seriously jeopardize the precariously-maintained British superiority on the seas. As for France, Laval was determined oil sanctions should not be applied, for they would surely ruin his Italian accord. It was such factors as these that led the British Foreign Secretary Hoare to conclude an agreement with Laval in which it was proposed to allow Mussolini a part of Ethiopia without further opposition and halt the brutal war. The agreement was a betrayal of League principles, and its premature revelation by Laval brought forth a storm of public indignation. Further consideration of oil sanctions became impracticable in view of the apparent willingness of the two leading League powers to sacrifice its principles. The Italian invasion against the ill-equipped Ethiopian army, marred by the use of poison gas and other practices in violation of international treaties, moved to its logical conclusion and Ethiopia was added to the Italian empire.

The failure of this effort of the League to employ its really formidable machinery for halting aggression was convincing evidence of the decline of the collective security idea. There still remained the possibility that the aggressive plans of the dictator states might be foiled if a firm stand were taken by the other leading powers. Further daring acts of aggression, however, soon proved that idea unfounded. On the heels of the Ethiopian crisis civil war broke out in Spain between the republican government and a group of insurgents led by General Franco. The republican régime represented a coalition of radical and liberal parties, supported by a large number of peasant and industrial proletarian elements and committed to a program of land distribution and anti-clericalism. Franco's insurgents represented the propertied classes who were the butt of the republican reform program, supported by most of the regular army, which had marked royalist leanings. They represented the revolt to be a war against communism and atheism. It would probably have been suppressed had it not been for liberal assistance from Italy and Germany which included foreign "volunteers" for Franco's army. Both Mussolini and Hitler made the Spanish Civil War (1936-39) a proving ground for officers, men, and equipment from their regular armies. Russia sent aid to the republican government, though in less quantity because of difficulties in getting it into Spain, and a general European war became a distinct possibility.

To avoid it, Great Britain and France took the lead in the formation of a non-intervention committee to prevent assistance to either side. The practical result was to prevent aid from reaching the beleaguered Loyalist forces, while Franco got whatever he needed. The neutrality policy of the United States contributed to the success of the non-intervention committee. France and Great Britain resolutely refused to notice the acts of open piracy committed by the fascist powers in preventing aid to the republican government; although public opinion in Britain and France was strongly republican, the industrial, banking, and other conservative elements were pro-Franco because he stood for the preservation of the interests of private property. The indescribable ferocity of the Spanish Civil War left Spain desolate when the conflict finally ended with Franco's victory, after vast destruction of material wealth, leaving a bitter legacy of hatred, and hundreds of thousands of political prisoners whose labor was desperately needed for reconstruction.

During the Spanish war Hitler and Mussolini made an agreement which they called the Rome-Berlin Axis. Hitler allied himself with Japan, and Mussolini joined both countries in a league against Communism (Anti-Comintern Pact). The initiative in the early acts of aggression had been largely that of Mussolini, but in 1938 his fellow-dictator, Hitler, assumed the leading role. The weakness of the League was plain. The supineness of the leading western democracies was amply demonstrated in the Spanish Civil War. For some time Hitler had, on every occasion, denounced the Versailles Treaty and declared his resolution to reunite all German peoples. He began to remilitarize the Rhineland. There was some acquiescence because of a widespread belief that the treaty of Versailles had been unjust and because of an acceptance of the principle of self-determination proclaimed at the Paris Peace Conference. And so the world watched while Austrian Nazis admitted German troops who overthrew the government at Vienna and annexed Austria to the Third Reich (1938).

In an effort to absorb all Germans into the Reich, Hitler began to make demands on Czechoslovakia, whose boundaries had been guaranteed by Great Britain and France and had been drawn on the basis of strategy rather than nationality. The greater part of the large German population lived in western districts along the Sudeten mountains; and to detach those areas would not only destroy the strategically-defensible Czech frontier but interfere with Czech economy by taking away much of the country's industrial production.

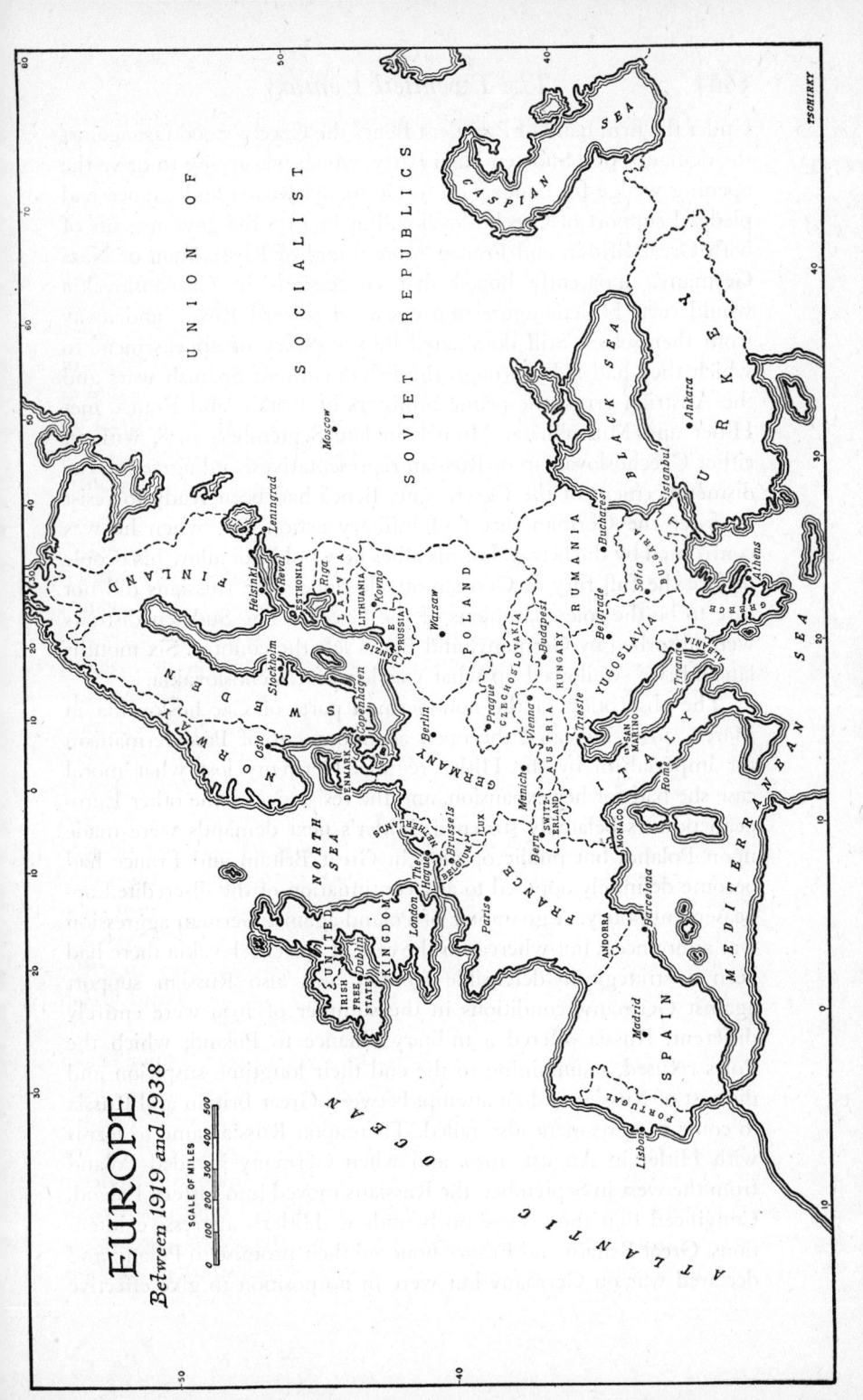

Under the firm hand of President Beneš the Czechs stood fast against the demands of a Sudeten Nazi Party, which was trying to drive the opening wedge for annexation to Germany. Russia and France had pledged support of Czechoslovakia, but in 1938 the governments of both Great Britain and France, more afraid of Russia than of Nazi Germany, apparently hoped that concessions in Czechoslovakia would turn Hitler's aggression eastward toward Russia and away from themselves. Still dominated by the policy of appeasement to which they had held through the Ethiopian and Spanish wars and the Austrian crisis, the prime ministers of Britain and France met Hitler and Mussolini at Munich in late September, 1938, without either Czechoslovakian or Russian representatives, and agreed to the dismemberment of the Czech state. Beneš had been ready to resist by force the German threat of military action, but when he was confronted by the betrayal of his allies he would not allow his people to face the full fury of German attack alone. The Russians did not care to be the sole champions of the Czechs. The Sudeten districts were absorbed by Germany, and Beneš left the country. Six months later Hitler swallowed up what was left of Czechoslovakia.

The absorption of the non-German parts of Czechoslovakia in March, 1939, indicated the open abandonment of Pan-Germanism for imperialism by the Hitler régime. Germany lost what moral case she had for her expansion, and the resistance of the other European powers belatedly stiffened. Hitler's next demands were made upon Poland, but public opinion in Great Britain and France had become definitely opposed to any continuation of the discredited appeasement policy. A guarantee of Poland against German aggression was announced, but whereas in the case of Czechoslovakia there had been a strategically-defensible frontier and also Russian support against Germany, conditions in the summer of 1939 were entirely different. Russia offered a military alliance to Poland, which the Poles refused, maintaining to the end their longtime suspicion and distrust of Russia; and an attempt between Great Britain and Russia to come to agreement also failed. Thereupon Russia came to terms with Hitler in August, 1939, and when Germany invaded Poland from the west in September, the Russians moved into eastern Poland. Convinced that there were no bounds to Hitler's aggressive intentions, Great Britain and France honored their promise to Poland and declared war on Germany but were in no position to give effective military aid. Within three weeks the mechanized German forces, meeting no natural obstacles in the broad Polish plains, crushed Polish resistance.

After the rapid conquest of western Poland Hitler spent several months consolidating his position. In the spring of 1940 he occupied Denmark and sent armies into Norway, where traitors had prepared for his seizure of the country. The French had remained on the defensive, relying on the heavily fortified Maginot line to stop German attacks if and when they should come. Hitler quickly crushed Holland and Belgium, his forces entered France from the north, and the French army, honeycombed with weakness, collapsed. The British succeeded in evacuating a large part of their expeditionary forces from the port of Dunkirk; Italy entered the war, apparently believing the end in sight; and the French government, expecting the British would be subdued, signed an armistice. It allowed the Germans to occupy two-thirds of France, including Paris and the entire Atlantic coast, and promised a huge sum for payment of the occupation forces. Vichy, the capital of unoccupied France, came increasingly under Nazi influence.

The striking German successes in the early phase of the war had been accomplished by an unprecedented tactical use of airpower and motorized equipment in smashing concentrations that penetrated fixed lines of defense and never gave the enemy time to recover. Halted at the English Channel, the Germans shifted to strategic bombing in an effort to compel the English to capitulate, but the British heroically took prolonged bombardment from the air and steadily prepared for the long road back toward victory. The German military effort was then directed to the remaining Continental areas, which were occupied one by one until there remained only Sweden, Switzerland, Spain—which was benevolently neutral—and Russia. The conquest of Russia had been a part of Hitler's plan from the beginning and in June, 1941, the invasion began. The heartbreaking ordeal of 1915 was repeated on a larger scale, but deep though the German penetration of Russia was, the vastness of the Russian theater, the unlimited Russian manpower, and the ability of the Russian armies to counter-attack with Hitler's own military tactics, foiled all German efforts to force a surrender. World War II did not witness a collapse of Russian morale: Stalin had used his period of respite well.

The execution of Hitler's policy toward the Jews accustomed his followers to the brutalities that were a part of his war plans. With ruthless force he used the manpower and resources of each occupied country to produce material for further conquests. The American people looked on, horrified. President Roosevelt, realizing that ultimately the United States would be forced into the struggle, began to prepare American forces and undertook to provide the countries fighting Germany with supplies from the "arsenal of democracy." Increasing tension in the Far East (caused by American resistance to the Japanese efforts to conquer China) finally brought a surprise attack by the Japanese upon the American naval base at Pearl Harbor in Hawaii. According to agreement, Hitler declared war on the United States, which openly entered the war on both sides of the globe. The Japanese thereupon duplicated the German successes by seizing an immense Far Eastern empire which stretched their military resources to the limit.

One of the notable features of World War I had been the superiority of defense to offense. In the most recent war, however, the situation was reversed; nations capable of sustained offensive action were successful until compelled to halt and to consolidate the position they had won. Once the limit of their capacity for sustained large-scale attack was reached, they were forced upon the defensive and the tide turned. Russia during the war transported war factories to the Urals. Substantially aided by American lend-lease supplies, she pushed the Germans back across Europe into Poland, while American and British heavy bombers, operating as a strategic air force, systematically destroyed the German industrial plants, grounded their planes, and undermined the German power for resistance.

While forces and supplies were being gathered in the British Isles for an invasion of Western Europe, Allied forces landed in North Africa in November, 1942. Later, in a slow and costly campaign, Sicily and southern Italy were invaded, and against strong German resistance Rome was reached. The Italians drove Mussolini from power and an armistice was agreed upon. Before that time, however, British and American expeditionary forces had landed on the Continent and, crushed under a three-pronged movement from east, south, and west, Germany was overrun. Paris was liberated the same week that Rome fell. Determined not to allow any basis for a revival of the legend that the German army could not be beaten in the field, the Allied powers refused to grant terms and insisted on a complete military occupation of Germany. Much the same results were evident in the Japanese aspect of the war; operating from a succession of bases always closer to the Japanese home islands, strategic bombing weakened the power of resistance and the overextended communication lines were gradually cut.

The work of emancipation of occupied countries was aided by the guerilla warfare which groups of men, women, and even children carried on against the occupation forces. The hopes of the enslaved peoples were sustained by the Atlantic Charter, which President Roosevelt and the British prime minister, Winston Churchill, had issued on August 14, 1941, before the entry of the United States into the war. In the spirit of Wilson's Fourteen Points it declared respect for "the right of all peoples to choose the form of government under which they will live" and envisaged the ultimate "establishment of a wider and permanent system of general security." Roosevelt knew that the conflicting aims and interests of peoples would survive the war, and that unless a really effective world organization were formed another war was inevitable. He insisted that such an organization must be set up before the end of hostilities, so that it might lay the foundations of the peace. Accordingly a conference of representatives was summoned to meet in San Francisco in the spring of 1945. Roosevelt had written an opening speech but, worn out by the strain of the war years, he died suddenly on April 12. The conference assembled a few days later and drew up the charter of the United Nations.

The United Nations was made an organization of sovereign states, for it was not believed that the great powers would agree to the surrender of sovereignty necessary for a world government. Final authority was vested in the delegates of the United States, Russia, Great Britain, France, and China, sitting continuously in a Security Council to deal at once with any danger to peace. Since no great power would be likely to join an organization which could use force against it, the members of the Security Council were given the veto power. The General Assembly, where each power had an equal vote, was to meet at definite intervals.

Before the first meeting of the new organization, the atom bomb fell. Scientific research, backed by government money, had made great progress during the war. A number of important discoveries were made, but the really epoch-making advance was the solution of the problem of atomic fission by the United States, in collaboration with Britain and Canada—a discovery which put at the service of man a source of power of unlimited possibilities. Russia had promised to come into the war against Japan when the Germans should yield. The German collapse came at the end of May, and in early August Russia declared war on Japan. Shortly after this the Japanese surrender was assured by the dropping of atomic bombs on two Japanese cities, Hiroshima and Nagasaki.

After the war the Americans assumed control of Japan. Germany had already been divided into zones occupied by Russia, Great Britain, France, and the United States. Each nation had a different policy, and before many months a situation developed singularly like that which had followed World War I. There was the same suspicion of Soviet Russia on the part of her former allies, the same distrust of the other powers on the part of Russia, and the same divergencies as to the extent to which Germany should be allowed to recover.

Post-war elections withdrew Winston Churchill from the direction of British policy, and of the three statesmen who had co-operated in the war years only Stalin was left. The new Labor government in Britain followed traditional foreign policy and opposed Russian aims in the Mediterranean. The Jews found that anti-Semitism was still rife in Europe and that Arab nationalism made them unwelcome in Palestine where a Jewish homeland had been established after World War I. The natives of the former Dutch colonies resisted the return of Netherland dominion. India seethed. Soviet Russia was spreading her influence westward, and the shadow of the atomic bomb was over all. The United States offered to put manufacture of the bomb ultimately under the control of the United Nations, but American and Russian plans for safeguarding this control differed widely. America followed her post-war custom of changing parties in Congress midway in a presidential term. Under these circumstances the early meetings of the United Nations exhibited the old division along lines of national interest; even the necessity of feeding the hungry in devastated countries was used as a political football. The peoples of the world were still in the clutches of national illusions and jealousies, colonial rivalries, competing industrialism and armaments.

The road toward unity is long and hard. The cathedral of Chartres presents the symbol of unity as far as the Middle Ages attained it: the cathedral raised by the co-operative effort of a community. Endowed by its craftsmen and beautified by its artists, it was meeting place, theatre, museum, and picture gallery as well as place of worship. All over Europe the bells of cathedrals summoned the people to the worship of one God; cathedral towers and spires directed thought to a common Heaven. In the days when the cathedrals were built the old ideal of political unity, the Roman empire, was falling into decay; plain folk looked to their feudal lords for protection; kings made bids for support; Germans and Slavs encroached on each others' lands; and students gathered in "nations" to hear familiar speech, talk of home cooking, and wonder if, for example, the English really did have tails.

Today peoples of many faiths seek unity, sending their national representatives to sit together as the United Nations. This organization was formed to fulfill the hopes of Roosevelt's Four Freedoms—freedom of religion, freedom of speech, freedom from want, and freedom from fear—and to redeem the pledges of the Atlantic Charter, whose promises looked back as well as forward. The Charter spoke of national sovereignty, but it also spoke of freedom of trade and of travel, of food to meet the needs of all. Much of the most important work for unity must be done in those committees which aim to reach mutual understanding, to bridle competing industrialism and colonial rivalries by economic agreements, and to turn atomic energy away from destruction and into fields where it can liberate human beings from heartbreaking toil; to cope with disease; to disseminate knowledge of differing cultures; and to do away with rivalry in armaments. Progress in these directions will lead to the waning of national jealousies, for nothing dispels national illusions more surely than mutual undertakings by people who owe allegiance to different flags. Progress will be slow—much slower than the building of a cathedral—and it will be subject to setbacks. Cathedrals sometimes stood for centuries with unfinished naves and unsightly humps of towers; they were not always symmetrical—the builders of Chartres sacrificed symmetry to balance—but the final result was a harmonious blending of opposites. The charter of the

United Nations, fortunately, is open to amendment when need arises. If in the course of time the work of abolishing the causes of war is accomplished and the Four Freedoms are enjoyed by all mankind, it will be because the peoples have unceasingly reminded themselves that

"Above all nations is humanity."

OFFICIAL SEAL AND EMBLEM OF THE
UNITED NATIONS

(Used by permission of the Department of Public Information of the United Nations.)

Nikolai Lenin

LETTERS *

[These extracts show Lenin's policy of educating the masses for participation in the government, his ruthlessness, his propaganda policy, his zeal for modernization, and his belief that the dictatorship was a temporary stage.]

To I. V. Stalin

[Moscow], 24th January, 1920

On the basis of the directive, given by the Central Committee, I think that all three projects ought to be amalgamated into one.

In my opinion, the following should be added:

1. The "Section" of the Worker-Peasant inspection, attached to the Goskon [State Control], should be temporary, with the object of introducing the worker-peasant inspection *into all* sections of the Goskon, and then for it to cease to function as a separate section.

2. The object: to pass the *whole* of the toiling masses, both men and (*particularly*) women, through participation in the worker-peasant inspection.

3. To compile lists (according to the constitution) locally, and to exclude those who are serving etc. and the rest in turn should all be passed through participation in the worker-peasant inspection.

4. To make this participation varied according to the stage of development of the participators, beginning with the rôle of "eavesdropper," or witness, or a hired informant or a learner, for those workers and peasants, who are illiterate and undeveloped, and ending with full privileges (or almost all) for the literate, educated, and those who in one way or another have been tested.

* From *The Letters of Lenin,* translated and edited by Elizabeth Hill and Doris Mudie, copyright, 1937, by Harcourt, Brace and Company, Inc. Reprinted by permission of the publishers.

5. Particular attention should be paid (and organised with exact rules) to the introduction of a *wider* control of the worker-peasant inspection over the checking of provisions, goods, stores, ammunition, raw materials, fuel etc. etc. (especially workers' kitchens etc.) It is absolutely essential to make use of women, indeed every woman for this.

6. It is necessary to establish a gradual interest among the women, so that there need not be any confusion in encouraging these masses of participators. It is also essential to consider carefully the kind of participators (two to three, and occasionally more, but only in special circumstances, so that those who are working are not unnecessarily removed from their work).

7. Detailed instructions must be worked out.

8. The workers in the Goskon must be compelled (by special instructions) firstly, to attract to their activities representatives, or groups, of the worker-peasant inspection, and secondly, to lecture to non-Party Conferences of workers and peasants (lectures according to a specially agreed programme; popular and on the principles and methods of the Goskon; or the lectures might be substituted by the reading of a pamphlet which we will publish i.e. the Goskon. Stalin and Avanesov will publish it with the special aid of the Party, and also a commentary on this pamphlet).

9. To call up peasants *gradually* (and they must be non-Party peasants) to participate in the Central Goskon: one might begin with one or two from each Province (if it is impossible to get more), and then later to *expand* this according to transport and other conditions; also for non-Party workers.

10. To introduce gradually the checking of participation of the masses in the Goskon on the part of those workers, through the Party and through Professional Unions i.e. to check whether everybody is participating and what is the result of such participation from the point of view of teaching the participators the business of Government.

Lenin

To the Members of the Council of Defence

[Moscow], 1st February, [1920]
[The Bolsheviks were fighting the armies of Kolchak and Yudenich.]

The railway transport position is catastrophic. Bread transport to

Moscow has ceased. Special measures are essential to save the situation. The following measures should be passed (and others of a similar character carefully considered) for two months (February and March):

1. *Decrease* the individual bread ration for those workers, who are not transport workers; *increase* it for transport workers. Let thousands perish, but the country must be saved. . . .

To Gosizdat (State Publishing House) and to E. A. Preobrazhensky and N. I. Bukharin

Moscow, 8th August, 1920

Both in our own and in foreign newspapers (not only Communist, but the *bourgeois* papers of *various* countries) there accumulates *weekly* a gigantic amount of material, *especially relating to the foreign policy* of the Entente.

This extremely valuable material is lost, so far as Communist agitation is concerned. (See also "Bulletin of the N. K. Foreign Department.")

I suggest that a Commission be formed to collate this material and for the *monthly* publication of small pamphlets.

Their contents: *facts* about the foreign policy of the Entente (plunder, wars, risings and *financial* strangulation).

The number of copies: the least possible, for the main purpose will be the translation *into other languages.*

A Sub-Commission consisting of a few professors must (under strict control) collect *everything* valuable, *especially from bourgeois newspapers* (which best denounce their rivals).

A Commission consisting of *Party* comrades will read the manuscripts of the professors, will correct them, and will *compel* the professors to correct them.

Newspapers get lost; the pamphlets, however, will be kept and they will *help our comrades abroad.*

Please reply.

Lenin

A Note to A. I. Elizarova

[Moscow, Autumn, 1920]

The basic principle of Government in the spirit of all the decisions of the Russian Communist Party and the Central Soviet institutions is that a definite person is wholly responsible for conducting a definite piece of work.

I have been conducting the work (for such and such a length of time) and I am responsible. A certain person is in my way, since he is not responsible and is not in control.

That is confusion! That is chaos! It is the interference of a person *unsuitable* for responsible work, and I demand his *removal*.

To N. A. Semashko

Moscow, 24th October, 1921

Comrade Semashko,

Having today signed the decision of the Maly S.N.K. to vote two milliard roubles (I believe that is correct, although I do not remember the actual figure) for the cleaning of Moscow, and having read the regulations of the Narkomsdrav about the week of dwelling-house resanitation ("Izvestia," 12th July), I have come to the conclusion that my suspicions (concerning the complete rottenness in the way the whole of this business is being organised) is increasing.

Milliards of roubles will be taken, pilfered and stolen, and the work will not be done.

We must get model (or to begin with *tolerable*) cleanliness in Moscow, for there can be no greater disgrace than the "Soviet" dirt, which is to be found in first class houses. It simply cannot be imagined. And what is it like in those houses which are not first class?

Please send me a report, brief, but accurate and businesslike, showing what was the result of the week devoted to cleaning. Can you tell me of one single Province, where something was done, that was not inefficient?

Further, what is being done (and what has been done) in Moscow? Who is responsible for this work? Are they mere clerks with pompous Soviet titles who understand nothing, do not know their jobs, and can only sign bits of paper? Or are there some *efficient* people in charge? And who are they?

The most important thing of all is to see that there are reliable people, who can take on responsibility.

What is being done to encourage personal responsibility?

Who inspects the work? Inspectors? And how many are there? Who are they?

Detachments of youth? (Komsomol?) Are there any? How many? Where and how have they proved themselves?

What other means are there for *real* control?

Is money being spent on buying valuable things (Carbolic? Cleaning implements? How much has been bought?), or is the money going towards the maintenance of official do-nothings?

President of the Sovnarkom,

V. Ulianov (Lenin)

To I. I. Skvortsov-Stepanov

[Moscow, 15th November, 1922]

My dear Ivan Ivanovich,

I have read your article on "Specialists" ["Pravda," No. 244].

I disagree on two points:

First, at the beginning (third column): "The proletarian dictatorship will fail if, firstly . . . (that is correct), and secondly "if these specialists are not their own specialists, namely those *who realise that their task is to consolidate and develop the dictatorship of the proletariat.*"

The italicized is wrong. We will not get such specialists for a long time, not until the *bourgeois* specialists have disappeared, also the *petit-bourgeois* specialists, and certainly not before *all* the specialists become *Communists*. Meanwhile, the proletarian dictatorship must not fail. The *lesser* condition is sufficient, namely, the first. The second does not ruin us. It is sufficient "to have it under control."

For a long time to come there will be doubts, uncertainty, suspicion, treachery etc. The second condition will last until the *end* of the dictatorship, and it is, therefore, *not a condition of the dictatorship*. . . .

∽ ∽ ∽

Winston Churchill

DUNKIRK*

[The first extracts are from Churchill's speech in Parliament June 4, 1940, after the rescue of the British expeditionary force from Dunkirk. The speech from which the second series of extracts are taken was made on June 18, after the fall of France. These speeches reflect the impact upon the public of the events of the war when the initiative was still with the Germans, and when the invasion of England seemed imminent. They show the extraordinary skill of Churchill in awaking people to the situation and eliciting the spirit which was to withstand the bombings. These passages are excellent examples of Churchill's style, with its scriptural overtones.]

When, a week ago today, I asked the House to fix this afternoon as the occasion for a statement, I feared it would be my hard lot to announce the greatest military disaster in our long history. I thought —and some good judges agreed with me—that perhaps 20,000 or 30,000 men might be re-embarked. But it certainly seemed that the whole of the French First Army and the whole of the British Expeditionary Force north of the Amiens-Abbeville gap would be broken up in the open field or else would have to capitulate for lack of food and ammunition. These were the hard and heavy tidings for which I called upon the House and the nation to prepare themselves a week ago. The whole root and core and brain of the British Army, on which and around which we were to build, and are to build, the great British Armies in the later years of the war, seemed about to perish upon the field or to be led into an ignominious and starving captivity.

That was the prospect a week ago. . . . Suddenly the scene has cleared, the crash and thunder has for the moment—but only for the moment—died away. A miracle of deliverance, achieved by valor, by perseverance, by perfect discipline, by faultless service, by resource, by skill, by unconquerable fidelity, is manifest to us all. The enemy was hurled back by the retreating British and French troops. He was so roughly handled that he did not hurry their departure seriously. The Royal Air Force engaged the main strength of the German Air Force, and inflicted upon them losses of at least four to

---

*The selections quoted are from *Blood, Sweat and Tears* by Winston Churchill (1941). Reprinted by permission of G. P. Putnam's Sons, New York, Cassell and Company, Ltd., London, and McClelland and Stewart, Ltd., Toronto.

one; and the Navy, using nearly 1,000 ships of all kinds, carried over 335,000 men, French and British, out of the jaws of death and shame, to their native land and to the tasks which lie immediately ahead. . . .

Nevertheless, our thankfulness at the escape of our Army and so many men, whose loved ones have passed through an agonizing week, must not blind us to the fact that what has happened in France and Belgium is a colossal military disaster. The French Army has been weakened, the Belgian Army has been lost, a large part of those fortified lines upon which so much faith had been reposed is gone, many valuable mining districts and factories have passed into the enemy's possession, the whole of the Channel ports are in his hands, with all the tragic consequences that follow from that, and we must expect another blow to be struck almost immediately at us or at France. We are told that Herr Hitler has a plan for invading the British Isles. This has often been thought of before. When Napoleon lay at Boulogne for a year with his flat-bottomed boats and his Grand Army, he was told by someone, "There are bitter weeds in England." There are certainly a great many more of them since the British Expeditionary Force returned.

The whole question of home defense against invasion is, of course, powerfully affected by the fact that we have for the time being in this Island incomparably more powerful military forces than we have ever had at any moment in this war or the last. But this will not continue. We shall not be content with a defensive war. . . .

Turning once again, and this time more generally, to the question of invasion, I would observe that there has never been a period in all these long centuries of which we boast when an absolute guarantee against invasion, still less against serious raids, could have been given to our people. In the days of Napoleon the same wind which would have carried his transports across the Channel might have driven away the blockading fleet. There was always the chance, and it is that chance which has excited and befooled the imaginations of many Continental tyrants. Many are the tales that are told. We are assured that novel methods will be adopted, and when we see the originality of malice, the ingenuity of aggression, which our enemy displays, we may certainly prepare ourselves for every kind of novel stratagem and every kind of brutal and treacherous maneuver. I think that no idea is so outlandish that it should not be considered and viewed with a searching, but at the same time, I hope, with a steady eye. We must never forget the solid assurances of sea power and those which belong to air power if it can be locally exercised.

I have, myself, full confidence that if all do their duty, if nothing is neglected, and if the best arrangements are made, as they are being made, we shall prove ourselves once again able to defend our Island home, to ride out the storm of war, and to outlive the menace of tyranny, if necessary for years, if necessary alone. At any rate, that is what we are going to try to do. That is the resolve of His Majesty's Government—every man of them. That is the will of Parliament and the nation. The British Empire and the French Republic, linked together in their cause and in their need, will defend to the death their native soil, aiding each other like good comrades to the utmost of their strength. Even though large tracts of Europe and many old and famous States have fallen or may fall into the grip of the Gestapo and all the odious apparatus of Nazi rule, we shall not flag or fail. We shall go on to the end, we shall fight in France, we shall fight on the seas and oceans, we shall fight with growing confidence and growing strength in the air, we shall defend our Island, whatever the cost may be, we shall fight on the beaches, we shall fight on the landing grounds, we shall fight in the fields and in the streets, we shall fight in the hills; we shall never surrender, and even if, which I do not for a moment believe, this Island or a large part of it were subjugated and starving, then our Empire beyond the seas, armed and guarded by the British Fleet, would carry on the struggle, until, in God's good time, the New World, with all its power and might, steps forth to the rescue and the liberation of the old.

THEIR FINEST HOUR

During the first four years of the last war the Allies experienced nothing but disaster and disappointment. That was our constant fear: one blow after another, terrible losses, frightful dangers. Everything miscarried. And yet at the end of those four years the morale of the Allies was higher than that of the Germans, who had moved from one aggressive triumph to another, and who stood everywhere triumphant invaders of the lands into which they had broken. During that war we repeatedly asked ourselves the question: How are we going to win? and no one was able ever to answer it with much precision, until at the end, quite suddenly, quite unexpectedly, our terrible foe collapsed before us, and we were so glutted with victory that in our folly we threw it away.

We do not yet know what will happen in France or whether the

French resistance will be prolonged, both in France and in the French Empire overseas. The French government will be throwing away great opportunities and casting adrift their future if they do not continue the war in accordance with their Treaty obligations, from which we have not felt able to release them. The House will have read the historic declaration in which, at the desire of many Frenchmen—and of our own hearts—we have proclaimed our willingness at the darkest hour in French history to conclude a union of common citizenship in this struggle. However matters may go in France or with the French Government, or other French Governments, we in this Island and in the British Empire will never lose our sense of comradeship with the French people. If we are now called upon to endure what they have been suffering, we shall emulate their courage, and if final victory rewards our toils they shall share the gains, aye, and freedom shall be restored to all. We abate nothing of our just demands; not one jot or tittle do we recede. Czechs, Poles, Norwegians, Dutch, Belgians have joined their causes to our own. All these shall be restored.

What General Weygand called the Battle of France is over. I expect that the Battle of Britain is about to begin. Upon this battle depends the survival of Christian civilization. Upon it depends our own British life, and the long continuity of our institutions and our Empire. The whole fury and might of the enemy must very soon be turned on us. Hitler knows that he will have to break us in this Island or lose the war. If we can stand up to him, all Europe may be free and the life of the world may move forward into broad, sunlit uplands. But if we fail, then the whole world, including the United States, including all that we have known and cared for, will sink into the abyss of a new Dark Age made more sinister, and perhaps more protracted, by the lights of perverted science. Let us therefore brace ourselves to our duties, and so bear ourselves that, if the British Empire and its Commonwealth last for a thousand years, men will still say, "This was their finest hour."

Bibliography

Suggestions for Reading

BECAUSE history is recorded by human beings, the record is never entirely satisfactory. Contemporary history is incomplete and full of inaccuracies due to faulty observation, insufficient knowledge, prejudice, and bias. From such testimony the historian must assemble what appear to be the facts, weigh them, and interpret them. He tries more or less successfully to avoid being influenced by his own bias and prejudices, but he cannot escape from expressing the point of view of the time in which he lives. Hence history is constantly being re-interpreted and rewritten. A student reading books representing different periods and points of view will find himself developing a critical attitude which will enable him to use history as a tool and not as a basis for prejudice.

He will also get an insight into the method of the historian, which is scientific and can be applied to any study. The first requisite is to keep a record of the books consulted. This should be done on separate slips or cards in the form used in the following lists. If the student notes on each card the ground covered by the book and something about the author's competence and point of view, and if he keeps the slips alphabetically arranged, he will find them useful for reference during the course. In the end, he will have an annotated bibliography of European history.

In dealing with any period the student will find it useful, after reading one or two works which give him a general survey, to decide upon those aspects of the period about which he is most curious to know more, and to spend the rest of his time reading books that deal specifically with these aspects. He will find it useful to take notes on some of his reading, though much he will simply read currently. Notes are most convenient for later use if taken on separate slips, with a subject heading and an exact page reference to the book from which the note is taken. Arranged by subjects, these notes provide useful material for papers or for topics.

The term *topic* as here used means a study of a particular subject complete except for the final writing. The material has been collected, on slips, has been analyzed and a plan worked out which acts as a table of contents. The notes are arranged according to the plan and a conclusion written which gives the student's analysis of the subject in the light of the evidence collected. A list of sources and authorities, arranged in proper form, is appended. The student has devoted all his available time to the purely historical aspects of his task, and has the material assembled for a paper which can be reduced to literary form, perhaps to fulfill a requirement in an English course.

It is customary to call contemporary material source material, and works written at a later time secondary authorities. (These terms are now generally used instead of primary and secondary sources.) In the following lists the sources are distinguished by asterisks. The reading of the sources gives the flavor of a period as no secondary authority can. Many of the sources are well worth reading as literature and can usually be purchased in inexpensive editions. Extracts from the sources are given in source books, and a list of these is appended. Source books, however, are mentioned in chapter lists only occasionally, for it is assumed that the student will know that extracts from the sources will be found in them for all periods covered by this book.

A textbook can list only samplings of the secondary authorities and the more obvious sources. The student will soon master the technique of looking for further material in bibliographies and footnotes. The most generally useful bibliographies are:

DUTCHER, G. M., et al.: *Guide to Historical Literature*. New York, 1936.

PAETOW, L. J.: *Guide to the Study of Medieval History*. New York, 1931.

THOMPSON, J. W.: *Reference Studies in Medieval History*. Chicago, 1923.

Brief bibliographies are appended to articles in the following reference works:

Allgemeine deutsche Biographie. Leipsig, 1875–1912.

Biographie universelle, ancienne et moderne. Paris, 1811–62.

The Catholic Encyclopedia (Roman Catholic). New York, 1907–22.

Dictionary of National Biography (British biography). London, 1885–1901.

Encyclopaedia Britannica. Eleventh edition. New York, 1911.

Encyclopaedia of the Social Sciences. New York, 1930–34.

Schaff-Herzog Encyclopaedia of Religious Knowledge (Protestant). New York, 1908.

A valuable guide is LANGER, W. L., Ed.: *An Encyclopaedia of World History*. Boston, 1940.

An historical atlas is indispensable. The most convenient is SHEPHERD, W. R.: *Atlas of Medieval and Modern History.* New York, 1932.

The works listed below cover extensive periods and the student will find that they repay regular investigation. Many of them contain useful suggestions for further reading.

CO-OPERATIVE WORKS

BERR, H., Ed.: *L'évolution de l'humanité.* Paris, 1915 ff.
The Cambridge Medieval History. London and New York, 1911-36. 8 vols.
The Cambridge Modern History. London and New York, 1904-31. 13 vols.
LAVISSE, E., Ed.: *Histoire de France depuis les origines jusqu'à la révolution.* Paris, 1900-11. 9 vols.
LAVISSE, E., and RAMBAUD, A., Ed.: *Histoire générale du IVe siècle à nos jours.* Paris, 1893-1901. 12 vols.

INDIVIDUAL WORKS

ADAMS, HENRY: *Mont Saint Michel and Chartres.* Boston, 1936.
BOISSONADE, P.: *Life and Work in Mediaeval Europe.* New York, 1937.
BRYCE, JAMES: *The Holy Roman Empire.* Enl. edition. London, 1907.
BURY, J. B.: *A History of the Eastern Roman Empire.* London, 1912.
CHAMBERS, SIR E. K.: *The Mediaeval Stage.* Oxford, 1903. 2 vols.
FAURE, ELIE: *History of Art.* New York, 1921-30. 5 vols.
GIBBON, EDWARD: *Decline and Fall of the Roman Empire.* J. B. Bury, Ed. Eighth edition. London, 1930. 7 vols.
HARTLEY, DOROTHY, and HARTLEY, ELLIOT, Ed.: *Life and Work of the People of England.* London, 1925-31. 6 vols.
HEATON, H.: *Economic History of Europe.* New York, 1936.
LANG, P. H.: *Music in Western Civilization.* New York, 1941.
LEICHTENTRITT, HUGO: *Music, History and Ideas.* Cambridge, 1938.
MÂLE, EMILE: *L'Art religieux en France.* Paris, 1924-25. 3 vols.
MERRIMAN, ROGER B.: *The Rise of the Spanish Empire in the Old World and the New.* New York, 1918-34. 4 vols.
MOREY, C. R.: *Mediaeval Art.* New York, 1942.
PORTER, A. K.: *Mediaeval Architecture; its Origins and Development.* New York, 1912. 2 vols.
POWER, EILEEN: *Medieval People.* Boston and New York, 1924.
RANDALL, J. H.: *The Making of the Modern Mind.* Revised edition. Boston, 1940.
SARTON, GEORGE: *An Introduction to the History of Science.* Baltimore, 1927-31. 3 vols.

SINGER, CHARLES: *A Short History of Science to the Nineteenth Century.* Oxford, 1941.
SMITH, PRESERVED: *A History of Modern Culture.* New York, 1930.
TAYLOR, H. O.: *The Classical Heritage of the Middle Ages.* Second edition. New York, 1903.
——, *Freedom of the Mind in History.* London, 1923.
——, *The Medieval Mind.* Fourth edition. New York, 1925. Vol. 1.
THOMPSON, J. W.: *An Economic and Social History of the Middle Ages (300–1300).* New York and London, 1928.
——, *Economic and Social History of Europe in the Later Middle Ages, 1300–1530.* New York, 1931.
WAUGH, W. T.: *History of Europe from 1378 to 1494.* New York, 1932.
DE WULF, M.: *History of Medieval Philosophy.* New York, 1926.

SOURCE BOOKS

BUTTERFIELD, H., Ed.: *Select Documents of European History, 1715–1920.* London, 1931.
CHEYNEY, E. P., Ed.: *Readings in English History drawn from the Original Sources.* Boston, 1922.
Contemporary Civilization Source Book. Prepared by the Contemporary Civilization Staff of Columbia College. New York, 1941. (Covers the whole period)
COOKE, W. H. and STICKNEY, E. P., Ed.: *Readings in European International Relations since 1879.* New York, 1931.
COULTON, G. G., Ed.: *Life in the Middle Ages.* New York, 1935.
CUBBERLY, E. P., Ed.: *Readings in the History of Education.* Boston 1920.
HENDERSON, E. F., Ed.: *Select Historical Documents of the Middle Ages.* London, 1892.
LAFFAN, R. G. D., Ed.: *Select Documents of European History, 800–1492.* New York, 1929.
LANGSAM, W. D., Ed.: *Documents and Readings in the History of Europe since 1918.* Chicago, 1939.
MORGAN, R. B., Ed.: *Readings in English Social History from Contemporary Literature.* Cambridge, England, 1921–22. 5 vols.
OGG, F. A., Ed.: *A Source Book of Mediaeval History.* New York, 1907.
ROBINSON, J. H., Ed.: *Readings in European History.* Boston, 1904. 2 vols.
ROBINSON, J. H., and BEARD, C. A., Ed.: *Readings in Modern European History.* Boston, 1909. 2 vols.
SCOTT, J. F., and BALTZLY, A., Ed.: *Readings in European History since 1814.* New York, 1934.

STEPHENSON, C. and MARCHAM, F. C., Ed.: *Sources of English Constitutional History.* New York, 1937.
THATCHER, O. J. and McNEAL, E. H., Ed.: *A Source Book of Mediaeval History.* New York, 1905.

REFERENCES
FOR FURTHER READING
[N.B. Source material indicated by asterisks]

PART I

The Fourth and Fifth Centuries

ABBOTT, F. F., and JOHNSON, A. C.: *Municipal Administration in the Roman Empire*. Princeton, 1926.
ARRAGON, R. F.: *The Transition from the Ancient to the Mediaeval World*. New York, 1936. (Berkshire Studies)
BAILEY, C., Ed.: *The Legacy of Rome*. Oxford, 1923.
BAKER, ARCHIBALD G., et al.: *A Short History of Christianity*. Chicago, 1940.
BURY, J. B.: *History of the Later Roman Empire*. London, 1923. 2 vols. Pp. 395–565.
——, *The Invasion of Europe by the Barbarians*. London, 1928.
Cambridge Economic History of Europe. Vol. I. Cambridge, 1941.
CHARANIS, PETER: *Church and State in the Later Roman Empire*. Madison, Wis., 1939.
CHARLESWORTH, M. P.: *Trade Routes and Commerce of the Roman Empire*. Cambridge, 1924.
DILL, SAMUEL: *Roman Society in the Last Century of the Western Empire*. London, 1921.
DOPSCH, ALFONS: *The Economic and Social Foundations of European Civilization*. New York, 1937.
GIBBON, EDWARD: *The History of the Decline and Fall of the Roman Empire*. J. B. Bury, Ed. Eighth edition, London: 1930. 7 vols.
GOODENOUGH, E. R.: *The Church in the Roman Empire*. New York, 1931. (Berkshire Studies)
HAYES, CARLETON J. H.: *An Introduction to the Sources Relating to the Germanic Invasions*. New York, 1909.
HODGKIN, THOMAS: *Italy and her Invaders*. Oxford, 1880. 8 vols.
* HOWLAND, A. C., Ed.: "The Early Germans," vol. VI, no. 3, *Translations and Reprints from the Original Sources of European History*. The Department of History of the University of Pennsylvania. Philadelphia, n.d.
* ——, "Ordeals, Compurgation, Excommunication and Interdict," ibid., vol. IV, no. 4.
HUTTMAN, M. A.: *The Establishment of Christianity and the Proscription of Paganism*. New York, 1914.

LABRIOLLE, PIERRE DE: *History and Literature of Christianity from Tertullian to Boethius.* New York, 1925.
LATOURETTE, K. S.: *History of the Expansion of Christianity.* New York, 1937–43. 5 vols.
* LOOMIS, LOUISE R., Ed.: *The Book of the Popes, I.* New York, 1916. (*Records of Civilization*)
LOT, F.: *The End of the Ancient World and the Beginnings of the Middle Ages.* London, 1931.
MCILWAIN, C. H.: *The Growth of Political Thought in the West.* Chapter 5. New York, 1932.
MCNEILL, J. T., et al., Ed.: *Environmental Factors in Christian History.* Chicago, 1939.
MONTALEMBERT, RÉNÉ DE: *The Monks of the West.* Edinburgh, 1861–79. 7 vols.
MOREY, C. R.: *Christian Art.* New York, 1933.
MOSS, H. S. and L. B.: *The Birth of the Middle Ages,* pp. 395–814. Oxford, 1935.
PIJOAN, J.: *History of Christianity in the Light of Modern Knowledge.* New York, 1929.
WOODWARD, E. L.: *Christianity and Naturalism in the Later Roman Empire.* London, 1916.

Ch. 1: *The World of St. Augustine*

ALBERTIN, E.: *L'Afrique Romaine.* Algiers, 1922.
* ST. AUGUSTINE: *The City of God.* Introduction by Ernest Barker. London, 1934. Other editions.
* ———, *Confessions.* Many editions.
* ———, *Letters.* London, 1930.
* ———, *Soliloquies.* Boston, 1910.
* AYER, J. C.: *Source Book for Ancient Church History.* New York, 1913.
BERTRAND, L.: *St. Augustin.* New York, 1914.
CARLYLE, A. J.: *St. Augustine and* The City of God (in Hearnshaw, *Social and Political Ideas*).
CARTER, JESSE B.: *The Religious Life of Ancient Rome.* Boston, 1911.
CUNNINGHAM, W.: *St. Augustine.* London, 1886.
CUTTS, E. L.: *St. Augustine.* London, 1909.
DARCY, M. C., et al.: *A Monument to St. Augustine.* London, 1930.
DUCHESNE, L.: *Early History of the Christian Church.* New York, 1920–24. 3 vols.
FIGGIS, J. N.: *Political Aspect of* The City of God. London, 1921.
LEIGH-BENNETT, ERNEST: *Handbook of the Early Christian Fathers.* London, 1920.

McCabe, J.: *St. Augustine and His Age.* London, 1902.
Pickman, E. M.: *The Mind of Latin Christianity.* Oxford, 1937.
Rand, E. K.: *Founders of the Middle Ages.* New York, 1928.
Reese, G.: *Music in the Middle Ages.* New York, 1940.
Rostovtzeff, M.: *Social and Economic History of the Roman Empire.* Oxford, 1926.
Singer, Charles: *A Short History of Science.*
* Tacitus: *De Germania.* Henry Fourneaux, Ed., Oxford, 1894. (Clarendon Press Series)
Taylor, H. O.: *The Medieval Mind.* Fourth edition, New York, 1925. 2 vols.

Ch. 2: *The World of Apollinaris Sidonius*

Allard, P.: *Saint Sidoine Apollinaris.* Paris, 1909.
Collingwood, R. G., and Myres, J. N. L.: *Roman Britain and the English Settlements.* Oxford, 1936.
Frank, Tenney: "Recent works on the economic history of ancient Rome," *Journal of Economic and Business History,* I (1928) pp. 105–18.
Huntington, Ellsworth: "Climatic change and agricultural exhaustion as elements in the fall of Rome," *Quarterly Journal of Economics,* XXXI (1917), pp. 173–208.
* Jordanes: *Origin and Deeds of the Goths.* Princeton, 1915.
Monceaux, P.: *Histoire de la Littérature Latine Chrétienne.* Paris, 1924.
Moss, H.: "The economic consequences of the barbarian invasions," *Economic History Review* (1937).
Rostovtzeff, M.: "Decay of the ancient world and its economic explanations," *Economic History Review,* II (1930), pp. 197–214.
Sandys, J. E.: *A History of Classical Scholarship.* Cambridge, 1903–8. 3 vols.
Shumway, D. B., Ed. and Tr.: *The Nibelungenlied.* Boston, 1909.
* Sidonius, Apollinaris: *Letters.* O. M. Dalton, Tr. Oxford, 1915. 2 vols.
* Sidonius, Apollinaris: *Poems and Letters.* Cambridge, Mass., 1936, (Loeb Classical Library).
Simkhovitch, V. G.: "Rome's fall reconsidered," *Political Science Quarterly,* XXXI (1916), pp. 201–43.
Stevens, C. E.: *Apollinaris Sidonius and His Age.* Oxford, 1933.
Toutain, J.: *The Economic Life of the Ancient World.* London, 1930.
Westermann, W. L.: "The economic basis of the decline of ancient culture," *American Historical Review,* XX (1915), 723–43.

PART II

The Sixth Century

BAYNES, N. H.: *The Byzantine Empire.* New York, 1925.
BUCKLAND, W. W.: *Roman Law from Augustine to Justinian.* Cambridge, 1932.
BURY, J. B.: *History of the Later Roman Empire.*
BYRON, ROBERT: *The Byzantine Achievement, A.D. 330–1453.* London, 1929.
DALTON, O. M.: *Byzantine Art and Archaeology.* Oxford, 1911.
——, *Introduction to* History of the Franks, *by Gregory of Tours.* Oxford, 1927. 2 vols.
HARRISON, FREDERIC: *Byzantine History in the Early Middle Ages.* London, 1900.
HOLMES, W. G.: *The Age of Justinian and Theodora.* London, 1912.
* JORDANES: *Origin and Deeds of the Goths.*
LABRIOLLE, PIERRE DE: *History and Literature of Christianity.*
LAISTNER, M. L. W.: *Thought and Letters in Western Europe, A.D. 500–900.* New York, 1931.
PATCH, HOWARD R.: *The Tradition of Boethius.* Oxford, 1935.
PEIRCE, HAYFORD, and TYLER, ROYALL: *Byzantine Art.* New York, 1926.
RICE, D. TALBOT: *Byzantine Art.* Oxford, 1935.
RUNCIMAN, STEVEN: *Byzantine Civilization.* London, 1933.
SCHEVILL, FERDINAND: *History of the Balkan Peninsula.* Revised edition. New York, 1933.
VASILIEV, A. A.: *History of the Byzantine Empire.* Madison, Wis., 1928–30. 2 vols.
VEN, PAUL VAN DEN: "When did the Byzantine empire and civilization come into being?" *American Historical Association, Annual Report for 1916.* Washington, 1919. Pp. 299–309.
WHITE, LYNN: "The Byzantinization of Sicily," *American Historical Review,* XLII (1936), pp. 1–21.
WRIGHT, F. A., and SINCLAIR, T. A.: *A History of the Later Latin literature from the middle of the Fourth to the End of the Seventeenth Century.* London, 1931.

Ch. 3: *The World of Justinian*

BAKER, G. P.: *Justinian.* New York, 1931.
BARRETT, H. M.: *Boethius: Some Aspects of His Times and Works.* Cambridge, 1940.

* ST. BENEDICT: *Rule*. F. A. Gasquet, Ed. London, 1908. Other editions.
* BOETHIUS: *The Consolations of Philosophy*. London, 1918. (Loeb Library) Also in Temple Classics, London, 1902.
BUTLER, E. C.: *Benedictine Monachism*. New York, 1919.
* CASSIODORUS: *Letters*. London, 1886.
CHAPMAN, JOHN: *Saint Benedict and the Sixth Century*. London, 1929.
DIEHL, CHARLES: *History of the Byzantine Empire*. Princeton, 1925.
——, *Byzantine Portraits*. New York, 1927.
——, *Manuel d'art Byzantin*. Paris, 1910.
——, *Théodora impératrice de Byzance*. Paris, 1904.
DUCKETT, E. S.: *The Gateway to the Middle Ages*. New York, 1938.
HODGKIN, THOMAS: *Theodoric the Goth*. London, 1923.
JACKSON, T. G.: *Byzantine and Romanesque Architecture*. Chicago, 2 vols.
MILLINGTON, A. VAN: *Byzantine Churches in Constantinople*. New York, 1912.
* PROCOPIUS OF CAESAREA: *Procopius with an English Translation*. New York, 1914-40. 7 vols.
SCHROLL, M. A.: *Benedictine Monachism*. New York, 1941.
SWIFT, E. H.: *Hagia Sophia*. New York, 1940.
WORKMAN, H. B.: *The Evolution of the Monastic Ideal*. London, 1913.

Ch. 4: *The World of Gregory I*

ST. ADAMNAN: *Life of St. Columba*. London, 1929. Other translations.
BALDWIN, SUMMERFIELD: *The Organization of Medieval Christianity*. New York, 1929. (Berkshire Studies)
BARMBY, JAMES: *Gregory the Great*. London, 1892.
BARRY, WILLIAM: *The Papal Monarchy (590-1303)*. Second Edition. London, 1906.
THE VENERABLE BEDE: *Ecclesiastical History of England*. (Everyman's Library and many other editions.)
CARLYLE, A. J.: "The sources of medieval political theory and its connection with medieval politics," *American Historical Review*, XIX (1913), pp. 1-12.
CHURCH, R. W.: *Miscellaneous Essays*. New York, 1904.
DUDDEN, F. H.: *Gregory the Great*. London, 1905. 2 vols.
GASQUET, F. A., Ed.: *A Life of Pope St. Gregory the Great*. Westminster, 1904.
GREGOROVIUS, F.: *History of the City of Rome in the Middle Ages*. Fourth edition. London, 1894-1902. 13 vols.
* ST. GREGORY: *Dialogues*. E. G. Gardner, Ed. London, 1911.

* St. Gregory: *Letters and Pastoral Rule.* Collected in *A Select Library of Nicene and Post-Nicene Fathers.* Second Series, Vols. XII–XIII. New York, 1890–1900.
* Gregory, Bishop of Tours: *History of the Franks.* New York, 1916. Another edition, Oxford, 1927. 2 vols. (*Records of Civilization*).
Hadow, W. H., Ed.: *The Oxford History of Music.* Oxford, 1901. 6 vols.
Howorth, H. H.: *St. Augustine of Canterbury.* London, 1913.
Villari, Pasquale: *The Barbarian Invasions of Italy.* New York, 1902. 2 vols.

ഗ ഗ ഗ

PART III

The Seventh Century

Ahmad ibn Yahya: *The Origins of the Islamic State.* New York, 1916–24. 2 vols.
Ameer, A. S.: *Short History of the Saracens.* London, 1921.
* Beowulf. Many translations
Dawson, Christopher: *The Making of Europe.* London, 1939.
Dopsch, Alfons: "Agrarian institutions of the Germanic kingdoms from the fifth to the ninth century," *Cambridge Economic History of Europe,* vol. I, ch. 4. Cambridge, 1941.
The Encyclopedia of Islam: a Dictionary of the Geography, Ethnography and Biography of the Mohammadan Peoples. London, 1913–36. 4 vols. Supplement, 1938.
Fustel de Coulanges, N. D.: *Histoire des institutions politiques de l'ancienne France.* Paris, 1888–92. 6 vols.
Guignebert, Charles: *A Short History of the French People.* New York, 1930. 2 vols.
Henderson, E. F.: *A Short History of Germany.* London, 1916. 2 vols.
Lavisse, E., Ed.: *Histoire de France.*
O'Leary, D.: *Arabia before Mohammed.* New York, 1927.
Oman, C.: *Story of the Byzantine Empire.* London, 1911.
Porter, A. K.: *The Crosses and Culture of Ireland.* New Haven, 1931.
Pirenne, Henri: *Economic and Social History of Mediaeval Europe.* I. E. Clegg, Ed. London, 1936.
Seignobos, C.: *The Feudal Regime.* E. W. Dow, Tr. New York, 1902.
Thompson, James Westfall: *The Economic and Social History of the Middle Ages.* New York, 1932.

Ch. 5: The World of Mohammed

AMIR ALI: *Islam.* London, 1906.
——, *The Spirit of Islam.* New edition. London, 1935.
ANDRAE, TOR: *Mohammed, the Man and His Faith.* London, 1936.
ARNOLD, SIR T. W.: *The Caliphate.* Oxford, 1924.
——, *The Preaching of Islam: a History of the Propagation of the Muslim Faith.* Westminster, 1896.
ARNOLD, SIR T. W., and GUILLAUME, A., Ed.: *The Legacy of Islam.* Oxford, 1931.
BREHAUT, ERNEST: *An Encyclopedist of the Dark Ages: Isidore of Seville.* New York, 1912.
ESSAD BEY: *Mohammed.* New York, 1936.
GRUNEBAUM, G. E. VON: *Medieval Islam.* Chicago, 1946.
HITTI, PHILIP K.: *History of the Arabs.* London, 1937.
HOGARTH, D. B.; *Arabia.* Oxford, 1922.
IKBAL ALI SHAH, *Sirdar: Mohammed: the Prophet.* London, 1932.
* *The Koran.* New York, 1929. (Everyman's Library)
LAMMENS, H.: *Islam: Beliefs and Institutions.* London, 1929.
LANE-POOLE, STANLEY: *The Mohammedan Dynasties.* Westminster, 1894.
MARGOLIOUTH, D. S.: *Mohammed and the Rise of Islam.* New York, 1905.
——, *Mohammedanism.* London, 1928.
* *The Meaning of the Glorious Koran.* Pickthall, Ed. New York, 1930.
* MOHAMMED: *The Sayings.* London, 1941.
* ——, *Speeches and Table Talk.* London, 1882.
MUIR, W.: *The Life of Mohammed from Original Sayings.* Revised edition. Edinburgh, 1912.
STOBART, J. W. H.: *Islam and Its Founder.* London, 1901.
THOMAS, BERTRAM: *The Arabs.* New York, 1937.

✧ ✧ ✧

PART IV

The Eighth Century

ABRAHAM, I., et al.: *The Legacy of Israel.* Oxford, 1927.
BERTRAND, LOUIS: *The History of Spain.* New York, 1934.
* ST. BONIFACE: *The English Correspondence.* London, 1911.
* ——, *Letters,* New York, 1940. (*Records of Civilization*)

Bibliography

BURKE, U. P.: *History of Spain.* Second edition. London, 1900. 2 vols.
BURY, J. B.: *History of the Later Roman Empire.*
CHAPMAN, C. E.: *A History of Spain.* New York, 1927.
CRESWELL, K. A. C.: *Early Muslim Architecture.* Oxford, 1932-40. 2 vols.
DILL, S.: *Roman Society in Gaul in the Merovingian Age.* London, 1926.
DUCHESNE, L.: *Les premiers temps de l'Etat pontifical.* Third edition. Paris, 1914.
* EDDIUS STEPHANUS: *The Life of Bishop Wilford.* Cambridge, 1927.
GOLDSCHMIDT, ADOLPH: *German Illumination.* New York, 1928. 2 vols.
HINKS, ROGER P.: *Carolingian Art.* London, 1935.
KRAUTHEIMER, RICHARD: "The Carolingian revival of early Christian architecture," *Art Bulletin,* March, 1942.
LAISTNER, M. L. W.: *Thought and Letters in Western Europe, A.D. 500-900.* London, 1931.
LANE-POOLE, STANLEY, and GILMAN, A.: *The Story of the Moors in Spain.* New York, 1886.
LEVISON, WILHELM: *England and the Continent in the Eighth Century.* Oxford, 1946.
RICHARD, ERNST: *History of German Civilization.* New York, 1911.
* WILLIBALD: *The Life of St. Boniface.* Cambridge, 1916.

Ch. 6: *The World of the Venerable Bede*

ABBOTT, W. C.: "An Uncanonized Saint," in *Conflicts with Oblivion.* New Haven, 1924.
* BEDE: *Ecclesiastical History of the English Nation.* Many editions.
BOISSONADE, P.: *Life and Work in Medieval Europe.* E. Power, Tr. New York, 1927.
BROWN, G. B.: *The Arts in Early England.* London, 1903-37. 6 vols.
BROWNE, G. F.: *The Venerable Bede, His Life and Writings.* London, 1919.
* CAEDMON: *Poems.* C. W. Kennedy, Tr. New York, 1916.
CHADWICK, H. M.: *The Heroic Age.* Cambridge, 1912.
CHAMBERS, R. W.: "Bede." British Academy. *Proceedings,* vol. XXII (1936).
CLAPHAM, A. W.: *English Romanesque Architecture before the Conquest.* Oxford, 1930.
CLARK, J. M.: *The Abbey of St. Gall as a Center of Literature and Art.* Cambridge, 1926.
FUHRMANN, J. P.: *Irish Mediaeval Monasteries on the Continent.* Washington, 1927.
GRAHAM, H.: *The Early Irish Monastic Schools.* Dublin, 1923.

HODGKIN, R. H.: *A History of the Anglo-Saxons.* Oxford, 1935. 2 vols.
MILLAR, E. G.: *The Lindisfarne Gospels.* London, 1923.
PFLUGK-HARTTUNG: "The Old Irish on the Continent." *Transactions of the Royal Historical Society* (n.s.) Vol. 75.
SARTON, GEORGE: *Introduction to the History of Science.* Vol. 1.
* SMITH, A. H., Ed.: *Three Northumberland Poems.* London, 1933.
SULLIVAN, E.: *The Book of Kells.* London, 1914.
THOMPSON, A. H., Ed.: *Bede, His Life, Times, and Writings.* Oxford, 1935.
THORNDIKE, LYNN: *History of Magic and Experimental Science.* London, New York, 1929–34. 4 vols.
* *Widsith.* Kemp Malone, Ed. London, 1936.

Ch. 7: *The World of Charlemagne*

BITTERMAN, H. R.: "Harun Ar-Raschid's gift of an organ to Charlemagne," *Speculum,* IV (1929), pp. 215–17.
BROWNE, G. F.: *Alcuin of York.* London, 1908.
BRYCE, JAMES: *The Holy Roman Empire.* Revised edition. London, 1928.
BURY, J. B.: *A History of the Eastern Roman Empire (802–867).* London, 1912.
CUTTS, E. L.: *Charlemagne.* London, 1882.
DAVIS, H. W. C.: *Charlemagne.* London, 1929.
* DUNCALF, FREDERIC and KREY, A. C.: *Parallel Source Problems in Medieval History.* New York, 1912.
* EINHARD (or EGINHARD): *Life of Charlemagne.* S. E. Taylor, Tr. New York, 1880. (Other Translations)
* EINHARD: *Letters.* Henry Preble, Tr. (American Society of Church History, *Papers.* Second series, I [1913]).
* FALKNER, R. P., Ed.: "Statistical Documents of the Middle Ages," *Translations and Reprints,* vol. III, no. 2. Philadelphia, n.d.
* GRANT, A. J., Ed. and tr.: *Early Lives of Charlemagne,* London, 1926.
HENDERSON, E. F.: *A History of Germany in the Middle Ages.* London, 1894.
HODGKIN, THOMAS: *Charles the Great.* London, 1897.
* HOWELL, W. S., Ed. and tr.: *The Rhetoric of Alcuin and Charlemagne.* Princeton, 1941.
KLEINCLAUSZ, A. J.: *Charlemagne.* Paris, 1934.
LOPEZ, ROBERT S.: "Mohammed and Charlemagne: a Revision," *Speculum,* XVIII (1943), pp. 14–38.
MCILWAIN, C. H.: *The Growth of Political Thought in the West from the Greeks to the End of the Middle Ages.* New York, 1932.
MOMBERT, J. I.: *A History of Charles the Great.* New York, 1888.

MULLINGER, J. B.: *The Schools of Charles the Great.* New York, 1911.
* MUNRO, DANA CARLETON, Ed.: "Laws of Charles the Great," *Translations and Reprints,* vol. VI, no. 5. Philadelphia, n.d.
PIRENNE, HENRI: *Mohammed and Charlemagne.* New York, 1939.
POWER, EILEEN: *Medieval People.* London, 1924.
RUSSELL, CHARLES E.: *Charlemagne, First of the Moderns.* Boston, 1930.
VILLARI, PASQUALE: *Mediaeval Italy from Charlemagne to Henry VII.* London, 1910.
WEST, ANDREW F.: *Alcuin and the Rise of the Christian Schools.* New York, 1892.

ᘓ ᘓ ᘓ

PART V

The Ninth Century

ANDERSON, SVEN AXEL: *Viking Enterprise.* New York, 1936.
* ANNALS: See Robinson, *Readings,* and Thatcher and McNeal, *Source Book.*
* ARABIAN NIGHTS. Lane or Burton Translation.
BEAZLEY, C. R.: *The Dawn of Modern Geography.* London, 1897–1906. 3 vols.
DASENT, SIR G. W., Ed.: *The Story of Burnt Njal.* (Everyman's Library).
DU CHAILLU, P. B.: *Viking Age.* New York, 1889. 2 vols.
* ERMOLD LE NOIR: *Poeme sur Louis le Pieux et Epitres au Roi Pepin.* Paris, 1932.
GJERSET, KNUT: A *History of Iceland.* London, 1924.
———, *A History of the Norwegian People,* New York, 1915. 2 vols.
HASKINS, C. H.: *The Normans in European History.* Boston, 1915.
JORANSON, E.: *The Danegeld in France.* Rock Island, Illinois, 1923.
KENDRICK, T. D.: *A History of the Vikings.* London, 1930.
KOHT, HALVDAN: *The Old Norse Sagas.* New York, 1931.
NICHOLSON, R. A.: *A Literary History of the Arabs.* Second edition. London, 1930.
OLRIK, AXEL: *Viking Civilization.* Revised edition. New York, 1930.
SARTON, GEORGE: *Introduction to the History of Science.* Vol. 1.
SCHEVILL, F.: *The History of the Balkan Peninsula.*
SCOTT, S. P.: *History of the Moorish Empire in Europe.* Philadelphia, 1904. 3 vols.
* SNORRI, STURLUSON: *Heimskringla.* Various translations.

STEPHENSON, CARL: *Mediaeval Feudalism.* Ithaca, 1942.
THOMPSON, J. W.: "The Commerce of France in the Ninth Century." *Journal of Political Economy,* XXIII (1915), pp. 857–87.
Viking Tales of the North. Fourth edition. Chicago, 1901.
WILLIAMS, MARY W.: *Social Scandinavia in the Viking Age.* New York, 1920.

Ch. 8: *The World of John Scotus Erigena*

BETT, H.: *Scotus Erigena.* Cambridge, 1925.
GARDNER, ALICE: *Studies in John the Scot.* London, 1900.
LOT, F., and HALPHEN, L.: *La Règne de Charles le Chauve.* Paris, 1909.
MACDONALD, A. J.: *Authority and Reason in the Early Middle Ages.* Oxford, 1933.
* NITHARD: *Histoire des Fils de Louis le Pieux.* Paris, 1926.
POOLE, REGINALD L.: *Illustrations of the History of Mediaeval Thought.* Revised edition. New York, 1920.
ROY, J.: *St. Nicholas I.* London, 1901.
STEPHENSON, C.: *Mediaeval Feudalism.*
TAYLOR, H. O.: *The Mediaeval Mind.*
THOMPSON, J. W.: *The Decline of the Missi Dominici in Frankish Gaul.* Decennial Publications of the University of Chicago, IV (1903), pp. 291–310.
——, *The Literacy of the Laity in the Middle Ages.* Berkeley, 1939.
TOWNSEND, W. J.: *The Great Schoolmen.*
VÁMBÉRY, A.: *The Story of Hungary.* New York, 1886.
* WILLIAM OF MALMESBURY: *Chronicle.* London, 1847.

Ch. 9: *The World of Alfred*

* ALFRED: *Version of the Consolations of Boethius.* Oxford, 1900.
* ——, *Works.* J. A. Giles, Ed. Oxford, 1858.
* ——, *Soliloquies of St. Augustine.* Hargrave, Tr. New York, 1904.
* THE ANGLO-SAXON CHRONICLE. London, 1934. (Everyman's Library)
* ASSER: *Life of King Alfred.* Boston, 1906. (Also in GILES, J. A.: *Old English Chronicles*)
BOWKER, ALFRED, Ed.: *Alfred the Great.* London, 1899.
BROOKS, S. A.: *King Alfred as Educator of His People.* London, 1907.
BROWNE, G. F.: *King Alfred's Books.* London, 1920.
CALVERT, A. F.: *Moorish Remains in Spain.* London, 1906.
CAPPER, D. P.: *The Vikings of Britain.* London, 1937.
* GILES, J. A., Ed.: *Memorials of King Alfred.* London, 1863.

HODGKIN, ROBERT H.: *A History of the Anglo-Saxons.* Second edition. Oxford, 1939. 2 vols.
HODGKIN, T.: *The Political History of England.* Vol. 1, London, 1906.
KERNER, ROBERT J.: *The Urge to the Sea; the Course of Russian History.* Berkeley, 1942.
LE BON, G.: *Le Civilisation des Arabes.* Paris, 1884.
LEES, BEATRICE A.: *Alfred the Great.* London, 1919.
LIPSON, E.: *An Introduction to the Economic History of England.* London, 1915–31. 3 vols.
OMAN, C. W. C.: *England before the Norman Conquest.* London, 1910.
PLUMMER, C.: *The Life and Times of Alfred the Great.* Oxford, 1902.
RAMSAY, SIR J. H.: *The Foundations of England.* London, 1898. 2 vols.
STENTON, F. M.: *Anglo-Saxon England.* Oxford, 1943.

ശ ശ ശ

PART VI

The Tenth Century

BARING, M.: *The Russian People.* London, 1911.
BEAZLEY, C. R.: *Russia from the Varangians to the Bolsheviks.* Oxford, 1918.
FINLAY, G.: *History of the Byzantine Empire.* New York, 1906. (Everyman's Library)
GJERSET, K.: *History of the Norwegian People.* 2 vols. New York, 1915.
GRAS, N. S. B. and E. C.: *The Economic and Social History of an English Village, A.D. 909–1928.* Cambridge, Mass., 1930.
HASKINS, C. H.: *Studies in Norman Institutions.* Cambridge, 1919.
* HELMHOLDUS: *Chronicle of the Slavs.* New York, 1935. (*Records of Civilization*)
HOVGAARD, W.: *The Voyages of the Northmen to America.* New York, 1914.
KLUCHEVSKY, V. O.: *A History of Russia.* London, 1911–31. 5 vols.
* LIUDPRAND OF CREMONA: *Works.* New York, 1930.
LÜTZOW, F. H. H. VON: *Bohemia, an Historical Sketch.* London, 1909. (Everyman's Library)
MUNRO and SELLERY: *Medieval Civilization.* Pp. 137–52.
NOWAK, FRANK: *Medieval Slavdom and the Rise of Russia.* New York, 1930. (Berkshire Studies.)
* REEVES, A. M., Tr.: *The Finding of Vineland the Good.* New York,

1906. (*Original Narratives of American History: Columbus and Cabot*)
* THE RUSSIAN PRIMARY CHRONICLE. Cambridge, Mass., 1930.
SAMUELSON, J.: *Bulgaria Past and Present.* London, 1888.

Ch. 10: The World of Otto I

BARRACLOUGH, GEOFFREY, Ed. and tr.: *Mediaeval Germany, 911–1250.* Oxford, 1938. 2 vols.
BLASHFIELD, E. W.: *Portraits and Backgrounds.* New York, 1917.
CALMETTE, J.: *La Société Féodale.* Paris, 1923.
CUTTS, E. L.: *Scenes and Characters of the Middle Ages.* Sixth edition. London, 1925.
EVANS, JOAN: *Life in Mediaeval France.* Oxford University Press, 1925.
FUNDENBURG, G. B.: *Feudal France in the French Epic.* Princeton, 1919.
GREGOROVIUS, F.: *History of the City of Rome.*
JOHNSON, EDWARD N.: *The Secular Activities of the German Episcopate, 919–1024.* Lincoln, Nebraska, 1932.
PETIT-DUTAILLIS, CHARLES: *The Feudal Monarchy in France and England.* London, 1936.
* RICHER: *Histoire de France (883–995).* Paris, 1930.
ROBINSON, J. A.: *The Times of St. Dunstan.* Oxford, 1923.
* ROSWITHA: *Plays.* London, 1923. (Another translation, HROSWITHA, London, 1923.)
SABINE, G. H.: *A History of Political Theory.* New York, 1937.
THOMPSON, JAMES W.: *Feudal Germany.* Chicago, 1928.
TOUT, T. F.: *The Empire and the Papacy, 918–1273.* Eighth edition. London, 1932.
ZEYDEL, E. H.: *The Holy Roman Empire in German Literature.* New York, 1918.

Ch. 11: The World of Gerbert

ALLEN, R.: "Pope Sylvester II," *English Historical Review,* VII (1892), pp. 625–68.
* BELL, C. H., Tr.: *Peasant Life in Old German Epics, Meier Helmbrecht und der Arme Heinrich.* New York, 1931. (*Records of Civilization*)
BURKE, U. R.: *A History of Spain from the Earliest Times to the Death of Ferdinand the Catholic.* Second edition, London, 1900. 2 vols.
BURR, G. L.: "The Year 1000," *American Historical Review,* VI (1900–1901), pp. 429–439. Reprinted in BURR, G. L.: *Life and Writings.* Ithaca, 1943.

CHAPMAN, C. E.: *A History of Spain, founded on the* Historia of Altamira. New York, 1918.
CUNNINGHAM, W.: *Western Civilization in its Economic Aspects: Medieval and Modern.* Cambridge, 1900.
DARLINGTON, O. G.: "Gerbert," *Speculum,* XI (1936), pp. 509–20.
——, "Gerbert, the Teacher," *American Historical Review,* LII (1947), pp. 456–76.
DÖLLINGER, J. J. IVAN: *Silvester II,* in *Fables Respecting the Popes of the Middle Ages.* London, 1871.
* GERBERT: *Lettres.* Havet, Ed. Paris, 1889.
LASALLE DE ROCHEMAURE, LE DUC DE: *Gerbert, Silvestre II.* Paris, 1914.
LUCHAIRE, ACHILLE: *Manuel des Institutions Françaises.* Paris, 1892.
NEILSON, NELLIE: *Medieval Agrarian Economy.* New York, 1936. (Berkshire Studies)
PARAIN, CHARLES: "The Evolution of Agricultural Technique," *Cambridge Economic History,* vol. I., ch. 3. Cambridge, 1941.
PETIT-DUTAILLIS, C.: *La Monarchie Féodale en France et en Angleterre, X^e–XIIIe Siècle.* Paris, 1933. (Also in English translation.)
PICAVET, F. J.: *Gerbert: un Pape Philosophe.* Paris, 1897.
PIRENNE, HENRI: *Economic and Social History of Medieval Europe.* London, 1936.
SARTON, G.: *Introduction to the History of Science.*
TAYLOR, H. O.: *The Medieval Mind.*
THOMPSON, J. W.: *An Economic and Social History of the Middle Ages.*
THORNDIKE, LYNN: *History of Magic and Experimental Science.*

෴ ෴ ෴

PART VII

The Eleventh Century

ADAMS, HENRY: *Mont-Saint Michel and Chartres.* Boston, 1913.
BALDWIN, SUMMERFIELD: *Business in the Middle Ages.* New York, 1937. (Berkshire Studies)
BATESON, MARY: *Mediaeval England.* London, 1904.
CLAPHAM, A. W.: *Romanesque Architecture in Western Europe.* Oxford, 1936.
* COULTON, G. G., Ed.: *Life in the Middle Ages.* New York, 1935.
CURTIS, E.: *Roger of Sicily and the Normans in Lower Italy.* New York, 1912.

* DAVIES, R. T., Ed.: *Civilization in Mediaeval England*. New York, 1935.
* FULCHER OF CHARTRES: *Chronicle of the First Crusade*. Philadelphia, 1941. (*Translations and Reprints,* Third series)
GROS, N. S. B., and E. C.: *The Economic and Social History of an English Village, 909-1928*.
* KREY, A. C., Ed.: *The First Crusade*. Princeton, 1921.
LARSON, L. M.: *Canute the Great*. New York, 1912.
LEA, H. C.: *A History of Sacerdotal Celibacy*. Third edition. New York, 1907.
LECKY, W. E. H.: *History of the Rise and Influence of the Spirit of Rationalism*. Revised edition. London, 1870. 2 vols.
LIPSON, E.: *An Introduction to the Economic History of England*. Vol. I.
MILLER, W.: *The Latin Orient*. London, 1920.
MUNRO, D. C.: "Speech of Pope Urban II," *American Historical Review,* XI (1905-06), pp. 231-42.
NEWHALL, R. A.: *The Crusades*. New York, 1927. (Berkshire Studies)
PAETOW, L. J., Ed.: *The Crusades and Other Historical Essays Presented to Dana C. Munro*. New York, 1928.
PORTER, A. W.: *Lombard Architecture*. New Haven, 1915-17. 4 vols.
STENTON, F. M.: *The First Century of English Feudalism*. Oxford, 1932.
STEPHENSON, CARL: "Feudalism and its antecedents in England," *American Historical Review,* XLVIII (1943), pp. 245-65.
STEVENSON, W. B.: *The Crusades in the East*. Cambridge, 1907.
VILLARI, P.: *Mediaeval Italy*. London, 1910.
VINOGRADOFF, P.: *English Society in the Eleventh Century*. Oxford, 1908.
WAERN, CECILIA: *Mediaeval Sicily*. New York, 1911.

Ch. 12: *The World of Lanfranc*

BELLOC, HILAIRE: *The Book of the Bayeux Tapestry, presenting the complete work in a series of colour facsimiles*. London, 1914.
BROOKE, Z. N.: *The English Church and the Papacy*. Cambridge, 1931.
CHURCH, R. W.: *Life of St. Anselm*. New York, 1905.
DAVIES, H. W. C.: *England under the Normans and Angevins*. London, 1905.
DUFF, NORA: *Matilda of Tuscany*. London, 1909.
* DUNCALF and KREY: *Parallel Source Problems*.
GALBRAITH, V. H.: "The Making of Domesday Book" *European History Review* LIX (1942) pp. 166-77.
* GREGORY VII: *A Selection of the Letters of Hildebrand*. London, 1853.
* ———, *Correspondence*. New York, 1932. (*Records of Civilization*)
MACDONALD, A. J.: *Lanfranc*. Oxford, 1926.

——, *Authority and Reason in the Early Middle Ages.* Oxford, 1933.
MAITLAND, F. W.: *Domesday Book and Beyond.* Cambridge, 1897.
MATHEW, H.: *The Life and Times of Hildebrand.* London, 1910.
SMITH, LUCY M.: "Cluny and Gregory VII," European History Review, XXVI (1911), pp. 20–33.
STENTON, F. M.: *The First Century of English Feudalism, 1066–1166.* Oxford, 1932.
STEPHENS, W. R. W.: *Hildebrand and His Times.* London, 1914.
TELLENBACH, G.: *Church, State and Christian Society at the Time of the Investiture Contest.* Oxford, 1940.
VILLEMAIN, A. F.: *The Life of Gregory VII.* London, 1874. 2 vols.
VINCENT, M. R.: *Age of Hildebrand.* New York, 1896.
WEBB, C. C. J.: *Studies in the History of Natural Religion.* Oxford, 1915.

ড় ড় ড়

PART VIII

The Twelfth Century

CHAPIN, ELIZABETH: *Les Villes des Foires de Champagne, des Origines au Début du XIV° Siècle.* Paris, 1937.
CLARKE, M. V.: *The Medieval City State.* London, 1926.
GILSON, ETIENNE: *The Spirit of Mediaeval Philosophy.* New York, 1936.
GIRY, A. and REVILLE, A.: *The Emancipation of the Mediaeval Towns.* New York, 1907.
HASKINS, C. H.: *The Renaissance of the Twelfth Century:* Cambridge, Mass., 1927.
HEARNSHAW, F. J. C., Ed.: *Mediaeval Contributions to Modern Civilization.* London, 1921. (Chapters 4, 7.)
* HITTI, P. K., Tr.: *An Arab-Syrian Gentleman.* New York, 1929. (*Records of Civilization*)
LANG, P. H.: *Music in Western Civilization.*
LUCHAIRE, A.: *Les Communes Françaises à L'époque des Capetiens Directs.* New edition. Paris, 1911.
MILLER, W.: *The Latins in the Levant.* Cambridge, 1921.
* OTTO OF FREISING: *The Two Cities.* New York, 1928. (*Records of Civilization*)
* OUSAMA (USAMAH IBN MURSHID): *Autobiography.* New York, 1929.
POOLE, ARTHUR LANE: *Obligations of Society in the Twelfth and Thirteenth Centuries.* Oxford, 1946.
SALZMAN, L. F.: *English Industries of the Middle Ages.* London, 1913.

TAYLOR, H. O.: *The Medieval Mind.*
* WILLIAM OF MALMESBURY: *Chronicle.*
* WADDELL, HELEN, Tr.: *Mediaeval Latin Lyrics.* New York, 1930.

Ch. 13: The World of St. Bernard of Clairvaux

* ABELARD: *Historia Calamitatum.* St. Paul, 1922.
BARKER, E.: *The Crusades.* London, 1923.
* ST. BERNARD: *Letters.* Ed. F. A. Gasquet. London, 1904.
* ——, *On the Love of God.* London, 1906.
* ——, *The Steps of Humility.* Cambridge, 1940.
CARRÉ, M. H.: *Realists and Nominalists.* Oxford, 1946.
COULTON, G. G.: *Five Centuries of Religion,* Vol. 1. Cambridge, 1927.
DAVID, C. W.: *Robert Curthose, Duke of Normandy.* Cambridge, Mass., 1920.
GARDINER, ALICE: *Medieval Sculpture in France.* Cambridge, 1937.
GILSON, ETIENNE: *The Spirit of Mediaeval Philosophy.* New York, 1936.
LA MONTE, JOHN L.: *Feudal Monarchy in the Latin Kingdom of Jerusalem, 1100–1291.* Cambridge, 1932.
MCCABE, J.: *Peter Abelard.* New York, 1901.
* MCKEON, R., Ed.: *Selections from Medieval Philosophers.* New York, 1929–30. 2 vols.
MORISON, J. C.: *St. Bernard.* Second edition. London, 1901.
MUNRO, D. C.: *The Kingdom of the Crusaders.* New York, 1935.
NEWHALL, R. A.: *The Crusades.* New York, 1927. (Berkshire Studies)
PAETOW, L. J., Ed. "The Crusades." Essays presented to D. C. Munro. New York, 1928.
* SCOTT-MONCRIEFF, C. K., Tr.: *The Letters of Abelard and Heloise.* New York, 1926.
* SIKES, J. G.: *Peter Abailard.* Cambridge, 1932.
STEVENSON, W. B.: *The Crusaders in the East.* Cambridge, 1907.
STORRS, R. S.: *Bernard of Clairvaux.* New York, 1892.
VACANDARD, E.: *Vie de St. Bernard.* Fourth edition. Paris, 1910. 2 vols.
WADDELL, HELEN: *The Wandering Scholars.* London, 1907.
WILLIAMS, W. W.: *Saint Bernard of Clairvaux.* Manchester, 1935.
WORKMAN, H. B.: *The Evolution of the Monastic Ideal.* London, 1913.
WRIGHT, J. K.: *The Geographical Lore of the Time of the Crusades.* New York, 1925.
YEWDALE, RALPH B.: *Bohemond I, Prince of Antioch.* Princeton, 1924.

Ch. 14: The World of Frederick Barbarossa

BALZANI, UGO: *The Popes and the Hohenstaufen.* London, 1901.
BUTLER, W. F.: *The Lombard Communes.* New York, 1906.

COULTON, G. G.: *Medieval Panorama, the English Scene from the Conquest to the Reformation.* New York, 1938.
GREEN, ALICE: *Henry II.* Boston, 1916.
HALL, HUBERT: *Court Life under the Plantagenets.* London, 1890. (See plates)
HASKINS, C. H.: *The Normans in European History.* Boston, 1915.
——, *Studies in Medieval Culture.* Oxford, 1929.
* HUTTON, W. H., Ed.: *St. Thomas of Canterbury.*
——, *Thomas Becket.* Cambridge, 1926.
KNAPPEN, M. M.: *Constitutional and Legal History of England.* New York, 1942.
* OTTO OF FREISING: *The Two Cities.* New York, 1928. (*Records of Civilization*)
POLLOCK, F. and MAITLAND, F. W.: *The History of English Law.* Second edition. Cambridge, 1898.
PREVITÉ-ORTON, C. W.: *Outlines of Medieval History.* Second edition. Cambridge, 1929.
SALZMAN, L. F.: *Henry II.* Boston, 1914.
* SUGER: *Vie de Louis VI.* Paris, 1929.
TURBERVILLE, A. S.: *Mediaeval Heresy and the Inquisition.* London, 1920.
VACANDARD, E.: *The Inquisition: a Critical and Historical Study of the Coercive Power of the Church.* New York, 1908.

ᔐ ᔐ ᔐ

PART IX

The Thirteenth Century

ARNOLD, H.: *Stained Glass of the Middle Ages in England and France.* New York, 1913.
CHEYNEY, E. R.: *The Dawn of a New Era.* New York, 1936.
* COULTON, G. G., Ed.: *From St. Francis to Dante. The Chronicle of Salimbene.* London, 1907.
D'ARCY, M. C.: *Thomas Aquinas.* Boston, 1930.
DAVIS, W. S.: *Life on a Mediaeval Barony.* New York, 1923.
FISHER, H. A. L.: *The Mediaeval Empire.* London, 1898. 2 vols.
GRAFMANN, M.: *Thomas Aquinas.* New York, 1928.
HARRISON, FREDERIC: *The Thirteenth Century.* In *The Meaning of History.* New York, 1908.

HASKINS, C. H.: *Rise of Universities.* New York, 1923.
——, *Studies in Mediaeval Culture.*
HOMANS, G. C.: *English Villages of the Thirteenth Century.* Cambridge, Mass., 1941.
JARRETT, BEDE: *Social Theories of the Middle Ages, 1200–1500.* Boston, 1926.
JESSOP, A.: *The Coming of the Friars.* London, 1928.
KIMBLE, G. H. T.: *Geography in the Middle Ages.* London, 1938.
LAMB, H.: *Genghis Khan.* New York, 1927.
MÂLE, EMILE: *L'art Religieux en France.* Paris, 1924. 3 vols.
MELLER, W. C.: *A Knight's Life in the Days of Chivalry.* London, 1924.
MOORMAN, J. R. H.: *Church Life in England in the Thirteenth Century.* Cambridge, 1946.
* NORTON, A. O.: *Readings in the History of Education: Mediaeval Universities.* Cambridge, 1909.
OMAN, C. W. C.: *Castles.* London, 1926.
* PARIS, MATTHEW: *History.* London, 1852–54. 3 vols.
RAIT, R. S.: *Life in the Mediaeval University.* Cambridge, 1912.
RASHDALL, HASTINGS: *The Universities of Europe in the Middle Ages.* New edition. Oxford, 1936. 3 vols.
* ROGER OF WENDOVER: *Flores Historiarum.* London, 1894.
* SEYBOLT, R. F., Ed.: *Manuale Scholarium.* Cambridge, 1921.
* ST. THOMAS AQUINAS: *Basic Works.* New York, 1945. 2 vols.
* VILLARD DE HONNECOURT: *Album de Villard de Honnecourt, Architecte du XIIIe Siècle.* Paris, 1906.
WHITE, LYNN, JR.: "Natural Science and Naturalistic Art in the Middle Ages," *American Historical Review*, LII (1947), pp. 421–35.

Ch. 15: The World of Innocent III

* ADAMS, G. B. and STEPHENS, H. M., Ed.: *Select Documents of English Constitutional History.* New York, 1933.
ADAMS, HENRY: *Mont St. Michel and Chartres.*
* AMBROISE: *The Crusade of Richard the Lion-Heart.* New York, 1941. (Records of Civilization)
* ARCHER, T. A., Ed.: *The Crusade of Richard I, 1189–1192.* New York, 1889.
* ST. BONAVENTURA: *Life of St. Francis.* London, 1926.
COULTON, G. G.: *The Death Penalty for Heresy from 1184 to 1921.* London, 1924.
FATHER CUTHBERT: *Life of St. Francis of Assisi.* Second edition. New York, 1933.

* DAVIES, R. TREVOR, Ed.: *Documents Illustrating the History of Civilization in Medieval England (1066–1500)*. New York, 1926.
HUTTON, W. H.: *Philip Augustus*. London, 1896.
* JOINVILLE: "Chronicle of the Crusade of St. Louis," *Memoirs of the Crusades*. London, 1908. (Everyman's Library)
LEA, HENRY C.: *A History of the Inquisition in the Middle Ages*. New York, 1888. 3 vols.
* BROTHER LEO: *The Mirror of Perfection*. London, 1902.
LUCHAIRE, ACHILLE: *Innocent III*. Paris, 1905–8. 6 vols.
—— *Social Life in the Reign of Philip Augustus*. New York, 1912.
MCKECHNIE, W. S.: *Magna Carta*. Second edition. Glasgow, 1914.
MALDEN, W. E., Ed.: *Magna Carta Commemoration Essays*. London, 1917.
MORRIS, W. A.: *The Constitutional History of England to 1216*. New York, 1930.
NORGATE, KATE: *England under the Angevins*. London, 1887. 2 vols.
—— *John Lackland*. London, 1902.
—— *Richard the Lion Heart*. London, 1924.
* OKEY, T., Ed.: *The Little Flowers and the Life of St. Francis, with the Mirror of Perfection*. London, 1910. (Everyman's Library)
PACKARD, SIDNEY K.: *Europe and the Church under Innocent III*. New York, 1927. (Berkshire Studies)
PEARS, SIR EDWIN: *The Fall of Constantinople: Being the Story of the Fourth Crusade*. New York, 1886.
—— *The Destruction of the Greek Empire*. London, 1903.
PORTER, A. K.: *Mediaeval Architecture*. New York, 1912. 2 vols.
* ROBERT OF CLARI: *Conquest of Constantinople*. New York, 1936. (*Records of Civilization*)
SABATIER, PAUL: *Life of St. Francis of Assisi*. London, 1922.
VASILIEV, A. A.: *History of the Byzantine Empire*. Madison, 1928–30. 2 vols.
YOUNG, KARL: *The Drama of the Medieval Church*. Oxford, 1933.

Ch. 16: The World of Frederick II

ADAMS, HENRY: *Mont St. Michel and Chartres*.
* ANDRÉ LE CHAPELAIN: *The Art of Courtly Love*. New York, 1941. (*Records of Civilization*)
* *The Book of the Knight of Latour Landry*. London, 1930.
CHAYTOR, H. J.: *The Troubadours*. Cambridge, 1912.
* DICKINSON, C., Ed.: *Troubadour Songs*. New York, 1920.
DUNN, PATTISON: *Leading Figures*, pp. 114–43.

* FREDERICK II: *The Art of Falconry.* London, 1943.
HASKINS, C. H.: *Medieval Science.*
* JOINVILLE, JEHAN, SIRE DE: "Chronicle of the Crusade of St. Louis," *Memoirs of the Crusades.* London, 1908. (Everyman's Library)
KANTOROWICZ, ERNEST: *Frederick II.* London, 1931.
KINGTON, T. L.: *History of Frederick II.* London, 1862. 2 vols.
* LA VIE DU SAINT ROI LOUIS. Paris, 1928.
* MARZIALS, SIR FRANK, Ed.: *Memoirs of the Crusades by Villehardouin and de Joinville.* London, 1908. (Everyman's Library)
PERRY, F.: *St. Louis.* New York, 1901.
PRESTAGE, E., Ed.: *Chivalry: a Series of Studies to Illustrate Its Historical Significance and Civilizing Influence.* London, 1928.
SEDGWICK, H. D.: *Italy in the Thirteenth Century.* Boston, 1912. 2 vols.
SHEARER, CRESWELL: *The Renaissance of Architecture in Southern Italy.* Cambridge, 1935.
SLAUGHTER, GERTRUDE: *The Amazing Frederick.* New York, 1937.
STALEY, E.: *The Guilds of Florence.* London, 1906.
* VILLANI, G.: *Selections from the Croniche Fiorentine.* London, 1936.
WICKSTEED, P. H.: *Dante and Aquinas.* New York, 1913.
* YULE, H., Ed.: *Cathay and the Way Thither.* London, 1913–16. (Hakluyt Society)

Ch. 17: The World of Dante

CHEYNEY, E. P.: *The Dawn of a New Era.*
CLARKE, MAUD V.: *The Medieval City State.* London, 1926.
* DANTE: *Divine Comedy.* Norton, Tr. Boston, 1891–92. 3 vols. (prose). H. W. Longfellow, Tr. Boston, 1867–71, 3 vols. H. F. Cary, Tr. (Everyman's Library)
* ——, *Convivio.* London, 1903.
* ——, *Vita Nuova.* Many editions.
* ——, *De Monarchia.* Boston, 1914.
GEBHART, E.: *Mystics and Heretics in Italy.* New York, 1923.
GIERKE, O.: *Political Theories of the Middle Ages.*
HODGSON, F. C.: *Venice in the Thirteenth and Fourteenth Centuries.* London, 1910.
MATHER, F. J.: *A History of Italian Painting.* Revised edition. New York, 1938.
MCILWAIN, C. H.: *The Growth of Political Thought in the West.* Chapter 6.
OLIPHANT, MARGARET: *Makers of Florence.* Third edition. London, 1889.
* POLO, MARCO: *Travels.* Everyman's Library and many other editions.

Bibliography [611

SALVEMINI, G.: "Florence in the Time of Dante," *Speculum*, XI (1936), pp. 317-26.
SCARTAZZINI: *A Companion to Dante*. London, 1893.
SCHEVILL, FERDINAND: *History of Florence*. London, 1936.

⚘ ⚘ ⚘

PART X

The Fourteenth Century

* BOCCACCIO: *Decameron*. Many editions.
EMERTON, E.: *The* Defensor Pacis *of Marsiglio of Padua*. Cambridge, 1920.
—— *Humanism and Tyranny: Studies in the Italian Trecento*. Cambridge, Mass., 1925.
GARDNER, E. G.: *St. Catherine of Siena*. London and New York, 1907.
GASQUET, FRANCIS A.: *Black Death of 1348 and 1349*. London, 1908.
GIBBONS, H. A.: *The Foundation of the Ottoman Empire, 1300-1403*. Oxford, 1916.
HECKSCHER, E. F.: *Mercantilism*. Vol. I. New York, 1935.
HENDERSON, E. F.: *A Short History of Germany*. Vol. I. New York, 1937.
HOBSON, J. A.: *Evolution of Modern Capitalism*. New York, 1926.
HUIZINGA, JOHAN: *Waning of the Middle Ages: a Study of the Forms of Life, Thought, and Art in France and the Netherlands in the XIVth and XVth Centuries*. London, 1924.
JUSSERAND, J. J.: *English Wayfaring Life in the Middle Ages*. London, 1889.
LODGE, R.: *The Close of the Middle Ages, 1273-1494*. London, 1922.
MERRIMAN, R. B.: *The Rise of the Spanish Empire in the Old World and the New*. Vols. I and II. New York, 1918.
MUZZEY, D. S.: *The Spiritual Franciscans*. New York, 1907.
NOWAK, F.: *Medieval Slavdom and the Rise of Russia*. New York, 1930.
PACKARD, L. B.: *The Commercial Revolution*. New York, 1927.
PAINTER, SIDNEY: *French Chivalry*. Baltimore, 1940.
POWER, EILEEN: *Medieval People*. London and New York, 1924.
* ROBINSON, F. N., Ed.: *The Complete Works of Geoffrey Chaucer*. Cambridge, 1933.
* ROBINSON, J. H., and ROLFE, H. W.: *Petrarch, the First Modern Scholar and Man of Letters; a selection from his correspondence with Boc-*

caccio and other friends, designed to illustrate the beginnings of the Renaissance. New York and London, 1914.
SALEMBIER, LOUIS: *Great Western Schism.* London, 1907.
SÉE, H.: *Modern Capitalism.* Adelphi, 1928.
SNELL, F. J.: *The Fourteenth Century.* Edinburgh, 1923.
THORNDIKE, LYNN: *A History of Magic and Experimental Science During the Fourteenth and Fifteenth Centuries.* New York, 1934. 2 vols.
WADDELL, HELEN: *Wandering Scholars.* Glasgow and Boston, 1927.
ZIMMERN, H.: *Hansa Towns.* New York, 1889.

Ch. 18: *The World of John Wycliffe*

BOASE, T. S. R.: *Boniface VIII.* London, 1933.
COULTON, G. G.: *Chaucer and His England.* London, 1908.
* FROISSART: *Chronicles.* (Everyman's Library)
GAIRDNER, JAMES: *Lollardry and the Reformation in England.* London, 1908–13. 4 vols.
LORIMER, P. J.: *John Wycliffe and His English Precursors.* London, 1884.
LUCAS, H. S.: *The Low Countries and the Hundred Years' War.* Ann Arbor, 1929.
OMAN, SIR CHARLES: *Great Revolt of 1381.* Oxford, 1906.
PATTISON, R. P. D.: *The Black Prince.* London, 1910.
POOLE, R. L.: *Wycliffe and Movements for Reform.* New York, 1896.
STODDARD, E. V.: *Bertrand du Guesclin.* New York, 1897.
TERRY, S. B.: *Financing the Hundred Years' War, 1337–1369.*
TREVELYAN, G. M.: *England in the Age of Wycliffe.* London, 1909.
WORKMAN, H. B.: *John Wyclif.* Oxford, 1926.

∽ ∽ ∽

PART XI

The Fifteenth Century

ABBOTT, WILBUR C.: *Expansion of Europe, A History of the Foundations of the Modern World.* New York, 1924.
* ARCHER-HIND, MRS., Ed.: *Paston Letters.* London and New York, 1924. 2 vols.
BERENSON, B.: *The Italian Painters of the Renaissance.* Oxford, 1930.
BURCKHARDT, JAKOB C.: *Civilization of the Period of the Renaissance in Italy.* London, 1929.

CLARKE, MAUDE V.: *The Medieval City State.* London, 1926.
* CUST, R. H. H., Tr.: *Life of Benvenuto Cellini.* London and New York, 1910. 2 vols.
FERGUSON, W. K.: *The Renaissance.* New York, 1940.
HULME, E. M.: *The Renaissance, the Protestant Revolution, and the Catholic Reformation.* New York, 1915.
HYMA, ALBERT: *Christian Renaissance*: *A History of the* Devotio moderna. Grand Rapids, 1924.
KITTS, E. J.: *In the Age of the Councils.* London, 1908.
MOORE, C. H.: *The Character of Renaissance Architecture.* New York, 1905.
PRESTAGE, E.: *Portuguese Pioneers.* New York, 1933.
ROOSES, M.: *Art in Flanders.* New York, 1927.
SCHEVILL, F.: *The First Century of Italian Humanism.* New York, 1928.
SICHEL, EDITH: *The Renaissance.* New York, 1914.
THOMPSON, J. W., et al.: *Civilization of the Renaissance.* Chicago, 1929.
WAUGH, W. T.: *A History of Europe from 1378–1494.* London, 1932.
* WHITCOMB, MERRICK: *Literary Source Book of the Renaissance.* Philadelphia, 1903.
WOODWARD, WILLIAM H.: *Studies in Education During the Age of the Renaissance.* Cambridge, 1914.
WYLIE, JAMES H.: *Council of Constance.* New York, 1900.

Ch. 19: *The World of Jacques Coeur*

BEAZLEY, C. R.: *Prince Henry the Navigator.* New York, 1895.
BOOTH, CECILY: *Cosimo I.* Cambridge, 1921.
BOUVIER, R.: *Un Financier Colonial au xve Siècle*: *Jacques Coeur.* Paris, 1928.
CASEY, R. J.: *The Last Kingdom of Burgundy.* London, 1924.
CLEMENT, PIERRE: *Jacques Coeur et Charles VII.* Paris, 1865. 2 vols.
HERBEN, JAN: *Hus and His Followers.* London, 1926.
KING, WILSON: *Chronicles of Three Free Cities, Hamburg, Bremen, Lübeck.* London and New York, 1914.
KINGSFORD, C. L.: *The Life of Henry V.* London, 1902.
LANE, F. C.: *Venetian Ships and Shipping of the Renaissance.* Baltimore, 1934.
LOWELL, FRANCIS C.: *Joan of Arc.* New York, 1896.
LUTZOW, F.: *The Life and Times of John Huss.* New York, 1909.
MAIN, E.: *The Emperor Sigismund.* Oxford, 1903.
MIJATOVICH, C.: *Constantine, the Last Emperor of the Greeks.* London, 1892.
* MONSTRELET, E. DE: *Chronicles.* London and New York, 1867. 2 vols.

NEWHALL, RICHARD A.: *English Conquest of Normandy, 1416–24; A Study in Fifteenth-century Warfare.* New Haven, 1924.
PAINE, A. B.: *Joan of Arc.* New York, 1925.
PEARS, EDWIN: *The Destruction of the Greek Empire and the Story of the Capture of Constantinople by the Turks.* New York, 1903.
PUTNAM, RUTH: *A Medieval Princess.* New York, 1904. (Holland and Burgundy)
SCHAFF, D. S.: *John Huss, His Life, Teachings, and Death.* New York, 1915.
WYLIE, J. H.: *Reign of Henry V.* Cambridge, 1914. 2 vols.

Ch. 20: *The World of Lorenzo dei Medici*

ADY, CECILIA M.: *History of Milan under the Sforza.* London, 1907.
ARMSTRONG, EDWARD: *Lorenzo the Magnificent and Florence of the Fifteenth Century.* London and New York, 1896.
BODE, W.: *Florentine Sculptors of the Renaissance.* London, 1928.
CHAMPION, PIERRE: *Louis XI.* Paris, 1927. 2 vols.
* COMINES, PHILIPPE DE: *Memoirs.* London, 1901–04. 2 vols.
EHRENBERG, R.: *Capital and Finance in the Age of the Renaissance.* New York, 1928.
HARE, C.: *Life of Louis XI.* London, 1907.
HYETT, FRANCIS A.: *Florence, Her History and Art to the Fall of the Republic.* London and New York, 1903.
MORISON, S. E.: *Admiral of the Ocean Sea.* Boston, 1942.
PLUNKET, IRENE L.: *Isabel of Castile and the Making of the Spanish Nation, 1451–1504.* New York, 1919.
PUTNAM, RUTH: *Charles the Bold, Last Duke of Burgundy, 1433–1477.* New York and London, 1908.
RICCI, CORRADO: *Architecture and Decorative Sculpture of the High and Late Renaissance in Italy.* New York, 1923.
SMEATON, W. H. O.: *The Medici and the Italian Renaissance.* New York, 1901.
STRIEDER, J.: *Jacob Fugger the Rich, Merchant and Banker of Augsburg.* New York, 1931.
YOUNG, GEORGE F.: *The Medici.* London, 1909. 2 vols.

PART XII

The Sixteenth Century

ALLEN, JOHN W.: *History of Political Thought in the Sixteenth Century.* London, 1928.
BOEHMER, H.: *The Jesuits.* Philadelphia, 1928.
* CASTIGLIONE, BALDASSARE: *Book of the Courtier.* London, 1900.
CHAPMAN, C. E.: *Colonial Hispanic America.* New York, 1937.
CHEYNEY, EDWARD P.: *European Background of American History, 1300–1600.* New York and London, 1904.
DAVIES, R. T.: *The Golden Century of Spain.* New York, 1937.
DUNNING, WILLIAM A.: *History of Political Theories from Luther to Montesquieu.* New York, 1905.
* GUICCIARDINI, F.: *Counsels and Reflections.* N. H. Thomson, Tr. London, 1890.
HANNAY, D.: *The Great Chartered Companies.* London, 1926.
HAYES, CARLTON J. H.: *A Political and Cultural History of Modern Europe.* New York, 1939. 2 vols.
HEARNSHAW, F. J. C., Ed.: *Social and Political Ideas of Some Great Thinkers of the Renaissance and the Reformation.* London, 1925.
KIDD, B. J.: *Counter-Reformation.* London, 1933.
KIRKPATRICK, F. A.: *The Spanish Conquistadores.* New York, 1934.
* LINGELBACH, WILLIAM E.: *Merchant Adventurers of England, Their Laws and Ordinances, with Other Documents.* Philadelphia, 1902.
* MACHIAVELLI, N.: *The Prince.* Various editions.
O'BRIEN, GEORGE: *Essay on the Economic Effects of the Reformation.* London, 1923.
OMAN, SIR CHARLES: *The Sixteenth Century.* London, 1937.
READ, C.: *The Tudors.* New York, 1936.
ROTH, CECIL: *The Spanish Inquisition.* London, 1938.
SMITH, PRESERVED: *Age of the Reformation.* New York, 1920.
* TANNER, JOSEPH R.: *Tudor Constitutional Documents.* Cambridge, 1922.
TAWNEY, RICHARD H.: *Religion and the Rise of Capitalism.* London and New York, 1926.
TROELTSCH, E.: *Social Teachings of the Christian Churches.* New York, 1931.
UNWIN, G.: *Industrial Organization in the Sixteenth and Seventeenth Centuries.* London, 1904.
WARD, ADOLPHUS W.: *Counter Reformation.* London, 1910.

WEBER, M.: *The Protestant Ethic and the Spirit of Capitalism*. London, 1930.

Ch. 21: *The World of Erasmus*

ALLEN, PERCY S.: *Age of Erasmus*. Oxford, 1914.
——, *Erasmus' Services to Learning*. London, 1926.
* BRANT, SEBASTIAN: *Ship of Fools*. Edinburgh and New York, 1874. 2 vols.
* DRUMMOND, ROBERT B.: *Erasmus; His Life and Character, as Shown in His Correspondence and Works*. London, 1873. 2 vols.
* ERASMUS, D.: *The Praise of Folly*. Various editions.
* ——, *Familiar Colloquies*. New York, 1900.
HACKETT, FRANCIS: *Francis I*. New York, 1935.
JOURDAN, GEORGE V.: *Movement Towards Catholic Reform in the Early Sixteenth Century*. London, 1914.
MCELWEE, W. L.: *The Reign of Charles V*. New York, 1936.
MERRIMAN, R. B.: *Suleiman the Magnificent*. Cambridge, 1944.
* MORE, THOMAS: *Utopia*. Various editions.
* NICHOLS, FRANCIS M.: *Epistles of Erasmus from His Earliest Letters to His Fifty-First Year*. London and New York, 1901–18. 3 vols.
PASCAL, R.: *The Social Basis of the German Reformation*. London, 1933.
* PIGAFETTA, ANTONIO: *Magellan's Voyage around the World*. Cleveland, 1906.
PRESCOTT, W. H.: *History of the Reign of Ferdinand and Isabella the Catholic*. Philadelphia, 1904. 3 vols.
ROEDER, RALPH: *The Man of the Renaissance*. New York, 1933.
SMITH, PRESERVED: *Erasmus, A Study of His Life, Ideals and Place in History*.
—— *The Life and Letters of Martin Luther*. Cambridge, 1914.
* STOKES, FRANCIS G., Ed.: *Epistolae Obscurorum Virorum: The Latin Text with an English Rendering, Notes, and an Historical Introduction*. London, 1909.
TILLEY, A. A.: *The Literature of the French Renaissance*. Cambridge, 1904.
VEDDER, H. C.: *The Reformation in Germany*. New York, 1914.
VILLARI, P.: *Life and Times of Girolamo Savonarola*. London, 1888.
——, *Life and Times of Niccolo Machiavelli*. London, 1898. 2 vols.
WILLIAMS, C. H.: *The Making of the Tudor Despotism*. London, 1935.

Ch. 22: *The World of John Calvin*

BAX, E. B.: *The Peasants' War in Germany*. London, 1899.
BREEN, Q.: *John Calvin*. Grand Rapids, Mich., 1931.

Bibliography [617]

* CALVIN, JOHN: *The Institutes of the Christian Religion.* Various editions.
DENIFLE, H. S.: *Luther and Lutherdom.* Somerset, Ohio, 1917.
GASQUET, FRANCIS A.: *Henry VIII and the English Monasteries.* London, 1906.
GRANT, A. J.: *The Huguenots.* London, 1934.
HARKNESS, G. E.: *John Calvin.* New York, 1931.
HUNT, R. N. C.: *Calvin.* London, 1933.
JACKSON, S. M.: *Zwingli.* New York, 1900.
MACKINNON, J.: *Calvin and the Reformation.* New York, 1936.
MCGIFFERT, A. C.: *Martin Luther, the Man and His Work.* New York, 1911.
POLLARD, A. F.: *Henry VIII.* London, 1905.
—— *Thomas Cranmer and the English Reformation.* London, 1904.
SEDGWICK, H. D.: *Ignatius Loyola.* New York, 1923.
* SMITH, PRESERVED: *Life and Letters of Martin Luther.* Boston, 1914.
WALKER, W.: *John Calvin.* New York, 1906.
WATSON, P. B.: *Swedish Revolution under Gustavus Vasa.* Boston, 1889.

Ch. 23: *The World of Elizabeth*

BAIRD, H. M.: *The Huguenots and Henry of Navarre.* New York, 1909.
BELL, D.: *Elizabethan Seamen.* Philadelphia, 1936.
BLACK, J. B.: *The Reign of Elizabeth.* Oxford, 1936.
CORBETT, J. S.: *Drake and the Tudor Navy.* New York, 1898. 2 vols.
EINSTEIN, LEWIS: *Italian Renaissance in England.* New York, 1902.
* *Fugger News-Letters.* New York, 1924-26.
GEHL, P.: *The Revolt of the Netherlands.* London, 1936.
HURST, Q.: *Henry of Navarre.* New York, 1938.
MARIEJOL, J. H.: *Philip II, the First Modern King.* New York, 1934.
MUIR, EDWIN: *John Knox.* London, 1929.
NEALE, J. E.: *Queen Elizabeth.* New York, 1934.
PALM, F. C.: *Calvinism and the Religious Wars.* New York, 1932.
—— *Politics and Religion in Sixteenth-century France, A Study of the Career of Henry of Montmorency-Damville.* Boston, 1927.
* PAYNE, EDWARD J., Ed.: *Voyages of the Elizabethan Seamen to America, Select Narratives from the Principal Navigations of Hakluyt.* Oxford, 1907.
STAFFORD, H. G.: *James VI of Scotland and the Throne of England.* New York, 1940.
THOMPSON, J. W.: *Wars of Religion in France, 1559-1576, the Huguenots, Catherine de Medici, and Philip II.* Chicago, 1914.
TILLEY, A. A.: *The French Wars of Religion.* New York, 1919.

WEDGWOOD, C. V.: *William the Silent*. New Haven, 1944.
WILLIAMS, C. H.: *Queen Elizabeth*. London, 1936.
WRIGHT, L. B.: *Middle Class Culture in Elizabethan England*. Durham, 1935.

PART XIII

The Seventeenth Century

BAKER, C. H. C.: *Dutch Painting of the XVII Century*. London, 1926.
BELL, E. T.: *Men of Mathematics*. New York, 1937.
BLOOM, H. I.: *The Economic Activities of the Jews of Amsterdam in the Seventeenth and Eighteenth Centuries*. Williamsport, Pa., 1937.
BOULENGER, J.: *The Seventeenth Century*. New York, 1920.
CLARK, G. N.: *The Seventeenth Century*. Oxford, 1929.
CORBETT, J. S.: *England in the Mediterranean, 1603–1713*. London, 1904. 2 vols.
FIGGIS, J. N.: *Theory of the Divine Right of Kings*. Cambridge, 1914.
GODFREY, E.: *Home Life under the Stuarts*. New York, 1903.
GOOCH, G. P.: *English Democratic Ideas in the Seventeenth Century*. Cambridge, 1927.
* GROTIUS, HUGO: *Law of War and Peace*. London, 1939.
OGG, D.: *Europe in the Seventeenth Century*. London, 1931.
ORNSTEIN, MARTHA: *Role of Scientific Societies in the Seventeenth Century*. Chicago, 1928.
PARKMAN, FRANCIS: *Works*. Boston, 1922. 13 vols. (Many titles: French in North America in the seventeenth and eighteenth centuries)
SCHNEIDER, H. W.: *The Puritan Mind*. New York, 1930.
SHIPLEY, A. E.: *Revival of Science in the Seventeenth Century*. Princeton, 1914.
SMITH, PRESERVED: *History of Modern Culture*. Vol. I, New York, 1930.
TREVELYAN, G. M.: *England under the Stuarts*. London, 1925.
TROTTER, E.: *Seventeenth Century Life in the Country Parish*. Cambridge, 1919.

Ch. 24: *The World of Galileo*

AHNLUND, N. G.: *Gustav Adolf, the Great*. Princeton, 1940.
* BACON, FRANCIS: *The Advancement of Learning*. Oxford, 1876.

BAILLY, A.: *The Cardinal Dictator: A Portrait of Richelieu.* London, 1936.
EDMUNDSON, GEORGE: *Anglo-Dutch Rivalry During the First Half of the Seventeenth Century.* Oxford, 1911.
FLETCHER, G. R. L.: *Gustavus Adolphus.* New York, 1890.
* GARDINER, S. R.: *Constitutional Documents of the Puritan Revolution.* London, 1899.
——, *History of England from the Accession of James I to the Outbreak of the Civil War, 1603–1642.* London, 1901. 10 vols.
HALDANE, E. S.: *Descartes, His Life and Times.* New York, 1905.
HASSAL, A.: *Mazarin.* New York, 1934.
HUTTON, W. H.: *William Laud.* London, 1895.
LEA, HENRY C.: *Moriscos of Spain, Their Conversion and Expulsion.* Philadelphia, 1901.
MCMUNN, G. F.: *Gustavus Adolphus, the Northern Hurricane.* London, 1930.
PERKINS, J. B.: *Richelieu and the Growth of French Power.* New York, 1926.
* *Political Works of James I.* Cambridge, 1918.
READE, H. G. R.: *Sidelights on the Thirty Years' War.* London, 1924. 3 vols.
TRAILL, H. D.: *Lord Strafford.* London, 1889.
TYLER, L. G.: *England in America, 1580–1652.* New York, 1904.
WATSON, F.: *Wallenstein, Soldier under Saturn.* New York, 1938.
WEDGWOOD, C. V.: *Thirty Years' War.* London, 1938.
WILLIAMSON, H. R.: *King James I.* London, 1935.

Ch. 25: The World of Isaac Newton

AIRY, OSMUND: *Charles II.* London, 1901.
ATKINSON, C. T.: *Marlborough and the Rise of the British Army.* New York, 1921.
BRAITHWAITE, W. C.: *Beginnings of Quakerism.* London, 1912.
* CLARENDON, EARL OF: *History of the Rebellion and Civil Wars in England.* Oxford, 1888.
CLARK, GEORGE N.: *Dutch Alliance and the War Against French Trade, 1688–1697.* London, 1923.
FARMER, JAMES: *Versailles and the Court under Louis XIV.* New York, 1905.
FIRTH, C. H.: *Oliver Cromwell.* New York, 1933.
GARDINER, S. R.: *History of the Great Civil War, 1642–49.* London, 1901. 4 vols.
——, *History of the Commonwealth and Protectorate.* London, 1903. 4 vols.

——, *Oliver Cromwell*. London, 1901.
GREENSTREET, W. J., Ed.: *Isaac Newton*. London, 1927.
MASSON, F.: *Robert Boyle, a Biography*. London, 1914.
MIMS, STEWART L.: *Colbert's West India Policy*. New Haven, 1912.
MORE, L. T.: *Isaac Newton*. New York, 1934.
* NEWTON, I.: *Principia*. New York, 1848.
O'BRIEN, LOUIS: *Innocent XI and the Revocation of the Edict of Nantes*. Berkeley, 1930.
PACKARD, L. B.: *Age of Louis XIV*. New York, 1929.
* PEPYS, SAMUEL: *Diary*. Various editions.
PERKINS, J. B.: *France under Mazarin*. New York, 1886. 2 vols.
SARGENT, A. J.: *Economic Policy of Colbert*. London, 1899.
SCHUYLER, EUGENE: *Peter the Great*. New York, 1884. 2 vols.

ᛌ ᛌ ᛌ

PART XIV

The Eighteenth Century

ACTON, LORD: *Lectures on Modern History*. London, 1906.
BEALES, H. L.: *The Industrial Revolution, 1750–1850*. London, 1938.
BECKER, CARL: *The Heavenly City of the Eighteenth Century Philosophers*. New Haven, 1932.
BOEHM, MAX VON: *Modes and Manners: the Eighteenth Century*. London, 1935.
BOTSFORD, J. B.: *English Society in the Eighteenth Century as Influenced from Oversea*. New York, 1924.
BOURNE, HENRY E.: *Revolutionary Period in Europe, 1763–1815*. New York, 1914.
BRUFORD, W. H.: *Germany in the Eighteenth Century*. New York, 1935.
BRUUN, G.: *The Enlightened Despots*. New York, 1929.
DUNNING, W. A.: *History of Political Theories from Rousseau to Spencer*. New York, 1920.
FAŸ, BERNARD: *The Revolutionary Spirit in France and America*. New York, 1927.
FEILING, KEITH: *The Second Tory Party, 1714–1832*. London, 1938.
GOTTSCHALK, LOUIS: *Era of the French Revolution (1715–1815)*. Boston, 1929.

KRONENBERGER, L.: *Kings and Desperate Men.* New York, 1942.
LASKI, H. J.: *Political Thought in England from Locke to Bentham.* New York, 1920.
LAMBERT, R. S., Ed.: *Grand Tour, a Journey in the Tracks of Aristocracy.* New York, 1937.
MAHAN, ALFRED THAYER: *Influence of Sea Power Upon History, 1660–1783.* Boston, 1928.
MANTOUX, P.: *The Industrial Revolution in the Eighteenth Century.* New York, 1928.
MARTIN, K.: *French Liberal Thought in the Eighteenth Century.* New York, 1929.
MAXWELL, C., Ed.: *The English Traveler in France, 1698–1815.* London, 1932.
McCLOY, S. T.: *Government Assistance in Eighteenth Century France.* Durham, 1946.
MOHRENSCHILDT, D. S. VON: *Russia in the Intellectual Life of Eighteenth Century France.* New York, 1936.
* MORITZ, P.: *Travels through Various Parts of England in 1782.* London, 1886.
MOSES, BERNARD: *Spain's Declining Power in South America, 1730–1806.* Berkeley, 1919.
MOWAT, R. B.: *The Age of Reason.* New York, 1934.
SÉE, H.: *Economic and Social Conditions in France During the Eighteenth Century.* New York, 1927.
SMITH, PRESERVED: *History of Modern Culture.* Vol. II. New York, 1934.
WOLF, A.: *A History of Science, Technology and Philosophy in the Eighteenth Century.* New York, 1939.
WROTH, L. E., and ANNAN, G. L.: *Acts of the French Royal Administration Concerning Canada, the West Indies, and Louisiana.* New York, 1930.

Ch. 26: *The World of Benjamin Franklin*

DAKIN, D.: *Turgot and the Ancient Regime in France.* London, 1939.
DOBSON, AUSTIN: *William Hogarth.* London, 1907.
DODWELL, H. H.: *Dupleix and Clive.* London, 1920.
EASUM, C. V.: *Prince Henry of Prussia, Brother of Frederick the Great.* Madison, 1942.
ERGANG, R. E.: *The Potsdam Fuehrer.* New York, 1942.
* FRANKLIN, BENJAMIN: *Autobiography.* (Everyman's Library)
GAXOTTE, P.: *Frederick the Great.* New Haven, 1942.
GILL, F. C.: *The Romantic Movement and Methodism.* London, 1937.

GREIG, J. Y. T.: *David Hume.* New York, 1931.
HODGETTS, E. A. B.: *The Life of Catherine the Great of Russia.* London, 1914.
HYSLOP, B. F.: *A Guide to the General Cahiers of 1789.* New York, 1936.
MAESTRO, M. T.: *Voltaire and Beccaria as Reformers of Criminal Law.* New York, 1942.
* MONTESQUIEU, BARON DE: *Persian Letters.* London, 1923.
MORLEY, JOHN: *Diderot and the Encyclopedists.* London, 1878.
PADOVER, S. K.: *The Revolutionary Emperor: Joseph II.* New York, 1934.
PARES, RICHARD: *War and Trade in the West Indies.* Oxford, 1936.
* REDDAWAY, W. F., Ed.: *Documents of Catherine the Great.* New York, 1931.
* ROUSSEAU, J. J.: *Confessions.* New York, 1935. 2 vols.
* ———, *The Political Writings of Jean Jacques Rousseau.* C. E. Vaughan, Ed. Cambridge, 1915. 2 vols.
* SMITH, ADAM: *Inquiry into the Nature and Causes of the Wealth of Nations.* Various editions.
SOREL, A.: *Montesquieu.* Chicago, 1888.
TAYLOR, S. R. STIRLING: *Walpole and His Age.* London, 1931.
TORREY, N. L.: *The Spirit of Voltaire.* New York, 1938.
TUNSTALL, BRIAN: *William Pitt, Earl of Chatham.* London, 1939.
VEALE, F.: *Frederick the Great.* London, 1935.
* VOLTAIRE: *Candide.* Various editions.
* ———, *History of Charles XII.* Various editions.
WICKWAR, W. A.: *Baron d'Holbach, A Prelude to the French Revolution.* London, 1935.

Ch. 27: *The World of Napoleon Bonaparte*

ARIS, R.: *History of Political Thought in Germany from 1789–1815.* New York, 1936.
AULARD, A.: *French Revolution; A Political History, 1789–1804.* New York, 1910. 4 vols.
BARTHOU, LOUIS: *Mirabeau.* London, 1913.
BRINTON, C. C.: *Decade of Revolution, 1789–1799.* New York, 1934.
——— *The Lives of Talleyrand.* New York, 1936.
* BURKE, E.: *Reflections on the French Revolution.* (Everyman's Library.)
CLAUSEWITZ, K. VON: *On War.* London, 1908. 3 vols.
DEUTSCH, HERMAN: *Genesis of Napoleonic Imperialism.* Cambridge, 1938.
FISHER, H. A. L.: *Napoleon.* London, 1912.
FORD, G. S.: *Stein and the Era of Reform in Prussia, 1807–1815.* Princeton, 1922.

GERSHOY, LEO: *French Revolution.* New York, 1932.
GOTTSCHALK, LOUIS: *Jean Paul Marat, A Study in Radicalism.* New York, 1927.
GUEDALLA, PHILIP: *Wellington.* New York, 1930.
HECKSHER, E. F.: *Continental System; an Economic Interpretation.* Oxford, 1922.
KIRCHEISEN, F. M.: *Napoleon I.* New York, 1932.
LANGSAM, W. C.: *Napoleonic Wars and German Nationalism in Austria.* London, 1930.
MADELIN, LOUIS: *Danton.* London, 1921.
MAHAN, ALFRED THAYER: *Influence of Sea Power Upon the French Revolution and Empire, 1793–1812.* Boston, 1898. 2 vols.
—— *Life of Nelson.* Boston, 1899.
MATHIEZ, A.: *The French Revolution.* New York, 1928.
—— *The Thermidorean Reaction.* New York, 1931.
ROSEBERY, ARCHIBALD: *Pitt.* London, 1892.
THAYER, A. W.: *Life of Ludwig van Beethoven.* New York, 1921.
THOMPSON, J. M.: *Leaders of the French Revolution.* New York, 1929.
VAN DEUSEN, G. G.: *Abbé Sieyes and French Nationalism.* London, 1932.
WEBSTER, C. K.: *The Foreign Policy of Castlereagh, 1812–1815.* London, 1934.

PART XV

The Nineteenth Century

BUER, M. C.: *Health, Wealth, and Population in the Early Days of the Industrial Revolution.* London, 1926.
CLAPHAM, J. H.: *The Economic Development of France and Germany, 1815–1914.* Cambridge, 1928.
CLARKE, H. B.: *Modern Spain, 1815–98.* Cambridge, 1906.
CLOUGH, S. B.: *France, A History of National Economics, 1789–1939.* New York, 1939.
CORTI, E.: *Rise of the House of Rothschild.* New York, 1928.
EGERTON, HUGH E.: *Short History of British Colonial Policy.* London, 1918.
FISHER, H. A. L.: *Bonapartism.* Oxford, 1908.
* HEINE, H.: *Selected Works.* (Everyman's Library)
HOBSON, JOHN A.: *Imperialism.* New York, 1905.

KNOWLES, L. C. A.: *Economic Development in the Nineteenth Century: France, Germany, Russia, and the United States.* London, 1932.
FUETER, E.: *World History, 1815–1920.* London, 1922.
* MARX, KARL, and ENGELS, FRIEDERICH: *Communist Manifesto.* Various editions.
MASARYK, T. G.: *The Spirit of Russia.* London, 1919. 2 vols.
MILLER, WILLIAM: *The Ottoman Empire and Its Successors, 1801–1934.* Cambridge, 1934.
MURRAY, R. H.: *Studies in the English Social and Political Thinkers of the Nineteenth Century.* Cambridge, 1929. 2 vols.
NUSSBAUM, F. A.: *A History of the Economic Institutions of Modern Europe.* New York, 1933.
* OAKES, SIR A., and MOWAT, ROBERT B.: *Great European Treaties of the Nineteenth Century.* Oxford, 1918.
KARPOVICH, MICHAEL: *Imperial Russia, 1801–1917.* New York, 1932.
SKRINE, F. H.: *The Expansion of Russia, 1815–1900.* Cambridge, 1915.
SOLTAU, R.: *French Political Thought in the Nineteenth Century.* London, 1931.
WARNER, W. J.: *The Wesleyan Movement in the Industrial Revolution.* London, 1930.

Ch. 28: *The World of Charles Darwin*

ARTZ, F. B.: *France Under the Bourbon Restoration.* Cambridge, 1931.
BARZUN, JACQUES: *Darwin, Marx, Wagner, the Fatal Legacy of "Progress."* Boston, 1941.
BRINTON, C. C.: *Nietzsche.* Cambridge, 1941.
* BUCKLE, G. E., Ed.: *Letters of Queen Victoria.* London, 1926–32. 6 vols.
CARR, E. H.: *Michael Bakunin.* London, 1937.
COLE, G. D. H.: *Life of Robert Owen.* London, 1930.
* DARWIN, CHARLES: *On the Origin of Species by Means of Natural Selection.* Various editions.
DILKE, SIR CHARLES: *Greater Britain.* London, 1876.
DORLODOT, H. DE: *Darwinism and Catholic Thought.* London, 1914.
HAMLEY, E. B.: *War in the Crimea.* London, 1890.
HECKER, J. F.: *Russian Sociology.* New York, 1915.
HOVELL, M.: *The Chartist Movement.* Manchester, 1925.
ILTIS, HUGO: *Life of Mendel.* New York, 1932.
KAYSER, E. L.: *Great Social Adventure, Contributions of Jeremy Bentham to Liberal Nationalism.* New York, 1932.
LICHTERVELDE, COUNT LOUIS DE: *Leopold of the Belgians.* New York, 1929.
LORD, ROBERT H.: *Origins of the War of 1870.* London, 1924.

MAUDE, AYLMER: *The Life of Tolstoy.* Oxford, 1930. 2 vols.
MONYPENNY, W. F., and BUCKLE, G. E.: *Life of Benjamin Disraeli, Earl of Beaconsfield.* London, 1910–20. 6 vols.
NABOKOV, V.: *Nikolai Gogol.* New York, 1944.
PEARSON, KARL: *National Life from the Standpoint of Science.* London, 1901.
STRACHEY, LYTTON: *Queen Victoria.* New York, 1921.
WEST, GEOFFREY: *Charles Darwin, A Portrait.* New Haven, 1938.

Ch. 29: The World of Jean Jaurès

CARROLL, E. M.: *French Public Opinion and Foreign Affairs, 1870–1914.* New York, 1931.
CROCE, B.: *A History of Italy, 1871–1915.* Oxford, 1929.
DAWSON, W. H.: *The German Empire, 1867–1914.* London, 1919. 2 vols.
DICKINSON, G. L.: *International Anarchy, 1904–1914.* London, 1926.
FAY, S. B.: *Origins of the World War.* New York, 1930. 2 vols.
* GREY, SIR EDWARD: *Twenty-five Years, 1892–1916.* London, 1925. 2 vols.
HACKETT, FRANCIS: *Ireland, A Study in Nationalism.* New York, 1918.
HALE, O. J.: *Publicity and Diplomacy, with Special Reference to England and Germany, 1890–1914.* New York, 1940.
HOLLS, F. W.: *The Peace Conference at The Hague.* New York, 1900.
JELLINEK, F.: *The Paris Commune of 1871.* New York, 1937.
EARLE, E. M.: *Turkey, the Great Powers and the Bagdad Railway.* New York, 1923.
LANGER, W. L.: *The Diplomacy of Imperialism, 1890–1902.* New York, 1935. 2 vols.
———, *Franco-Russian Alliance, 1890–1914.* Cambridge, 1929.
* MORLEY, JOHN: *Memorandum on Resignation.* New York, 1928.
REDLICH, JOSEPH: *Emperor Francis Joseph of Austria.* New York, 1929.
ROSENBERG, ARTHUR: *The Birth of the German Republic, 1871–1918.* New York, 1931.
SCHUMAN, F. L.: *War and Diplomacy in the French Republic.* New York, 1931.
* SCOTT, J. B., Ed.: *The Hague Peace Conferences of 1899 and 1907.* Vol. II. Baltimore, 1909.
SETON-WATSON, R. W.: *The Southern Slav Question and the Habsburg Monarchy.* London, 1911.
TOWNSEND, MARY E.: *The Rise and Fall of Germany's Colonial Empire, 1884–1918.* New York, 1930.
WEINSTEIN, H. R.: *Jean Jaurès, A Study of Patriotism in the French Socialist Movement.* New York, 1936.

PART XVI

The Twentieth Century

ANGELL, NORMAN: *Great Illusion.* London, 1913.
BENNS, F. L.: *Europe Since 1870.* New York, 1941.
BOWMAN, ISAIAH: *New World: Problems in Political Geography.* Yonkers, 1928.
BRUCK, W. F.: *Social and Economic History of Germany from William II to Hitler, 1888–1938.* London, 1938.
CHAMBERS, FRANK P., GRANT, C. P., and BAYLEY, C. C.: *Age of Conflict.* New York, 1943.
* CLARK, J. M., HAMILTON, WALTON H., and MOULTON, HAROLD G., Eds.: *Readings in the Economics of War.* Chicago, 1918.
* *Collected Diplomatic Documents Relating to the Outbreak of the European War.* London, 1915.
DOMINIAN, LEON: *Frontiers of Language and Nationality in Europe.* New York, 1917.
HAYES, CARLTON J. H.: *Essays in Nationalism.* New York, 1926.
JASZY, O.: *The Dissolution of the Hapsburg Monarchy.* Chicago, 1929.
MILNE, A. A.: *Peace with Honour.* London, 1934.
MOON, PARKER T.: *Imperialism and World Politics.* New York, 1926.
NICOLAI, GEORG F.: *Biology of War.* New York, 1918.

Ch. 30: The World of Nikolai Lenin

ANDERSON, PAUL B.: *People, Church and State in Modern Russia.* London, 1944.
BERGSON, ABRAM: *The Structure of Soviet Wages; A Study in Socialist Economics.* Cambridge, 1944.
BIENSTOCK, GREGORY, et al.: *Management in Russian Industry and Agriculture.* New York, 1944.
* BUCHANAN, GEORGE: *My Mission to Russia and other Diplomatic Memories.* Boston, 1923. 2 vols.
* BUNYAN, JAMES, and FISHER, H. H., Eds.: *The Bolshevik Revolution, 1917–1918; Documents and Materials.* Stanford University, Calif., 1934.
CALLCOTT, MARY S.: *Russian Justice.* New York, 1935.
* CENTRAL COMMITTEE OF THE COMMUNIST PARTY OF THE SOVIET UNION: *The Political and Social Doctrine of Communism: Report . . . by J. Stalin.* New York, 1934.
CHAMBERLIN, WILLIAM HENRY: *Russia's Iron Age.* Boston, 1934.

Bibliography

CROWTHER, J. G.: *Soviet Science.* New York, 1936.
CURTISS, JOHN SHELTON: *Church and State in Russia; the Last Years of the Empire, 1900–1917.* New York, 1940.
DALLIN, DAVID J.: *The Real Soviet Russia.* New Haven, 1944.
DAVIES, JOSEPH E. *Mission to Moscow.*
FISCHER, LOUIS: *The Soviets in World Affairs.* London, 1930. 2 vols.
FISHER, H. H.: *The Famine in Soviet Russia, 1919–1923; the Operations of the American Relief Administration.* New York, 1927.
FÜLOP-MILLER, RENE: *Rasputin, the Holy Devil.* New York, 1928.
* GOLDER, FRANK ALFRED: *Documents of Russian History, 1914–1917.* New York, 1927.
HARPER, SAMUEL N.: *Civic Training in Soviet Russia.* Chicago, 1929.
——, *The Government of the Soviet Union.* New York, 1938.
——, *Making Bolsheviks.* Chicago, 1931.
HAZARD, JOHN N.: *Soviet Housing Law.* New Haven, 1939.
HINDUS, MAURICE: *Red Bread.* New York, 1931.
* KNOX, SIR ALFRED: *With the Russian Army, 1914–1917, Being Chiefly Extracts from the Diary of a Military Attache.* London, 1921.
KOHN, HANS: *Nationalism in the Soviet Union.* New York, 1933.
KOVALEVSKY, M. M.: *Russian Political Institutions.* Chicago, 1902.
* LENIN, V. I., and STALIN, JOSEPH: *The Russian Revolution.* New York, 1938. (Writings and speeches, Feb.–Oct. 1917)
* LENIN, N., and TROTSKY, LEON: *The Proletarian Revolution in Russia.* New York, 1918.
MASARYK, THOMAS G.: *The Spirit of Russia; Studies in History, Literature and Philosophy.* London, 1919. 2 vols.
MAVOR, JAMES: *An Economic History of Russia.* London, 1925.
MILYUKOV, P.: *Russia and Her Crisis.* Chicago, 1903.
* OBOLENSKY-OSSINSKY, V. V., et al.: *Social Economic Planning in the Union of Soviet Socialist Republics: Report of Delegation from the USSR to the World Social Economic Congress, Amsterdam, August 23–29, 1931.* Schiedam, 1931.
OLGIN, M.: *The Soul of the Russian Revolution.*
PARES, BERNARD: *The Fall of the Russian Monarchy, A Study of Evidence.*
REED, JOHN: *Ten Days that Shook the World.* New York, 1919.
ROBINSON, G. T.: *Rural Russia Under the Old Regime.* New York, 1932.
SCHUMAN, FREDERICK L.: *Soviet Politics: At Home and Abroad.* New York, 1946.
SIGERIST, HENRY E.: *Socialized Medicine in the Soviet Union.* New York, 1937.
STALIN, J.: *Building Collective Farms.* London, 1931.
* TROTSKY, LEON: *My Life; an Attempt at an Autobiography.* New York, 1931.

WEBB, SIDNEY and BEATRICE: *Soviet Communism: A New Civilisation?* New York, 1938. 2 vols.
* YARMOLINSKY, A., Ed.: *The Memoirs of Count Witte.* New York, 1921.
YUGOW, A.: *Russia's Economic Front for War and Peace, An Appraisal of the Five Year Plans.* New York, 1942.

Ch. 31: The World of Winston Churchill

CHURCHILL, WINSTON L. S.: *World Crisis 1918–1928: The Aftermath.* New York, 1929.
——, *Roving Commission: My Early Life.* New York, 1930.
——, *World Crisis 1911–1918.* New York, 1931.
——, *Great Contemporaries.* New York, 1937.
——, *Marlborough, His Life and Times.* New York, 1937.
——, *Blood, Sweat and Tears.* New York, 1941.
——, *War Memoirs,* Vol. I. Boston, 1948.

Ch. 32: Our World

BRUUN, G.: *Clemenceau.* Cambridge, 1944.
CHURCHILL, WINSTON: *World Crisis 1915, 1916–18.* London, 1923–27. 3 vols.
COON, C. S.: *The Races of Europe.* New York, 1939.
HAYES, CARLTON J. H.: *Brief History of the Great War.* New York, 1920.
HUDSON, MANLEY O.: *Permanent Court of International Justice.* Cambridge, 1925.
KEYNES, JOHN M.: *Economic Consequences of the Peace.* London, 1920.
* LLOYD GEORGE, DAVID: *Memoirs of the Peace Conference.* New Haven, 1939. 2 vols.
MADARIAGA, S. DE: *Spain.* New York, 1943.
MONTGELAS, MAX: *Case for the Central Powers, An Impeachment of the Versailles Verdict.* London, 1925.
MOULTON, H. G., and McGUIRE, C. E.: *Germany's Capacity To Pay.* New York, 1923.
NOTESTEIN, FRANK W., et al.: *The Future Population of Europe and the Soviet Union.* New York, 1944.
* POINCARE, RAYMOND: *Memoirs.* London, 1926.
SCHMITT, BERNADOTTE E., Ed.: *Poland.* Berkeley, 1944.
SCOTT, ARTHUR P.: *Introduction to the Peace Treaties.* Chicago, 1920.
* *Source Book on European Governments.* New York, 1938.
WEBSTER, C. K.: *The League of Nations in Theory and Practice.* Boston, 1933.

Index

Abelard, Peter, 227, 234-5, 236, 237, 239
Absolute monarchy, 401-4, 406, 408, 412, 413-17, 420, 440, 445-8
Abu Bekr, 87
Académie des Sciences, 413
Adalbero of Rheims, 176, 177, 178
Addison, Joseph, 436
Address to the Christian Nobility of the German Nation (Luther), 360-1
Adrian IV, Pope, 246
Agincourt, battle of, 330
Agriculture, Germanic tribes, 8, 48; in Middle Ages, 198-9; Roman Empire, 19
Aids, 164
Alaric, 20, 24, 25, 27
Albertus Magnus, 275, 280
Albigenses, 271, 272, 274; Albigensian crusade, 262
Alcuin, 109, 116
Aldus Manutius, 338
Alexander of Macedon, 4, 6, 7
Alexander II, Pope, 204
Alexander VI, Pope, 340, 359
Alexander I, Tsar, 466-7
Alexander II, Tsar, 529
Alexander III, Tsar, 528
Alfonso of Aragon, 337
Alfred, King of England, 134, 135, 141, 142-6, 152-7, 161, 162, 170
Alsace-Lorraine, 495, 507, 525
Ambrose, 18, 20, 22, 25, 30, 107
Anabaptists, 365, 405

Anagni, 282, 304
Angles, 8, 29, 30, 47, 64, 80, 104
Anglo-Saxon Chronicle, 144, 227
Anne of Bohemia, 311
Anne of Brittany, 339
Anne of England, 420, 422, 423
Anselm of Bec, 234, 236
Anti-Comintern Pact, 564
Apollinaris Sidonius, 15, 26-32, 40-3, 65, 89, 179
Aquinas, Thomas, 261, 280, 283
Aquitaine, 47, 55
Arabian Nights, 113
Arabs, 79, 83-85, 87, 88, 90, 97, 102, 105
Architecture, 442, 487; Gothic, 219, 230, 239-40, 264, 328, 332; Romanesque, 199, 200, 219, 230, 239-40, 264
Arianism, 30, 47, 63
Aristotle, 18, 35, 56, 264, 280, 283, 399
Armada, defeat of, 1588, 373
Arminius, 404
Arnulf, 145
Arthur, King, 29
Asia Minor, 58, 194, 195, 198
Asquith, Herbert, 547
Asser, 144
Assignats, 452
Astronomy, 367, 392, 398, 400, 413
Athanasius, 29
Attila, 27, 28, 134
Augustine, of Canterbury, 64, 89, 104

[i

Index

Augustine, of Hippo, 14, 17–25, 26, 29, 33–9, 41, 52, 107, 138, 144, 360, 416, 485
Augsburg, Diet of, 365
Augsburg, League of, 421
Aurelian, 9, 22
Austen, Jane, 492
Austrasia, 80, 88, 107
Austria-Hungary, 494, 502–3, 507, 512–13, 525, 540, 541, 548, 550
Austrian Succession, War of, 443
Avars, 48, 80, 87, 112, 113, 134
Averroës, 264, 273
Avignon, 282–3, 306, 307, 308, 310, 325, 332
Axis, Rome-Berlin, 564

Babylonian Captivity, *see* Avignon
Bach, J. S., 435, 446
Bacon, Francis, 355, 392, 412, 485
Bacon, Roger, 264, 280, 308
Bagdad Railway, 509
Baillis, 268
Balkan Union, 550–1
Banalities, 165
Basel, Council of, 333
Basques, 47, 80, 113
Bavarians, 112
Becket, Thomas, 245
Bede, 64, 103, 104–10, 118–24, 144
Beethoven, Ludwig van, 435, 454, 466, 487
Benedict Biscop, 90, 105
Benedict, of Nursia, 51, 55, 56, 61, 65
Benedictine Rule, 51, 52, 57, 63, 90, 107
Beneš, Edward, 566
Beowulf, 227
Berengar of Tours, 201, 202
Berlin, Congress of, 496–7
Bernard, of Clairvaux, 230–1, 233–42, 247, 252–4, 268
Bismarck, Otto von, 494, 506–7, 508
Black Death, 304, 307–8, 309, 310, 325, 352
Black Prince, 309
Bobbio, monastery of, 177, 178, 180

Boccaccio, Giovanni, 303, 308, 312, 324
Bodin, Jean, 373
Boethius, 55ff., 61
Bohemia, 80, 283, 302, 358, 403
Boleyn, Anne, 366
Bologna, University of, 280, 368
Bolsheviks (Russian Social Democratic Party), 531, 537–9, 542–4, 548
Bonaparte, Joseph, 462, 476–7
Bonaparte, Napoleon, *see* Napoleon I
Boniface, 106, 107, 109, 110
Boniface VIII, Pope, 262, 280, 281, 282, 284
Book of Common Prayer, 367, 407
Book of Martyrs (Foxe), 373, 406
Book of the Courtier (Castiglione), 357
Botticelli, Sandro, 337
Bourbon, House of, 372, 391, 410, 418, 423, 464
Bouvines, Battle of, 261
Boyle, Robert, 393
Brahe, Tycho, 392, 400
Brandenburg, 171, 407, 410, 421
Brescia, Arnold of, 239, 246
Brest-Litovsk, Treaty of, 539
Brethren of the Common Life, 361
Brétigny, Treaty of, 307, 310
Bretons, 80
Bright, John, 491
British Empire, in the 19th and 20th centuries, 503–4, 506, 547, 551–2
Britons, 7, 29, 47, 80
Brittany, 47
Brunelleschi, Filippo, 324, 337
Bruno, Giordano, 400, 485
Bruno of Cologne, 173, 206
Buchanan, George, 373, 404
Buffon, Georges-Louis Leclerc de, 485
Bulgarian National Church (Exarchate), 496
Bulgars, 82, 114
Burgundians, 9, 13, 27, 40, 42–3, 47
Burgundy, County of, 80, 244
Byron, George Gordon, Lord, 490
Byzantine architecture, 59ff.
Byzantine culture, 61

Index

Byzantine Empire, 79, 81, 87, 90, 106, 193–4, 195, 196, 198, 222, 265, 271, 302, 337

Cabot, John, 371
Caesar, Augustus, 6
Caesar, Julius, 6
Caliphate, Bagdad, 145, 194, 195, 233
Caliphate, Spanish, 145, 194, 195
Calvin, John, 355, 362, 363–9, 371, 373, 379–83, 398
Cambrai, League of, 359
Cambrai, Treaty of (1529), 364
Canary Islands, 262
Canterbury, 64
Canterbury Tales, 305
Capitalism, 328–9
Carlsbad decrees, 490
Carnot, Lazare, 462
Carolingian Empire, 98, 100, 101, 102, 103; ecclesiastical policy, 106
Cartier, Jacques, 402
Cassiodorus, 55, 56, 61, 109
Castlereagh, Viscount, 467
Castiglione, Baldassare, 357
Cathari, *see* Albigenses
Catharine of Aragon, 366, 370
Cathedrals, 229–30
Catherine II, Empress of Russia, 446–8
Cavour, Camillo, 493
Celestial Hierarchy, 138
Cellini, Benvenuto, 364
Celts, 7, 80; Celtic Christianity, 82, 83, 89, 90, 104
Cervantes, Miguel de, 354
Charlemagne, 100, 101, 102, 110, 111–17, 124–8, 133, 142, 144, 145, 163, 170, 173, 175, 203, 220; capitularies, 116–17; Carolingian renaissance, 116; court, 115–16; marches, 113
Charles, duke of Lorraine, 178
Charles IV, Emperor, 332, 333
Charles V, Emperor, 353, 359, 363, 364, 366, 367, 369, 405
Charles V, King of France, 310
Charles VI, King of France, 310, 330

Charles VIII, King of France, 330, 334, 338, 339, 341–3, 358, 359
Charles IX, King of France, 372
Charles X, King of France, 490
Charles I, King of England, 404, 405, 406, 408, 409
Charles II, King of England, 409, 412, 420, 423
Charles III, King of Spain, 448
Charles Martel, 98, 100, 101, 105, 106, 109, 111
Charles the Bald, 134, 136, 137, 138, 139, 141, 143, 145, 170
Charles the Bold, Duke of Burgundy, 338
Charles the Fat, 145
Charles the Simple, 145, 161, 170
Chansons de geste, 227
Chartered companies, 354, 372, 397, 403, 404; East India, 371, 458; Muscovy, 371
Chartres, Cathedral of, 275
Chartres, School of, 201, 225
Chaucer, Geoffrey, 305, 308, 312
China, 493, 505, 532, 561, 568
Christian of Denmark, 403
Chivalry, 227–8, 301
Chrysoloras, Manuel, 331
Churchill, John, duke of Marlborough, 547
Churchill, Lord Randolph, 547
Churchill, Winston, 547–54, 569, 570, 578–81
Cicero, 18, 41
Cistercians, 224, 235, 236
City of God (Augustine), 24, 36–9
Clement VII, Pope, 364
Clergy, Benefit of, 245
Clericis laicos, Bull, 281
Clermont, Council of, 234
Clovis, 32, 47, 49, 54, 60, 64, 65, 80, 98, 106
Cluniac movement, 168, 177, 195, 197, 206, 235
Cnut, 202, 204, 208
Cobbett, William, 489
Cobden, Richard, 491

Coeur, Jacques, 321, 327, 328–35, 337, 341–4
Colbert, J. B., 418–19
Coleridge, S. T., 454, 484
Colet, John, 361
Coligny, Admiral Gaspard de, 372
Cologne, 276
Colonial policy, Spanish, 352–3
Colonies, English, 371
Columba, 64
Columbus, Bartholomew, 340
Columbus, Christopher, 339, 340
Common Lot, Brethren of the, 331
Communes (Italian), 224, 239, 246, 303, 324
Communism, 499, 537, 542, 561, 563, 564; war communism (Russia), 544
Communist Manifesto, 490
Communist Party (Russia), 537, 543, 556, 557, 558
Comnenus, Alexis, 233
Compurgation, 49
Conceptualism, 235
Conciliar movement, 325–6, 332–3
Confessions (Augustine), 21, 33–6
Conrad II, Emperor, 206
Conrad III, Emperor, 238, 240, 243
Conrad IV, Emperor, 278
Conrad of Franconia, 171
Conradin, 279
Consolation of Philosophy (Boethius), 56, 144, 146
Constance, Council of, 333
Constantine, 9, 11, 12, 14, 16, 19, 29
Constantinople, 14, 27, 31, 32, 55, 58, 59, 79, 87, 88, 90, 98, 100, 106, 141, 162, 173, 180, 198, 222, 223, 262, 265, 271, 327, 328, 333, 334, 337, 369, 493, 495, 496, 530, 548
Cognac, League of (1526), 364
Concordat of 1516, 363, 415
Concordat of 1801, 460
Continental System, 462
Copernicus, 368, 392, 398, 400
Corneille, Pierre, 423
Corn Laws, 489
Corot, J. B., 487
Corvée, 166

Cracow, University of, 368
Cranmer, Thomas, 367
Crécy, battle of, 307
Crimean War, 493, 530
Croats, 81, 113
Cromwell, Oliver, 408, 409
Crucé, 410
Crusade, First, 194, 198, 234
Crusade, Fourth, 265, 271
Crusade, Second, 240, 241
Curia regis, 237
Czechoslovakia, partition of, 564–6
Czechs, 112

Danegeld, 202
Danelaw, 135, 143, 161, 171
Danes, 134
Dante, 264, 265, 267, 279–84, 294–8, 303, 305, 308, 331, 360
Danton, Jacques, 455
Danzig, 302
Darwin, Erasmus, 489
Darwin, Charles, 485, 487, 489–98, 515–17
David, Louis, 454
Decameron, 303, 308
Declaration of the Gallican Clergy (1682), 415, 416
Declaration of the Rights of Man and the Citizen, 451–52
Decline and Fall of the Roman Empire (Gibbon), 14
De Divisione Naturae (Erigena), 139, 202
De Monarchia (Dante), 283
De Natura Rerum (Bede), 108
De Temporum Ratione (Bede), 108
Defensor Pacis, 309
Delegation of powers, 322, 324
Demarcation, Papal bulls of, 340
Descartes, René, 393, 412, 413, 424, 485
Descent of Man (Darwin), 497
Despots, rule of, in Italian cities, 324, 331
Dialogue on the Two Principal Systems of the Universe (Galileo), 403
Dialogues (Gregory the Great), 144

Index [v

Diderot, Denis, 440
Diocletian, 9, 10, 11, 12, 14
Dionysian Code, 51
Dionysius, 51
Dionysius the Areopagite, 139
Dionysius, the pseudo-, 138, 141
Disraeli, Benjamin, 493
Divine Comedy (Dante), 267, 283, 295-8, 308
Dominic, 274
Dominions, British, 503, 506
Don Quixote (Cervantes), 354
Donatello, 324, 336
Donation of Constantine, 115, 179, 331
Donatus, 55
Doomsday Book, 205
Dowry, 228
Dreyfus, Alfred, 500-1
Dushan, Stephen, 302

Ealdorman, 143
Earl, 202
Ecclesiastical History of the English Nation (Bede), 64, 105, 108, 144
Eckhardt, Meister, 331
Eden, Richard, 374
Edict of Nantes, 372, 401-2, 415, 416
Edward I, King of England, 261, 262, 280, 281, 282, 284
Edward II, King of England, 306, 329
Edward III, King of England, 306, 307, 309, 310
Edward IV, King of England, 338
Edward VI, King of England, 367
Edward the Confessor, 204
Edward the Elder, 171, 172
Education, nine liberal arts, 55; Justinian, 60; popular, 361, 362, 439, 440, 452, 461, 463, 464
Egbert, King of Wessex, 116, 142
Egbert of York, 109
Einhard, 111, 115, 116, 124-8
Einstein, Albert, 424
Eleanor of Aquitaine, 237, 241
Electors, College of, 244, 332-3
Elizabeth, consort of Henry VII, 338

Elizabeth, Empress of Russia, 447-8
Elizabeth, Queen of England, 354, 356, 366, 370-5, 384-8, 404, 405, 419, 446
Encyclopédie, 440
Engels, Friedrich, 490
England, Christianity in, 64, 82, 89, 104; vernacular literature, 107
Enlightenment, 436-40, 445, 446, 448, 449, 450, 484
Erasmus of Rotterdam, 355, 357-62, 376-9, 391
Ericson, Leif, 161
Erigena, John Scotus, 134, 136-41, 143, 148-52, 201, 202, 485
Escorial, 372
Estates, the three feudal, 162
Estates general, 310, 450, 451
Ethelwulf, 142
Ethiopia, Italian conquest of, 562-3
Etruscans, 6
Etymologies (Isidore of Seville), 89
Eudes, count of Paris, 145, 170
Eugenius III, Pope, 240, 241
Eugenius IV, Pope, 333
Evesham, battle of, 281

Faerie Queen, 354
False Decretals, 140
Ferdinand I, Emperor, 367
Ferdinand II, Emperor, 403
Ferdinand of Aragon, 339, 358, 359, 360, 366
Ferrara-Florence, Council of, 333, 337
Feudalism, 80, 81, 101, 102, 116, 117, 131-3, 135, 162-8, 220, 223, 261, 311
Fichte, J. G., 464, 500, 506
Ficino, Marsiglio, 336
Fielding, Henry, 436
Finns, 112
Flanders, 222, 224, 306, 307, 325, 326, 330, 332, 358
Florence, 279-80, 308, 324, 331, 336, 337, 359, 360, 391, 400, 401, 403, 407
Foxe, John, 373, 406
Francis, of Assisi, 268, 272, 273, 274, 284, 286-8

Francis Ferdinand, 512
Francis Joseph, 494, 502
Francis I, King of France, 353, 359, 363, 364, 365, 369, 372, 402, 415
Francis II, King of France, 371, 372
Franco, Francisco, 563, 564
Franco-Russian Alliance, 507, 508
Franklin, Benjamin, 442-53, 469-73, 489
Frankfort Assembly, 491
Franks, 8, 13, 27, 30, 32, 40, 47, 49, 65, 83, 90, 98, 100, 106; Frankish kingdoms, 80, 88, 89, 98, 101
Frederick, Elector Palatine, 403
Frederick I, Emperor, 231, 232, 243-7, 255-8, 275
Frederick II, Emperor, 247, 261, 265, 270, 272, 275-8, 279, 281, 282, 284, 289-93
Frederick II, King of Prussia, 421, 443, 445, 446, 448
Frederick William, the Great Elector, 407, 410
Frederick William I, King of Prussia, 445
Frederick William II, King of Prussia, 421
Frederick William III, King of Prussia, 463
Frederick William IV, King of Prussia, 491
Friends of God, 331
Frisians, 112
Froissart, John, 301, 307, 329
Fronde, 412
Fulbert, 201, 202

Gainsborough, Thomas, 436
Galileo, 391, 393, 396, 397, 398-407, 408, 413, 425-8, 492
Garibaldi, 493
Gaul, 47
Genghis Khan, 265
Genoa, 196, 223, 233, 240, 279, 326
Geoffrey of Anjou, 237
George I, King of England, 423, 436, 442
George II, King of England, 436, 443

George III, King of England, 436, 444, 489
Gerbert, see Silvester II
German Empire, 495, 501-2, 512-13, 534, 540, 541, 550
German unification, 494-5
Germanic law, 48, 49
Germanic tribes and customs, 7, 8, 13, 28, 29, 47, 48, 49, 80, 104, 107, 112
Ghiberti, Lorenzo, 324, 336, 337
Ghirlandaio, Domenico, 337
Gibbon, Edward, 14
Giotto, 284, 324, 332
Girondins, 455-6
Gladstone, William, 493
Gneisenau, Count von, 463
Gobineau, J. A. de, 506
Godwin, Earl, 204
Goethe, J. W., 435, 454, 484, 485
Golden Bull of 1356, 332
Goldsmith, Oliver, 436
Goliardic songs, 275
Goths, 9, 30, 47; Ostrogoths, 9; Visigoths, 9, 13, 14, 27, 28, 28, 89, 97
Gottschalk, 138, 352
Government, town, 322
Granada, fall of, 339
Greek Orthodox Church and Balkan nationalism, 495-6
Greeks, ancient, 4, 6; city state, 4, 6; literature, 98; science, 90
Gregory I, Pope, 50, 56, 62-6, 72, 83, 89, 107
Gregory II, Pope, 106
Gregory VII, Pope, 193, 194, 200, 204, 205, 206, 207, 208, 214, 233, 236, 280
Gregory of Tours, 64
Gregorian chant, 66
Grosseteste, Robert, 264, 273
Grotius, Hugo, 410
Guelph, house of, 238
Guesclin, Bertrand de, 310
Guilds, 223, 224, 225, 227, 263-4, 322
Guiscard, Robert, 204, 207, 238
Guise, house of, 372

Index [vii

Gustavus Adolphus, 403
Gustavus III, King of Sweden, 448

Hadrian, and English Church, 89, 90, 105
Haeckel, Ernest, 492
Haendel, G. F., 442
Hakluyt's *Voyages*, 374
Hampton Court, 366
Hanseatic League, 302
Hapsburg, House of, 283, 338, 358, 367, 391, 403, 409, 410, 418, 422, 466, 493, 494, 502, 512, 550
Hardenberg, C. A. von, 463
Harold, King of England, 204
Harold Bluetooth, 172
Haroun al-Raschid, 113
Harrington, James, 394
Harvey, William, 393
Hastings, battle of, 204
Hegel, G. W. F., 484, 506
Heliocentric theory, 368, 400, 403
Heloise, 236
Henrietta Maria of England, 404, 406
Henry II, Emperor, 206
Henry III, Emperor, 206
Henry IV, Emperor, 193, 194, 206, 207, 208, 236, 238
Henry V, Emperor, 236, 238, 242
Henry VI, Emperor, 269, 270
Henry VII, Emperor, 284
Henry I, King of England, 236, 237, 238, 241, 242
Henry II, King of England, 232, 241, 244–5, 247, 270, 284
Henry III, King of England, 276, 280–1
Henry IV, King of England, 329, 330
Henry V, King of England, 329, 330
Henry VI, King of England, 329, 330, 338
Henry VII, King of England, 338, 359, 371
Henry VIII, King of England, 353, 354, 357, 359, 363, 366, 370
Henry II, King of France, 372
Henry III, King of France, 372

Henry IV, King of France, 372, 394, 400, 401, 402, 404, 406, 409
Henry the Fowler, 171, 206
Henry the Lion, 244
Henry the Navigator, Prince, 340
Heraclius, 81, 87, 88
Hildebrand, *see* Gregory VII, Pope
Hincmar, bishop of Rheims, 138
Hindu mathematics and numerical notation, 145
Historia Calamitatum (Abelard), 237
History of the Franks (Gregory of Tours), 64
Hitler, Adolph, 551, 552, 561, 562, 563, 564, 566, 567, 568
Hoare, Samuel, 563
Hobbes, Thomas, 394, 424
Hogarth, William, 436, 454
Hohenstaufen, house of, 238
Hohenzollern, house of, 410, 445, 446, 494
Holbein, Hans, 362
Holy Alliance, 466–7
Holy Places, 194, 195, 196, 197, 198, 233, 276
Holy Roman Empire of the German Nation, 175, 244, 395, 410, 461
Honoratus, 51
Honorius III, Pope, 276
Hrotswitha, 174
Hugh the Great, count of Paris, 170, 178
Huguenots, 371, 372, 373, 401, 402, 415, 416, 437
Humanism, 324, 325, 331, 332, 336, 337, 351, 352, 355, 357, 361, 392
Humphrey, duke of Gloucester, 354
Hundred Years' War, 302, 305–7, 309–10, 312, 321, 329, 330, 331, 334, 338, 357
Hungary, 225
Huns, 9, 13, 27, 28, 29, 47, 79, 134
Huss, John, 311, 333
Huxley, Thomas, 492
Huygens, Christian, 393

Iberians, 7
Immunities, 131–2, 165, 203

Index of forbidden books, 365, 403
India, 504, 547, 551-2
Indies, Spanish, 352, 353, 367, 372, 373, 408-9, 443, 467, 490
Indulgences, 351-2, 360, 361
Industrial revolution, 442, 481-3, 486
Innocent II, Pope, 237, 239
Innocent III, Pope, 261, 265, 266, 268-74, 276, 280, 285-6, 304, 305
Innocent XI, Pope, 416
Inquisition, 272, 326, 354, 365, 398, 400, 403
Institutes of the Christian Religion (Calvin), 365
International Labor Office, 560
Interregnum, Great, 283
Inventions, 265, 303-4
Investiture, 236
Irene, Empress, 101
Isabella of Castile, 339, 340, 358, 359, 366
Isidore of Seville, 89, 90, 108
Islam, 66
Italian language, 283, 308
Italian unification, 493-4
Italy, invasion by Lombards, 48, 50; invasions, Renaissance, 358-60; intervention by Justinian, 56
Ivan IV, Tsar, 371, 446

Jacobins, 455-8
Jacquerie, 310, 322
Jagello, house of, 358
Jahn, F. L., 464
James I, King of England, 403, 404, 405, 406
James II, King of England, 420, 421
James V, King of Scotland, 371
Jansen, Cornelius, 416
Japan, 505, 530, 532, 533, 561, 564, 568, 569, 570
Jaurès, Jean, 499-514, 518-20, 524
Jefferson, Thomas, 445
Jerome, 25, 107
Jerome of Prague, 333
Jerusalem, kingdom of, 234
Jesuits, 367, 373, 393, 398, 400, 416

Jews, 85, 239, 272, 302, 321, 462, 502, 530, 551, 561, 568, 570
Joan of Arc, 330
John of England, 269, 270, 276, 302, 305, 306
John II, King of France, 309
John XII, Pope, 173
John XXII, Pope, 308
John XXIII, Pope, 333
John of Gaunt, 310, 311, 329
Joinville, Sieur de, 267
Joseph II, Emperor, 448
Julian, 14
Julius II, Pope, 359
Junkers, 463, 494, 556
Jury system, 203, 204
Justice, feudal, 164, 165, 166
Justin, Emperor, 56
Justinian, 49, 54-61, 67, 68, 87
Justinian code, 49, 60
Jutes, 8, 29, 64, 104

Kant, Emmanuel, 484, 500
Karageorge, 495, 496
Keats, John, 484
Kellogg-Briand Pact, 560
Kemal, Mustapha, 549, 550
Kepler, Johann, 392, 393, 400, 413
Kerensky, Alexander, 537, 538
Knights Hospitaller, 234
Knights Templar, 231, 234, 238, 263
Knox, John, 371, 373
Koran, 86-8, 91-4
Kossovo, battle of, 302

Laborers, Statute of, 308
Laissez-faire, 439, 441, 449, 483, 486
Lamarck, J. B., 485, 492
Lanfranc, 200, 201-8, 210-14, 234, 236
Langton, Stephen, 269, 270
Lateran, Council of the, 272
Latin, 10, 107
Latin Christianity, 6, 10, 11, 12, 14, 16, 21, 24; and heresy, 22, 23, 24, 30, 31; church architecture, 102; councils, 30; development of pa-

Latin Christianity (*continued*)
  pacy, 29, 30, 31, 32, 89, 106, 107; rise of bishops, 19, 20, 21
Latin education, liberal arts, 23
Latini, Brunetto, 280
La Tour Landry, *Book of the Knight*, 301
Laud, William, 405
Lausanne, Treaty of, 549
Laval, Pierre, 562, 563
Law, codification, France, 439, 452, 457; *Code Napoléon*, 459–60
League, Holy, 359, 360
League of Nations, 527, 541, 559–60, 561, 562, 563
Leagues of cities, federative, 321
Lechfeld, battle of, 172
Lefèvre d'Etaples, Jacques, 363
Legnano, battle of, 246
Leibnitz, G. W., 393, 423
Lenin, Nikolai, 528–46, 556, 573–7
Leo the Isaurian, 106
Leo III, Pope, 114
Leo IX, Pope, 206
Leonardo da Vinci, 325, 332, 355, 392, 399
Leonin, 275
Lepanto, battle of, 372
Lerins, monastery of, 51
Lessing, G. E., 484
Letts and Lithuanians, 112
Leviathan (Hobbes), 394
L'Hopital, Michel de, 372
Lindisfarne, 105, 108, 109, 133
Liudprand of Cremona, 173, 175, 182–5
Linnaeus, Charles, 485
Lithuania, colonization of by Germans, 302
Lloyd George, David, 548
Locke, John, 394, 420, 436, 437, 440, 443, 445, 449
Logic (Aristotle), 56
Lollards, 311
Lombard League, 271, 302
Lombards, 48, 61, 63, 100, 112, 113, 114
Longbow, 307

Lothair, 137
Lothair II, Emperor, 140, 178, 238, 240
Louis V, King of France, 178
Louis VI, King of France, 232, 237, 242, 243
Louis VII, King of France, 237, 240, 241, 242, 243, 245
Louis IX, King of France, 261, 262, 275, 276, 278, 293–4
Louis XI, King of France, 338, 357, 360
Louis XII, King of France, 359
Louis XIII, King of France, 402, 407
Louis XIV, King of France, 393, 394, 396, 397, 403, 409, 410, 412, 413, 414, 415, 416, 417, 418, 419, 420, 421, 422, 423, 424, 435, 437, 457, 547
Louis XVI, King of France, 449, 453, 454, 455, 457, 466
Louis XVIII, King of France, 466
Louis d'Outremer, 171
Louis Philippe, 490
Louis the German, 137, 145
Louis the Great, of Hungary, 302
Louis the Pious, 136, 137
Louvois, Michel Le Tellier, marquis de, 417, 418, 419
Loyola, Ignatius, 367
Lübeck, 244
Luther, Martin, 138, 352, 353, 355, 360, 361, 362, 364, 365, 377–8
Luxeuil, monastery of, 64
Lyell, Charles, 492

Machiavelli, Niccolo, 359–60
Magna Carta, 270, 272, 276, 281
Magyars, 134, 171–2, 225
Mainz, 276
Malleus Maleficarum, 326
Malthus, Thomas, 492
Manor, 164, 167
Manzikert, battle of, 198
Marat, J. P., 455
Marcel, Etienne, 309, 310
Marguerite d'Angoulême, Queen of Navarre, 363

Mariana, Juan de, 373
Maria Theresa, consort of Louis XIV, 419
Maria Theresa, Empress, 443, 448
Marignano, battle of, 359
Marriage of Mercury and Philosophy, 55
Marsiglio of Padua, 309, 311
Martianus Capella, 55
Martin, of Tours, 50, 65
Martin V, Pope, 333
Martinet, Jean, 417
Marx, Karl, 483, 486, 490, 499, 500, 501, 524
Mary of Burgundy, 339
Mary of Guise, Queen of Scotland, 371
Mary Stuart, Queen of Scotland, 371, 373, 403
Mary Tudor, Queen of England, 367, 370, 406
Mary, Queen of England, 420
Masaccio, Thomas, 324, 332, 336
Massacre of St. Bartholomew, 372
Matilda, countess of Tuscany, 238
Matilda of England, 237, 241
Maximilian I, Emperor, 339, 358, 359, 363
Mazarin, Cardinal, 409, 410, 412
Mazzini, Giuseppe, 491, 493
Mecklenburg, 244
Medici, 324, 327, 336, 338, 359, 360
Medici, Catherine de', Queen of France, 372
Medici, Cosimo de', 336, 337, 338
Medici, Lorenzo de' (the Magnificent), 327, 336–40, 344–8
Medici, Lorenzo de', Duke of Florence, 360
Mendelssohn, Felix, 487
Mercantilism, 418–19, 422, 449
Merchant class, rise of, 222–4, 225, 328, 329, 354
Mesco, 161
Metternich, Prince, 464, 466, 490, 502
Meung, Jean de, 267, 275
Mirandola, Pico della, 331

Michelangelo Buonarroti, 332, 355, 360, 392, 398
Middle class, 352, 448; in France, 414–15, 449, 450, 455, 458, 490; rise of English, 354, 436, 442, 448
Military institutions, artillery, 329, 331; Louis XIV, 417–18; in French Revolution, 457; Napoleon, 462–3; Nineteenth Century and World War of 1914–1918, 500–1, 507–8, 534, 535; World War of 1939–1945, 567–70
Mill, James, 485
Milton, John, 394, 404, 405
Mining, 224, 225
Ministerial responsibility, 436, 501–2
Minnesingers, 227
Mithraism, 9, 22
Milyukov, Paul, 530
Mohammed, 66, 83, 84–8, 90
Mohammedan art and architecture, 83, 145
Mohammedan Empire, 79, 83, 87, 88, 90, 97, 106, 194
Mohammedanism, 79, 85, 86; sects, 88
Molière, 423
Monasteries, dissolution of English, 366
Monasticism, 50; codification of rules, 51; in England, 90; missions, 106, 107, 110; scholarship, 101, 104, 105, 108, 109, 110
Montaigne, Michel de, 355
Monte Cassino, monastery of, 56
Montesquieu, baron de, 438
Montfort, Simon de, 271, 272
Montfort, Simon de, the younger, 281, 282
Montpelier, University of, 280
Montreux Straits Convention, 549
More, Hannah, 489
More, Thomas, 357, 361, 366
Moscow, Principality of, 302, 358
Mozart, W. A., 435
Muscovy, Grand Duchy of, 446–7
Mussolini, Benito, 559, 560, 562, 563, 564, 566, 568

Naples, University of, 278
Napoleon I, 454–68, 473–7, 489, 490, 500
Napoleon III, 490, 493, 494
Nation state, 394–7
Nationalism in 19th and 20th century, 484–6, 495–8, 503, 505–6, 510–12, 523, 524–5, 548–51; economic nationalism, 542, 552, 560; self-determination for nationalities, 540–1, 555–6
Natural law, 438–40
Natural rights, 438–40
Nelson, Horatio, 459, 461
Neo-Platonism, 22
NEP, 545–6, 556, 558
Netherlands, revolt of, 372–3
Neustria, 80, 89, 107, 114
Newcomen, Thomas, 440
Newton, Isaac, 393, 397, 405, 407, 408–24, 428–31, 436, 442, 443, 492
Nibelungenlied, 227
Nicea, council of, 29, 30
Nicholas I, Pope, 140
Nicholas V, Pope, 331, 334, 337, 390
Nicholas I, Tsar, 529
Normans, 161, 170, 203; in Sicily, 196, 207, 238, 270

Obrenovich, Milosh, 495
Occam, William of, 308, 309
Odoacer, 32, 54, 55
Omar, 87
Ommiad dynasty, 88
On the Law of Peace and War (Grotius), 410
Opium War, 493
Ordeal, 49
Origin of Species, 492, 493
Orosius, *Seven Books of History against the Pagans,* 144
Othman, 88
Otto I, Emperor, 169, 170–4, 176, 177, 243; intervention in Italy, 173; secularization of ecclesiastical offices, 172–3
Otto II, Emperor, 173, 176, 177, 246

Otto III, Emperor, 168, 178, 179, 180, 181, 206
Otto IV, Emperor, 270, 272
Oxford, Provisions of, 281
Oxford, University of, 308, 309

Padua, University of, 280, 393, 399, 400, 401
Paine, Thomas, 445
Palestine, 58, 551
Palestrina, 355
Palissy, Bernard, 392
Papacy, 50, 62, 63, 66, 272, 281, 282, 304, 310, 311, 325, 326, 337, 367, 415–16, 460; and Crusades, 193, 231, 233, 265–6, 271; and eastern emperor, 114; and Lombards, 114; and Normans, 196–7, 200, 205; papal monarchy, 229; temporal position, 100, 114, 117
Papal provisions, 281, 304, 309, 311, 312
Paris, Treaty of (1763), 444
Paris, University of, 275
Parlements, 450
Parliament, growth of, 282, 308, 309, 310, 312, 329, 330, 366, 371, 374–5, 394, 406, 407, 408, 420, 422; Reform Bill of 1832, 490; Chartists, 491; 2nd Reform Bill, 493
Pascal, Blaise, 393, 416, 424
Pastoral Care (Gregory the Great), 144
Patrick, 64
Patrimony of St. Peter, 63
Paul, 12, 22
Paul III, Pope, 364
Paul the Deacon, 62
Pavia, battle of (1525), 364
Pavia, University of, 368
Peace of God, 167, 195, 233
Peasants, commutation of services, 308, 311
Peasants' Revolt in England (1381), 311, 322
Peasants' Revolt in Germany (1524), 364
Pepin of Heristal, 88, 98, 106

Pepin of Landen, 88
Pepin the Short, 100, 111, 114
Permanent Court of International Justice, see World Court
Perotin, 275
Peter, 31
Peter I, Tsar, 446–7, 421–2
Peter's Pence, 304
Petrarch, 303, 308, 312, 324
Philip II, King of France, 231, 232, 247, 268, 269, 270, 271, 275
Philip IV, King of France, 262, 280, 281, 282, 305, 506
Philip V, King of France, 306
Philip II, King of Spain, 353, 367, 372, 373, 405
Philip V, King of Spain, 421
Philip the Good, duke of Burgundy, 338
Philosophes, 436–40, 448, 449, 450, 484
Physiocrats, 449
Picard, Abbé, 393
Pilgrimage, 135, 142, 146, 195, 197, 204, 245
Pisa, 196, 233
Pisa, Council of, 333
Pisa, University of, 399
Pisano, Noccolo, 284
Pitt, William (the elder), 443
Pius V, Pope, 400
Pius IX, Pope, 494
Plato, 18, 22, 41, 56
Platonic Academy (Florence), 336
Plekhanov, George, 528
Poggio Bracciolini, 333
Poitiers, battle of, 307, 309
Poor laws, England, 373–4
Poland, colonization of by Germans, 302; German-Russian partition 1939, 566–7
Polo, Marco, 265
Population, Middle Ages, 223
Praemunire, Statute of, 309
Prague, University of, 332
Praise of Folly (Erasmus), 361
Prestations, 165, 166
Prince, 360

Principia (Newton), 420–1, 424, 428–31
Printing, 331–2
Priscian, 55
Procopius of Caesarea, 67
Propaganda in wartime, 540
Protestant revolt, 360–2; antecedents, 351–2
Provincial Letters (Pascal), 416
Provisors, Statute of, 309
Prudentius, 41
Prussia, 421, 443, 445–6, 448, 461, 462, 463, 464, 466, 491
Prussians, 302
Ptolemaic geography, 339, 340
Ptolemaic system, 283
Purchas' *Pilgrims,* 374
Puritans, English, 370, 404, 405, 406, 408
Purveyance, 164

Quadrivium, 55
Quadruple Alliance, 466
Quintuple Alliance, 466–7, 489

Rabelais, François, 355
Race, 8n
Racine, Jean, 423
Radich, Stephen, 551
Raeburn, Henry, 436
Ramus, Peter, 399
Raphael, 355
Rationalism, 437–40
Ravenna, Theodoric's capital, 55; architecture, 60
Raymond of Aurillac, 176
Redevances, 165
Reformation, Protestant, in England, 366–7, 370; in France, 365; in Germany, 364–5; in Switzerland, 365–6
Regalian rights, 245–6
Reliefs, 164
Renaissance, English, 374
Renaissance, Italian, 324, 325, 327, 331–2, 336–7, 351
Revolution of 1789, France, 450–61
Revolutionary movement of 1830, 490

Revolutionary movement of 1848, 490-1
Revolutionary Tribunal, 456
Richard I, King of England, 231, 268, 269
Richard II, King of England, 310, 311, 329
Richard III, King of England, 338
Richelieu, Cardinal, 402, 407, 409, 410
Richer, 177, 178, 185-7
Robbia, Luca della, 336
Robespierre, Max., 455
Rodin, Auguste, 487
Roemer, Ole, 393
Roland, Song of, 227
Rolf the Ranger, 170
Rome, ancient, 6; commerce, 17; expansion, 6; Germanic invasions, 21, 27, 28, 29, 47, 48, 49, 50; imperial decline, 18, 19, 20, 21, 27; imperial organization, 6, 7, 9, 10, 14; imperial tradition, 98, 100; republic, 6
Roman law, 48, 49, 60, 61
Roman society, 48, 65
Romulus Augustulus, 32
Roncaglia, diet of, 246
Roosevelt, F. D., 568, 569, 571
Roscellinus of Compiègne, 226, 234
Rose, Romaunt of the, 267, 275
Rostovzeff, Michael, 15
Rousseau, J. J., 438
Royal Society (England), 412, 413, 423, 442, 444
Rudolf of Hapsburg, Emperor, 283, 284
Russia, 358, 421-2, 446-8, 462, 463, 464, 466, 493, 496-7, 502, 507, 508, 512-13, 525, 528-37

Sacraments, 228-9
St. Clement Danes, 202
St. Denis, Abbey of, 237, 239
St. Peter's, Rome, 337, 355
Saladin, 269
Salerno, school of medicine at, 278
Salimbene, 290-4

Santiago de Compostella, 146, 195, 197, 233
Saracen civilization, 97, 98, 113, 145, 176, 219, 220, 227, 264
Sardinia, 233
Savonarola, 340, 359
Saxons, 9, 29, 30, 43, 47, 64, 80, 104; Charlemagne's campaigns, 112, 113
Scharnhorst, G. von, 463
Schiller, Friedrich, 454
Schism, eastern and western churches, 197, 206
Schism, Great, 304, 310, 311, 325, 332-3, 337
Schmalkaldic League, 364
Schola Cantorum, 66
Scholasticism, 226-7
Schubert, Franz, 487
Scott, Reginald, 355
Scutage, 232, 245
Sens, Council of, 239
Serbs, 81, 87, 113
Serfdom (Russia), 446-8, 529, 530
Servetus, Michael, 366
Seven Weeks' War (1866), 494
Seven Years' War, 443
Sèvres, Treaty of, 549
Seymour, Jane, 366
Sforza, Francesco, 336, 337
Shakespeare, William, 354, 374
Shelley, P. B., 454, 484
Sigismund, Emperor, 333
Silvester II, Pope, 169, 176-81, 187-90, 201, 234
Simeon (Bulgar Tsar), 134
Simony, 168, 177, 206
Slave trade, African, 372, 484, 492
Slavs, 47, 58, 80, 82, 112, 134, 162, 171; and Byzantine Christianity, 162, 180; and Kiev, 162; and Roman Christianity, 180
Slovenes, 81, 82
Sluys, battle of, 306, 307
Smith, Adam, 449, 483
Social contract, theory, 438
Socialism, 483, 486, 490, 499-500, 501-2, 514, 524, 553-4; in Russia, 531-2, 534, 536, 544, 553, 556-9

Society of Jesus, see Jesuits
Soissons, Synod of, 236
Soliloquies (Augustine), 144
Song of Roland, 114
Sorel, Agnes, 334
Soviet Union, 526, 543-6, 551, 552, 553, 564, 566, 567, 568, 570
Spain, 58, 89, 97, 98, 101, 105
Spanish Civil War (1936-1939), 563-4
Spanish Succession, War of, 421, 422, 423, 435
Spectator, 442
Spenser, Edmund, 354
Spinning-wheel, 265
Stalin, Joseph, 556, 558, 567, 570, 573-4
Stambulisky, Alexander, 551
Steele, Richard, 436, 442
Stein, H. von, 463
Stephen, King of England, 243, 244
Stephen of Blois, 241
Stilicho, 27
Stolypin, Peter, 533
Strasburg, Oath of, 137
Sueves, 47
Suger, 237, 239, 250-1
Suleiman I, Sultan, 369
Sully, duc de, 402
Summa Theologiae (Thomas Aquinas), 280
Sun Yat-Sen, 505
Swedes, 134
Sweyn, 172, 193, 202
Swiss, confederacy, 284
Symbolism, medieval religious architecture, 230
Syria, 58

Tacitus, 8, 80
Talleyrand, 464, 475-6
Tatars, 358, 446
Tennyson, Alfred, 492
Teutonic Knights, 276-7, 302, 358
Theodora, 54, 59, 67, 68, 70
Theodore of Tarsus, 89, 90, 105
Theodoric the Ostrogoth, 55, 56, 57, 61

Theodosius I, 13, 22, 25, 27
Theophano, 173, 176, 179
Thirty Years' War, 403, 404, 409, 410, 421, 435, 445
Thuringians, 112
Tithes, 229
Titian, 355
Toleration, religious, 365, 396, 400-2, 403, 410, 415-17, 438
Torricelli, E., 393
Torture, 166
Toscanelli, 326
Toulouse, Raymond of, 272
Toulouse, University of, 280
Towns, rise of commercial, 199, 201, 220, 222, 223, 224, 225, 231, 237, 263, 279, 302, 306, 321, 322, 324, 328, 329, 331, 354
Trade, growth in middle ages, 220, 222, 223, 224, 225, 240, 262, 279, 280, 328, 329, 333-4
Trade, with Orient, 339-40
Trafalgar, battle of, 461
Transubstantiation, 201-2, 272, 311
Treatise of Civil Government (Locke), 394
Trent, Council of, 364-5, 367
Trier, 276
Triple Alliance, 507, 508, 509, 513
Triple Entente, 508, 509
Trivium, 56
Trotsky, Leon, 537, 538, 556
Troubadours, 227-8
Trouvères, 227
Troyes, Synod of, 238
Troyes, Treaty of, 330
Truce of God, 195, 233
Turgot, 449
Turkey, 548-9, 550
Turkish Empire in 19th and 20th centuries, 484, 493, 495-7, 503, 509, 548
Turks, Ottoman, 302, 327, 332-3, 335, 337, 340, 364, 369, 372, 422, 423
Turks, Seljuk, 197, 198, 233
Turner, William, 487

Unam Sanctam, Bull, 282
United Nations, 527, 569, 570-2
Universals, controversy over, 234-5
Universities, 225-6
Urban II, Pope, 198, 233, 235, 248-9
Urban VIII, Pope, 400, 403
U. S. S. R., *see* Soviet Union
Utilitarianism, 485
Utopia (More), 366
Utrecht, Treaty of, 421

Valla, Lorenzo, 331
Vandals, 21, 25, 29, 47, 58
Varro, 18, 22, 41
Vatican library, 337
Vauban, marquis de, 418
Venice, 198, 201, 222, 223, 240, 265, 270, 279, 302, 326, 328, 337, 359, 399, 400, 494
Verdun, Treaty of, 137, 171
Vergil, 18
Verrazano, Giovanni, 402
Verrochio, Andrea del, 337
Versailles, Treaty of (1919), 541, 564
Vesalius, 392
Victor Emmanuel II, 493, 494
Victoria, Queen of England, 493
Vienna, Congress of, 464-6, 467
Vikings, 132-5, 136, 137, 140, 142, 143, 144, 145
Village (*mir,* Russian), 447-8, 529, 533
Villehardouin, 267, 275
Villein, 132
Virgin, cult of, 227-8, 276, 301
Visconti family, 337
Vision of Piers the Plowman, 309
Vita Nuova (Dante), 283
Voltaire, 437, 443, 446
Vulgate, 25

Wagner, Richard, 487, 498
Waibling, *see* Hohenstaufen
Waldo, Peter, 271
Wales, 47
Wallace, Alfred, 492

Wallingford, Treaty of, 241
Walpole, Robert, 442, 443
Wardship, 164
Water power, 303
Waterloo, battle of, 464
Watt, James, 440, 489
Wealth of Nations, 449, 483
Wedgwood, Josiah, 489
Welf, *see* Guelph
Wellington, duke of, 462
Wenceslas, 161
Wergeld, 48
Westphalia, Treaties of, 409, 410, 412
Weyer, John, 355
Whistler, James, 487
Whitby, Synod of, 83, 89, 90, 104
Wilde, Oscar, 498
Wilkes, John, 444
William, duke of Aquitaine, 168
William II, Emperor of Germany, 502, 540
William I, King of England, 193, 196, 204, 205, 207, 208, 214, 216, 241, 244
William II, King of England, 207, 236, 237
William III, King of England, 420, 421, 422
William I, King of Sicily, 246
William of Champeaux, 234, 235, 236
William of Malmesbury, 141, 210-14
William (the Silent) of Orange, 373
Willibrord, 106
Wilson, Woodrow, 540, 541, 569
Windmill, 303
Witan, 202, 203, 204
Witchcraft persecutions, 325, 326, 355
Wolsey, Cardinal, 366
Women, political enfranchisement, 526; status of, middle ages, 227-8
Wool trade, 306-7
Wordsworth, William, 454
World Court, 560
World War (1914-1918), 534-5, 539-40; background, 507-14
World War (1939-1945), 566-70; background, 561-6

Worms, Concordat of, 236, 242
Worms, Diet of (1521), 360, 364
Wren, Christopher, 441
Wycliffe, John, 304, 305–17, 328, 333

Yuan Shik-k'ai, 505

Zollverein, 491
Zwingli, Ulrich, 365

A NOTE ON THE TYPE

This book is set in GRANJON *a type named in compliment to Robert Granjon, type-cutter and printer—Antwerp, Lyons, Rome, Paris—active from 1523 to 1590. The boldest and most original designer of his time, he was one of the first to practise the trade of type-founder apart from that of printer.*

This type face was designed by George W. Jones, who based his drawings upon a type used by Claude Garamond (1510–61) in his beautiful French books, and more closely resembles Garamond's own than do any of the various modern types that bear his name.

The book was composed, printed, and bound by Kingsport Press, Inc., Kingsport, Tennessee.